SECOND EDITION

LEADERSHIP
Research Findings, Practice, and Skills

Andrew J. DuBrin
Rochester Institute of Technology

Houghton Mifflin Company   Boston   New York

Senior Associate Editor: Susan M. Kahn
Associate Project Editor: Rachel D'Angelo Wimberly
Production/Design Coordinator: Carol Merrigan
Senior Manufacturing Coordinator: Priscilla Bailey
Marketing Manager: Juli Bliss

Cover design: Diana Coe
Cover image: Tim Davis, Penguins running down iceberg in line to water—
© Tony Stone Images.

To Melanie

Printed in the U.S.A.

Library of Congress Catalog Card Number: 97-72462

ISBN: 0-395-85664-7

23456789-DH 01 00 99 98

Brief Contents

Contents

v

9 *Developing Teamwork*   217

13   *Strategic Leadership*   *332*

Preface

*W*elcome to the Second Edition of *Leadership: Research Findings, Practice, and Skills*. The new edition of this text is an expansion and updating of the first edition that has been used widely in both graduate and undergraduate courses in leadership. Some of the changes in this edition are based on my intuition about what recent information on leadership should be included in the new edition. The majority of the changes, though, reflect suggestions made by adopters and reviewers. For example, many professors and students found the skill-building exercises so useful that I have expanded them in this edition. Further information about changes to the text is presented later in this preface.

Leadership has always been a key topic in management, organizational behavior, and industrial and organizational psychology. In recent years, however, leadership has become an important new course in schools and colleges of business, business administration, and public administration. Teaching and research about leadership have surged. Many business school faculty are convinced that effective leadership is required to meet most organizational challenges. Without effective leadership at all levels in private and public organizations, it is difficult to sustain profitability, productivity, quality, and good customer service. In dozens of different ways, researchers and teachers have demonstrated that leadership does make a difference. Many business school curricula therefore now emphasize the development of leadership skills.

More so than previously, business organizations recognize that leadership transcends senior executives. As a result, they require people with appropriate leadership skills to inspire and influence others in small teams, task forces, and units at all organizational levels.

PURPOSE OF THE TEXT

The purpose of this text is implied by its title—*Leadership: Research Findings, Practice, and Skills*, Second Edition. It is designed for undergraduate and graduate courses in leadership that give attention to research findings about leadership, the practice of leadership, and skill development. The text is also designed to fit courses in management development that emphasize the leadership function of management. In addition, it can serve as a supplement to organizational behavior or management courses that emphasize leadership.

The student who masters this text will acquire an overview of the voluminous research literature about leadership. The student will also acquire a feel for how leadership is practiced and gain insights and information to enhance her or his leadership skills.

What the text is *not* also helps define its nature and scope. This book does not attempt to duplicate the scope and purpose of a leadership handbook by integrating theory and research from several thousand studies. At the other extreme, it is not an evangelical approach to leadership espousing one leadership technique. I have attempted to find a midpoint between a massive synthesis of the literature and a trade book promoting a current leadership fad. *Leadership: Research Findings, Practice, and Skills*, Second Edition is designed to be a mixture of scholarly integrity, examples of effective leadership in action, and skill development.

It is important to note that this book is not intended to duplicate or substitute for an organizational behavior text. Because almost all organizational behavior texts are survey texts, they will mention many of the topics covered here. My approach, however, is to emphasize skill development and prescription rather than to duplicate basic descriptions of concepts and theories. I have tried to minimize overlap by emphasizing the leadership aspects of any concept presented here that might also be found in an organizational behavior or management text.

One area of intentional overlap with organizational behavior and management texts does exist: a review of all basic leadership theories. In such instances, however, I emphasize skill development and ideas for leadership practice stemming from these older theories.

FEATURES OF THE BOOK

To accomplish its purpose, this text incorporates nine features into each chapter in addition to summarizing and synthesizing relevant information about leadership:

1. **Self-assessment exercises** relating both to skills and personal characteristics
2. **Leader in Action** inserts describing the leadership practices, behaviors, and personal attributes of real-life leaders
3. Boldfaced **key terms,** listed at the end of the chapter and defined in a **glossary** at the back of the text

4. Real-life and hypothetical **examples** throughout the text
5. **Skill development** and **application exercises,** including role plays, to emphasize the activities and skills of effective leaders
6. **Discussion questions** and **activities** suited for individual or group analysis
7. End-of-chapter **Guidelines for Action,** giving additional suggestions for improving leadership skill and practice
8. End-of-chapter **summaries** that integrate all key topics and concepts
9. **Leadership Case Problems,** which illustrate the major theme of the chapter, for individual or group analysis
10. **Learning objectives** to help focus the reader's attention on major outcomes

FRAMEWORK OF THE TEXT

The text is a blend of description, skill development, insight development, and prescription. Chapter 1 describes the meaning, importance, and nature of leadership including leadership roles. Chapter 2 identifies personal attributes associated with effective leaders, a subject that has experienced renewed importance in recent years. Charismatic and transformational leadership, an extension of understanding the personal attributes of leadership, is the subject of Chapter 3.

Chapter 4 surveys behaviors and practices associated with effective leadership in a variety of situations. Chapter 5 shifts to a description of various approaches to classifying leadership styles. Chapter 6 extends the style approach to leadership by describing the contingency and situational aspects of leadership. After Chapter 7 describes how leaders use power and politics, Chapter 8 extends the topic through an analysis of tactics leaders use to influence others. Chapter 9 describes how leaders foster teamwork and empower team members.

The next five chapters deal with specific leadership skills: motivating and coaching skills (Chapter 10), which constitute the basics of many leadership positions; creative problem solving (Chapter 11); communication (including nonverbal and cross-cultural communication) and conflict resolution skills (Chapter 12); skills for providing vision and strategy (Chapter 13); and leadership skills and attitudes required for providing effective leadership in international and culturally diverse settings (Chapter 14).

Chapter 15 concludes the book with an overview of approaches to leadership development and learning. In addition, it covers a group of leading-edge and future challenges facing the leader, such as providing leadership in a reengineered workplace and in a virtual corporation.

CHANGES IN THE SECOND EDITION

The Second Edition of *Leadership: Findings, Practice, and Skills* is an expansion and extension of the first edition in several important ways. First, I focus more on the visionary and direction-setting aspect of leadership by adding to the text a new chapter on strategic leadership (Chapter 13). Included in the chapter is information about quality and technology management. In response to the high acceptance of the skill-building exercises in the first edition, each chapter now contains at least one more activity of this type. The framework for understanding leadership presented in Chapter 1 of the previous edition has been replaced by a briefer, more conceptual model. The information about leadership succession presented in Chapter 15 has been substantially expanded.

New topics for the second edition include the leadership aspects of 360-degree feedback, goal setting, delegation, and neurolinguistic programming. I have also added information about the contribution of good followership to leadership and the importance of value-driven leadership. About 85 percent of the cases and Leader in Action inserts in the second edition are new.

SUPPLEMENTS

An instructor's manual with test bank accompanies the text. Among its features are chapter outline and lecture notes, possible answers to discussion questions and case questions, comments on exercises in the text, and a comprehensive list of leadership videos. The instructor's manual also describes how to use Computer-Assisted Scenario Analysis (CASA). Especially designed for helping students develop a contingency point of view, CASA is a user-friendly technique that can be used with any word-processing software. It allows the student to insert a new scenario into the case and then re-answer the questions based on the new scenario. CASA helps to develop an awareness of contingency factor in making leadership decisions, as well as creative thinking. A brief version of CASA was published in the October 1992 issue of *The Journal of Management Education*.

ACKNOWLEDGMENTS

Any project as complex as this one requires a team of dedicated and talented people to see that it achieves its goals. First, I thank the professors listed below who either offered suggestions for improving the first draft of the first edition or reviewed and made suggestions for improving the second edition. Second, I thank the many effective leaders I have observed in action for improving my understanding of leadership.

John Bigelow
Boise State University

Felipe Chia
Harrisburg Area Community College

Barry Gold
Pace University

George B. Graen
University of Cincinnati

Stephen G. Green
Purdue University

James R. Harris
North Carolina Agricultural and
    Technical State University

Nell Hartley
Robert Morris College

Winston Hill
California State University—Chico

Avis L. Johnson
University of Akron

David Lee
University of Dayton

Ralph Mullin
Central Missouri State University

Linda L. Neider
University of Miami

Joseph Petrick
Wright State University

Randall G. Sleeth
Virginia Commonwealth University

Ahmad Tootoonchi
Frostburg State University

John Warner
University of New Mexico

David Van Fleet
Arizona State University West

The editorial and production team at Houghton Mifflin Company also receives my gratitude. By name they are Jennifer Speer, Susan Kahn, and Rachel Wimberly. Writing without loved ones would be a lonely task. My thanks therefore also go to my family members—Drew, Douglas, Melanie, Rosie, and Clare.

The Nature and Importance of Leadership

LEARNING OBJECTIVES

After studying this chapter, you should be able to

1. explain the meaning of leadership and how it differs from management.
2. describe how leadership influences organizational performance.
3. pinpoint several important leadership roles.
4. identify the major satisfactions and frustrations associated with the leadership role.
5. identify the major approaches to understanding leadership.
6. recognize how leadership skills are developed.

Arthur G. Martinez walks down the aisles of Sears, Roebuck and Co.'s newest hardware store, carrying a shovel and occasionally stopping to weigh a sack of nails. Nobody who understands Martinez's leadership style is surprised to see him at the opening of yet another hardware store in the Sears chain. Martinez is a hands-on manager. Industry analysts agree that the Sears hardware store venture will encounter tough competition in the United States and Canada. Martinez, however, is the affable but tough executive who brought Sears back from close to collapse—who turned water into wine, and an Edsel into a hot-selling vehicle. Before Martinez came on the scene, many Wall Street investors regarded Sears as an overpriced, out-of-touch dinosaur.

Martinez is an extraordinary fix-it person in the eyes of anyone familiar with the retail industry. "He is, without a shadow of a doubt, the most able, imaginative, competitive, and creative retail executive in the country today," contends an industry analyst. "Up until Martinez stepped in, I felt that Sears had maybe one or two more years and that would be the end. He not only rescued Sears, not only saved it from demise, he turned it into one of the most formidable rivals in the retail marketplace."

1

Martinez has shown strong determination in tightening Sears' focus and getting customers to appreciate the giant retailer's soft side. Now his target is for Sears to become the dominant player in the hardware store business, and also make a major impact in the do-it-yourself home improvement business.[1]

Our introductory chapter to the study of leadership begins with an explanation of what leadership is and is not. We then examine how leaders make a difference, the various roles they occupy, and the major satisfactions and frustrations they experience. The next section presents a framework of leadership, which identifies the major approaches to understanding leadership. The chapter concludes with an explanation of how reading this book and doing the exercises will enhance your leadership skills.

THE MEANING OF LEADERSHIP

By helping to revitalize Sears, Martinez exerted leadership. He made a difference in company performance through a combination of winning business strategies and personal influence. The fact that Martinez inspired, influenced, and motivated people to achieve constructive change means that he exercised leadership. To be a leader, one has to make a difference and facilitate positive changes.

You will read about many other effective organizational leaders throughout this text. The common characteristic of these leaders is their ability to inspire and stimulate others to achieve worthwhile goals. The people who can accomplish these important deeds practice leadership. Compatible with the theme of this text, **leadership** is the ability to inspire confidence and support among the people who are needed to achieve organizational goals.[2]

About 30,000 research articles, magazine articles, and books have been written about leadership so far this century. As a consequence, leadership has been defined in many ways. Several other representative definitions of leadership are as follows:

- Interpersonal influence directed through communication, toward goal attainment.
- The influential increment over and above mechanical compliance with directions and orders.
- An act that causes others to act or respond in a shared direction.
- The art of influencing people by persuasion or example to follow a line of action.
- The principal dynamic force that motivates and coordinates the organization in the accomplishment of its objectives.[3]

Leadership as a Partnership

An important current thrust in understanding leadership is to regard it as a long-term relationship, or partnership, between leaders and group members. According to Peter Block, in a **partnership** the leader and the group members are connected in such a way that the power between them is approximately balanced. Block also describes partnership as the opposite of parenting (in which one person—the parent—takes the responsibility for the welfare of the other—the child). Partnership occurs when control shifts from the leader to the group member, in a move away from authoritarianism and toward shared decision making.[4] Four things are necessary for a valid partnership to exist:

1. *Exchange of purpose.* In a partnership, every worker at every level is responsible for defining vision and values. Through dialogue with people at many levels, the leader helps articulate a widely accepted vision.

2. *A right to say no.* The belief that people who express a contrary opinion will be punished runs contrary to a partnership. Rather, a person can lose an argument but never a voice.

3. *Joint accountability.* In a partnership, each person is responsible for outcomes and the current situation. In practice, this means that each person takes personal accountability for the success and failure of the organizational unit.

4. *Absolute honesty.* In a partnership, not telling the truth to one another is an act of betrayal. When power is distributed, people are more likely to tell the truth because they feel less vulnerable.[5]

Block's conception of leadership as a partnership is an ideal to strive toward. Empowerment and team building—two major topics in this book—support the idea of a partnership.

Leadership Versus Management

To understand leadership, it is important to grasp the difference between leadership and management. We get a clue from the standard conceptualization of the functions of management: planning, organizing, directing (or leading), and controlling. Leading is a major part of a manager's job, yet a manager must also plan, organize, and control. Broadly speaking, leadership deals with the interpersonal aspects of a manager's job, whereas planning, organizing, and controlling deal with the administrative aspects. According to current thinking, leadership deals with change, inspiration, motivation, and influence. In contrast, management deals more with maintaining equilibrium and the status quo. Table 1–1 explains other differences between management and leadership.

TABLE 1–1   Leadership Versus Management

	Leadership	*Management*
Creating an Agenda	Establishes direction: develops a vision and the strategies needed for its achievement	Plans and budgets: establishes detailed steps and timetables for achieving needed results; allocates necessary resources
Developing a Network for Achieving the Agenda	Involves aligning people: Communicates direction by words and deeds to all those whose cooperation may be needed to help create teams and coalitions that understand the vision and strategies, and accept their validity.	Organizes and staffs: Establishes structure for achieving the plans; staffs; delegates responsibility and authority for implementation; develops policies and procedures to guide people; creates monitoring systems
Execution	Motivates and inspires: Energizes people to overcome major political, bureaucratic, and resource barriers to change by satisfying basic human needs.	Controls and solves problems: Monitors results against plans, and then plans and organizes to close the gap.
Outcomes	Produces change, often to a dramatic degree: Has the potential of producing extremely useful change, such as new products desired by managers.	Produces a degree of predictability and order: Has the potential to consistently produce key results expected by various stakeholders (such as meeting deadlines for customers and paying dividends to stockholders)

Source: John P. Kotter, *A Force for Change: How Leadership Differs from Management* (New York: The Free Press, 1990); Wayne K. Kirchner, book review of "A Force for Change," *Personnel Psychology*, Autumn 1990, p. 655.

According to John P. Kotter, a prominent leadership theorist, today's managers must know how to *lead* as well as manage. Without leading as well as managing, organizations face the threat of extinction. Kotter draws the following distinction between management and leadership:

- Management is more formal and scientific than leadership. It relies on universal skills such as planning, budgeting, and controlling. Management is an explicit set of tools and techniques, based on reasoning and testing, that can be used in a variety of situations.

- Leadership, in contrast to management, involves having a vision of what the organization can become.

- Leadership requires eliciting cooperation and teamwork from a large network of people and keeping the key people in that network motivated, using every manner of persuasion.[6]

Another key distinction has been drawn between leadership and management. The key function of the *leader* is to create a vision (mission or agenda) for the organization. The leader specifies the far-reaching goal as well as the strategy for goal attainment. In contrast to the leader, the key func-

LEADER IN ACTION

Rebecca Mark of Enron Development

Rebecca P. Mark, age 43, is the chairman and chief executive of Enron Development, the international ventures unit of Enron Corp., based in Houston, Texas. In her days at Harvard Business School, she was nicknamed Mark the Shark for her exceptional ambition. By building pipelines and power plants, Mark and her company deliver electricity to underdeveloped sections of the world.

She began her business career as a lending specialist for the First City National Bank in Houston, lending money to energy companies for huge, high-risk development projects. After a few years she joined a natural-gas company that later became a unit of Enron. Acquiring new responsibility rapidly, Mark eventually became the manager of power-plant development. She persuaded her boss to create a separate company to build in Third World markets. She and her group have built power plants in Guatemala, China, and the Philippines. Power plants are now in the works in twenty-seven other countries, with Mark being a driving force behind this continuous expansion.

Mark's biggest deal to date is a $2.8 billion project in Dabhol, India. After Hindu nationalists and their allies overturned the deal, Mark used her personal influence to resuscitate it. A major part of bringing back the deal was testifying before the parliament of the Maharashtra government. "I enjoy being a world-class problem solver," she says. "I'm constantly asking, 'How far can I go? How much can I do?'" (*Fortune*, p. 42).

Source: As reported in Patricia Sellers, "Women, Sex & Power," *Fortune*, August 5, 1996, pp. 42, 50; "Enron: Maybe Megadeals Mean Megarisk," *Business Week*, September 4, 1995, pp. 52–53.

tion of the *manager* is to implement the vision. The manager and his or her team thus choose the means to achieve the end that the leader formulates.[7]

If these views are taken to their extreme, the leader is an inspirational figure and the manager is a stodgy bureaucrat mired in the status quo. But we must be careful not to downplay the importance of management. Effective leaders have to be good managers themselves, or be supported by effective managers. A germane example is the inspirational entrepreneur who is so preoccupied with motivating employees and captivating customers that internal administration is neglected. As a result, costs skyrocket beyond income and such matters as funding the employee pension and paying bills and taxes on time are overlooked. Also, recall that Arthur Martinez's approach to turning around Sears was to emphasize the soft side in the traditional stores and also open freestanding hardware stores. Such strategizing is part of the planning function of management.

THE IMPACT OF LEADERSHIP ON ORGANIZATIONAL PERFORMANCE

An assumption underlying the study of leadership is that leaders affect organizational performance. Leaders, through their actions and personal influence, bring about change. People who control organizations—the very top executives—make the same assumption. A frequent antidote to major organizational problems is to replace the leader, in the hope that the newly appointed leader will reverse performance problems. An example of this assumption in action is the frequent replacement of athletic coaches after one or two losing seasons. The owners, or school officials, assume that the leadership acumen of the new coach will vastly improve the ratio of wins to losses.

Here we will review some of the evidence and opinion, pro and con, about the ability of leaders to affect organizational performance. The accompanying Leader in Action vignette provides a positive example of the importance of effective leadership.

Research and Opinion: Leadership Does Make a Difference

The belief that leaders actually influence organizational performance and morale is so plausible that there is very little research and opinion that even deals with this issue. Let us look at a sampling of what research and opinion there are.[8]

Psychoanalyst Michael Maccoby conducted in-depth interviews with business executives over eighteen years ago. He concluded that organizations required a higher level of leadership than ever before to survive and prosper. Among the challenges Maccoby saw confronting organizations were increasing competition, technological advances, changing governmental regulations, and changing worker attitudes. These observations are relevant because they persist today.

Two researchers examined the evolution of a retail firm over a sixty-year period. They found that a senior executive could successfully reorient the firm by changing strategies and organizational structures. For example, in the mid-1970s top management at J. C. Penney decided to upgrade the store's quality and fashion image. In the mid-1990s, company management shifted its emphasis to appeal strongly to the youth market. As a result of these visionary decisions, Penney's has attracted a more upscale and youthful clientele, and the giant retailer has remained highly profitable. A study of executive succession corroborated these results with retailing firms: A change in an executive accounts for up to 45 percent of the organization's performance. For example, within a year after a new CEO is appointed, profits might increase 45 percent. In another firm, profits might plunge by the same amount in the year following executive succession.

Another study compared selected factors relating to senior managers in better-performing minicomputer firms and those in poorer-performing firms. The senior management in the more successful firms had previous experience in the electronics industry. In fact, the founder of the firm was likely to be the chief executive officer. The study implies that knowledge of the business *does* make a difference in leadership effectiveness. This leadership attribute will be pursued in detail in Chapter 2.

In addition to tangible evidence that leadership makes a difference, the perception of these differences is also meaningful. An understanding of these perceptions derives from **attribution theory,** the process of attributing causality to events. Gary Yukl explains that organizations are complex social systems of patterned interactions among people. In their efforts to understand (and simplify) organizational events, people interpret these events in simple human terms. One especially strong and prevalent explanation of organizational events is to attribute causality to leaders. They are viewed as heroes and heroines who determine the fates of their organizations.[9] The extraordinary success of Ford Motor Co. during the early 1990s is thus attributed largely to its top executive, Harold A. Poling. If we accept the logic of attribution theory in a positive way, most organizational successes are attributed to heroic leaders.

Research and Opinion: Formal Leadership Does Not Make a Difference

Leadership has a smaller impact on organizational outcomes than do forces in the situation, according to the antileadership argument. To personalize this perspective, imagine yourself appointed as the manager of a group of highly skilled investment bankers. How well your group performs could be attributed as much to their talent and to economic conditions as to your leadership. The two major arguments against the importance of leadership are substitutes for leadership, and leadership irrelevance.

Substitutes for Leadership.   At times competent leadership is not necessary, and incompetent leadership can be counterbalanced by certain factors in the work situation. Under these circumstances, leadership itself is of little consequence to the performance and satisfaction of team members. According to this viewpoint, many organizations have **substitutes for leadership.** Such substitutes are factors in the work environment that provide guidance and incentives to perform, making the leader's role almost superfluous.[10] Figure 1–1 shows four leadership substitutes: closely knit teams, intrinsic satisfaction, computer technology, and professional norms.

Closely knit teams of highly trained individuals.   When members of a cohesive, highly trained group are focused on a goal, they may require almost no leadership to accomplish their task. Several researchers have studied air traffic controllers who direct traffic into San Francisco, and pilots who land jet fighters on a nuclear aircraft carrier. With such groups, directive (decisive and task-oriented) leadership is seemingly unimportant. When danger is the highest, these groups rely more on each other than on a leader.

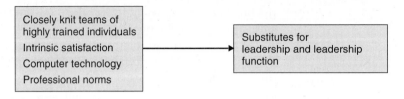

FIGURE 1–1

Substitutes for Leadership

Intrinsic satisfaction.   Employees engaged in work they find strongly self-motivating, or intrinsically satisfying, require a minimum of leadership. Part of the reason is that the task itself grabs the worker's attention and energy. The worker may require a minimum of leadership as long as the task is proceeding smoothly. Consultants observed a unique example of this principle at a manufacturer of camping equipment. The company manufactures sleeping bags of various qualities. At the top of the line are lightweight backpackers filled with down. At the other end are low-cost models filled with floor sweepings from a mattress factory.

Production workers must rotate among all the lines so that no one group claims exclusive rights to working on one product. Management contends that supervisory direction is almost unnecessary for production employees assigned to the top-of-the-line product, yet product quality exceeds expectation. Workers say they are proud to work on this line and often team together to solve production problems. The production of bottom-of-the-line sleeping bags, on the other hand, is fraught with both quality problems and below-standard output. Close supervision is required to deal with these problems, thus raising indirect costs. Consultants to this company have concluded that when assigned to produce the low-quality backpackers, the workers lose intrinsic satisfaction. As a consequence, they require considerable supervision and leadership.

Computer technology.   Some companies today use computer-aided monitoring and computer networking to take over many of the supervisor's leadership functions. The computer provides productivity and quality data, and directions for certain tasks are entered into the information system. Even error detection and goal setting are incorporated into some interaction systems. Instead of asking a supervisor for assistance, some employees use the computer network to ask for assistance from other workers. (We could argue here that the computer is being used to control rather than to lead workers.)

Professional norms.   Workers who incorporate strong professional norms often require a minimum of supervision and leadership.[11] A group of certified professional accountants may not need visionary leadership to inspire them to do an honest job of auditing the books of a client, or advising against tax fraud.

Although the leadership substitute concept has some merit, it reflects naiveté about the role of organizational leadership. Bass notes that self-management by groups and individuals requires delegation by a higher authority. In addition, higher-ranking managers provide guidance, encouragement, and support.[12]

Leader Irrelevance.   According to the theorizing of Jeffrey Pfeffer, leadership is irrelevant to most organizational outcomes. Rather, it is the situation that must be carefully analyzed. Pfeffer argues that factors outside the leader's control have a larger impact on business outcomes than do leadership actions.[13] During the early 1990s the trend toward many people working at home created a surge in demand for personal computers and related telecommunications equipment. The sales boom in this electronic equipment could be better attributed to an outside force than to inspirational leadership within computer companies.

Another aspect of the leader irrelevance argument is that high-level leaders have unilateral control over only a few resources. Furthermore, the leader's control of these resources is limited by obligations to stakeholders such as consumers and stockholders. Finally, firms tend to choose new organizational leaders whose values are compatible with those of the firm. The leaders therefore act in ways similar to previous leaders.

The leader irrelevance argument would have greater practical value if it were recast as a *leader constraint theory,* which would hold that leaders are constrained in what they can do, but still have plenty of room to influence others.

LEADERSHIP ROLES

Another way to gain an understanding of leadership is to examine the various roles carried out by leaders. A *role* in this context is an expected set of activities or behaviors stemming from one's job. Leadership roles are a subset of the managerial roles studied by Henry Mintzberg and others.[14] Before reading ahead to the summary of leadership roles, you are invited to do the accompanying leadership self-assessment exercise.

Leading is a complex activity, so it is not surprising that the researchers identified eight roles that can be classified as part of the leadership function of management.

1. *Figurehead.* Leaders, particularly high-ranking managers, spend some part of their time engaging in ceremonial activities, or acting as a figurehead. Four specific behaviors fit the figurehead role of a leader:
   a. entertaining clients or customers as an official representative of the organization
   b. making oneself available to outsiders as a representative of the organization

LEADERSHIP SELF-ASSESSMENT
EXERCISE 1–1   Readiness for the Leadership Role

Instructions: Indicate the extent to which you agree with each of the following statements, using the following scale: 1, disagree strongly; 2, disagree; 3, neutral; 4, agree; 5, agree strongly.

1. It is enjoyable having people count on me for ideas and suggestions.   1   2   3   4   5

2. It would be accurate to say that I have inspired other people.   1   2   3   4   5

3. It's a good practice to ask people provocative questions about their work.   1   2   3   4   5

4. It's easy for me to compliment others.   1   2   3   4   5

5. I like to cheer people up even when my own spirits are down.   1   2   3   4   5

6. What my team accomplishes is more important than my personal glory.   1   2   3   4   5

7. Many people imitate my ideas.   1   2   3   4   5

8. Building team spirit is important to me.   1   2   3   4   5

9. I would enjoy coaching other members of the team.   1   2   3   4   5

10. It is important to me to recognize others for their accomplishments.   1   2   3   4   5

11. I would enjoy entertaining visitors to my firm even if it interfered with my completing a report.   1   2   3   4   5

12. It would be fun for me to represent my team at gatherings outside our department.   1   2   3   4   5

13. The problems of my teammates are my problems too.   1   2   3   4   5

14. Resolving conflict is an activity I enjoy.   1   2   3   4   5

15. I would cooperate with another unit in the organization even if I disagreed with the position taken by its members.   1   2   3   4   5

16. I am an idea generator on the job.   1   2   3   4   5

17. It's fun for me to bargain whenever I have the opportunity.   1   2   3   4   5

18. Team members listen to me when I speak.   1   2   3   4   5

19. People have asked to me to assume the leadership of an activity several times in my life.　　1　2　3　4　5

20. I've always been a convincing person.　　　　1　2　3　4　5

Total score: _____

Scoring and interpretation: Calculate your total score by adding the numbers circled. A tentative interpretation of the scoring is as follows:

- 90–100　　high readiness for the leadership role
- 60–89　　moderate readiness for the leadership role
- 40–59　　some uneasiness with the leadership role
- 39 or less　low readiness for the leadership role

If you are already a successful leader and you scored low on this questionnaire, ignore your score. If you scored surprisingly low and you are not yet a leader, or are currently performing poorly as a leader, study the statements carefully. Consider changing your attitude or your behavior so that you can legitimately answer more of the statements with a 4 or a 5. Studying the rest of this text will give you additional insights that may be helpful in your development as a leader.

---

    c. serving as an official representative of the organization at gatherings outside the organization
    d. escorting official visitors

2. *Spokesperson.* When a manager acts as a spokesperson, the emphasis is on answering letters or inquiries and formally reporting to individuals and groups outside the manager's direct organizational unit. As a spokesperson, the managerial leader keeps five groups of people informed about the unit's activities, plans, capabilities, and possibilities (vision):
    a. upper-level management
    b. clients or customers
    c. other important outsiders such as labor unions
    d. professional colleagues
    e. the general public

Dealing with outside groups and the general public is usually the responsibility of top-level managers.

3. *Negotiator.* Part of almost any manager's job description is trying to make deals with others for needed resources. Three specific negotiating activities are:
    a. bargaining with superiors for funds, facilities, equipment, or other forms of support

      b. bargaining with other units in the organization for the use of staff, facilities, equipment, or other forms of support

      c. bargaining with suppliers and vendors for services, schedules, and delivery times

4. *Coach.* An effective leader takes the time to coach team members. Specific behaviors in this role include

      a. informally recognizing team members' achievements

      b. providing team members with feedback concerning ineffective performance

      c. ensuring that team members are informed of steps that can improve their performance

5. *Team builder.* A key aspect of a leader's role is to build an effective team. Activities contributing to this role include

      a. ensuring that team members are recognized for their accomplishments, such as through letters of appreciation

      b. initiating activities that contribute to group morale, such as giving parties and sponsoring sports teams

      c. holding periodic staff meetings to encourage team members to talk about their accomplishments, problems, and concerns

6. *Team player.* Related to the team-builder role is that of the team player. Three such behaviors are

      a. displaying appropriate personal conduct

      b. cooperating with other units in the organization

      c. displaying loyalty to superiors by supporting their plans and decisions fully

7. *Technical problem solver.* It is particularly important for supervisors and middle managers to help team members solve technical problems. Two such specific activities are

      a. serving as a technical expert or advisor

      b. performing individual contributor tasks on a regular basis, such as making sales calls or repairing machinery

8. *Entrepreneur.* Although not self-employed, managers who work in large organizations have some responsibility for suggesting innovative ideas or furthering the business aspects of the firm. Three entrepreneurial leadership role activities are

      a. reading trade publications and professional journals to keep up with what is happening in the industry and profession

      b. talking with customers or others in the organization to keep aware of changing needs and requirements

      c. getting involved in situations outside the unit that could suggest ways of improving the unit's performance, such as visiting other firms, attending professional meetings or trade shows, and participating in educational programs

A common thread in the leadership roles of a manager is that the managerial leader in some way inspires or influences others. A recent analysis in the *Harvard Business Review* concluded that the most basic role for corporate leaders is to release the human spirit that makes initiative, creativity, and entrepreneurship possible.[15] An important practical implication is that managers at every level can exercise leadership. For example, a team leader can make an important contribution to the firm's thrust for quality by explaining to team members how to minimize duplications in a mailing list. Leadership Skill-Building Exercise 1–1 provides additional insights into the various leadership roles.

Up to this point we have described the meaning of leadership, how leadership affects organizational performance, and the many activities carried out by leaders. You have had an opportunity to explore your attitudes toward occupying the leadership role. Let's now further personalize information about leadership.

LEADERSHIP SKILL-BUILDING
EXERCISE 1–1   Identifying Leadership Roles

Robert J. Eaton had distinguished himself as the president of General Motors Europe. He then was recruited to succeed Lee A. Iacocca as chief executive of Chrysler Corp. At the outset, Eaton was confident that he would be successful. "I have a strong background in product and manufacturing, and at least enough marketing and finance to run a successful business," he said (*Fortune*, p. 63). Within days of being appointed as the new chief executive, Eaton dispelled rumors that his low-key demeanor was a sign of indecisiveness or wimpiness.

At the outset, Eaton informed key staffers at Chrysler that he believed in participatory management, not consensus management. The message was that Eaton would be calling the shots. Chrysler's president, Robert A. Lutz, said in 1995 that Eaton was a strong, effective leader who knew when using an authoritarian style was more appropriate than encouraging participation.

A former colleague said that Eaton laid out broad objectives, but he gave group members the freedom to choose how to achieve the objectives. Eaton's preference for the team-leader management style had helped him attract and keep a high-caliber staff in Europe. He knew how to pump up profits in an automotive company that was already making a comeback.

Eaton faced a serious challenge in the spring of 1995 when investor Kirk Kerkorian teamed with Lee Iacocca in an attempt to buy a controlling interest in Chrysler. The deal would have been close to a $23 billion takeover. Included in Kerkorian's takeover strategy was a plan to finance part of the takeover with a $7.5 billion cash reserve that Chrysler had on hand. When Kerkorian first announced his intentions, Eaton attempted to placate him by raising Chrysler's dividend. He also agreed to start a $1 billion stock-buyback program designed to increase the price of Chrysler shares. However, he decided to fight the takeover. One of his arguments for opposing the bid was that Chrysler needed a huge reserve to cope with the uncertainties in the automobile business.

Skill development: Jot down all the leadership roles you perceived in the vignette. Specify the activity and the role it reflects. Refer to the eight leadership roles described previously.

_____

_____

_____

_____

Source: As reported in John Templeton, "Bob Eaton Is No Lee Iacocca—But He Doesn't Need to Be," *Business Week,* November 9, 1992, p. 96; "Iacocca's Last Stand at Chrysler," *Fortune,* April 20, 1992, p. 63; Gabriella Stern, "Chrylser's President Rejects Kerkorian's Reaching Out, Says He Isn't Interested," *The Wall Street Journal,* September 20, 1995, p. A4; Richard Lacayo, "The Sunshine Boys," *Time,* April 24, 1995, p. 55.

THE SATISFACTIONS AND FRUSTRATIONS OF BEING A LEADER

The term *leader* has a positive connotation for most people. To be called a leader is generally better than to be called a follower or a subordinate. (Note that the term *follower* is rapidly falling into disuse in modern organizations. The term *subordinate* is also being used less frequently. The preferred term for a person who reports to a leader has become *team member* or *group member.*) Yet being a leader, such as a team leader, vice president, or CEO, does not always bring personal satisfaction. Some leadership jobs are more fun than others. The leader of a high-performing group has more fun than the leader of a low-performing one. The owner of a large, successful restaurant has more fun than the owner of a small restaurant facing bankruptcy.

Because most of you are contemplating becoming a leader or moving further into a leadership role, it is worthwhile to examine some of the potential satisfactions and frustrations many people find in being an organizational leader.

Satisfactions of Leaders

The type of satisfactions that you might obtain from being a formal leader depends on your particular leadership position. Factors such as the amount of money you are paid and the type of people in your group influence your satisfaction. Following are seven sources of satisfaction that leaders often experience.

1. *A feeling of power and prestige.* Being a leader automatically grants you some power. Prestige is forthcoming because many people think highly of people who are leaders. In many organizations, top-level leaders are addressed as Mr., Mrs., or Ms., whereas lower-ranking people are referred to by their surnames.

2. *A chance to help others.* A leader works directly with people, often teaching them job skills, serving as a mentor, and listening to personal problems. Part of a leader's job is to help other people become managers and leaders. A leader often feels as much of a "people helper" as does a human resources manager or a counselor.

3. *High income.* Leaders, in general, receive higher pay than team members, and executive leaders in major business corporations typically earn several million dollars per year. If money is an important motivator or satisfier, being a leader has a built-in satisfaction. In some situations a team leader earns virtually the same amount of money as other team members. Occupying a leadership position, however, is a starting point on the path to high-paying leadership positions.

4. *Respect and status.* A leader frequently receives respect from group members. He or she also enjoys a higher status than people who are not occupying a leadership role. Status accompanies being appointed to a leadership position on or off the job. When an individual's personal qualifications match the position, his or her status is even higher.

5. *Good opportunities for advancement.* Once you become a leader, your advancement opportunities increase. Obtaining a leadership position is a vital first step for career advancement in many organizations. Staff or individual contributor positions help broaden a person's professional experience, but most executives rise through a managerial path.

6. *A feeling of "being in on" things.* A side benefit of being a leader is that you receive more inside information. For instance, as a manager you are invited to attend management meetings. In those meetings you are given information not passed along to individual contributors. One such tidbit might be plans for expansion or downsizing.

7. *An opportunity to control money and other resources.* A leader is often in the position of helping to prepare a department budget and authorize expenses. Even though you cannot spend this money personally, knowing that your judgment on financial matters is trusted does provide some satisfaction. Many leaders in both private and public organizations control annual budgets of several million dollars.

Dissatisfactions and Frustrations of Leaders

About one out of ten people in the work force is classified as a supervisor, administrator, or manager. Not every one of these people is a true leader. Yet the problems these people experience often stem from the leadership portions of their job. Many individual contributors refuse to accept a leadership role because of the frustrations they have seen leaders endure. The frustrations experienced by a wide range of people in leadership roles center around the problems described next.

1. *Too much uncompensated overtime.* People in leadership jobs are usually expected to work longer hours than other employees. Such unpaid hours are called *casual overtime.* People in organizational leadership positions typically spend about fifty-five hours per week working. During peak periods of peak demands, this figure can surge to eighty hours per week.

2. *Too many "headaches."* It would take several pages to list all the potential problems leaders face. Being a leader is a good way to discover the validity of Murphy's law: "If anything can go wrong, it will." A leader is subject to a batch of problems involving people and things. Many people find that a leadership position is a source of stress, and many managers experience burnout.

3. *Not enough authority to carry out responsibility.* People in managerial positions complain repeatedly that they are held responsible for things over which they have little control. As a leader, you might be expected to work with an ill-performing team member, yet you lack the power to fire him or her. Or you might be expected to produce high-quality service with too small a staff and no authority to become fully staffed.

4. *Loneliness.* The higher you rise as a leader, the more lonely you will be in a certain sense. Leadership limits the number of people in whom you can confide. It is awkward to confide negative feelings about your employer to a team member. It is equally awkward to complain about one group member to another. Some people in leadership positions feel lonely because they miss being "one of the gang."

5. *Too many problems involving people.* A major frustration facing a leader is the number of human resources problems requiring action. The lower your leadership position, the more such problems you face. For example, the office supervisor spends more time dealing with problem employees than does the chief financial officer.

6. *Too much organizational politics.* People at all levels of an organization, from the office assistant to the chairperson of the board, must be aware of political factors. Yet you can avoid politics more easily as an individual contributor than you can as a leader. As a leader you have to engage in political byplay from three directions: below, sideways, and upward.

Political tactics such as forming alliances and coalitions are a necessary part of a leader's role.

7. *The pursuit of conflicting goals.* A major challenge leaders face is to navigate among conflicting goals. The central theme of these dilemmas is attemptimg to grant others the authority to act independently, yet still getting them aligned or pulling together for a common purpose. As identified by a group of senior bank executives, these dilemmas are listed in Table 1–2.[16] Many of the topics relating to these conflicting goals are discussed at later points in the text.

A FRAMEWORK FOR UNDERSTANDING LEADERSHIP

Many different theories and explanations of leadership have been developed because of the interest in leadership as a practice and as a research topic. Several attempts have been made to integrate the large number of leadership theories into one comprehensive framework.[17] The framework presented

TABLE 1-2   The Nine Dilemmas Leaders Face

Broad-based leadership versus high-visibility leadership. Should the leader share leadership responsibilities widely, or be a highly visible charismatic leader?

Independence versus dependence. Should the organizational units work competitively against one another, or should they cooperate highly in a team mode?

Long term versus short term. Should the leader invest in projects with a long-term payout at the expense of actions that bring immediate results and profits?

Creativity versus discipline. Should imaginative thinking be encouraged at the expense of disciplined activities such as meeting budgets and deadlines?

Trust versus change. To maintain a high level of trust, it is important for the leader not to make too many changes, yet change is necessary to move the organization forward.

Bureaucracy busting versus economies of scale. If the leader decentralizes, there is less hierarchy, yet the organization may lose out on the cost savings possible from manufacturing or purchasing on a large scale.

Productivity versus people. To attain high productivity, it may be necessary to push people to a point where their health and personal lives are disrupted.

Leadership versus managerial and technical capability. The people-and-vision skills that produce good leadership are quite different from the managerial and technical skills required for efficient operations.

Revenue growth versus cost containment. Organizational growth requires free spending, but an organization must still control costs.

Source: Assembled and adapted from information in Thomas A. Stewart, "The Nine Dilemmas Leaders Face," *Fortune*, March 18, 1996, pp. 112–113.

here focuses on the major sets of variables that influence leadership effectiveness. The basic assumption underlying the framework can be expressed in terms of a simple formula with a profound meaning:

$$L = f (l, gm, s)$$

The formula means that the leadership process is a function of the leader, group members (or followers), and other situational variables.[18] In other words, leadership does not exist in the abstract but takes into account factors related to the leader, the person or persons being led, and a variety of forces in the environment. A charismatic and visionary leader might be just what a troubled organization needs to help it achieve world-class success. Yet a group of part-time telemarketers might need a more direct and focused type of leader to help them when their telephone calls mostly meet with abrupt rejection from the people solicited.

The model presented in Figure 1–2 extends this situational perspective.[19] According to this model, leadership can best be understood by examining its key variables: leader characteristics and traits, leader behavior and style, group member characteristics, and the internal and external environment. At the right side of the framework, **leadership effectiveness** refers to attaining desirable outcomes such as productivity, quality, and satisfaction in a given situation. Whether or not the leader is effective depends on the four sets of variables in the box.

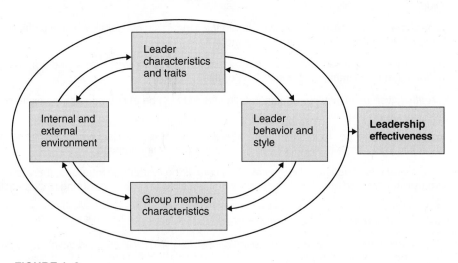

FIGURE 1–2

A Framework for Understanding Leadership

Source: An extension and adaptation of Stephen P. Robbins, Managing Today! *(Upper Saddle River, N.J.: Prentice-Hall, 1997), p. 419.*

Beginning at the top of the circle, *leader characteristics and traits* refers to the inner qualities, such as self-confidence and problem-solving ability, that help a leader function effectively in many situations. *Leader behavior and style* refers to the activities engaged in by the leader, including his or her characteristic approach, that relate to his or her effectiveness. A leader who frequently coaches group members and practices participative leadership, for example, might be effective in many circumstances. *Group member characteristics* refers to attributes of the group members that could have a bearing on how effective the leadership attempt will be. Intelligent and well-motivated group members, for example, facilitate the leader's doing an outstanding job. The *internal and external environment* also influences leadership effectiveness. A leader in a culturally diverse environment, for example, will need to have multicultural skills to be effective. All of the topics in this text fit somewhere into this model, and the fit will be more obvious at some places than at others. Table 1–3 outlines how the elements of the leadership model line up with chapters in the text.

The arrows connecting the four sets of variables in the model suggest a reciprocal influence among them. Some of these linkages are stronger than others. The most pronounced linkage is that a leader's characteristics and traits will typically influence the leader's style. If a given individual is

TABLE 1–3 Relationship Between Chapter Topics and the Framework for Understanding Leadership

Component of the Model	Relevant Chapter or Chapters
Leader characteristics and traits	Chapter 2, "Traits, Motives, and Characteristics of Leaders"
	Chapter 3, "Charismatic and Transformational Leadership"
	Chapter 11, "Creative Problem Solving and Leadership"
	Chapter 12, "Communication and Conflict Resolution Skills"
Leader behavior and style	Chapter 4, "Effective Leadership Behaviors and Attitudes"
	Chapter 5, "Leadership Styles"
	Chapter 8, "Influence Tactics of Leaders"
	Chapter 9, "Developing Teamwork"
Group member characteristics	Chapter 6, "Contingency and Situational Leadership"
	Chapter 10, "Motivation and Coaching Skills"
Internal and external environment	Chapter 13, "Strategic Leadership"
	Chapter 14, "International and Culturally Diverse Aspects of Leadership"
	Chapter 7, "Power, Politics, and Leadership"
	Chapter 15, "Leadership Development, Succession, and the Future"

extroverted, warm, and caring, it will be natural for him or her to adopt a people-oriented leadership style. Another linkage is that the group members' characteristics might influence the leader's style. If the members are capable and self-sufficient, the leader is likely to choose a style of leadership that grants freedom to the group. It will be easier for the leader to empower these people. A final linkage is that the internal and external environment can influence or mediate the leader's traits to some extent. In an environment in which creativity and risk taking is fostered, leaders are more likely to give expression to their tendencies toward creative problem solving and risk taking.

SKILL DEVELOPMENT IN LEADERSHIP

Developing leadership skills is more complex than developing a structured skill such as conducting an inventory audit or driving a golf ball. Nevertheless, you can develop leadership skills by reading this text, which follows a general learning model:

1. Conceptual knowledge and behavioral guidelines. Each chapter in this text presents useful information about leadership, including a section titled "Guidelines for Action and Skill Development."

2. Conceptual information demonstrated by examples and brief descriptions of leaders in action.

3. Experiential exercises. The text provides an opportunity for practice and personalization through cases, role plays, and self-assessment exercises. Self-quizzes are emphasized here because they are an effective method of helping you personalize the information, that is, link conceptual information to yourself. For example, you will read about the importance of assertiveness in leadership and also complete an assertiveness scale. Readers who look for opportunities to practice some of the leadership skills outside the classroom will acquire new skills more quickly.

4. Feedback on skill utilization, or performance, from others. Feedback exercises appear at several places in the text. Implementing some of the skills outside of the classroom will provide additional opportunities for feedback.

Chapter 15, about leadership development, provides more information about how leadership skills are developed. As you work through the text, keep the four-part learning model in mind.

SUMMARY

Leadership is the ability to inspire confidence in and support among the people who are needed to achieve organizational goals. Leading is a

major part of a manager's job, but a manager also plans, organizes, and controls. Leadership is said to deal with change, inspiration, motivation, and influence. In contrast, management deals more with maintaining equilibrium and the status quo. An important new development is to regard leadership as a long-term relationship, or partnership, between leaders and group members.

Some research evidence supports the widely accepted view that the leader affects organizational performance. It is also observed that many people attribute organizational performance to leadership actions. The concept of substitutes for leadership argues that factors in the work environment make the leader's role almost superfluous. Among these factors are closely knit teams of highly trained workers, intrinsic satisfaction with work, computer technology, and professional norms. Another antileadership argument is that the leader is irrelevant in most organizational outcomes because the situation is more important. Part of the leadership irrelevance argument is that the leader has unilateral control over only a few resources. Another part is that new leaders are chosen whose values are compatible with those of the firm.

Examining the roles carried out by leaders contributes to an understanding of the leadership function. Eight such leadership roles are the figurehead, spokesperson, negotiator, coach, team builder, team player, technical problem solver, and entrepreneur. An important implication of these roles is that managers at every level can exert leadership.

A leadership position is often a source of satisfaction to its holder, stemming from such factors as power, prestige, the opportunity to help others, high income, and the opportunity to control resources. At other times being a leader carries with it a number of frustrations, such as insufficient authority, dealing with human problems, and too much organizational politics. The leader also faces many dilemmas centering around the theme of granting organizational members independence versus getting them aligned.

The framework for understanding leadership presented here is based on the idea that the leadership process is a function of the leader, group members, and other situational variables. According to the model, leadership can best be understood by examing its key variables: leader characteristics and traits, leader behavior and style, group member characteristics, and the internal and external environment. Leadership effectiveness is dependent on all four sets of variables.

KEY TERMS

Leadership	Attribution theory	Leadership effectiveness
Partnership	Substitutes for leadership	

GUIDELINES FOR ACTION AND SKILL DEVELOPMENT

Vast amounts of information have been gathered about leaders and leadership, and many different leadership theories have been developed. A definitive review of leadership research, *Bass & Stogdill's Handbook of Leadership: Theory, Research, & Managerial Applications*, contains approximately 7,560 references.[20] Moreover, these references include very few magazine articles and trade books about leadership. Many leadership research findings and theories are confusing and contradictory. Nevertheless, from this thicket of information emerge many useful leadership concepts and techniques to guide you toward becoming a more effective leader.

As you work toward leadership effectiveness, first be familiar with the approaches to leadership described in this text. Then choose the formulation that seems best to fit the leadership situation you face. For example, if you are leading a team, review the information about team leadership. Typically an effective leader needs to combine several leadership approaches to meet the demands of a given situation. For instance, a leader might need to combine creative problem solving and emotional support to members to help the team rebound from a crisis.

DISCUSSION QUESTIONS AND ACTIVITIES

1. What would be a practical problem stemming from the idea that the leader creates a vision, whereas the manager implements it?

2. For what reasons are the terms *subordinate* and *follower* used less frequently than previously?

3. After reading this chapter, do you believe that a person who is not a "born leader" still has a chance of becoming an effective leader?

4. Identify a sports or business leader who you think is very effective. Present your observations to the class.

5. Why are persuasive skills so important for a leader?

6. Why are leaders often the highest-paid workers within an organization?

7. To what extent do you think the current emphasis on teamwork in business and government is a fad?

8. How might a leader apply the framework for understanding leadership presented in this chapter?

9. Several surveys have indicated that leadership is the most important topic in organizational behavior and management. How do you explain this finding?

10. Why are you or are you not suited for a leadership role at this stage in your career?

LEADERSHIP CASE PROBLEM

Phasedown at Park Fashions

For seventy-five years Park Fashions has been a leading manufacturer of men's and women's suits. The average retail price for the company's suits has been around $650 for several years. Demand for Park Fashions' suits peaked in 1988, when the company's gross revenues exceeded $100 million. Current annual sales have slipped to about $65 million. The Vermont plant of Park Fashions has a work force of 350, and the Tennessee plant employs 500. Four years ago, Park Fashions was sold by its founders to a publicly owned clothing manufacturer, Melrose Industries.

Park Fashions' president, Martha Albright, offered this explanation for the declining sales of Park Fashions' suits: "Unfortunately, we're part of a national trend. The demand for fine men's and women's suits has declined dramatically. Many suit manufacturers have closed up shop or been forced to diversify into other lines of clothing. Some clothing industry analysts have estimated that dress-down days alone have created a 20 percent decline in the demand for suits. They figure that if suits are worn four instead of five days per week, they will last 20 percent longer. Even if you don't take that arithmetic seriously, there has still been a deemphasis on wearing fine suits. Professionals wear less formal clothing to work than they did previously.

"Foreign competition has also hurt our business. At first it was low-priced competitors from Asia. Then came formidable competition from Eastern Europe. A smaller contributor to the decline of our business has been the fact that most people do not wear suits when dining in restaurants. On a recent Saturday night I dined at a restaurant near our Vermont location. I was the only person in the restaurant wearing a suit."

When asked why Park Fashions did not diversify into casual wear, Albright said, "We would have diversified if we were still an independent company. But our parent company is calling the shots. Melrose owns several companies in the casual wear business. They don't want competition from us in an already crowded field.

"Another diversification strategy that we turned away from was to develop a line of lower-priced suits. We would be cannibalizing sales from our flagship, high-price line. It's very difficult to sell both a high-price and a low-price line. After we have spent so many years developing an image of a high-fashion company, selling low-price suits would confuse our customers."

Shortly after giving the above analysis, Albright met with several members of the top management team from Melrose headquarters. After two somber planning sessions, top management laid out a plan for closing the Vermont plant. According to the plan, the plant would be shuttered in three years. In the meantime, the work force at the plant would be allowed to dwindle through attrition. At the same time, the work force at the Tennessee plant would be expanded. An undetermined number of supervisors and professionals from the Vermont plant would be offered positions in Tennessee. A Melrose executive explained carefully, "Martha, we want your plant to go down in a blaze of glory. While you are phasing down, I want you and Al [Al Bedouin, the plant manager in Vermont] to keep productivity and quality at the highest possible level.

"I want the rest of the world to know that Melrose is a high-class operation. We are keeping a plant going at close to full steam while it is being phased out. No other company in the industry could match that performance."

Albright and Bedouin both questioned the feasibility of a plant's being phased out in such a blaze of glory. The executive said that they should use their imagination. "Think of the possibilities," he said. "If your people develop an industry reputation, many opportunities may surface. Maybe another company will want to buy the Vermont plant. In such a case, you will all have jobs. Also, think of the skill you will develop in phasing down a plant."

1. What are several of the leadership challenges facing Albright and Bedouin?

2. How might Albright and Bedouin make use of the framework for understanding leadership presented in this chapter?

3. What evidence of excuse making by Albright have you observed?

The names of the managers and other identifying data have been changed at the request of the company.

LEADERSHIP SKILL-BUILDING EXERCISE 1–2

The Inspirational Leader

An important leadership characteristic is the ability to inspire others. To develop a preliminary feel for what it means to inspire a group, conduct the following role play. One person plays the role of a leader who is attempting to inspire a work group toward some important end, such as increasing sales or attaining new heights of quality. About five other people play the role of the inspirees (the people being inspired). After the leader makes his or her inspirational appeal, a group discussion is held of how well the appeal might have worked in reality.

Although it is early in the course to have learned how to inspire people, use this exercise as a baseline experience. Attempt to use whatever persuasive appeals you can.

Traits, Motives, and Characteristics of Leaders

LEARNING OBJECTIVES

After studying this chapter, you should be able to

1. identify general and task-related personality traits of leaders that contribute to leadership effectiveness.
2. identify key motives that contribute to leadership effectiveness.
3. describe cognitive factors associated with effective leadership, and summarize key points of the cognitive resource theory.
4. discuss the heredity versus environment issue in relation to leadership effectiveness.
5. summarize strengths and weaknesses of the trait approach to understanding leadership.

A seasoned company manager was describing the difference between George Fisher, the CEO of Eastman Kodak Company, and other heads of large corporations. "The difference is his unassuming manner," said the manager. "He walks into a room with his shirt sleeves rolled up. He brings his Midwestern style to management; he's down-to-earth, direct, and open. And he brings with him a high sense of urgency, and adheres to high standards in everything he does."[1]

This anecdote illustrates a workplace reality: When managers are evaluated by others in terms of their leadership effectiveness, their traits and personal characteristics are scrutinized. Instead of focusing only on the results the leader achieves, or the adequacy of his or her planning, those making the evaluation assign considerable weight to the leader's attributes, such as adhering to high standards. Many people believe intuitively that personal characteristics strongly determine leadership effectiveness.

The belief that certain personal characteristics and skills contribute to leadership effectiveness in many situations is the **universal theory of lead-**

ership. According to this theory, certain leadership traits are universally important—that is, they apply in all situations. This and the following chapter concentrate on the personal characteristics aspect of the universal theory; Chapter 4 describes the behaviors and skills that are part of the universal theory. Recognize, however, that personal characteristics are closely associated with leadership skills and behaviors. For example, creative thinking ability (a characteristic) helps a leader formulate an exciting vision (leadership behavior).

Characteristics associated with leadership can be classified into three broad categories: personality traits, motives, and cognitive factors. These categories of behavior serve as helpful guides but are not definitive. A convincing argument can often be made that an aspect of leadership placed in one category could be placed in another. Nevertheless, no matter how personal characteristics are classified, they point toward the conclusion that effective leaders are made of the *right stuff*. Published research about the trait (*great person*) approach first appeared at the turn of the century; it continues today. A full listing of every personal characteristic ever found to be associated with leadership would take several hundred pages. Therefore, included here are the major and most consistently found characteristics related to leadership effectiveness.

PERSONALITY TRAITS OF EFFECTIVE LEADERS

Observations by managers and human resource specialists, as well as dozens of research studies, indicate that leaders have certain personality traits.[2] These characteristics contribute to leadership effectiveness in many situations as long as the leader's style fits the situation reasonably well. For example, an executive might perform admirably as a leader in several different high-technology companies with different organizational cultures. However, his intellectual style might make him a poor fit with production workers. Leaders' personality traits can be divided into two groups: general personality traits, such as self-confidence and trustworthiness, and task-related traits, such as an internal locus of control.

General Personality Traits

We define a general personality trait as a trait that is observable both within and outside the context of work. That is, the same general traits are related to success and satisfaction in both work and personal life. Figure 2–1 lists the general personality traits that contribute to successful leadership.

Self-confidence. In virtually every leadership setting, it is important for the leader to be realistically self-confident. A leader who is self-assured

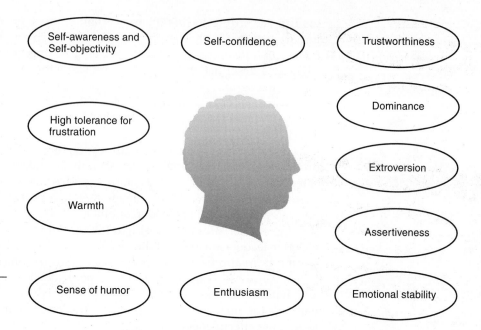

FIGURE 2–1

General Personality Traits of Effective Leaders

(Self-awareness and Self-objectivity · Self-confidence · Trustworthiness · High tolerance for frustration · Dominance · Warmth · Extroversion · Assertiveness · Sense of humor · Enthusiasm · Emotional stability)

without being bombastic or overbearing instills confidence in team members. Self-confidence was among the first leadership traits researchers identified. Recent research with leaders in many situations has continued to underscore the importance of this trait. In addition to being self-confident, the leader must project that self-confidence to the group. Quite often he or she can do so by using unequivocal wording, maintaining good posture, and making appropriate gestures, such as pointing an index finger outward.

Self-confidence is not only a personality trait; it also refers to the behavior a person exhibits in a number of situations. It is akin to being cool under pressure. We can conclude that a person is a self-confident leader when he or she retains composure during a crisis such as managing a large product recall.

CEO John Reed of Citicorp exemplifies a self-confident leader. He has worked his way into and out of poor company performance and engineered a comeback that quieted his critics. Asked at one time by a business journalist why he deserved to remain CEO, Reed said, "Well, you know my sense of it is, I know what has to be done. I think I understand the problem. I think I have the right sort of response to it, and it is likely that I will get it done."[3]

Trustworthiness.   Group members consistently believe that leaders must display honesty, integrity, and credibility, thus engendering trust. Leaders themselves believe that honesty makes a difference in their effectiveness. Warren G. Bennis, a noted leadership authority, interviewed more than one hundred corporate leaders and fifty private-sector leaders during a thirteen-year period. One of the common threads he found was the capacity of leaders to generate and sustain trust. Under the umbrella term of *trust*, Bennis included competence, caring, reliability, predictability, and integrity. He observed a consistency among what leaders think, feel, and do. Bennis said that it drives people crazy when bosses do not walk their talk.[4]

Trust can be eroded in ways other than inconsistency and dishonesty. Bennis believes that the large disparity between the pay of top executives and that of lower-ranking workers damages trust. He contends that when CEOs of large corporations make 187 times the pay of average workers, it creates an "us versus them" mentality within the work force rather than promoting teamwork.[5]

The importance of honesty also emerged in a study by the Center for Creative Leadership. Research showed that managers who become executive leaders are likely to espouse the following formula: "I will do exactly what I say I will do when I say I will do it. If I change my mind, I will tell you in advance so you will not be harmed by my actions."[6]

Dominance.   A dominant person imposes his or her will on others. As a consequence, a dominant leader is often seen as domineering or bossy. Whereas dominance was considered almost synonymous with leadership in the early days of leadership research, the more modern viewpoint recognizes that many other traits are involved.

Extroversion.   Extroversion has been recognized for its contribution to leadership effectiveness because it is helpful for leaders to be gregarious and outgoing in most situations. Also, extroverts are more likely to want to assume a leadership role and participate in group activities.[7] Even though it is logical to think that extroversion is related to leadership, many effective leaders are laid-back and even introverted. AT&T executive Bob Allen, for example, is quiet and reserved.

Assertiveness.   In recent years more attention has been paid to assertiveness as a leadership trait than to dominance and extroversion. **Assertiveness** refers to being forthright in expressing demands, opinions, feelings, and attitudes. Assertiveness helps leaders perform many tasks and achieve goals. Among them are confronting group members about their mistakes, demanding higher performance, setting high expectations, and making legitimate demands on higher management.

To be assertive differs significantly from being aggressive or passive. Aggressive people express their demands in an overly pushy, obnoxious, and abrasive manner; passive people suppress their own ideas, attitudes, feelings, and thoughts as if they were likely to be perceived as controversial. As a result of being passive, a person might not be recommended for large salary increases, good assignments, and promotions.

To determine how assertive you are, do the accompanying leadership self-assessment exercise.

LEADERSHIP SELF-ASSESSMENT
EXERCISE 2–1   The Assertiveness Scale

Directions: Indicate whether each of the following statements is mostly true or mostly false as it applies to you. If in doubt about your reaction to a particular statement, think of how you would *generally* respond.

	Mostly True	Mostly False
1. It is extremely difficult for me to turn down a sales representative when he or she is a nice person.	____	____
2. I express criticism freely.	____	____
3. If another person is being very unfair, I bring it to that person's attention.	____	____
4. Work is no place to let your feelings show.	____	____
5. It's no use asking for favors; people get what they deserve.	____	____
6. Business is not the place for tact; say what you think.	____	____
7. If a person looks as if he or she is in a hurry, I let that person in front of me in a supermarket line.	____	____
8. A weakness of mine is that I'm too nice a person.	____	____
9. If my restaurant bill is even 50 cents more than it should be, I demand that the mistake be corrected.	____	____
10. If the mood strikes me, I will laugh out loud in public.	____	____
11. People would describe me as too outspoken.	____	____
12. I am quite willing to have the store take back a piece of furniture that was scratched upon delivery.	____	____
13. I dread having to express anger toward a coworker.	____	____
14. People often say that I'm too reserved and emotionally controlled.	____	____
15. Nice people finish last in business.	____	____

16. I fight for my rights down to the last detail. ____ ____

17. I have no misgivings about returning an overcoat to the store if it doesn't fit me right. ____ ____

18. After I have an argument with a person, I try to avoid him or her. ____ ____

19. I insist that my spouse (or roommate or partner) do his or her fair share of undesirable chores. ____ ____

20. It is difficult for me to look directly at another person when the two of us are in disagreement. ____ ____

21. I have cried among friends more than once. ____ ____

22. If someone near me at a movie keeps up a conversation with another person, I ask him or her to stop. ____ ____

23. I am able to turn down social engagements with people I do not particularly care for. ____ ____

24. It is in poor taste to express what you really feel about another individual. ____ ____

25. I sometimes show my anger by swearing at or belittling another person. ____ ____

26. I am reluctant to speak up at a meeting. ____ ____

27. I find it relatively easy to ask friends for small favors such as giving me a ride to work while my car is being repaired. ____ ____

28. If another person is talking very loudly in a restaurant and it bothers me, I inform that person. ____ ____

29. I often finish other people's sentences for them. ____ ____

30. It is relatively easy for me to express love and affection toward another person. ____ ____

Scoring Key

1. Mostly false	6. Mostly true	11. Mostly true
2. Mostly true	7. Mostly false	12. Mostly true
3. Mostly true	8. Mostly false	13. Mostly false
4. Mostly false	9. Mostly true	14. Mostly false
5. Mostly false	10. Mostly true	15. Mostly true

16. Mostly true	21. Mostly true	26. Mostly false
17. Mostly true	22. Mostly true	27. Mostly true
18. Mostly false	23. Mostly true	28. Mostly true
19. Mostly true	24. Mostly true	29. Mostly true
20. Mostly false	25. Mostly true	30. Mostly true

Interpretation: Score +1 for each of your answers that agrees with the scoring key.

0–15	Nonassertive
16–24	Assertive
25+	Aggressive

Do this exercise again about thirty days from now to give yourself some indication of the stability of your answers. You might also discuss your answers with a close friend to determine if that person has a similar perception of your assertiveness.

Emotional Stability.   Anyone who has ever worked for an unstable boss will attest to the importance of emotional stability as a leadership trait. **Emotional stability** refers to the ability to control emotions to the point that one's emotional responses are appropriate to the occasion. Emotions associated with low emotional stability include anxiety, depression, anger, embarrassment, and worry.

Emotional stability is an important leadership trait because group members expect and need consistency in the way they are treated. A sales manager had this to say about her boss, the vice president of marketing: "It was difficult to know whether to bring problems to Larry's attention. Some days he would compliment me for taking customer problems seriously. Other times he would rant and rave about the ineffectiveness of the sales department. We all worry about having our performance appraised on one of Larry's crazy days."

One study found that executive leaders who are emotionally unstable and lack composure are more likely to handle pressure poorly and give in to moodiness, outbursts of anger, and inconsistent behavior. Such inconsistency undermines their relationships with group members, peers, and superiors. In contrast, effective leaders are generally calm, confident, and predictable during a crisis.[8]

Enthusiasm.   In almost all leadership situations, it is desirable for the leader to be enthusiastic. Group members tend to respond positively to enthusiasm, partly because enthusiasm may be perceived as a reward for

LEADER IN ACTION

Robyn Holden of Emergency 911 Security

Robyn Holden openly expresses her enthusiasm for her business. "I love what I do," says the founder of Emergency 911 Security, based in Washington, D.C. The company designs and installs security systems for commercial, federal, and residential clients. She notes that people often say to her, "Well, Robyn, you're making a lot of money." Yet Holden contends that loving what she does is more important to her than the money. Her passion for her work helps inspire her small work force.

Holden thinks she knows why her enthusiasm for her work has not dwindled. Ensuring customer safety is a major part of the answer. "I know I'm protecting people," she says. "I'm saving people's lives. I'm giving them the opportunity to develop a comfort level within their businesses or within their homes." Holden is able to articulate this mission to her staff members, which helps them keep focused on the purpose of their work.

Source: Adapted from Debra Phillips, "The Joy of Business: Keeping the Passion Alive in Your Business," *Entrepreneur*, August 1995, p. 144.

constructive behavior. Enthusiasm is also a desirable leadership trait because it helps build good relationships with team members. A leader can express enthusiasm both verbally ("Great job"; "I love it") and nonverbally (making a "high five" gesture). An executive newsletter made an enthusiastic comment about enthusiasm as a leadership trait:

> People look to you for [enthusiasm] to inspire them. It is the greatest tool for motivating others and for getting things done. As a leader, you have to get out in front of your people. Even the most enthusiastic employee is loath to show more of it than his or her boss. If you don't project a gung-ho attitude, everybody else will hold back.[9]

The accompanying Leader in Action insert above presents a portrait of a leader known for her enthusiasm.

Sense of Humor.   Some see a sense of humor as a trait, and some as a behavior. However you classify it, the effective use of humor is considered an important part of a leader's role. Humor serves such functions in the workplace as relieving tension and boredom and defusing hostility. Because humor helps the leader dissolve tension and defuse conflict, it helps her or him exert power over the group. Psychologist Paul McGhee contends that "more companies now realize that people who are able to lighten up in stressful situations are a plus to their organizations."[10]

Self-effacing humor is the choice of comedians and organizational leaders alike. By being self-effacing, the leader makes a point without insulting or slighting anybody. A vice president of marketing at Sun Microsystems once said, "I want you people to design a work station so uncomplicated that even managers at my level could learn how to use it."

Warmth.   Being a warm person and projecting that warmth contribute to leadership effectiveness in several ways. First, warmth facilitates the establishment of rapport with group members. Second, the projection of warmth is a key component of charisma. Third, warmth is a trait that facilitates providing emotional support to group members. Giving such support is an important leadership behavior. Fourth, in the words of Kogan Page, "Warmth comes with the territory. Cold fish don't make good leaders because they turn people off."[11]

High Tolerance for Frustration.   Two researchers content-analyzed televised interviews of thirty business executives. Most of the executives showed **high tolerance for frustration,** or the ability to cope with the blocking of goal attainment.[12] This trait is important because a leader encounters a great many frustrations. For example, a manager might invest a year in developing a strategic plan and then be informed that top management does not want the plan implemented.

Self-awareness and Self-objectivity.   Effective leaders are aware of their strengths and limitations. This awareness enables them to capitalize upon their strengths and develop their weaknesses. A leader might realize, for example, that he or she is naturally distrustful of others. Awareness of this problem cautions the leader not to distrust people without good evidence. Self-awareness and self-objectivity will be described further in Chapter 15.

Task-Related Personality Traits

Certain personality traits of effective leaders are closely associated with task accomplishment even though they still seem to fall more accurately in the trait category rather than the behavior category. The task-related traits described here are outlined in Figure 2–2.

Initiative.   Exercising **initiative,** or being a self-starter, refers to taking action without support and stimulation from others. A person aspiring to leadership assignments should recognize that initiative is a personality trait sought in potential leaders. Initiative is also related to problem-finding ability—you need to exercise initiative to search for worthwhile problems. An example would be a team leader of a packing design group suggesting to the group that they hold a brainstorming session to identify services they could offer the company in addition to designing packages.

   Initiative refers to the proactive side of leadership. Rather than just reacting to events, effective leaders make choices and take action that leads to change.[13] The new president of a building supply company exemplifies such

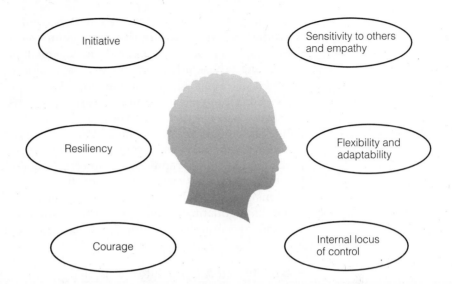

FIGURE 2–2

Task-Related Person-ality Traits of Leaders

proactive leadership. He was appointed after a larger company bought the supply company, allowing the former owner to retire. After four weeks on the job, the new president made some important changes:

> The company I was invited to run was doing quite well. But I wasn't there for more than ten days when I found out a lot of money was being thrown out the window. There were also a lot of good opportunities being neglected. Worst of all, the former owner had two relatives on the payroll who were being paid management salaries for doing practically nothing. One guy was called "customer relations coordinator," and did practically nothing but go to lunch and play golf with customers. A gal with the title "inventory manager" presided over a warehouse for basically unsalable merchandise. I offered both of these people honest jobs at much-reduced pay.
>
> I also found that nobody in the marketing department was cultivating new customers. The sales personnel stayed with their cozy relationships with established customers. New business development translated into waiting for the phone to ring. I immediately worked with the marketing people to set some tight quotas on pursuing new business leads.
>
> At first my changes brought me no love and admiration. Yet after awhile most people admitted that the changes I made were necessary. As bigger profits began to stream in, I became much more popular.

Sensitivity to Others and Empathy.   In an effort to influence others, it is instrumental for the leader to understand group members, their interests and attitudes, and how to reach them. According to Jeffrey Pfeffer, this type of **sensitivity to others** means understanding who the group members are, what their position on issues is, and how to best communicate with and influence them.[14] Achieving sensitivity to others requires **empathy,** the ability to place oneself in the other person's shoes.

To lack sensitivity to others is to risk becoming a failed leader. A series of studies spanning twenty-five years compared derailed executives with those who had progressed to senior management positions. A *derailed* executive is one whose advancement has been blocked because of a poor fit between job requirements and personal skills. Leaders in the United States and in Europe appear to derail for the same reasons. The leading category of fatal flaws was insensitivity to others, characterized by an abrasive, intimidating, bullying style.[15] Insensitivity to others is particularly self-defeating in a large, bureaucratic firm because such firms emphasize politeness. You can probably think of a tyrannical, yet powerful leader. It is important to realize, however, that such tyrants are the exception.

Sensitivity to others is an important leadership trait also because it enhances negotiating effectiveness. The sensitive leader can "read" the other side more accurately, thus doing a better job in the negotiator role. Union leaders who bargain effectively are particularly well respected.

Flexibility and Adaptability.   A leader is someone who facilitates change. It therefore follows that a leader must be flexible enough to cope with such changes as technological advances, downsizings, a shifting customer base, and a changing work force. **Flexibility**, or the ability to adjust to different situations, has long been recognized as an important leadership characteristic. Leaders who are flexible are able to adjust to the demands of different situations, much as antiblock brakes enable an automobile to adjust to changes in road conditions. Without the underlying trait of flexibility, a person could be an effective leader in only one or two situations. The public utility industry exemplifies a field in which situation adaptability is particularly important because top executives are required to provide leadership for both the regulated and nonregulated units within their organization.

Internal Locus of Control.   People with an **internal locus of control** believe that they are the prime mover behind events. Thus, an internal locus of control helps a leader in the role of a take-charge person because the leader believes fundamentally in his or her innate capacity to take charge. An internal locus of control is closely related to self-confidence. A strong internal locus facilitates self-confidence because the person perceives that he or she can control circumstances enough to perform well.

Supervisory leaders with an internal locus of control are favored by group members.[16] One reason is that an "internal" person is perceived as more powerful than an "external" person because he or she takes responsibility for events. The dean of a liberal arts college provides an example of how an internal locus of control contributes to effective leadership. Presented with declining enrollment figures, and the threat of a drastic cutback at her college, the dean said:

> Indeed, our enrollment has been declining. Yet there are many liberal arts colleges that have stabilized enrollments. Even better, there are many other liberal

arts colleges that are expanding in an era of declining enrollment. The reason these liberal arts colleges are succeeding is that they are offering something the world wants. Either their reputation is so glowing that a degree from them is worth the money, or they offer very useful, marketable degrees. We can't upgrade our prestige in the next year, but we can put together a program with a recession-proof demand.

The dean's pep talk, with its take-charge attitude, reflected the dean's internal locus of control and led to constructive change. The college developed a master's degree program in school psychology that met with high enough demand to stabilize enrollment and remove the environmental threat.

Leadership Skill-Building Exercise 2–1 provides you an opportunity to begin strengthening your internal locus of control. Considerable further work would be required to shift from an external to an internal locus of control.

LEADERSHIP SKILL-BUILDING EXERCISE 2–1   Developing an Internal Locus of Control

A person's locus of control is usually a deeply ingrained thinking pattern that develops over a period of many years. Nevertheless, you can begin developing a stronger internal locus of control by analyzing past successes and failures to determine how much influence you had on the outcome of these events. By repeatedly analyzing the relative contribution of internal versus external factors in shaping events, you may learn to feel more in charge of key events in your life. The events listed below are a good starting point.

1. A contest or athletic event that you either won or made a good showing in.

   What were the factors within your control that led to your winning or making a good showing?_____

   _____

   _____

   _____

   What were the factors beyond your control that led to your winning or making a good showing?_____

   _____

   _____

   _____

2. A course in which you received a poor grade

What were the factors within your control that led to this poor grade? _____

_____

_____

What were the factors beyond your control that led to this poor grade? _____

_____

_____

3. A group project to which you were assigned that worked out poorly

What were the factors within your control that led to this poor result? _____

_____

_____

What were the factors beyond your control that led to this poor result? _____

_____

_____

After you have prepared your individual analysis, you may find it helpful to discuss your observations in small groups. Focus on how people could have profited from a stronger internal locus of control in the situations analyzed.

Courage.   Leaders need courage to face the challenges of taking prudent risks and taking initiative in general. They must also face up to responsibility, and be willing to put their reputations on the line. It takes courage for a leader to suggest a new undertaking because if the undertaking fails, the leader is often seen as having failed. The more faith people place in the power of leaders to cause events, the more strongly they blame leaders when outcomes are unfavorable. Beyond these reasons for the importance of courage, Peter Koestenbaum emphasizes, "It is on the personal side of leadership—in the sense of greatness and inspiration, focus on people, their meanings, their souls and hearts, their destinies—that the next breakthrough in business will occur."[17]

Resiliency.   An important observation about effective leaders, as well as managers in general, is that they are resilient—they bounce back quickly

LEADER IN ACTION

Larry Ellison of Oracle Corp.

Lawrence J. Ellison founded Oracle Corp. and built it into the leading supplier of powerful database programs. Although less well known than rival Microsoft Corp., Oracle is the second largest company in the software business, and Ellison is the second richest software executive. Annual revenues for his company are projected to exceed $4 billion for the next several years. Ellison is among the two dozen wealthiest people in the United States, and leads an adventurous personal life. A divorced father and active parent, he lives in a sprawling Japanese-style estate in Atherton, California, and also owns a house in San Francisco. He is a high-fashion dresser, gourmet, wine connoisseur, and physical fitness buff, and dates a variety of stylish young women.

Before achieving his fantasylike success, Ellison bounced back from heavy adversity, including being abandoned by his mother as an infant. His adopted Russian immigrant parents stepped in to raise him in a modest Chicago neighborhood. Ellison's next major brush with adversity was dropping out of the University of Illinois after turning in a lackluster performance.

After eight years of working as a computer programmer, Ellison founded Oracle with a partner in 1973. The company experienced rapid growth after 1980. By around 1990, however, the company was in trouble, partly because it promised more in the way of products than it could deliver. At one point, accounts receivables rose to almost 50 percent of sales, in part because some of the company's software did not live up to expectations. The company announced a loss of close to $29 million, and the stock slid from $28 to $5. Oracle was close to bankruptcy, and the Securities and Exchange Commission was investigating suspected illicit accounting practices such as recording sales too far in advance of an actual commitment.

Ellison made the decision to stay with his company and bring it back to health. He replaced his management team, tightened financial controls, and introduced a new compensation system that paid sales commissions only after products were actually shipped. (This helped to reduce inflated claims of completed sales.) Part of the comeback strategy was to hire consultants to help install Oracle software at customer locations. During the company restructuring, Ellison took a vacation in Hawaii. While bodysurfing, he was smashed into coral by a giant wave. His injuries included a fractured neck and a punctured lung. Despite his brush with death, Ellison continued to lead his company on its comeback trail.

Ellison says he is inspired by Miyamoto Musashi, a sixteenth-century Japanese samurai who could kill if necessary but was also an artist and poet. Larry Ellison's most pressing career goal these days is for Oracle to become the world's leading software provider.

Source: Michael Warshaw, "10th Annual Great Comebacks," *Success*, August 1995, pp. 34–36; Richard Brandt, "Can Larry Beat Bill?" *Business Week*, May 15, 1995, pp. 88–90.

from setbacks such as budget cuts, demotions, and being fired. An intensive study of executive leaders revealed that they don't even think about failure; in fact, they don't even use the word. Instead, they rely on synonyms such as *mistake, glitch, bungle,* and *setback.*[18] In practice, this means that the leader sets an example for team members by not crumbling when something goes wrong. Instead, the leader tries to conduct business as usual. The accompanying Leader in Action insert above illustrates the resiliency of an influential figure in the software industry.

LEADERSHIP MOTIVES

Effective leaders, as opposed to nonleaders and less effective leaders, have frequently been distinguished by their motives and needs. In general, leaders have an intense desire to occupy a position of responsibility for others and to control them. Figure 2–3 outlines four specific leadership motives or needs. All four motives can be considered task-related.

The Power Motive

Effective leaders have a strong need to control resources. Leaders with high power motives have three dominant characteristics: (1) They act with vigor and determination to exert their power, (2) they invest much time in thinking about ways to alter the behavior and thinking of others; and (3) they care about their personal standing with those around them.[19] The power motive is important because it means that the leader is interested in influencing others. Without power, it is much more difficult to influence others. Power is not necessarily good or evil; it can be used for the sake of the power holder (personalized power motive), or for helping others (socialized power motive).[20]

Personalized Power Motive.   Leaders with a personalized power motive seek power mostly to further their own interests. They crave the trappings

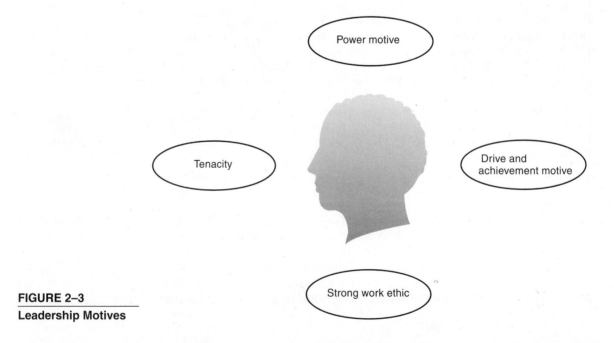

FIGURE 2–3

Leadership Motives

of power, such as status symbols, luxury, and money. In recent years, some leaders have taken up power boating, or racing powerful, high-speed boats. When asked how he liked his power boating experience, an entrepreneurial leader replied, "It's fun, but the start-up costs are about $350,000."

Donald Trump is seen as a leader with a strong personalized power motive because of his love of the trappings of power. He has a penchant for naming yachts, hotels, and office buildings after himself. Nevertheless, he gives his financial managers considerable latitude in managing his enterprises. In contrast to Trump, some leaders with strong personalized power motives typically enjoy dominating others. Their need for dominance can lead to submissive subordinates who are frequently sycophants and yes-persons.

Socialized Power Motive.   Leaders with a socialized power motive use power primarily to achieve organizational goals or a vision. In this context, the term *socialized* means that the leader uses power primarily to help others. As a result, he or she is likely to provide more effective leadership. Leaders with socialized power motives, in contrast to leaders with personalized power motives, tend to be more emotionally mature. Also, they exercise power more for the benefit of the entire organization and are less likely to manipulate others through the use of power. Leaders with socialized power motives are less defensive, and are more willing to accept expert advice. Finally, they have longer-range perspectives.[21]

It is important not to draw a rigid dichotomy between leaders with personalized power motives and those with socialized power motives. The distinction between doing good for others and doing good for oneself is often made on the basis of very subjective criteria. A case in point is H. Ross Perot, the highly successful business founder, social activist, and two-time candidate for U.S. president. Perot supporters attest to his genuine desire to create a good life for others and to serve them. His detractors, however, regard Perot as a leader obsessed with power and self-importance.

Drive and Achievement Motivation

Leaders are known for the strong effort they invest in achieving work goals. The importance of strong motivation for leadership is well accepted. **Drive** refers to a propensity to put forth high energy into achieving goals and to a persistence in applying that energy. Drive also includes **achievement motivation,** finding joy in accomplishment for its own sake. Entrepreneurs and high-level corporate managers usually have strong achievement motivations. A person with a strong achievement motivation has a consistent desire to:

1. achieve through one's own efforts and take responsibility for success or failure;

2. take moderate risks that can be handled through one's own efforts;

3. receive feedback on level of performance;

4. introduce novel, innovative, or creative solutions;

5. plan and set goals.[22]

To personalize the information just presented about the achievement motive, do Leadership Self-Assessment Exercise 2–2.

LEADERSHIP SELF-ASSESSMENT
EXERCISE 2–2   How Strong Is Your Achievement Motive?

Answer the following questions Yes or No to compare your traits to those of people with a strong achievement motive (or need).

_____ 1. am flexible enough to put work out of my mind when I am off the job.

_____ 2. I very much enjoy gambling, sports pools, lotteries, races, and so forth.

_____ 3. I dislike seeing things such as fuel and water wasted.

_____ 4. I give a good deal of respect to people in positions superior to mine.

_____ 5. I would prefer working with a congenial but somewhat incompetent partner to working with one who is difficult but highly competent.

_____ 6. I frequently have a compulsion to do things today rather than put them off until tomorrow.

_____ 7. I have a strong interest in the lives of successful people.

_____ 8. I feel secure enough to spend money without much planning for the future.

Explanation

Give yourself one point for each correct answer.

1. No. Whether you judge it as good or bad, strivers have a strong sense of involvement and continue to dwell on work problems long after quitting time.

2. No. Those with high aspirations rarely engage in the magical thinking that success comes through outside forces.

3. Yes. Achievers abhor waste in any form and try to avoid unnecessary motions.

4. Yes. Those with a strong need for achievement take on successful role models. If a person does not respect successful role models, he or she probably has a self-defeating attitude.

5. No. Most achievement-motivated people don't agree with this type of partner arrangement. They are willing to sacrifice congeniality for a partner who helps them make it to the top.

6. Yes. Achievers usually have a strong sense of time urgency. They keep ahead of their work by finishing assignments on time.

7. Yes. (See No. 4 above.)

8. No. Most achievers are good planners. They use money in the same manner as they use their personal resources.

Interpretation

7–8 points   high achievement motive; you think and act like a striver
4–6 points   achievement motive equal to that of most people
0–3 points   low achievement motive

If your score was low, remember that achievement is a relative term. We have largely been discussing success in the workplace. You may find that your sense of success lies elsewhere.

Source: Reprinted and adapted with permission from the files of psychologist Salvatore V. Didato, Ph.D., 1993.

Strong Work Ethic

Effective leaders typically have a strong **work ethic,** a firm belief in the dignity of work. People with a strong work ethic are well motivated because they value hard work; not to work hard clashes with their values. A strong work ethic helps the organizational leader believe that the group task is worthwhile. For example, the outside world might not think that a poultry-preparation factory is so important, but an effective leader of one of Frank Perdue's chicken factories said, "Everybody works hard here and I set the example. We are making it possible for thousands of families to eat nutritious food."

Tenacity

A final observation about the motivational characteristics of organizational leaders is that they are *tenacious.* Leaders are better at overcoming obstacles (as mentioned in relation to resiliency) than are nonleaders. Tenacity multiplies in importance for organizational leaders because it can take so long to implement a new program or consummate a business deal such as acquiring another company.

The Bennis study of 150 leaders reinforces the link between leadership effectiveness and tenacity. All interviewees embodied a strongly developed sense of purpose and a willful determination to achieve what they wanted. "Without that," said Bennis, "organizations and individuals are not powerful. The central ingredient of power is purpose."[23]

COGNITIVE FACTORS AND LEADERSHIP

Mental ability as well as personality is important for leadership success. To inspire people, bring about constructive change, and solve problems creatively, leaders need to be mentally sharp. Another mental requirement for leaders is the ability to sort out essential information from the less essential, and then store the most important in memory. Problem solving and intellectual skills are referred to collectively as **cognitive factors.** The term *cognition* refers to the mental process or faculty by which knowledge is gathered. Our discussion of cognitive factors and leadership begins with a description of mental ability and the cognitive resource theory. We then describe the specific cognitive factors shown in Figure 2–4.

Mental Ability and the Cognitive Resource Theory

A current theory of leadership supports what has been known for many years: Effective leaders have good problem-solving ability. **Cognitive resource theory** is based on two key assumptions: (1) Intelligent and competent leaders make more effective plans, decisions, and strategies than do leaders with less intelligence or competence. (2) Leaders of task groups communicate their plans, decisions, and action strategies primarily in the form of directive behavior. Cognitive resource theory is based on several hypotheses that focus on mental ability:

1. If a leader is experiencing stress, his or her intellectual abilities will be diverted from the task at hand. As a result, measures of leader intelligence and competence will not correlate with group performance when the leader is stressed.

2. The intellectual abilities of directive leaders will correlate more highly with group performance than will the intellectual abilities of nondirective leaders.

3. A leader's intellectual abilities will be related to group performance to the degree that the task requires the use of intellectual ability.[24]

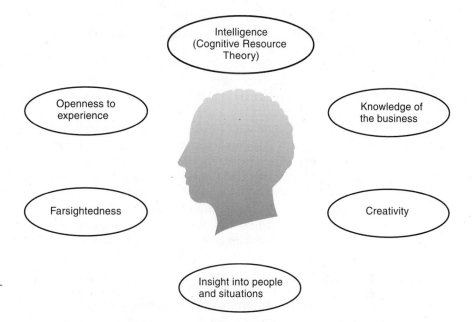

FIGURE 2–4

Cognitive Factors and Leadership

The general thrust of the cognitive resource theory is plausible, and highlights the importance of intelligence in many leadership situations. Robert P. Vecchio critically examined the theory and found support for the second hypothesis. Intelligence makes a bigger contribution with a directive leader because such a leader makes more problem-solving suggestions than does a nondirective leader.[25] For example, a group member might ask a directive leader, "What new projects for next year should we be working on?" The directive leader might reply, "Here's what I want you to be working on. I'll prepare a list right now." The nondirective leader might reply, "What projects do you think you should be working on?"

Strong problem-solving ability is an asset to leaders, who must collect, integrate, and interpret enormous amounts of data. Computers add to the intellectual demands of a leader's job as more data is brought to his or her attention. Managerial leaders also need intelligence to run complex software.

Despite the importance of problem-solving ability for leadership, an advanced capacity for solving abstract problems and an overly intellectual style can create problems. A leader with too strong a penchant for gathering and analyzing information may suffer from *analysis paralysis.* The leader might keep analyzing problems at the expense of taking decisive action.

Knowledge of the Business

Intellectual ability is closely related to having knowledge of the business. An effective leader has to be technically or professionally competent in some discipline, particularly when leading a group of specialists. It is difficult for the leader to establish rapport with group members when he or she does not know what they are doing and when the group does not respect the leader's technical skills. At a minimum, the leader of specialists must be "snow proof," that is, not readily bluffed about technical matters.

The importance of knowledge of the business is increasingly being recognized as an attribute of executive leadership. Leaders at every level are expected to bring forth useful ideas for carrying out the mission of the organization or organizational unit. A recent analysis of CEO leadership concluded that one of the basic ways in which top executives lead is through the **expertise approach.** Executives who lead by using this approach think that the leader's most important responsibility is providing an area of expertise that will be a source of competitive advantage. Such CEOs devote most of their time to continually improving their expertise through such means as studying new technological research, analyzing competitors' products, and conferring with customers and engineers.[26]

An otherwise capable leader can sometimes fail to meet expectations because he or she lacks the specialized functional knowledge necessary to move the organization forward. Such was the case when Robert Holland Jr., the Ben & Jerry's CEO, resigned, eighteen months after his much-publicized arrival at the company. Holland had achieved many of the goals he undertook, but it was thought that he lacked the expertise to effectively market ice cream, frozen yogurts, and sorbets. (An alternative analysis, however, is that Holland had clashes of opinion about marketing with cofounder Ben Cohen.)

Creativity

Many effective leaders are creative in the sense that they arrive at imaginative and original solutions to complex problems. Creative ability lies on a continuum, with some leaders being more creative than others. At one end of the creative continuum are business leaders who think of innovative products and services. One example is Steven Jobs of NeXT, Inc. (now a software firm), Pixar (a computer graphics firm specializing in cinema animation), and Apple. Another example is Michael Eisner, a senior executive whose chief duty is to lead the Disney empire creatively. At the middle of the creativity continuum are leaders who explore imaginative—but not breakthrough—solutions to business problems. At the low end of the creativity continuum are leaders who inspire group members to push forward with standard solutions to organizational problems.

Creativity is such an important aspect of the leader's role in the modern organization that the development of creative problem-solving skills receives chapter-length attention in this book (see Chapter 11).

Insight into People and Situations

Another important cognitive trait of effective leaders is **insight,** a depth of understanding that requires considerable intuition and common sense. Insight is related to creativity because of its intuitive component. Insight into people and situations involving people is an essential characteristic of managerial leaders. A manager with keen insight is able to make wise choices in selecting people for key assignments. Furthermore, insight enables a manager to make better work assignments and do a better job of training and developing team members. The reason is that such a manager makes a careful assessment of the strengths and weaknesses of team members. Another major advantage of being insightful is that the leader can size up the situation and adapt his or her leadership approach accordingly. For instance, in a crisis situation group members welcome directive and decisive leadership.

Insight is also closely linked to perceiving trends in the environment. Leaders must be able to process many different types of information, and use their perceptions to predict the direction of environmental forces. Leaders appear to be more effective than others in managing cognitive complexity. According to Manfred F. R. Kets de Vries, they are effective in searching out and structuring the kind of information they need. Leaders can make sense of a complex environment and then use the data for problem solving.[27] A basic example of this type of insight occurred several years ago. August A. Busch IV, the brand manager for Budweiser beer, proposed to develop clever ads that did not display scantily clad women. Despite the objection of beer wholesalers, Busch's insights told him that young people would welcome non-sexually oriented appeals.

You can gauge your insight by charting the accuracy of your hunches and predictions about people and business situations. For example, size up a new coworker or manager as best you can. Record your observations and test them against how that person performs or behaves many months later. The feedback from this type of exercise helps sharpen your insights.

Farsightedness

To develop visions and corporate strategy, a leader needs **farsightedness,** the ability to understand the long-range implications of actions and policies. Ray J. Friant, Jr., among many other critics, is concerned that too many business leaders are shortsighted. For example, the "get-rich-quick" philosophy of many business executives and investment bankers has left many companies with burdensome debt loads.

Friant recommends that to develop as future business leaders, junior executives should be given long-term assignments in long-range planning and implementation. At the same time, they should go through their usual developmental rotations such as intermediate-term assignments in marketing and manufacturing. In addition, they should spend at least five years doing projects that change the character of the business. Such assignments would help business leaders of the future understand both the need for and the difficulty of balancing long-term and short-term results.[28]

Openness to Experience

Yet another important cognitive characteristic of leaders is their openness to experience, or their positive orientation toward learning. People who have a great deal of openness to experience have well-developed intellects. Traits commonly associated with this dimension of the intellect include being imaginative, cultured, curious, original, broad-minded, intelligent, and artistically sensitive.

To help personalize the information about key leadership traits presented so far, do Leadership Skill-Building Exercise 2–2.

THE INFLUENCE OF HEREDITY AND ENVIRONMENT ON LEADERSHIP

Does heredity or environment contribute more to leadership effectiveness? Are leaders born or made? Do you have to have the right stuff to be a leader? Many people ponder these issues now that the study of leadership is more

---

LEADERSHIP SKILL-BUILDING
EXERCISE 2–2   Group Feedback on Leadership Traits

Your instructor will organize the class into groups of about seven people. A volunteer sits in the middle of each group. Each group member looks directly at the person in the "hot seat" and tells him or her what leadership trait, characteristic, or motives he or she seems to possess. It will help if the feedback providers offer a few words of explanation for their observations. For example, a participant who is told that he or she has self-confidence might also be told, "I notice how confidently you have told the class about your success on the job." The group next moves on to the second person, and so forth. (We assume that you have had some opportunity to observe your classmates prior to this exercise.)

Each member thus receives positive feedback about leadership traits and characteristics from all the other members in the group. After all members have had their turn at receiving feedback, discuss as a group the value of the exercise.

in vogue than ever. The most sensible answer is that the traits, motives, and characteristics required for leadership effectiveness are a combination of heredity and environment. Personality traits and mental ability traits are based on certain inherited predispositions and aptitudes that require the right opportunity to develop. Mental ability is a good example. We inherit a basic capacity that sets an outer limit to how much mental horsepower we will have. Yet people need the right opportunity to develop their mental ability so that they can behave brightly enough to be chosen for a leadership position.

The physical factor of energy also sheds light on the nature-versus-nurture issue. Some people are born with a biological propensity for being more energetic than others. Yet unless that energy is properly channeled, it will not help a person become an effective leader.

The nature-versus-nurture issue also surfaces in relation to the leadership characteristic of creativity and innovation. Important genetic contributors to imaginative thinking include brain power and emotional expressiveness. Yet these traits require the right environment to flourish. Such an environment would include encouragement from others and ample opportunity to experiment with ideas.

THE STRENGTHS AND LIMITATIONS OF THE TRAIT APPROACH

A compelling argument for the trait approach is that the evidence is convincing that leaders possess personal characteristics that differ from those of nonleaders. Based on their review of the type of research reported in this chapter, Kirkpatrick and Locke concluded: "Leaders do not have to be great men or women by being intellectual geniuses or omniscient prophets to succeed. But they do need to have the 'right stuff' and this stuff is not equally present in all people."[29]

Understanding the traits of effective leaders serves as an important guide to leadership selection. If we are confident that honesty and integrity, and creativity and imagination are essential leadership traits, then we can concentrate on selecting leaders with those characteristics. Another important strength of the trait approach to leadership is that it can help people prepare for leadership responsibility and all of the issues that accompany it. A person might seek experiences that enable him or her to develop vital characteristics such as self-confidence, good problem-solving ability, and assertiveness.

A limitation to the trait approach is that it does not tell us which traits are absolutely needed in which leadership situations. We also do not know how much of a trait, characteristic, or motive is the right amount. For example, some leaders get into ethical and legal trouble because they allow their ambition to cross the borderline into greed and gluttony. Too much focus on the trait approach can breed an elitist conception of leadership. People who are not outstanding on key leadership traits and characteristics might be discouraged from seeking leadership positions.

Peter Drucker, a key figure in the modern management movement, is skeptical about studying the qualities of leaders. He believes that a leader cannot be categorized by a particular personality type, style, or set of traits. Instead, a leader should be understood in terms of his or her constituents, results, example setting, and responsibilities. A leader must look in the mirror, and ask if the image is the kind of person the leader wants to be. (Without realizing it, Drucker in this instance is probably alluding to the leader's traits and values!)[30]

A balanced perspective on the trait approach is that certain traits, motives, and characteristics increase the probability that a leader will be effective. Yet they do not guarantee effectiveness, and the leadership situation often influences which traits will be the most important.[31]

SUMMARY

A universal theory of leadership contends that certain personal characteristics and skills contribute to leadership effectiveness in many situations. The trait approach to leadership studies the traits, motives, and other characteristics of leaders. General personality traits associated with effective leadership include the following: (1) self-confidence, (2) trustworthiness, (3) dominance, (4) extroversion, (5) assertiveness, (6) emotional stability, (7) enthusiasm, (8) sense of humor, (9) warmth, (10) self-awareness, and (11) a high tolerance for frustration.

Some personality traits of effective leaders are closely associated with task accomplishment. Among them are (1) initiative, (2) sensitivity to others, (3) flexibility and adaptability, (4) an internal locus of control, (5) courage, and (6) resiliency.

Certain motives and needs associated with leadership effectiveness are closely related to task accomplishment. Among them are (1) the power motive, either personalized or socialized, (2) drive and achievement motivation, (3) a strong work ethic, and (4) tenacity.

Cognitive factors are also important for leadership success. Cognitive resource theory underscores the contribution of intelligence to planning and decision making. The theory also emphasizes that plans, decisions, and action strategies are communicated through directive behavior. Good problem-solving ability is an asset to leaders because they must collect, integrate, and interpret enormous amounts of data.

Intellectual ability is closely related to the leadership requirement of possessing knowledge of the business or being technically competent. Creativity is another important cognitive skill for leaders, but effective leaders vary widely in their creative contributions. Insight into people and situations, including the ability to make effective judgments about business opportunities, also contributes to leadership effectiveness. The cognitive skill of farsightedness helps leaders understand the long-range implications of actions and policies.

The issue of whether leaders are born or bred frequently surfaces. A sensible answer is that the traits, motives, and characteristics required for leadership effectiveness are a combination of heredity and environment.

The trait approach to leadership is supported by many studies showing that leaders are different from nonleaders, and effective leaders different from less effective leaders. Nevertheless, the trait approach does not tell us which traits are the most important in which situations, or the amount of the trait required.

KEY TERMS

Universal theory of leadership	Empathy	Cognitive factors
Assertiveness	Flexibility	Cognitive resource theory
Emotional stability	Internal locus of control	Expertise approach
High tolerance for frustration	Drive	Insight
Initiative	Achievement motivation	Farsightedness
Sensitivity to others	Work ethic	

GUIDELINES FOR ACTION AND SKILL DEVELOPMENT

An important application of the trait theory of leadership is to choose a leadership trait as a personal development goal. Assertiveness is one such trait amenable to development. To become a more assertive person, follow these steps:

1. **Observe your own behavior.** Are you asserting yourself adequately? Or are you being pushy or abrasive? Do you believe you get what you want, when you want it, without stepping on the rights of others?

2. **Concentrate on a specific situation.** Imagine how you would handle a specific incident, such as asking to be considered for a task force assignment.

3. **Observe an effective model.** Observe another person who appears to be assertive. Observe the person's style as well as what he or she says.

4. **Try it out.** You are now prepared to try out an assertive behavior in a specific problem situation or two. Possibilities include asking for an interesting assignment, getting an error corrected by a bank, or turning down a luncheon request.

5. **Evaluate your performance.** Review how well you performed in behaving assertively, and therefore improving your trait of assertiveness.

6. **Practice and obtain social reinforcement.** Continue your assertive behavior in a variety of situations. Observe the beneficial consequences in order to receive reinforcement in a real situation (social reinforcement).[32]

DISCUSSION QUESTIONS AND ACTIVITIES

1. How much faith does the public place in the trait theory of leadership when they elect public officials?

2. When managers are polled, they claim honesty is an essential leadership trait. To what extent do you think these managers are just making a response they think the researchers want to hear?

3. Why is a high tolerance for frustration an important leadership trait?

4. Why is personal warmth an important leadership trait?

5. How does an internal locus of control help a leader become a good crisis manager?

6. A company president made the following comment about leadership and intelligence: "Sometimes a less than top IQ is an advantage because that person doesn't see all the problems. He or she sees the big problem and gets on and gets it solved. But the extremely bright person can see so many problems that he or she never gets around to solving any of them." What is your reaction to his comment?

7. Find an article or book about a successful executive leader, and look for evidence that knowl-edge of the business is an important success factor for that person.

8. Visualize the least effective leader you know. Identify the traits, motives, and personal characteristics in which that person might be deficient.

9. Many people who disagree with the trait approach to leadership nevertheless still conduct interviews when hiring a person for a leadership position. Why is conducting such interviews inconsistent with their attitude toward the trait approach?

10. Explain whether or not a person who lacks the "right stuff" should give up on ever holding a significant leadership position.

LEADERSHIP CASE PROBLEM

What Leadership Characteristics Does Wayne Huizenga Possess?

Success Magazine calls Wayne Huizenga the leading American entrepreneur. In building his vast empire, Huizenga's winning strategy has been to target cash-rich industries (such as waste removal) that are ready for rapid consolidation. His strategy of rapid acquisitions has led to incredible growth since 1995, when his small waste management company paid $100 million for Republic Industries, Inc. From that time forward, Huizenga's group has made eighteen acquisitions. The outstanding reputation Huzienga developed as head of Blockbuster Entertainment Corp. and WMX Technologies, Inc., has fueled a run-up of the price of Republic stock. The company is now a dominant player in three industries: electronic security, superstore chains of used-car dealerships, and waste disposal.

During his seven years in control of Block-buster, the company's stock soared 4,000 percent in value. Ultimately Viacom bought the company in a stock swap valued at $8.4 billion. Speaking after the shareholders' meeting, Huizenga was blunt, as usual. He explained that he would remain with the company only for six months to allow a smooth transition. His reasoning was that he cannot tolerate working for anyone else. Huizenga explained that either he is the lead person or he leaves a company. Yet on his way out of Blockbuster, Huizenga left stockholders with a vision of the company: "A global entertainment company that will make a movie, put it in our theaters, rent it in our video stores, sell it on our pay-per-view channels, show it on our cable networks, and play it on our television stations. And we'll publish the book, release the soundtrack, make the video game, and sell them in all our stores" (*Success*, p. 42).

At age 58, Huizenga is a hard-driving, hard-working entrepreneur whose net worth is at least $1 billion. His forte is building companies, making deals, and helping other managers become wealthy by rewarding them with part ownership of the companies they helped grow. Huizenga has now built three empires (videos, waste management, and Republic Industries). He also owns the Miami Dolphins, Florida Panthers, and Florida Marlins professional sports teams. Offers pour into his office every day. Hundreds of people submit résumés weekly, hoping to have some business connection to Huizenga. One man offered to work for Huizenga for a year without pay just to capture some of his expertise.

Huizenga's business career began with a garbage truck and a route worth $500 per month. His grandfather founded one of Chicago's first private services for collecting refuse. At age 14, Huizenga worked afternoons and weekends at his father's home-building business. During high school Wayne Huizenga developed the reputation of being strong-willed. He played linebacker on the high school football team. After attending Calvin College in Michigan, Huizenga moved to Florida and was convinced by a friend to manage a small garbage hauling company. Soon tired of working for somebody else, Huizenga began his own garbage route. He hauled garbage early in the morning and solicited for new accounts in the afternoon.

Huizenga's company grew rapidly, and he merged with another hauler to form WMX Technologies, Inc. At that time Huizenga developed the strategy of taking a small company public, then buying other companies with money from the stock sale. In its first decade, WMX Technologies, Inc. grew to become the largest garbage hauler in the world. The company and Huizenga faced charges of corruption during the rapid growth phase. Many critics assumed that the trash hauling business must be linked to organized crime. And the Securities and Exchange Commission accused WMX Technologies, Inc. of making illegal political contributions and price fixing.

According to one of Huizenga's sons, his happiest moments as a manager are when people come to him for advice, or with a problem they need solved. Huizenga's basic approach to growing his business is to gather his key staff members together and discuss ideas for expansion and possible deals. The staff members respond by pointing out weaknesses in Huizenga's proposals. At a given time, the company is working on a dozen possible deals. Huizenga's workday begins at 4 A.M. When talking to a person about a possible deal, he relates to him or her in a relaxed, chummy manner. When speaking to a group, Huizenga is engaging and direct, and wants to make sure he is clearly understood.

Another way Huizenga expands his empire is by meeting with a core group of friends who made loads of money with him at WMX Technologies, Inc. the "Old Pals' Club." The group shares leads, resources, and business strategy. Many of their deals have led to more riches for Huizenga and his buddies. Blockbuster Video began from discussions with his network of friends. Huizenga had the idea of creating a McDonald's of video, including the policy of not renting or selling pornographic videos.

Huizenga has developed the reputation of being a highly disciplined entrepreneur with world-class expertise in making companies grow. At the same time he is known to his close associates as a goofball on occasion. Part of his sense of humor includes sticking out his tongue at others while eating food.

Identify the traits, motives, and personal characteristics from the above description.

Source: Duncan Maxwell Anderson and Michael Warshaw, "The Number One Entrepreneur in America," *Success*, March 1995, pp. 32–43; "A Lollapalooza for Huizenga," *Business Week*, July 15, 1996, p. 29; "Conference Keynote Speaker: Wayne Huizenga," http://garnet.acns.fsu.edu/~jostery/wayne.html

LEADERSHIP SKILL-BUILDING EXERCISE 2–3

A Sense of Humor on the Job

One person plays the role of the company president who has scheduled a staff meeting. The president's task is to inform employees that the seventh top manager in the last year has just resigned. You want to make effective use of humor to relieve some of the tension and worry. Make a couple of humorous introductory comments. Five other people should play the roles of the remaining staff members. Make effective use of humor yourself in response to the president's comments.

Charismatic and Transformational Leadership

LEARNING OBJECTIVES

After studying this chapter, you should be able to

1. achieve a comprehensive understanding of the meaning and types of charismatic leadership.
2. describe many of the traits and behaviors of charismatic leaders.
3. explain the visionary component of charismatic leadership and display skill in creating a vision.
4. explain the communication style of charismatic leaders.
5. have an action plan for developing your charisma.
6. explain the nature of transformational leadership and how leaders create transformations.
7. describe the concerns about charismatic leadership from the scientific and moral standpoint.

*L*ewis Jordan, the CEO of the airline ValuJet, Inc., stood before the television cameras to announce that his company had cleared another regulatory hurdle in its bid to fly again. The FAA had suspended the airline after Flight 592 crashed in the Everglades in May 1996. Although Jordan announced only progress toward restarting the company, a crowd of about 100 ValuJet employees gave him a standing ovation.

Jordan was tapped to run ValuJet after a successful thirty-year career. He quickly became an industry favorite as the discount carrier enjoyed sensational growth. The company's rapid rise was credited mostly to Jordan's flair for frugality and attention-getting advertising. An animated airplane, known as The Critter, is painted on the outside of every ValuJet DC-9. A superhero, Captain Valu, is a major part of the advertising. Many company outsiders and insiders also attributed the company's rapid growth, and its rebound after the crash, to Jordan's magnetic effect on people.

Despite his successes, Jordan does have some detractors. Susan Clayton, a ValuJet flight attendant and local union representative, said that his strong personality has enabled him to brush aside problems. "He is very charismatic. He does have an open-door personality—it's open as long as you go in and say how wonderful he's doing."[1]

Lewis Jordan exemplifies leaders who are so exciting, so appealing, so dynamic, and visionary that most (not necessarily all) of their constituents eagerly accept their leadership. Such leaders are said to be charismatic. The same leaders are described as transformational when they facilitate major changes in organizations. The study of charismatic and transformational leadership is an extension of the trait theory, and has emerged as an important new way of understanding leadership.

In this chapter we examine the meaning and effects of charismatic leadership, the characteristics of charismatic leaders, how such leaders form visions, and how one develops charisma. We also describe the closely related and overlapping subject of transformational leadership. Finally, we look at the dark side of charismatic leadership.

THE MEANINGS OF CHARISMA

Charisma, like leadership itself, has been defined in various ways. Nevertheless, there is enough consistency among these definitions to make charisma a useful concept in understanding and practicing leadership. To begin, *charisma* is a Greek word meaning divinely inspired gift. In the study of leadership, **charisma** is a special quality of leaders whose purposes, powers, and extraordinary determination differentiate them from others.[2]

The various definitions of charisma have a unifying theme. Charisma is a positive and compelling quality of a person that makes many others want to be led by him or her. The term *many others* is chosen carefully. Few leaders are perceived to be charismatic by *all* their constituents. A case in point is Bill Gates, the chairman and cofounder of Microsoft Corp., whose name surfaces frequently in discussions of charisma. Despite his wide appeal, many people consider Gates to be brash, outspoken, too all-controlling, and obsessed with demolishing the competition—hardly the characteristics of an inspiring leader.

Table 3–1 presents a sampling of additional definitions of charisma. These definitions point to different subtleties of charisma.

Charisma: A Relationship Between the Leader and Group Members

A key dimension of charismatic leadership is that it involves a relationship or interaction between the leader and the people being led. (The same, of course, holds true for all types of leadership.) Furthermore, the people

TABLE 3–1   Definitions of Charisma and Charismatic Leadership

1. A devotion to the specific and exceptional sanctity, heroism, or exemplary character of an individual person, and of the normative patterns revealed or ordained by that person.

2. Endowment with the gift of divine grace.

3. The process of influencing major changes in the attitudes and assumptions of organization members, and building commitment for the organization's objectives.

4. Leadership that has a magnetic effect on people.

5. In combination with individualized consideration, intellectual stimulation, and inspirational leadership, a component of transformational leadership.

Sources: (1) Max Weber, cited in S. N. Eisenstadt, *Max Weber: On Charisma and Institution Building* (Chicago: University of Chicago Press, 1968); (2) Bernard M. Bass, "Evolving Perspectives on Charismatic Leadership," in *Charismatic Leaders,* eds. Jay A. Conger, Rabindra N. Kanungo, et al (San Francisco: Jossey-Bass, 1988), p. 40; (3) Gary A. Yukl, *Leadership in Organizations,* 3rd ed. (Upper Saddle River, N.J.: Prentice Hall, 1994), p. 207; (4) James M. Kouzes and Barry Z. Posner, *The Leadership Challenge: How to Get Extraordinary Things Done in Organizations* (San Francisco: Jossey-Bass, 1987), p. 123; Bernard M. Bass, cited in Kenneth E. Clark and Miriam B. Clark (eds.), *Measures of Leadership,* A Center for Creative Leadership Book (West Orange, N.J.: Leadership Library of America, 1990).

accepting the leadership must attribute charismatic qualities to the leader. John Gardner believes that charisma applies to leader-constituent relationships in which the leader has an exceptional gift for inspiration and nonrational communication. At the same time the constituent's response is characterized by awe, reverence, devotion, or emotional dependence.[3] The late Sam Walton, founder of Wal-Mart Stores, had this type of relationship with many of his employees. Walton's most avid supporters believed he was an inspired executive to whom they could trust their careers.

Charismatic leadership is possible under certain conditions. The beliefs of the constituents must be similar to those of the leader, and unquestioning acceptance of and affection for the leader must exist. The group members must willingly obey the leader, and they must be emotionally involved both in the mission of the charismatic leader and in their own goals. Finally, the constituents must have a strong desire to identify with the leader.[4]

The Effects of Charisma

Robert J. House developed a theory of charismatic leadership that defined charisma in terms of its effects. A charismatic leader, according to House, is any person who brings about certain outcomes to an unusually high degree. The nine charismatic effects are as follows:

1. Group member trust in the correctness of the leader's beliefs

2. Similarity of group members' beliefs to those of the leader

3. Unquestioning acceptance of the leader

4. Affection for the leader
5. Willing obedience to the leader
6. Identification with and emulation of the leader
7. Emotional involvement of the group members or constituents in the mission
8. Heightened goals of the group members
9. Feeling on the part of group members that they will be able to accomplish, or contribute to, the accomplishment of the mission[5]

Jane A. Halpert factor-analyzed (statistically clustered) these nine hypothesized outcomes into three groups or dimensions, as outlined in Figure 3–1. The first six effects refer to the power exerted by the leader. Three of them (similarity of beliefs, affection for the leader, identification with and emulation of the leader) are related to referent power. **Referent power** is the ability to influence others that stems from the leader's desirable traits and characteristics. Three other effects (group member trust, unquestioning acceptance, and willing obedience) are related to expert power. **Expert power** is the ability to influence others because of one's specialized knowledge, skills, or abilities.

The last three effects are perceptions related to the task or mission. Halpert noted also that the job-related effects (emotional involvement, heightened goals, and perceived ability to contribute) are concerned with *job*

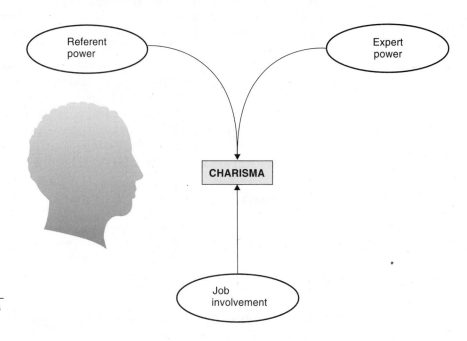

FIGURE 3–1
Halpert's Dimensions of Charisma

involvement. As a result, charismatic leaders will encourage group members to be job involved. A recent study provides more evidence of the relationship between charismatic leadership and job satisfaction. (Job involvement is a key component of satisfaction.) Using a sample of state government employees, the researchers found that managers who rated their own managers as high on charisma tended to have high satisfaction with supervision. Working for a charismatic leader also enhanced commitment to the organization.[6]

In summary, the nine charismatic effects in House's theory can be reduced to three dimensions: referent power, expert power, and job involvement.[7] Such information is useful for the aspiring charismatic leader. To be charismatic, one must exercise referent power and expert power and must get people involved in their jobs.

TYPES OF CHARISMATIC LEADERS

The everyday use of the term *charisma* suggests that it is a straightforward and readily understood trait. As already explained, however, charisma has different meanings and dimensions. As a result, charismatic leaders can be categorized into five types: socialized charismatics, personalized charismatics, office-holder charismatics, personal charismatics, and divine charismatics.[8]

Following the distinction made for the power motive, some charismatic leaders use their power for the good of others. A **socialized charismatic** is a leader who restrains the use of power in order to benefit others. This type of leader also attempts to develop a value congruence between himself or herself and constituents. The socialized charismatic formulates and pursues goals that fulfill the needs of group members and provides intellectual stimulation to them. Followers of socialized charismatics are autonomous, empowered, and responsible.

A second type of charismatic leader is the **personalized charismatic.** Such individuals exercise few restraints on their use of power so they may best serve their own interests. Personalized charismatics impose self-serving goals on constituents, and they offer consideration and support to group members only when it facilitates their own goals. Followers of personalized charismatics are typically obedient, submissive, and dependent.

Another type of charismatic leader is the office-holder charismatic. For this type of leader, charismatic leadership is more a property of the office occupied than of his or her personal characteristics. The chief executive officer of General Electric, for example, might have considerable luster but would lose much of it immediately after leaving office. By occupying a valuable role, office-holder charismatics attain high status. Office-holder charisma is thus a byproduct of being placed in a key position.

In contrast to office-holder charismatics, personal charismatics gain very high esteem through the extent to which others have faith in them as people. A personal charismatic exerts influence whether he or she occupies a low-or high-status position because he or she has the right traits, characteristics, and behaviors.

Former top-ranking U.S. Army general Colin H. Powell would qualify in the eyes of many as a personal charismatic. After leaving office, he was deluged with offers to serve on corporate boards and to make speaking appearances, and he was allegedly courted by both major political parties as a possible vice-presidential candidate. A former national security advisor said that Powell "has great judgment, common sense, and a skepticism that would be healthy on any board."[9]

A historically important type of charismatic leader is the divine charismatic. Originally, charismatic leadership was a theological concept: A divine charismatic is endowed with a gift of divine grace. In 1924 Max Weber defined a charismatic leader as a mystical, narcissistic, and personally magnetic savior who would arise to lead people through a crisis. When H. Ross Perot ran for U.S. president in 1992 and 1996, many of his constituents reacted to him as if he were a divine charismatic.

The accompanying Leader in Action portrayal describes a charismatic executive. After reading the excerpt, categorize this leader into one of the five types just described.

LEADER IN ACTION

Richard Branson of the Virgin Group

A huge silver ball slowly slides down a giant neon sign on a building in Times Square. As the ball has almost completed its journey, off leaps the wildly imaginative entrepreneur Richard Branson. The occasion is the opening of a 75,000-square-foot Virgin music-and-entertainment megastore. Along with four other stores planned for New York, the Virgin Group will have sixty-four of these new-wave entertainment centers in twelve countries. Among the more than 100 businesses headed by Branson are a transatlantic airline, a bridal service, a hotel chain, a book publisher, and a train service under the English Channel. Furthermore, Branson has spearheaded the introduction of Virgin Cola in the United States to battle Coca-Cola and Pepsi-Cola head on.

Branson has achieved extensive publicity through a gamut of goofball stunts and daredevil deeds such as ballooning around the world. Ever since the beginning of his career, he has valued the media. He looked upon a photo or an article as free advertising that multiplied in effectiveness if he were speedboating across the Atlantic or flying across the ocean in a hot-air balloon. To him, risking his life is part of doing business. Branson's reputation as a "adventure capitalist" has kept him in the spotlight as a glamour boy who mingles with the jet set and rules over an empire worth close to $2 billion. Branson's ability to spot a profitable business opportunity, as well as to know when to get out of a business when still on top, has perplexed the British financial community.

LEADERSHIP SKILL-BUILDING EXERCISE 3–1   Formulating a Vision

Along with your teammates, assume the role of the top management group of an organization or organizational unit that is in need of revitalization. Your revitalization tactic is to create a vision for the organization. Express the vision in not more than twenty-five words. Use the guidelines for developing a vision described in the text. Come to agreement quickly on the organization or large organizational unit that needs a vision. Or choose one of the following:

- The Jeep Division of Chrysler Corporation
- A sausage manufacturer
- A waste disposal company
- The human resources department of a large company
- A credit card company

- A group discussion of what it takes to delight the people your group serves.
- Annual reports, management books, and business magazines to uncover the type of vision statements formulated by others.
- Group members and friends; speak to them individually and collectively to learn of their hopes and dreams for the future.
- For a vision for an organizational unit, the organization's vision. You might get some ideas for matching your unit's vision with that of the organization.

Leadership Skill-Building Exercise 3–1 gives you an opportunity to practice vision formulation. Keep in mind that a critic of vision statements once said that it is often difficult to tell the difference between a vision and a hallucination.

THE COMMUNICATION STYLE OF CHARISMATIC LEADERS

Charismatic and transformational leaders communicate their visions, goals, and directives in a colorful, imaginative, and expressive manner. In addition, they communicate openly with group members and create a comfortable communication climate. To set agendas that represent the interests of their constituents, charismatic leaders regularly solicit constituents' viewpoints on critical issues. They encourage two-way communication with team members while still promoting a sense of confidence.[13] Here we describe two related aspects of the communication style of charismatic leaders: management by inspiration and management by anecdote.

Management by Inspiration

According to Jay A. Conger, the era of managing by dictate is being replaced by an era of managing by inspiration. An important way to inspire others is to articulate a highly emotional message. Roger Enrico, the dynamic CEO of Pepsico, directs a leadership development program for selected company managers. At the outset of the program, he knocks participants off balance by telling them that, "nobody in this room can look at the company's problems and blame the turkeys at the top. You're now one of them."[14] Conger has observed two major rhetorical techniques of inspirational leaders: the use of metaphors and analogies, and the ability to gear language to different audiences.[15]

Metaphors and Analogies.   A well-chosen analogy or metaphor appeals to the intellect, to imagination, and to values. The charismatic Mary Kay Ash, the founder of Mary Kay Cosmetics, made frequent use of metaphors during her career. To inspire her associates to higher performance, she often said: "You see, a bee shouldn't be able to fly; its body is too heavy for its wings. But the bumblebee doesn't know that and it flies very well." Mary Kay explains the message of the bumblebee metaphor in these terms: "Women come to us not knowing they can fly. Finally, with help and encouragement, they find their wings—and then they fly very well indeed."[16]

Gearing Language to Different Audiences.   Metaphors and analogies are inspiring, but effective leaders must also choose the level of language to suit the audience. The challenge of choosing the right level of language is significant because constituents vary widely in verbal sophistication. One day, for example, a CEO might be attempting to inspire a group of Wall Street financial analysts, and the next day she or he might be attempting to inspire first-level employees to keep working hard despite limited salary increases.

Conger has observed that an executive's ability to speak on a colloquial level contributes heavily to creating appeal. A person with the high status of an executive is expected to use an elevated language style. When the person unexpectedly uses the everyday language of an operative employee, it may create a special positive response.

Management by Anecdote

Another significant aspect of the communication style of charismatic and transformational leaders is that they make extensive use of memorable anecdotes to get messages across. **Management by anecdote** is the technique of inspiring and instructing team members by telling fascinating stories. The technique is a major contributor to building a strong company culture. David Armstrong, an executive at Armstrong International, uses the following anecdote to reinforce the importance of listening to customers:

Bill, our sales manager, wanted to add an obsolete feature to our company's new fish finder. We thought he was crazy. Bill knew that we preferred only to offer high-end, advanced products in order to hold on to our market share. The "flasher mode" he wanted to add to our fish finders was outdated, since it only told the fishers that fish were nearby—while our new computerized models would also indicate the fish's location and size.

Who on earth would want the old-fashioned fish finder? Our customers, as it turned out. Many of them were old-time fishermen and didn't feel comfortable with the newfangled model, which confused them. They wanted the kind of machine they were used to.

Nobody agreed with Bill at first, but eventually he got his way. We put the "flasher" back on the fish finder. Customers are still calling us to tell us how much they like this feature. We've sold a lot more units, because we listened to the market.

After Armstrong tells this story, he explains the lessons illustrated by the story. One is, "Listen, listen, listen to your salespeople and your customers. Get direct feedback and don't second-guess them." Another is, "Ask yourself if this feature is necessary. Technology is not an end in itself." The third lesson is that classic products can outsell new products. Experts told the Coca Cola Bottling Company to change its formula, but Coca-Cola drinkers didn't agree."[17]

To get started developing the skill of management by anecdote, do Leadership Skill-Building Exercise 3–2 (on page 66).

THE DEVELOPMENT OF CHARISMA

By developing some of the traits, characteristics, and behaviors of charismatic people, a person can increase his or her charisma. Several of the charismatic characteristics described earlier in the chapter are capable of development. For example, most people can enhance their communication skills, become more emotionally expressive, take more risks, and become more self-promoting. In this section we examine several behaviors of charismatic people that can be developed through practice and self-discipline.

Create Visions for Others. If you can create visions for others, this will be a major factor in your being perceived as charismatic. A vision uplifts and attracts others. To form a vision, use the guidelines presented previously in the chapter. The visionary person looks beyond the immediate future to create an image of what the organization or unit thereof is capable of becoming. A vision is designed to close the discrepancy between present and ideal conditions. The vision thus sees beyond present realities.

Be Enthusiastic, Optimistic, and Energetic. A major behavior pattern of charismatic people is their combination of enthusiasm, optimism, and high

LEADERSHIP SKILL-BUILDING
EXERCISE 3–2   **Charismatic Leadership by Anecdote**

Directions: Gather in a small problem-solving group to develop an inspiring anecdote about something that actually happened, or might have happened, at a present or former employer. Here are some guidelines:

1. Make up a list of core values the firm holds dear, such as quality, service, or innovation.

2. Think of an incident in which an employee strikingly lived up to (or violated) one of these values. Write it up as a story with a moral.

3. Share your stories with other members of the class, and discuss whether this exercise could make a contribution to leadership development.

Source: The guidelines are from "Management by Anecdote," *Success*, December 1992, p. 35.

energy. Without a high level of all three characteristics, a person is unlikely to be perceived as charismatic by many people. A remarkable quality of charismatic people is that they maintain high enthusiasm, optimism, and energy throughout their entire workday and beyond. Elevating your energy level takes considerable work, but here are a few feasible suggestions:

1. Get ample rest at night, and sneak in a fifteen-minute nap during the day when possible. If you have a dinner meeting where you want to shine, take a shower and nap before the meeting.

2. Exercise every day for at least 10 minutes, including walking. No excuses allowed, such as being too busy or too tired, or the weather being a handicap.

3. Switch to a healthy, energy-enhancing diet.

4. Keep chopping away at your To Do list so you do not have unfinished tasks on your mind, draining your energy.

An action orientation contributes to being enthusiastic, optimistic, and energetic. "Let's do it" is the battle cry of the charismatic person. An action orientation also means that the charismatic person prefers not to agonize over dozens of facts and nuances before making a decision.

Be Sensibly Persistent.   Closely related to the high energy level of charismatics is their almost-never-accept-no attitude. I emphasize the word *almost* because outstanding leaders and individual contributors know when to cut their losses. If an idea or a product will not work, the sensible charismatic absorbs the loss and moves in another, more profitable direction. An executive at a telecommunications company said, "A test of executive material in our company is whether the middle manager has the guts to kill a failed project. Some managers become so ego-involved in a product they sponsored, they fight to keep it alive long after it should have died. They twist and distort financial information to prove that there is still life left in their pet product. A person with executive potential knows when to fold his or her tent."

Be Candid.   Charismatic people, especially effective leaders, are remarkably candid with people. Although not insensitive, the charismatic person is typically explicit in giving his or her assessment of a situation, whether the assessment is positive or negative. Charismatic people speak directly rather than indirectly, so that people know where they stand. Instead of asking a worker, "Are you terribly busy this afternoon?" the charismatic leader will ask, "I need your help this afternoon. Are you available?"

Display an In-Your-Face Attitude.   The preferred route to being perceived as charismatic is to be a positive, warm, and humanistic person. Yet some people earn their reputation for charisma based on toughness and nastiness. An in-your-face attitude may bring you some devoted supporters, although it will also bring you many detractors. The tough attitude is attractive to people who themselves would like to be mean and aggressive.

Be Dramatic and Unique.   A final tactic for becoming more charismatic is really an amalgam of the ideas already introduced. Being dramatic and unique in significant, positive ways is a major contributor to charisma. Drama and uniqueness stem from a combination of factors mentioned in this list and at other places in the chapter. Among these factors are being energetic, engaging in self-promotion, and taking risks.

TRANSFORMATIONAL LEADERSHIP

The focus of transformational leadership is on what the leader accomplishes, rather than on the leader's personal characteristics and her or his relationship with group members. Here we describe three aspects of transformational leadership: how transformations take place, the key components of transformational leadership, and the impact of transformational (and charismatic) leadership on performance.

How Transformations Take Place

Leaders often encounter the need to transform organizations from low performance to acceptable performance, or from acceptable performance to high performance. At other times, a leader is expected to move a firm from a crisis mode to high ground. To accomplish these lofty purposes, the transformational leader attempts to overhaul the organizational culture or subculture. His or her task can thus be as immense as the process of organizational change. To focus our discussion specifically on the leader's role, let's look at several ways in which transformations take place.[18] (See Figure 3–2.)

1. *Raising people's awareness.* The transformational leader makes group members aware of the importance and values of certain rewards and how to achieve them. He or she might point to the pride workers would experience should the firm become number one in its field. At the same time, the leader should point to the financial rewards accompanying such success.

2. *Helping people look beyond self-interest.* The transformational leader helps group members look to "the big picture" for the sake of the team and the organization. The executive vice president of a bank told her staff members, "I know most of you dislike word processing your own memos and letters. Yet if we hire enough staff to makes life more convenient for you, we'll be losing money. Then the government might force us to be taken over by a larger bank. Who knows how many management jobs would then have to be cut."

3. *Helping people search for self-fulfillment.* The transformational leader helps people go beyond a focus on minor satisfactions to a quest for self-fulfillment. The leader might explain, "I know that making sure you take every vacation day owed you is important. Yet if we get this proposal out on time, we might land a contract that will make us the envy of the industry." (Being the envy of the industry satisfies the need for self-fulfillment.)

4. *Helping people understand the need for change.* The transformational leader must help group members understand the need for change both emotionally and intellectually. The problem is that change involves dislocation and discomfort. An effective transformational leader recognizes

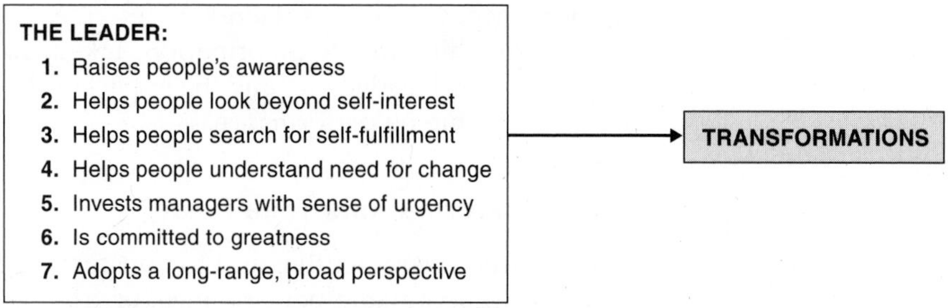

FIGURE 3–2
**How Transformations
Take Place**

THE LEADER:
1. Raises people's awareness
2. Helps people look beyond self-interest
3. Helps people search for self-fulfillment
4. Helps people understand need for change
5. Invests managers with sense of urgency
6. Is committed to greatness
7. Adopts a long-range, broad perspective

→ **TRANSFORMATIONS**

this emotional component to resisting change and deals with it openly. Organizational change is much like a life transition. Endings must be successfully worked through before new beginnings are possible. People must become unhooked from their pasts.

Dealing with the emotional conflicts of large numbers of staffers is obviously an immense task. One approach taken by successful leaders is to conduct discussion groups, in which managers and workers are free to discuss their feelings about the changes. This approach has been used quite effectively when firms are downsized. Many of the "survivors" feel guilty that they are still employed while many competent coworkers have lost their jobs. Clearly, conducting these sessions requires considerable listening skill on the manager's part.

5. *Investing managers with a sense of urgency.* To create the transformation, the leader assembles a critical mass of managers and imbues in them the urgency of change. The managers must also share the top leader's vision of what is both necessary and achievable. To sell this vision of an improved organization, the transformational leader must capitalize on available opportunities.

6. *Committing to greatness.* Peter Koestenbaum argues that business can be an opportunity for individual and organizational greatness. By adopting this greatness attitude, leaders can ennoble human nature and strengthen societies. Greatness encompasses striving for business effectiveness such as profits and high stock value, as well as impeccable ethics. An emphasis on ethical leadership instills a desire for customer service and quality and fosters feelings of proprietorship and involvement.[19] (A commitment to greatness is, of course, important for all leaders, not just those who are charismatic.)

7. *Adopting a long-range perspective and at the same time observing organizational issues from a broad rather than a narrow perspective.* Such thinking on the part of the transformational leader encourages many group members to do likewise. Unless many people think with a future orientation, and broadly, an organization cannot be transformed.[20]

Four Key Qualities of Transformational Leaders

Transformational leaders possess the personal characteristics of other effective leaders. In addition, four qualities of leaders are particularly helpful in enabling them to bring about transformations.[21] Above all, transformational leaders are *charismatic.* They have a vision and a sense of mission, and they have the respect, confidence, and loyalty of group members. As a result of experiencing a bond of identification with such leaders, many group members have faith, pride, enthusiasm, and a trust in what they are attempting to accomplish.

Closely linked to charisma, transformational leaders practice *inspirational leadership.* Part of the inspiration derives from communicating a vision with fluency and confidence. By giving emotional support and making emotional appeals, transformational leaders inspire group members to exceed their initial expectations. Transformational leaders also work within the cognitive domain. They provide *intellectual stimulation* by encouraging group members to examine old problems or methods in new ways. The transformational leader creates an atmosphere that encourages creative thinking and intuition. At the same time, he or she emphasizes methodical problem solving, rethinking, reexamining assumptions, and the use of careful reasoning rather than giving unsupported opinions. The net result of providing intellectual stimulation is that group members are willing to submit even fanciful ideas.

Transformational leaders demonstrate *individualized consideration* by giving personal attention to group members. Employees are treated as individuals and receive special attention regarding their individual concerns. The transformational leader invests time in one-on-one communication with group members and listens to them carefully, thereby helping group members to feel respected. Leaders of this type also emphasize the personal development of group members by such means as talking to them about career goals and developmental opportunities.

The Impact of Transformational and Charismatic Leadership on Performance

Although the present discussion deals primarily with transformational leadership, it would be artificial to separate its impact on performance from that of charismatic leadership. An important reason is that charismatic leadership, as already discussed, is a component of transformational leadership. A concern some scholars have about transformational leadership is that it sounds too mystical and "soft." Fortunately, several empirical studies have been conducted on the effects of charismatic and transformational leadership in work settings. We review three of them here.

Bass surveyed 1,500 general managers, leaders of technical teams, governmental and educational administrators, upper-middle managers, and senior U.S. Army officers.[22] One of the companies involved in the research was Federal Express Corp. A key research instrument was the Multifactor Leadership Questionnaire (MLQ), developed by Bass. To help you develop a firsthand feel for the research in question, the charisma scale of the MLQ is reproduced in Leadership Assessment Exercise 3-1.

Subordinates of leaders who described their managers as being more transformational were also more likely to respond that the organizational units their managers led were more highly effective. The leaders who were described as transformational were judged to be more effective than those

LEADERSHIP ASSESSMENT
EXERCISE 3–1   The MLQ Charismatic Leadership Scale

Rate your current manager, or any other manager you remember well, on the items below. Use the following 5-point scale: 0 (not at all), 1 (once in a while), 2 (sometimes), 3 (fairly often), and 4 (frequently).

1. Makes me feel good to be around him or her. 0 1 2 3 4

2. Commands respect from everyone. 0 1 2 3 4

3. Is a model for me to follow. 0 1 2 3 4

4. In my mind, he or she is a symbol of success and accomplishment. 0 1 2 3 4

5. I am ready to trust his or her capacity and judgment to overcome any obstacle. 0 1 2 3 4

6. Is an inspiration to us. 0 1 2 3 4

7. Makes me proud to be associated with him or her. 0 1 2 3 4

8. Has a special gift for seeing what is really important for me to consider. 0 1 2 3 4

9. Increases my optimism for the future. 0 1 2 3 4

10. Inspires my loyalty to the organization. 0 1 2 3 4

11. I have complete faith in him or her. 0 1 2 3 4

12. Excites us with his or her visions of what we may be able to accomplish if we work together. 0 1 2 3 4

13. Encourages me to express my ideas and opinions. 0 1 2 3 4

14. Encourages understanding of points of view of other members. 0 1 2 3 4

15. Gives me a sense of overall purpose. 0 1 2 3 4

16. Has a sense of mission that he or she transmits to me. 0 1 2 3 4

17. Makes everyone around him or her enthusiastic abut assignments 0 1 2 3 4

Interpretation:

0–17   Your manager has below-average charisma.

18–36 Your manager has about average charisma.

37–50 Your manager has above-average charisma.

51–68 Your manager is highly charismatic.

Source: Adapted with the permission of The Free Press, a Division of Simon & Schuster from *Leadership and Performance Beyond Expectations* by Bernard M. Bass. Copyright © 1985 by The Free Press.

described as transactional. First, they were judged to have better relationships with higher-ups. Second, their team members exerted more effort for them. If leaders were judged to be only transactional, the organizations were seen as less effective.

Leaders who were described as charismatic by their team members also tended to be appraised highly by their superiors. Being perceived as charismatic was significantly correlated with five dimensions of managerial performance, as shown in Table 3–2.

Another study demonstrated that the performance appraisals of group members were higher if their leaders had been described as transformational.[23] A possible bias here is that people who receive higher performance ratings may develop more positive perceptions of that leader. Have you noticed the same effect in student evaluation of faculty members?

As part of a larger study, Jane M. Howell and Bruce J. Avolio investigated the relationship of transformational leadership to business unit performance.[24] The sample included seventy-eight managers from the highest four levels of management in a large Canadian financial institution. At the time of the study, the firm was facing a turbulent external environment because of increased competition. A new form of the MLQ was developed to measure three aspects of transformational leadership: charisma, intellectual stimulation, and individualized consideration. The measure of business unit performance represented the degree to which the manager reached goals for the year, calculated in terms of the percentage of goals met. Each goal was measured against criteria for expected, superior, and outstanding performance.

Data analysis revealed that leaders who displayed more individualized consideration, intellectual stimulation, and charisma positively contributed to business unit performance. Leaders who used the techniques of management by exception and contingent rewards (positive reinforcement) were less likely to increase unit performance. The authors concluded that the

TABLE 3–2   Correlations Between Ratings of Charisma by Team Members and Appraisals by Superiors

Superior's Appraisal	Subordinates' Evaluation of Charisma
Judgment and decision making	.33*
Financial management	.36†
Communication	.32*
Persuasion	.33*
Risk taking	.45†

*$p < .05.$
†$p < .01.$

Source: Derived from data presented in John J. Hater and Bernard M. Bass, "Supervisors' Evaluations and Subordinates' Perceptions of Transformational and Transactional Leadership," *Journal of Applied Psychology,* November 1988, p. 701.

more positive contribution to business unit performance came from behaviors associated with transformational leadership.

The accompanying Leader in Action portrayal describes a charismatic person who is in the process of being a transformational leader. As you read the excerpt, look for examples of charismatic and transformational leadership.

CONCERNS ABOUT CHARISMATIC LEADERSHIP

Up to this point, an optimistic picture has been painted of both the concept of charisma and charismatic leaders. For the sake of fairness and scientific integrity, contrary points of view must also be presented. The topic of charismatic leadership has been challenged from two major standpoints: the validity of the concept, and the misdeeds of charismatic leaders.

Challenges to the Validity of Charismatic Leadership

One reason so few studies of charismatic leadership have been conducted is that most leadership researchers doubt that charisma can be accurately defined and measured. Conducting research about charisma is akin to conducting research about total quality: You know it when you see it, but it is difficult to define in operational terms. Furthermore, even when one leader is deemed to be charismatic, he or she has many detractors. According to the concept of **leadership polarity,** leaders are often either revered or vastly unpopular. People rarely feel neutral about them.

LEADER IN ACTION

Roy S. Roberts, The Force Behind Merging Two GM Divisions

Roy S. Roberts is experienced at taking charge of situations requiring a turnaround. In 1987, as a General Motors Corp. vice president, he was responsible for eliminating 40,000 jobs. As head of the GMC Division, Roberts is now a key figure in overseeing the delicate merger of the Pontiac Division with his division. To merge the two divisions, Roberts will have to eliminate overlapping positions in marketing and sales, and cut back on a large number of stand-alone Pontiac and GMC dealerships. Regarded as a charismatic leader by many GM managers and workers, Roberts thinks he can show even those people who are hurt that the cutbacks will benefit the company in the long term. He says, "I never minimize the people side of the business. That's one thing I learned as an hourly worker, a UAW member, and an employee coming up through the ranks" (*Business Week*, p. 38).

Getting people to accept the merger should be made easier by the fact that GMC's pickup trucks and sport-utility vehicles complement Pontiac's array of sporty cars. Also, nearly 60 percent of Pontiac franchises already share space with GMC dealerships. Roberts's new organizational unit is estimated to sell about 1 million vehicles annually. One automotive analyst thinks that adding Buick to the merger would make good business sense.

Roberts realizes that he is in a high-pressure position. Yet others feel that his ebullient personality should help him cope with the situation. A GM dealer from Minnesota thinks that Roberts has the right personality to be a Gospel minister because he attracts so many people to his way of thinking.

During the first seventeen years of his career, Roberts worked in an aerospace plant, working his way up from factory worker (and union steward) to plant manager. At GM he managed several factories before being appointed as a vice president for personnel in 1987. He then left for a three-year stint at Navistar. Roberts returned to GM as the chief of manufacturing at Cadillac. Next, he led GMC to three consecutive record-breaking years. Based on his accomplishments and his personality, Roy Roberts is regarded as the most visible black executive in the auto industry.

Source: "GM's Man in Merging Traffic," *Business Week*, March 4, 1996, p. 38; "African Americans on Wheels— Auto Briefs," October 28, 1996, //www.automag.com/autob/

Another problem with the concept of charisma is that it may not be necessary for leadership effectiveness. Warren Bennis and Burt Nanus have observed that very few leaders can accurately be described as charismatic. The organizational leaders the two researchers studied were "short and tall, articulate and inarticulate, dressed for success and dressed for failure, and there was virtually nothing in terms of physical appearance, personality, or style that set them apart from followers."

Based on these observations, Bennis and Nanus hypothesized that instead of charisma resulting in effective leadership, the reverse may be true. People who are outstanding leaders are granted charisma (perceived as charismatic) by their constituents as a result of their success.[25]

The Dark Side of Charismatic Leadership

Some people believe that charismatic leadership can be exercised for evil purposes. This argument was introduced previously in relation to personalized charismatic leaders. Years ago, Robert Tucker warned about the dark side of charisma, particularly with respect to political leaders:

> The magical message which mesmerizes the unthinking (and which can often be supplied by skilled phrase makers) promises that things will become not just better but perfect. Charismatic leaders are experts at promising Utopia. Since perfection is the end, often the most heinous actions can be tolerated as seemingly necessary means to that end.[26]

More recently it has been observed that some charismatic leaders are unethical and lead their organizations toward illegal and immoral ends. People are willing to follow the charismatic leader down a quasi-legal path because of his or her referent power.[27] For example, the legendary dealmaker Michael Milken was convicted of illegal securities transactions and sentenced to jail. Nevertheless, he inspired hundreds of people. Many of his admirers claimed that by promoting high-risk, high-yield bonds (junk bonds), Milken facilitated the growth of small business.

Charismatic leaders can also abuse power by virtue of their symbolic status as parent figures. According to Daniel Sankowsky, group members tacitly regard leaders, especially charismatic leaders, as parent figures. Given that charismatic leaders exert such strong influence, group members are particularly susceptible to being exploited. Abuse of this power can undermine group members' psychological well-being. Another important factor determining the extent of abuse is the leader's degree of narcissism. Leaders who are both charismatic and narcissistic are the most likely to induce group members to accept abusive behaviors.

According to Sankowsky, a leader abuses the power of symbolic status (representing a parent) when he or she convinces others that they were being mistreated for the good of the organization or for their own good. For example, the leader might abuse his or her position by berating group members and then making them think they deserved such treatment.[28] Whether or not you accept this psychoanalytic interpretation of leader-member relations, it does underscore the fact that charismatic leaders can abuse their power.

Another way of framing the issue of the dark side of charisma is that some charismatic and transformational leaders neglect their social responsibility. **Social responsibility** is an obligation to groups in society other than owners or stockholders and beyond that prescribed by law or union contract. When charismatic leaders behave in socially responsible ways, concerns about abusing the gift of charisma are lessened.

A charismatic leader's ability to influence constituents multiplies the importance of his or her having a strong sense of social responsibility. For example, a company president who invests substantial personal time in helping community groups will inspire workers throughout the firm to do the same. Leaders who are not particularly charismatic also have an obligation to behave in socially responsible ways, thus serving as a positive model.

SUMMARY

Charisma is a special quality of leaders whose purposes, powers, and extraordinary determination differentiate them from others. Charisma is also a positive and compelling quality of a person, which creates a desire in many others to be led by him or her. The relationship between group members and the leader is significant because the group members must attribute charismatic qualities to the leader.

Charismatic leadership can be understood in terms of its effects, such as group members' trust in the correctness of the leader's beliefs. One study showed that the effects of charismatic leadership can be organized into three dimensions: referent power, expert power, and job involvement. Charismatic leadership enhances job satisfaction.

Charismatic leaders can be subdivided into five types: socialized, personalized (self-interested), office-holder, personal (outstanding characteristics), and divine. Charismatic leaders have characteristics that set them apart from noncharismatic leaders. Charismatic leaders have a vision, have masterful communication skills, inspire trust, make group members feel capable, and have high energy and an action orientation. They are also emotionally expressive and warm, romanticize risk, use unconventional strategies, are self-promoting, tend to emerge during crises, and have minimum internal conflict about their roles.

The idea of vision is closely linked to charisma because charismatic leaders inspire others with their vision, and a vision uplifts and attracts others. In formulating a vision, it is helpful to gather information from a variety of sources, including intuition, futurists, and group members.

Charismatic and transformational leaders communicate their visions, goals, and directives in a colorful, imaginative, and expressive manner. Communication effectiveness allows for management by inspiration. One communication technique to inspire others is through metaphors, analogies, and organizational stories. Another is gearing language to different audiences. Charismatic and transformational leaders also extensively use memorable anecdotes to get messages across.

A person can increase his or her charisma by developing some of the traits, characteristics, and behaviors of charismatic people. The suggestions presented here include creating visions for others; being enthusiastic, optimistic, and energetic; being sensibly persistent; being candid; displaying an in-your-face attitude; and being dramatic and unique.

To bring about change, the transformational leader attempts to overhaul the organizational culture or subculture. The specific change techniques include raising people's awareness of the importance of certain rewards. and getting people to look beyond their self-interests for the sake of the team and the organization. The transformational leader also assembles a critical mass of managers who share his or her sense of urgency, makes a commitment to greatness, and takes a long-range perspective. Transformational leaders have characteristics similar to those of other effective leaders. In addition, they are charismatic, provide intellectual stimulation to others, and also demonstrate individualized consideration.

Empirical research indicates that leaders who are perceived to be charismatic are more likely to run highly effective units. Charismatic leaders are also more likely to be rated high on several important work dimensions such as judgment and decision making. It has also been demonstrated that leaders who display more individualized consideration, intellectual stimulation, and charisma (transformational leaders) have high business unit performance.

One concern about charismatic and transformational leadership is that the concept is murky. Many noncharismatic leaders are effective. Another concern is that some charismatic leaders are unethical and devious, suggesting that being charismatic does not necessarily help the organization. Charismatic leaders are often perceived as parent symbols, therefore setting up the possibility that they will abuse such power. By behaving in a socially responsible manner, charismatic leaders can avoid abusing their influence over others.

KEY TERMS

Charisma	Personalized charismatic	Leadership polarity
Referent power	Transformational leader	Social responsibility
Expert power	Vision	
Socialized charismatic	Management by anecdote	

GUIDELINES FOR ACTION AND SKILL DEVELOPMENT

Roger Dawson offers suggestions to help a person act in a charismatic manner, thus creating charismatic appeal. All of them relate to well-accepted human relations techniques.

1. **Be sure to treat everyone you meet as the most important person you will meet that day.**   For example, when at a company meeting, shake the hand of every person you meet.

2. **Multiply the effectiveness of your handshake.**   Shake firmly without creating pain, and make enough eye contact to notice the color of the other person's eyes. When you take that much trouble, you project care and concern. Think a positive thought about the person whose hand you shake.

3. **Give sincere compliments.**   Most people thrive on flattery particularly when it is plausible. Attempt to compliment only those behaviors, thoughts, and attitudes you genuinely believe merit praise. At times you may have to dig to find something praiseworthy, but it will be a good investment of your time.

4. **Thank people frequently, especially your own group members.**   Thanking others is still so infrequently practiced that it gives you a charismatic edge.

5. **Smile frequently, even if you are not in a happy mood.**   A warm smile seems to indicate a confident, caring person, which contributes to a perception of charisma. A smile generally sends a message to the effect, "I like you. I trust you. I'm glad we're together."

6. **Maintain a childlike fascination for your world.**   Express enthusiasm for and interest in the thoughts, actions, plans, dreams, and material objects of other people. Your enthusiasm directed toward others will engender enthusiasm in you.[29]

DISCUSSION QUESTIONS AND ACTIVITIES

1. Identify a business, government, education, or sports leader whom you perceive to be charismatic. Explain the basis for your judgment.

2. Can a first-level supervisor be charismatic?

3. Identify a well-known leader who is *not* charismatic.

4. Explain why the presence of a charismatic leader tends to enhance the job satisfaction of group members.

5. What does it say about the personality of Richard Branson when he declares that Virgin Cola will soon overtake Coca-Cola and Pepsi-Cola?

6. What should a leader do who is not effective at developing inspirational metaphors and anecdotes?

7. What similarities do you see between the goals of organization development practitioners and transformational leaders?

8. Furnish an example of how some workers need to transcend their self-interest for the good of the organization.

9. A concern has been expressed that leaders who are charismatic are often incompetent. They simply get placed into key positions because they create such a good impression. What do you think of this argument?

10. Design a research study or survey to determine if you are charismatic.

LEADERSHIP CASE PROBLEM

"I Have a Dream"

Martin Luther King, Jr., delivered the following address on the steps of the Lincoln Memorial in Washington, D.C. on August 28, 1963.

I say to you, my friends, that in spite of the difficulties and frustrations of the moment I still have a dream. It is a dream deeply rooted in the American Dream.

I have a dream that one day this nation will rise up and live out the true meaning of its creed: "We hold these truths to be self-evident; that all men are created equal."

I have a dream that one day on the red hills of Georgia the sons of former slaves and the sons of former slave owners will be able to sit down together at the table of brotherhood.

I have a dream that one day even the state of Mississippi, a desert state sweating in the heat of injustice and oppression, will be transformed into an oasis of freedom and justice.

I have a dream that my four little children will one day live in a nation where they will not be judged by the color of their skin but the content of their character.

I have a dream today.

I have a dream that one day the state of Alabama, whose governor's lips are presently dripping with the words of interposition and nullification, will be transformed into a situation where little black boys and girls will be able to join hands with little white boys and white girls and walk together as sisters and brothers.

I have a dream today.

I have a dream that one day every valley shall be exalted, every hill and mountain shall be made low, the rough places will be made plains, and the crooked places will be made straight, and the glory of the Lord shall be revealed, and all flesh shall see it together.

This is our hope. This is the faith with which I return to the South. With this faith we will be able to transform the jangling discords of our nation into a beautiful symphony of brotherhood. With this faith we will be able to work together, to pray together, to struggle together, to go to jail together, to stand up for freedom together, knowing that we will be free one day.

This will be the day when all of God's children will be able to sing with new meaning, "My country 'tis of thee, sweet land of liberty, of thee I sing. Land where my fathers died, land of the pilgrim's pride, from every mountainside, let freedom ring."

And if America is to be a great nation this

must become true. So let freedom ring from the prodigious hilltops of New Hampshire. Let freedom ring from the mighty mountains of New York. Let freedom ring from the heightening Alleghenies of Pennsylvania!

Let freedom ring from the snowcapped Rockies of Colorado!

Let freedom ring from the curvaceous peaks of California!

But not only that; let freedom ring from the Stone Mountains of Georgia.

Let freedom ring from every hill and mole-hill of Mississippi. From every mountainside, let freedom ring.

When we let freedom ring, when we let it ring from every village and every hamlet, from every state and every city, we will be able to speed up that day when all of God's children, black men and white men, Jews and Gentiles, Protestants and Catholics, will be able to join hands and sing in the words of that old Negro spiritual, "Free at last! Free at last! Thank God almighty, we are free at last!"

1. How would you rate the charismatic appeal of King's speech? (If feasible, listen to the speech on tape to better comprehend the nonverbal aspects of the speech.)

2. What specific charismatic elements can you identify in this famous speech?

3. Would a speech of this emotional intensity be appropriate in a work setting? Explain your reasoning.

_____

Reprinted by arrangement with The Heirs to the Estate of Martin Luther King, Jr., c/o Writers House, Inc. as agents for the proprietor. Copyright 1963 by Martin Luther King, Jr., copyright renewed 1991 by Coretta Scott King.

LEADERSHIP SKILL-BUILDING EXERCISE 3–3

Visionary Speech

Write a brief speech about a dream that you or someone else could use in a work setting. Make the dream so inspiring that workers will eagerly help the organization attain the vision you have articulated. Remember to make several emotional appeals to strengthen your speech.

ANSWERS TO LEADERSHIP SELF-ASSESSMENT EXERCISE 3–1

1. b; 2. a: 3. a; 4. b; 5. b; 6. b; 7. a; 8. b; 9. a: 10. b.

If you responded this way to four or fewer questions, you probably don't have much charisma. Seven or more? You ooze it!

CHAPTER FOUR

Effective Leadership Behaviors and Attitudes

LEARNING OBJECTIVES

After studying this chapter, you should be able to

1. summarize the pioneering research on leadership behaviors and attitudes conducted at the Ohio State University and the University of Michigan.
2. describe at least seven task-oriented leadership behaviors and attitudes.
3. describe at least seven relationship-oriented leadership attitudes and behaviors.
4. describe the meaning and significance of SuperLeadership.
5. explain how leaders use 360-degree feedback to fine-tune their behaviors and attitudes.
6. pinpoint possible limitations to understanding leadership through the leader's behaviors and attitudes.

*T*o New York City Police Commissioner William Bratton, high productivity and profit meant low crime. The simple goal he set for the entire department was to cut crime. To help fight crime and direct his police force, Bratton developed Comstat (a shortening of computer statistics) meetings. The statistics made the 76 precinct commanders and 38,000 police workers accountable for the city's crime rate. Precinct commanders who showed up for meetings without carefully prepared statistics, accompanied by crime-reduction strategies, were severely reprimanded by Bratton. The focus on measuring the crime rate contributed to a 27 percent reduction in crime in two years. Bratton introduced technology, including LAN systems and cellular phones in squad cars, to help police fight crime. His aggressive push for community policing and putting more police on the street also helped to reduce street crime. He also pushed for a crackdown on even minor offenses such as public drunkenness.

When Bratton first arrived in New York after being hired away from the Boston Police Department, he asked for an immediate 10 percent drop in crime. By 1995, Bratton raised the goal to a 15 percent reduction, and the crime rate was reduced by 17 percent. A criminologist from the University of Maryland says that Bratton spearheaded the most focused crime-reduction effort he had ever seen.[1]

The traits and personal characteristics described in the previous two chapters contribute substantially to effective leadership. Success as a leader, however, also depends on the right behaviors (including skills) and attitudes. For example, to be effective, William Bratton provided considerable direction and structure for his police force. This chapter describes a number of key behaviors and attitudes that contribute to a manager's ability to function as a leader. It also describes how the right leadership behaviors and attitudes can get team members to lead themselves, and how 360-degree feedback helps leaders adjust their attitudes and behaviors.

Frequent reference is made in this chapter, and at other places in the text, to leadership effectiveness. A working definition of an **effective leader** is one whose actions facilitate group members' attainment of productivity, quality, and satisfaction.

PIONEERING RESEARCH ON LEADERSHIP BEHAVIOR AND ATTITUDES

Over the period between the mid-1940s and mid-1950s, extensive research was conducted at the Ohio State University and the University of Michigan on effective leadership practices. This pioneering research laid the foundation for understanding the difference between successful and unsuccessful leaders. The same research led to modern conceptions of leadership styles. Despite the contributions of this early leadership research, it has limitations for a modern understanding of high-level leadership. Most of the surveys and interviews were conducted with bomber airplane commanders and production and office supervisors.

The Ohio State University Studies of Initiating Structure and Consideration

After World War II, a major leadership research program was conducted at the Bureau of Business Research at the Ohio State University. The study identified 1,800 specific examples of leadership behavior, which were reduced to 150 questionnaire items on leadership functions.[2] The functions are also referred to as *dimensions of leadership behavior.* A major thrust of the research was to ask team members to describe their supervisors by responding to questionnaires. Leaders were also asked to rate themselves on leadership dimensions.

Two Key Leadership Dimensions. A series of studies identified two leadership dimensions that accounted for 85 percent of the variance in descriptions of leadership behavior: initiating structure and consideration. For historical interest, the ten original dimensions that were later clustered into the final two dimensions are shown in Table 4–1. **Initiating structure** is the degree to which the leader organizes and defines relationships in the group by activities such as assigning specific tasks, specifying procedures to be followed, scheduling work, and clarifying expectations of team members.

Leaders who score high on the initiating structure dimension define the relationship between themselves and their staff members, as well as the role that they expect each staff member to assume. Such leaders also endeavor to establish well-defined channels of communication and ways of getting the job done. Five self-assessment items measuring initiating structure are as follows:

1. Try out your own new ideas in the work group.
2. Encourage the slow-working people in the group to work harder.
3. Emphasize meeting deadlines.
4. Meet with the group at regularly scheduled times.
5. See to it that people in the work group are working up to capacity.

TABLE 4–1   Dimensions of Leadership Behavior Based on Descriptions by Group Members

Original Dimensions	Four Factors Identified Next	Final Two Factors
1. Domination	I. Consideration 49.6*	I. Consideration
2. Initiation	II. Initiating structure 33.6*	II. Initiating structure
3. Membership	III. Production emphasis 9.8*	
4. Representation	IV. Sensitivity 7.0*	
5. Integration		
6. Organization		
7. Communication up		
8. Communication down		
9. Recognition		
10. Production		

*Refers to the percentage of common variance accounted for by the factors.

Source: Gathered from information in Ralph M. Stogdill and Alvin E. Coons, *Leader Behavior: Its Description and Measurement* (Columbus, Ohio: The Ohio State University Bureau of Business Research, 1957), pp. 40–42.

Consideration is the degree to which the leader creates an environment of emotional support, warmth, friendliness, and trust. The leader creates this environment by being friendly and approachable, looking out for the personal welfare of the group, keeping the group abreast of new developments, and doing small favors for the group.

Leaders who score high on the consideration factor typically are friendly, are trustful, earn respect, and have a warm relationship with team members. Leaders with low scores on the consideration factor typically are authoritarian and impersonal in their relationships with group members. Five questionnaire items measuring the consideration factor are as follows:

1. Do personal favors for people in the work group.
2. Treat all people in the work group as your equal.
3. Be willing to make changes.
4. Back up what people under you do.
5. Do little things to make it pleasant to be a member of the staff.

An important output of research on initiating structure and consideration was to categorize leaders with respect to how much emphasis they place on the two dimensions. As implied by Figure 4–1, the two dimensions are not mutually exclusive. A leader can achieve high or low status on both dimensions. For example, an effective leader might contribute to high productivity yet still place considerable emphasis on warm human relationships. The four-cell grid of Figure 4–1 is a key component of several approaches to describing leadership style. We return to this topic in Chapter 5.

Some Research Findings and Implications.   Many practical implications have been derived from research conducted on the relationship between

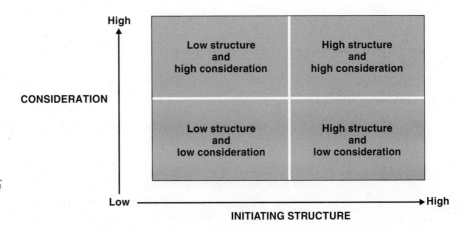

FIGURE 4–1

Four Combinations of Initiating Structure and Consideration

these two leadership dimensions and effectiveness criteria. A general finding is that the most effective leaders emphasize both initiating structure and consideration. In summarizing some of the earliest research, Andrew W. Halpin wrote, "In short, our findings suggest that to select a leader who is likely to satisfy both his men [only male aircraft pilots were studied], we do best by choosing an aircraft commander who is above average on both leader behavior dimensions."[3]

Another consistent finding from the Ohio State studies was that group members desire more in the way of consideration. In contrast, the managers to whom the supervisory leaders reported preferred a greater emphasis on initiating structure. The higher the level of management, the greater the emphasis on initiating structure. Additional data supported the idea that group members value consideration. It was discovered that employee turnover was lowest and job satisfaction highest under leaders who were rated high in consideration. Conversely, leaders who were rated low in consideration and high in initiating structure had high grievance and turnover rates among their employees. Research also indicated that leaders high on structure were generally rated highly by superiors. They also had higher-producing work groups than did leaders who scored lower in initiating structure.

Another important implication for organizational leaders is that the situation influences whether the leader should emphasize initiating structure or consideration. In some situations, group members rated leaders with a strong emphasis on initiating structure as being more effective. For example, Air Force commanders who rated high on consideration were rated as *less* effective than were commanders who rated high on structure. A plausible reason for this finding is that the organizational culture of the Air Force supports a demanding leader. The importance of leaders adapting to the situation will be mentioned later in this chapter and featured in Chapter 6, "Contingency and Situational Leadership."

The University of Michigan Studies of Effective Leadership Practices

During the time of the Ohio State studies, researchers at the Survey Research Center of the University of Michigan were also studying leadership effectiveness. Interviews and questionnaires were used extensively to contrast the behavior of leaders from high-producing units with that of leaders from low-producing units.[4]

Two Key Approaches to Leadership.   Supervisory leaders were categorized into two groups, depending on whether they emphasized production or employees. **Production-centered leaders** set tight work standards, organized tasks carefully, and prescribed the work methods to be followed. They also closely supervised the work of group members. **Employee-centered leaders** encouraged subordinate participation in goal setting and in other work decisions. They also helped to ensure high performance by engendering trust and mutual respect. The production-centered versus employee-centered difference parallels the distinction between initiating structure and consideration, with one exception. A leader is classified as either production-centered or employee-centered, which is a one-dimensional classification. The classification of structure and consideration is two-dimensional with four possible categories, as previously explained.

Some Research Findings and Implications.   A dominant finding of the University of Michigan studies was that most productive work groups tend to have leaders who are employee-centered rather than production-centered. Also, the most effective leaders are those who have supportive relationships with group members. They emphasize group rather than individual decision making, and encourage team members to set and achieve high performance goals. Despite the general consistency of the contribution of employee-centered leadership, the studies produced some mixed findings.

Later research by the Michigan group shed new light on the complexity of the relationship between the type of leadership and productivity. One group of employees in a life insurance company was managed by employee-centered leaders. A comparable group was managed by production-centered leaders. Contrary to expectations, both groups showed a significant increase in productivity. The employee-centered leadership approach, however, fostered an increase in favorable attitudes toward the supervisors and the company. In contrast, the production-centered group showed a marked decrease in favorable attitudes toward supervision and management. Another study was conducted with 20,000 employees in a firm that manufactures earth-moving equipment. It was concluded that supervisors with the best production records were both production- and employee-centered.

An important implication of both the Ohio State and Michigan studies is that effective leaders emphasize both high productivity and good interpersonal relationships. The same theme surfaces in many of the approaches to leadership studied throughout this book. In almost any leadership situation you face, you will need to juggle the two dimensions of task orientation and people orientation.

TASK-RELATED ATTITUDES AND BEHAVIORS

The task-related versus relationship-related classification remains useful as a framework for understanding leadership attitudes, behaviors, and practices. This section identifies and describes task-related attitudes and behaviors

TABLE 4–2   Task-Related Leadership Attitudes and Behaviors

1. Adaptability to the situation	5. Ability to interpret conditions
2. Direction setting	6. Frequent feedback
3. High performance standards	7. Stability of performance
4. Risk taking and bias for action	8. Strong customer orientation

characteristic of effective leaders, as outlined in Table 4–2. *Task-related* in this context means that the behavior, attitude, or skill focuses more on the task to be performed than on the interpersonal aspect of leadership. Most task-related activities would be included under initiating structure. Before reading further, do Leadership Self-Assessment Exercise 4–1.

Adaptability to the Situation.   Effective leaders adapt to the situation. Adaptability reflects the contingency viewpoint: A tactic is chosen based on the unique circumstances at hand. A leader who was responsible for psychologically immature group members would find it necessary to supervise them closely. If the group members were mature and self-reliant, they would require less supervision. The adaptive leader also selects an organization structure best suited to the demands of the situation, such as choosing between a brainstorming group and a committee.

The ability to size up people and situations, and adapt tactics accordingly, is a vital leadership behavior. It stems from insight and intuition, both of which reflect a talent for direct perception of a situation, unrelated to any specific reasoning process. Adaptability is a leadership behavior that includes attention to both task and interpersonal factors. The accompanying Leader in Action profile describes a heralded adaptive leader.

Direction Setting.   John Kotter reasons that since the function of leadership is to produce change, the leader must set the direction of that change. Setting the direction goes beyond planning, which is a management process designed to produce orderly results rather than change. Kotter explains that setting a direction is more inductive. Leaders gather voluminous data and search for patterns, relationships, and linkages that help explain events.[5]

Direction setting is part of creating a vision and strategy. The strategy describes a feasible way of achieving the vision. (Again, we emphasize the link between leadership and vision. Just in case you are not satiated with the topic, Chapter 13 has more information about visions and strategy.) A new buzzword to signify direction setting is the *northbound train*.

LEADERSHIP SELF-ASSESSMENT
EXERCISE 4–1   How Effective Are You as a Leader?

Directions: Circle the number on the 1–5 scale that best indicates how you really feel. If you are not now a manager, project how you would react if you were a manager.

1. I'll wait until things settle down.	1 2 3 4 5	I really like change.
2. Most of my staff meetings are about internal procedures and budgeting.	1 2 3 4 5	I spend much of my time talking to and about customers.
3. If there's a way, I'll find it.	1 2 3 4 5	Top management should make the first move.
4. I'll wait for orders from above.	1 2 3 4 5	Let's get it done right now.
5. I seek responsibility beyond my job description.	1 2 3 4 5	I fulfill my job description.
6. How can I enhance revenue? Add value?	1 2 3 4 5	I'll stay within my budget plan.
7. My people should "challenge the system."	1 2 3 4 5	I carefully review subordinates' work.
8. If I haven't been told *yes*, I can't do it.	1 2 3 4 5	If I haven't been told *no*, I can do it.
9. I'll take responsibility for my failures.	1 2 3 4 5	I usually make excuses for my failures.
10. I won't take risks because I may fail.	1 2 3 4 5	I'll take my risks although I may fail.
11. We've got to do things faster.	1 2 3 4 5	We can't turn things around that fast.
12. I want to know what other departments are doing and what their needs are.	1 2 3 4 5	I protect my own department.

13. I talk mainly to those people who are formally linked to me.   1 2 3 4 5   I'll go beyond the organization chart to share information and resources.

14. Leave my people and me alone and let us get our job done.   1 2 3 4 5   I'll cross department lines to get the job done.

15. I trust only a few people within the firm.   1 2 3 4 5   I volunteer to share ideas and resources with people in other departments.

Scoring and interpretation: Measure your effectiveness as a managerial leader as follows: For questions 1, 2, 4, 8, 10, 13, 14, and 15, simply add up the scores. For questions 3, 5, 6, 7, 9, 11 and 12, flip the scale so that a response score of 1 becomes 5, 2 becomes 4, 4 becomes 2, and 5 becomes 1. A total score of 60 means you have the mindset of an effective manager. If you scored below 45, you have some work to do.

Source: Adapted from Oren Harari and Linda Mukai, "A New Decade Demands a New Breed of Manager," *Management Review,* August 1990, p. 23. Used by permission of the authors.

Consultant and author Karl Albrecht contends that executives should tell their leadership team, "This is our northbound train. This is the direction we have chosen. If you don't feel you want to go north, there are other trains you can ride. But this particular train is going north, and I expect anyone who rides it to commit his or her energy fully to the journey." For example, the northbound train for the Australian Natural Gas Company is gaining market share by having more customers hook up to natural gas. The northbound train for the company became "Everything we do must help people choose natural gas."[6]

High Performance Standards.   Effective leaders consistently hold group members to high standards of performance. Setting such standards increases productivity, as people tend to live up to the expectations set for them by superiors. This is called the Pygmalion effect, and it works in a subtle, almost unconscious way. When a managerial leader believes that a group member will succeed, the manager communicates this belief without realizing that he or she is doing so. Conversely, when a leader expects a group member to fail, that person will not disappoint the manager. The manager's expectation of success or failure becomes a self-fulfilling prophecy. The manager's perceptions contribute to the success or failure.

LEADER IN ACTION

Chuck Daly, Basketball Coach

Chuck Daly is now head coach of the Orlando Magic. He joined Turner Broadcasting System during the 1994–95 season as an NBA game analyst. Prior to that he served as head coach of the New Jersey Nets for the 1992–93 and 1993–94 seasons, both times leading the team into the playoffs. Coach Daly says, "I've coached at every level. I know that you take what you have and you work with it." In college that may mean screaming and hollering and teaching. With the Detroit Pistons it meant pedal to the metal one night, foot covering the brake the next. With the "Dream Team" (the 1992 Olympic men's basketball team) it meant realizing that the best players ever just need a little nurturing.

"He's made the whole thing enjoyable," said Michael Jordan, a Dream Team player. "We needed someone to meld all these personalities together. He can put into words, and get a player to accept a certain responsibility. He makes it so

easy to accept a role without animosity. There's been no ego problem, and no ball-hogging either. . . . Even we were a little concerned about potential problems, but it's been smooth sailing from Day 1."

Daly said that when coaching a group of superstars, "You have to give them some structure, but that's about it. You don't diagram plays, you give them some ideas and they go from there. I learned when I coached the NBA all-star game that professional players have a great deal of pride."

Sportswriter Michael Wilbon adds that there never was a more logical choice for Dream Team coach than to pick the man who has the perfect touch for most every situation.

Source: © 1992 *The Washington Post*. Reprinted with permission.

A plausible explanation for the Pygmalion effect is that the leader sends nonverbal signals that indicate how much confidence he or she has in the group member. The signals, in turn, elevate or lower the group member's confidence level.

Gary C. Wendt, chief executive of General Electric Capital Services Inc., exemplifies an executive leader who sets high performance standards. Wendt is known to set a high bar for his managers to reach. Following his pattern, Wendt's staff managers set high standards for the people who report to them. The high standards set are considered the key reason that GE Capital has become the major finance company in the United States. Among these high standards are outwitting competitors by moving faster, buying cheaper, and servicing customers more rapidly. Another standard is to deal with problems the minute they arise.[7]

Risk Taking and Bias for Action. A bias for action rather than contemplation has been identified as a characteristic of a successful organization.[8] Combined with risk taking, a bias for action is also an important leadership behavior. To bring about constructive change, the leader must take risks and be willing to implement these risky decisions. Xerox Corp.'s performance appraisal includes risk taking and a bias for action as an evaluation characteristic. On the evaluation form, the characteristic is defined as follows:

> Willing to take personal risks to advance new ideas and programs for the success of the Company; has the courage to commit sizable resources based on a blend of analysis and intuition; is comfortable with making the percentages, rather than achieving success with each initiative; trusts own judgment and instincts without requiring definitive proof; prefers quick and approximate actions to slow and precise approaches.

Ability to Interpret Conditions.   According to the consulting firm Forum, leaders must interpret internal and external conditions that affect the leader and the organizational unit. A leader who interprets conditions is carrying out the management role of environmental sensing. When significant trends are observed, the leader helps the group develop an action plan to capitalize on or defend against the trends. The five interpreting practices are as follows:

1. Seeking information from as many sources as possible
2. Knowing how one's own work supports the organization's strategy
3. Analyzing how well the members of the group work together
4. Knowing the capabilities and motivations of the individuals in the work group
5. Knowing one's own capabilities and motivations[9]

John Sculley, formerly of Apple Computer, Inc., and currently a venture capitalist, exemplifies a leader who interprets conditions. He sensed that the consumer need for information handling has transcended single-use devices such as fax machines, E-mail, and cellular telephones. Sculley therefore spearheaded a strategic alliance of six companies called General Magic. The company is developing a "telephone for the year 2000" that combines the three personal communication devices just mentioned.[10]

Frequent Feedback.   Giving group members frequent feedback on their performance is another vital leadership behavior. The leader can rarely influence the actions of group members without appropriate performance feedback. Feedback of this nature has two aspects. First, group members are informed how well they are doing so that they can take corrective action if needed. Second, positive feedback serves as a reinforcer that prompts group members to continue favorable activities. Leadership Skill-Building Exercise 4–1 provides practice in developing feedback skills.

LEADERSHIP SKILL-BUILDING
EXERCISE 4–1   Feedback Skills

After small groups have completed an assignment such as answering the case questions or discussion questions, hold a performance feedback session. Also use observations you have made in previous problem-solving activities as the basis for your feedback. Each group member provides some feedback to each other member about how well he or she thinks the other person performed. To increase the probability of benefiting from this experience, feedback recipients must listen actively. Refer to the section in Chapter 10 about giving feedback and active listening.

A convenient way to do this exercise is for everyone to sit in a circle. Choose one feedback recipient to begin. Going clockwise around the circle, each group member gives that person feedback. After all people have spoken, the feedback recipient gives his or her reactions. The person to the left of the first recipient is the next one to get feedback.

After everyone has had a turn receiving performance feedback, hold a general discussion. Be sure to discuss three key issues:

1. How helpful was the feedback?
2. What was the relative effectiveness of positive versus negative feedback?
3. Were some group members better than others in giving feedback?

Stability of Performance.   Effective leaders are steady performers, even under heavy workloads and uncertain conditions. Remaining steady under conditions of uncertainty contributes to effectiveness because it helps team members cope with the situation. When the leader remains calm, group members are reassured that things will work out satisfactorily. Stability is helpful for another reason: It helps the managerial leader appear professional and cool under pressure.

In early 1993, a bomb exploded inside the underground garage of the World Trade Center. Key executives at Coopers & Lybrand, an accounting and consulting firm, provided steady performance to help workers cope with the situation. Almost overnight, operations from the Coopers & Lybrand offices in the World Trade Center were transferred temporarily to nearby offices of the firm. Without the calm leadership of the executives, company clients would have experienced severe disruption in services. Furthermore, the company would have lost substantial revenue.

Strong Customer Orientation.   Effective leaders are strongly interested in satisfying the needs of customers, clients, or constituents; this approach helps inspire employees to satisfy customers. A customer orientation is natural in a consumer products business but can be equally important for an industrial company. John W. Snow became the president of CSX, a financially troubled conglomerate, in 1988. Snow sold off all non-transportation-related businesses. In addition, he eliminated many jobs and helped the company develop a customer focus. Snow met with major shippers, listened to their complaints about poor service, and then made internal changes. CSX quickly returned to profitability, much of which has been attributed to Snow's customer focus.[11]

Now that you have studied various components of task-oriented behaviors and attitudes, do Leadership Self-Assessment Exercise 4–2. It will further sensitize you to the task activities of leaders and managers.

LEADERSHIP SELF-ASSESSMENT
EXERCISE 4–2   Task-Oriented Attitudes and Behaviors

Indicate whether you mostly agree or mostly disagree with the following statements. Relate the statements to any work situation, including sports, community activities, and school activities, in which you have been responsible for the work of others. If a work situation does not come to mind, imagine how you would act or think.

	Mostly Agree	Mostly Disagree
1. I keep close tabs on productivity figures, and interpret them to the group.	____	____
2. I send frequent E-mail messages to group members, giving them information about work procedures.	____	____
3. I clearly specify the quality goals our group needs to achieve.	____	____
4. I maintain clear-cut standards of performance.	____	____
5. When I conduct a meeting, the participants can count on a clear-cut agenda.	____	____
6. I feel good about my work week only if our team has met or exceeded its productivity goals.	____	____

7. People shouldn't be spending time with computers in the office unless the computers are actually increasing productivity.   ____   ____

8. I freely criticize work that does not meet standards.   ____   ____

9. I spend at least 20 percent of my work week either planning myself or helping team members with their planning.   ____   ____

10. I spend a good deal of time solving technical or business problems myself, or helping group members do the same.   ____   ____

If you responded "mostly agree" to eight, nine, or ten of the above statements, you have a strong task orientation. If you responded "mostly disagree" to four or more of the statements, you have below-average task-oriented behaviors and attitudes.

RELATIONSHIP-ORIENTED ATTITUDES AND BEHAVIORS

Leadership involves influencing people, so it follows that many effective leadership attitudes, behaviors, and practices deal with interpersonal relationships. Table 4–3 lists eight relationship-oriented attitudes and behaviors, which we will discuss next. (Most other parts of this book describe the interpersonal aspects of leadership.)

Alignment of People.   According to John Kotter, aligning people is more of a communications challenge than a problem of organization design. To get people pulling together, it is necessary to talk to more people than are required in organizing. The target population can involve many different stakeholders. Among them are immediate subordinates, higher-ups, peers, and workers in other parts of the organization, as well as suppliers, government officials, and even customers. Anyone who can help implement the vision and strategies or who can block implementation must be aligned.[12]

Another perspective on alignment is that it represents organizational members pulling together toward a higher purpose. This stands in contrast to being organized into units in which people stay within the confines of tight job descriptions. Alignment enables people to have a clear sense of direction because they are pursuing a vision. As long as their behavior supports the vision, they are less likely to be reprimanded by superiors.

TABLE 4–3   Relationship-Oriented Attitudes and Behaviors

1. Alignment of people	5. Satisfaction of human needs
2. Mobilization	6. Making work meaningful for people
3. Concert building	7. Emotional support and encouragement
4. Inspiration	8. Promotion of principles and values

During his seventeen-month stay as CEO of Apple Computer, Inc., in 1996–97, Gilbert F. Amelio invested considerable time in aligning company stakeholders. This included mending fences with dealers, asking them for feedback, and articulating his long-range vision for Apple. Amelio also kept open lines of communication with suppliers and corporate customers in an attempt to reinvigorate their faith in the company.[13]

Mobilization.   Whereas alignment of people takes place at almost a spiritual level, mobilization is more involved with getting the group working together smoothly. Mobilizing people is getting individuals with different ideas, skills, and values to carry out the work of the group. Mobilizing practices include:

1. Communicating expectations clearly
2. Appealing to people's hearts and minds to lead them in a new direction
3. Demonstrating care for team members
4. Demonstrating confidence in the abilities of others
5. Letting people know how they are progressing toward the group's goal.[14]

Concert Building.   A new concept of the leader's role, **concert building,** involves both aligning and mobilizing. The concert builder functions as an orchestra leader. His or her goal is to produce a system that is self-evaluating, self-correcting, self-renewing, and ongoing. David S. Brown describes concert-building leadership in these terms:

> The system can be thought of as a large modern orchestra with a number of professionals playing quite different instruments and performing separate—and often very difficult—tasks. Each instrumentalist, like so many in large organizations, is indeed a specialist in a particular field whose work must be integrated with the work of others to make up the whole.[15]

Becoming an organizational concert builder requires many of the skills and insights described throughout this book. Building teamwork, as described in Chapter 9, is particularly relevant.

Inspiration.   As described in the discussion of charismatic and transformational leadership, inspiring others is an essential leadership practice. Based on surveys and focus groups, the Forum Group has identified five inspiring practices:

1. Promoting the development of people's talents
2. Recognizing the contribution of others
3. Enabling others to feel like leaders
4. Stimulating others' thinking
5. Building enthusiasm about projects and assignments[16]

What it takes to inspire people depends considerably on the characteristics of the group members being inspired. The accompanying Leader in Action vignette describes a tactic the wealthiest man in America once used to inspire a well-educated, highly intelligent work force.

Satisfaction of Human Needs.   To inspire people, effective leaders motivate people by satisfying higher-level needs. John Kotter explains that motivation and inspiration energize people by satisfying needs for achievement, a sense of belonging, recognition, self-esteem, and a feeling of control over one's life. A strictly managerial—rather than leadership—approach would be

LEADER IN ACTION

Bill Gates, Software Mogul

Microsoft Corp. founder Bill Gates inspires employees by holding out the promise of a great future such as a global marketing strategy. In 1996 he vowed to his employees that Microsoft would soon become the dominant provider of Internet services even though Microsoft was a late entrant into this aspect of information technology. Gates also inspires employees with dramatic stunts. For example, one day 5,000 Microsoft employees were assembled in the Kingdome in Seattle, Washington. While the houselights dimmed, a spotlight followed a red Corvette with the word "Windows" written across its door. The executive vice president stepped out from the car. He pumped his fist into the air, and led the crowd in a boisterous chant: "Windows, Windows, Windows, Windows." The spotlight then shifted to an Edsel making its way into the arena. "OS/2," the name of IBM's competing software, emblazoned the failed automobile.

Next, as the song "Leader of the Pack" blared from the loudspeakers, ten motorcyclists clad in leather roared into the Kingdome on Harleys. The crowd greeted lead biker Bill Gates with the same roar typically reserved for rock stars. After his flamboyant entrance, the 36-year-old chairman presented his overview of the computer market and Microsoft for the current year and beyond.

Source: Joshua Cooper Ramo, "Winner Take All," *Time,* September 16, 1996, pp. 56–64; "Microsoft: Bill Gates' Baby Is On Top of the World. Can It Stay There?" *Business Week,* February 24, 1992, pp. 60–61; "Microsoft: Mark II," *The Economist,* March 19, 1994, p. 81.

to push people in the right direction through control mechanisms.[17] An example would be suspending people who did not achieve sales or quality quotas. Specific motivational skills used by leaders are described in Chapter 10.

Providing Meaning for People.   A major approach to providing meaning to people is to formulate the right vision and strategy. Formulating a vision and strategy helps involve group members in goal accomplishment. One of the purposes of Bill Gates's address after his motorcycle entrance was to provide specifics about what his vision of Microsoft would mean to employees. This vision formulating includes maintaining the most stringent hiring standards for employees. Employees can also find meaning in their work if the leader employs a basic tactic such as explaining how a particular job helps the company or society. Allegedly, Coca-Cola employees have found their work more meaningful upon learning that the real business of Coca-Cola is to bring a moment of pleasure to people whose days would otherwise be humdrum. Do you now look at producing soft drinks from a new perspective?

Emotional Support and Encouragement.   Supportive behavior toward team members usually increases leadership effectiveness. A supportive leader gives frequent encouragement and praise. One of the many work-related ways of encouraging people is to allow them to participate in decision making. Emotional support generally improves morale and sometimes improves productivity. In the long term, emotional support and encouragement may bolster a person's self-esteem.[18] Being emotionally supportive comes naturally to the leader who has empathy for people and who is a warm person.

Promotion of Principles and Values.   A major part of a top leader's role is to help promote values and principles that contribute to the welfare of individuals and the organizations. The promotion of values and principles can be classified as relationship-oriented because it deals directly with the emotions and attitudes of people, and indirectly with the task. Steven Covey, who is widely quoted for his uplifting messages, advises that an organization's mission statement must be for all good causes.[19] Leaders who believe in these good causes will then espouse principles and values that lead people toward good deeds in the workplace. Almost every leader or manager—even the most devious—claims to harbor values and principles that promote human welfare and the general good. Yet not all leaders and managers actually implement such values and principles.

To encourage managers and all other employees to conduct their work affairs at a high moral level, many companies put their values in written form. At Eastman Kodak Company, managers are evaluated partially on the basis of how well they have engaged in activities that support company values. Kodak values are as follows:

- ■ Respect for individual dignity
- ■ Uncompromising integrity
- ■ Trust
- ■ Credibility
- ■ Continuous learning and personal renewal

Leadership Skill-Building Exercise 4–2 gives you an opportunity to think through your work-related values, thus enhancing your ability to provide moral leadership to others. The reason is that providing moral leadership to others begins with understanding one's own values.

SUPERLEADERSHIP: LEADING OTHERS TO LEAD THEMSELVES

Charles C. Manz and Henry P. Sims, Jr. have formulated what they refer to as the SuperLeadership Theory. A **SuperLeader** is one who leads others to lead themselves, by acting as a teacher and a coach, not a director.[20] Unlike a charismatic leader, who maintains a high profile indefinitely, a SuperLeader inspires others to motivate themselves. And when people are self-directing, they require a minimum of external control.

SuperLeadership requires the leader to take a risk on people—to believe that if given a chance to be self-directing, workers will rise to the occasion. Over a decade ago, Lincoln Electric Co., a renowned welding equipment manufacturer, faced a severe sales slump. To maintain its no-layoff policy, company leadership asked production workers for some help. Fifty production workers volunteered to help out in sales. After a brief sales training program, the workers called on body shops throughout the United States to sell a small welder. The new temporary sales representatives brought in $10 million in new sales and established the small arc welder as an industry leader. The SuperLeadership in this example centers on taking a risk with workers and showing faith in their resourcefulness.

The key aspect of SuperLeadership deals with teaching the right thought patterns. Manz and Sims contend that the leader must teach team members how to develop productive thinking. The purpose of productive, or constructive, thinking is to enable workers to gain control over their own behavior. The SuperLeader serves as a model of constructive thought patterns. For example, the leader should minimize expressing pessimistic, self-critical thoughts to team members. Instead, he or she should reward employees when they think constructively.[21]

Manz recommends several specific ways of establishing and altering thought patterns in desirable ways, as outlined in Figure 4–2 and described next. Leaders and individual contributors alike should be able to practice self-leadership by incorporating the following attitudes and behaviors:

1. *Identification and replacement of destructive beliefs and assumptions.* Negative thoughts are identified and then replaced with more accurate and

LEADERSHIP SKILL-BUILDING
EXERCISE 4–2   Clarifying Your Work Values

To provide effective value leadership, it is essential that you first understand your own values with respect to dealing with others. Rank from 1 to 12 the importance of the following values to you as a person. The most important value on the list receives a rank of 1; the least important, a rank of 12. Use the space next to "Other" if we have left out an important value in your life.

____   Respect for the dignity of others

____   Ensuring that others have interesting work to perform

____   Earning the trust of others

____   Earning the respect of others

____   Impressing others with how well my group performs

____   Giving others proper credit for their work

____   Continuous learning on the part of each member in our group, myself included

____   Holding myself and others accountable for delivering on commitments

____   Helping others grow and develop

____   Inspiring others to achieve high productivity and quality

____   Developing the reputation of being a trustworthy person

____   Other

1. Compare your ranking of these values with that of the person next to you, and discuss.

2. Perhaps your class, assisted by your instructor, might arrive at a class average on each of these values. How does your ranking compare to the class ranking?

3. Look back at your own ranking. Does your ranking surprise you?

4. Are there any surprises in the class ranking? Which values did you think would be highest and lowest?

constructive ones. For example, an employee might regard the manager's criticism as an indicator of personal dislike. A more productive way to view the criticism is to think that the manager is just trying to help him or her perform at a higher level.

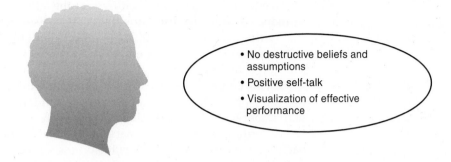

FIGURE 4–2

Productive Thinking as Part of SuperLeadership

2. *Positive and constructive self-talk.* Negative thoughts are converted into positive ones. For example, instead of saying, "My communication skills are too poor to make a presentation to higher management," one would say, "In order to make an impressive presentation to management, I will have to improve my oral communication skills. I'll get started tonight."

3. *Visualization of methods for effective performance.* One imagines oneself moving effortlessly through a challenging assignment, using methods that have worked in the past. Visualize making a hard-hitting presentation to management, similar to a presentation of lesser stake that you have made in the past. The idea is that the visualization is practice for the real event and will help one believe in one's capacity to be effective.

In summary, the SuperLeader helps create conditions whereby team members require very little leadership. Achieving such a goal is important because organizations have reduced the number of managers. Also, organizational structures such as work teams and horizontal structures require a high degree of self-management.

360-DEGREE FEEDBACK FOR FINE-TUNING LEADERSHIP APPROACH

In many organizations, leaders not only provide feedback to group members, they also receive feedback that gives them insight into the efficacy of their attitudes and behaviors. The feedback is systematically derived from a full sampling of parties who interact with the leader. In particular, **360-degree feedback** is a formal evaluation of superiors based on input from people who work for and with them, sometimes including customers and suppliers. Often, 360-degree feedback includes an optional self-evaluation. When self-evaluation is used, the individual completes the same structured evaluations that all others used to evaluate his or her performance. The feedback is communicated to the leader (as well as to others being evaluated by 360-degree evaluation) and interpreted with the assistance of a company human resources professional or an external consultant.

In addition to using the feedback for the administrative purposes of performance evaluation, the same data can be used to help leaders fine-tune their attitudes and behavior. For example, if all the interested parties gave the leader low ratings on "empathy toward others," the leader might be prompted to improve his or her ability to empathize. Action plans for improving empathy would include reading about empathy, attending a seminar, and simply making a conscious attempt to empathize when involved with a conflict of opinion with another person.

According to Robert Hoffman, a major reason for using 360-degree feedback is that it can detect barriers to success.[22] Feedback sometimes indicates that a leader perceived as a hurdle by those working with or for him or her is stalling organizational or unit growth. Success can be limited by such restricted behaviors as inflexibility, hostility, refusing to give information, lack of initiative, and inappropriate leadership style. A Colgate-Palmolive Co. human resources manager explains, "Three-hundred sixty-degree feedback on a departmental basis is an effective method that determines how we can be better as an individual and an organization. We use the results to plan departmental training needs. How can we expect people to meet our objectives if the necessary skills are underdeveloped?"[23]

Also, 360-degree feedback is a key component of *Benchmarks,* a widely used leadership training program developed by the Center for Creative Leadership. The leader and a good sampling of work associates complete a lengthy questionnaire about dozens of specific behaviors. (It easily takes two hours to respond to all the questions.) Self-ratings are then compared to ratings by others. Assume that a leader rates himself in the 90th percentile on "Putting people at ease: Displays warmth and a good sense of humor." If others rated him at the 15th percentile on this dimension, the leader might be counseled about how to put others at ease.

The example just cited hints at the importance of professionally trained counselors being involved in 360-degree feedback. Some people feel emotionally crushed when they find a wide discrepancy between their self-perception on an interpersonal skill dimension and the perception of others. A middle manager involved in a 360-degree evaluation prided herself on how well she was liked by others. The feedback that emerged, however, depicted her as intimidating, hostile, and manipulative. Upon receiving the feedback, the woman went into a rage (proving the feedback true!) followed by despondency. Professional counseling can sometimes help a person benefit from critical feedback and place it in perspective.

LIMITATIONS TO STUDYING LEADERSHIP THROUGH BEHAVIORS AND ATTITUDES

For over fifty years a basic approach to understanding the leadership aspects of management has been to examine the behaviors and attitudes of leaders. Categorizing these behaviors and attitudes as either task- or relationship-oriented has proved to be sensible and workable as a means of both under-standing leadership and training leaders. As you have seen in this chapter, a wide variety of behaviors and attitudes can be included under that task ver-sus relationship dichotomy.

The task versus relationship categorization is at its weakest when lead-ership activity is simply described by these two broad dimensions. The spe-cific behaviors included under each dimension (such as those described in this chapter) need to be highlighted to provide useful guidelines for leader-ship practice. For example, the specific behavior "emotional support and encouragement" tells more about leadership activity than the broad behav-ior "relationship-oriented." The discussion of leadership roles in Chapter 1 is another example of identifying specific behaviors that contribute to lead-ership effectiveness.

Gary Yukl raises another important problem with understanding leader-ship through the behavior and attitudes of leaders. He notes that relatively few studies have attempted to identify situations in which specific types of leadership behaviors are relevant. It would be useful to know, for example, the circumstances under which maintaining high performance standards or providing inspiration would achieve the best results. The contingency theo-ries discussed in Chapter 6 are a step in this direction.[24]

A needed refinement of the behaviors and attitudes approach to study-ing leadership would be to identify which clusters of behaviors and atti-tudes will achieve the intended results in a given situation. For example, for a leader faced with the challenge of getting the highest productivity from a work group experiencing job insecurity, which combination of behaviors and attitudes would be best for achieving high productivity, high quality, and high morale?

In evaluating any one approach to understanding leadership, the reader is advised to remember the general framework presented in Chapter 1. From the various approaches, choose the one or more that best fit the circum-stances. For example, in some situations a leader might want to emphasize charisma and inspiration, while in others he or she might emphasize provid-ing considerable structure to group members.

SUMMARY

Effective leadership requires the right behav-iors, skills, and attitudes, as emphasized in two pioneering sets of studies. The Ohio State Uni-versity studies identified two major dimensions of leadership behavior, initiating structure and consideration.

Initiating structure is the degree to which the leader organizes and defines relationships in the group by such activities as assigning tasks and specifying procedures. Consideration is the de-gree to which the leader creates an environment of emotional support, warmth, friendliness, and trust. The most effective leaders emphasize both initiating structure and consideration. The situa-tion, however, often influences which leadership dimension should be emphasized.

The University of Michigan studies classified leaders as production-centered versus employee-centered. Among the key findings were that employee-centered leaders were the most effective. Yet it was also found that emphasizing both types of leadership can lead to high productivity.

Many task-related attitudes and behaviors of effective leaders have been identified. Among them are (1) adaptability to the situation, (2) direction-setting, (3) high performance standards, (4) risk taking and a bias for action, (5) ability to interpret environmental conditions, (6) frequent feedback, (7) stability of performance, and (8) strong customer orientation.

Many relationship-oriented attitudes and behaviors of leaders have also been identified. Among them are (1) alignment of people, (2) mobilization, (3) concert building, (4) inspiration, (5) satisfaction of human needs, (6) making work meaningful for people, (7) emotional support and encouragement, and (8) promotion of principles and values.

A SuperLeader is one who leads others to lead themselves. Teaching team members to develop productive thought patterns helps develop self-leadership. For example, the leader encourages people to talk to themselves positively and constructively.

Many leaders today are receiving extensive feedback on their behaviors and attitudes in the form of 360-degree feedback, whereby people who work for or with the leader provide the feedback. Such feedback is helpful in detecting barriers to success. The leadership training program Benchmarks makes extensive use of 360-degree feedback.

Understanding leadership through behaviors and attitudes has its limitations. The specific behaviors included under the task and relationship dimensions need to be highlighted to provide useful guidelines for leadership practice. It would also be helpful to understand which combination of behaviors and attitudes is likely to be the most effective in a given situation.

KEY TERMS

Effective leader	Production-centered leader	SuperLeader
Initiating structure	Employee-centered leader	360-degree feedback
Consideration	Concert building	

GUIDELINES FOR ACTION AND SKILL DEVELOPMENT

One practical way to increase your leadership effectiveness is to select appropriate leadership behaviors to implement when you carry out a leadership assignment. Here is a checklist of the leadership behaviors described in this chapter. Choose several that would appear to be relevant to the leadership situation you face. Remember, however, that all leadership situations call for some combination of initiating structure and consideration. Adapting to the situation is the essence of situational leadership and is required almost universally.

Develop an action plan for developing each leadership behavior or attitude you choose. Typically the action plan will call for first understanding the meaning of the attitude or behavior, then using appropriate self-discipline or monitoring to engage in such behavior. Assume, for example, that you perceive "showing a strong customer orientation" as an area for growth. To achieve a stronger customer orientation, you might engage in such behaviors as the following:

- Reviewing your daily work activities and asking, "How would this help our customers?"

- Holding brief discussions with group members to review the importance of satisfying customer needs.

- Accompanied by a group member, calling on customers to discuss the quality of your firm's service.

Leadership Behaviors and Attitudes

1. Initiating structure
2. Showing consideration
3. Showing adaptability to the situation
4. Setting a direction
5. Setting high performance standards
6. Giving frequent feedback
7. Exhibiting performance stability
8. Showing a strong customer orientation
9. Aligning people
10. Mobilizing people
11. Engaging in concert building
12. Inspiring people
13. Satisfying human needs
14. Making work meaningful
15. Giving emotional support
16. Promoting principles and values
17. Being a SuperLeader

DISCUSSION QUESTIONS AND ACTIVITIES

1. How is initiating structure related to planning, organizing, and controlling?
2. How would a high standing on initiating structure help a manager do an effective job of reengineering?
3. Why is consideration so closely associated with a leader's having good interpersonal skills?
4. Explain how a leader could realistically be both production-centered and employee-centered.
5. Why is direction setting still an important leadership activity in an era of empowerment?
6. What would be the likely focus of an organizational leader who did not have a customer orientation?

7. How does a leader go about aligning people?
8. Ask an experienced leader how he or she gives emotional support to team members. Be prepared to report your findings in class.
9. Assume that you are assigned the task of managing the work of a group of housekeepers at a hotel, most of whom have no prior work experience. What combination of task and relationship behaviors and attitudes would it be important for you to emphasize? Why?
10. What about the ethics of SuperLeadership? Is the leader's attempt to modify the thought patterns of group members justified from an ethical standpoint?

LEADERSHIP CASE PROBLEM

What Kind of a Leader Is Aaron Feuerstein?

Malden Mills of Lawrence, Massachusetts, manufactures textiles for upholstery and durable outdoor wear. In early 1996, Aaron Feuerstein, the company owner, became a national celebrity. His heroic efforts to keep his company operating after a fire loss estimated at $400 million led to Feuerstein's being featured in newspapers, magazines, and television shows throughout the country and abroad. Even the Land's End catalog (the company is a Malden Mills customer) featured his story. The disaster took place the morning of December 12, 1995. After returning home from a party celebrating his seventieth birthday, Feuerstein received a telephone call from one of his top managers telling him that fire was consuming the entire mill.

After Feuerstein arrived at the mill, another fire broke out. Even worse, the fire victim count was mounting. Twenty-three workers were caught in the blaze, and nine of them were near death. Later, Feuerstein made numerous visits to the hospitals to help comfort the burn victims and their families. The fire was so ferocious that police evacuated residences and businesses in the immediate area. As the multiple fires finally died down, Feuerstein stood outside with his family, close associates, and mill employees. It appeared that only one or two of the buildings in the mill complex would be usable again. "No, I'll not weep," he stated emphatically. "There will be a Malden Mills tomorrow."

Feuerstein reasoned that if there was enough remaining of the Finishing 2 building to get production going, and that if the insurance manager could assure him of adequate coverage, Malden Mills would make a comeback. Both conditions were met; the insurance coverage was estimated at $300 million, and Finishing 2 could be brought back into partial operation quickly. Many union members and officials were skeptical that even a smart businessperson like Feuerstein could bring much of the mill back into operation. Two thousand jobs were at stake in a geographic area where the textile industry was rapidly becoming extinct. Malden Mills also had another 1,000 employees in locations outside of Lawrence.

Malden Mills, under Feuerstein, had faced near disaster in the past. The company had chosen bankruptcy protection in 1992 when one of its main product lines, artificial fur, suddenly went out of fashion. Feuerstein's rebound strategy was to restructure the mill around two innovative fabrics, Polartec and Polarfleece. These wool-like synthetics, developed by Malden employees out of recycled plastic, were light and warm, thus achieving a huge demand. Sales of the two products were about $200 million in 1995, one-half the company's total sales.

Before the fire, Feuerstein was phasing down his day-to-day involvement in the company. The decision to rebuild reenergized him. He pushed his cadre of managers to be decisive and take risks. A lot of the responsibility for quick rebuilding fell on the shoulders of his 35-year-old manufacturing manager, Patti Fitzpatrick. Another challenge facing the Lawrence operation was that until it was back in operation, Malden's other plants could not operate because they fed raw material to Lawrence. Each day the management team met for crisis meetings to plan the comeback. In less than one week, at least some of the Polartec product began to flow from Finishing 2.

Inside a makeshift office, Feuerstein made an announcement that catapulted him and the company to fame. He committed to paying all 3,100 employees for ninety days even if they were not called back. (Ultimately about 1,000 employees received three months wages while unemployed.) The potential $15 million tab shocked the Malden Mills managers and outside analysts. The insurance reimbursement, which was coming in slowly, was estimated to be $40 million short of covering the losses. Feuerstein insisted that he was right. In his mind, it was his high-quality employees who made possible the high-quality product that had enabled Malden Mills to compete successfully against lower-price foreign competition. Feuerstein explained, "We need to keep our people together."

In September 1996, Malden Mills introduced a broad new line of high-end upholstery fabrics at a trade show in Brussels. The comeback was now complete for a company that had experienced one of the biggest industrial fires in New England history. Yet the skeptics remain. Some observers have criticized Feuerstein, saying that he reacted irrationally. They think he should have taken the insurance money, sold the property, and enjoyed the rest of his life in leisure. Another sensible alternative, said many critics, would have been to rebuild the factories in a low-wage area, perhaps overseas. Why continue to run a union operation?

Feuerstein believes that he has good arguments to counter all his critics. For example, he says that textile manufacturers who search for low-wage workers may be sacrificing quality, thus eroding their customer base. He says his business philosophy is to create so much quality that his customers would not think of choosing another supplier. Feuerstein also believes that his concern for workers, combined with heavy investments in technology, has spearheaded success for his company. The employee retention rate at Malden Mills is 95 percent. During the period from 1982 to 1995, revenues in inflation-adjusted dollars have tripled while the work force has doubled. In comparison, the overall productivity increase for U.S. manufacturers has been just over 1 percent per year.

1. What leadership behaviors has Feuerstein demonstrated?

2. What leadership attitudes has Feuerstein demonstrated?

3. What criticisms can you offer of Feuerstein as a leader and a manager?

Source: Bruce D. Butterfield, "There Will Be a Malden Mills Tomorrow," *The Boston Sunday Globe*, September 8, 1996, pp. A28–29; Thomas Teal, "Not a Fool, Not a Saint," *Fortune*, November 11, 1996, pp. 201–204; http://www.boston.com (keyword Malden Mills).

LEADERSHIP SKILL-BUILDING EXERCISE 4–3

Effective and Ineffective Leaders

Prepare a written description of either the best boss or the worst boss you have ever had. Relate your description to the behaviors and attitudes described in this chapter. After all class members have completed their descriptions, assemble into groups of "bad bosses" or "good bosses." Working in groups, search for patterns of behaviors, skills, and attitudes characteristic of very good or very bad leaders. To help prepare your descriptions, use the checklist presented in the "Guidelines for Action and Skill Development."

Leadership Styles

*D*urk Jager is the president and chief operating officer of the consumer-products giant Procter & Gamble. He and CEO John Pepper are regarded as the two major leaders at P&G. At one time he was considered to be Pepper's chief rival for the top slot. Jager is the first executive in company history to hold the title of COO (chief operating officer). All four of the company's global regions report directly to Jager. When he was promoted to this position, Jager had to deal with the many problems created by his brusque predecessor, Edwin Artzt, who was nicknamed the Prince of Darkness. Jager is regarded by his team members as a decisive leader who makes sure that decisions are implemented and projects are completed. Before he makes a decision, however, he gets input from the managers of all four regions. For this reason he is regarded by people around him as a consensus builder.[1]

The perceptions of managers working closely with Durk Jager illustrate the widespread acceptance of thinking about leadership in terms of style. Phrases such as "he's a real autocrat" and "she's a consensus manager" have become commonplace. Most experienced workers are thus familiar with the concept of **leadership style,** the relatively consistent pattern of behavior that characterizes a leader. The study of leadership style is an extension of an understanding of leadership behaviors and attitudes. As described in Chapter 4, most classifications of leadership style are based on the dimensions of initiating structure and consideration.

This chapter describes two well-known classifications of leadership style, the leadership continuum and the Leadership Grid. It then examines other style-related issues such as the entrepreneurial leadership style, sex differences in leadership style, and choosing the best style. Chapter 6 continues the exploration of leadership style by presenting several leadership theories that sharply focus on contingency factors. Two chapters about leadership style are presented to enhance leadership effectiveness through the understanding of one's style and adapting it to circumstances.

THE LEADERSHIP CONTINUUM: CLASSICAL LEADERSHIP STYLES

The original concept of leadership style traces back to research conducted with Boy Scout leaders. In 1938, Lewin and Lippitt suggested that leadership behavior could be classified in terms of how much involvement leaders have with people-related versus work-related issues.[2] Research into initiating structure and consideration, and work-centered versus employee-centered leadership extended these ideas. Here we examine two related explanations of the leadership continuum: the boss-centered versus employee-centered continuum, and the autocratic–participative–free-rein continuum.

The Boss-Centered Versus Employee-Centered Leadership Continuum

Robert Tannenbaum and Warren H. Schmidt advised managers how to choose a leadership pattern from among a range of leadership behaviors.[3] The behaviors chosen characterize different leadership styles. As shown in Figure 5–1, the selection is made along a continuum of boss-centered versus employee-centered leadership. To select the most appropriate style, the leader takes into account certain forces in the manager, the subordinates, and the situation, as well as time constraints.

Forces in the Manager. Managers who believe strongly that team members should have a say in decision making will move toward the right side of the continuum. Managers who have confidence in the capabilities of team members will grant them more freedom. A leader's natural inclinations are also important. Some people are directive by nature, whereas others feel comfortable sharing decision making. Emotionally secure leaders are more comfortable releasing decision making to team members.

Forces in the Subordinates. Each team member, similar to the leader, is influenced by many personality variables. Generally speaking, team members can be granted more decision-making latitude if they are independent, can tolerate ambiguity, are competent, and identify with organizational goals. Team members who expect to share in decision making can be more readily granted authority.

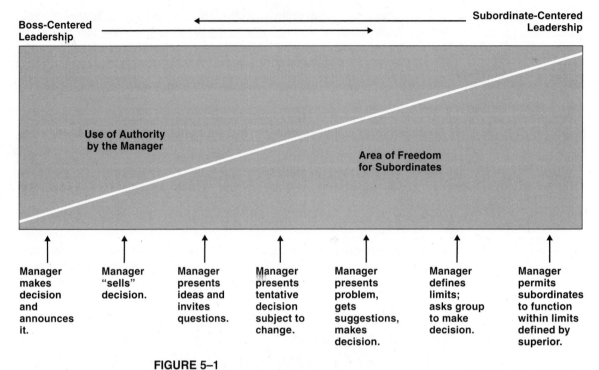

**Boss-Centered
Leadership**

**Subordinate-Centered
Leadership**

Use of Authority
by the Manager

Area of Freedom
for Subordinates

| Manager makes decision and announces it. | Manager "sells" decision. | Manager presents ideas and invites questions. | Manager presents tentative decision subject to change. | Manager presents problem, gets suggestions, makes decision. | Manager defines limits; asks group to make decision. | Manager permits subordinates to function within limits defined by superior. |

FIGURE 5–1

Continuum of Leadership Behavior

Source: Reprinted by permission of Harvard Business Review. *"Continuum of Leadership Behavior" from "How to Choose a Leadership Pattern" by Robert Tannenbaum and Warren H. Schmidt,* Harvard Business Review, *May/June 1973. Copyright © 1973 by the President and Fellows of Harvard College; all rights reserved.*

Forces in the Situation.   The values and traditions of the organization with regard to shared decision making influence how much authority can be granted to team members. Effective work groups can handle more freedom. At times the team has the requisite knowledge to handle the problem; at other times only the manager has enough competence to solve the problem. For example, the manager might have a network contact that enables him or her to get a budget issue resolved.

The Pressure of Time.   The more the manager feels the need for an immediate decision, the more difficult it is to involve others in decision making. Employee-centered leadership is time consuming despite its merits.

Tannenbaum and Schmidt's leadership continuum summarizes a wealth of knowledge about participative decision making. Other leadership theories, such as the normative decision model described in Chapter 6, incorporate many of its basic ideas.

The Autocratic–Participative–Free-Rein Continuum

The Schmidt and Tannenbaum model gradually evolved into a leadership continuum with more specific anchor points on the continuum. Three key points on the continuum represent autocratic, participative, and free-rein styles of leadership, as shown in Figure 5–2.

Autocratic Leadership Style.   **Autocratic leaders** retain most of the authority for themselves. They make decisions confidently and assume that group members will comply; they usually are not concerned with group members' attitudes toward a decision. Autocratic leaders are considered task-oriented because they place heavy emphasis on getting tasks accomplished. Typical autocratic behaviors include telling people what to do, asserting themselves, and serving as a model for team members.

Albert J. Dunlap, on current assignment as the CEO of Sunbeam Corp., is an extreme example of an authoritarian manager. He has developed a reputation for achieving excellent results for shareholders, yet he has been described as having a brutal, take-no-prisoners approach to management. Two of his nicknames are Chainsaw Al and Rambo in Pinstripes. During an eighteen-month stint at Scott Paper, he laid off 35 percent of the work force, paid down debt, refocused the firm, and then sold it to Kimberly-Clark Corporation. By exercising his stock options and receiving special grants, Dunlap earned $100 million. Shortly after joining Sunbeam, he laid off half the work force. Dunlap makes big decisions with a minimum of input from others, partly because he is convinced of his own greatness. Dunlap is highly critical of others, including executives who do not follow his slash-and-burn style of management.

When asked, "Are you a tough, hard-nosed guy?" Dunlap replied, "I'm a piece of cake. I do turnarounds. You have to be tough; otherwise you don't get it done—and I've had to get rid of a lot of people. I've always held the

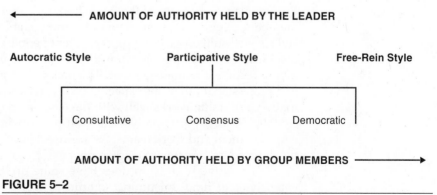

FIGURE 5–2

The Authoritarian–Participative–Free-Rein Continuum

view that I'm not willing to sacrifice 100 percent of the people for 30 percent."[4] As reflected in these comments, Dunlap does not perceive himself as brutal, but as a leader who makes the best decisions possible to accomplish his mission.

Participative Leadership Style.   **Participative leaders** share decision making with group members. Participative leadership encompasses so many behaviors that it can be divided into three subtypes: consultative, consensus, and democratic. **Consultative leaders** confer with group members before making a decision. However, they retain the final authority to make decisions. **Consensus leaders** are called that because they strive for consensus: They encourage group discussion about an issue and then make a decision that reflects general agreement and will be supported by group members. All workers who will be involved in the consequences of a decision have an opportunity to provide input. A decision is not considered final until all parties involved agree with the decision. Another criterion of consensus is that the group members are willing to support the final decision even if they do not agree with it totally.

Russell Salzman, the executive director of the chamber of commerce charged with representing Chicago's entertainment and shopping district, believes that consensus and decisive leadership must be carefully blended. He says that to interpret consensus and then provide the leadership to accomplish the goal is an art and a skill. According to Salzman, broad consensus can sometimes find that the loudest voice receives the most weight. Strong leadership, on the other hand, can sometimes minimize participants' involvement or the sense of reward.[5]

Democratic leaders confer final authority on the group. They function as collectors of group opinion and take a vote before making a decision. Some observers see very little differentiation between democratic leadership and free-rein leadership, which will be described later.

The participative leadership style encompasses the teamwork approach. Predominant behaviors of the participative leader include coaching team members, negotiating their demands, and collaborating with others. This style is well suited to managing competent people who are eager to assume responsibility. Such people want to get involved in making decisions and giving feedback to management. The majority of graduates from business and professional programs expect to be involved in decision making. Participative leadership works well with the new breed of managers and professionals. Finally, participative leadership is an important component of empowerment and work teams. As a consequence, participative leadership fits the modern thrust in managing people.

Participative leadership does have some problems. It often results in extensive and time-consuming committee work. Sometimes participative management is carried to extremes. Team members are consulted about trivial things that management could easily handle independently. Another problem is that many managers still believe that sharing decision making with team members reduces their power.[6]

Maryellen Kelly and Bennett Harrison conducted a study of how well the employee involvement form of participative management worked in more than 1,000 factories. They discovered that involvement programs often failed in large, bureaucratic firms, because these programs were unable to intervene in rule making and decision making at many levels.[7] Such evidence, however, does not negate the importance of participative management in most work settings.

Free-Rein Leadership Style.   **Free-rein leaders** turn over virtually all authority and control to the group. (A synonym for free rein is *laissez-faire*, a French term meaning "do not interfere.") Leadership is provided to the group indirectly rather than directly. Group members are presented a task to perform and are given free rein to figure out how to perform it best. The leader does not get involved unless requested. Team members are allowed all the freedom they want as long as they do not violate policy. In short, the free-rein leader delegates completely.

The free-rein leadership style sometimes works effectively with well-motivated and experienced employees. These people are self-sufficient and may not need help or emotional support from the manager. A problem with free-rein leadership, however, is that group members perceive the free-rein leader as uninvolved and indifferent. Yet free-rein leaders believe they are helping subordinates develop self-sufficiency.

Part of your skill development as a leader is to attain insight into your own leadership style or potential style. To this end, do Leadership Self-Assessment Exercise 5–1 (on pages 112–114).

The leadership continuum and the other approaches to describing leadership styles presented in this and the next chapter provide useful suggestions for being an effective leader. Most approaches to classifying leadership styles, however, overlook a major aspect of leadership: inspiring people, being innovative, and initiating positive change.

THE LEADERSHIP GRID® STYLES

A popular method of classifying leadership styles suggests that the best way to achieve effective leadership is to integrate the task and relationship orientations. The **Leadership Grid**® (formerly known as the Managerial Grid) is a framework for simultaneously specifying the concern for the production and people dimensions of leadership. The grid is also a comprehensive system of leadership training and organization development. Grid leadership styles are based on the extent of a person's concern for production and people (see Figure 5–3).[8]

LEADERSHIP SELF-ASSESSMENT
EXERCISE 5–1   What Type of Leader Are You or Would You Be?

Directions: Answer the following questions, keeping in mind what you have done, or think you would do, in the situations described.

	Mostly Yes	Mostly No
1. Do you enjoy the authority leadership brings?	____	____
2. Do you think it is worth the time and effort for a manager to explain the reasons for a decision or policy before putting the policy into effect?	____	____
3. Do you tend to prefer the planning functions of leadership, as opposed to working directly with team members?	____	____
4. A stranger comes into your work area, and you know the person is a new employee. Would you first ask, "What is your name?" rather than introduce yourself?	____	____
5. Do you keep team members up to date on developments affecting the work group?	____	____
6. Do you find that in giving out assignments, you tend to state the goals, and leave the methods up to your team members?	____	____
7. Do you think leaders should keep aloof from team members, because in the long run familiarity breeds lessened respect?	____	____
8. It comes time to decide about a company event. You have heard that the majority prefer to have it on Wednesday, but you are pretty sure Thursday would be better for all concerned. Would you put the question to a vote rather than make the decision yourself?	____	____
9. If you had your way, would you make communication an employee-initiated affair, with personal consultation held only on request?	____	____
10. Do you find it fairly easy to give negative performance evaluations to group members?	____	____
11. Do you feel that you should be friendly with the members of your work group?	____	____

12. After considerable time, you determine the answer to a tough problem. You pass along the solution to your team members, who find many errors. Would you be annoyed that the problem is still unsolved, rather than become upset with the employees? _____ _____

13. Do you agree that one of the best ways to avoid discipline problems is to provide adequate punishment for rule violations? _____ _____

14. Your employees are criticizing the way you handled a situation. Would you sell your view-point, rather than make it clear that as the manager, your decisions are final? _____ _____

15. Do you generally leave it up to the team members to contact you as far as informal, day-to-day communications are concerned? _____ _____

16. Do you feel that everyone in your work group should have a certain amount of personal loyalty to you? _____ _____

17. Do you favor the practice of using task force teams and committees rather than making decisions alone? _____ _____

18. Do you agree that differences of opinion within work groups are healthy? _____ _____

Scoring and skill development: On the scoring matrix below, place a check mark next to each question you answered Mostly Yes.

1. _____	2. _____	3. _____
4. _____	5. _____	6. _____
7. _____	8. _____	9. _____
10. _____	11. _____	12. _____
13. _____	14. _____	15. _____
16. _____	17. _____	18. _____
Authoritarian total _____	Participative total _____	Free-rein total _____

You favor one of the three styles if your total for that style is three or more points higher than your total for either of the other styles. The quiz you just completed is also an opportunity for skill development. Review the eighteen questions and look for implied suggestions for engaging in leadership and management practices. For example, question 17 might prompt you to make better use of task forces and committees.

Source: Adapted and updated from George Manning and Kent Curtis, *Leadership: Nine Keys to Success* (Cincinnati: South-Western, 1988), pp. 51–53; Naomi Miller, Northern Kentucky University, 1981; Auren Uris, *Techniques of Leadership* (New York: McGraw-Hill, 1953), pp. 49–52; 78–89.

Concern for production, rated on the horizontal axis, includes such matters as results (including high quality), the bottom line, performance, profits, and mission. Concern for people, rated on the vertical axis, is reflected in such matters as showing support for team members, getting results based on trust and respect, and worrying about employees' job security. Each concern is rated on a 1–9 scale.

Key Grid Positions

The benchmark styles on the Leadership Grid are described here and also defined in Figure 5–3.

Authority-Compliance (9,1). The authority-compliance style, in the lower right corner, is characterized by a maximum concern for production combined with a minimum concern for people. A leader with this orientation concentrates on maximizing production by exercising power and authority, and dictating to people.

Country Club Management (1,9). The "country club" style, in the top left corner, shows a minimum concern for production and a maximum concern for people. Primary attention is placed on good feelings among team members and coworkers, even at the expense of achieving results.

Impoverished Management (1,1). The lower left position is impoverished management: a minimum concern for both production and people. Such a leader does only the minimum required to remain a member of the firm. (According to the current definition of leadership, this type of manager does not qualify as a leader.)

Middle-of-the-Road Management (5,5). In the center is the 5,5 orientation. Leaders with this middle-of-the-road style do their job but avoid making waves and conform to the status quo.

Team Management (9,9). In the upper right corner is the 9,9 orientation, team management, which integrates concern for production and people. It is a goal-directed team approach that seeks to gain optimum results through participation, involvement, and commitment.

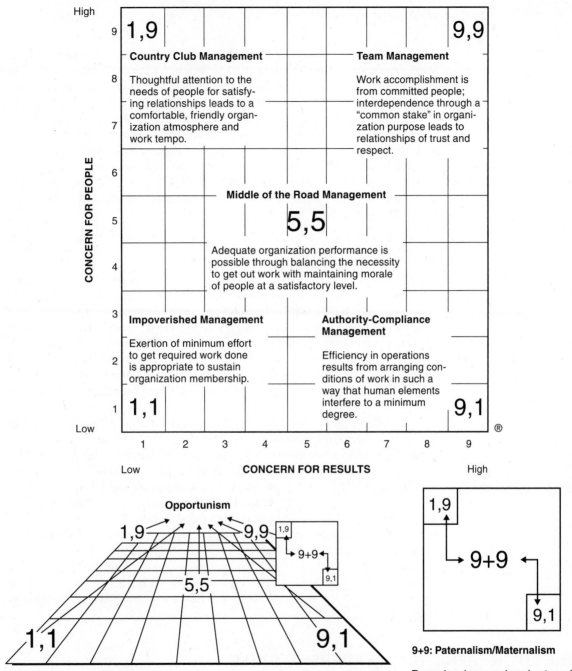

High

9 1,9
Country Club Management

8 Thoughtful attention to the needs of people for satisfying relationships leads to a comfortable, friendly organization atmosphere and work tempo.

7

6

5 Middle of the Road Management
5,5

4 Adequate organization performance is possible through balancing the necessity to get out work with maintaining morale of people at a satisfactory level.

3 Impoverished Management

2 Exertion of minimum effort to get required work done is appropriate to sustain organization membership.

1 1,1

9,9
Team Management

Work accomplishment is from committed people; interdependence through a "common stake" in organization purpose leads to relationships of trust and respect.

Authority-Compliance Management

Efficiency in operations results from arranging conditions of work in such a way that human elements interfere to a minimum degree.

9,1

CONCERN FOR PEOPLE

Low

1   2   3   4   5   6   7   8   9

Low   **CONCERN FOR RESULTS**   **High**

Opportunism

1,9 → → ← 9,9

1,9
→ 9+9
9,1

5,5

1,1   9,1

In Opportunistic Management, people adapt and shift to any Grid style needed to gain the maximum advantage. Performance occurs according to a system of selfish gain. Effort is given only for an advantage for personal gain.

1,9

→ 9+9 ←

9,1

9+9: Paternalism/Maternalism

Reward and approval are bestowed to people in return for loyalty and obedience; failure to comply leads to punishment.

FIGURE 5–3

The Leadership Grid

Source: From Leadership Dilemmas—Grid Solutions, *p. 29 by Robert R. Blake and Anne Adam McCanse. Copyright 1991 © by Robert R. Blake and the Estate of Jane S. Mouton. Used with permission. All rights reserved.*

Managers generally have one dominant leadership style and a backup style. Leaders tend to use the backup style when the dominant style does not achieve the desired results. For instance, you might use the 9,9 approach, only to find that most team members are unenthusiastic about implementing a total quality program. It might then be necessary to shift to a 9,1 approach.

Leaders can also combine their concern for people and production in a way that is either opportunistic or paternalistic/maternalistic. The opportunistic leader shifts to any Grid style needed to achieve personal gain and self-promotion. The paternalistic/maternalistic leader takes the high 9 level of concern from 9,1 and 1,9 to create a combined style of controlling with parentlike behavior.

Which Style Is Best?

The creators of the Grid argue strongly for the value of team management (9,9). They present evidence that the team management orientation usually results in improved performance, low absenteeism and turnover, and high employee satisfaction. In one study, two matched subsidiaries of the same parent company were compared on performance. Measures were taken of profitability before and after a ten-year period. One subsidiary engaged in an extensive Grid program emphasizing team management. The experimental subsidiary increased its profitability four times more than did the comparison subsidiary.[9]

A synthesis of a number of studies indicates that effective leaders score highly on concern for both people and production. The researchers who analyzed the studies caution, however, that each leadership situation should be investigated before prescribing the best leadership style.[10] Similarly, the Leadership Grid does not dictate that the manager mechanically use one style in trying to lead very different groups. Instead, he or she should use principles of human behavior to size up the situation. Many researchers criticize the Leadership Grid for dictating one best style, yet the team style includes adapting to the situation.

The accompanying Leader in Action vignette portrays a successful manager who emphasizes concern for people in his leadership and management style. After reading the insert, place the executive on the Leadership Grid.

THE ENTREPRENEURIAL LEADERSHIP STYLE

Many entrepreneurs use a similar leadership style that stems from their key personality characteristics and circumstances. (The same is true to a lesser extent for *intrapreneurs,* company employees who take on entrepreneurial projects for the firm, such as a business start-up.) The general picture that

LEADER IN ACTION

Philip M. Condit of The Boeing Co.

Only the seventh executive to lead The Boeing Co. in its eighty-year history, Phil Condit is in tune with the times with respect to his education, experience, and demeanor. In contrast to his more formal predecessor, Condit is comfortable in engineering meetings, on the factory floor, and in the executive suite. A versatile manager and professional, he has had assignments in aircraft design, marketing, sales, and project management. Among his notable achievements was leading the early development of the computer-designed 777 widebody. Based on his visibility in his field, the AIAA has designated him a fellow of the society, a honor given to persons of distinction in aeronautics or astronautics who have made valuable contributions to the arts, sciences, or technology thereof.

The aspect of Condit's leadership approach that distinguishes him the most from former Boeing CEOs is his strong interest in the human resources aspects of the business. He is adamant that Boeing focus strongly on the contribution people make to the organization. Outside observers believe that such an emphasis on people will help motivate a work force of 118,000 employees at a time when the company is at the top of a business cycle. In the fall of 1996, contracts for new aircraft were being signed faster than the company could build aircraft. New employees were arriving at a rate of more than 1,000 per month.

In his quest to manage all the change and growth taking place at Boeing, Condit is paying careful attention to the people side of the business. Selecting and training 1,000 employees a month is a formidable task. The present work force, which is being pushed to its limits, must be led with sensitivity. In 1995, Boeing workers conducted a successful sixty-nine-day strike for improved wages and job security. Condit, of course, is also facing business and technological challenges, such as doubling the rate of production in less than two years and streamlining production. Furthermore Boeing plans to merge with McDonnell Douglas Corp.

Condit drives an ordinary sports utility vehicle, lunches in the company cafeteria on occasion, and often makes spontaneous visits to the shop floor to talk to workers. During his first 100 days in office, Boeing introduced a $1 billion stock-grant program for employees and opened its first day-care center. Condit also increased the training budget and assured employees that productivity improvements would result in job reassignments, not job cuts.

Source: Based on facts reported in "Booming Boeing," *Business Week*, September 30, 1996; "AIAA's Honorary Fellows and Fellows," www.aiaa.information/professional/fellow.html, November 9, 1996.

emerges is of a task-oriented and charismatic leader. Entrepreneurs drive themselves and others relentlessly, yet their personalities inspire others.

This entrepreneurial leadership style often incorporates certain behaviors described in the following paragraphs.[11] Recognize, however, that authorities disagree about whether an entrepreneurial personality exists. For example, Howard H. Stevenson of Harvard Business School says, "You can't build a single psychological profile of the entrepreneur because there are too many examples that break the rules." Instead, Stevenson regards entrepreneurship as a behavior focusing on the pursuit of opportunity without regard to the resources currently under control.[12]

1. *Strong achievement motive and sensible risk taking.* Entrepreneurs have stronger achievement motives than do most leaders (see Chapter 2). Building a business is an excellent vehicle for accomplishment and risk taking. The theory surrounding achievement motivation indicates that the entrepreneur would take sensible risks or pursue realistic goals. Because they take sensible risks, many entrepreneurs do not perceive themselves as being risk takers—just as many tightrope walkers believe they are not taking risks because they are in control. Wilson L. Harrell, a consultant to entrepreneurs, expresses it this way: "When we ask entrepreneurs if they are risk takers, they say no! Entrepreneurs are so sure they'll succeed that, to them, there's no risk." By solving problems creatively they reduce risk.[13] Leadership Self-Assessment Exercise 5–2 gives you the opportunity to think about your risk-taking tendencies.

LEADERSHIP SELF-ASSESSMENT
EXERCISE 5–2   What Is Your Propensity for Taking Risks?

Indicate how well each of the following statements reflects your attitudes or behavior, using the following scale: very inaccurately (VI); inaccurately (I); moderately well (MW); accurately (A); very accurately (VA).

	VI	I	MW	A	VA
1. If I had a serious illness, I would purchase generic instead of brand-name drugs.	1	2	3	4	5
2. I invest (or would invest) much more money in bonds or CDs (certificates of deposit) than in stocks.	5	4	3	2	1
3. The thought of starting my own business appeals to me.	1	2	3	4	5
4. I am (or was) willing to go on blind dates frequently.	1	2	3	4	5
5. My career advice to young people is to pursue a well-established occupation with a high demand for newcomers to the field.	5	4	3	2	1
6. I would be willing to relocate to a city where I had no family or friends.	1	2	3	4	5

7. During the last few years, I have taken up a new sport, dance, or foreign language of my own.   1   2   3   4   5

8. My preferences are to have at least 90 percent of my compensation based on guaranteed salary.   5   4   3   2   1

9. From time to time I buy jewelry, clothing, or food from street vendors.   1   2   3   4   5

10. The idea of piloting my own single-engine plane over the ocean appeals to me.   1   2   3   4   5

Total score _____

Scoring and interpretation: Obtain your score by adding the numbers you have circled.

46 – 50   You are a heavy risk taker, bordering on reckless at times. You are most likely not assessing risk carefully enough before proceeding.

38 – 45   You probably are a sensible risk taker, and an adventure-some person in a way that enhances your leadership appeal to others.

5 – 37   You have a propensity to avoid risks. Your conservatism in this regard could detract from an entrepreneurial leadership style.

2. *High degree of enthusiasm and creativity.* Related to the achievement need are enthusiasm and creativity. Entrepreneurs' enthusiasm, in turn, makes them persuasive. As a result, they are often perceived as charismatic. Some entrepreneurs are often so emotional that they are regarded as eccentric.

3. *Tendency to act quickly when opportunity arises.* Entrepreneurs are noted for seizing upon opportunity. When a deal is on the horizon, they push themselves and those around them extra hard. As the founder of an information systems firm told his staff after receiving an important inquiry, "Cancel all your weekend plans. We work until this proposal is completed to my satisfaction and that of our prospect."

4. *Constant hurry.* Entrepreneurs are always in a hurry. When engaged in one meeting, their minds typically begin to focus on the next meeting. Their flurry of activity rubs off on group members and those around

them. Entrepreneurs often adopt a simple dress style in order to save time, and they typically allow very little slack time between appointments.

5. *Visionary perspective.* Entrepreneurs and intrapreneurs, at their best, are visionaries. They see opportunities others fail to observe. Specifically, they have the ability to identify a problem and arrive at a solution.

6. *Dislike of hierarchy and bureaucracy.* Entrepreneurs are not ideally suited by temperament to working within the mainstream of a bureaucracy. Many successful entrepreneurs are people who were frustrated by the constraints of a bureaucratic system. Intrapreneurs, by definition, fit reasonably well into a bureaucracy, yet they do not like to be restrained by tight regulations. The implication for leadership style is that entrepreneurs and intrapreneurs deemphasize rules and regulations when managing people.

7. *Preference for dealing with external customers.* One of the reasons why entrepreneurs and intrapreneurs have difficulty with bureaucracy is that they focus their energies on products, services, and customers, rather than on employees. Some entrepreneurs are gracious to customers and money lenders but brusque with company insiders.

To practice one aspect of entrepreneurial leadership, do Leadership Skill-Building Exercise 5–1.

GENDER DIFFERENCES IN LEADERSHIP STYLE

Controversy over whether men and women have different leadership styles continues. Several researchers and observers argue that women have certain acquired traits and behaviors that suit them for relations-oriented leadership. Consequently, women leaders frequently exhibit a cooperative, empowering style that includes nurturing team members. According to this same perspective, men are inclined toward a command-and-control, militaristic leadership style. Women find participative management more natural than do men because they feel more comfortable interacting with people. Furthermore, it is argued that women's natural sensitivity to people gives them an edge over men in encouraging group members to participate in decision making.

Let us look briefly at some of the evidence and reasoning that shows that gender differences do and do not exist between the leadership styles of today's organizational leaders. We emphasize the present because many more women hold formal leadership positions today than in previous decades. Also, sex roles are less rigid today.

A significant side issue here is that the terms *sex* and *gender* arouse controversy for both scientific and political reasons. As the term is used by many researchers, *gender* refers to perceptions about the differences among

LEADERSHIP SKILL-BUILDING
EXERCISE 5–1   Entrepreneurial Leadership

An important part of the entrepreneurial role is to convince others of the merit of your idea so that they will invest in your company or lend you money. Two students play the role of a team of entrepreneurs who have a new product or service and want to launch a business. (The two entrepreneurs choose the product or service.) About five other students play the role of a group of venture capitalists or bankers listening to the presentation to decide whether to invest or lend money. The entrepreneurs will communicate excitement and commitment about their product, along with a good business plan. (You might want to quickly review the material about persuasive communication in Chapter 12.) The students who are not participating will evaluate how well the two entrepreneurs displayed aspects of the entrepreneurial leadership style.

males and females.[14] An example would be believing that women managers tend to be better listeners than their male peers. Sex differences, however, refer to actual (objective and quantitative) differences, such as the fact that the mean height of men exceeds that of women. Despite these observations, the terms *gender* and *sex* are still used interchangeably in general usage and to some extent in scholarly writings. In this era of celebrating diversity, we hope no reader will be offended by either term.

The Argument for Male-Female Differences in Leadership Style

In an article that stimulated considerable debate, Judy Rosener concluded that men and women do tend toward opposite styles. Based on self-reports, she found that men tended toward a command-and-control style. In contrast, women tended toward a transformational style, relying heavily on interpersonal skills.[15] Reporting from Britain, Cary Cooper contends that men tend to manage by punishment and women by rewards. He observes that women are socialized to manage people and relationships in the home, and have taken their skills from the home and transformed them to the workplace. Relying more on data, Cooper reports:

> Our studies have shown that women tend to be more participatory in their management style and they are seen by both male and female subordinates to be much more caring than male counterparts. In practical terms, this means that men's style of management contributes to stress, by putting much pressure on people and stopping them from producing their best.[16]

Based on some of his more recent research, Bass has found some specific male-female differences in leadership style. Data collected from subordinates suggest that women are less likely to practice management-by-exception (intervening only when something goes wrong). Yet women and men appear to use contingent recognition with equal frequency. Even when the women leaders studied do practice management-by-exception, they typically temper criticism with positive feedback. Bass also found that women leaders are slightly more likely to be described as charismatic. In a survey of sixty-nine world-class leaders (nine women included), women scored higher on the transformation factor than did men.[17] The Leader in Action vignette on page 123 describes a leader who is charismatic and task-oriented.

Based on his experiences in conducting workshops on caring leadership, James Autry thinks that women get the idea of caring more quickly than men. He contends that women are more willing to reach out, to reveal their feelings, to connect, and to bond. From Autry's perspective, men fear such approaches. The differences in caring can surface in such ways as women managers giving more reassurance to group members.[18] A related perspective is that women entrepreneurs are more likely than their male counterparts to perceive their business as a family. As corporate managers, women tend to place a greater emphasis on forming caring, nurturing relationships with employees. Women are also more likely than men to praise group members. And when an employee falls short of expectations, women are more likely to buffer criticism by finding something praiseworthy.[19]

The Argument Against Gender Differences in Leadership Style

Based on a literature review, Jan Grant concluded that there are apparently few, if any, personality or behavioral differences between men and women managers. Also, as women move up the corporate ladder, their identification with the male model of managerial success becomes important; they consequently reject even the few managerial feminine traits they may have earlier endorsed.[20] Studies reviewed by Bass (other than his own research) indicate no consistent pattern of male-female differences in leadership style.[21]

To what extent these stereotypes of men and women leaders are true is difficult to judge. Even if male and female differences in leadership style do exist, they must be placed in proper perspective. Both men and women leaders differ among themselves in leadership style. Plenty of male leaders are relations-oriented, and plenty of women practice command and control (the extreme task orientation). Many women believe that women managers can be more hostile and vindictive than men managers. A case in point is Linda Wachner, the chairman and CEO of Warnaco Inc. (a major manufacturer of intimate apparel), who could qualify for the nickname Chainsaw Linda. As a manager, Wachner once made the *Fortune* list of the "Toughest Bosses" based on her disdain for poor performers. She once told a newly arrived executive, "You'd better start firing people so they'll understand you're serious."[22]

LEADER IN ACTION

Donna Karan of Donna Karan International Inc.

Donna Karan, founder, CEO, and co-owner with her husband of an apparel conglomerate, stalks the models' runway where she is presenting her spring collection to fashion buyers. As the models prepare to move down the runway, Karan stays on top of every detail. She is in constant motion behind the curtain, tucking, smoothing, and adjusting angles unnoticeable to others. She has been described by a fashion reporter as "a combination of Auntie Mame, Everywoman and personal shopper extraordinaire—a woman who *knows* her merchandise" (Agins, p. 66).

Karan's devotion to detail and her insatiable drive have made her a powerful executive in the fashion business. She is the only well-known woman in the male-dominated group of U.S. clothing designers. Karan has shaped a sexy yet comfortable, distinctive style. She has also built a full-line apparel conglomerate. Her business units include top-of-the-line fashion for both men and women, and sportswear.

Karan attracts talented people who become fiercely loyal to her and who are willing to put up with her incessant demands. She has unusually devoted employees. Two of her key executives have been with her since her days at Anne Klein. Her executive assistant says, "Donna draws you in. She is this irresistible force" (*Time*, p. 57). Most of the staff has developed something of a Donna Karan cult. A vice president for design says,

"There's no question that everyone loves what she does and wants to dress like her and be like her" (*Time*, p. 57).

Karan uses her energy, flair, and enthusiasm to carry the company over rough spots. In 1994, for example, the company fired its CFO, suing him for sexual harassment and gross negligence. A controversy ensued, and the executive charged that the real trouble was his refusal to cover up what he perceived to be the company's deteriorating financial condition. Around the same time, the company closed its DKNY children's division because of low profit margins. By 1996 sales had increased 20 percent to $550 million, and total sales using the Karan brand name (e.g., licensing agreements) reached $1 billion. Donna Karan, the personality, was hotter than ever. Oprah Winfrey, for example, devoted an entire show to her. Karan also launched a "Woman to Woman" intensive marketing campaign that includes a Web site and newsletter.

Source: Based on facts in "Donna Inc.," *Time*, December 21, 1992, pp. 54–57; Janet Bamford, "The Top 50: America's Top Women Business Owners," *Working Woman*, May 1995, p. 41; Eric Schmuckler and Janet Mumford, "The Top 50 Women Business Owners," *Working Woman*, May 1996, Julia Carty, "Look Magazine—Donna Karan Interview," p. 35; www.tempestco.com/karan.html November 9, 1996; Teri Agins, "Woman on the Verge," *Working Woman*, May 1993, p. 66.

A more important issue is how to capitalize on both male and female leadership tendencies. Connie Glaser believes that the best approach to leadership takes advantage of the positive traits of both men and women. She sees a new management style that blends the male and female sides:

> While the female may impart that sense of nurturing, the sensitivity to individual and family needs, that's offset by certain traits that the male brings to the table. The ability to make decisions quickly, the sense of humor, the risk-taking—those are qualities that traditionally have been associated with the male style of management.[23]

SELECTING THE BEST LEADERSHIP STYLE

An underlying theme of this chapter and the following chapter is that there is no one best or most effective style of leadership. As explained in the Tannenbaum and Schmidt leadership continuum, the leader examines certain forces to determine which style best fits the situation. Although the Leadership Grid has been accused of touting one style, the one style espoused includes adaptability to the situation. Paul Hersey, Kenneth H. Blanchard, and Dewey E. Johnson explain that there is no one best way to lead because leadership is situational.[24] Over twenty years ago Ralph Stogdill made a statement about selecting a leadership style that still holds today:

> The most effective leaders appear to exhibit a degree of versatility and flexibility that enables them to adapt their behavior to the changing and contradictory demands made on them.[25]

More recently, Thomas R. Horton has observed that CEOs practice many different styles to achieve their objectives. Among these styles are public person or private, loose cannons or reflective thinkers, and autocrats or participative leaders.[26]

Table 5–1 presents useful information for choosing among the autocratic, participative, and free-rein styles depending on the needs of the group members and other forces in the situation. As implied in Chapters 4, 5, and 6, the most successful leaders typically find the right blend of a task and a

TABLE 5–1   Choosing a Leadership Style to Fit the Situation

Consider Being Autocratic Under These Conditions:	
Leader/manager	Has high power and limited restraints on its use
	Has a way of saving matters in an emergency
	Has some unique knowledge
	Is firmly entrenched in her or his position
Group members	Are leader-dependent
	Are rarely asked for an opinion
	Are readily replaced by other workers
	Recognize emergencies
	Are autocrats themselves
	Have low need for independence
Work situation	Features tight discipline
	Is characterized by strong controls
	Is marked by low profit margins or tight cost controls
	Includes physical dangers
	Requires low skills from workers
	Requires that changes be made frequently and quickly

Source: Reprinted by permission of the publisher, from *Personnel*, July/August 1981. © 1981 American Management Association, New York. All rights reserved.

TABLE 5–1 Choosing a Leadership Style to Fit the Situation *(Cont.)*

Consider Being Participative Under These Conditions:	
Leader/manager	Has limited power and authority, and restraints on its use Risks rejection of his or her authority Has few existing time pressures Has limited sanctions that he or she can exert
Group members	Expect to have some control over methods used Have predominantly middle-class values Possess relatively scarce skills Like system, but not authority
Work situation	Is characterized by overall organizational objectives Involves shared responsibility for controls Has some time pressures Consists of gradual changes or regularly spaced changes Involves actual or potential hazards occasionally Values teamwork skills

Consider Being Free Rein Under These Conditions:	
Leader/manager	Has very limited power and authority Believes his or her authority will be rejected Has many work projects of his or her own to perform Lacks charisma
Group members	Expect to lead themselves Are professionally competent and psychologically mature Dislike hierarchy and formal authority
Work situation	Is characterized by clear organizational objectives Does not have major time pressures or budgetary constraints Involves shared responsibilities for controls

relationship orientation. A case in point is Alan F. Shugart, the CEO of Seagate Technology, Inc., a dominant manufacturer of computer hard drives. His colleagues attribute much of his outstanding business success to his leadership style, which is a blend of taskmaster and caring buddy. Shugart demands hard work but also understands the restorative power of rest and play.[27]

Leadership Self-Assessment Exercise 5–3 (on page 126) provides an opportunity to think about your own willingness to adapt to circumstances as a leader. By developing such flexibility, you increase your chances of becoming an effective leader—one who achieves high productivity, quality, and satisfaction.

Before moving on to the end-of-chapter activities, do Leadership Skill-Building Exercise 5–2 (on pages 126–127). It provides an opportunity to implement the most important differences in leadership style.

LEADERSHIP SELF-ASSESSMENT
EXERCISE 5–3   How Flexible Are You?

To succeed as a managerial leader, a person needs a flexible style: an ability to be open to others and a willingness to listen. Where do you stand on being flexible? Test yourself by answering often, sometimes, or rarely to the following questions.

___ 1. Do you tend to seek out only those people who agree with your analysis of issues?

___ 2. Do you ignore most of the advice from coworkers about process improvements?

___ 3. Do your team members go along with what you say just to avoid an argument?

___ 4. Have people referred to you as "rigid" or "close-minded" on several occasions?

___ 5. When presented with a new method, do you immediately look for a flaw?

___ 6. Do you make up your mind early on with respect to an issue, and then hold firmly to your opinion?

___ 7. When people disagree with you, do you tend to belittle them or become argumentative?

___ 8. Do you often feel you are the only person in the group who really understands the problem?

Check Your Score: If you answered "rarely" to seven to eight questions, you are unusually adaptable. If you answered "sometimes" to at least five questions, you are on the right track, but more flexibility would benefit your leadership. If you answered "often" to more than four questions, you have a long way to go to improve your flexibility and adaptability. You are also brutally honest about your faults, which could be an asset.

LEADERSHIP SKILL-BUILDING
EXERCISE 5–2   Contrasting Leadership Styles

One student plays the role of a new associate working for a financial services firm that sells life insurance and other investments. The associate has completed a six-week training program and is now working full-time. Four weeks have passed, and the associate still has not made a sale. The associate's boss is going to meet with him or her today to discuss progress. Another student plays the role of a task-oriented leader. The two people participate in the review session.

Before playing (or assuming) the role of the associate or the boss, think for a few minutes how you would behave if you were placed in that role in real life. Empathize with the frustrated associate or the task-oriented leader. A good role-player is both a script writer and an actor.

Another two students repeat the same scenario except that this time the manager is a strongly relationship-oriented leader. Two more pairs of students then have their turn at acting out the task-oriented and relationship-oriented performance reviews. Another variation of this role play is for one person to play the roles of both the task-oriented and the relationship-oriented boss. Other class members observe and provide feedback on the effectiveness of the two styles of leadership.

SUMMARY

Leadership style is the relatively consistent pattern of behavior that characterizes a leader. The concept of leadership style is an extension of understanding leadership behaviors. One of the earliest classifications of leadership style places the style on a boss-centered through employee-centered continuum. The leader selects a style by taking into account forces in the manager, the subordinates, and the situation, and also time pressures. For example, a more employee-centered style is appropriate if team members are independent, can tolerate ambiguity, and are competent.

A related leadership continuum has three key anchor points: autocratic, participative, and free rein leadership. Autocratic leaders retain most of the authority for themselves. Participative leaders share decision making with group members. The participative style can be subdivided into consultative, consensus, and democratic leadership. The participative style is well suited to managing competent people, eager to assume responsibility. Yet the process can be time consuming, and some managers perceive it to be a threat to their power. The free-rein leader turns over virtually all authority and control to the group.

The Leadership Grid styles classify leaders according to how much concern they have for both production (task accomplishment) and people. Leaders can also combine their concern for people and production to be either opportunistic or paternalistic/maternalistic. Team management, with its high concern for both production and people, is considered the best.

Another important style of leader is the entrepreneur (and to some extent, intrapreneur). The entrepreneurial style stems from the leader's personal characteristics and the circumstances of self-employment. The entrepreneurial style includes these elements: strong achievement motivation and sensible risk taking, high degree of enthusiasm and creativity, rapid response to opportunity, hurriedness, visionary perspective, dislike of hierarchy and bureaucracy, and preference for dealing with external customers.

Male-female differences in leadership style have been observed. Women have a tendency toward relationship-oriented leadership, whereas men tend toward command and control. Some people argue, however, that male-female differences in leadership are inconsistent and not significant.

Rather than searching for the one best style of leadership, managers are advised to diagnose the situation and then choose an appropriate leadership style to match. To be effective, a leader must be able to adapt his or her style to the circumstances.

KEY TERMS

Leadership style
Autocratic leaders
Participative leaders

Consultative leaders
Consensus leaders
Democratic leaders

Free-rein leaders
Leadership Grid®

GUIDELINES FOR ACTION AND SKILL DEVELOPMENT

Most leadership style classifications are based on the directive (task-oriented) dimension versus the nondirective (relationship-oriented) dimension. In deciding which of these two styles is best, consider the following questions:

1. **What is the structure of your organization and the nature of your work?** You might decide, for example, that stricter control is necessary for some types of work, such as dealing with proprietary information.

2. **Which style suits you best?** Your personality, values, and beliefs influence how readily you can turn over responsibility to others.

3. **Which style suits your boss and organization?** For example, a boss who is highly direc-

tive may perceive you as weak if you are too nondirective.

4. **How readily will you be able to change your style if good results are not forthcoming?** Morale can suffer if you grant too much latitude today and have to tighten control in the future.

5. **Is there high potential for conflict in the work unit?** A directive leadership style can trigger conflict with independent, strong-willed people. A more nondirective style allows for more freedom of discussion, which defuses conflict.[28]

DISCUSSION QUESTIONS AND ACTIVITIES

1. How would you characterize the leadership style of your favorite executive, athletic coach, or instructor?

2. Where would you place the leadership and management practice of empowerment on the leadership continuum? Explain your reasoning.

3. Using the dimensions of task and relationships, how would you characterize the style of a highly charismatic leader?

4. Have you ever worked with people who would respond poorly to participative leadership? Describe the situation.

5. Describe an example of the 9,9 style of leader from personal experience or from your reading.

6. What would be some of the dysfunctional consequences to the organization if the vast majority of managers were 5,5 leaders?

7. Find an article on a business entrepreneur (or think of one from personal experience). Report

to the class how well that person fits the entrepreneurial leadership style.

8. Why does an individual's basic personality have such a strong influence on his or her leadership style?

9. What are the practical implications of knowing that men and women typically have different leadership styles?

10. How might being a free-rein leader damage your career?

LEADERSHIP CASE PROBLEM

What Kind of a Leader Is Sue Wong?

Sue Wong, an office manager at Great Western Mutual, recently took a leadership development course sponsored by her company. The major thrust of the course was to teach supervisors how to implement participative management. In the words of the course leader, "Today, almost all employees want to get involved. They want a say in all important decisions affecting them. The era of the industrial dictator is over."

Wong was mildly skeptical about the course leader's universal endorsement of participative management. Yet she decided that if this was what the company wanted, she would adopt a more participative style. Wong took extensive notes on how to implement participative management.

Six months after the leadership development program was completed, the human resources department attempted to evaluate its impact. One part of the evaluation consisted of interviews with the managers who had attended the program. Managers were asked how they liked the program and how it had helped them. Another part of the program eval-

uation was to speak to employees about how the course had influenced their boss's approach to supervision.

Rick Alluto, the company training director, conducted several of the interviews with employees. He spoke first with Amy Green, a claims processor who reported to Sue Wong. Alluto told Green that her answers would be kept confidential. He said that the purpose of these interviews was to evaluate the leadership effectiveness training program, not to evaluate the manager.

Green responded, "It would be okay with me if Sue did hear my comments. I have nothing very critical to say. I think that the leadership training program was very useful. Sue is a much better manager now than she was before. She's much more aware that the people in her group have something useful to contribute. She asks our opinion on everything.

"I'll give you an example," Green continued. "Sue was going to order a new office copier. In the past she might have just ordered a new copier and told us when it was going to be delivered. Instead, we held three meetings to decide which copier to purchase. Three of us formed a committee to study the problem. We finally chose a copier that everybody in the office agreed would be okay. We even obtained approval from the new office assistant. It sure made him feel good."

Green concluded, "I think that every manager at Great Western should learn how to be a participative manager."

Alluto then spoke to Kent Nelson, another claims analyst reporting to Sue Wong. Nelson said he appreciated the fact that the interviews would be confidential. However, he hoped that the drift of his comments would get back to Wong, as long as he was not identified. Nelson offered this evaluation:

"Sue has gone downhill as a manager ever since she took your training program. She has become lazier than ever. Sue always did have a tendency to pass off too much work to employees. Now she's gone overboard. The recent purchase of a photocopy machine is a good example. Too many people spent too much time deciding which machine to purchase. To make matters worse, a committee of three people was formed to research the matter. It seems to me that we can make better use of working time.

"If Sue keeps up this approach to leadership much longer, she won't have a job. We will be doing all of her work. How can you justify a supervisor's salary if other people are doing her work?"

Alutto thought, "I wonder if Amy and Kent are talking about the same supervisor. Their comments make it difficult for me to know whether the development program is getting the job done."

1. What does this case tell us about choosing the right leadership style?

2. How do you explain the different perceptions of Green and Nelson?

3. What might be wrong with the leadership development program?

4. Can you offer Sue Wong any suggestions for making better use of consensus decision making?

5. What is the counterargument to Nelson's point about Wong's not justifying her pay?

Contingency and Situational Leadership

LEARNING OBJECTIVES

After studying this chapter, you should be able to

1. describe how the situation influences the choice of leadership objectives.
2. present an overview of the contingency theory of leadership effectiveness.
3. explain the path-goal theory of leadership effectiveness.
4. explain the situational leadership theory.
5. use the normative decision model to determine the most appropriate decision-making style in a given situation.
6. describe an approach to contingency management for leading an entire enterprise.

*U*ntil recently, Bill Fields had seemed to be in line to become the CEO of retailing giant Wal-Mart Stores, Inc. Therefore, close friends and work associates were surprised when Fields announced that he was resigning to become CEO of Blockbuster Entertainment Corp., a company one-thirtieth the size of Wal-Mart. From the outset, Fields began making major changes at Blockbuster to broaden its scope. The former video-rental stores are now entertainment variety stores that sell home videos, CDs, books, and computer software in addition to renting videos. The concept failed and Fields has left Blockbuster.

Fields uses a variety of approaches in his dealings with work associates. Typically he has a stiff facial expression and a reserved demeanor. Yet at times he can be intimidating and melodramatic like a basketball coach. An executive vice president at Blockbuster says he has heard Fields say on several occasions, "When the rate of external change exceeds the rate of internal change, disaster is imminent."

When Fields visits Blockbuster outlets, he is warm and supportive toward store personnel. He makes a special effort to ensure that employees feel that they are critical to the company's future. At an annual franchisee meeting in Palm Springs, California, Fields spontaneously danced the Macarena with the franchisees.[1]

131

The variety of behaviors exhibited by Fields points to a major component of contingency and situational leadership—adjusting one's approach based on factors in the situation. The former Blockbuster CEO can be intimidating or warm and supportive, depending upon the demands of the situation. Contingency and situational leadership builds further upon the study of leadership styles. It does so by adding more specific guidelines about which style to use under which circumstances.

In this chapter we first present an overview of the situational perspective on leadership. We then describe the four best-known contingency theories of leadership: Fiedler's contingency theory, path-goal theory, the Hersey-Blanchard situational leadership theory, and the normative decision-making model. We also summarize a contingency model that is especially useful for CEOs. Although the presentation of five theories about the same topic may appear baffling, you will notice that these theories share many elements.

SITUATIONAL INFLUENCES ON EFFECTIVE LEADERSHIP BEHAVIOR

As mentioned in relation to leadership attitudes and behavior and leadership styles, the situation can influence which leadership behavior or style a leader emphasizes. The essence of a **contingency approach to leadership** is that leaders are most effective when they make their behavior contingent upon situational forces, including group member characteristics. Both the internal and the external environment have a significant impact on leader effectiveness. For example, the quality of the work force and the competitiveness of the environment could influence which behaviors the leader emphasizes. A manager who supervises competent employees might be able to practice SuperLeadership readily. And a manager who faces a competitive environment might find it easier to align people to pursue a new vision.

Current research comparing entrepreneurial leaders with those from large corporations illustrates situational influences on leadership. One of the research questions asked was whether chief executive officers from different corporate environments differ in the attributes, skills, and abilities they possess. A sample of thirty-five *Fortune* 500 (large-company) CEOs and thirty-five *Inc.* (small-company) CEOs was assessed on a psychological assessment battery of nine different inventories. The battery evaluates higher-level personnel ranging from supervisors and nonmanagerial professionals to presidents and chief executive officers.

The profiles of the large-company and small-company CEOs were then compared. Many significant differences between the two groups were found. The skills of small-company CEOs appeared to be centered primarily on production-oriented areas. For example, *Inc.* CEOs significantly exceeded *Fortune* 500 CEOs on a measure of developing and implementing technical ideas. Small-company CEOs were significantly stronger in measures of coping with difficulties and emergencies, and in handling outside contacts. The researchers explained that the environment of the entrepreneurs requires them to perform tasks that their *Fortune* 500 counterparts delegate to others.

The large-company CEOs had a significantly better developed subset of interpersonal skills. They scored higher than their small-company counterparts on measures of communications, developing group cooperation and teamwork, developing employee potential, and supervisory practices. The large-company CEOs also scored better on a measure of leadership and group participation.[2]

FIEDLER'S CONTINGENCY THEORY OF LEADERSHIP EFFECTIVENESS

Fred E. Fiedler developed a widely researched and quoted contingency model that holds that the best style of leadership is determined by the situation in which the leader is working.[3] Here we examine how the style and situation are evaluated, the overall findings of the theory, and how leaders can modify situations to their advantage.

Measuring Leadership Style: The Least Preferred Coworker (LPC) Scale

Fiedler's theory classifies a manager's leadership style as relationship-motivated or task-motivated. The intermediate style—which receives little mention—is labeled socioindependent. According to Fiedler, leadership style is a relatively permanent aspect of behavior and thus difficult to modify. He reasons that once leaders understand their particular leadership style, they should work in situations that match their style. Similarly, the organization should help managers match leadership styles and situations.

The least preferred coworker (LPC) scale measures the degree to which a leader describes favorably or unfavorably his or her least preferred coworker—that is, an employee with whom he or she could work the least well. A leader who describes the least preferred coworker in relatively favorable terms tends to be relationship-motivated. In contrast, a person who describes a coworker in an unfavorable manner tends to be task-motivated. You can use this scale to measure your leadership style by doing Leadership Self-Assessment Exercise 6–1.

Measuring the Leadership Situation

Fiedler's contingency theory classifies situations as high, moderate, and low control. The more control exercised by the leader, the more favorable the situation is for him or her. The control classifications are determined by rating the situation on its three dimensions, as follows: (1) *Leader-member relations*

LEADERSHIP SELF-ASSESSMENT
EXERCISE 6–1   The Least Preferred Coworker (LPC) Scale for Measuring Leadership Style

Throughout your life you will have worked in many groups with a wide variety of different people—on your job, in social groups, in church organizations, in volunteer groups, on athletic teams, and in many other situations. Some of your coworkers may have been very easy to work with in attaining the group's goals, while others were less so.

Think of all the people with whom you have ever worked, and then think of the person with whom you could work *least well.* He or she may be someone with whom you work now or someone with whom you have worked in the past. This does not have to be the person you liked least well, but should be the person with whom you had the most difficulty getting a job done, the *one* individual with whom you could work *least well.*

Describe this person on the scale that follows by placing an "X" in the appropriate space. Look at the words at both ends of the line before you mark your "X." *There are no right or wrong answers.* Work rapidly: Your first answer is likely to be the best. Do not omit any items, and mark each item only once.

Now describe the person with whom you can work least well.

Scoring

	8	7	6	5	4	3	2	1		
Pleasant									Unpleasant	____
Friendly	8	7	6	5	4	3	2	1	Unfriendly	____
Rejecting	1	2	3	4	5	6	7	8	Accepting	____
Tense	1	2	3	4	5	6	7	8	Relaxed	____
Distant	1	2	3	4	5	6	7	8	Close	____
Cold	1	2	3	4	5	6	7	8	Warm	____
Supportive	8	7	6	5	4	3	2	1	Hostile	____
Boring	1	2	3	4	5	6	7	8	Interesting	____
Quarrelsome	1	2	3	4	5	6	7	8	Harmonious	____
Gloomy	1	2	3	4	5	6	7	8	Cheerful	____
Open	8	7	6	5	4	3	2	1	Guarded	____
Backbiting	1	2	3	4	5	6	7	8	Loyal	____
Untrustworthy	1	2	3	4	5	6	7	8	Trustworthy	____
Considerate	8	7	6	5	4	3	2	1	Inconsiderate	____
Nasty	1	2	3	4	5	6	7	8	Nice	____
Agreeable	8	7	6	5	4	3	2	1	Disagreeable	____
Insincere	1	2	3	4	5	6	7	8	Sincere	____
Kind	8	7	6	5	4	3	2	1	Unkind	____
									Total	____

Scoring and interpretation: To calculate your score, add the numbers in the right column. If you scored 64 or higher, you are a high LPC leader, meaning that you are relations-motivated. If you scored 57 or lower, you are a low LPC leader, meaning that you are task-motivated. A score of 58 to 63 places you in the intermediate range, making you a socioindependent leader. Compare your score to your score in Leadership Self-Assessment Exercise 5–1.

Source: Adapted from Fred E. Fiedler, Martin M. Chemers, and Linda Mahar, *Improving Leadership Effectiveness*. Copyright © 1976. Reprinted by permission of John Wiley & Sons, Inc.

measure how well the group and the leader get along; (2) *task structure* measures how clearly the procedures, goals, and evaluation of the job are defined; and (3) *position power* measures the leader's authority to hire, fire, discipline, and grant salary increases to group members.

Leader-member relations contribute as much to situation favorability as do task structure and position power combined. The leader therefore has the most control in a situation in which his or her relationships with members are the best.

The Leader-Match Concept and Overall Findings

The major proposition in contingency theory is the **leader-match concept:** Leadership effectiveness depends on matching leaders to situations in which they can exercise more control. It states that task-motivated leaders perform the best in situations of both high control and low control. Relationship-motivated leaders perform the best in situations of moderate control. Socioindependent leaders tend to perform the best in situations of high control.

Task-motivated leaders perform better in situations that are highly favorable for exercising control, because they do not have to be concerned with the task. Instead, they can work on relationships. In moderately favorable situations, the relationship-motivated leader works well because he or she can work on relationships and not get involved in overmanaging. Also, in very low-control situations, the task-motivated leader is able to structure and make sense out of confusion, whereas the relationship-motivated leader wants to give emotional support to group members or call a committee meeting.[4]

Figure 6–1 presents a summary of the findings on which the leader-match concept is based. To interpret the model, look first at the situational characteristics at the top of the figure. Leader-member relations can be good or poor; task structure can be high or low; and position power may be strong or weak. The eight possible situations (labeled i through viii) range from very favorable for exercising control (cells i through iii) to very unfavorable for exercising control (cell viii). Note that cell iii is classified as favorable

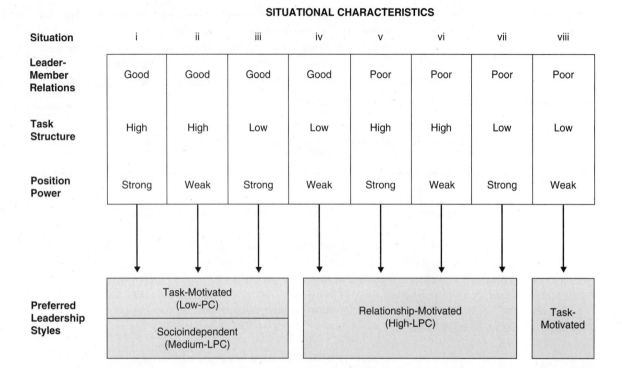

FIGURE 6–1

Fiedler's Findings on Leadership Performance and Favorability of the Situation

even though the leader has to deal with an unstructured task. This is because leader-member relations and position power are so favorable.

The bottom portion of the figure shows the leadership style most strongly associated with effective group performance in each situation. For example, task-motivated (low LPC) leaders perform the best in situations of high control and low control (cells i, ii, iii, and viii), and relationship-motivated leaders are the most effective when the situation gives the leader moderate control.

Making the Situation More Favorable for the Leader

A practical implication of the contingency theory is that leaders should modify situations to best match their leadership style, thereby enhancing their chances of being effective. Imagine the scenario of leaders who are either task-motivated or socioindependent who decide that they need to exercise more control over the situation to achieve higher productivity in their work units. To increase control over the situation, the leader can do one or more of the following:

- Improve leader-member relations through such means as displaying an interest in the personal welfare of group members, having meals with them, actively listening to their concerns, telling anecdotes, and in general being a "nice person."

- Increase task structure by engaging in behaviors related to initiating structure, such as being more specific about expectations, providing deadlines, showing samples of acceptable work, and providing written instructions.

- Exercise more position power by requesting more formal authority from higher management. For example, the leader might let it be known that he or she has the authority to grant bonuses and make strong recommendations for promotion.

Now imagine a scenario in which a relationship-motivated leader wanted to create a situation of moderate favorability, so that his or her interests in being needed by the group could be satisfied. It might be far-fetched to create poor leader-member relations; however, the leader might give the group tasks of low structure and deemphasize his or her position power. In effect, the leader would be creating the type of situation depicted in Octant iv of Figure 6–1. A final scenario, and the least plausible, would be for a task-motivated leader to purposely create a situation of low control (Octant viii). The leader would communicate poorly with group members, provide low task structure, and deemphasize position power. Then a task-motivated style would be required in order to grab hold of the leadership situation.

Evaluation of Fiedler's Contingency Theory

A major contribution of Fiedler's work is that it has prompted others to conduct studies about the contingency nature of leadership. Fiedler's theory has been one of the most widely researched theories in industrial psychology, and at one time was used extensively as the basis for leadership training programs. The model has also alerted leaders to the importance of sizing up the situation to gain control. Despite its potential advantages, however, the contingency theory is too complicated to have much of an impact on most leaders. A major problem centers on matching the situation to the leader. In most situations, the amount of control the leader exercises varies from time to time. For example, if a relationship-motivated leader were to find the situation becoming too favorable for exercising control, it is doubtful that he or she would be transferred to a less favorable situation or attempt to make the situation less favorable.

Research support for Fiedler's model has been mixed. In general, laboratory studies provide more support than do those conducted in the workplace. A meta-analysis was conducted of close to 1,300 studies dealing with contingency theory. The conclusion reached was that studies of leadership effectiveness conducted within the various octants often found positive results. For example, the evidence does suggest that there is a negative correlation between LPC score and group performance in Octants i, ii, iii, and viii. This means that there is a tendency for relationship-motivated leaders to perform less well than task-motivated leaders in the situations depicted by the octants. The negative conclusion reached by the study is that it is difficult to make generalizations about leadership performance when leaders are compared from one situation to another (across-octant comparisons). For example, contingency theory predicts equal performance for high-LPC leaders in Octants i, ii, iii, and viii (combined) and equal but higher performance in Octants iv, v, and vii (combined). Such across-octant differences were rarely found in the studies reviewed.[5]

THE PATH-GOAL THEORY OF LEADERSHIP EFFECTIVENESS

The **path-goal theory** of leadership effectiveness, as developed by Robert House, specifies what the leader must do to achieve high productivity and morale in a given situation. In general, a leader attempts to clarify the path to a goal for a group member so that he or she receives personal payoffs. At the same time, job satisfaction and performance increase.[6] Like the expectancy theory of motivation, on which it is based, path-goal theory is complex and has several versions. Its key features are summarized in Figure 6–2.

The major proposition of path-goal theory is that the manager should choose a leadership style that takes into account the characteristics of the group members and the demands of the task. Two key aspects of this theory will be discussed: matching the leadership style to the situation, and steps the leader can take to influence performance and satisfaction.

Matching the Leadership Style to the Situation

Path-goal theory emphasizes that the leader should choose among four different leadership styles to achieve optimum results in a given situation. Two important sets of contingency factors are the type of subordinates and the type of work they perform. The type of subordinates is determined by how much control they think they have over the environment (locus of control) and by how well they think they can do the assigned task.

Environmental contingency factors consist of factors that are not within the control of group members but that influence satisfaction and task accomplishment. Three broad classifications of contingency factors in the environment are (1) the group members' tasks, (2) the authority system within the organization, and (3) the work group.

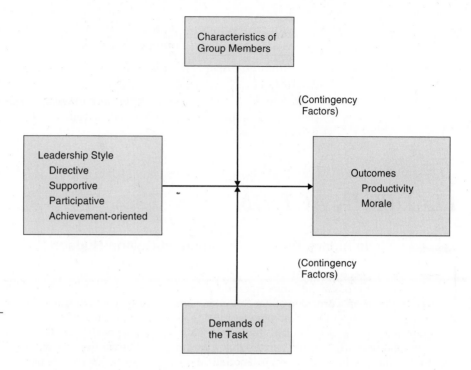

FIGURE 6–2

The Path-Goal Contingency Theory of Leadership

To use path-goal theory, the leader must first assess the relevant variables in the environment. Second, she or he selects the one of the four styles listed next that fits those contingency factors best.

1. *Directive style.* The leader who is directive (similar to task-motivated) emphasizes formal activities such as planning, organizing, and controlling. When the task is unclear, the directive style improves morale.

2. *Supportive style.* The leader who is supportive (similar to relationship-motivated) displays concern for group members' well-being and creates an emotionally supportive climate. He or she enhances morale when group members work on dissatisfying, stressful, or frustrating tasks. Group members who are unsure of themselves prefer the supportive leadership style.

3. *Participative style.* The leader who is participative consults with group members to gather their suggestions, and then takes these suggestions seriously when making a decision. The participative leader is best suited for improving the morale of well-motivated employees who perform nonrepetitive tasks.

4. *Achievement-oriented style.* The leader who is achievement-oriented sets challenging goals, pushes for work improvement, and sets high expectations for team members. Group members are also expected to assume responsibility. The achievement-oriented leadership style works well

with achievement-oriented team members, and also with those working on ambiguous and nonrepetitive tasks.

Although not specified in path-goal theory, a leader can sometimes successfully combine more than one of the four styles. The accompanying Leader in Action vignette illustrates a manager who generally uses a participative style with group members yet is quite directive in making some business decisions.

LEADER IN ACTION

Linda Ahlers, Division President at Dayton-Hudson

Several years ago Linda Ahlers was promoted to head of hard goods at the Target Stores division of Dayton-Hudson Corp. One of her first merchandising decisions was to banish pink-handled tools from the shelves. Ahlers liked the idea of hammers and screwdrivers with handles that conform to a woman's hand. She knew enough about ergonomics to sell tools that met the physical requirements of her majority group of customers. However, she thought that having pink-handled tools for women was too patronizing. The Pepto-Bismol-colored grips were replaced by strong colors such as red and blue. As a result of Ahlers's quick decision, tool sales increased at a double-digit rate.

As the new president of Dayton-Hudson's department store division, Ahlers's charge is to rapidly increase sales and profits. Although she has spent nineteen years in the discount end of retailing, Ahlers believes that the merchandising savvy she developed in that field will carry over to a more upscale retailing environment. She believes that the core elements of successful retailing are the same in both discount and full-price stores. Part of the pressure that Ahlers faces comes from shareholders, who believe that their return on investment badly needs boosting. The year before she was named division president, profits plunged 32 percent at Dayton-Hudson department stores. (These include the Marshall Field's, Dayton's, and Hudson chains.)

When Ahlers assumed her new position, she was under heavy pressure to slash costs. Her problem-solving approach was to spend hours in meetings to gather information, and also to pore over spreadsheets. Company insiders believe that the strengths that will enable Ahlers to accomplish the job include her persistence, merchandising intuition, and team-building skills.

Ahlers approaches her leadership responsibilities in a low-key style. She wears glasses instead of contacts and wears pantsuits in the office. Colleagues describe her as unpretentious and reserved. Part of Ahlers's strategy for bringing about a turnaround is to work with the present staff rather than bring in outsiders. She told her team, "I want you to figure out the solutions. That empowers you."

Within her first two months on the job, Ahlers began to make major merchandising decisions. She brought in a larger assortment of men's lines, and also upgraded other apparel. She has also upgraded customer-service training to help make store associates more knowledgeable about merchandise. The new term for shoppers is "guests" following the lead of The Walt Disney Company.

Source: Susan Chandler, "Under the Gun at Dayton Hudson," *Business Week,* May 20, 1996, pp. 66, 70.

How the Leader Influences Performance

In addition to recommending the leadership style to fit the situation, the path-goal theory offers other suggestions to leaders. Most of them relate to motivation and satisfaction, including the following:

1. Recognize or activate group members' needs over which the leader has control.

2. Increase the personal payoffs to team members for attaining work goals. The leader might give high-performing employees additional recognition.

3. Make the paths to payoffs (rewards) easier by coaching and providing direction. For instance, a manager might help a team member be selected for a high-level project.

4. Help group members clarify their expectations of how effort will lead to good performance, and how performance will lead to a reward. The leader might say, "Anyone who has gone through this training in the past came away knowing how to implement an ISO 9000 (quality standards) program. And most people who learn how to meet these standards wind up getting a good raise."

5. Reduce frustrating barriers to reaching goals. For example, the leader might hire a temporary worker to help a group member catch up on paperwork and electronic mail.

6. Increase opportunities for personal satisfaction if the group member performs effectively. The "if" is important because it reflects contingent behavior on the leader's part.

7. Be careful not to irritate people by giving them instructions on things they already can do well.

8. To obtain high performance and satisfaction, the leader must provide structure if it is missing, and must also supply rewards contingent upon adequate performance. To accomplish this, leaders must clarify the desirability of goals for the group members.[7]

As a leader, you can derive specific benefit from path-goal theory by applying these eight methods of influencing performance. A contribution of path-goal theory is that it highlights the importance of achievement-oriented leadership, which is becoming more important in high-technology organizations.[8] Despite the theory's potential contributions, however, the criticisms of Fiedler's contingency theory apply. Path-goal theory contains so many nuances and complexities that it has attracted little interest from managers.

THE HERSEY–BLANCHARD SITUATIONAL LEADERSHIP® MODEL

The two contingency approaches to leadership presented so far take into account collectively the task, the authority of the leader, and the nature of the subordinates. Another explanation of contingency leadership places its primary emphasis on the characteristics of group members. The **situational leadership model** of Paul Hersey and Kenneth H. Blanchard explains how to match the leadership style to the readiness of the group members. The term *model* rather than *theory* is deliberately chosen because situational leadership does not attempt to explain why things happen (as a theory would). Instead, the situational leadership model offers some procedures that can be repeated.[9]

Before delving further into the situational leadership model, do Leadership Self-Assessment Exercise 6–2. It will help alert you to the specific acts of behavior involved in regarding the characteristics of group members as key contingency variables in choosing the most effective leadership style.

Basics of the Model

Leadership style in the situational model is classified according to the relative amount of task and relationship behavior the leader engages in. The

---

LEADERSHIP SELF-ASSESSMENT
EXERCISE 6–2   Measuring Your Situational Perspective

Indicate how well you agree with the following statements, using the following scale: DS = disagree strongly; D = disagree; N = neutral; A = agree; AS = agree strongly. Circle the most accurate answer.

1. Workers need to be carefully trained
   before you can place high expectations
   on them.   DS   D   N   A   AS

2. The more knowledgeable the worker,
   the less he or she needs a clear
   statement of objectives.   DS   D   N   A   AS

3. "Hand holding" is an ineffective
   leadership technique for anxious
   group members.   DS   D   N   A   AS

4. The same well-delivered pep talk
   will usually appeal to workers at
   all levels.   DS   D   N   A   AS

5. As a manager, I would invest the
   least amount of time supervising the
   most competent workers.   DS   D   N   A   AS

6. It is best not to put much effort into supervising unenthusiastic staff members.   DS   D   N   A   AS

7. An effective leader delegates equal kinds and amounts of work to group members.   DS   D   N   A   AS

8. Even the most effective workers need frequent reassurance and emotional support.   DS   D   N   A   AS

9. If I noticed that a group member seemed insecure and anxious, I would give him or her extra clear instructions and guidelines.   DS   D   N   A   AS

10. Many competent workers get to the point where they require relatively little leadership and supervision.   DS   D   N   A   AS

Total score _____

Scoring:

1. DS = 1, D = 2, N = 3; A = 4, AS = 5
2. DS = 1, D = 2, N = 3, A = 4, AS = 5
3. DS = 5, D = 4, N = 3, A = 2, AS = 1
4. DS = 5, D = 4, N = 3, A = 2, AS = 1
5. DS = 1, D = 2, N = 3, A = 4, AS = 5
6. DS = 5, D = 4, N = 3, A = 2, AS = 1
7. DS = 5, D = 4, N = 3, A = 2, AS = 1
8. DS = 5, D = 4, N = 3, A = 2, AS = 1
9. DS = 1, D = 2, N = 3, A = 4, AS = 5
10. DS = 1, D = 2, N = 3, A = 4, AS = 5

45 – 50 points: You have (or would have) a strong situational perspective as a leader and manager.

30 – 44 points: You have (or would have) an average situational perspective as a leader and manager.

10 – 29 points: You rarely take (or would take) a situational perspective as a leader and manager.

differentiation is akin to initiating structure versus consideration. **Task behavior** is the extent to which the leader spells out the duties and responsibilities of an individual or group. It includes giving directions and setting goals. **Relationship behavior** is the extent to which the leader engages in two-way or multiway communication. It includes such activities as listening, providing encouragement, and coaching. As Figure 6–3 shows, the situational model places combinations of task and relationship behaviors into four quadrants. Each quadrant calls for a different leadership style.

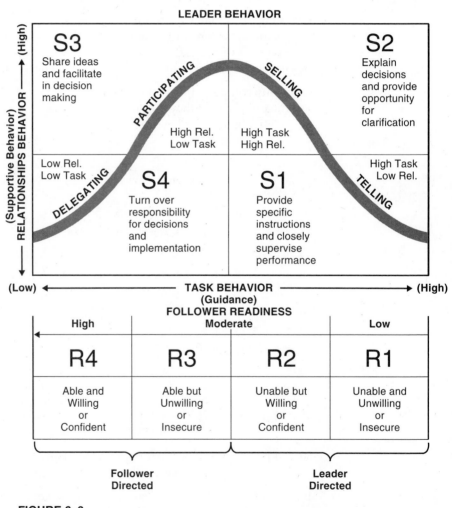

FIGURE 6–3

Situational Leadership Model

Situational Leadership® is a registered trademark of the Center for Leadership Studies. All rights reserved.

Style 1—High task and low relationship. The "telling" style is very directive because the leader produces a lot of input but a minimum amount of relationship behavior. An autocratic leader would fit here.

Style 2—High task and high relationship. The "selling" style is also very directive, but in a more persuasive, guiding manner. The leader provides considerable input about task accomplishment but also emphasizes human relations.

Style 3—High relationship and low task. In the "participating" leadership style, there is less direction and more collaboration between leader and group members. The consultative and consensus subtypes of participative leader generally fit into this quadrant.

Style 4—Low relationship and low task. In the "delegating" leadership style, the leader delegates responsibility for a task to a group member and is simply kept informed of progress. If carried to an extreme, this style would be classified as free-rein.

The situational leadership model states that there is no one best way to influence group members. The most effective leadership style depends on the readiness level of group members.

Readiness in situational leadership is defined as the extent to which a group member has the ability and willingness or confidence to accomplish a specific task. The concept of readiness is therefore not a characteristic, trait, or motive—it relates to a specific task.

Readiness has two components, ability and willingness. *Ability* is the knowledge, experience, and skill an individual or group brings to a particular task or activity. *Willingness* is the extent to which an individual or group has the confidence, commitment, and motivation to accomplish a specific task.

The key point of situational leadership theory is that as group member readiness increases, a leader should rely more on relationship behavior and less on task behavior. When a group member becomes very ready, a minimum of task or relationship behavior is required of the leader. Guidelines for the leader, outlined in Figure 6–3, can be summarized as follows:

Situation R1—Low readiness. When followers are unable, unwilling, or insecure, the leader should emphasize task-oriented behavior and be very directive and autocratic, using a *telling* style.

Situation R2—Moderate readiness. When group members are unable but willing or confident, the leader should focus on being more relationship-oriented, using a *selling* style.

Situation R3—Moderate-to-high readiness. Group members are able but unwilling or insecure, so the leader needs to provide a high degree of relationship-oriented behavior but a low degree of task behavior, thus engaging in a *participating* style.

Situation R4—High readiness. When followers are able, willing, or confident, they are self-sufficient and competent. Thus the leader can grant them considerable autonomy, using a *delegating* style.

Evaluation of the Situational Model

The situational model represents a consensus of thinking about leadership behavior in relation to group members: competent people require less specific direction than do less competent people. The model is also useful because it builds on other explanations of leadership that emphasize the role of task and relationship behaviors. As a result, it has proved to be useful as the basis for leadership training. The situational model also corroborates common sense and is therefore intuitively appealing. You can benefit from this model by attempting to diagnose the readiness of group members before choosing the right leadership style.

Nevertheless, the model presents categories and guidelines so precisely that it gives the impression of infallibility. In reality, leadership situations are less clear-cut than the four quadrants suggest. Also, the prescriptions for leadership will work only some of the time. For example, many supervisors use a telling style with unable and unwilling or insecure team members (R1) and still achieve poor results.

Research evidence for the situational model has been mixed. A major concern is that there are few leadership situations in which a high-task, high-relationship orientation does not produce the best results.[10] Robert P. Vecchio conducted a comprehensive test of the Hersey-Blanchard model involving 303 teachers and their principals. The results were mixed, suggesting that

LEADERSHIP SKILL-BUILDING
EXERCISE 6–1   Applying the Situational Leadership Model

One student plays the role of a team leader whose team is given the responsibility of improving customer service at a consumer electronics megastore. Before jumping into this task, the team leader decides to use the situational leadership model. Today you are going to meet with three group members individually to estimate their *readiness* to perform the customer-service-improvement task. You will want to estimate both the *ability* and the *willingness* of team members to perform the task. Three different people will play the role of group members whose readiness is being assessed. After the brief interviews (about five minutes) are conducted, the team leader will announce which leadership style he or she intends to use with each of the people interviewed. Class members not directly involved in the role play will offer feedback on how well readiness was assessed.

the model may hold for only certain types of employees. For one thing, Vecchio found that more recently hired employees may need and appreciate greater task behavior from superiors.[11]

Leadership Skill-Building Exercise 6–1 provides you the opportunity to practice implementing the situational leadership model. The same exercise also supports other contingency and situational models.

THE NORMATIVE DECISION MODEL OF VROOM, YETTON, AND JAGO

Another contingency viewpoint is that leaders must choose a style that elicits the correct degree of group participation when making decisions. This perception makes sense because much of a leader's relationships with team members involves decision making. The **normative decision model** views leadership as a decision making process and specifies what a leader ought to do in a given situation.[12] The model was originally developed by Victor H. Vroom and Philip W. Yetton, and later refined by Vroom and Arthur G. Jago, and is often referred to as the Vroom–Yetton–Jago model. *Normative* refers to the idea that the leader should follow certain prescriptions indicated in the model. A leader examines certain factors in the situation to determine which decision-making style will be the most effective. Two major factors influencing decision making in this model are decision quality and decision acceptance.

Decision Quality and Decision Acceptance

Not all decisions are of the same quality. Linda Ahlers's decision to stop selling tools with pink handles was a high-quality decision because it boosted sales of the tools to women. Decision quality refers to the objective aspects of a decision that affect group or individual performance. When an effective alternative is chosen, decision quality is said to be high. If the consequences for choosing various alternatives are about the same, or if the consequences of the decision are unimportant, decision quality is not important. For example, decision quality is generally not a major factor when the leader or manager must choose among five different suppliers of photocopy paper. Any brand paper of the right grade will get the job done. The normative model assumes that decision quality will be higher when group members possess relevant information and are willing to cooperate with the leader in making a good decision.

Decision acceptance refers to how committed group members are to implementing a decision effectively. At times group members will be strongly committed to implementing a decision made by the leader because it is in their self-interest. A manager, for example, might make the decision to purchase laptop computers for the entire sales force. Most of the sales representatives would eagerly implement the decision because they think that using laptops will boost their productivity and commissions. If group members are responsible for implementing a decision, acceptance is crucial. Many intelligent decisions result in no organizational improvement because group members resist their implementation. A wellness program, for example, will not improve employee health unless employees actively participate in the program and supervisors encourage such participation—even during peak workloads.

At times decision acceptance is not an issue because very few employees are involved in implementation or would have a strong opinion about which decision should have been made. At one company, a bank president joined the board. Shortly thereafter, the president and chief financial officer made the decision to use the board member's bank as the company's primary bank. Although this decision involved the transfer of millions of dollars, and some paperwork on the part of employees who had direct payroll deposits, there was minimal reaction to the decision.

Decision-Making Styles and the Decision Tree

The Vroom–Yetton–Jago model identifies five decision-making styles, each reflecting a different degree of participation by group members. As shown in Table 6–1, the decision-making styles follow the leadership continuum closely. The first two styles, AI and AII, are autocratic because the leader makes the decision with a minimum of group input. The second two styles, CI and CII, are consultative. The fifth style, GII, is group-directed because the leader turns over considerable authority to the group, and group consensus is achieved before a decision is reached.

The manager diagnoses the situation in terms of several variables. Based on those variables, the manager follows the paths through a decision tree to a recommended course of action. The model includes four decision trees: two for group-level decisions and two for individual-level decisions. (An

TABLE 6–1   Decision-Making Styles in the Normative Decision Model

Decision-Making Style	Description
Autocratic I (AI)	Leader solves problem alone, using information that is readily available.
Autocratic II (AII)	Leader obtains additional information from group members, then makes decision alone. Group members may or may not be informed.
Consultative I (CI)	Leader shares problem with group members individually, and asks for information and evaluation. Group members do not meet collectively, and leader makes decision alone.
Consultative II (CII)	Leader shares problem with group members collectively, but makes decision alone.
Group II (GII)	Leader meets with group to discuss situation. Leader focuses and directs discussion, but does not impose will. Group makes final decision.

Key: A—autocratic, C—consultative, G—group

individual-level decision involves only one subordinate.) One of each pair of trees is for use when time is critical. The other member of each pair is for use when time is less important and when the leader wants to develop a group member's decision-making capabilities.

Figure 6–4 depicts the decision tree for time-given group problems, that is, those for which time is a critical factor. The situational variables, or problem attributes, are listed above the decision tree. To use the model, the decision maker begins at the left side of the diagram and asks the first question, regarding the quality requirement (QR). He or she asks, "How important is the technical quality of this decision?" If the answer is "high," the manager proceeds to CR, the commitment requirement, and answers another question: "How important is subordinate commitment to the decision?" The answer to each question takes the user to another node. The process continues until the group leader reaches a terminal node. At that point, the leader is told which decision-making (or leadership) style is best. Assume that following the right paths took the group leader to CII. He or she would make the second type of consultative decision described in Table 6–1.

The complete normative decision model is more complex than the version just described. Several of the questions allow for more than yes or no answers. Because of its complexity, the authors of the model have also developed a software version to help managers diagnose a situation. As with the decision trees, the manager then makes an appropriate decision about the correct amount of group participation.

An Illustrative Use of the Model

Assume that you are vice president of the claims division of a medical insurance company. You think it would benefit the company and the employees involved to begin a telecommuting (work-at-home) program for claims specialists. You wonder how much to involve the group in this decision. You decide to use the normative decision model for time-driven group problems. Referring to Figure 6–4, proceed as follows:

1. You begin at the QR node: "How important is the quality of the decision?" You decide that quality importance is high. The wrong decision could result in poor-quality claims service. Answering "high" takes you to the CR node.

2. At the CR node, you ask: "How important is subordinate commitment to the decision?" Again, you answer "high," because the magnitude of a telecommuting program necessitates commitment on the part of all staffers concerned. Your "high" response takes you to the LI node.

3. At the LI node, you ask: "Do I have sufficient information to make a high-quality decision?" You answer "no" because you need to gather many facts before you can decide whether a telecommuting program will work for the division. Your "no" response takes you to node ST.

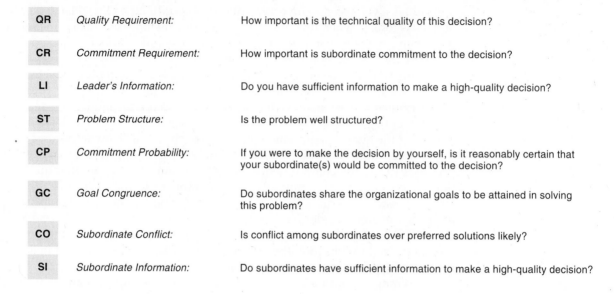

QR	*Quality Requirement:*	How important is the technical quality of this decision?
CR	*Commitment Requirement:*	How important is subordinate commitment to the decision?
LI	*Leader's Information:*	Do you have sufficient information to make a high-quality decision?
ST	*Problem Structure:*	Is the problem well structured?
CP	*Commitment Probability:*	If you were to make the decision by yourself, is it reasonably certain that your subordinate(s) would be committed to the decision?
GC	*Goal Congruence:*	Do subordinates share the organizational goals to be attained in solving this problem?
CO	*Subordinate Conflict:*	Is conflict among subordinates over preferred solutions likely?
SI	*Subordinate Information:*	Do subordinates have sufficient information to make a high-quality decision?

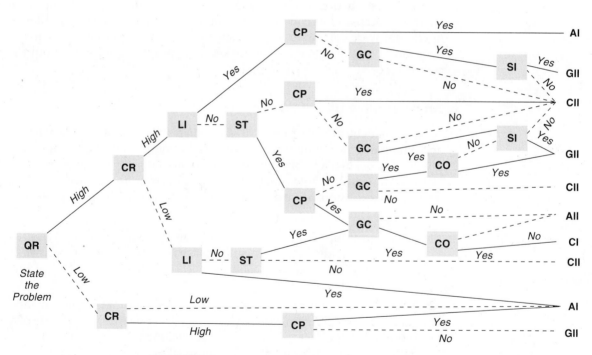

FIGURE 6–4

The Vroom–Yetton–Jago Model for Time-Driven Group Problems

Source: Reprinted from The New Leadership: Managing Participation in Organizations *by Victor H. Vroom and Arthur G. Jago, 1988, Englewood Cliffs, N.J.: Prentice-Hall. Used with permission.*

4. At the ST node, you ask: "Is the problem well structured?" You respond "no" because a telecommuting program involves many nuances, including determining what format the program will take. Your "no" answer takes you to node CP.

5. At the CP node, you ask: "If I were to make the decision by myself, is it reasonably certain that my subordinate(s) would be committed to the decision?" You answer "yes" because you believe you have a cohesive team who will make a commitment to any rational decision from above. Your "yes" response takes you directly to the terminal node, CII. Your action plan, as defined in Table 6–1, is to share the decision with team members, obtain their ideas and suggestions, and so forth.

Now try Leadership Skill-Building Exercise 6–2 for additional practice with the normative decision model.

Evidence and Opinion About the Model

Researchers and managers have reacted positively to the Vroom–Yetton–Jago model and its earlier versions. Managers who follow the step-by-step procedures of the model are likely to increase their decision-making effectiveness. The model also predicts accurately the type of decisions practicing managers make. Furthermore, managers who make decisions consistent with the model are more likely to be perceived as effective managers.[13]

The Vroom–Yetton–Jago model provides a valuable service to practicing managers and leaders. It prompts them to ask intelligent and perceptive

---

LEADERSHIP SKILL-BUILDING
EXERCISE 6–2 **Using a Decision Tree to Select an Appropriate Leadership Style**

Directions: You are the president of a chain of ten deep-discount drug stores. Sales have increased 20 percent in the previous year, but profits are down by 110 percent. You have actually lost money. One of the problems you see is that some of your discounts have been too deep and employee turnover has been too high. You are thinking about offering no salary increases next year in order to bring the chain back to profitability. You have four vice presidents reporting to you, all of whom have a financial stake in the business.

Take this problem through the normative decision model by yourself. Next, meet in a group with classmates and discuss your conclusions about which decision-making style you reached. If group members disagree, discuss the answers given at each node to learn why you pursued different branches on the decision-making tree.

questions about decision-making situations. Although the decision tree appears formidable at first glance, a person with answers to the eight diagnostic questions can work through it in fewer than ten minutes.

Despite the utility of the normative decision model, it can be criticized on the same grounds as other contingency models. All of them pay scant attention to the major elements of leadership—inspiring and influencing others, and bringing about change. Because of this, they are more about *management* than about leadership. Nevertheless, contingency theories and models provide supervisors and middle managers with precise guidelines for selecting an appropriate leadership style and making the right decisions. As such, they make an important contribution to the less glamourous aspects of leadership.

CONTINGENCY LEADERSHIP IN THE EXECUTIVE SUITE

An interview investigation of the approaches to leading their organizations taken by top executives provides additional insight into the contingency approach to leadership.[14] The approach these leaders take lies on the borderline between style and strategy. We include the information here under contingency leadership because each approach is chosen based on an analysis of the requirements of the situation. A leadership approach is defined as a coherent, explicit style of management, not a personal style. However, the style of management centers around leadership behaviors.

Charles M. Farkas, Philippe De Backer, and Suzy Wetlaufer interviewed 163 top executives on six continents to learn how these leaders delivered consistently extraordinary results. They scrutinized 12,000 pages of interview transcripts to reach their conclusions. Five distinct approaches were revealed by the interview analysis: strategic, human assets, expertise, box, and change agent. The overriding conclusion from the study is that successful CEOs assess their companies' needs, then adapt their leadership style to fit the particular situation. Here we will summarize each approach, including its associated contingency factors and leadership behaviors. Table 6–2 provides an outline of the approaches and accompanying contingency factors.

The *strategic approach* is a systematic, dispassionate, and structured analysis of a company's strengths and weaknesses, and its mission. CEOs using this approach perceive their major contribution as creating, testing, and designing the implementation of a long-term business strategy. Much of their workday is devoted to activities intended to analyze their organization's current situation and most advantageous business position in the future. CEOs using this approach devote about 80 percent of their time to external factors such as customers, competitors, technological advances, and market trends. An example is Michael Dell of Dell Computer, who logs on to the Internet each day to track information and opinions about market trends and reactions to his company's products and those of competitors. Day-to-day operation of the business is delegated extensively to trusted subordinates.

TABLE 6–2   Contingency Factors for Five Approaches to CEO Leadership

CEO Leadership Approach	Contingency Factors
Strategic (create, test, and design long-term strategy)	Unstable environment, high rate of change, complexity
Human assets (add value through hiring, retention, and development programs)	Business units are better positioned than headquarters to make strategy
Expertise (design and implement programs around specific expertise such as technology)	Certain expertise can be source of significant competitive advantage
Box (add values through controls that set boundaries for employee performance)	Presence of government examiners who insist on strict controls to protect consumer and company
Change agent (create an environment of continual reinvention)	Company wants to remain a leader in the field, and status quo is unacceptable

Source: Gathered from information in Charles M. Farkas and Suzy Wetlaufer, "The Ways Chief Executive Officers Lead," *Harvard Business Review*, May–June 1996, pp. 110–122; Farkas and Philippe De Backer, *Maximum Leadership: The World's Leading CEOs Share Their Five Strategies for Success* (New York: Henry Holt, 1996)

CEOs should use the strategic approach in unstable environments where the volume and pace of change is high. Significant complexity in terms of technology, geography, or functions is another contingency factor calling for the strategic approach. For example, the CEO of Coca-Cola uses a strategic approach because the company has 32,000 employees in approximately 200 countries worldwide. The strategic approach is often chosen by CEOs who must frequently make decisions of enormous consequence.

In the *human assets approach*, the CEO and the corporate staff add value to the organization through hiring, retention, and development programs. CEOs using this approach believe that strategy formulation belongs in the business units. These CEOs believe that their most important job is to impart selected values, behaviors, and attitudes by managing the growth and development of individuals. To implement this approach, these executives travel extensively and spend most of their time in human resource activities such as recruiting, performance evaluation, and career planning. An important goal of the human assets approach is to develop business unit managers to the point where they act and make decisions the way the CEO would. The human assets CEO believes that good employees should do things the *company way*. Herb Kelleher, the colorful CEO of Southwest Airlines, says, "We hire great attitudes, and we'll teach them any functionality they need."[15]

The human assets approach is most frequently used when a company has such far-flung operations that managers in the business units are better equipped to formulate strategy than people in the corporate group. Consistency in running the geographically remote businesses is achieved by the CEO's imparting corporate values to employees worldwide. Consistency in values is also enhanced when the CEO is involved in hiring key people. Another contingency factor favoring the human assets approach is if key executives strongly believe that the company values and standards of behavior are necessary for the success of the business.

Executives who use the *expertise approach* believe that the CEO's key responsibility is selecting and disseminating throughout the organization an area of expertise that will give the firm a competitive advantage. The majority of their working time is devoted to activities that foster the cultivation and continual improvement of this expertise. Among these activities are studying new technological research, analyzing competitors' products, and meeting with engineers and customers. Areas of expertise include marketing, manufacturing, technology, and distribution. Organizational members who have good technical expertise and share it across organizational units are rewarded. A key contingency factor for favoring the expertise approach is if a certain expertise can give the firm a significant competitive advantage. A historically important example is that an emphasis on quality gave Motorola a competitive advantage for many years.

A *box approach* occurs when the corporate group adds value by creating, communicating, and overseeing an explicit set of controls. The controls can take a variety of forms, including financial measures, rules, procedures, and values that define boundaries for the performance of all employees. The purpose of these controls is to ensure uniform and predictable experiences for employees and customers, and to lower risk. CEOs who use the box approach devote much of their workdays to attending to deviations from standard, such as quarterly results that are below forecast. They also devote time to rewarding employees whose behavior and performance match the control standards.

The key contingency factor favoring the box approach is a regulated environment such as banking or nuclear power plants in which the government insists on strict controls to protect employees and customers. The purpose of the controls is to strive for consistency. Claude Bébéar, the president of AXA group, an international insurance company, has invented a language of words and symbols to enhance uniform behavior among the company's 50,000 employees in twelve countries. For example, employees are encouraged to use "TNT action" to express the rapid implementation of decisions.

CEOs who use the *change agent approach* believe that their most critical role is to create an environment of continual reinvention, even if such an emphasis on change creates short-term disturbances such as anxiety, confusion, and poorer financial results. Change agent CEOs spend up to 75 percent of their time using speeches, meetings, and other forms of communication to motivate members to embrace change. They meet regularly with a variety of stakeholders to beat the drums for change. Change agent executives regularly visit factories, create and answer E-mail, and attend company picnics. (It's a good thing these CEOs have a strong internal staff to run the business!) Employees who embrace change receive the biggest rewards. At the investment bank Goldman, Sachs, a talented young banker was promoted to partner two years ahead of his class because he was willing to accept an assignment in Asia. At the time, few U.S. employees were willing to work abroad.

The change agent approach appears to be triggered when the CEO believes that the status quo will lead to the company's undoing, such as a software development company being content with its current lineup of products. The contingency factor is not obvious, such as a troubled organization needing change; rather, the CEO has the vision to recognize that trouble lies ahead unless changes are made now.

The five leadership approaches just described are not mutually exclusive, and sometimes a CEO will emphasize more than one approach. For example, the change agent approach might be needed to implement a radical business strategy. Yet in the most effectively run organizations, the CEO usually has a dominant approach or style that serves as a compass and rudder for all corporate decisions. In general, emphasizing one of these approaches, at least for a period in a firm's history, can help a CEO to lead with clarity, consistency, and commitment.

SUMMARY

Theories of contingency and situational leadership build further upon the study of leadership style by adding more specific guidelines about which style to use under which circumstances. The essence of a contingency approach to leadership is that leaders are most effective when they make their behavior contingent upon situational forces, including group member characteristics. One study suggested that entrepreneurial leaders are faced with an environment that prompts them to emphasize production-oriented behaviors. In contrast, large-company CEOs work in an environment more conducive to emphasizing interpersonal behaviors and skills.

Fiedler's contingency theory states that the best style of leadership is determined by the situation in which the leader is working. Style, in Fiedler's theory, is measured by the least preferred coworker (LPC) scale. You are relationship-motivated if you have a reasonably positive attitude toward your least preferred coworker. You are task-motivated if your attitude is negative, and you are socioindependent if your attitude is neutral. Situational control, or favor- ability, is measured by a combination of the quality of leader-member relations, the degree of task structure, and the leader's position power.

The key proposition of Fiedler's theory is the leader-match concept: In situations of high control or low control, leaders with a task-motivated style are the most effective. In a situation of moderate control, a relationship-motivated style works best. In a high-control situation, a socioindependent style can also be effective. Leaders can improve situational control by modifying leader-member relations, task structure, and position power.

The path-goal theory of leadership effectiveness specifies what the leader must do to achieve high productivity and morale in a given situation. Effective leaders clarify the paths to attaining goals, help group members progress along these paths, and remove barriers to goal attainment. Leaders must choose a style that best fits the two sets of contingency factors—the characteristics of the subordinates and the tasks. The four styles in path-goal theory are directive, supportive, participative, and achievement-oriented.

The situational leadership model (developed by Hersey and Blanchard) explains how to match leadership style to the readiness of group members. The model classifies leadership style according to the relative amounts of task and relationship behavior the leader engages in. The four styles are different combinations of task and relationship behavior, both rated as high versus low. *Readiness* refers both to ability and to willingness to accomplish a specific task. As group member readiness increases, a leader should rely more on relationship behavior and less on task behavior. When a group member becomes very ready, however, minimum task or relationship behavior is required.

According to the normative decision model of Vroom, Yetton, and Jago, leadership is a deci-sion-making process. Two major factors influencing decision making in this model are decision quality and decision acceptance by those responsible for implementation. To follow the model, a leader examines certain factors in the situation to determine which decision-making style will be the most effective. The model identifies five decision-making styles: two autocratic, two consultative, and one group-centered. By answering a series of eight diagnostic questions in a decision tree, the manager follows the path to a terminal node that recommends one of the five styles.

An interview-based study indicates that CEOs who are successful assess their companies' needs, then adapt their leadership style to fit the particular situation. The five approaches or styles are strategy, human assets, expertise, box (emphasis on controls), and change agent. Each of these approaches is emphasized under different circumstances; for example, the human assets approach is used when business units are better positioned than headquarters to make strategy.

KEY TERMS

Contingency approach to leadership
Leader-match concept

Path-goal theory
Situational leadership model
Task behavior

Relationship behavior
Readiness
Normative decision model

GUIDELINES FOR ACTION AND SKILL DEVELOPMENT

1. To apply contingency and situational theory, a leader typically has to make choices involving two related considerations. The first is to achieve the right balance between a task and a relationship orientation. Unless there is strong evidence to the contrary, the leader should strive to emphasize both tasks and relationships. The second consideration is to choose a decision style at some place on the leadership continuum, from autocratic to democratic. A consultative decision-making style is called for when a decision is complex, technical accuracy is important, and group acceptance is necessary.

2. Consider four factors as a shortcut to deciding whether a decision is best made by a group. The stronger the need for *buy-in* or

commitment, the more important is group participation. When a *creative solution* is important, group input is valuable because varied viewpoints ordinarily enhance creativity. When *time is scarce*, it is better for the leader to make the decision. When a decision is needed that *reflects the bigger picture*, the leader will often be in the best position to make the decision.[16]

DISCUSSION QUESTIONS AND ACTIVITIES

1. In what way does contingency theory go beyond stating that the best leadership approach depends on the situation?
2. What differences in leadership approach have you noticed between top executives and first-level supervisors?
3. After studying Fiedler's contingency theory, what would you now do differently as a leader?
4. Which of the four path-goal styles do you think would be best for managing a professional football team? Justify your answer.
5. What kind of personal payoffs would the members of most groups want?
6. To which Leadership Grid style does the achievement-oriented style correspond most closely?
7. Linda Ahlers appeared to autocratically make the decision about discontinuing the sale of tools with pink handles. Explain whether or not you think she should have used a group decision.
8. According to the situational model of leadership, which style is likely to be the most effective for leading a strongly motivated group of stockbrokers (investment counselors)?
9. In what way does the situational model of leadership take an optimistic view of leadership ability?
10. Show the normative model of decisions to an experienced leader. Obtain his or her opinion on its practicality, and be ready to discuss your findings in class.

LEADERSHIP CASE PROBLEM

Hard-Driving Pfeiffer

Eckhard Pfeiffer is president and CEO of Compaq Computer Corp., the world's largest supplier of desktop and portable PCs, and also the dominant player in PC servers. In his first two years in office, Pfeiffer engineered a stunning turnaround for his company. In 1993, Compaq made more money than its two major rivals, Apple Computer, Inc., and IBM, combined. When Pfeiffer was appointed CEO in 1991, sales were $3 billion. By 1995, sales had reached $14.8 billion, and Pfeiffer was hoping for yearly worldwide sales of $30 billion by 2000. In a four-year period Pfeiffer has helped Compaq improve its ranking from fifth to first place in worldwide PC industry market share. The company now manufactures and sells a wide range of computers, including mainframes, and is getting into networking on a large scale. Compaq is even entering the children's software market.

Company insiders contend that it has been Pfeiffer's ability to communicate his vision and a sense of urgency that has made the turnaround and sustained growth possible. He convinces staffers with statements such as "We've seen the power of the PC, and we've seen that it is unstoppable" (*Fortune,* p. 122). Pfeiffer moves at a fast pace, inside and outside the office. Most weekday mornings he leaves his Houston high-rise apartment and drives to work in a black Porsche convertible, often reaching speeds of 100 mph. At company meetings he parties with the intensity of a college student on spring break in Fort Lauderdale, Florida. During one company meeting in a sports arena he had himself hoisted seventy feet up to the ceiling on a cable.

Pfeiffer is a perfectionist who conducts his work as fast as he drives his convertible. His new mandate to Compaq managers and other employees is to capture double the market share of its nearest competitor in every market it serves. He wants Compaq to become one of the top three computer companies in the world, moving up from its present standing of number five. Pfeiffer stays focused on his major goals despite occasional glitches. In the first quarter of 1996, for example, sales were below analysts' forecasts, and the price of the company stock dropped 18 percent. Pfeiffer and his staff responded by reducing PC prices up to 21 percent and beefing up promotions. The plan worked; revenues for the next quarter increased by 42 percent, and the stock price recovered almost completely. One reason that the company can reduce prices is the emphasis Pfeiffer places on tightly controlling manufacturing costs, and other operating costs as well. Pfeiffer's personal staff consists of one secretary. Compaq's operating profits in PCs are 9 percent, significantly higher than those of competitors.

The German-born and -raised Pfeiffer emphasizes speed in running the business: speed in revenue growth, market share gains, entrance into new businesses, and cycle times in manufacturing. Managers throughout the organization recognize that they must constantly change their operations. The division head of desktop PCs for business says, "Nothing's sacrosanct around here. We don't assume that what

worked one year will work the next. The environment is changing and you'd better be innovative—not just in your products but in every part of your business" (*Fortune,* p. 122).

Pfeiffer is on the job about seventy hours per week. He drives himself as hard as he drives his staff. He is known as a person who is never satisfied, even with the best efforts of others. One of his key managers recently resigned, citing burnout as the reason. Yet Pfeiffer is patient, calm, and self-assured in high-pressure situations. He thoroughly analyzes a situation before making a decision. He asks probing questions about how customers will respond to a proposed innovation.

Pfeiffer was originally an accountant but then switched to sales and marketing. Eventually he headed European marketing for Texas Instruments before launching Compaq's European operations in 1983. He was enormously successful in that position, and European sales accounted for 54 percent of Compaq's business by 1990. Pfeiffer was then chosen by the board to replace company founder Rod Canion as the CEO. The issue in replacing Canion was that he did not want to bend on lowering the manufacturing cost of PCs. Pfeiffer immediately championed cost cutting. He reasoned that the company had erred by focusing heavily on improving PC performance instead of moving into the lower end of the market.

When speaking to outsiders, Pfeiffer emphasizes how Compaq is headed toward becoming a full-line information technology company, a complete provider of hardware, software, and services. He dubs this being a provider of both razors and razor blades. Along with his interest in diversification, Pfeiffer continues to hammer away at the importance of efficiency in operations. People who know Pfeiffer well think that he has the tenacity to lead the company toward his goals. A former colleague of Pfeiffer's said, "I never, ever, saw Eckhard miss a forecast. He'd sell the electricity out of the building before he'd miss a forecast" (*Business Week,* July 22, 1966, p. 72).

1. What evidence of contingency leadership do you find in Pfeiffer's approach?

2. Which of the five CEO approaches to leadership does Pfeiffer appear to emphasize?

3. What recommendations can you offer to make Pfeiffer an even more effective leader?

4. Would you want to work for Pfeiffer? Why or why not?

Source: Gary McWilliams, "Compaq at the 'Crossroads,'" *Business Week,* July 22, 1996, pp. 70–72; David Kirkpatrick, "Fast Time Compaq," *Fortune,* April 1, 1996, pp. 120–128; "Eckhard Pfeiffer: Compaq Computer Corporation," www.cspp.org/organize/pfeiffer.html, November 15, 1996; "Compaq: How It Made Its Impressive Move out of the Doldrums," *Business Week,* November 2, 1992, pp. 146–151.

Power, Politics, and Leadership

LEARNING OBJECTIVES

After studying this chapter you should be able to

1. recognize the various types of power.
2. identify tactics used for becoming an empowering leader.
3. know how to use delegation to support empowerment.
4. pinpoint factors contributing to organizational politics.
5. describe both ethical and unethical political behaviors.
6. explain how a leader can control dysfunctional politics.

*I*n June 1995, Pat Riley, the New York Knicks coach at the time, was angry. He resigned from the team because the owners rejected his bid to become part owner. Riley walked away with a year left on his contract, and turned down a $15 million extension. The popular and charismatic coach said, "I emphasize that the decision to leave the Knicks had absolutely nothing to do with money. The financial package which we had been discussing was extremely generous. Regrettably there were serious differences and questions about authority and final decision-making.

"I do not believe that any team can realize its potential when its head coach, the person most intimately involved with the players, cannot make final, critical decisions on matters bearing directly and intensely on the team, its performance and its future."[1]

Agree with Coach Riley's decision or not, it dramatizes how much importance some leaders place on having the formal authority (a type of power) to accomplish their mission. To exercise influence, a leader must have **power,** the potential or ability to influence decisions and control resources. To acquire and retain power, a leader must often skillfully use politics. No matter how meritorious a leader's ideas for constructive change, without political backing those ideas will not be implemented.

As used here, the term **organizational politics** refers to informal approaches to gaining power through means other than merit or luck. Politics are played to achieve power, either directly or indirectly. The power may be achieved in such diverse ways as being promoted, receiving a larger budget or other resources, obtaining more resources for one's work group, or being exempt from undesirable assignments.

The definition of organizational politics here is nonevaluative, except that we shall draw a distinction between ethical and unethical political behavior. Many other writers regard organizational politics as emphasizing self-interest at the expense of others, or engaging in mysterious activities. Two researchers, for example, said "Politics are the observable, but often covert, actions by which executives enhance their power to influence a decision."[2]

This chapter covers the nature of power, the ways leaders acquire power and empower others, and the use and control of organizational politics. Chapter 8 continues the discussion of organizational politics by examining influence tactics.

SOURCES AND TYPES OF POWER

Organizational power can be derived from many sources, as shown in Table 7–1. How a person obtains power depends to a large extent on the type of power he or she seeks. Therefore, to understand the mechanics of acquiring power, one must also understand what types of power exist and the sources and origins of these types of power. The seven types or sources of power listed in Table 7–1 are described in the following sections.

TABLE 7–1 Types or Sources of Power

1. Power granted by the organization (position power)

2. Power stemming from characteristics of the person (personal power)

3. Power stemming from ownership

4. Power stemming from providing resources

5. Power derived from capitalizing upon opportunity

6. Power stemming from managing critical problems

7. Power stemming from being close to power

Position Power

Power is frequently classified according to whether it stems from the organization or the individual.[3] Four such bases of power—legitimate power, reward power, coercive power, and information power—stem from the person's position in the organization.

Legitimate Power.   Power granted by the organization is called **legitimate power.** People at the highest levels in the organization have more power than do people below them. However, organizational culture helps establish the limits to anyone's power. Newly appointed executives, for example, are often frustrated with how long it takes to effect major change. A chief financial officer (CFO) recruited to improve the profitability of a telecommunications firm noted: "The company has been downsizing for three years. We have more office space and manufacturing capacity than we need. Yet whenever I introduce the topic of selling off real estate to cut costs, I get a cold reception."

Reward Power.   The authority to give employees rewards for compliance is referred to as **reward power.** If a vice president of operations can directly reward supervisors with cash bonuses for achieving quality targets, this manager will exert considerable power. Of course, leaders can use reward power effectively only when they have meaningful rewards at their disposal.

Coercive Power.   **Coercive power** is the power to punish for noncompliance; it is based on fear. A common coercive tactic is for an executive to demote a subordinate manager if he or she does not comply with the executive's plans for change. Coercive power is limited, in that punishment and fear achieve mixed results as motivators. The leader who relies heavily on coercive power runs the constant threat of being ousted from power.

The heavy emphasis on downsizing in recent years has given managers an opportunity to use coercive power more extensively. Managers with an inclination toward mistreatment of employees now have a new weapon. According to Harvey Hornstein, downsizing has given many managers broad, blunt, and often unrestrained power to eliminate jobs. He notes that more than half the cases of abusive bosses he has uncovered in his research can be attributed to the nineties work environment, in which workers are readily dismissed to reduce costs.[4]

Information Power.   **Information power** is power stemming from formal control over the information people need to do their work.[5] A sales manager who controls the leads from customer inquiries holds considerable power. As the branch manager of a real estate agency put it: "Ever since the leads were mailed directly to me, I get oodles of cooperation from my agents. Before that they would treat me as if I were simply the office manager."

Personal Power

Three sources of power stem from characteristics or behaviors of the power actor: expert power, referent power, and prestige power. All are classified as **personal power,** because they are derived from the person rather than from the organization. Expert power and referent power contribute to charisma. Expert power is the ability to influence others through specialized knowledge, skills, or abilities—for example, like a marketing manager who is adept at identifying new markets. Referent power is the ability to influence others through desirable traits and characteristics.

Another important form of personal power is **prestige power,** the power stemming from one's status and reputation.[6] A manager who has accumulated important business successes acquires prestige power. Executive recruiters, for example, identify executives who could readily be placed in key CEO positions because of their excellent track record.

According to a new analysis, personal power is **leadership power,** the exercise of position power. To make effective use of position power, the leader should have such characteristics as integrity, initiative, the desire to lead, communication skills, and emotional security.[7] Outstanding leaders such as Donna Karan (described previously) exercise leadership power.

Leadership Self-Assessment Exercise 7–1 on pages 164–165 provides a sampling of the specific behaviors associated with five of the sources of power: three kinds of position power and two kinds of personal power.

Power Stemming from Ownership

Executive leaders accrue power in their capacity as agents acting on behalf of shareholders. The strength of ownership power depends on how closely the leader is linked to shareholders and board members. A leader's ownership power is also associated with how much money he or she has invested in the firm.[8] An executive who is a major shareholder is much less likely to be fired by the board than one without an equity stake. The New Golden Rule applies: The person who holds the gold, rules.

Power Stemming from Providing Resources

A broad way to view power sources is from the **resource dependence perspective.** According to this perspective, the organization requires a continuing flow of human resources, money, customers and clients, technological inputs, and materials to continue to function. Organizational subunits or individuals who can provide these key resources accrue power.[9]

LEADERSHIP SELF-ASSESSMENT
EXERCISE 7–1   Rating a Manager's Power

Directions: If you currently have a supervisor or can clearly recall one from the past, rate him or her. Circle the appropriate number of your answer, using the following scale: 5 = strongly agree, 4 = agree, 3 = neither agree nor disagree, 2 = disagree, 1 = strongly disagree. (The actual scale presents the items in random order. They are classified here according to the power source for your convenience.)

My manager can (or former manager could) . . .	Strongly Agree				Strongly Disagree
Reward Power	◄──				──►
1. increase my pay level.	5	4	3	2	1
2. influence my getting a pay raise.	5	4	3	2	1
3. provide me with specific benefits.	5	4	3	2	1
4. influence my getting a promotion.	5	4	3	2	1
Coercive Power					
5. give me undesirable job assignments.	5	4	3	2	1
6. make my work difficult for me.	5	4	3	2	1
7. make things unpleasant here.	5	4	3	2	1
8. make being at work distasteful.	5	4	3	2	1
Legitimate Power					
9. make me feel that I have commitments to meet.	5	4	3	2	1
10. make me feel like I should satisfy my job requirements.	5	4	3	2	1
11. give me the feeling that I have responsibilities to fulfill.	5	4	3	2	1
12. make me recognize that I have tasks to accomplish.	5	4	3	2	1
Expert Power					
13. give me good technical suggestions.	5	4	3	2	1
14. share with me his or her considerable experience and/or training.	5	4	3	2	1

15. provide me with sound job-related advice.   5   4   3   2   1

16. provide me with needed technical knowledge.   5   4   3   2   1

Referent Power

17. make me feel valued.   5   4   3   2   1

18. make me feel that he or she approves of me.   5   4   3   2   1

19. make me feel personally accepted.   5   4   3   2   1

20. make me feel important.   5   4   3   2   1

Total score: ____

Scoring and interpretation: Add all the circled numbers to calculate your total score. You can make a tentative interpretation of the score as follows:

90+:   high power

70–89:   moderate power

below 70:   low power

Also, see if you rated your manager much higher on one type of power than on the others.

Source: Adapted from "Development and Application of New Scales to Measure the French and Raven (1959) Bases of Social Power," by Thomas R. Hinkin and Chester A. Schriescheim, *Journal of Applied Psychology*, August 1989, p. 567. Copyright © 1989 by the American Psychological Association. Adapted with permission.

An important consequence of resource-related power is that when leaders start losing their power to control resources, their power declines. A case in point is Donald Trump. When his vast holdings were generating a positive cash flow and his image was one of extraordinary power, he found many willing investors. The name *Trump* on a property escalated its value. As his cash-flow position worsened, however, Trump found it difficult to find investment groups willing to buy his properties at near the asking price. However, by mid-1993, Trump's cash-flow position had improved again and investors showed renewed interest. By 1996 Trump had regained all of his power to control resources, and money from investors flowed freely in his direction.

Power Stemming from Capitalizing on Opportunity

Power can be derived from being at the right place at the right time and taking the appropriate action. A person also needs to have the right resources to capitalize on the opportunity.[10] It pays to be "where the action is" in order to gain power through capitalizing on opportunity. For example, the best opportunities in a diversified company lie in one of its growth divisions.

Leaders can escalate their power by meeting the needs of the time. William Rothschild has identified four types of leaders, each of whom exercises the most power when his or her type matches the times. A *risk taker* is a visionary, such as Bill Gates of Microsoft, who starts the business. A *caretaker* institutionalizes the business so it can run smoothly. Quite often the caretaker is a key executive hired by a risk taker to manage the business professionally. An *undertaker* phases down a failed business and is sometimes hired after a company has declared bankruptcy. *Surgeon leaders* are analytical and objective with no ties to the past. Nothing is sacred to them, so they can surgically remove unprofitable lines of business even if these lines are sentimental favorites. A surgeon leader accrues the most power when a large business has become overweight, complacent, and slow.

Jack Welch of General Electric is a legendary surgeon leader. He had the courage to trade GE's RCA consumer electronics division for medical systems, and later sell the aerospace business to Martin Marietta. By carefully creating a "new" General Electric, Jack Welch has become an enormously powerful leader.[11] The accompanying Leader in Action vignette gives more information on the power orientation of Jack Welch.

Power Stemming from Managing Critical Problems

A simple but compelling theory has been developed to explain why some organizational units are more powerful than others. The **strategic contingency theory** of power suggests that units best able to cope with the firm's critical problems and uncertainties acquire relatively large amounts of power.[12] The theory implies, for example, that when an organization faces substantial lawsuits, the legal department will gain power and influence over organizational decisions. The sudden power and influence of the legal department is based on its exclusive ability to handle the particular problem of lawsuits.

Another important aspect of the strategic contingency theory concerns the power a subunit acquires by virtue of its centrality. **Centrality** is the extent to which a unit's activities are linked into the system of organizational activities. A unit has high centrality when it is an important and integral part of the work done by another unit. The second unit is therefore dependent on the first subunit. A sales department would have high centrality, whereas an employee credit union would have low centrality.

A study conducted by Herminia Ibarra provides some empirical evidence that holding a position of centrality does influence the power a worker, and therefore his or her subunit, can exert. The research setting was an advertising and public relations agency with ninety-four employees. The firm had recently gone through a period of turbulence, and needed to

LEADER IN ACTION

Jack Welch of General Electric

Ever since he became the top executive at GE, Jack Welch has set his sights on turning the industrial conglomerate into the most globally competitive company in the world. He expounded his greatly expanded vision of the company at management training sessions held at the Crotonville management development center. In a sense, Welch conducted a political campaign to gain supporters for his vision.

By 1996, GE had a capitalization (value of all the company's stock) of over $157 billion, the highest in the world. Its range of products and services includes the ubiquitous light bulbs and home appliances as well as jet engines, power generating systems, and an industrial finance company. An angioplasty in 1995 has not stopped Welch's zeal for expanding the market domination of GE businesses. He regularly warns employees about the dangers of complacency, believing that other multinational companies pose a constant competitive threat. "We've just got to be faster. We come to work every day on the razor's edge of a competitive battle" (*Business Week*, July 8, 1996, p. 48).

A major component of Welch's strategy for growing GE's business has been expansion into international markets. Overseas sales are now approaching one-half of the company's revenues. Welch has spearheaded the company effort to invest heavily in fast-growing markets such as India and China. He defines success in terms of GE's being a dominant power in whatever market it enters. "We're sitting here fighting like (expletive) to be No. 1 next year," he said recently (*Business Week,* July 8, 1996, p. 48).

Welch believes strongly that the way to increase the company's impact is to aim for his version of a stretch goal. To Welch, a stretch goal means attempting to achieve a huge gain, yet not knowing how to get there. This forces people to figure out the path to goal accomplishment. Welch admires the way Toshiba was able to produce a VCR in half the time, with half the

parts, and at half the cost by establishing stretch goals.

Welch believes the way he can contribute best as an executive is to allocate resources, people, and dollars. He reasons that his contribution is to detect opportunities, assign the right people to pursue them, and give those people the funds they need. Welch says, "I don't go to a major appliance review and pick out the colors or the crisper trays or all that sort of stuff. That's not my job" (*Fortune*, p. 146).

Welch's current goal is to make GE the world's only $70 billion growth company. Part of the thrust is to push GE deeper into services, such as management training, servicing jet engines, and helping utilities run power plants. The company is at the forefront of the new trend of regarding the products it sells as only one component of the business, with helping the customer make the best use of the product being another key component. Welch remains vigilant for new opportunities. A current possibility for expansion is consulting with other companies to show them how to cut costs and boost efficiency, using GE as a model.

Welch has been willing to take dramatic steps to achieve what he thinks is best for the company. At one time many people referred to him as Neutron Jack because of his penchant for laying off thousands of workers. (A neutron bomb kills people without destroying physical property.) He also closed many factories and sold old-line businesses. Such moves, however, gave GE the cash flow it needed to fuel the growth Welch's competitive spirit demanded.

Source: Tom Brown, "Politics and Managerial Leadership," *Management Review,* November 1996, p. 12; Marshall Loeb, "Jack Welch Lets Fly on Budgets, Bonuses, and Buddy Boards," *Fortune,* May 29, 1995, pp. 145–147; Tim Smart, "Jack Welch's Encore: How GE's Chairman Is Remaking His Company—Again," *Business Week,* October 28, 1996, pp. 154–160; Smart, "Fighting Like Hell to Be No. 1," *Business Week,* July 8, 1996, p. 48.

acquire many new clients to replace those that had defected. Centrality was measured in terms of the number of links a given individual had to others in the firm. Although this is not the same measure of centrality as closeness to power, it does indicate the extent to which a person is involved with others in making important decisions. Like formal authority, network centrality indicates a high position in a status hierarchy. Power was measured as bringing new administrative and technical ideas to life.

Among the findings in the study was that being at the center of a network was a strong determinant of individual involvement in administrative innovation. Two examples of such innovations are media training and the creation of a conflict management program. Having a position of centrality, however, did not contribute much to technical innovation (such as a new strategy for generating clients). Bringing forth technical innovations was related as much to informal as to formal power. Being a member of senior management, for example, would give a person the formal authority to create technical innovations.[13]

Power Stemming from Being Close to Power

The closer a person is to power, the greater the power he or she exerts. Likewise, the higher a unit reports in a firm's hierarchy, the more power it possesses. In practice, this means that a leader in charge of a department reporting to the president has more power than one in charge of a department reporting to a vice president. Leaders in search of more power typically maneuver toward a higher-reporting position in the organization. Many managers of quality assurance now report at a higher organizational level than previously. Part of this enhanced power can be attributed to the increasing attention organizations are paying to quality as part of their strategy.

Bases of Power and Transformational and Transactional Leadership

One justification for studying bases of power is that they have direct application to understanding and applying leadership. Leanne E. Atwater and Francis J. Yammarino investigated how the bases of power, both personal and positional, relate to transformational and transactional leadership.[14] Consistent with the definition provided in Chapter 3, transformational leadership is depicted as the influence a leader acquires through being respected and admired by group members. In contrast, transactional leadership is largely based on exchanges between the leader and group members, such as using rewards and punishments to control behavior. Two hundred and eighty employees reporting to 118 supervisors in forty-five organizations of many different types provided data for the study. Questionnaires were used to measure bases of power as well as perceptions of transformational and transactional leadership. (The Multifactor Leadership Questionnaire, mentioned in Chapter 3, was used to measure the perceptions of leader behavior.)

Of particular interest here, analysis of the data revealed that personal power, both referent and expert, was related to transformational leadership. Leaders who behave in a transformational manner (being charismatic, inspirational, intellectually stimulating, and considerate of individuals) are perceived to possess referent and expert power. Transformational leadership also showed a positive correlation with reward and legitimate power, yet was unrelated to coercive power. The message is that punitive bosses are rarely perceived as transformational. A less strong finding was that perceptions of power were not clearly linked to transactional leadership.

An important implication of the study derived from regression analysis is that leaders who behave in a transformational manner are likely to be perceived as having a variety of positive bases of power. The data also suggest that transformational leaders are able to influence group members by virtue of the referent power attributed to them. Another implication justifies studying power in relation to leadership: The researchers conclude that power and leader behavior are interrelated.

TACTICS FOR BECOMING AN EMPOWERING LEADER

A leader's power and influence increase when he or she shares power with others. A partial explanation for this paradox is that as team members receive more power, they can accomplish more. And because the manager shares credit for their accomplishments, he or she becomes more powerful. A truly powerful leader makes team members feel powerful and able to accomplish tasks on their own. To empower others is to be perceived as an influential person. Here we look briefly at the nature of empowerment before describing a group of empowering practices.

The Nature of Empowerment

In its basic meaning, **empowerment** refers to passing decision-making authority and responsibility from managers to group members. Almost any form of participative management, shared decision making , and delegation can be regarded as empowerment. Several attempts have been made to explore the nature of empowerment beyond its basic meaning.[15] Gretchen M. Spreitzer conducted research in several work settings to develop a psychological definition of empowerment. Her work provides useful insights for leaders and also builds on the work of other inquiries into the nature of empowerment.[16] Four components of empowerment were identified: meaning, competence, self-determination, and impact. Full-fledged empowerment includes all four dimensions.

Meaning is the value of a work goal, evaluated in relation to a person's ideals or standards. Work has meaning when there is a fit between the requirements of a work role and a person's beliefs, values, and behaviors. A person who is doing meaningful work is likely to feel empowered. *Competence,* or *self-efficacy,* is an individual's belief in his or her capability to perform a particular task well. The person who feels competent feels that he or she has the capability to meet the performance requirements in a given situation, such as a credit analyst saying, "I've been given the authority to evaluate credit risks up to $10,000 and I know I can do it well."

Self-determination is an individual's feeling of having a choice in initiating and regulating actions. A high-level form of self-determination occurs when a worker feels that he or she can choose which is the best method to solve a particular problem. Self-determination also involves such considerations as choosing the work pace and work site. A highly empowered worker might choose to perform the required work while on a cruise rather than remain in the office. *Impact* is the degree to which the worker can influence strategic, administrative, or operating outcomes on the job. Instead of feeling there is no choice but to follow the company's course, he or she might have a say in the future of the company. A middle manager might say, "Here's an opportunity for recruiting minority employees that we should exploit. And here's my action plan for doing so."

Empowering Practices

The practices that foster empowerment described here supplement standard approaches to participative management such as conferring with team members before reaching a decision. Many of them are based on direct observations of successful leaders, including a study by Jay Conger.[17] Before reading these practices, you are invited to do Leadership Self-Assessment Exercise 7–2.

Providing a Positive Emotional Atmosphere.   Conger identified an unusual empowering practice: executives providing emotional support to team members, especially through play or drama. For example, every few months several executives would hold a day-long event devoted to confidence building. Among the activities were inspirational speeches and films about mountain climbing. The message conveyed in such activities is that the person featured is finding extraordinary satisfaction in work, and is performing superbly.

Providing a positive emotional atmosphere contributes to empowerment indirectly by helping group members develop greater self-confidence. As their self-confidence grows, they are more willing to assume the responsibilities required of an empowered worker.

Rewarding and Encouraging in Visible and Personal Ways.   The majority of executives in the Conger study rewarded the achievements of team members by praising them and by giving them rewards in visible and confidence-building ways. For example, one executive established the "I Make a Difference Club." Each year staff members who have performed exceptionally well are invited to a company dinner in which they are inaugurated into this exclusive club.

LEADERSHIP SELF-ASSESSMENT
EXERCISE 7–2   Becoming an Empowering Manager

Directions: To empower employees successfully, the leader has to convey appropriate attitudes and develop effective interpersonal skills. To the best of your ability, indicate which skills and attitudes you now have, and which ones require further development.

Empowering Attitude or Behavior	Can Do Now	Would Need to Develop
1. Believe in team members' ability to be successful	___	___
2. Have patience with people and give them time to learn	___	___
3. Provide team members with direction and structure	___	___
4. Teach team members new skills in small, incremental steps so they can easily learn those skills	___	___
5. Ask team members questions that challenge them to think in new ways	___	___
6. Share information with team members, sometimes just to build rapport	___	___
7. Give team members timely feedback and encourage them throughout the learning process	___	___
8. Offer team members alternative ways of doing things	___	___
9. Exhibit a sense of humor and demonstrate care for workers as people	___	___
10. Focus on team members' results and acknowledge their personal improvement	___	___

Source: Reprinted by permission of the publisher, from *Supervisory Management*, April 1991, © 1991, American Management Association, New York. All rights reserved.

Expressing Confidence.   The empowering leaders in the study invested considerable time in expressing their confidence in team members' abilities. They did so daily in speeches, at meetings, and even during chance encounters in the hallways.

Fostering Initiative and Responsibility.   A leader can empower team members simply by fostering greater initiative and responsibility in their assignments. For example, one bank executive transformed what had been a constricted branch manager's job into a branch "president" role. Managers were then evaluated on the basis of deposits because they had control over them. After the transformation, branch managers were allowed to stay with one branch rather than being rotated every three years.

Building on Success.   Empowering executives often introduce organizational change by starting small. If the change proves successful in the pilot run, it then proceeds on a larger scale. For example, a new technology might be introduced in one plant rather than throughout the organization. In Conger's study, the managers who launched such new projects successfully reported feelings of self-efficacy (or competence).

Praising Initiative.   To reinforce empowerment, leaders praise workers who take risks and display initiatives that lead to success. They also recognize workers who make honest and thoughtful efforts yet fall short of achieving worthwhile results.

Establishing Limits to Empowerment.   One of the major situations in which empowerment creates disharmony, dissatisfactions, and dysfunctions is when workers do not have a clear perception of the boundaries of empowerment. Limits to empowerment might mean explaining to employees that they have more authority than before, but still they cannot engage in such activities as the following:

- Set their own wages
- Set the wages of top management
- Decide on dividends to shareholders
- Make downsizing decisions
- Hire mostly friends and relatives
- Work less than forty hours for full pay
- Take two-hour lunch breaks
- Devote three hours per day to Internet surfing for recreational purposes

As facetious as a few of the above may appear, many employees justify dysfunctional actions by saying, "I'm empowered to do what I want." It is management's responsibility to guide empowerment toward activities that support the organization.

Practicing SuperLeadership

Encouraging team members to practice self-leadership is the heart of empowerment. When employees lead themselves, they feel empowered. At W. L. Gore and Associates, a manufacturer of insulated material including GORE-TEX®, a popular buzzword is *unmanagement*—no bosses or managers but many leaders. One example of unmanagement takes place during salary reviews. Each associate's (employee's) salary is periodically reviewed by a compensation team drawn from individuals at the associate's work site. Each associate has a sponsor who acts as his or her advocate during the reviews. The sponsor gathers data about the associate's performance by speaking to internal and external customers.

Effective Delegation and Empowerment

A major contributor to empowerment is **delegation,** the assignment of formal authority and responsibility for accomplishing a specific task to another person. Delegation is more narrow than empowerment because delegation deals with a specific task, whereas empowerment covers a broad range of activities and a mental set about assuming more responsibility. The intensive exploration of delegation is usually more a part of studying management than of studying leadership. Our purposes are served here by briefly discussing guidelines for effective delegation.[18]

An excellent starting point in effective delegation is to *assign duties to the right people.* The chances for successful delegation and empowerment improve when it is capable, responsible, self-motivated group members who are assigned the tasks in question. Vital tasks should not be assigned to ineffective performers. When feasible, *delegate the whole task.* In the spirit of job enrichment, a manager should delegate an entire task to one group member rather than dividing it among several. So doing gives the group member complete responsibility and enhances his or her motivation, and also gives the manager more control over results. *Give as much instruction as needed,* depending upon the characteristics of the group member. Some people will require highly detailed instructions, whereas others can operate effectively with general instructions.

As a leader or manager, *retain some important tasks for yourself.* In general, the manager should handle some high-output or sensitive tasks, and any tasks that involve the survival of the unit. However, which tasks the manager should retain always depends on the circumstances. A basic management principle is to *obtain feedback on the delegated task.* A responsible manager does not delegate a complex assignment to a group member, then wait until the assignment is completed before discussing it again. Managers must establish checkpoints and milestones to obtain feedback on progress. A morale-building suggestion is to *delegate both pleasant and unpleasant tasks to group members.* When group members are assigned a mixture of pleasant and unpleasant responsibilities, they are more likely to believe they are being treated fairly. Few group members expect the manager to handle all the

LEADERSHIP SKILL-BUILDING
EXERCISE 7–1   Conducting an Empowerment Session

A profound cliché floating around organizations is that to empower group members, a leader must do more than say, "Pfft, you're empowered." The description of empowering practices has provided you some useful ideas to get started empowering others if you are already a manager. The role-assuming exercise described here gives you a chance to practice your empowering skills. One person plays the role of a leader, and six other people play the role of group members. You are meeting with your group today to get them started on the road toward empowerment. You will need to engage in dialogue with the group to begin the empowerment process. The empowerment scenarios described next should be staffed by different groups of students:

Information technology customer-service center. You are in charge of an information technology customer-service center whose primary activity is to respond to telephone inquiries from around the country from customers who are having problems in using the company's software. Visualize the help line of Microsoft or Corel to get an idea of this type of operation. The workers who answer the phone are full-time professionals, many of whom are recent college graduates. A major goal of yours is to empower your workers to do as much as they can to satisfy the demands of the callers. You want your staff to take more personal responsibility for customer problems.

Vision-care proprietors. You are the CEO of a nationwide chain of vision-care stores that sell both eyeglasses and contact lenses. You believe strongly that one of the constraining forces in your business is that your store managers, as well as franchise owners, do not take enough responsibility for running their operations. They rely too heavily on the corporate group for guidance and problem resolution. Today you are holding an empowerment meeting with the seven vision-care proprietors in your region. If your approach to empowerment works well, you will expand to other regions. Six other students play the role of store managers and franchise owners who generally believe that the corporate group should take the initiative to lead the stores toward greater prosperity. After all, why be a manager within a corporation or a franchise owner? Without corporate assistance, you might as well open your own vision-care store.

undesirable jobs. A related approach is to rotate undesirable tasks among group members. One or two group members should not be "empowered" to handle all the nasty assignments.

A fundamental part of effective delegation is to *step back from the details.* Many managers are poor delegators because they get too involved with technical details. If a manager cannot let go of details, he or she will never be effective at delegation or empowerment. As in virtually all leadership endeavors, it is important to *evaluate and reward performance.* After the task is completed, the manager should evaluate the outcome. Favorable outcomes should be rewarded, and unfavorable outcomes may either not be rewarded or be punished. It is important, however, not to discourage risk taking and initiative by punishing all mistakes.

A final point is that the leader and manager should *prevent reverse delegation.* A reverse delegator is an employee who tosses assignments back to the manager. Common excuses include employees complaining that they are overwhelmed or stressed out, or that they lack the right background to perform the task. Most of the suggestions for effective delegation already presented will help with reverse delegation. In addition, Joseph T. Straub recommends that the manager create an implied contract with the group members. Make sure employees understand that the tasks are theirs for the duration, and obtain their agreement and commitment. As part of empowerment and delegation, the group members must recognize that accountability lies with them.[19]

Before moving on to a study of organizational politics, you are invited to gain some practice in the realities of empowerment by doing Leadership Skill-Building Exercise 7–1. Also, keep in mind suggestions about delegation when doing the exercise.

FACTORS THAT CONTRIBUTE TO POLITICAL BEHAVIOR

People want power for many different reasons, which is why political behavior is so widespread in organizations. By definition, politics is used to acquire power. A number of individual and organizational factors contribute to political behavior, as outlined in Table 7–2.

Pyramid-Shaped Organization Structure

Organizations have been described as political structures that operate by distributing authority and setting the stage for the exercise of power. The very shape of large organizations is the most fundamental reason why organizational members are motivated toward political behavior. A pyramid concentrates power at the top. Only so much power is therefore available to distribute among the many people who would like more of it. Each successive layer on the organization chart has less power than the layer above. At the

TABLE 7–2   Factors Contributing to Political Behavior in Organizations

1. Pyramid-shaped organization structure

2. Subjective standards of performance

3. Environmental uncertainty and turbulence

4. Emotional insecurity

5. Machiavellian tendencies

6. Disagreements that prevent rational decision making

very bottom of the organization, workers have virtually no power. Since most organizations today have fewer layers than they previously had, the competition for power has become more intense. Although empowerment may be motivational for many workers, it is unlikely to satisfy the quest to hold a formal position of power.

In one study, every member of the top management team in eight micro-computer firms was asked about decision making and politics. The finding suggested that a pyramid-shaped structure fosters politics. According to the study, politics arises from power centralization (the consequence of a pyra-mid). Furthermore, autocratic executives (those who prefer to centralize power) engage in politics and generate political behavior among their team members.[20]

A pyramid-shaped organization creates competition for the limited resource of high-level positions. Competition for other limited resources also breeds political behavior. As Gregory Moorhead and Ricky W. Griffin note, whenever resources are scarce, some people will fail to attain what they want or deserve. Consequently, they may behave politically as a means of inflating their share of resources.[21]

Recognizing that budgets were tight, a director of training predicted dire consequences if her request for funding a training program were denied. She told top management, "If we are not fully funded, the board of directors will be very unhappy. We will not be able to make the quality improvements the board wants."

Subjective Standards of Performance

People often resort to organizational politics because they do not believe that the organization has an objective and fair way of judging their performance and suitability for promotion. Similarly, when managers have no objective way of differentiating effective people from the less effective, they will resort to favoritism. The adage "It's not what you know but who you know" applies to organizations that lack clear-cut standards of performance.

Environmental Uncertainty and Turbulence

When people, or the organizational subunits they represent, operate in an unstable and unpredictable environment, they tend to behave politically. They rely on organizational politics to create a favorable impression because uncertainty makes it difficult to determine what they should really be accomplishing.

The uncertainty, turbulence, and insecurity created by corporate downsizings is a major contributor to office politics. Many people believe intuitively that favoritism plays a major role in deciding who will survive the downsizing. In response to this perception, organizational members attempt to ingratiate themselves with influential people.

Emotional Insecurity

Some people resort to political maneuvers to ingratiate themselves with superiors because they lack confidence in their talents and skills. As an extreme example, a pension fund manager who had directed the firm toward investments with an annualized 35 percent return does not have to be overly political because he or she will have confidence in his or her capabilities. A person's choice of political strategy may indicate emotional insecurity. For instance, an insecure person might laugh loudly at every humorous comment the boss makes.

Machiavellian Tendencies

Some people engage in political behavior because they want to manipulate others, sometimes for their own personal advantage. The term *Machiavellianism* traces back to Niccolo Machiavelli (1469–1527), an Italian political philosopher and statesman. His most famous work, *The Prince,* describes how a leader may acquire and maintain power. Machiavelli's ideal prince was an amoral, manipulating tyrant who would restore the Italian city-state of Florence to its former glory.

Research conducted by Gerald Biberman provided the evidence for the relationship between Machiavellianism and political behavior. He found a high correlation between scores on a test of Machiavellian attitudes and an organizational politics scale.[22] An updated version of this scale is presented in Leadership Self-Assessment Exercise 7–3 (on pages 178–180). Recent research also demonstrates that people with a strong disposition to dominate other people are more likely to seek power and feel powerful in an organizational setting. Marshall Schminke used a computer-based experimental job simulation to study the effects of a need for dominance on perceived power. Structural characteristics of the job were held constant, and the success or failure of individuals on job performance was varied. People with a high need to dominate perceived themselves to be more powerful independent of their job success.[23]

1

LEADERSHIP SELF-ASSESSMENT
EXERCISE 7–3   The Organizational Politics Questionnaire

Directions: Answer each question "mostly agree" or "mostly disagree," even if it is difficult for you to decide which alternative best describes your opinion.

	Mostly Agree	Mostly Disagree
1. The boss is always right.	___	___
2. It is wise to flatter important people.	___	___
3. If you do somebody a favor, remember to cash in on it.	___	___
4. Given the opportunity, I would cultivate friendships with powerful people.	___	___
5. I would be willing to say nice things about a rival in order to get that person transferred from my department.	___	___
6. If it would help me get ahead, I would take credit for someone else's work.	___	___
7. Given the chance, I would offer to help my boss build some shelves for his or her den.	___	___
8. I laugh heartily at my boss's jokes, even if I do not think they are funny.	___	___
9. Dressing for success is silly. Wear clothing to work that you find to be the most comfortable.	___	___
10. Never waste lunch time by having lunch with somebody who can't help you solve a problem or gain advantage.	___	___
11. I think using E-mail to zap somebody for his or her mistakes is a good idea (especially if you want to show that person up).	___	___
12. If somebody higher up in the organization offends you, let that person know about it.	___	___
13. Honesty is the best policy in practically all cases.	___	___
14. Power for its own sake is one of life's most precious commodities.	___	___

15. If I had a legitimate gripe against my employer, I would air my views publicly (such as writing a letter to the editor of a local newspaper).   ____ ____

16. I would invite my boss to a party at my home, even if I didn't like him or her.   ____ ____

17. An effective way to impress people is to tell them what they want to hear.   ____ ____

18. Having a high school or skyscraper named after me would be an incredible thrill.   ____ ____

19. Hard work and good performance are usually sufficient for career success.   ____ ____

20. Even if I made only a minor contribution to a project, I would get my name listed as being associated with that project.   ____ ____

21. I would never publicly correct mistakes made by the boss.   ____ ____

22. I would never use my personal contacts in order to gain a promotion.   ____ ____

23. If you happen to dislike a person who receives a big promotion in your firm, don't bother sending that person a congratulatory note.   ____ ____

24. I would never openly criticize a powerful executive in my organization.   ____ ____

25. I would stay in the office late just to impress my boss.   ____ ____

Scoring and interpretation: Give yourself a plus one for each answer that agrees with the keyed answer. Each question that receives a score of plus one shows a tendency toward playing organizational politics. The scoring key is as follows:

1. Mostly agree	7. Mostly agree	13. Mostly disagree
2. Mostly agree	8. Mostly agree	14. Mostly agree
3. Mostly agree	9. Mostly disagree	15. Mostly disagree
4. Mostly agree	10. Mostly agree	16. Mostly agree
5. Mostly agree	11. Mostly agree	17. Mostly agree
6. Mostly agree	12. Mostly disagree	18. Mostly agree

19. Mostly disagree	22. Mostly disagree	24. Mostly agree
20. Mostly agree	23. Mostly disagree	25. Mostly agree
21. Mostly agree		

Based on a sample of 750 men and women managers, professionals, administrators, sales representatives, and business owners,* the mean score is 10.

1–7:   below-average tendency to play office politics
8–12:   average tendency to play office politics
13 and above: above-average tendency to play office politics; strong need for power.

---

*Andrew J. DuBrin, "Career Maturity, Organizational Rank, and Political Behavior Tendencies: A Correlational Analysis of Organizational Politics and Career Experience," *Psychological Reports,* Vol. 63, 1988, pp. 531–537; DuBrin, "Sex Differences in Endorsement of Influence Tactics and Political Behavior Tendencies," *Journal of Business and Psychology,* Fall 1989, pp. 3–14.

Disagreement over Major Issues

Many executives attempt to use rational criteria when making major decisions, but rational decision making is constrained by major disagreements over employees' preferences and theories of what the organization should be doing. Unless strategy and goals are shared among key organizational members, political motivation is inevitable in organizational decision making. Jeffrey Pfeffer analyzes this contributor to organizational politics in this manner:

> In some ways the relative weighting of the various demands and criteria must be determined. Since there is no way of rationalizing away the dissensus, political strength within the coalition comes to determine which criteria and whose preferences are to prevail.[24]

An example of disagreement over major issues leading to political behavior took place at a savings bank. Substantial inner turmoil occurred because of power struggles between the consumer loan and home mortgage departments. Each department saw itself as the most important future thrust of the bank. Representatives of both groups often diverted marketing and customer service efforts while they waged their internal power struggle.

POLITICAL TACTICS AND STRATEGIES

To make effective use of organizational politics, leaders must be aware of specific political tactics and strategies. To identify and explain the majority of political tactics would require years of study and observation. Leaders so frequently need support for their programs that they search for innovative types of political behaviors. Furthermore, new tactics continue to emerge as the workplace becomes increasingly competitive. Let's look at a representative group of political tactics and strategies, categorized as to whether they are ethical or unethical. (Several of the influence tactics described in Chapter 8, such as ingratiation, might also be considered political behaviors.)

Ethical Political Tactics and Strategies

So far we have discussed organizational politics without pinpointing specific tactics and strategies. This section describes a sampling of ethical political behaviors, divided into three related groups: tactics and strategies aimed directly at (1) gaining power, (2) building relationships with superiors and coworkers, and (3) avoiding political blunders. All of these approaches help the leader gain or retain power. They also help the leader cope with the fact that organizations are not entirely rational. In the words of Gerald R. Ferris and Thomas R. King, "Politics is what takes place between the perfect workings of the rational model (efficiency) and the messiness of human interaction. The greater the gap, the more political behavior becomes necessary."[25]

Strategies and Tactics Aimed Directly at Gaining Power.   All political tactics are aimed at acquiring and maintaining power, even the power to avoid a difficult assignment. Tom Peters points to a fundamental reason that gaining power can justify the effort. He says that although power can often be abused, it can also be used to benefit many people. "And as a career building tool, the slow and steady (and subtle) amassing of power is the surest road to success."[26] Here are six techniques aimed directly at gaining power.

1. *Develop power contacts.* After powerful people have been identified, alliances with them must be established. Cultivating friendly, cooperative relationships with powerful organizational members and outsiders can make the leader's cause much easier to advance. These contacts can benefit a person by supporting his or her ideas in meetings and other public forums. One way to develop these contacts is to be more social, for example, throwing parties and inviting powerful people and their guests. Some organizations and some bosses frown on social familiarity, however. And powerholders receive many invitations, so they might not be available.

2. *Control vital information.* Power accrues to those who control vital information, as indicated in the discussion of personal power. Many former government or military officials have found power niches for themselves in industry after leaving the public payroll. Frequently such an individual will be hired as the Washington representative of a firm that does business with the government. The vital information they control is knowledge of whom to contact to shorten some of the complicated

procedures in getting government contracts approved. The Clinton administration has attempted to decrease this blatant use of vital information by establishing a lag time between departure from a government post and assumption of certain types of jobs.

3. *Keep informed.* In addition to controlling vital information, it is politically important to keep informed. Management consultant Eugene Schmuckler writes that we are all aware of the significance of having our name removed from a distribution list. Even if the information is not accurate, being able to tap into the corporate grapevine is power-enhancing. Successful leaders develop a pipeline to help them keep abreast, or ahead, of developments within the firm. For this reason, a politically astute individual befriends the president's assistant. No other source offers the potential for obtaining as much information as the executive administrative assistant.[27]

4. *Control lines of communication.* Related to controlling information is controlling lines of communication, particularly access to key people. Administrative assistants and staff assistants frequently control an executive's calendar. Both insiders and outsiders must curry favor with the *conduit* in order to see the important executive. The administrative assistant can also control how quickly the executive responds to telephone and fax messages.

5. *Bring in outside experts.* To help legitimate their positions, executives will often hire a consultant to conduct a study or cast an opinion. Consciously or unconsciously, many consultants are hesitant to "bite the hand that feeds them." A consultant will therefore often support the executive's position. In turn, the executive will use the consultant's findings to prove that he or she is right. This tactic might be considered ethical because the executive believes he or she is obtaining an objective opinion.

6. *Make a quick showing.* A display of dramatic results can help gain acceptance for one's efforts or those of the group.[28] Once a person has impressed management with his or her ability to solve that first problem, that person can look forward to working on problems that will bring greater power. For instance, the manager of a systems analysis group volunteered to take on a mundane assignment of reducing paperwork in the accounts payable department. Within two weeks, paperwork was reduced 75 percent through electronic information storage and retrieval. The group next received a series of plum assignments without having to volunteer.

Strategies and Tactics Aimed at Building Relationships.   Much of organizational politics involves building positive relationships with network members who can be helpful now or later. This network includes superiors, subordinates, other lower-ranking people, coworkers, external customers, and suppliers. The following are several representative strategies and tactics:[29]

1. *Display loyalty.* A loyal worker is valued because organizations prosper more with loyal than with disloyal employees. Blind loyalty—the belief that the organization cannot make a mistake—is not called for; most rational organizations welcome constructive criticism. An obvious form of loyalty to the organization is longevity. The average chief executive of the nation's largest firms has spent 22.5 years with the firm. In some companies, 90 percent of the senior staff is promoted from within.[30]

2. *Manage your impression.* Impression management includes behaviors directed at enhancing one's image by drawing attention to oneself. Often the attention of others is directed toward superficial aspects of the self, such as clothing and grooming. Yet impression management also deals with deeper aspects of behavior, such as speaking well and presenting one's ideas coherently. Another part of impression management is to tell people about your success or imply that you are an "insider." E-mail is used extensively today to send messages to others for the purpose of impressing them with one's good deeds. Displaying good business etiquette has received renewed attention as a key part of impression management, with companies sending staff members to etiquette classes to learn how to create favorable impressions on key people. Many management scholars take a dim view of impression management, yet the topic has been carefully researched.[31] Self-Assessment Exercise 7–4 (on pages 184–185) provides you with an opportunity to relate impression management to yourself.

3. *Ask satisfied customers to contact your boss.* A favorable comment by a customer receives considerable weight because customer satisfaction is a top corporate priority. If a customer says something nice, the comment will carry more weight than one from a coworker or subordinate. The reason is that coworkers and subordinates might praise a person for political reasons. Customers' motivation is assumed to be pure because they have little concern about pleasing suppliers.

4. *Be courteous, pleasant, and positive.* According to employment specialist Robert Half, courteous, pleasant, and positive people are the first to be hired and the last to be fired (assuming they are also technically qualified).[32]

5. *Ask advice.* Asking advice on work-related topics builds relationships with other employees. Asking another person for advice—someone whose job does not require giving it—will usually be perceived as a compliment. Asking advice transmits a message of trust in the other person's judgment. The accompanying Leader in Action insert illustrates the effective use of asking advice.

6. *Send thank-you notes to large numbers of people.* One of the most basic political tactics, sending thank-you notes profusely, is simply an

LEADERSHIP SELF-ASSESSMENT
EXERCISE 7–4   **The Manager Impression Survey**

Respond to each of the following statements on the following scale: VI = very infrequently; I = infrequently; S = sometimes; F = frequently; VF = very frequently. The VI to VF categories correspond to a 1-to-5 scale. If you do not have a manager currently, think of a previous relationship with a manager, or how you would behave if you were placed in the situation being described.

To what extent do you	**Frequency**
1. Do personal favors for your manager (such as getting him or her coffee or a soft drink)	VI I S F VF
2. Offer to do something for your manager that you were not required to do, but are doing as a personal favor	VI I S F VF
3. Compliment your immediate manager on his or her dress or appearance	VI I S F VF
4. Praise your immediate manager on his or her accomplishments	VI I S F VF
5. Take an interest in your manager's personal life	VI I S F VF
6. Try to be polite when interacting with your manager	VI I S F VF
7. Try to be a friendly person when interacting with your manager	VI I S F VF
8. Try to act as a "model" employee, such as never taking longer than the established time for lunch	VI I S F VF
9. Work hard when you know the results will be seen by your manager	VI I S F VF
10 Let your manager know that you try to do a good job in your work	VI I S F VF

Total Score: _____

Scoring and interpretation: Score each circled response 1, 2, 3, 4, or 5 according to the scale indicated above. Use the following interpretative guide:

45 – 50   You are working diligently at creating a good impression with your manager. You show good political savvy.

30 – 44 You show moderate concern for creating a good impression with your manager. Become more sensitive to the impression you are making on your boss.

10 – 29 You are not making enough effort to create a good impression with your manager. If you want to be recognized, do a more effective job of managing your impression.

Source: Adapted and expanded from Sandy J. Wayne and Robert C. Liden, "Effects of Impression Management on Performance Ratings: A Longitudinal Study," *Academy of Management Journal*, February 1995, p. 246.

application of sound human relations. Many successful people take the time to send handwritten notes to employees and customers to help create a bond with those people. In the words of Tom Peters, "The power of a thank you (note or otherwise) is hard—make that impossible—to beat."[33]

Avoiding Political Blunders. A strategy for retaining power is to refrain from making power-eroding blunders. Committing these politically insensitive acts can also prevent one from attaining power. Several leading blunders are described next.

1. *Criticizing the boss in a public forum.* The oldest saw in human relations is to "praise in public and criticize in private." Yet in the passion of the moment, we may still surrender to an irresistible impulse to criticize the boss publicly. In the early days of President Bill Clinton's administration, Senator Richard Shelby (D-Ala.) crossed Clinton publicly by criticizing his economic plan. Clinton promptly yanked federal money from a Huntsville, Alabama, project.

2. *Bypassing the boss.* Protocol is still highly valued in a hierarchical organization. Going around the boss to resolve a problem is therefore hazardous. You might be able to accomplish the bypass, but your career could be damaged and your recourses limited. Courts upheld an oil company's dismissal of a manager because the manager had repeatedly ignored the chain of command. The manager would go over his superior's head, directly to the president.[34]

3. *Declining an offer from top management.* Turning down top management, especially more than once, is a political blunder. You thus have to balance sensibly managing your time against the blunder of refusing a request from top management. An increasing number of managers and professionals today decline opportunities for promotion when the new job requires geographic relocation. For these people, family and lifestyle preferences are more important than gaining political advantage on the job.

LEADER IN ACTION

■ Felicia Anderson, Bank Manager and Input Seeker

Felicia Anderson was brought in from another bank to be the manager of small business loans for a bank in Indianapolis. The three previous incumbents had lasted fewer than two years. Each was transferred to another position because of poor investment decisions. Because the bank executives thought poorly of the performance of the small business loan department, morale was low and turnover was high.

Anderson recognized that she was moving into a sensitive situation. Her mandate was to improve the performance of the unit as quickly as possible without creating any additional morale problems. She wanted to implement certain changes, but she decided to move slowly. She scheduled full-hour interviews with all seventeen members of the department. During these meetings, Anderson expressed considerable interest in learning about each worker's job responsibilities. Furthermore, she asked each person how the unit could make better loans and how morale could be improved.

Anderson took four of the best suggestions offered by the group and added several of her own. Immediate support was found for these new procedures. As the suggestions for improvement proved to be effective, top management at the bank was willing to give the department more resources. One of Anderson's suggestions for improving the performance of loans was to actively solicit loans to small businesses with good track records. A bank representative called on these firms and offered to lend them money for expansion. In the past, the bank had relied heavily on start-up firms seeking funds to open a business.

In 1996, Anderson added a program that ran counter to the successful program with the credit-worthy small businesses. Based upon a suggestion from a loan officer who was a self-proclaimed champion of the underdog, Anderson agreed to an experimental program of lending money to small businesses with poor credit. The bank would select the better risks among the applicants with the worst credit histories. In addition to charging these applicants the highest loan rates, the bank offered them counseling on debt management. Anderson says that preliminary evidence shows that the program will be profitable for the bank.

The leader described above and management at the bank she represents chose to remain anonymous.

4. *Burning your bridges.* A potent political blunder is to create ill will among former employers or people who have helped you in the past. The most common type of bridge burning occurs when a person departs from an organization. A person who leaves involuntarily is especially apt to express anger toward those responsible for the dismissal. Venting your anger may give a temporary boost to your mental health, but it can be detrimental in the long run.

Unethical Political Tactics and Strategies

Any technique of gaining power can be devious if practiced in the extreme. A person who supports a boss by feeding him or her insider information that could affect the price of company stock is being devious. Some approaches are unequivocally unethical, such as those described next. In the long run they erode a leader's effectiveness by lowering his or her credibility. Devious tactics might even result in lawsuits against the leader, the organization, or both.

Back Stabbing.   The ubiquitous back stab requires that you pretend to be nice, but all the while plan someone's demise. A frequent form of back stabbing is to initiate a conversation with a rival about the weaknesses of a common boss, encouraging negative commentary and making careful mental notes of what the person says. When these comments are passed along to the boss, the rival appears disloyal and foolish. E-mail has become a medium for back stabbing. The sender of the message documents a mistake made by another individual and includes key people on the distribution list. A sample message sent by one manager to a rival began as follows, "Hi, Ted. I'm sorry you couldn't make our important meeting. I guess you had some other important priorities. But we need your input on the following major agenda item we tackled. . . ."

Embrace or Demolish.   The ancient strategy of "embrace or demolish" suggests that you remove from the premises rivals who suffered past hurts through your efforts; otherwise the wounded rivals might retaliate at a vulnerable moment. This kind of strategy is common after a hostile takeover; many executives lose their jobs because they opposed the takeover.

     A variation of embrace or demolish is to fire people who disagree with you on important policy issues. In this way, antagonists are removed from the scene, helping you maintain total support. Joseph A. Graziano, the former chief financial officer of Apple Computer, Inc., appeared to fall victim to this, being banished because he disagreed with the boss. Graziano insisted that Apple could best prosper by selling off all or part of the company, while his boss, Chief Executive Michael H. Spindler, thought otherwise. The board supported Spindler and accepted the resignation of Graziano.[35] As Apple's troubles continued, the board later dismissed Spindler.

Setting a Person Up for Failure.   The object of a setup is to place a person in a position where he or she will either fail outright or look ineffective. For example, an executive whom the CEO dislikes might be given responsibility for a troubled division whose market is rapidly collapsing. The newly assigned division president cannot stop the decline and is then fired for poor performance.

Divide and Rule.   An ancient military and governmental strategy, this tactic is sometimes used in business. The object is to have subordinates fight among themselves, therefore yielding the balance of power to another person. If team members are not aligned with one another, there is an improved chance that they will align with a common superior. One way of getting subordinates to fight with one another is to place them in intense competition for resources—for example, asking them to prove why their budget is more worthy than the budget requested by rivals.

Doing Leadership Skill-Building Exercise 7–2 will give you further practical insights into political behavior. Since the material deals with a sensitive issue, we recommend that you proceed in a good-spirited mood.

EXERCISING CONTROL OVER DYSFUNCTIONAL POLITICS

Carried to excess, organizational politics can hurt an organization and its members. Too much politicking can result in wasted time and effort, thereby lowering productivity. For example, a highly political environment was said to contribute to IBM's decline under the leadership of former CEO John Akers. It was politically unwise for top executives to suggest that the company deemphasize mainframe computers. (The market had shifted away from mainframes and toward smaller computers.) The human consequences of excessive politics can also be substantial; examples are lowered morale and the loss of people who intensely dislike office politics. Leaders are therefore advised to combat political behavior when it is excessive and dysfunctional.

In a comprehensive strategy to control politics, organizational leaders must be aware of its causes and techniques. For example, during a downsizing the CEO can be on the alert for instances of back stabbing and transparent attempts to please him or her. Open communication also can constrain the impact of political behavior.[36] For instance, open communication can let everyone know the basis for allocating resources, thus reducing the amount of politicking. If people know in advance how resources are allocated, the effectiveness of attempting to curry favor with the boss will be reduced. When communication is open, it also makes it more difficult for some people to control information and pass along gossip as a political weapon.

Avoiding favoritism—giving the best rewards to the group members you like the most—is a potent way of minimizing politics within a work

LEADERSHIP SKILL-BUILDING
EXERCISE 7–2   Classroom Politics

Gather in groups of about five students. Each group's task is to identify student political behaviors you have observed in this or other classes. Label the tactics you have observed, and indicate what you think the political actor hoped to achieve by the tactic. Also attempt to indicate what the political behavior achieved. Finally, summarize the leadership implications of what you have observed. If time permits, each team appoints a leader who presents the team's findings to the rest of the class.

LEADERSHIP SKILL-BUILDING
EXERCISE 7–3 Controlling Office Politics

One student plays the role of a corporate executive visiting one of the key divisions. Six other students play the roles of managers within the division, each of whom wants to impress the boss during their meeting. The corporate executive gets the meeting started by asking the managers in turn to discuss their recent activities and accomplishments. Each division-level manager will attempt to create a very positive impression on the corporate executive. After about fifteen minutes of observing them fawning over him or her, the executive decides to take action against such excessive politicking. Review the information on political tactics and their control before carrying out the role-assuming exercise.

group. If group members believe that getting the boss to like them is much less important than good job performance in obtaining rewards, they will kiss up to the boss less frequently. In an attempt to minimize favoritism, the manager must reward workers who impress him or her through task-related activities.

Setting good examples at the top of the organization can help reduce the frequency and intensity of organizational politics. When leaders are non-political in their actions, they demonstrate in subtle ways that political behavior is not welcome. It may be helpful for the leader to announce during a staff meeting that devious political behavior is undesirable and unprofessional.

Finally, politics can sometimes be constrained by a threat to discuss questionable information in a public forum. People who practice devious politics usually want to operate secretly and privately. They are willing to drop hints and innuendoes and make direct derogatory comments about someone else, provided they will not be identified as the source. An effective way of stopping the discrediting of others is to offer to discuss the topic publicly.[37] The person attempting to pass on the questionable information will usually back down and make a statement closer to the truth.

Leadership Skill-Building Exercise 7–3 provides an opportunity to practice the subtle art of discouraging excessive political behavior on the job.

SUMMARY

To acquire and retain power, a leader must skillfully use organizational politics—informal approaches to gaining power through means other than merit or luck. Organizational power is derived from many sources, including position power (legitimate, reward, coercive, and information) and personal power (expert, reference, and prestige). Power also stems from ownership, providing resources, capitalizing upon opportunity, and being close to power. A study cited here shows that referent power, expert power, and reward power contribute to the leader's being perceived as transformational.

Full-fledged empowerment includes the dimensions of meaning, competence, self-determination, and impact. Certain actions can be taken to become an empowering leader. These include providing a positive emotional atmosphere, giving visible rewards, expressing confidence, fostering initiative and responsibility, building on success, praising initiative, and establishing limits to empowerment. Super-Leadership is also helpful because it encourages team members to practice self-leadership. Delegation is another important part of empowerment. To be effective, delegation should follow certain guidelines, including assigning tasks to the right people, delegating whole tasks, and preventing reverse delegation.

The quest for power causes political behavior. Specific contributing factors include the pyramidal shape of organizations, competition for limited resources, subjective performance standards, and environmental uncertainty. Emotional insecurity and Machiavellianism also contribute to political behavior.

To make effective use of organizational politics, leaders must be aware of specific political tactics and strategies. Ethical methods can be divided into those aimed directly at gaining power, building relationships, and avoiding political blunders. Unethical and devious tactics, such as the embrace-or-demolish strategy, constitute another category of political behavior.

Carried to an extreme, organizational politics can hurt an organization and its members. Being aware of the causes and types of political behavior can help leaders deal with the problem. Setting good examples of nonpolitical behavior is helpful, as is threatening to publicly expose devious politicking.

KEY TERMS

Power
Organizational politics
Legitimate power
Reward power
Coercive power
Information power

Personal power
Prestige power
Leadership power
Resource dependence
    perspective

Strategic contingency theory
Centrality
Empowerment
Delegation

GUIDELINES FOR ACTION AND SKILL DEVELOPMENT

The information presented throughout this chapter can be used by leaders to acquire and maintain power for the purpose of influencing people. Gary A. Yukl has prepared suggestions for using five standard power sources to gain commitment. An adaptation and abridgement of these suggestions is as follows:

1. Referent power will likely lead to commitment if the request is believed to be important to the

leader. The leader must therefore enthusiastically convey the importance of the request.

2. Expert power will likely lead to commitment if the request is persuasive and group members share the leader's task goals. The leader is therefore advised to be persuasive and hold a group discussion about the relevance of task goals.

3. Legitimate power will possibly lead to commitment if the request is polite and very appropri-

ate. The leader should therefore be mannerly and explain the appropriateness of the request.

4. Reward power will possibly lead to commitment if rewards are used in a subtle, very personal way. The leader must therefore avoid the appearance of offering bribes.

5. Coercive power is very unlikely to lead to commitment, so another type of power should be used.[38]

Related to the above discussion, the manner in which a leader uses power mediates how well exercising power will result in positive outcomes. A leader who exercises power in a blunt, abrasive, and mean-spirited manner will usually achieve less effective long-range results than a leader who wields power gracefully.

DISCUSSION QUESTIONS AND ACTIVITIES

1. How can a leader occupy a top-level executive position and still have relatively little power?

2. What does it really mean to describe a leader as a "slick politician"?

3. Shortly after being appointed as CEO of Sunbeam Corporation, Al Dunlap laid off half the work force, closed thirty production and warehouse sites, and reduced the number of products by 81 percent. What various kinds of powers was he exercising?

4. With so many people in the workplace having similar educational backgrounds, how can a person acquire information power?

5. Empowerment has been criticized because it leaves no one in particular accountable for results. What is your opinion of this criticism?

6. Which styles of leader are the most likely to delegate easily? You might want to review the

information in Chapters 5 and 6 to help you answer this question.

7. Why are entrepreneurial leaders often poor delegators?

8. Assume a leader received a maximum score of twenty-five on the organizational politics questionnaire. How would this affect his or her ability to lead?

9. After listening to an after-dinner talk on organizational politics, a member of the audience asked the speaker, "Isn't office politics just for incompetents?" What is your answer to this person's question?

10. Read a current report about an organizational leader, and identify at least one political tactic he or she has used.

LEADERSHIP CASE PROBLEM

The Computerization Power Failure

Jerry Falvo was an information systems manager for a life insurance and financial services company. The firm planned to computerize all its operating systems. Such a sweeping change meant that 40 percent of the work force would have to learn new skills. Jerry thought that a program to help all employees become computer literate would be beneficial because the employees would become more versatile. He

therefore developed a curriculum, gathered materials, and performed a cost-benefit analysis. He also surveyed 200 employees on their computer knowledge.

Armed with convincing information, Jerry secured approval from his boss to establish a training program. He then went to the director of corporate training to discuss obtaining instructors. Jerry was taken aback when the director said that her group was already aware of the need for expanded training. The director also said that the training department had already upgraded the course content of its computer literacy program.

After reviewing the training director's program, Jerry concluded that it was of low quality. After listening to Jerry's analysis, his boss ordered the training department to cooperate. The director agreed, as long as a pilot program proved Jerry's program to be worthwhile. Jerry enlisted the cooperation of a manager to volunteer his people for the pilot program. Only six out of a possible twenty-three showed up for the first class.

With such a poor turnout, Jerry's boss ordered the program terminated. He also gave Jerry a poor performance evaluation for having spent so much time on a failed effort.

1. What political mistakes did Jerry make? ·

2. How might Jerry have improved his program's chances of success?

3. What political behavior does it appear the training director used to hamper Jerry's program?

Source: Based on information in William H. Fonvielle, *From Manager to Innovator: Using Information to Become an Idea Entrepreneur* (Trevose, Pa: Administrative Management Society Foundation, 1991).

Influence Tactics of Leaders

LEARNING OBJECTIVES

After studying this chapter, you should be able to

1. describe the relationship between power and influence.
2. identify a set of honest and ethical influence tactics.
3. identify a set of less honest and ethical influence tactics.
4. summarize some empirical research about the effectiveness and sequencing of influence tactics.

---

*I*n 1996 Louis V. Gerstner Jr., chairman and chief executive of IBM, was leading the company toward spectacular success, rebounding from the previous decade, in which many critics had thought Big Blue was in big trouble. After a few years with Gerstner at the helm, the company was booming. Computer service sales had reached their highest level ever. IBM also showed excellent growth in its core business of selling computers and information technology to business and industry. Furthermore, demand for its new home PC far exceeded supply. Thousands of talented and dedicated people had contributed to the resurgence of IBM, but a particularly visible success factor was Gerstner's personal appeals to major customers and potential customers. According to his estimate, he spends 40 percent of his time with customers, listening to their concerns and plans. A case in point was a visit to Toronto, where Gerstner held a conference with twenty top executives. Seated at a horseshoe-shaped table, and dressed in shirt sleeves, the IBM top executive held forth for 90 minutes in a casual, but powerful presentation. There were no slides, no computerized overheads, and no prepared speech. Gerstner chatted about a wide range of subjects, including the changes that technology is bringing to business and society. Most of the CEOs in the room were impressed by the relevance of his discourse to their companies. In the words of the chairman and CEO of Rubbermaid, "He's able to connect."[1]

Lou Gerstner is fulfilling a leader's quintessential responsibility—he influences key people to think and act in ways that benefit his organization. Leadership, as oft repeated, is an influence process. To become an effective leader, a person must be aware of the specific tactics leaders use to influence others. Here we discuss a number of specific influence tactics, but other aspects of leadership also concern influence. Being charismatic, as described in Chapter 3, influences many people. Leaders influence others through power and politics, as described in Chapter 7. Furthermore, motivating and coaching skills, as described in Chapter 10, involve influencing others toward worthwhile ends.

The terms *influence* and *power* have understandable, everyday meanings yet present complexities to the scholar. The two terms are sometimes used interchangeably, whereas at other times power is said to create influence and vice versa. In this book, let's distinguish between power and influence as follows: **Influence** is the ability to affect the behavior of others in a particular direction,[2] whereas power is the potential or capacity to influence. Keep in mind, however, that recognizing power as the ability to influence others will not interfere with learning how to use influence tactics.

Leaders are influential only when they exercise power. A leader therefore must acquire power to influence others. Assume that a worker is the informal leader among a group of quality technicians. The worker exerts a modicum of influence because of his talent, charm, and wit. Move the person into the position of vice president of quality assurance (more formal authority), and his or her influence will multiply.

This chapter presents some underlying theories, a description and explanation of influence tactics (both ethical and less ethical), and a summary of research about the relative effectiveness and sequencing of influence tactics.

A MODEL OF POWER AND INFLUENCE

The model shown in Figure 8–1, as developed by Gary Yukl, explains that leader power, influence behavior, and influence skills interact in various ways to determine how much influence a leader has with target people.[3] Although the model is complex, it is useful because it illustrates that what a leader can accomplish depends on many internal and external factors. Beginning at the left, the leader's choice of an influence tactic depends to some extent on how much personal power and position power he or she can exercise in relation to the target person (arrow 1 in Figure 8–1). The choice of influence behavior also depends somewhat on which traits the leader possesses, such as self-confidence and extroversion (arrow 2). Which influence tactic is chosen also depends on certain situational factors, such as the anticipated reaction of the influence target (arrow 3).

A leader's influence behavior has a direct impact on how the target responds to the influence attempt, with the three possible outcomes being

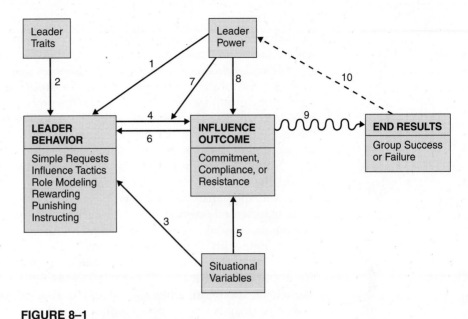

FIGURE 8–1

A Model of Power and Influence

Source: Leadership in Organizations, 3/E *by Yukl, Gary, © 1997. Reprinted by permission of Prentice-Hall, Inc., Upper Saddle River, NJ.*

commitment, compliance, and resistance (arrow 4). The outcomes can be regarded as anchor points on a continuum. **Commitment** indicates the highest degree of success: The target of the influence attempt is enthusiastic about carrying out the request and makes a full effort. **Compliance** means that the influence attempt is partially successful: The target person is apathetic (not overjoyed) about carrying out the request and makes only a modest effort. **Resistance** is an unsuccessful influence attempt: The target is opposed to carrying out the request and finds ways to either not comply or do a poor job. How the target person reacts also depends on some aspects of the situation, such as the relevance of the request to achieving the task and the feasibility of the request (arrow 5).

The outcome of the influence attempt provides the leader some feedback (arrow 6). For example, if the target resists the first attempt, the influence agent might try again, using another influence tactic. Depending on the target's reaction, the leader might also modify the proposal, much as Lou Gerstner would switch the topic in his conference if the CEOs present did not appear interested. The effect of leader power is contingent upon how the leader attempts to influence the target. Leader power enhances the impact of the influence attempts when the power is relevant (arrow 7). For example, threats have more clout when the influence target believes that the agent has sufficient coercive power to follow through on the threats. Leader power may directly affect target attitudes and behavior (arrow 8). For example, when a leader has high reward and coercive power, people are more likely to comply with requests in hopes of gaining rewards and avoiding punishment.

Influence outcomes are intervening variables that affect end results, such as the success of the agent's proposal or the group success or failure. Commitment by group members will enhance the probability of success, whereas resistance will decrease the probability. The wavy line (arrow 9) indicates that the relationship is not strong because many factors in addition to the commitment of target persons determine the end results. The end results provide some feedback regarding the leader's power (arrow 10). If the leader is successful, the target people perceive him or her to have more expert power. Failure lowers the perception of expert power. Over the long term, success may result in increased position power for the leader because the success may lead to promotion and the acquisition of more resources.

The model attributes the outcome of an influence attempt to the combined effect of the leader's influence skills, influence behavior, and power. For example, an influence attempt using inspirational appeal is the most likely to be successful when the leader has good charisma and high expert power. An inspirational appeal will sometimes work without good expert power, but success is much more likely when the leader is both charismatic and knowledgeable.

Although Yukl's model has not been proven to work in its entirety, it serves as a useful framework for understanding the specific role influence tactics play in leadership. The rest of this chapter concentrates on identifying and describing influence tactics, with some mention of situational variables. Leader traits and power have been described in previous chapters. Leadership Self-Assessment Exercise 8–1 gives you an opportunity to think about which influence tactics you use.

LEADERSHIP SELF-ASSESSMENT EXERCISE 8–1   Survey of Influence Tactics

Directions: Indicate how frequently you use the influence tactics listed below. VI = very infrequently or never; I = infrequently; S = sometimes; F = frequently; VF = very frequently. The VI to VF categories correspond to a 1-to-5 scale.

	1 VI	2 I	3 S	4 F	5 VF
1. I am a team player.	—	—	—	—	—
2. I am personally charming.	—	—	—	—	—
3. I make a good personal appearance.	—	—	—	—	—

4. I manipulate the situation. ___ ___ ___ ___ ___

5. I manipulate people. ___ ___ ___ ___ ___

6. I am assertive (open and forthright
   in my demands). ___ ___ ___ ___ ___

7. I joke with or kid other people. ___ ___ ___ ___ ___

8. I exchange favors with the other
   person. ___ ___ ___ ___ ___

9. I promise to reward the person. ___ ___ ___ ___ ___

10. I threaten to punish the person. ___ ___ ___ ___ ___

11. I get the other person to like me. ___ ___ ___ ___ ___

12. I make an appeal to logic or reason. ___ ___ ___ ___ ___

13. I form an alliance with the other
    person. ___ ___ ___ ___ ___

14. I threaten to go over the person's
    head to the boss. ___ ___ ___ ___ ___

15. I compliment the other person. ___ ___ ___ ___ ___

16. I offer to compromise with the other
    person. ___ ___ ___ ___ ___

Interpretation: The more of the above tactics you use frequently or very frequently, the more influential you probably are. You might also want to compare your scores to normative data. Listed below are the mean scores on each tactic for a group of 523 working adults (292 men and 231 women). The sample was composed of mostly managers and professionals. You will recall that the scale runs from 1 for *very infrequently* to 5 for *very frequently.*

Influence Tactic	Men	Women
1. Team play	4.1	4.2
2. Charm	3.3	3.5
3. Appearance	3.3	3.5
4. Manipulation of situation	3.1	2.7*
5. Manipulation of person	2.6	2.3*
6. Assertiveness	3.9	3.9
7. Joking or kidding	3.7	3.5
8. Exchange of favors	2.9	3.0

9. Promise of reward	2.5	2.2*
10. Threat of punishment	1.8	1.5*
11. Ingratiation	3.2	3.2
12. Logic or reason	4.3	4.1*
13. Alliances	3.3	3.5
14. Threat of appeal	1.5	1.6
15. Compliments	3.6	3.5
16. Compromise	3.4	3.5

Suggestions for skill development: In comparing your profile to the norms, it could be apparent that you are neglecting to use, or are overusing, one or more influence tactics. For example, being a team player is used "frequently" by men and women. If you are not using team play to influence others, you could be at a competitive disadvantage. Observe also that both men and women make "very infrequent" use of threats of appeal. If you are making threats of appeal very frequently, you could be perceived as using an unacceptable influence tactic.

*Differences between the means is significant at or beyond the 1 percent level of significance.
Source: Andrew J. DuBrin, "Sex and Gender Differences in Tactics of Influence," *Psychological Reports*, Vol. 68, 1991, pp. 635–646.

DESCRIPTION AND EXPLANATION OF INFLUENCE TACTICS

Influence tactics are often viewed from an ethical perspective. Following this perspective, the influence tactics described here are classified into those that are essentially ethical and honest versus those that are essentially manipulative and dishonest.

Several guidelines, or ethical screens, have been developed to help the influence agent decide whether a given act is ethical or unethical. The Center for Business Ethics at Bentley College has developed six questions to evaluate the ethics of a specific decision. Before engaging in a particular influence act or political tactic, a person should seek answers to the following questions:

- *Is it right?* (based on absolute principles of moral rights)
- *Is it fair?* (based on absolute principles of justice)
- *Who gets hurt?* (the fewer the better)
- *Would you be comfortable if the details of your decision or actions were made public in the media or through electronic mail?* (based on the principle of disclosure)

- *What would you tell your child, sibling, or young relative to do?* (based on the principle of reversibility)
- *How does it smell?* (based on common sense and intuition)[4]

The categorization of the influence tactics presented here is far from absolute. Except for the extremes, most of the tactics could conceivably be placed in either category, depending on how they are used. For example, the tactic "joking and kidding" can be either good-spirited or mean-spirited. Joking and kidding could therefore be classified as "essentially ethical" or "essentially manipulative."

Essentially Ethical and Honest Tactics

This section describes essentially ethical and honest tactics and strategies for influencing others, outlined in Table 8–1. Used with tact, diplomacy, and good intent, these strategies can facilitate getting others to join you in accomplishing a worthwhile objective. Because these influence tactics vary in complexity, they also vary with respect to how much time is required to develop them.

Leading by Example.   A simple but effective way of influencing group members is **leading by example,** or leading by acting as a positive role model. The ideal approach to leading by example is to be a "do as I say and do" manager—that is, one whose actions and words are consistent. Also, actions and words confirm, support, and often clarify each other. For example, if the firm has a dress code and the manager explains the code and dresses accordingly, he or she provides a role model that is consistent in

TABLE 8–1   Essentially Ethical and Honest Influence Tactics

1. Leading by example

2. Rational persuasion

3. Developing a reputation as a subject matter expert (SME)

4. Exchanging favors and bargaining

5. Developing a network of resource persons

6. Legitimating a request

7. Inspirational appeal and emotional display

8. Consultation

9. Forming coalitions

10. Team play

words and actions. The action of following the dress code provides an example that supports and clarifies the words used in the dress code.[5]

Rational Persuasion.   Rational persuasion is an important tactic for influencing people. Rational persuasion involves using logical arguments and factual evidence to convince another person that a proposal or request is workable and likely to result in goal attainment.[6] Assertiveness combined with careful research is necessary to make rational persuasion an effective tactic. Rational persuasion is likely to be most effective with people who are intelligent and rational. Chief executive officers typically use rational persuasion to convince their boards that an undertaking, such as product diversification, is mandatory.

A major intervening variable in rational persuasion is the credibility of the influence agent. The obvious link between credibility and persuasiveness is that influence targets are more likely to be influenced by people they believe. A less obvious moderating effective of credibility is that credible people are perceived as having higher social power. Mitchell S. Nesler et al. conducted an experiment with college students in which the credibility and power of a manager were manipulated in vignettes. The results indicated that credibility had a direct effect on ratings of five bases of power: reward, coercive, expert, referent, and legitimate. When the subjects in the experiment were given evidence that the manager was credible, they tended to give the manager higher ratings than a counterpart who was portrayed in the vignettes as having low credibility.[7]

In short, credibility helps an individual be more persuasive in two ways. First, credibility makes a person more convincing. Second, credibility contributes to a person's perceived power, and the more power one is perceived to have, the more targets will accept an influence attempt.

Developing a Reputation as a Subject Matter Expert.   Becoming a subject matter expert (SME) on a topic of importance to the organization is an effective strategy for gaining influence. Being an SME can be considered a subset of rational persuasion. A series of interviews conducted by Bernard Keys and Thomas Case support this observation. Managers who possess expert knowledge in a relevant field and who continually build on that knowledge can get others to help them get work accomplished.[8]

Exchanging Favors and Bargaining.   Offering to exchange favors if another person will help you achieve a work goal is another standard influence tactic. By making an exchange, you strike a bargain with the other party. The exchange often translates into being willing to reciprocate at a later date. The exchange might also be promising a share of the benefits if the other person helps you accomplish a task. For example, you might promise to place a person's name on a report to top management if that person helps analyze the data and prepare the tables.

Another perspective on exchange and bargaining is that you are building a favor bank. In other words, you do favors for people today with the expectation that you can make a withdrawal from the favor bank when needed. A human resources manager took the initiative to help a colleague in another company recruit a physically disabled compensation analyst. Several months later the same human resources professional called on the colleague to nominate her for office in their professional society.

Robert Dilenschneider, the CEO of the worldwide public relations firm of Hill and Knowlton, describes how middle managers can build favor banks: "At any level, it's a matter of knowing who needs you and whom you need. You should build good will. If you are a middle manager, look around you. You interact with a money specialist, with a lawyer, with a variety of operations people. Use them and let them use you."[9]

Developing a Network of Resource Persons.   Networking is an important strategy for career management, including becoming an influential person. The ability to establish a network and call on support when needed helps a manager or professional exert influence. A branch bank manager used his network of resource persons when he needed additional space for his operation. He felt that part of providing the right leadership was to expand the operation physically.

> My strategy was to convince my immediate superior that the current facilities were too small to not only manage the current volume of business, but too small to allow us to increase our market share in a rapidly growing area. First, I persuaded my manager to visit the branch more often, especially when the branch was very busy. I also solicited my accountant's help to provide statistical reports on a regular basis that communicated the amount of overall growth in the area, as well as the growth of our competitors. These reports showed that our market share had increased.
>
> I then asked my superior to visit with me as I called on several prospects in the area. This would let him know the types of potential business in the area. During this time I kept pushing to increase all levels of business at the branch.
>
> Finally, I encouraged key bank customers to say favorable things about my branch when they visited with my senior managers. Eventually my boss got behind my proposal. We were able to build an addition to the building which allowed me to add several new employees.[10]

Legitimating a Request.   To legitimate is to verify that an influence attempt is within your scope of authority. Another aspect of legitimating is to show that your request is consistent with organizational policies, practices, and expectations of professional people. Making legitimate requests is an effective influence tactic because most workers are willing to comply with regulations. A team leader can thus exert influence with a statement such as this one: "Top management wants a 25 percent reduction in customer complaints by next year. I'm therefore urging everybody to patch up any customer problems he or she can find." According to research conducted by Gary Yukl, behavior intended to establish the legitimacy of a request includes the following:

Providing evidence of prior precedent.

Showing consistency with organizational policies that are involved in the type of request being made.

Showing consistency with the duties and responsibilities of the person's position or role expectations.

Indicating that the request has been endorsed by higher management or by the person's boss.[11]

Inspirational Appeal and Emotional Display.   A leader is supposed to inspire others, so it follows that making an inspirational appeal is an important influence tactic. As Jeffrey Pfeffer notes, "Executives and others seeking to exercise influence in organizations often develop skill in displaying, or not displaying, their feelings in a strategic fashion."[12] An inspirational appeal usually involves an emotional display by the leader. It also involves appealing to group members' emotions.

In 1983, the Gary Works of U.S. Steel (a division of USX) was threatened with extinction. Major customers such as General Electric, Westinghouse, and General Motors were on the verge of eliminating the Gary plant as a steel supplier. To help turn around this crisis situation, Thomas Usher, president of U.S. Steel, made an emotional appeal. He asked the steelworkers how long they were going to put up with being insulted for their shoddy quality, their high costs, and their smug attitude toward customers. Usher's emotionally charged appeal helped start a process of constructive change that brought success to the Gary Works.

For an emotional appeal to be effective, the influence agent must understand the values, motives, and goals of the influence target. The U.S. Steel executive believed that the once-proud steelworkers still had some pride. An emotional appeal will also be more effective when the leader displays emotion. Indicators of emotion include talking about feelings, raising and lowering voice tone, showing moist eyes or a few tears, and pounding a table. As described in Chapter 3, charismatic leadership relies heavily on making inspirational appeals.

Consultation.   Consulting with others before making a decision is both a leadership style and an influence technique. The influence target becomes more motivated to follow the agent's request because the target is involved in the decision-making process. Yukl explains that consultation is most effective as an influence tactic when the objectives of the person being influenced are consistent with those of the leader.[13]

An example of such goal congruity took place in a major U.S. corporation. The company had decided to shrink its pool of suppliers to form closer partnerships with a smaller number of high-quality vendors. As a way of influencing others to follow this direction, a manufacturing vice president told his staff, "Our strategy is to reduce dealing with so many suppliers to improve quality and reduce costs. Let me know how we should implement this strategy." The vice president's influence attempt met with excellent reception, partially because the staff members also wanted a more streamlined set of vendor relationships.

Forming Coalitions. At times it is difficult to influence an individual or group by acting alone. A leader will then have to form coalitions, or alliances, with others to create the necessary clout. A **coalition** is a specific arrangement of parties working together to combine their power. Coalition formation works as an influence tactic because, to quote an old adage, "there is power in numbers." Coalitions in business are a numbers game—the more people you can get on your side, the better.

The more powerful the leader, the less need exists for coalition formation. Yet there are times when even a powerful leader needs an extraordinary amount of power to accomplish a major goal. Recall that John Sculley formed the Magic Six coalition to help shape the future of telecommunications.

Team Play. Influencing others by being a good team player is an important strategy for getting work accomplished. Refer to Leadership Self-Assessment Exercise 8–1. Observe that team play, along with logic or reason, was the influence tactic most frequently chosen by men and women. Another study of influence tactics compared the frequency of use of seven influence tactics. Men and women endorsed team play more frequently than the other six tactics (personal charm, manipulation, personal appearance, assertiveness, exchange of favors, and upward appeal).[14]

The accompanying Leader in Action profile (page 205) describes a manager who successfully uses ethical and honest influence tactics. As you read the description, attempt to identify several of her tactics.

Essentially Dishonest and Unethical Tactics

The tactics to be described in this section are less than forthright and ethical, yet they vary in intensity with respect to dishonesty. Most people would consider the first four influence strategies presented here as unethical and devious, yet they might regard the last five tactics as still within the bounds of acceptable ethics, even though less than fully candid. The tactics in question are outlined in Figure 8–2.

Deliberate Machiavellianism. Almost 500 years ago, Niccolo Machiavelli advised that princes must be strong, ruthless, and cynical leaders because people are self-centered and self-serving. People in the workplace who ruthlessly manipulate others have therefore come to be called **Machiavellians.** They tend to initiate actions with others and control the interactions. Machiavellians regularly practice deception, bluff, and other manipulative tactics.[15]

A current example of deliberate Machiavellianism is the practice of forcing managerial and professional employees into working many extra hours of uncompensated overtime. The employees are told that if they refuse to

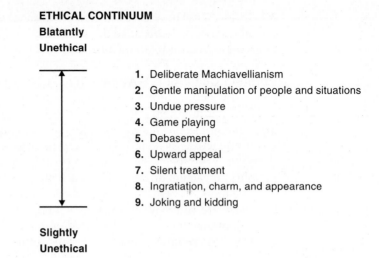

ETHICAL CONTINUUM
Blatantly
Unethical

1. Deliberate Machiavellianism
2. Gentle manipulation of people and situations
3. Undue pressure
4. Game playing
5. Debasement
6. Upward appeal
7. Silent treatment
8. Ingratiation, charm, and appearance
9. Joking and kidding

Slightly
Unethical

FIGURE 8–2

Essentially Dishonest and Unethical Influence Tactics

work extra hours, they will be fired. Because jobs in some categories are scarce, the employees comply. The person profiled in the next Leader in Action essay (page 206) would be perceived by many as Machiavellian.

Gentle Manipulation of People and Situations.   Some people who attempt to influence others are manipulative, but to a lesser extent than an outright Machiavellian. By making untrue statements or faking certain behaviors, they gain the compliance of another person. For example, a leader might imply that if a colleague supports his position in an intergroup conflict, the person *might* be recommended for promotion. A widely used manipulative approach is the **bandwagon technique,** in which one does something simply because others are doing likewise. An example is a manager who informs the vice president that she wants an enlarged budget for attendance at Internet seminars because "all other companies are doing it."

Undue Pressure.   Effective leaders regularly use motivational techniques such as rewards and mild punishments. Yet when rewards become bribes for compliance, and threats of punishment become severe, the target person is subjected to undue pressure or coercion. An example of a bribe by a manager might be, "If you can work eighty hours on this project this week, I'll recommend you for the highest pay grade." Several specific behaviors labeled coercive in a research study were as follows:

I demand that she do it.

I yell at her until she does it.

I criticize her for not doing it.

I curse at her until she does it.

I threaten her with something if she doesn't do it.[16]

LEADER IN ACTION

Ann M. Fudge, Maxwell House Chief

As the president of Maxwell House Coffee, Ann M. Fudge runs a $1.4 billion business within the Kraft Foods division of Philip Morris. She has followed a marketing track in her career, going from General Electric to General Mills to General Foods (now part of Kraft). She is one of the twenty highest-ranking women in American industry. Her accomplishments at Maxwell House make her a strong candidate to be chosen as a company CEO. An executive search firm representative said about Fudge, "She has shown that she can take a product and reposition it and increase the bottom line. She could be chairwoman and CEO of a company about the same size, or she could be president and chief operating officer of a larger company" (*The New York Times*, p. 6).

Fudge is a determined competitor who regarded the riots that followed the assassination of Martin Luther King, Jr., as a formative experience in her life. "They made me incredibly determined," she said. "I wanted to do something that black people hadn't done before. When I hit roadblocks, that was what kept me going" (*The New York Times*, p. 6). In recent years, Fudge has applied her determination to fighting the competition from specialty coffee makers such as Starbucks. Under her leadership, new ads have been introduced to create a mystique for Maxwell House, and the division has introduced flavored ground coffees such as Swiss Cocoa and French Vanilla.

An advertising executive who works with Fudge says that she has an extremely focused approach to problem solving. She has been described as having single-minded determination. Her attitude is that if you dig hard enough, you will find an idea someplace in a problem-solving discussion. She always looks for the best idea, whether hers or somebody else's, to solve a business problem. The energy she brings to the table helps other people get focused on the problem.

Several people who work closely with Fudge perceive her as a team player and team builder who can ignite enthusiasm in others. A former chief executive at Philip Morris says that she is a low-key and confident manager who gets the most out of group members.

Fudge's advertising strategy of emphasizing the Maxwell House brand image is controversial within her company. Her superiors think that dramatizing bean quality is a more effective approach to sales growth. However, she has convinced her management team through her passion. Fudge uses a similar approach to managing people—passion and teamwork rather than directives. Among her initiatives have been problem-solving meetings of employees from different levels and disciplines, and a Shape Up program designed to jettison unnecessary reports and processes. She has also created a Blue Sky Room for brainstorming, and an awards program for innovative suggestions.

The only hint of negative feedback about Fudge is that she is too consistently nice, and never loses her temper or pounds the table. Like Maxwell House Coffee, Fudge is good to the last drop and keeps perking along.

Source: Based on information in Judith H. Dobrzynski, "Way Beyond the Glass Ceiling: Is a C.E.O. Job in the Maxwell House Chief's Future?" *The New York Times*, Themes of the Times, Fall 1995, p. 6; Tom Dunkel, "The Front Runners," *Working Woman*, April 1996, pp. 35, 72.

Game Playing.   Leaders, as well as others, often play games in order to influence others. A **game** in this context is a repeated series of exchanges between people that seems plausible but has a hidden agenda or purpose. Influence is exerted in a game because the person whom the game is played against is made to feel humble.

LEADER IN ACTION

Paul Kazarian, Investment Banker and Internet Corporate Raider

Back in 1993, Paul Kazarian, then 37 years old and the chairman of Sunbeam, was attending a consumer products trade show. Late that night, a company director entered Kazarian's hotel room and fired him, despite his excellent business performance. Kazarian was perplexed by his firing, but Sunbeam employees and outside contacts could not understand why.

The chairman had developed the reputation of intentionally abusing and humiliating employees, suppliers, and people with whom he negotiated. So many employees complained of Kazarian's insensitivity and hostility that the board conducted an independent investigation of his handling of people. The results showed that the chairman was so hostile that he could no longer provide effective leadership at Sunbeam.

Kazarian, an investment banker, came into power during a hostile takeover. Executives who knew him said he was far better with numbers than with people. One former executive says Kazarian's comments to people were often "obscene, vulgar, and haranguing. Every other word was the F word." During one negotiation session involving the takeover, Kazarian spit a cigar butt on the floor and nearly came to blows with an attorney.

Kazarian defends his blunt, intimidating style in this way: "You don't change a company in bankruptcy without making a few waves. I wasn't there to be a polite manager. I was there to create value for shareholders." Because Kazarian was not fired for poor performance, he was to receive five years' worth of compensation, approximately $8.75 million. Kazarian, however, did not settle for this compensation. He denied the many charges against him, including sexual harassment of female employees, and filed a wrongful termina-

tion suit. He ultimately won a $180 million settlement from Sunbeam's largest shareholders.

After Sunbeam, Kazarian returned to investment banking. In one grueling battle, he lost out to a rival investment banking firm in his bid to purchase Borden, Inc. In another buyout attempt, Kazarian turned to the Internet as a takeover tool. He launched a World Wide Web site to gather intelligence on possible targets, including the E-mail addresses of their directors and employees. His tactic was to send electronic messages to shareholders and board members, supplying them with information he thought would persuade them to his way of thinking. Kazarian regards the Internet as a powerful tool for corporate activism. He says, "It's democracy, freedom of speech, and the power to advocate a point of view" (*Business Week*, October 23, 1995, p. 35).

A major purpose of Kazarian's Internet activities is to help people lobby company directors. People enter their messages, which are then forwarded to the appropriate director. In this way, the directors might be swayed into accepting a takeover bid that many constituents, as well as Kazarian, think is in the best interest of shareholders. Some observers are concerned that communicating on the Web about takeover attempts could create some legal problems, such as violating insider trading rules. Yet Kazarian believes he has a powerful new tool to facilitate takeovers. "The beauty of the Internet is that everyone has instant access," he says (*Business Week*, October 23, 1995, p. 35).

Source: Based on facts in "How to Lose Friends and Influence No One," *Business Week*, January 25, 1993, pp. 42–43; Geoffrey Smith, "Raider on the Net: Paul Kazarian Is on the Prowl—Online," *Business Week*, October 23, 1995, p. 35.

Blemish is an example of a simple game often used by managers to keep team members in line. All that is required is for the leader to find some flaw in every assignment completed by team members. The game-playing boss stays one up with comments such as "You did a great job on that report except in your conclusion. It just didn't seem to fit the body of the report."

One-time transactions between the influence agent and the influence target sometimes resemble a game. One such tactic is the door-in-the-face technique. The person attempting to exert influence makes a major request that will most likely be rejected. Shortly thereafter comes a more modest request, which was really intended in the first place.[17] In rejecting the first request, the target person may feel guilty and thus be responsive to a future request. For example, a security manager wanted a larger budget for cellular telephones and pagers for her group. At the time the company was carefully controlling expenditures. The security manager approached her manager and requested authorization for new office space for her staff. Her budget request was rejected quickly. She returned two weeks later with a request for an increased cellular telephone and paging system budget to compensate for the denial of new offices. Her request was granted within one week.

Debasement.   A subtle manipulative tactic is **debasement,** demeaning or insulting oneself to control the behavior of another person. For example, the security manager just mentioned might say, "I realize our department just contributes to overhead, but we do need more cellular telephones and pagers to get our job done." Specific debasing tactics revealed by research include the following:

> I allow myself to be debased so she'll do it.
>
> I lower myself so she'll do it.
>
> I act humble so she'll do it.[18]

Upward Appeal.   In **upward appeal,** the leader exerts influence on a team member by getting a person with more formal authority to do the influencing. An example: "I sent the guy to my boss when he wouldn't listen to me. That fixed him." More than occasional use of upward appeal weakens the leader's stature in the eyes of group members and superiors, thus eroding his or her effectiveness.

Leaders can apply upward appeal in other ways. A leader might attempt to persuade another staff member that his or her request is approved by higher management. The target of the influence event is thus supposed to grant acceptance automatically. Or the leader can request higher management's assistance in gaining another person's compliance with the request. The influence target thus feels pressured.[19]

Silent Treatment.   A leader uses the **silent treatment** through saying nothing, sulking, or other forms of passivity until the influence target complies.
Research questionnaire items related to sulking are as follows:

I don't respond to him until he does it.

I ignore him until he does it.

I am silent until he agrees to do it.

I refuse to do something he likes until he does it.[20]

Ingratiation, Charm, and Appearance.   Getting somebody else to like you
can be considered a mildly manipulative influence tactic—particularly if you
do not like the other person. Ingratiating tactics identified in a study about
influence tactics included the following:

Made him or her feel important. (For example, "Only you have the
brains and talent to do this.")

Acted very humbly toward him or her while making my request.

Praised him or her.

Sympathized with him or her about the added problems that my
request caused.

Waited until he or she appeared in a receptive mood before asking.

Asked in a polite way.

Pretended I was letting him or her decide to do what I wanted. (Acted
in a pseudo-democratic manner.)[21]

Another way of being ingratiating is through charm and appearance.
Charm contributes to ingratiation because many people like a charming person. Being charming includes such behaviors as complimenting others profusely, expressing thanks, and displaying impeccable etiquette. Appearance
in this context means dressing professionally and fashionably. In the survey
referred to in the self-assessment exercise, men gave both charm and appearance a frequency rating of 3.3 on a 1-to-5 scale. Women gave charm and
appearance frequency ratings insignificantly different from those given by
men.

Joking and Kidding.   Good-natured kidding is especially effective when
a straightforward statement might be interpreted as harsh criticism. Joking
or kidding can thus get the message across and lower the risk that the influence target will be angry with the influence agent. Joking and kidding
might be interpreted either as dishonest or as extraordinarily tactful
because the criticizer softens the full blow of the criticism. A vice president
of manufacturing successfully used joking and kidding to influence his team

to improve quality. After examining what he thought were low-quality components for the company's power tools, he commented, "I appreciate your effort, but I'm afraid you misinterpreted my message. I wanted you to produce a component we could use as a positive model of quality. You went out of your way to produce a negative model. Otherwise you did a great job."

In studying the most severe unethical influence (and political) tactics, recognize that the use of these influence approaches can bring about human suffering. For example, bullying and intimidating tactics may not be illegal, but they are unethical. If Paul Kazarian and his attorneys pressure his former employer into paying him $180 million for wrongful job loss, think of the damage to the organization. Even if much of that money was paid by an insurance company, $180 million could have been used for more constructive purposes than giving it to an abrasive investment banker and his attorneys. Cruelty in the organization creates many problems. As one observer notes, "Cruelty is blatantly unethical and erodes the organizational character through intellectual, emotional, moral and social vices that reduce the readiness of groups to act ethically (organizational cynicism)."[22]

Leadership Skill-Building Exercise 8–1 will help your recognize several of the influence tactics described in this chapter. Another tactic, assertiveness, is mentioned in the exercise but was described previously.

RELATIVE EFFECTIVENESS AND SEQUENCING OF INFLUENCE TACTICS

Although we have described influence tactics separately, they must also be understood in relation to one another. Two ways of comparing influence tactics is to examine their relative effectiveness and the order in which they might be used to achieve the best result.

A Study of the Relative Effectiveness of Influence Tactics

Influence tactics are a major component of leadership. Research about their relative effectiveness is therefore worth noting. A study by Gary Yukl and J. Bruce Tracey provides insights about the relative effectiveness of influence tactics.[23] One hundred and twenty managers participated in the study, along with 526 subordinates, 543 peers, and 128 superiors, who also rated the managers' use of influence tactics. The proportion of men and women in the study is unknown because respondents were not asked to reveal demographic information. (Some people prefer to remain anonymous in such

LEADERSHIP SKILL-BUILDING
EXERCISE 8–1   Identifying Influence Tactics

Directions: After reading each tactic listed here, label it as being mostly an example of one of the following: I = Ingratiation; E = Exchange of Favors; R = Rationality; A = Assertiveness; U = Upward Appeal.

Tactic	Code
1. I sympathized with the person about the added problems that my request caused.	____
2. I offered to help if the person would do what I wanted.	____
3. I set a time deadline for the person to do what I asked.	____
4. I obtained the informal support of higher-ups.	____
5. I used logic to convince him or her.	____
6. I made a formal appeal to higher levels to back up my request.	____
7. I had a showdown in which I confronted the person head-on.	____
8. I offered to make a personal sacrifice if the person would do what I wanted (for example, work late or harder).	____
9. I made him or her feel good about me before making my request.	____
10. I explained the reasons for my request.	____

Answers: 1. I   6. U
2. E   7. A
3. A   8. E
4. U   9. I
5. R   10. R

Source: Based on information in Chester A. Schriescheim and Timothy R. Hinkin, "Influence Tactics Used by Subordinates: A Theoretical and Empirical Analysis and Refinement of the Kipnis, Schmidt, and Wilkinson Subscales," *Journal of Applied Psychology*, June 1990, p. 246.

studies.) Half the managers worked for manufacturing companies, and half worked for service companies.

The people who worked with the managers completed a questionnaire to identify which of nine influence tactics the managers used. Defined for the participants, the tactics were as follows:

1. Rational persuasion
2. Inspirational appeal
3. Consultation
4. Ingratiation
5. Exchange
6. Personal appeal
7. Coalition
8. Legitimating
9. Pressure

Another question asked how many influence attempts by the agent resulted in complete commitment by the target respondent. The seven response choices were (1) None of them; (2) A few of them; (3) Some (less than half); (4) About half of them; (5) More than half of them; (6) Most of them; and (7) All of them. Respondents were also asked to rate the overall effectiveness of the manager in carrying out his or her job responsibilities. The item had nine response choices, ranging from the least effective manager I have ever known (1) to the most effective manager I have ever known (9).

The results suggested that the most effective tactics were rational persuasion, inspirational appeal, and consultation. (An effective tactic was one that led to task commitment, and that was used by managers who were perceived to be effective by the various raters.) In contrast, the least effective were pressure, coalition, and appealing to legitimate authority (legitimating). Ingratiation and exchange were moderately effective for influencing team members and peers. The same tactics, however, were not effective for influencing superiors.

Inspirational appeal, ingratiation, and pressure were used primarily in a downward direction. Personal appeal, exchange, and legitimating were used primarily in a lateral direction. It was also found that coalitions were used most in lateral and upward directions, and that rational persuasion was used most in an upward direction.

The researchers concluded that some tactics are more likely to be successful. Yet they caution that the results do not imply that these tactics will always result in task commitment. The outcome of a specific influence attempt is determined by factors in addition to influence attempts, such as the target's motivation and the organizational culture. Also, any tactic can trigger target resistance if it is not appropriate for the situation or if it is applied unskillfully. Tact, diplomacy, and insight are required for effective application of influence tactics.

The Sequencing of Influence Tactics

Another important consideration in using influence tactics is the sequence or order in which they should be applied. In general, begin with the most positive, or least abrasive, tactic. If you do not gain the advantage you seek, proceed to a stronger tactic. For example, if you want a larger salary increase than that initially assigned you, try rational persuasion. If persuasion doesn't work, move on to exchange. Use a more abrasive tactic such as upward appeal only as a last resort. The reason is that abrasive tactics trigger revenge and retaliation. Many people who have brought their complaints to an outside agency such as a governmental office have found themselves with a limited future in their organization. Although the appeal is legally justified, it is politically unwise.

The sequencing of tactics can also be considered in terms of cost and risk. A sensible approach is to begin with low-cost, low-risk tactics. If the outcome is important enough to the influence agent, he or she can then proceed to higher-cost and higher-risk influence tactics. An example of a low-cost, low-risk tactic would be joking and kidding. An accounting manager who was disappointed with the budget offered her group might say to her boss, "Does the new budget mean that our group will have to pay for our own floppy disks and green eyeshades?" It would be much more costly in terms of time and potential retaliation to form a coalition with another underbudgeted group to ask for an enlarged budget.

Some research evidence supports the importance of sequencing of influence attempts. Significant differences were found for the following:

- Rational persuasion is used more for an initial request.

- Ingratiation is used more for an initial request.

- Personal appeal is used more for an initial request.

- Exchange is used more for immediate follow-up.

- Coalition formation is used more for delayed follow-up.

- Legitimating is used most for immediate follow-up.

- Undue pressure is used most for delayed follow-up.[24]

LEADERSHIP SKILL-BUILDING
EXERCISE 8–2   Applying Influence Tactics

Divide the class into small teams. Each group assigns one leadership influence tactic to each team member. During the next week or so, each team member takes the opportunity to practice the assigned influence tactic in a work or personal setting. Hold a group discussion with the same class teams after the influence attempts have been practiced. Report back the following information: (1) under what circumstances the influence tactic was attempted; (2) how the influence target reacted; and (3) what results, both positive and negative, were achieved.

In addition to the sequencing of tactics, the influence agent must also consider the direction of the influence attempt as a contingency factor. In general, the more position power an individual exerts over another, the less the need for being cautious in the use of influence tactics. For example, a vice president can more readily use undue pressure against a supervisor than vice versa. When you have more power, there are likely to be fewer negative consequences from using more powerful tactics.

Leadership Skill-Building Exercise 8–2 provides an opportunity to practice implementing various influence tactics. As with any other skill, influence skills need to be practiced under field conditions.

SUMMARY

To become an effective leader, a person must be aware of specific influence tactics. Influence is the ability to affect the behaviors of others in a particular direction. Power, in contrast, is the potential or capacity to influence. A model presented here indicates that a leader's power, influence behavior, and influence skills interact in various ways to determine how much influence the leader has with target people. A leader's choice of influence tactic depends to some extent on how much personal power he or she can exercise in relation to the target person. The outcomes of influence attempts are commitment, compliance, or resistance, all of which influence end results such as group success or failure.

Influence tactics are often viewed from an ethical perspective. Some tactics are clearly ethical, but others are clearly unethical. Used with tact, diplomacy, and good intent, ethical influence tactics can be quite effective. The essentially ethical tactics described here include leading by example, rational persuasion, developing a reputation as an expert, exchanging of favors and bargaining, developing a network of resource persons, and legitimating a request. Also included are inspirational appeal and emotional display, consultation, forming coalitions, and team play.

Essentially dishonest and unethical tactics presented here were divided into two groups: clearly unethical and borderline. The more clearly unethical and devious tactics are deliberate Machiavellianism, gentle manipulation of people and situations, undue pressure, and game playing. The five borderline influence tactics are debasing oneself to gain advantage; upward appeal; silent treatment; ingratiation, charm, and appearance; and joking and kidding (hardly devious at all).

A study of influence tactics concluded that the most effective were rational persuasion, inspirational appeal, and consultation. The least effective were pressure, coalition, and appealing to legitimate authority. Certain tactics are more effective for exerting influence upward, whereas others are better suited for downward influence. For example, inspirational appeal, ingratiation, and exchange are moderately effective for influencing subordinates and peers. Yet the same tactics are not effective for influencing superiors.

Sequencing of influence tactics is another important consideration. In general, begin with the most positive, or least abrasive, tactic. If you do not gain the advantage you seek, proceed to a stronger tactic. Also, begin with low-cost, low-risk tactics.

KEY TERMS

Influence	Leading by example	Blemish
Power	Coalition	Debasement
Commitment	Machiavellians	Upward appeal
Compliance	Bandwagon technique	Silent treatment
Resistance	Game	

GUIDELINES FOR ACTION AND SKILL DEVELOPMENT

A starting point in choosing influence tactics to help you lead others is to select those that fit your ethical code. For example, a person might say, "Being a team player and ingratiation fit my ethics, but I can't use undue pressure."

Another major consideration is to choose the correct combination of influence tactics. You must choose these tactics carefully on the basis of the influence target and your objectives. For example, ingratiation and joking and kidding might not work well with superiors. Quite often it is best to begin with a gentle influence tactic, then strengthen your approach as needed. Keys and Case found that most first influence attempts by managers involved gentle approaches such as requests or logical persuasion. Later attempts included firmer tactics when the influence target was reluctant to comply.[25] (In days of old, this was referred to as tightening the thumbscrews!)

A person must also choose influence tactics to fit the influence objectives. Kipnis and his associates have observed that managers should not rely on a single influence tactic, such as assertiveness, to achieve both organizational and personal objectives. It may be appropriate to insist that one's boss be mindful of cost overruns. It is inappropriate, however, to insist that one be granted time off to golf with network members.[26]

Good communication skills are required to implement influence tactics. As Keys and Case note, "Managers who choose rational ideas based on the needs of the target, wrap them with a blanket of humor or anecdotes, and cast them in the language of the person to be influenced, are much more likely to see their influence objectives achieved."[27]

DISCUSSION QUESTIONS AND ACTIVITIES

1. According to the model presented in Figure 8–1, how does leader behavior affect influence outcomes?

2. Which of the tactics described in this chapter help explain the widespread use by leaders of person-to-person meetings when they want to accomplish a major objective?

3. Identify two exchanges of favors you have seen or can envision on the job.

4. Why is being a team player regarded as an influence tactic?

5. Give an example of how a first-level manager could use legitimating a request to influence group members.

6. Interpret the significant differences found among the data presented in Leadership Self-Assessment Exercise 8–1.

7. How does a leader build credibility so that he or she can be more effective at influencing people inside and outside the work group?

8. Which of the influence tactics described in this chapter is a charismatic leader the most likely to use? Explain.

9. Identify two influence tactics used by Ann Fudge, the Maxwell House executive.

10. Get the opinion of an experienced leader as to the most effective influence tactic. Share your findings with class members.

LEADERSHIP CASE PROBLEM

Big Challenges Ahead for Ron Sommer at Deutsche Telekom

Ron Sommer feels that he is under considerable pressure to make things happen in a hurry in his new assignment as CEO of Deutsche Telekom. The night before his first official day on the job (in May 1995), he was tied up in negotiations in Paris for a deal necessary to the success of Telekom, the largest telecommunications company in Europe. The plan involved European companies taking a 20 percent stake in Sprint so they could launch a global telecommunications service for corporate customers.

Sommer needs a sense of urgency to be successful in his new position, considered the toughest in Europe. A major challenge is to spark a competitive spirit in workers long coddled by Germany's biggest monopoly. Sommer also has to prepare workers for massive cost cutting, and motivate the company to give good service to customers it has long taken for granted. Furthermore, he must entice investors. All of these activities must be accomplished by January 1, 1998, when the European Union intends to create open competition in telecommunications throughout the continent.

As Telekom begins privatization with a $10 billion stock offering, Sommer must convince investors that his company can compete favorably against telecommunications giants such as AT&T and British Telecommunications, and against new German rivals. If the stock offering fails, the government will be humiliated and Telekom will be hard-pressed to achieve its expansion plans.

Sommer is accustomed to both challenges and accomplishments. He received a doctorate in mathematics in 1971 from the University of Vienna. By 1986 he had become president of Sony Deutschland, and then in 1990 he became president and chief operating officer of Sony USA. In 1993 he took on the same functions as the top executive in Sony Europe. He achieved dramatic results at Sony's U.S. and European operations. Sommer's strongest areas of expertise are information technology and marketing strategy.

Other challenges facing Sommer at Telekom include laying off 60,000 workers, a quarter of the company's work force. As a result of privatization, he will have to increase profits sufficiently to cover $86 billion in debt and still pay dividends to stockholders. Prices for services may have to be reduced 50 percent to meet the new competition. Telekom will also have to modernize its product line to offer the multimedia services that are now considered standard for telecommunication companies.

One of the many reasons Sommer was chosen for this demanding leadership assignment is that he has exceptional international credentials. He speaks fluent German (his native tongue), French, and English and has worked for European and Japanese employers in the United States and in Europe.

According to Sommer's analysis, one of Telekom's key strengths is its customer-friendliness. Among its weaknesses is the long time required to install telephones. It takes Telekom a long time to process orders for equipment and to perform service upgrades. Sommer's initial thrust for moving the company forward is to conduct a broad-based attack. Early in his assignment, he sought regulatory approval for joint ventures with French Télécom and Sprint. Following this course of action should help meet his goal of generating 20 percent of sales from international business before 2000. Inside the company, Sommer is letting workers know that the company must ready itself to compete on price and service. He is urging branch managers to shorten the cycle time for phone installation from twelve days to next-day installation.

. Sommer has told employees he wants Deutsche Telekom to become a well-known company like IBM or Coca-Cola. A telecommunications executive said that for Telekom to become such a well-known company, Sommer would have to motivate his employees to blossom in a deregulated company. Many managers at lower levels in the company, however, would prefer to remain in a noncompetitive environment.

Word is out within the company that Telekom senior executives must meet the new performance criteria based on growth and profitability to retain their positions. Despite such hard-nosed proclamations, Sommer believes that his spirit of optimism will help motivate workers. He prefers setting the tone from a distance rather than managing by mingling with people throughout the company.

One of Sommer's biggest hurdles in achieving his goals for the company is to deal effectively with a major labor issue. The labor union may be hesitant to accept his plan to boost productivity more than 50 percent, in part because it involves getting 60,000 workers to accept early retirement and severance packages. So far, the union has agreed to cut only 30,000 jobs. Without a major reduction in force, Telekom might not earn high enough profits to attract investors to its stock.

Sommer's philosophy for achieving outstanding results is straightforward: "It's not magic. You just have to do it." (*Business Week*, October 9, 1995, p. 53)

(To help answer the following questions, consider finding information about Telekom published within the last few months.)

1. Which influence tactics is Sommer using to achieve his corporate goals?

2. What other influence tactics do you think Sommer should be using?

3. What suggestions can you offer Ron Sommer to enhance his leadership effectiveness at Deutsche Telekom?

Source: Based on facts reported in "The Toughest Job in Europe: Can Ron Sommer Transform the Bloated Deutsche Telekom in Time?" *Business Week*, October 9, 1995, pp. 52–53; "Dr. Ron Sommer—Président du Directoire de Deutsche Telekom AG," www.DTAG.DE/telekom/sommer_fr.html (April 18, 1996).

Developing Teamwork

LEARNING OBJECTIVES

After studying this chapter you should be able to

1. explain the difference between team leadership and solo leadership.
2. present an overview of the advantages and disadvantages of working in groups.
3. understand the leader's role in a team-based organization.
4. list and describe leader behaviors and attitudes that foster teamwork.
5. explain the potential contribution of outdoor training to the development of team leadership.
6. describe how the leader-member exchange model contributes to an understanding of teamwork.

A Coca-Cola syrup plant in Baltimore, Maryland, had committed itself to continuous improvement even though the plant was to be closed in about two years and its operations merged into another plant in town. Coca-Cola's manufacturing operation identified three key criteria for the operation's success: employees' quality of work life, customer service, and product cost. General Manager Harrison Bentley said that he wanted employees to feel as if they were partners: "We wanted to move past simple compliance. We wanted people to begin asking, 'What can I do to make this a better workplace?' We felt this eventually would lead to a better product." After pondering the situation, senior management decided that a team structure would be the best vehicle for improving quality of work life and productivity at the plant.

Under the new team structure, much of the leadership for running the plant was turned over to employees. Top management took on the role of a steering team by carrying out such activities as defining the scope of the design team's work and providing resources and rewards. Members of the design team were chosen on the basis of a vote by fifty employees who volunteered to be on the selection committee.

To create an environment favorable for cooperation, the design team members spent time together during the first two weeks in orientation and

217

team-building activities. Two of the goals were to strengthen relationships among team members themselves and with the steering team. A lab assistant and team member said, "We quickly discovered that the eight of us on the design team had to first learn how to function as a team. We knew that if we failed as a team, our high-performance team culture would be doomed." After the design team became cohesive, it carried out its plan to develop the team structure at Baltimore Coca-Cola. Ultimately the design team established three types of teams. Functional teams included shipping, maintenance, and administration. Process teams would be responsible for an entire work process, from input of raw materials to delivery of a product to an external customer. Satellite teams—such as a safety satellite—were formed to work together to address specific issues affecting everybody in the operation.

Senior management was happy with the new structure because they saw it as an opportunity to reduce cycle times and costs. At the same time, quality of work life would improve because employees took a more active role in leadership.[1]

As implied by the above case history, teams are becoming a dominant form of organization. The careful attention paid to the development of teams at Coca-Cola suggests that it takes careful planning and implementation to create smooth-functioning teams composed of individuals who work well together. Developing teamwork is such an important leadership role that team building is said to differentiate successful from unsuccessful leaders.[2]

A difficulty in understanding teams is that the words *teams* and *teamwork* are often overused and applied loosely. For some people, a team is simply another term for a group. As used here, a **team** is a small number of people with complementary skills who are committed to a common purpose, set of performance goals, and approach, for which they hold themselves accountable.[3] **Teamwork** is an understanding and commitment to group goals on the part of all team members. All teams are groups, but not all groups are teams. Jon R. Katzenbach and Douglas K. Smith, based on extensive research in the workplace, make a clear differentiation between teams and groups.[4] A team is characterized by a common commitment, whereas the commitment within a group might not be as strong. A team accomplishes many collective work products, whereas group members sometimes work slightly more independently. Members of a group have a strong leader, whereas a team has shared leadership roles. In a team there is individual and mutual accountability; in contrast, a group emphasizes individual accountability.

Team members produce a collective work product, whereas group members sometimes produce individual work products. A team leader is likely to encourage open-ended discussion and active problem-solving meetings, whereas a group leader is more likely to run an efficient meeting.

Also, teams discuss, decide, and do real work together, and a group is more likely to discuss, decide, and delegate.

Although the distinction between a group and a team may be valid, it is difficult to cast aside the practice of using the terms *group* and *team* interchangeably. For example, a customer service team is still a team even if its teamwork is poor.

As background for this chapter, we first examine how team leadership is different from more traditional leadership, followed by a brief look at the advantages and disadvantages of working in groups. The central focus of this chapter is a description of specific leader behaviors and attitudes that foster teamwork. We also describe outdoor training, a widely used method of teamwork development. In addition, we summarize a leadership theory that provides some insights into how teamwork emerges within a work group.

TEAM LEADERSHIP VERSUS SOLO LEADERSHIP

Various writers have touted the importance of team leadership. Meredith Belbin, for one, contrasts the team leader and the solo leader[5] (see Figure 9–1). Team leaders share power and deemphasize individual glory. They are flexible and adaptable, thus welcoming change. Team leaders function as facilitators who bring out the best in others while still being inspirational. The team leader conforms closely to the consensus and 9,9 (Leadership Grid) styles. William D. Hitt has observed related characteristics and behaviors of team leaders. In his analysis, team leaders place considerable emphasis on team building, and then evaluate their own performance on the basis of how well they have developed the team. Team leaders intuitively recognize that the whole is greater than the sum of the parts. Based on this belief, they look for linkages (members working closely with each other) among team

SOLO LEADER	TEAM LEADER
1. Plays unlimited role (interferes)	1. Chooses to limit role (delegates)
2. Strives for conformity	2. Builds on diversity
3. Collects acolytes	3. Seeks talent
4. Directs subordinates	4. Develops colleagues
5. Projects objectives	5. Creates mission

FIGURE 9–1

The Solo Leader and the Team Leader

Source: From Meredith Belbin, "Solo Leader/Team Leader: Antithesis in Style and Structure," in Michel Syrett and Clare Hogg, Frontiers of Leadership, *p. 271. Copyright © 1992. Used by permission of Blackwell Publishers, Oxford, England.*

members to help multiply productivity.[6] According to Hitt, team leaders understand that sharing power with group members multiplies their own power. As the team members become stronger, so does the leader. A related attitude is that team leaders are not threatened by sharing power. They are therefore willing to surround themselves with capable people in order to multiply the effectiveness of the team.

The solo leader is the traditional leader in a bureaucracy. Basically an autocrat, the solo leader receives much of the credit for the success of his or her firm. Frequently, some of the credit is undeserved. The solo leader may not recognize how dependent he or she is on the team. Leonard "Boogie" Weinglass, the entrepreneur who built the now-defunct Merry-Go-Round Enterprises, appears to have been a solo type of leader. During Merry-Go-Round's best years, Weinglass was a spectacular success in selecting fashions that appealed to adolescents and teenagers. Among these fads were Sgt. Pepper jackets and Madonna-style clothing. Weinglass relied heavily on his own intuition when making major merchandising decisions, instead of using the team approach. He also ignored the advice of market researchers. The beginning of Merry-Go-Round's demise was when Weinglass insisted on stocking his stores with hip-hop-style clothing, which had limited national appeal in an era (circa 1991) when young people were becoming anti-style[7] (unless you consider grunge to be a style!).

ADVANTAGES AND DISADVANTAGES OF GROUP WORK AND TEAMWORK

Groups have always been the building blocks of organizations. Yet as Peter Drucker, and more recently Richard S. Wellins and his associates, have observed, groups and teams have recently grown in importance as a fundamental unit of organization structure.[8] In an attempt to adapt to rapidly changing environments, many work organizations have granted teams increased autonomy and flexibility. Cross-functional teams have been formed in many firms to achieve a broader perspective on problem solving, and simultaneously to help downplay intergroup rivalries. Teams are also asked to span traditional boundaries by working more closely with groups from other disciplines. Furthermore, teams are often required to work more closely with customers and suppliers.

The increased acceptance of teams suggests that group work offers many advantages. Nevertheless, it is useful to specify several of these advantages and also examine the potential problems of groups.

Advantages of Group Work and Teamwork

Group work and group decision making offer several advantages over individual effort. If several knowledgeable people are brought into the decision-making process, a number of worthwhile possibilities may be uncovered. It is also possible to achieve synergy, whereby the group's total output exceeds the sum of the various individuals' contribution. For example, it would be a rare person working alone who could build an automobile. Group decision making is helpful in gaining acceptance and commitment, as described in the context of the normative decision model in Chapter 6.

Group members often evaluate one another's thinking, so the team is likely to avoid major errors. The information systems manager in one company was formulating plans to install a computer network that would make electronic mail feasible. Shortly before a contract was signed with a vendor, one of the committee members asked, "Are you sure the PCs we have throughout the company have sufficient memory to run that system?" A quick review of equipment revealed that they did not. The electronic mail system had to be postponed until the PCs were upgraded.

Another key advantage of teams is that they can contribute well to continuous improvement and innovation. An example is the Customer Assistance Center for imaging products that was formerly a part of Eastman Kodak Company, and is now owned by Danka Business Systems. Teams at the Center are organized regionally around specialized or unique customer groups. In the past, team members were assigned a quota of telephone calls per hour and directed those calls to the proper source. Now, team members are both trained and empowered to provide total customer support and look for continuous improvement in their work processes. Self-management responsibilities of the team include scheduling shift and work assignments, training and coaching other team members, appraising the call handling of coworkers, and monitoring customer satisfaction. The results from the empowered team structures were outstanding. Within one year the number of calls handled per hour doubled, and so did the accuracy with which customer problems were handled. Employee turnover dropped to one-half the industry average. An exceptional amount of training, however, was required to achieve these results.[9]

Top management teams, as well as teams at lower levels in the organization, can often produce results superior to those attributed to individual managers. Milan Moravec notes that a group of top executives becomes a resource that is often richer, more textured and diverse, and more accessible than an individual leader could be.[10]

Working in groups also enhances many members' job satisfaction. Being a member of a work group makes it possible to satisfy more needs than if one worked alone. Among these needs are needs for affiliation, security, self-esteem, and self-fulfillment. For example, playing a key role in a successful team effort can be fulfilling because of the job challenge and the recognition.

Disadvantages of Group Activity

Group activity has some potential disadvantages for both organizations and individuals. A major problem is that members face pressure to conform to group standards of performance and conduct. Some work groups might ostracize a person who is much more productive than his or her coworkers. Shirking of individual responsibility is another problem frequently noted in groups. Unless work is assigned carefully to each group member, an under-motivated person can often squeeze by without contributing his or her fair share to a group effort.

Social loafing is the psychological term for shirking individual responsibility in a group setting. The social loafer risks being ostracized by the group but may be willing to pay the price rather than work hard. Loafing of this type is sometimes found in groups such as committees and project teams. Many students who have worked on team projects have encountered a social loafer.

At their worst, groups foster conflict on the job. People within the work group often bicker about such matters as doing a fair share of the undesir-able tasks within the department. Cohesive work groups can also become xenophobic (fearful of outsiders); that is, they may grow to dislike other groups and enter into conflict with them. A marketing group might devote considerable effort into showing up the finance group because the latter often puts financial brakes on marketing activities.

A well-publicized disadvantage of group decision making is **group-think,** a deterioration of mental efficiency, reality testing, and moral judgment in the interest of group solidarity. Simply put, groupthink is an extreme form of consensus. The group atmosphere values getting along more than getting things done. The group thinks as a unit, believes it is impervious to outside criticism, and begins to have illusions about its own invincibility. As a consequence, the group loses its own powers of critical analysis.[11]

Groupthink took place at one of the failed savings and loan associations. The senior management group voted themselves extraordinary salaries and bought art collections that they frequently borrowed for personal use. In addition, they purchased a corporate jet to fly around the country looking for investments, and also to take vacations. Not one of the savings and loan association executives expressed a dissenting opinion.

Another concern about teams is that teamwork is an unstable arrange-ment because team leaders soon revert to exercising most of the authority. As Kenneth Labich observes, "All too often team leaders revert to form and claim the sandbox for themselves, refusing to share authority with the other kids. Everyone else, meanwhile, sets to bickering about peripheral things like who gets credit for what the team produces. Old habits cling to life."[12]

To evaluate how well any work team or group familiar to you is functioning as a team, do Leadership Self-Assessment Exercise 9–1. The exercise will help sensitize you to important dimensions of team effectiveness.

LEADERSHIP SELF-ASSESSMENT
EXERCISE 9–1   The Teamwork Checklist

This checklist serves as an informal guide to diagnosing teamwork. Base your answers on whatever experiences you have in leading a team, at work or outside of work. Indicate whether your team has (or had) the following characteristics:

	Mostly Yes	Mostly No
1. Definite goals that each member knows and understands	____	____
2. Clearly established roles and responsibilities	____	____
3. Members who work together very well without strong egos or personalities creating problems	____	____
4. Well-documented guidelines for behavior and ground rules	____	____
5. After a consensus is reached, every team member supporting it	____	____
6. Team being aware when it has achieved success	____	____
7. Open communication in an atmosphere of trust	____	____
8. Continuous learning and training in appropriate skills	____	____
9. Team members who are flexible, open-minded, and dependable	____	____
10. Team members who have an "all in it together" attitude	____	____
11. Higher management's patience and support	____	____
12. Each member having pride in his or her work	____	____
13. Rewards tied to individual as well as team results	____	____
14. Team members who automatically provide backup and support for one another without the team leader's stepping in	____	____

Scoring and interpretation: The larger the number of statements answered "mostly yes," the more likely it is that good teamwork is present, thus contributing to productivity. The answers will serve as discussion points among team members for improving teamwork and group effectiveness. Negative responses to the statements can be used as suggestions for taking action to improve teamwork in your group.

Source: Based on material gathered from Mark Kelly, *The Adventures of a Self-Managing Team* (San Diego, CA: Pfeiffer & Company, 1991); brochure for "Team Leadership: How to Inspire Commitment, Teamwork & Cooperation," Seminars International, Olathe, KS, 1996.

THE LEADER'S ROLE IN THE TEAM-BASED ORGANIZATION

Although an important goal of a team-based organization is for group members to participate in leadership and management activities, leaders still play an important role. Instead of the leader's job disappearing, leaders learn to lead in new ways. Organizations need leaders who are knowledgeable in the team process and who can help with the interpersonal demands of teams. For example, giving feedback and resolving conflict is important in a team structure. Quite often the leader is a facilitator who works with two or three teams at a time. He or she helps them stay focused when personality and work-style differences create problems.[13] Without effective leadership, teams can get off course, go too far or not far enough, lose sight of their mission, and become blocked by interpersonal conflict. Effective leadership is particularly important early in the history of a group to help it reach its potential. Key roles of a leader in a team-based organization include the following:

- Building trust and inspiring teamwork
- Coaching team members and group members toward higher levels of performance
- Facilitating and supporting the decisions made by the team
- Expanding the team's capabilities
- Creating a team identity
- Anticipating and influencing change
- Inspiring the team toward higher levels of performance
- Enabling and empowering group members to accomplish their work
- Encouraging team members to eliminate low-value work[14]

Several of these roles have already been alluded to in this book, and several others, such as coaching, are described later. All of these roles contribute to effective leadership in general. The enabling role, for example, centers around empowerment. Yet properly motivating team members also enables, or facilitates, work accomplishment. The empowering processes described in Chapter 7 are a major part of enabling. Group members who are empowered are enabled to accomplish their work. The leader behavior and attitudes that foster teamwork, to be described in the next section, might also be interpreted as part of the leader's role in a team-based organization.

LEADER BEHAVIOR AND ATTITUDES THAT FOSTER TEAMWORK

Sometimes a leader's inspiring personality alone can foster teamwork. Yet inspirational leaders, as well as less charismatic ones, can encourage teamwork through certain behaviors and attitudes. Table 9–1 lists the teamwork-enhancing behaviors that are described in the following pages. (The suggestions for becoming an empowering leader offered in Chapter 8 also contribute to teamwork, but less directly.)

TABLE 9–1   Leader Behavior and Attitudes That Foster Teamwork

1. Defining the team's mission

2. Developing a norm of teamwork

3. Emphasizing pride in being outstanding

4. Holding a powwow

5. Serving as a model of teamwork

6. Using a consensus leadership style

7. Designing physical structures that facilitate communication

8. Establishing urgency, demanding performance standards, and providing direction

9. Emphasizing group recognition and rewards

10. Challenging the group regularly with fresh facts and information

11. Encouraging competition with another group

12. Encouraging the use of jargon

13. Initiating ritual and ceremony

14. Soliciting feedback on team effectiveness

15. Minimizing micromanagement

Defining the Team's Mission

A starting point in developing teamwork is to specify the team's mission. Commitment to a clear mission has recently been identified as a key practice of a highly effective team.[15] The mission statement for the group helps answer the question "Why are we doing this?" To answer this question, the mission statement should contain a specific goal, purpose, and philosophical tone. Here are two examples:

> "To plan and implement new manufacturing approaches to enhance our high-performance image and bolster our competitive edge."

> "To enhance our expert systems capability so we can provide decision makers throughout the organization with an advanced decision-making tool."

The leader can specify the mission when the team is first formed or at any other time. Developing a mission for a long-standing team breathes new life into its activities. Being committed to a mission improves teamwork, as does the process of formulating a mission. The dialogue necessary for developing a clearly articulated mission establishes a climate in which team members can express feelings, ideas, and opinions. Participative leadership is required in developing a mission, as in most other ways of enhancing teamwork.

Developing a Norm of Teamwork

A major strategy of teamwork development is to promote the attitude among group members that working together effectively is an expected standard of conduct. Developing a norm of teamwork will be difficult for a leader when a strong culture of individualism exists within the firm. A belief in cooperation and collaboration rather than competitiveness as a strategy for building teamwork has been referred to as **cooperation theory**.[16] Individuals who are accustomed to competing with one another for recognition, salary increases, and resources must now collaborate. Despite the challenge of making a culture shift, the leader can make progress toward establishing a teamwork norm.

Some leaders encourage team members to treat one another as if they were customers, thus encouraging cooperative behavior and politeness. The leader can also foster the norm of teamwork by explicitly stating its desirability. The manager of a group of financial analysts used the following comments, with good results, to promote teamwork:

> My manager is concerned that we are not pulling together as a cohesive team. I do see some merit in her argument. We are performing quite well as a group of individuals. Yet I see a need for an improved united effort in our group. We need to share ideas more frequently and to touch base with each other. It would

also help if we picked each other's brains more frequently. From now on when I evaluate performance, I'm going to give as much weight to group effort as I do to individual contribution.

The leader can also communicate the norm of teamwork by making frequent use of words and phrases that support teamwork. Emphasizing the words *team members* or *teammates,* and deemphasizing the words *subordinates* and *employees,* helps communicate the norm of teamwork. Group incentives are typically used to supplement, rather than replace, individual incentives.

Normative statements about teamwork by influential team members are also useful in reinforcing the norm of teamwork. A team member might say to coworkers, for example: "I'm glad this project is a joint effort. I know that's what earns us merit points around here."

Emphasizing Pride in Being Outstanding

A standard way to build team spirit, if not teamwork, is to help the group realize why it should be proud of its accomplishments. William A. Cohen argues that most groups are particularly good at some task. The leader should help the group identify that task or characteristic, and promote it as a key strength. A shipping department, for example, might have the best on-time shipping record in the region. Or a claims processing unit might have the least overpayments in an insurance company.[17] To try your hand at being an outstanding team, do Leadership Skill-Building Exercise 9–1.

LEADERSHIP SKILL-BUILDING
EXERCISE 9–1   Shelters for the Homeless

This exercise should take about one hour; it can be done inside or outside of class. Organize the class into teams of about six people. Each team takes on the assignment of formulating plans for building temporary shelters for the homeless. The dwellings you plan to build, for example, might be two-room cottages with electricity and indoor plumbing. During the time allotted to the task, formulate plans for going ahead with Shelters for the Homeless. Consider dividing up work by assigning certain roles to each team member. Sketch out tentative answers to the following questions: (1) How will you obtain funding for your venture? (2) Which homeless people will you help? (3) Where will your shelters be? (4) Who will do the actual construction?

After your plan is completed, evaluate the quality of the teamwork that took place within the group. Search the chapter for techniques you might have used to improve it.

Holding a Powwow

An informal approach to laying the groundwork for cooperation among people who will be working together as a team is to hold a *powwow*. Disney Studios began using the term when Walt Disney was asked if he conducted brainstorming sessions. He answered that he preferred to hold a powwow in which people "get together, beat the drum, light a fire, smoke a pipe, and socialize." As practiced at Disney, the powwow is intentionally informal, friendly, and unstructured. It is intended to lay the groundwork for a cooperative working relationship among team members assigned to a new project. Each powwow has three parts. A *skills inventory* gives each group member a chance to describe his or her task-relevant skills, experience, and aptitudes. An *interest inventory* gives group members an opportunity to describe their off-the-job interests. The interests revealed can serve as connectors among group members. During the *data dump*, each group member expresses his or her thoughts and feelings about the project. Other members listen without interrupting the person dumping data. An effective data dump reduces complaining because each member of the group has an opportunity to air any concerns about the project.

Powwows give each group member an opportunity to be heard, thus establishing open communication.[18] As a consequence, the group of people assigned to the project takes an important step toward becoming a team.

Serving as a Model of Teamwork

A powerful way for a leader to foster teamwork is to be a positive model of team play. And one way to exemplify teamwork is to reveal important information about ideas and attitudes relevant to the group's work. As a result of this behavior, team members may follow suit. A leader's self-disclosure fosters teamwork because it leads to shared perceptions and concerns.[19]

Interacting extensively with team members serves as a model of teamwork because it illustrates the mechanism by which team development takes place—frequent informal communication. While interacting with team members, the team leader can emphasize that he or she is a team member. For example, he or she might say, "Remember the deadline. We must all have the proposal in the mail by Thursday." A less team-member-oriented statement would be, "Remember the deadline. I need the proposals in the mail by Thursday."[20]

Using a Consensus Leadership Style

Teamwork is enhanced when a leader practices consensus decision making. Contributing input to important decisions helps group members feel that they are valuable team members. Consensus decision making also leads to an exchange of ideas within the group, including supporting and refining one another's suggestions. As a result, the feeling of working jointly on problems is enhanced.

The Japanese approach to human resource management is ground in the philosophy of teamwork and group harmony. To help achieve such harmony, many Japanese managers use consensus leadership. When all group members contribute to and finally support a decision, teamwork is enhanced. Because each person has contributed important input, he or she

LEADER IN ACTION

Brian Wilson at General Electric, Charlottesville, VA

Brian Wilson remembers what it was like working for General Electric when management called the shots and gave orders in one-way communiqués. That was the situation when he began working for the company in the early 1980s. But at the Charlottesville, Virginia, plant, those days have long passed. General Electric has since merged the Charlottesville plant with a Japanese company to form GE Fanuc Automation North America, Inc. The U.S. Department of Labor has cited the company as a clearinghouse workplace for its outstanding leadership.

Over the past five years, traditional managerial and leadership roles have shifted dramatically. Formerly a supervisor, Wilson is now a *team developer* of production operations. He is responsible for three teams with a total of forty-three associates. "Today, management works to support the associates," he says. "We go directly to the people on the front lines—those responsible for implementing the ideas. That's been good for the teams and for business."

The gains have not been achieved without significant challenges. When the program first began, consultants and supervisors recruited representatives from manufacturing, marketing, engineering, human resources, and production. Led by Robert Collins (the CEO of GE Fanuc), the group discussed how to develop GE into a team-based work force. "In the beginning, we had a number of people who wanted to opt out. But we wouldn't let them. You hate to say something was

mandatory, but it was. We knew there couldn't be gains without some pain. So we stuck with it.

"We had a situation where some people had been working together side by side for ten to fifteen years, and hadn't had to speak to each other. Suddenly, they had to. Many people were used to taking orders. We had to learn that when we made decisions as a team, we had to stick with them. And when things didn't happen the way we had planned, we had to bring it back to the meetings and discuss it."

Progress is charted through weekly meetings, for which associates set the agenda. In the beginning, associates and team developers were given hours of training in problem solving, conflict management, and goal setting. Continuous education is still available, and once a month, the entire work force gathers for an operations review led by CEO Collins.

"In January, one of my work teams presented at the operations review," said Wilson. "They were asked to share some of their best practices." The team was commended for a newly created cross-training program in which the associates rotate jobs every three weeks. "I'm really proud of them," Wilson says, "And this is just the beginning. The sky's the limit."

is less likely to be in conflict with other group members. The accompany-ing Leader in Action vignette illustrates how practicing consensus leader-ship can foster teamwork. Recognize, however, that consensus decision making alone does not create good teamwork. Many of the other ingredi-ents described here must also be included to bring about a cohesive team effort.

Another way of framing the consensus leadership style is that it reflects a belief in shared governance and partnerships instead of patriarchal care-taking.[21] The team, rather than hierarchical departments, becomes the focus of organizational activity. As with the other tactics and techniques for enhancing teamwork, people have to participate in a cultural shift to fully accept shared governance.

Designing Physical Structures That Facilitate Communication

Group cohesiveness, and therefore teamwork, is enhanced when team mem-bers are located close together and can interact frequently and easily. In con-trast, people who spend most of their time in private offices or cubicles are less likely to interact. Frequent interaction often leads to camaraderie and a feeling of belongingness. A useful tactic for achieving physical proximity is to establish a shared physical facility, such as a conference room, research library, or beverage lounge. This area should be decorated differently from other areas in the building and a few amenities should be added, such as a coffeepot, microwave oven, and refrigerator. Team members can then use this area for refreshments and group interaction. Recognizing the contribu-tion of a shared physical facility to promoting teamwork, many organiza-tions today have incorporated more open working space into the work place, often eliminating private offices. So far information has not been pub-lished about the productivity loss stemming from limited time for quiet reflection on the job.

Establishing Urgency, Demanding Performance Standards, and Providing Direction

As management consultants, Jon R. Katzenbach and Douglas K. Smith have studied work teams in many organizations. They have observed that team members need to believe that the team has urgent, constructive purposes. Team members also want to have a list of explicit expectations. The more urgent and relevant the rationale, the more likely it is that the team will achieve its potential. A customer service team was told that further growth for the corporation would be impossible without major improvements in providing service to customers. Energized by this information, the team met the challenge.[22]

Emphasizing Group Recognition and Rewards

Giving rewards for group accomplishment reinforces teamwork because people receive rewards for what they have achieved collaboratively. The recognition accompanying the reward should emphasize the team's value to the organization rather than that of the individual. Recognition promotes team identity by enabling the team to take pride in its contributions and progress. The following are examples of team recognition:

- A display wall for team activities such as certificates of accomplishment, schedules, and miscellaneous announcements
- Team logos on items such as identifying T-shirts, athletic caps, mugs, jackets, key rings, and business cards
- Celebrations to mark milestones such as first-time activities, cost savings, and safety records
- Equipment painted in team colors
- Athletic team events such as softball, volleyball, and bowling
- Team-of-the-Month award, with gifts from the organization to team members or to the entire team

Saturn Corporation believes that team compensation is an important contributor to the success of its self-managing teams. Its self-directed work teams accomplish tasks in their area of responsibility without outside direction. Each unit is authorized to make its own job assignments, plan its work, and perform its own maintenance, among other responsibilities. Team leadership is rotated. Total compensation is made up of base pay, risk pay, and reward pay. The base pay is lower than the market rate by 10 percent, which represents the risk part. Team members have to earn the risk portion back. Team members can go beyond market pay through rewards. The rewards are linked to company goals and training goals, and the rewards are based on a blend of individual and group performance.[23]

Returning to the general situation of team rewards, as the team evolves, some individuals will be more worthy of recognition than others. Rather than denying the reality of individual effort, the team might present an award to an outstanding performer. Consultant Gerald Graham suggests that recognizing an outstanding performer is likely to build teamwork.[24]

Challenging the Group Regularly

A leader can enhance teamwork by feeding the team valid facts and information that motivate team members to work together to modify the status quo. According to Katzenbach and Smith, new information prompts the team to redefine and enrich its understanding of the challenge it is facing. As a result, the team is likely to focus on a common purpose, set clearer goals, and work together more smoothly. Feeding the group relevant facts and information is also valuable because it helps combat groupthink.

A quality improvement team in a manufacturing plant recognized the high cost of poor quality. Nevertheless, they did not know what to do next until they researched the different types of defects and established the price on each one. In contrast, teams err when they assume that all the information they need exists within the group.[25]

Encouraging Competition with Another Group

One of the best-known methods of encouraging teamwork is rallying the support of the group against a real or imagined threat from the outside. Beating the competition makes more sense when the competition is outside your organization. When the enemy is within, the team spirit within may become detrimental to the overall organization, and we–they problems may arise.

When encouraging competition with another group, the leader should encourage rivalry, not intense competition that might lead to unethical business practices. One factor contributing to the success of the Saturn automobile is the rivalry created with competitive brands. One of the marketing executives asked his staff several times, "How much longer are you going to take the insult that Americans can't make a world-class car in the low-price range? The Japanese are great automakers, but I know you people from Tennessee can be just as good." Observe that the executive encouraged rivalry with a formidable opponent but did not bash the competition.

Encouraging the Use of Jargon

An analysis by Lee G. Bolman and Terrence E. Deal suggests that the symbolic and ritualistic framework of a group contributes heavily to teamwork. An important part of this framework is a specialized language that fosters cohesion and commitment. In essence, this specialized language is in-group jargon. The jargon creates a bond among team members and sets the group apart from outsiders. It also reinforces unique values and beliefs, thus contributing to corporate culture. Jargon also allows team members to communicate easily, with few misunderstandings.

Bolman and Deal analyzed reports contained in Tracy Kidder's book about the computer industry, *The Soul of a New Machine* (Little, Brown, 1981). The Eagle Group outperformed all other Data General divisions to produce a new, state-of-the-art computer. Here is some of the jargon the highly cohesive Eagle Group used:

A kludge: something to be avoided, such as a machine with loose wire held together with duct tape.

A canard: anything false.

Give me a core dump: tell me your thoughts.

A stack overflow: an engineer's memory compartments are suffering from communication overload.[26]

The accompanying Team in Action vignette illustrates the colorful, jargon-laden speech of an organization known for its teamwork.

Initiating Ritual and Ceremony

According to Bolman and Deal, another way to enhance teamwork is to initiate ritual and ceremony. Ritual and ceremony afford opportunities for reinforcing values, revitalizing spirit, and bonding workers to one another and to the team. An example would be holding a team dinner whenever the group achieves a major milestone, such as making a winning bid on a major contract. Leadership in Data General's Eagle Group encouraged ritual and ceremony from the beginning of the project. Bolman and Deal provide an example:

> Eagle's leaders met regularly, including a meeting every Friday afternoon. But their meetings dealt more with symbols, gossip, and play than substance and decisions. Friday afternoon was a traditional time for winding down and relaxing. Honoring such a tradition was all the more important for a group whose members often worked all week and then all weekend.[27]

TEAM IN ACTION

A Technical Group at Microsoft Corp.

Microsoft organization members, headed by the charismatic Bill Gates, are known for their cohesiveness and team spirit. Part of the organizational culture is to learn and use *Microspeak,* as sampled in the following representative comments made by a software development team within the firm.

Person A: "He's very bandwidth."

Person B: "Bill sent me some wicked flame mail."

Person C: "Your idea has no granularity."

Person D: "She's hardcore about spreadsheets."

Person E: "He went nonlinear on me."

Person F: "That's the most random thing I've ever heard."

Translation:

Bandwidth: a measure of a person's intelligence, much like IQ.

Flame mail: hypercritical, emotional, and inflammatory electronic mail, often containing vulgarisms.

Granularity: fineness of detail.

Hardcore: serious about work.

Nonlinear: out of control, angry.

Random: illogical.

Source: "Microsoft: Bill Gates' Baby Is on Top of the World. Can It Stay There?" *Business Week,* February 24, 1992, p. 63.

Soliciting Feedback on Team Effectiveness

Yet another approach to building teamwork is for the leader to systematically collect feedback on how well the team is working together. After rating its performance as a team, the team can discuss areas for improvement. Working together in this manner enhances cooperation. Edward Glassman recommends that after a meeting, each member rate on a scale of 1 to 10 (with 10 the highest) the performance of the leader and the team in several key areas, including the following:

1. Was participation in the discussion equally balanced among all members?
2. Were your opinions and thoughts solicited by the team?
3. Do you feel you influenced the final outcome?
4. Do you feel others influenced the final product?
5. Do you feel the final outcomes were creative?[28]

Meeting participants can also be asked to write a one-sentence comment about their ratings. They discuss the feedback at the next meeting, with the anticipation of bringing about constructive change and stronger team spirit.

Minimizing Micromanagement

A strategic perspective on encouraging teamwork is for the leader to minimize **micromanagement,** the close monitoring of most aspects of group member activities. To be a good team leader, the manager must give group members ample opportunity to manage their own activities. Avoiding micromanagement is a core ingredient of employee empowerment because empowered workers are given considerable latitude to manage their own activities.[29] Research has shown that leaders of self-managing teams encourage self-reinforcement, self-goal setting, self-criticism, self-observation/evaluation, self-expectation, and rehearsal (mental review of upcoming events).[30]

The extreme argument against micromanagement was made by a member of a successful empowered team at a Hewlett-Packard distribution center: "People in leadership shouldn't think about what they can do to make people productive, happier, etc.—they should think about what they can stop doing."[31] Despite the enthusiasm of this team member, a caveat is in order. For empowerment to work (the opposite of micromanaging), team members must have the appropriate skills, job knowledge, and education in addition to motivation. Would you want an empowered group of production associates to design an airplane in which you would be a passenger? Team or group members must also be ready to accept empowerment in the sense of being willing to assume more responsibility and be accountable for their results.

OUTDOOR TRAINING AND TEAM DEVELOPMENT

Cognitive information about strategies and tactics for improving teamwork is potentially valuable. The person reading such information can selectively apply the concepts, observe the consequences, and then fine-tune his or her approach. Another approach to developing teamwork is to participate in experiential activities.

One popular experiential approach to building teamwork and leadership skills is outdoor training. Wilderness training is closely associated with outdoor training, except that the setting is likely to be much rougher—perhaps in the frozen tundra of northernmost Minnesota. Some forms of outdoor training take place in city parks.

Both outdoor and wilderness training are forms of learning by doing. Participants are supposed to acquire leadership and teamwork skills by confronting physical challenges and exceeding their self-imposed limitations. The goals of outdoor training are reasonably consistent across different training groups. The Big Rock Creek Camp, which offers team building and leadership training, specifies these representative goals:

- Discover your strengths and weaknesses.

- Test your limits (they're far broader than you imagine).

- Work together as a team.

- Have fun.

- Face the essence of who you are and what you are made of.

- Have the opportunity to break through barriers within yourself.

- Have the opportunity to break through barriers between yourself and others.

Features of Outdoor Training Programs

Program participants are placed in a demanding outdoor environment. They have to rely on skills they did not realize they had, and on one another, to complete the program. The emphasis is on building not only teamwork but also self-confidence for leadership. Sometimes lectures on leadership, self-confidence, and teamwork precede the outdoor activity.

Outward Bound is the best known and largest outdoor training program. The program offers more than 500 courses in wilderness areas in twenty states and provinces. The courses typically run from three days to four weeks; one course in North Carolina lasts eighty-eight days. Worldwide, Outward Bound runs about forty-eight schools on five continents, with a total annual enrollment of about 28,000.

The Outward Bound Professional Development Program is geared to organizational leaders because it emphasizes teamwork, leadership, and risk taking. The wilderness is the classroom, and the instructors draw analogies between each outdoor activity and the workplace. Among the courses offered are dogsledding, skiing and winter camping, desert backpacking, canoe expeditioning, sailing, sea kayaking, alpine mountaineering, mountain backpacking and horsetrailing, and cycling.

Rope activities are typical of outdoor training. Participants are attached to a secure pulley with ropes, then climb up a ladder and jump off to another spot. Sometimes the rope is extended between two trees. Another activity is a "trust fall," in which each person takes a turn standing on a platform and falling backwards into the arms of coworkers. The trust fall can also be done on ground level.[32] To examine a trust fall first hand, do Leadership Skill-Building Exercise 9–2.

Outdoor training enhances teamwork by helping participants examine the process of getting things done through working with people. Participants practice their communication skills in exercises such as rappeling down a cliff by issuing precise instructions to one another about how to scale the cliff safely. At the same time, they have to learn to trust one another more because survival appears to depend on trust. The accompanying Team in Action vignette provides more details about how outdoor training is used for team building.

LEADERSHIP SKILL-BUILDING
EXERCISE 9–2   The Trust Fall

Perhaps the most widely used team-building activity is the trust fall, which may be familiar to many readers. Nevertheless, each application of this exercise is likely to produce new and informative results. The class organizes itself into teams. In each team, each willing member stands on a chair and falls backwards into the arms of teammates. A less frightening alternative to falling off a chair is to simply fall backwards standing up. Those team members who for whatever physical or mental reason would prefer not to fall back into others or participate in catching others are unconditionally excluded. However, they can serve as observers. After the trust falls have been completed, a team leader gathers answers to the following questions, and then shares the answers with the rest of the class.

1. How does this exercise develop teamwork?

2. How does this exercise develop leadership skills?

3. What did the participants learn about themselves?

Evaluation of Outdoor Training for Team Development

Many outdoor trainers and participants believe strongly that they derived substantial personal benefits from outdoor training. Among the most important are developing greater self-confidence, appreciating hidden strengths, and learning to work better with people. Strong proponents of outdoor training believe that those who do not appreciate the training simply do not understand it. Many training directors also have positive attitudes toward outdoor training. They believe that a work team that experiences outdoor training will work more cooperatively back at the office.

Many people have legitimate reservations about outdoor training, however. Although outdoor trainers claim that almost no accidents occur, a

TEAM IN ACTION

■ Evart Employees Attend Outdoor Training

Employees at the Evart Glass Plant, a division of Chrysler Corp., strive to work together. Division management decided to help workers achieve this goal by sending all 257 employees to team-building training. The idea for the training stemmed from a corporate interest in improving organizational culture and climate. Bert Burtolozzi, the plant manager, commented, "As we move toward a team-focused approach in our operation, team effort is what counts. As a society we have focused on the individual, but in the workplace no one individual can do it themselves [meaning himself or herself]—we must focus on our greatest asset: our teams."

The outdoor training took place through the New Horizons program of Eagle Village, an experiential-based adventure center, a twenty-minute drive from the plant. Several key aspects of the program made it distinctive. The program took place during regular work hours, and employees received their regular pay for participating in the program. Throughout June 1995, employees from a variety of work areas were brought together during their respective shifts for an eight-hour session of seven cooperative and problem-solving activities. Line workers, supervisors, and management

were assembled into mixed groups of ten to fifteen participants for this experience. Ninety-five percent of Evart employees participated.

Teams were formed with cross-functional groupings so that employees were outside their normal work groups for the training. During one of the exercises, participants attempted to maneuver through a carpet-square maze under time-limit pressure. The group had to find the hidden path through the maze and then safely move each member through it in a limited amount of time. A line worker noted that to get through the maze and reach the objective, employees had to say when something didn't work and offer ways to fix it. The intended lesson is that by allowing each individual's strength to come out (such as a good memory or physical strength), the group discovers hidden leaders. Either the entire group finds success by making the deadlines, or the group pays the consequence of starting a new maze from the beginning.

Another of the team-building experiences was the tube-pass activity. Participants had to pass a bicycle inner tube around a circle of people who were holding hands, without either breaking the circle or letting the tube touch the ground. The activity is meant to show that what one person does affects the group as a whole. It also shows that people must be willing to go out of their way to help one another in order to complete a task at a high quality level.

After completing an activity, the group gathered together to discuss the experience and compare it to workplace challenges of cooperating to produce a quality product. Facilitators prodded participants to think about how they could apply their team-building experiences to the job. Ruth A. Moore, the human resources director, noted: "Everybody was equal in their group. It allowed people to get to know those in different work areas and feel more comfortable about going to each other to talk, and solve a work-related problem and share information."

Leadership at Evart was careful to ease concern about the training by starting to provide information six months beforehand. Eagle Village

representatives made a preprogram presentation that included suggesting attire for training day. A post-team-building survey indicated that employees generally liked the program, and many wanted to repeat it with their regular work groups. Many workers noticed that back on the job, employees were more cooperative and showed a how-can-I-help-you attitude. The human resources director believed that overall the program was beneficial. She said, "This type of training seems to break down personal walls that people build around themselves. It gets them out into the open and contributing rather than just existing and doing their jobs."

Source: Adapted and excerpted from Heidi Campbell, "Adventures in Teamland," *Personnel Journal*, May 1996, pp. 56–62.

threat to health and life does exist. (To help minimize casualties, participants usually need medical clearance.) Another concern is that the teamwork learned in outdoor training does not spill over into the job environment. As Jay Conger explains, the workplace is a different environment from the wilderness. And real workplace teams tend to gain and lose their members rapidly as teammates are transferred, promoted, terminated, or quit. This mobility often negates all the team-building efforts that take place during the wilderness experience. Another problem is that when teams return to work, they often revert to noncollaborative behavior.[33]

One way to facilitate the transfer of training from outdoors to the office is to hold debriefing and follow-up sessions. Debriefing takes place at the end of outdoor training. The participants review what they learned and discuss how they will apply their lessons to the job. Follow-up sessions can then be held periodically to describe progress in applying the insights learned during outdoor training.

For a quick trip to team-building and leadership training, do Leadership Skill-Building Exercise 9–3. If you have done this exercise previously, please do not solve the problem for the group. Instead, you be the timer or an observer.

THE LEADER-MEMBER EXCHANGE MODEL AND TEAMWORK

Research and theory about the development of teamwork lag far behind research and theory about many other aspects of leadership. Nevertheless, the leader-member exchange model, developed by George Graen and asso-

LEADERSHIP SKILL-BUILDING
EXERCISE 9–3   Learning Teamwork Through Ball Handling

The exercise to be described next is used to develop leadership, and also to practice brainstorming. If the class has twenty-five or fewer students, the entire class can participate. Otherwise, divide the class into groups of about fifteen people. One person in the group is handed a ball, who then hands it to the adjacent person, who hands it to the next, and so on, until everyone has had a chance to have the ball. Each person tries to remember who gave him or her the ball, and who the ball was handed to. A timekeeper records how long the passing along of the ball takes.

The process begins all over again, with the goal of cutting the ball-passing time in half. The one rule is that the ball must touch everyone's hand. With each new round, the goal is to cut the time again by one-half. A point will quickly be reached where the team has only several seconds to pass the ball along to all the participants. Use brainstorming to find a way of reducing the time required for passing the ball to all of the participants.

ciates, helps explain why one subgroup in a unit is part of a cohesive team and another subgroup is excluded.[34] The **leader-member exchange model** (also called the **vertical dyad linkage model**) proposes that leaders develop unique working relationships with subordinates. By so doing, they create in-groups and out-groups. The in-groups become part of a smoothly functioning team headed by the formal leader. Out-group members are less likely to experience good teamwork. Figure 9–2 depicts the major concept of the leader-member exchange model.

Graen and his associates argue that leaders do not typically use the same leadership style in dealing with all group members. Instead, they treat each member somewhat differently. According to the model, the linkages (relationships) that exist between the leader and each individual team member probably differ in quality. In theory, the differences lie on a continuum of low quality to high quality. With group members on the top half of the continuum, the leader has a good relationship; with those on the lower half of the continuum, the leader has a poor relationship. Each of these pairs of relationships, or dyads, must be judged in terms of whether a group member is "in" or "out" with the leader.

Members of the in-group are invited to participate in important decision making, are given added responsibility, and are privy to interesting gossip. Members of the out-group are managed according to the requirements of their employment contract. They receive little warmth, inspiration, or encouragement. Robert Vecchio explains that an in-group member is elevated to the unofficial role of trusted assistant.[35] An out-group member is treated much like a hired hand. In-group members tend to achieve a higher

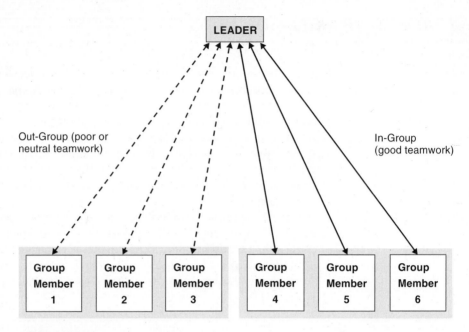

FIGURE 9–2

The Leader-Member Exchange Model

Source: Adapted from Gregory Moorhead and Ricky W. Griffin, Organizational Behavior: Managing People and Organizations, *4/e, p. 314. Copyright © 1995 by Houghton Mifflin Company. Used by permission.*

level of performance, commitment, and satisfaction than do out-group members. Furthermore, they are less likely to quit.

The in-group versus out-group status also includes an element of reciprocity or exchange. The leader grants more favors to the in-group member, who in turn works harder to please the leader. Two recent studies provide more specific information about the consequences of a positive exchange between a supervisor and group members. In a hospital setting, positive exchanges involved group members engaging in increased good citizenship behavior and also in-role behaviors such as putting extra effort into performing duties.[36] As a result, the leader then would feel justified in granting the in-group members more resources, such as a larger salary increase or a larger budget.

In a study conducted in diverse industrial settings, it was also found that high-quality exchanges between supervisors and employees contribute to employees' engaging in extra-role behavior, or being cooperative in ways that were not expected of them. Helping behaviors were measured by supervisors rating their employees on altruism. An example would be for an accountant to help a sales representative prepare a sales forecast. The researchers concluded that through the development of high-quality relationships with group members, supervisors are able to motivate the group members and enable them to engage in helping behaviors that benefit them as well as their coworkers.[37]

Being part of the in-group can facilitate a member's future promotional opportunities. Unfortunately, choices about who becomes an in-group or out-group member are sometimes based on factors unrelated to job performance. Leaders sometimes form bonds with group members who play golf with them, or who belong to the same ethnic, religious, or racial group, or who are the same sex.

The leader's first impression of a group member's competency plays an important role in placing the group member into the in-group or the out-group. Another key linking factor is whether the leader and team member have positive or negative chemistry. We can assume that group members who make effective use of influence and political tactics increase their chances of becoming members of the in-group.

A field study seems to confirm that first impressions make a difference. The researchers gathered ratings of six aspects of the manager–group member dyad. One measure was the group members' perceived similarity with the leader. For example, "My supervisor and I are alike in a number of ways." A second measure was feelings about the manager, such as "I like my supervisor very much as a friend." A third rating dealt directly with the member's view of the leader-member exchange (LMX). An example is "I can count on my supervisor to 'bail me out,' even at his or her expense, when I really need it."

A fourth rating measured the leader expectation of the member, such as "I think my new employee will be an excellent employee." A fifth rating measured leader liking of the member, such as "I like my subordinate very much as a person." A sixth rating was the leader's view of the LMX, including a rating of the statement, "I would be willing to 'bail out' my subordinate, even at my own expense, if he or she really needed it."

Results showed that the initial leader expectations of members and member expectations of the leader were good predictors of the leader-member exchanges at two weeks and at six weeks. Member expectations of the leader also accurately predicted member assessments of the quality of the leader-member exchange at six months. An important interpretation of these results is that the leader-member exchange is formed in the first several days of the relationship.[38] As the adage states, "You have only one chance to make a first impression."

In summary, the leader-member exchange model provides a partial explanation of teamwork development. Members of the in-group work smoothly together and with the leader because they feel privileged. Being a member of the out-group may not diminish teamwork, but it certainly does not make a positive contribution.

SUMMARY

Leaders are required to build teamwork because it is needed for such key activities as group problem solving and achieving high quality. Teamwork is an understanding of and commitment to group goals on the part of all group members. Team leaders share power, deemphasize individual glory, and understand that power sharing increases their own power. The solo style of leader is the traditional autocratic leader in a bureaucracy.

Group work and group decision making offer several advantages, including the possibility of synergy, catching major errors, continuous improvement, and innovation. Working in groups often enhances job satisfaction, and many personal needs can be satisfied. Group activity also has some potential disadvantages, including pressures toward conformity, social loafing, the breeding of conflict, and groupthink.

Leaders still play an important role in a team-based organization, such as being expert in the team process, being facilitators, building trust and inspiring teamwork, and enabling and empowering group members to accomplish their work. The enabling role centers around empowerment.

A wide range of leader behaviors and attitudes contribute directly to teamwork: (1) defining the team's mission; (2) developing a norm of teamwork; (3) emphasizing pride in being outstanding; (4) holding a powwow; (5) serving as a model of teamwork; (6) using a consensus leadership style; (7) designing physical structures that facilitate communication; (8) establishing urgency, demanding performance standards, and providing direction; (9) emphasizing group recognition and rewards; (10) challenging the group regularly with fresh facts and information; (11) encouraging competition with another group; (12) encouraging the use of jargon; (13) initiating ritual and ceremony; (14) soliciting feedback on team effectiveness; and (15) minimizing micromanagement. For empowerment to work, team members must have the appropriate skills, job knowledge, and education in addition to motivation.

In outdoor training, a popular experiential approach to building teamwork and leadership skills, emphasis is placed on building self-confidence. Outdoor training enhances teamwork by helping participants examine the process of getting things done collaboratively. The Outward Bound Professional Development Program is particularly geared toward organization leaders. Opinion about the effectiveness of outdoor training for developing teamwork and leadership skills is mixed. Concern has been expressed that the skills learned in the field do not carry over to the workplace.

The leader-exchange model helps explain why one subgroup in a work unit is part of a cohesive team and another unit is excluded. According to the model, leaders develop unique working relationships with subordinates. As a result, in-groups and out-groups are created. Members of the in-group tend to perform better, have higher satisfaction, and exhibit more teamwork. The leader's first impression of a group member's competency plays an important role in placing that person into the in-group or the out-group.

KEY TERMS

Team
Teamwork
Social loafing
Groupthink

Cooperation theory
Micromanagement
Leader-member exchange
   model

(or vertical dyad linkage-
   model)

GUIDELINES FOR ACTION AND SKILL DEVELOPMENT

Management consultant Robert J. Waterman, Jr., offers many suggestions for strengthening teamwork throughout the organization. Among those not already described in this chapter are the following:

1. **Hire people who both qualify for the job and fit into the culture.** Too many like-minded team players could create problems. Nevertheless, attempt to hire the best people for your business, not necessarily for any business.

2. **Destroy at least one "we–they" barrier a year.** Encourage your team to be loyal to broader groups than your own. People have the capacity to identify with at least several larger groups than their own, including the division and region.

3. **Use training programs to build relationships.** When people are being trained and retrained, they are also forging new cross-organization bonds.

4. **Share the facts.** Sharing information engenders trust, and trust is a major contributor to teamwork. Sharing facts is also a way of sharing power.

5. **Come down hard on political infighting.** Political squabbles hamper teamwork, so it is advisable to confront team members who continually engage in conflict with each other.

6. **Do not tolerate lack of integrity or of trustworthy behavior.** An atmosphere low in trust breeds negative politics and poor cooperation. Confront instances of low trustworthiness.[39]

In addition to the positive suggestions above, certain behaviors should be avoided if you are to lead a successful team. Deborah Harrington-Mackin recommends that during a team meeting the leader should avoid arguing with team members. Being too casual about the leadership role, such as neglecting to facilitate or showing lack of involvement, can also hamper teamwork. Also watch out for manipulating and controlling discussion. Be careful not to neglect the needs of team members by such acts as failing to protect a team member who is under attack.[40]

DISCUSSION QUESTIONS AND ACTIVITIES

1. Why should leaders be concerned with developing teamwork?

2. Identify several *collective work products* from any group you have worked in.

3. If you were applying for a position in a modern, high-tech company, would it be better for you to describe yourself as a team leader or a solo leader? Why?

4. In what way might a leader engage in *social loafing*?

5. Identify and describe any team you have been a member of, or know about otherwise, that has a strong norm of teamwork.

6. Is there a role for decisive, creative, and independent-thinking leaders in a team-based organization? Explain.

7. What forces for and against being a good team player are embedded in American culture?

8. How effective are team symbols such as athletic caps and coffee mugs in building teamwork among managers and professionals?

9. You have probably been told many times to minimize jargon in speech and writing in order to enhance communication, yet this chapter advocated jargon for teamwork. How do you reconcile the difference between the two pieces of advice?

10. How can political skill help a person avoid being adversely affected by the leader exchange model?

LEADERSHIP CASE PROBLEM

The Unbalanced Team

Mercury Printing is one of the largest commercial printing companies in San Diego, California, with annual sales of $25 million. Two years ago, Alvero Velasquez, the vice president of marketing, reorganized the sales force. Previously the sales force had consisted of inside sales representatives (who took care of phone-in orders) and outside sales representatives (who called on accounts). The reorganization divided the outside sales force into two groups: direct sales and major accounts. The direct sales representatives were made responsible for small and medium-size customers. As before, they would service existing customers and prospect for new accounts.

Four of the direct sales representatives were promoted to major account executives. The account executives would service the company's largest accounts, including prospecting for new business within those accounts. To promote teamwork and cooperation, Velasquez assigned a group sales quota to the account executives. Collectively, their goal was to bring in sixteen new large accounts per month.

Because the sales quota was a group quota, the account representatives were supposed to work together on strategy for acquiring new accounts. If a particular account exec did not have the expertise to handle his or her customer's problems, another account executive was supposed to offer help. For example, Darcy Wentworth was the resident expert on printing packages and inserts for packages. If invited, Darcy would join another account executive to call on a customer with a complex request for package printing.

After the new sales organization had been in place for eighteen months, Ann Osaka, an account executive, was having lunch with George Lewis, a production superintendent at Mercury Printing. "I've about had it," said Ann. "I'm tired of singlehandedly carrying the team."

"What do you mean you are singlehandedly carrying the team?" asked George.

"You're a trusted friend, George. So let me lay out the facts. Each month the group is supposed to bring in sixteen new sales. If we don't average those sixteen sales per month, we don't get our semiannual bonus. That represents about 25 percent of my salary. So a big chunk of my money comes from group effort.

"My average number of new accounts brought in for the last twelve months has been nine. And we are averaging about fourteen new sales per month. This translates into the other three account execs averaging five sales among them. I'm carrying the group, but overall sales are still below quota. This means I didn't get my bonus last month.

"The other account execs are friendly and helpful in writing up proposals. But they just don't bring in their share of accounts."

George asked, "What does your boss say about this?"

"I've had several conversations with him about the problem. He tells me to be patient and to remember that the development of a fully balanced team requires time. He also tells me that I should develop a stronger team spirit. My problem is that I can't pay my bills with team spirit."

1. What does this case illustrate about teamwork?

2. What steps should Alvero Velasquez take, if any, to remedy the situation of unequal contribution of the account representatives?

3. What type of leadership input might help this situation?

4. To what extent are Ann Osaka's complaints justifiable?

Motivation and Coaching Skills

Whit Garson is a plant superintendent at a Chrysler minivan assembly plant in Windsor, Ontario. A visitor to his office inquired about a glass-encased whistle on a bookshelf adjacent to his desk. Garson replied, "The whistle is a constant reminder to me that a good leader has to be a good coach. You have to cheer people on when they are doing something right. When they make a mistake, you have to blow the whistle and show them how to improve. Even when they don't make a mistake, it helps to blow the whistle to show them how to reach new heights."

As the manager of a highly successful automotive plant just explained, effective leaders are outstanding motivators and coaches. They influence others in many of the ways previously described. In addition, they often use specific motivational and coaching skills. These techniques are important because not all leaders can influence others through formal authority or charisma and inspirational leadership alone. Face-to-face, day-by-day motivational skills are also important. As explained by Roger D. Evered and James C. Selman, good coaching is the essential feature of effective management.[1] Many organizations today, including Xerox Corp., believe that the

245

manager should function as a coach. Team leaders in particular function more like coaches than like managers in a hierarchy.

In this chapter we approach motivation and coaching skills from various perspectives. We examine first how leaders make effective use of expectancy theory, behavior modification, and goal setting to motivate group members. Second, we describe coaching as a leadership philosophy, followed by a description of specific coaching skills, including coaching people through difficult times.

EXPECTANCY THEORY AND MOTIVATIONAL SKILLS

Expectancy theory is a good starting point in learning how leaders can apply systematic explanations of motivation for two major reasons. First, the theory is comprehensive because it incorporates and integrates features of other motivation theories, including goal theory and behavior modification. Second, it offers the leader many guidelines for triggering and sustaining constructive effort from group members.

The **expectancy theory** of motivation is based on the premise that the amount of effort people expend depends on how much reward they expect to get in return. In addition to being broad, the theory deals with cognition and process. Expectancy theory is cognitive because it emphasizes the thoughts, judgments, and desires of the person being motivated. It is a process theory because it attempts to explain how motivation takes place.

The theory is really a group of theories based on a rational, economic view of people.[2] In any given situation, people want to maximize gain and minimize loss. The theory assumes that people choose among alternatives by selecting the one they think they have the best chance of attaining. Furthermore, they choose the alternative that appears to have the biggest personal payoff. Given a choice, people will select the assignment that they think they can handle the best and that will benefit them the most.

Basic Components of Expectancy Theory

Expectancy theory contains three basic components: valence, instrumentality, and expectancy. Because of these three components, the theory is often referred to as VIE theory. Figure 10–1 presents a basic version of expectancy theory. All three elements must be present for motivation to take place. To be motivated, people must value the reward, think they can perform, and have reasonable assurance that performance will lead to a reward.

Valence. The worth or attractiveness of an outcome is referred to as **valence.** As shown in Figure 10–1, each work situation has multiple outcomes. An **outcome** is anything that might stem from performance, such as a reward. Each outcome has a valence of its own. For example, potential

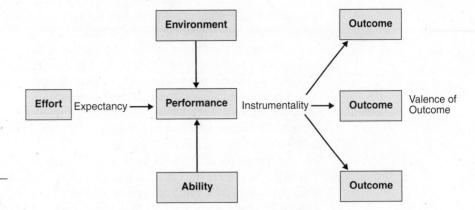

FIGURE 10–1

The Expectancy Theory of Motivation

second-level outcomes for a successful franchise operator include high income, an opportunity to purchase another franchise from the same company, and a feeling of independence. The sum of all the valences must be positive for the person to work hard. If the sum of all the valences is negative, the person will probably work hard to avoid the outcome.

Valences range from –100 to +100 in the version of expectancy theory presented here. (The usual method of placing valences on a –1.00 to +1.00 scale does not do justice to the true differences in preferences.) A valence of +100 means that a person intensely desires an outcome. A valence of –100 means that a person is strongly motivated to avoid an outcome such as being fired or declaring bankruptcy. A valence of zero signifies indifference to an outcome and is therefore of no use as a motivator.

Instrumentality. The probability assigned by the individual that performance will lead to certain outcomes is referred to as **instrumentality**. (An instrumentality is also referred to as a *performance-to-outcome expectancy* because it relates to the outcome people expect from performing in a certain way.) When people engage in a particular behavior, they do so with the intention of achieving a desired outcome or reward. Instrumentalities range from 0 to 1.0, where 0 is no chance of receiving the desired reward, and 1.0 is a belief that the reward is certain to follow. For example, an hourly worker might say, "I know for sure that if I work overtime, I will receive overtime pay."

Expectancy. The probability assigned by the individual that effort will lead to correct performance of the task is referred to is **expectancy**. (The same concept is also referred to as *effort-to-performance expectancy*.) An important question people ask themselves before putting forth effort to accomplish a task is, "If I put in all this work, will I really get the job done properly?" Expectancies range from 0 to 1.0, where 0 is no expectation of performing the tasks correctly, and 1.0 signifies absolute faith in being able to perform the task properly. Expectancies thus influence whether a person will even strive to earn a reward. Self-confident people have higher expectancies than do less self-confident people. Being well trained increases a person's subjective hunch that he or she can perform the task.

A seeming contradiction in expectancy theory requires explanation. Some people will engage in behaviors with low expectancies, such as trying to invent a successful new product or become the CEO of a major corporation. The compensating factor is the large valences attached to the second-level outcomes associated with these accomplishments. The payoffs from introducing a successful new product or becoming a CEO are so great that people are willing to take a long shot.

The performance aspect of expectancy is a first-level outcome. It is rooted in the job itself. If people work hard, they expect to accomplish such outcomes as producing goods, supplying a service, or achieving quality standards. Instrumentality, on the other hand, deals with second-level outcomes—the rewards associated with performing. Instrumentality can also be regarded as a hunch that a first-level outcome will lead to a second-level outcome. For example, you might have a strong belief that if you produce high-quality work, you will receive recognition from the organization.

A Brief Look at the Evidence.   The application of expectancy theory, especially the VIE version, to work motivation has been the subject of research for over thirty years. Two researchers recently performed a meta-analysis of seventy-seven studies of how well various aspects of expectancy theory were related to workplace criteria such as performance and effort. Although the results were not consistent, the general conclusion reached was that the three components of expectancy theory are positively related to workplace criteria. For example, job performance showed a positive correlation with valence, instrumentality, expectancy, and the total VIE model. The total VIE model typically refers to a multiplication of the values for valence, instrumentality, and expectancy. Another finding was that effort expended on the job was positively correlated with valence, instrumentality, expectancy, the VIE model, and performance.[3] The last correlation helps verify the justification for leaders and managers being concerned about motivating employees: People who try harder perform better!

Despite the utility of expectancy theory, leaders need to supplement it with other approaches to understanding motivation. Two very applied explanations of motivation, behavior modification and goal theory, are presented later.

Leadership Skills and Behaviors Associated with Expectancy Theory

Expectancy theory has many implications for leaders and managers with respect to motivating others.[4] Some of these implications would also stem from other motivational theories, and they fit good management practice in general. As you read each implication, reflect on how you might apply the skill or behavior during a leadership assignment.

1. *Determine what levels and kinds of performance are needed to achieve organizational goals.* Motivating others proceeds best when workers have a clear understanding of what needs to be accomplished. At the same time, the leader should make sure that the desired levels of performance are possible. For example, sales quotas might be set too high because the market is already saturated with a particular product or service.

2. *Make the performance level attainable by the individuals being motivated.* If the group members believe that they are being asked to perform extraordinarily difficult tasks, most of them will suffer from low motivation. A task must generally be perceived as attainable to be motivational.

3. *Train and encourage people.* Leaders should give group members the necessary training and encouragement to be confident they can perform the required task. (We will return to the encouragement aspect of leadership in the discussion of coaching.) Some group members who appear to be poorly motivated simply lack the right skills and self-confidence.

4. *Make explicit the link between rewards and performance.* Group members should be reassured that if they perform the job up to standard, they will receive the promised reward.

5. *Make sure the rewards are large enough.* Some rewards fail to motivate people because although they are the right kind, they are not in the right amount. The promise of a large salary increase might be motivational, but a 1 percent increase will probably have little motivational thrust for most workers.

6. *Analyze what factors work in opposition to the effectiveness of the reward.* Conflicts between the leader's package of rewards and other influences in the work group may require the leader to modify the reward. For example, if the work group favors the status quo, a large reward may be required to encourage innovative thinking.

7. *Explain the meaning and implications of second-level outcomes.* It is helpful for employees to understand the value of certain outcomes, such as receiving a favorable performance appraisal. (For example, it could lead to a salary increase, assignment to a high-status task force, or promotion.)

8. *Understand individual differences in valences.* To motivate group members effectively, leaders must recognize individual differences or preferences for rewards. An attempt should be made to offer workers rewards to which they attach a high valence. One employee might value a high-adventure assignment; another might attach a high valence to a routine, tranquil assignment. Cross-cultural differences in valences may also occur. For example, many (but not all) Asian workers prefer not to be singled out for recognition in front of the group. According to their cultural values, receiving recognition in front of the group is insensitive and embarrassing. Leadership Skill-Building Exercise 10–1 on page 250 deals further with the challenge of estimating valences.

9. *Use the Pygmalion effect to increase expectancies.* By communicating confidence that group members can perform at a high level, they will gradually raise their levels of expectation. (As described in Chapter 4, this phenomenon is called the Pygmalion effect.) As the levels of expectation increase, so will performance. The high expectations thus become a self-fulfilling prophecy.

10. *Ensure that the system is equitable for everyone.* Workers who achieve the same level of performance should receive comparable rewards. Similarly, workers who fail to attain certain levels of performance should receive comparable punishment.

GOAL-SETTING THEORY

Goal setting is a basic process that is directly or indirectly part of all major theories of work motivation. Goal setting is accepted widely by leaders and managers as a means to improve and sustain performance. A vision, for example, is really an exalted goal. The core finding of goal-setting theory is that individuals who are provided with specific hard goals perform better than those who are given easy, nonspecific, "do your best" goals or no goals. At the same time, however, the individuals must have sufficient ability, accept the goals, and receive feedback related to the task.[5] Our overview of goal-setting theory elaborates on this basic finding.

LEADERSHIP SKILL-BUILDING EXERCISE 10–1 Estimating Valences for Applying Expectancy Theory

Directions: A major challenge in applying expectancy theory is estimating what valence attaches to possible outcomes. A leader or manager also has to be aware of the potential rewards or punishment in a given work situation. Listed below are a group of rewards and punishments, along with a space for rating the reward or punishment on a scale of –100 to +100. Work with about six teammates, with each person rating all the rewards and punishments.

Potential Outcome	**Rating** **(–100 to +100)**
1. Promotion to vice president	____
2. One-step promotion	____
3. Above-average performance rating	____
4. Top-category performance rating	____
5. $5,000 performance bonus	____

6. $1,000 performance bonus   ____

7. $50 gift certificate   ____

8. Employee-of-the-month plaque   ____

9. Note of appreciation placed in file   ____

10. Luncheon with boss at good restaurant   ____

11. Lunch with boss in company cafeteria   ____

12. Challenging new assignment   ____

13. Allowed to do more of preferred task   ____

14. Allowed to purchase software of choice   ____

15. Assigned new equipment for own use   ____

16. Private corner office with great view   ____

17. Assigned a full-time administrative assistant ____

18. Documentation of poor performance   ____

19. Being fired   ____

20. Being fired and put on industry "bad-list"   ____

21. Demoted one step   ____

22. Demoted to entry-level position   ____

23. Being ridiculed in front of others   ____

24. Being suspended without pay   ____

25. Being transferred to undesirable location   ____

After completing the ratings, discuss the following issues:

1. Which rewards and punishments received the most varied ratings?

2. Which rewards and punishments received similar ratings?

Another analytical approach would be to compute the means and standard deviations of the valences for each outcome. Each class member could then compare his or her own valence ratings with the class norm. To add to the database, each student might bring back two sets of ratings from employed people outside of class.

To apply this technique to the job, modify the above form to fit the outcomes available in your situation. Explain to team members that you are attempting to do a better job of rewarding and disciplining, and that you need their input. The ratings made by team members might provide fruitful discussion for a staff meeting.

The premise underlying goal-setting theory is that behavior is regulated by values and goals. A **goal** is what a person is trying to accomplish. Our values create within us a desire to behave in a way that is consistent with them. For example, if a leader values honesty, she will establish a goal of hiring only honest employees. The leader would therefore have to make extensive use of reference checks and honesty testing. Edwin A. Locke and Gary P. Latham have incorporated hundreds of studies about goals into a theory of goal setting and task performance.[6] Figure 10–2 summarizes some of the more consistent findings, and the information that follows describes them. A leader should keep these points in mind when motivating people through goal setting.

To begin, remember that *specific goals lead to higher performance than do generalized goals.* Telling someone to "do your best" is a generalized goal. A specific goal would be, "Increase the number of new hires to our management training program to fifteen for this summer." Another key point is that *performance generally improves in direct proportion to goal difficulty.* The harder one's goal, the more one accomplishes. An important exception is that when goals are too difficult, they may lower performance. Difficulty in reaching the goal leads to frustration, which in turn leads to lowered performance (as explained in relation to expectancy theory).

For goals to improve performance, the group member must accept them. If a group member rejects a goal, he or she will not incorporate it into planning. This is why it is often helpful to discuss goals with group members, rather than imposing the goals on them. Participating in goal setting has no major effect on the level of job performance except when it improves goal acceptance. Yet the leader should recognize that participation is valuable because it can lead to higher satisfaction with the goal-setting process. *Goals are more effective when they are used to evaluate performance.* When workers know that their performance will be evaluated in terms of how well they attain their goals, the impact of goals increases.

Keep in mind the key principle that *goals should be linked to feedback and rewards.* Rewarding people for reaching goals is the most widely accepted principle of management. A final goal-setting principle here is that *group*

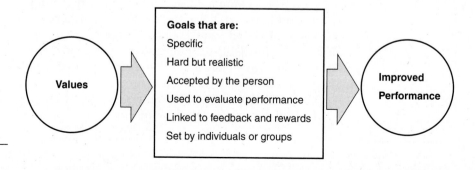

FIGURE 10–2
Goal-Setting Theory

Values

Goals that are:

Specific

Hard but realistic

Accepted by the person

Used to evaluate performance

Linked to feedback and rewards

Set by individuals or groups

Improved
Performance

goal setting is as important as individual goal setting. Having employees work as teams with a specific team goal, rather than as individuals with only individual goals, increases productivity. Furthermore, a combination of compatible group and individual goals is more effective than either individual or group goals alone.

Despite their contribution to performance, goals are not, technically speaking, motivational in themselves. Rather, the discrepancies created by what individuals do and what they aspire to creates self-dissatisfaction. This dissatisfaction, in turn, creates a desire to reduce the discrepancy between the real and the ideal.[7] When a person has a desire to attain something, the person is in a state of arousal. The tension created by not having already achieved a goal spurs the person to reach the goal. As a leader, you can sometimes create this tension by suggesting possibilities that group members might strive for.

The accompanying Leader in Action insert describes a leader who makes active use of a motivation theory familiar to every reader, Maslow's need hierarchy. Without realizing it specifically, the leader also makes use of some aspects of expectancy theory, goal-setting theory, and behavior modification.

Goal setting is widely practiced by leaders and managers, but they typically do not give careful consideration to goal-setting theory. Leadership Skill-Building Exercise 10–2 gives you an opportunity to apply what you have learned about goal setting.

LEADER IN ACTION

Joe Raymond of Transworld Home Healthcare

"I relate everything back to Maslow's theory," says Joseph J. Raymond, a Red Bank, New Jersey, entrepreneur who founded Transworld Home Healthcare Inc., now a company with $70 million in annual sales. Employee placement is one area in which Raymond applies the need hierarchy. Raymond routinely puts new employees into key positions on the basis of an extensive posthiring interview in which he asks questions about the kind of house and neighborhood they live in. He also makes inquiries about their tastes in movies, food, recreation, and reading.

Workers are often confused and uneasy about the unusual questions, Raymond admits. Yet he asks them anyway because he believes it is important to know where each person is on the need hierarchy. "One you get a good inkling as to where they're at, you try to apply the Maslow theory to motivate them," Raymond explains.

He typically finds his management-level hires to be somewhere between the social or belonging need level and the esteem level, which relates to the need to achieve and gain recognition. For those people, money is frequently less important as a motivator than symbols of status or membership. "The yuppies are in that category," says Raymond. "That's why they want to have the keys to the executive washroom, the window office, or the country club membership."

Source: Adapted from Mark Henricks, "Motivating Force: What Motivates Your Employees? Find Out—and Unlock New Doors for Your Business," *Entrepreneur*, December 1995, pp. 68–71.

LEADERSHIP SKILL-BUILDING
EXERCISE 10–2 **The Application of Goal-Setting Theory**

Working in a group of about five to six people, visualize your group as a task force whose mission is to make and implement suggestions for reducing water consumption in your company, a manufacturer of camping equipment. Water is a major company expense, and there is a distinct possibility that the county in which you are located will soon be rationing water. One of the group members plays the role of the task force leader. The leader must help the group establish goals that are likely to be motivational, following the principles of goal-setting theory. The goal of today's meeting is to establish four goals that are likely to lead to high performance. After each team has established its goals, present them to other class members. Students listening to the goals of the other groups should be willing to offer whatever constructive feedback comes to mind.

BEHAVIOR MODIFICATION AND MOTIVATIONAL SKILLS

Behavior modification, a well-known system of motivation, is an attempt to change behavior by manipulating rewards and punishment. Behavior modification stems directly from reinforcement theory. Since many readers are already familiar with reinforcement theory and behavior modification (often shortened to "behavior mod"), we will limit our discussion to a brief summary of the basics of behavior modification, and focus instead on its leadership applications.

An underlying principle of behavior modification is the law of effect: Behavior that leads to a positive consequence for the individual tends to be repeated. In contrast, behavior that leads to a negative consequence tends not to be repeated. Leaders typically emphasize linking behavior with positive consequences, such as expressing enthusiasm for a job well done.

Behavior Modification Strategies

The techniques of behavior modification apply to both learning and motivation; they can be divided into four strategies. *Positive reinforcement*, which rewards the right response, increases the probability that the behavior will be repeated. The phrase *increases the probability* means that positive reinforcement improves learning and motivation but is not 100 percent effective. The phrase *the right response* is also noteworthy. When positive reinforcement is used properly, a reward is contingent upon the person doing something right. If the company achieves a high-quality award, the company president might recognize the accomplishment through a bonus to all. Authorizing a bonus for no particular reason might be pleasant, but it is not positive reinforcement.

Avoidance motivation (or *negative reinforcement*) is rewarding people by taking away an uncomfortable consequence of their behavior. It is the withdrawal or avoidance of a disliked consequence. A leader offers avoidance motivation when he or she says, "We have performed so well that the wage freeze will now be lifted." Removal of the undesirable consequence of a wage freeze was contingent upon performance above expectation. Be careful not to confuse negative reinforcement with punishment. Negative reinforcement is the opposite of punishment: It involves rewarding someone by removing a punishment or an uncomfortable situation.

Punishment is the presentation of an undesirable consequence, or the removal of a desirable consequence, because of unacceptable behavior. A leader or manager can punish a group member by demoting him or her for an ethical violation such as lying to a customer. Or the group member can be punished by losing the opportunity to attend an executive development program.

Extinction is decreasing the frequency of undesirable behavior by removing the desirable consequence of such behavior. Company leaders might use extinction by ceasing to pay employees for making frivolous cost-saving suggestions. Extinction is sometimes used to eliminate annoying behavior. Assume that a group member persists in telling ethnic jokes. The leader and the rest of the group can agree to ignore the jokes and thus extinguish the joke telling.

Rules for the Use of Behavior Modification

Behavior modification in organizations, often called OB Mod, frequently takes the form of a companywide program administered by the human resources department.[8] Our focus here is on leaders' day-by-day application of behavior mod, with an emphasis on positive reinforcement. The coaching role of a leader exemplifies the application of positive reinforcement. Although using rewards and punishments to motivate people seems straightforward, behavior modification requires a systematic approach. The rules presented here are specified from the standpoint of a leader or manager trying to motivate an individual or a group.[9]

Rule 1: Target the desired behavior. An effective program of behavior modification begins with specifying the desired behavior—that which will be rewarded. The target or critical behaviors chosen are those that have a significant impact on performance, such as asking to take an order, conducting performance appraisals on time, or troubleshooting a customer problem. According to Fred Luthans, the critical behaviors are the 5 to 10 percent of behaviors that may account for as much as 70 or 80 percent of the performance in the area in question.[10]

Rule 2: Choose an appropriate reward or punishment. An appropriate reward or punishment is one that is (1) effective in motivating a given group member or group and (2) feasible from the company standpoint. If one reward does not work, try another. Feasible rewards include money, recognition, challenging new assignments, and status symbols such as a private work area. When positive motivators do not work, it may be necessary to use negative motivators (punishment).

It is generally best to use the mildest form of punishment that will motivate the person or group. For example, if a group member reads a newspaper during the day, the person might simply be told to put away the newspaper. Motivation enters the picture because the time not spent on reading the newspaper can now be invested in company work. If the mildest form of punishment does not work, a more severe negative motivator is selected. Written documentation placed in the person's personnel file is a more severe form of punishment than a mere mention of the problem.

Rule 3: Supply ample feedback. Behavior modification cannot work without frequent feedback to individuals and groups. Feedback can take the form of simply telling people when they have done something right or wrong. Brief paper or electronic messages are another form of feedback. Be aware, however, that many employees resent seeing a message with negative feedback flashed across their video display terminals.

Rule 4: Do not give everyone the same size reward. Average performance is encouraged when all forms of accomplishment receive the same reward. Say one group member makes substantial progress in providing input for a strategic plan. He or she should receive more recognition (or other reward) than a group member who makes only a minor contribution to solving the problem.

Rule 5: Find some constructive behavior to reinforce. This rule stems from **behavior shaping,** rewarding any response in the right direction and then rewarding only the closest approximation. Using this approach, the desired behavior is finally attained. Behavior shaping is useful to the manager because the technique recognizes that you have to begin somewhere in teaching a worker a new skill or motivating a worker to make a big change. For example, if you were attempting to motivate a group member to make exciting computer graphics (such as Powerpoint), you would congratulate the first step forward from preparing a mundane overhead transparency. You would then become more selective about what type of presentation received a reward.

Rule 6: Schedule rewards intermittently. Rewards for good performance should not be given on every occasion. *Intermittent* rewards sustain desired behavior longer, and also slow the process of behavior fading away when it is not rewarded. If a person is rewarded for every instance of good performance, he or she is likely to keep up the level of performance until the reward comes, then slack off. Another problem is that a reward that is given continuously may lose its impact. A practical value of intermittent reinforcement is that it saves time. Few leaders have enough time to dispense rewards for every good deed forthcoming from team members.

Rule 7: Rewards and punishments should follow the behavior closely in time. For maximum effectiveness, people should be rewarded shortly after doing something right, and punished shortly after doing something wrong. A built-in feedback system, such as a computer program working or not working, capitalizes on this principle. Many effective leaders get in touch with people quickly to congratulate them on outstanding accomplishment.

Rule 8: Change the reward periodically. Rewards do not retain their effectiveness indefinitely. Team members lose interest in striving for a reward they have received many times in the past. This is particularly true of a repetitive statement such as "Nice job" or "Congratulations." Plaques for outstanding performance also lose their motivational appeal after a group receives many of them. It is helpful for the leader or manager to formulate a list of feasible rewards and try different ones from time to time.

The accompanying Leader in Action vignette (page 258) illustrates the successful application of positive reinforcement to achieve an important organizational outcome. As you read the case history, attempt to identify the principles and rules of behavior modification being applied.

COACHING AS A LEADERSHIP PHILOSOPHY

As mentioned at the outset of this chapter, effective leaders who deal directly with people are good coaches. The coaching demands are much less rigorous for leaders who have little face-to-face contact with organization members. Among such leaders would be financial dealmakers, chairpersons of the board, and high-ranking government officials. The chairperson of the board is not expected to coach the board members, and the president of the United States does not coach cabinet members.

The quality of the relationship between the coach and the person coached distinguishes coaching from other forms of leader-member interactions. The person being coached trusts the leader's judgment and experience and will listen to advice and suggestions. Similarly, the coach believes in the capacity of the group member to learn and profit from his or her advice. The coach is a trusted superior, and the person being coached is a trusted subordinate. Several of the points made here about coaching as a philosophy of management present more details about the quality of the relationship between the coach and the team member.

As noted by Florence M. Stone and Randi T. Sachs, a major purpose of coaching is to achieve enthusiasm and high performance in a team setting. One mechanism for achieving this end is for the manager, acting as a coach, to provide praise and positive feedback to team members. Another coaching responsibility is to make sure that responsibilities are clear. Team members need to know why the task should be accomplished, when it must be completed, how the completed work will be measured, and how the task contributes to the team's mission. Another relevant coaching approach here is for the leader to demonstrate respect for the knowledge, skills, and abilities that team members bring to the effort. Empowering team members is an effective vehicle for demonstrating such respect.[11]

LEADER IN ACTION

Martin Edelson of Boardroom Reinforces I-Power

Most business leaders do not think of dollar bills as motivators for sparking creativity among group members. But Martin Edelson, the president of Boardroom Inc., a publishing company based in Greenwich, Connecticut, discovered that basic rewards can get ideas flowing. He calls his approach "I-Power," short for Ideas Power, a management technique designed to bring continuous improvement to organizations. With this technique, employees are asked to come up with at least two ideas a week for improving their own work or the company's performance.

Edelson started I-Power six years ago as a way of making Boardroom meetings more productive. Today the system is being used by hundreds of companies looking to increase productivity, improve performance, or elevate morale. The idea for I-Power came out of a meeting with Peter Drucker, the long-time management guru. Drucker once asked Edelson, "How are the meetings at your company?" Edelson replied that his meetings were bad, but so were those at most companies. Drucker suggested that Edelson have everyone who came to a meeting be prepared to give two ideas for making his or her own work or the department's work more productive.

Edelson started the program at Boardroom by handing out dollar bills and candy bars for good ideas. The rewards now range from $5 or $10 for a single idea to $50 for the most good ideas in a month. The best idea each month, selected by a committee of three managers, earns the winner two tickets to a show or concert. If an idea is a big money saver, the submitter also receives a special cash award. "There is this fantastic drive within individuals to show they are individuals and that they can think of ideas, and there's virtually nothing in society that recognizes that," said Edelson (Associated Press story).

The program has generated thousands of ideas at all levels of the company. At one time a worker suggested that the company could reduce costs by finding a way to produce books that weighed less than four pounds. Boardroom accomplished the feat, and started out by saving half a million dollars a year in postage. All the company had to do was make its books one-eighth of an inch shorter.

Edelson said that when he began the I-Power meetings, he expected the employees to be wary of the idea. So he showed up at the meetings with a stack of dollar bills and a bag of candy to hand out. He brought along a big gong and a huge hunter's horn to salute ideas as they surfaced. One strike of the gong was for a $1 idea, and two strikes for a $2 idea. Weak ideas received a honk of the hunter's horn, yet they were rewarded with candy. The honking didn't work because it raised negative feelings. Edelson now uses the gong and the horn interchangeably, and awards at least $1 for each idea. He believes that even a $1 payout helps to create a bright, positive atmosphere.

Edelson explains that an essential part of the program is feedback and reward. Everyone who submits an idea gets a response. Team members who submit ideas that are not acted on immediately receive handwritten notes of thanks for making a contribution. Some action is taken on every feasible idea.

Source: "Small Rewards Can Make Companies More Productive: I-Power New Technique to Get Employees Involved," Associated Press story, January 22, 1996; "Come to Each Meeting with Three Ideas," http://newciv.org/GIB/BI/BI-67.html (December 15, 1996).

A description of coaching offered by Tom Peters and Nancy Austin provides a good starting point for framing coaching as a leadership philosophy. As they see it, to coach is to facilitate accomplishment, in the sense of being less discouraging and removing excessive controls and complications.

Coaching is a way of enabling others to act, and to build on their strengths. To coach is to care enough about people to invest time in building personal relationships with them.[12]

Roger D. Evered and James C. Selman regard coaching as a paradigm shift from traditional management, which focuses heavily on control, order, and compliance. Coaching, in contrast, focuses on uncovering actions that enable people to contribute more fully and productively. Furthermore, people feel less alienated than when working under the control model.[13] Coaching is also seen as a partnership for achieving results. At the same time, it represents a commitment to collaborating in accomplishing new possibilities rather than holding on to old structures. Figure 10–3 depicts coaching as a philosophy of management.

When coaching is elevated to a philosophy of leadership, it becomes more complex than a handy technique leaders and managers use to rev up and

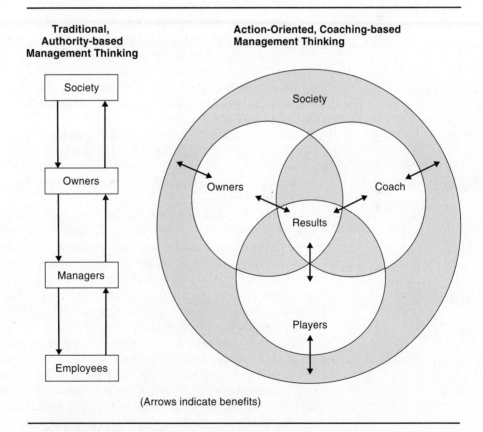

FIGURE 10–3

Coaching Versus the Traditional Way of Thinking about Management

Source: Reprinted, by permission of the publisher, from Organizational Dynamics, *Autumn 1989, © 1989, American Management Association, New York. All rights reserved.*

sustain performance. Evered and Selman have observed a number of characteristics of coaching that contribute to its close relationships with leadership.[14]

Coaching is a comprehensive and distinctive way of being linked to
others in the organization. The type of relationship inherent in coaching
facilitates the accomplishments of coaching. Mentoring is one example
of this unique relationship. Protégés are inspired to greater achievement
partially because of the quality of their relationship with their mentors.
More will be said about mentoring in Chapter 15, which covers leadership
development.

Coaching in the workplace might ordinarily be explained as the "art of
management." Because of the uniqueness of a coaching relationship, the person being coached is better motivated to accomplish goals for the good of
the organization. Unfortunately, in most firms coaching is not ordinarily
understood as a way of working and relating. As a result, most management
development programs do not give enough attention to developing the
skills and qualities of effective coaching.

Coaching is often overlooked as a result of a cultural blind spot that
emphasizes control and order rather than the development of people. A
good leader/coach is more concerned about developing team members than
about controlling their behavior. Recognize also that coaching is a two-way
process, suggesting that to be a great coach, one needs formidable team
members. The people coached must also be good listeners, open to suggestions, and eager to develop.

Coaching produces results only through the process of communication.
The actions of coaches are found in the messages they send, both verbally
and nonverbally, and in their listening and noticing. During the game on the
athletic field or in the workplace, coaches influence action by how they listen and what they say.

Coaching is a dyad—that is, like leader/group member, or director/actor,
it cannot exist without at least two participants. The interaction of the two
personalities influences the coaching outcome. Some leaders, for example,
can successfully coach certain people but not others. An executive vice president of finance was highly regarded as a good coach. Yet a newly appointed
special assistant asked to be transferred after she worked for him for several
months. The explanation she offered was, "My working relationship with
Marty (the executive vice president) is just flat."

Coaching requires a high degree of interpersonal risk and trust on the
part of both people in the relationship. The coach might give the person
being coached wrong advice. Or the person being coached might reject the
coach's encouragement. Think of the risk involved when a basketball player
asks the coach for advice on how to correct a shot that is not working well.
As a result of the coaching, the player might shoot more poorly, to the
embarrassment of both. Similarly, an organizational leader might coach a
team member in a direction that backfires—for example, by resulting in even
fewer sales than before.

An important advantage of coaching is that it generates new possibilities for action and facilitates breakthroughs in performance. A vice president might say to a lower-ranking manager, "Had you thought of getting your people more involved in setting objectives? If you did, you might find greater commitment and follow-through." The middle manager begins to involve managers more in setting objectives, and performance does increase. Coaching has achieved substantial results.

Coaching requires the transformation of traditional models of management, organization, work, and society. A coaching philosophy calls for a more dynamic organization based to a large extent on relationship, commitment, purpose, and results. In contrast, the very traditional organization is based more on role, hierarchical position, and authority.

Despite all the exalted statements made about coaching as a philosophy of leadership, it is still useful to specify a few concrete contributions of coaching. One advantage is higher motivation. An effective coach keeps up the spirit and administers praise and recognition frequently. Good coaching also leads to personal development. Group members are encouraged to cross-train and serve as backups for each other. Good coaching also improves group performance. The effective coach makes team members aware of one another's skills and how these skills can contribute to attaining the group's goals.[15]

COACHING SKILLS AND TECHNIQUES

Leaders and managers have varied aptitudes for coaching. One way to acquire coaching skill is to study basic principles and suggestions, and then practice them. Another way is to attend a training program for coaching that involves modeling (learning by imitation) and role playing. Here we examine a number of suggestions for coaching. If implemented with skill, the suggestions will improve the chances that coaching will lead to improved performance.

1. *Communicate clear expectations to group members.* For people to perform well and to continue to learn and grow, they need a clear perception of what is expected of them. The expectations of a position become the standards by which performance will be judged, thus serving as a base point for coaching. If a team member is supposed to contribute three new ideas for improvement of operations per month, coaching is justified when an average of only one idea per month is forthcoming. It is not unusual for group members and managers to have only 50 percent overlap in their perceptions of the group member's job responsibilities.[16]

2. *Provide specific feedback.* To coach a group member toward higher levels of performance, the leader pinpoints what specific behavior, attitude, or skill requires improvement. A good coach might say, "I read the

product-line expansion proposal you submitted. It's okay, but it falls short of your usual level of creativity. Each product you mentioned is already being carried by competitors. Have you thought about. . . ."

3. *Listen actively.* Listening is an essential ingredient in any coaching session. An active listener tries to grasp both facts and feelings. Observing the group member's nonverbal communication is another part of active listening. The leader must also be patient and not poised for a rebuttal of any difference of opinion between him or her and the group member.

Part of being a good listener is encouraging the person being coached to talk about his or her performance. Asking open-ended questions facilitates a flow of conversation. For example, ask: "How did you feel about the way you handled conflict with the marketing group yesterday?" A close-ended question covering the same issue would be "Do you think you could have done a better job of handling conflict with the marketing group yesterday?"

4. *Help remove obstacles.* To perform at anywhere near top capacity, individuals may need help in removing obstacles such as a maze of rules and regulations and rigid budgeting. An important role for the leader of an organizational unit is thus to be a "barrier buster." A leader-manager is often in a better position than a group member to gain approval from a higher-level manager, find money from another budget line, expedite a purchase order, or authorize hiring a temporary worker to provide assistance. Yet William D. Hitt cautions that deciding when to intervene requires considerable judgment on the manager's part. His advice to managers is: "Don't take your people's 'monkeys' when the monkeys should clearly rest with them."[17]

5. *Give emotional support.* By being helpful and constructive, the leader provides much-needed emotional support to the group member who is not performing at his or her best. A coaching session should not be an interrogation. An effective way of giving emotional support is to use positive rather than negative motivators. For example, the leader might say, "I liked some things you did yesterday, yet I have a few suggestions that might bring you closer to peak performance." The accompanying Leader-in-Action box (page 263) describes a leader who emphasizes emotional support and a coaching philosophy.

6. *Reflect feelings.* The counseling professional is adept at reflecting feelings. To reflect feelings is to give a person immediate feedback on the feelings and emotions that he or she is expressing. Some reflection of feelings is recommended in a job situation. Too much reflection, however, is inappropriate because the work situation may begin to feel like a continuous counseling session. Reflection-of-feeling responses typically begins with "You feel. . . ." For example, assume that a group member says to the leader, "The workload is too much for me. I can't cope!" The manager then responds, "You feel overwhelmed right now."

LEADER IN ACTION

Sam Rivera of Fel-Pro Inc.

Fel-Pro Inc., of Skokie, Illinois, is an international automotive parts manufacturer with about $450 million in annual sales and 3,000 employees globally. A pillar of its company philosophy is a belief in the growth and development of its people. The company is at the forefront of employee-friendly programs, one of which is an on-site career development center. The center is part of Fel-Pro's attempt to form partnerships with employees rather than having a paternalistic relationship with them. Outside consultants at the center provide career counseling to help workers assess their capabilities and make sound career choices from among their options. Employees at every level are using the center. An example of how the career center benefits employees is a clerical employee who wanted to become an administrative assistant and was coached in how to make the transition.

Many managers throughout the company contribute to the supportive organizational culture of Fel-Pro. One of them is Sam Rivera, a long-time company employee. He made up his mind early that he was going to become a manager who cared about people. For Rivera, caring about people meant such things as giving production worker Edwin Carrera three days of emergency leave so he and his son could meet with Fel-Pro's on-site psychologist. The production worker needed help in removing his son from Chicago's Latino gang culture.

Caring about people also meant finding another job for Pedro Hernandez, who wasn't able to operate a forklift truck, the job he was hired for. Sensing that the 45-year-old Hernandez would have a difficult time finding employment elsewhere, Rivera found him an assignment as a punch-press operator. Hernandez is now one of Fel-Pro's best punch-press operators.

Rivera attempts to place himself in the employee's shoes. He also gives workers ample flexibility and discretion. "As long as the job gets done, that's the bottom line," he says. According to Rivera and Fel-Pro top management, Rivera's unit exceeds objectives 95 percent of the time. Company management believes that Rivera's leadership style motivates workers to extend themselves. Carrera was so grateful that Rivera gave him time to help his son that he found a way to repay the company. In his spare time he developed a way to increase machine productivity and safety that the company found valuable enough to implement.

Rivera says that his leadership philosophy stems from his poor childhood in Puerto Rico. "I know what people have to do to survive," he says. Rivera's manager, Ricky Justus, believes that if Rivera has a limitation, it is that he hates to turn down special requests and to discipline people. Rivera agrees, but adds: "I'd rather be soft than hard, because hard people are hated and can't accomplish anything."

Source: Based on facts as reported in Ann Therese Palmer, "An Easygoing Boss—And a Master Motivator," *Business Week*, June 28, 1993, p. 84; "Chicago Company Does It Right with Career Counseling," Knight-Ridder News Service story, December 2, 1996.

Here is another example of reflection of feelings: An inventory-control analyst is asked why a report was late. She answers, "Those clods in manufacturing held me up again." The manager responds, "You are angry with manufacturing?" The inventory-control analyst, now feeling encouraged, might vent her anger about manufacturing. The manager's reflection of feelings communicates the fact that he or she understands the real problem. Because the analyst felt understood, she *might* be better motivated to improve.

7. *Reflect content or meaning.* Reflecting feelings deals with a person's emotions. Reflecting content or meaning deals with the person's intellectual or cognitive behavior. An effective way of reflecting meaning is to rephrase and summarize concisely what the group member is saying. A substandard performer might say, "The reason I've fallen so far behind is that our company has turned into a bureaucratic nightmare. We're being hit right and left with forms to fill out for quality improvement. My computer has twenty-five messages waiting to be read." You might respond, "You're falling so far behind because you have so many forms and messages that require attention." The group member might then respond with something like, "That's exactly what I mean. I'm glad you understand my problem."

8. *Give some constructive advice.* Too much advice-giving interferes with two-way communication, yet some advice can elevate performance. The manager should assist the group member in answering the question, "What can I do about this problem?"[18] Advice in the form of a question or suppositional statement is often effective. One example is, "Could the root of your problem be insufficient planning?" A direct statement—such as "The root of your problem is obviously insufficient planning"—often makes people resentful and defensive. By responding to a question, the person being coached is likely to feel more involved in making improvements.

9. *Allow for modeling of desired performance and behavior.* An effective coaching technique is to show the group member by example what constitutes the desired behavior. Assume that a manager has been making statements to customers that stretch the truth, such as falsely saying that the product met a zero-defects standard. In coaching him, the manager's boss might allow the manager to observe how she handles a similar situation with a customer. The manager's boss might telephone a customer and say, "You have been inquiring about whether we have adopted a zero-defects standard for our laser printers. Right now we are doing our best to produce error-free products. Yet, so far we do not have a formal zero-defects program. We stand by our printers and will fix any defect at no cost to you."

10. *Gain a commitment to change.* Unless the leader receives a commitment from the team member to carry through with the proposed solution to a problem, the team member may not attain higher performance. An experienced manager/coach develops an intuitive feel for when employees are serious about performance improvement. Two clues that commitment to change is lacking are (1) overagreeing about the need for change, and (2) agreeing to change without display of emotion.

Leadership Self-Assessment Exercise 10–1 will help you think through the development you might need to be an effective coach.

LEADERSHIP SELF-ASSESSMENT
EXERCISE 10–1 Characteristics of an Effective Coach

Directions: Below is a list of traits, attitudes, and behaviors characteristic of effective coaches. Indicate next to each trait, attitude, or behavior whether you need to develop along those lines (for example, whether you need to become more patient). Also, design an action plan for improvement for each trait, attitude, or behavior that you need to develop. An example of an action plan for improving patience might be, "I'll ask people to tell me when I appear too impatient. I'll also try to develop self-control about my impatience."

Trait, Attitude, or Behavior	Action Plan for Development
1. Empathy (putting self in other person's shoes)	_____
2. Listening skill	_____
3. Insight into people	_____
4. Diplomacy and tact	_____
5. Patience toward people	_____
6. Concern for welfare of people	_____
7. Low hostility toward people	_____
8. Self-confidence and emotional security	_____
9. Noncompetitiveness with group members	_____
10. Enthusiasm for people	_____
11. Take great satisfaction in helping others grow	_____
12. View development of group members as a major job function	_____
13. Have high expectations for each group member	_____
14. Give authentic feedback	_____
15. View people in terms of their potential	_____

Source: Items 1–10 adapted with permission from Andrew J. DuBrin, *Participant Guide to Module 10: Development of Subordinates*, p. 11. Copyright © 1985. Used by permission of Leadership Systems Corporation. Items 11–15 gathered from information in William D. Hitt, *The Leader-Manager: Guidelines for Action* (Columbus, Ohio: Battelle Press, 1988) pp. 183–186.

COACHING PEOPLE THROUGH DIFFICULT TIMES

The focus of our discussion about coaching has been helping adequate performers elevate their performance levels. Another important leadership responsibility is coaching group members who are going through difficult times. Marilyn J. Darling suggests that it is more constructive to view troubled work associates as people going through difficult times, rather than as difficult people.[19] An example of a worker going through difficult times would be a normally cheerful and productive group member who now appears sullen and whose productivity dips below standard. The suggestions for coaching already presented increase in importance when you are working with team members who are experiencing personal difficulty because a person in trouble needs more emotional support and skillful leadership. Although the leader-manager should not attempt to play the role of a mental health counselor, four aspects of the coaching relationship can help a group member through troubled times: validation, inquiry, possibility, and responsibility.

The coach must *validate* the individual by showing respect. A starting point in showing respect is willingness to invest time in helping the person rather than simply writing him or her off as a marginal performer. Another part of validation is a willingness to listen to the person's slant on the problem, such as an explanation for a temporary dip in productivity. *Inquiry* is essential because effective coaching is based on asking good questions to help understand the nature of the problem. Simple questions are the most effective:

- What are you trying to accomplish?
- How will you know if you have succeeded?
- What obstacles are you facing?
- How can I as your manager help you succeed?

The spirit of inquiry helps foster an environment that respects each person's experience and also conveys a helping attitude. *Possibility* refers to believing that the individual has the potential to improve, in contrast to labeling the person a poor performer with no prospects of improving. The person who is labeled a poor performer is too often excluded from assignments that will reestablish his or her reputation for good performance. *Responsibility* refers to working with the troubled individual to find a creative solution to the problem. Both the leader and the team member must take responsibility for dealing with the problem. Suppose a group member is experiencing such overwhelming financial problems that he is having difficulty concentrating on work. The coach and the group member might hold a joint problem-solving session to pinpoint sources of help with the problem.

Table 10–1 summarizes information about a coaching attitude that will help troubled individuals. Remember, however, that the leader as manager

TABLE 10–1   An Effective Coaching Attitude for Workers in Trouble

	If I Disrespect You	*If I Respect You*
Validation	I give orders without explanation.	I take time to set a context for our work.
Inquiry	I construct elaborate theories to explain your behavior.	I ask questions to understand you.
Possibility	I focus on short-term expectations.	I keep a long-term perspective.
Responsibility	I see "you" versus "me."	I become your committed partner.

From Marilyn J. Darling, "Coaching People Through Difficult Times," *HRMagazine*, November 1994, p. 73. Reprinted with the permission of *HRMagazine*, published by the Society for Human Resource Management, Alexandria, Va.

is still responsible for maintaining high standards of performance. If coaching, along with referral for professional assistance such as that offered by an Employee Assistance Program, does not facilitate performance improvement, it will be necessary for the manager to begin a formal discipline process.[20] In short, if coaching and leadership is not successful, more traditional bureaucratic procedures should be implemented.

SUMMARY

Effective leaders are outstanding motivators and coaches, and the role of the modern leader and manager emphasizes coaching. The expectancy theory of motivation is useful for developing motivational skills because it is comprehensive, building on other explanations of motivation.

Expectancy theory has three major components: valence, instrumentality, and expectancy. Valence is the worth or attractiveness of an outcome. Each work situation has multiple outcomes, and each outcome has a valence of its own. Valences range from –100 to +100 in the version of expectancy theory presented here. Zero valences reflect indifference and therefore are not motivational. Very high valences help explain why some people will persist in efforts despite a low probability of payoff. Instrumentality is the probability assigned by the individual that performance will lead to certain outcomes. (An outcome is anything that might stem from performance, such as a reward.) Performance is a first-level outcome because it is rooted in the job itself. Instrumentalities deal with second-level outcomes—the rewards associated with performing. Expectancy is the probability assigned by the individual that effort will lead to performing the task correctly.

Expectancy theory has implications and provides guidelines for leaders, including the following: (1) determine necessary performance levels; (2) make the performance level attainable; (3) train and encourage people; (4) make explicit the link between rewards and performance; (5) make sure the rewards are large enough; (6) analyze factors that oppose the effectiveness of the reward; (7) explain the meaning and implications of second-level outcomes; (8) understand individual differences in valences; (9) use the Pygmalion effect to increase expectancies; and (10) ensure that the system is equitable for everyone.

Goal setting is a basic process that is directly or indirectly part of all major theories of motivation. Goal-setting theory includes the following ideas: Specific and difficult goals result in high performance; goals must be accepted by group members; goals are more effective when they are linked to feedback and rewards; and the combination of individual and group goals is very effective. Behavior modification is a widely used motivational strategy. Its key principle is the law of effect: Behavior that leads to a positive effect tends to be repeated, and the opposite is also true. The basic behavior modification strategies are positive reinforcement, avoidance motivation, punishment, and extinction.

Rules for the effective use of behavior modification include the following: (1) target the desired behavior; (2) choose an appropriate reward or punishment; (3) supply ample feedback; (4) do not give everyone the same size reward; (5) find some constructive behavior to reinforce; (6) schedule rewards intermittently; (7) give rewards and punishments soon after the behavior; and (8) change the reward periodically.

A major purpose of coaching is to achieve enthusiasm and high performance in a team setting. Coaching can also be regarded as a paradigm shift from traditional management, which focuses heavily on control, order, and compliance. Coaching is a partnership for achieving results. Several characteristics of coaching contribute to its close relationship with leadership. Coaching is a comprehensive and distinctive way of being linked to others in the organization. Coaching is also a two-way process, suggesting that being a great coach requires having a talented team. Coaching requires a high degree of interpersonal risk and trust on the part of both people in the relationship. Also, coaching requires the transformation of traditional models of management, organization, work, and society.

Suggestions for improving coaching are as follows: (1) communicate clear expectations to group members; (2) provide specific feedback; (3) listen actively; (4) help remove obstacles; (5) give emotional support; (6) reflect feelings; (7) reflect content or meaning; (8) give some constructive advice; (9) allow for modeling of desired performance and behavior; and (10) gain a commitment to change.

Another important leadership responsibility is coaching group members who are going through difficult times. The coaching skills and techniques already mentioned are critically important. In addition, the leader should validate the individual by showing respect, and inquire to better understand the problem. The leader should also think in terms of the person's possibilities for the future, and share responsibility for a solution to the problem.

KEY TERMS

Expectancy theory	Instrumentality	Behavior modification
Valence	Expectancy	Behavior shaping
Outcome	Goal	

GUIDELINES FOR ACTION AND SKILL DEVELOPMENT

We have seen many suggestions for incorporating coaching into leadership. Gerald M. Sturman recommends that a leader should also engage in career coaching with team members. If executed properly, career coaching benefits the group member, the manager, and the organization. Career management, in Sturman's view, is the process by which individuals take responsibility for developing their ability to expand their contribution to the organization. The following five-point guide, AIM . . . CM, suggests that a career coach should aim employees at career management.

1. **Assess.** Encourage group members to assess their strengths and weaknesses, and provide feedback of your own. Suggest that group members also obtain feedback from others.

2. **Investigate.** Has the group member investigated all the needs and opportunities his or her organizational unit and the total organization have to offer?

3. **Match.** Group members should match their preferences and self-assessments with the organizational opportunities available.

4. **Choose.** Upon careful examination of the match between, on the one hand, capabilities and preferences and, on the other hand, opportunities, have group members chosen feasible targets?

5. **Manage.** Encourage group members to formulate a career development plan that can lead to the achievement of their goals.[21]

DISCUSSION QUESTIONS AND ACTIVITIES

1. Based on your own experiences, how important do you think coaching is for effective management and leadership?

2. Several companies have contemplated calling managers "coaches," or have actually done so. Do you think the change in job title is advisable? Explain.

3. Identify several outcomes you expect from occupying a leadership position. What valences do you attach to them?

4. In what way could a leader use the instrument presented in Leadership Skill-Building Exercise 10–1 to help motivate group members?

5. How can the influence exerted by a charismatic leader tie in with expectancy theory?

6. Explain how valence, instrumentality, and expectancy could relate to job performance.

7. What is a potential second-level outcome a person could gain from receiving an A grade in the course for which you are reading this text? From receiving an F grade?

8. What does goal-setting theory tell managers that they probably don't already know about using goals to motivate people?

9. Many big-name athletic coaches are hired by business organizations to give motivational speeches. Do you think athletic coaches are qualified to advise business leaders about motivation?

10. Ask a manager to describe the amount of coaching he or she does on the job. Be prepared to bring your findings back to class.

LEADERSHIP CASE PROBLEM

The Financial Services Coach

Jennifer Falcone is an account representative (stockbroker) at a branch office of an established financial services firm. Her manager, Derek Anderson, is concerned that Jennifer is 25 percent below quota in sales of a new index mutual fund offered by the company. Derek sets up an appointment with Jennifer to spur her to achieve quota. The conversation proceeds, in part, in this manner:

ANDERSON: My most important responsibility is to help team members work up to their potential. I wanted to get together with you today to see if there is any way I can help you.

During the last quarter you were 25 percent below quota in your sales of our new index fund. That displeases me and top management because our margin of profit on this fund is very high.

FALCONE: I know I'm under quota. But I can't help it. It's just tough pushing an index fund these days. Our clients are getting very conservative, and they don't want to jump into a new product they don't understand.

ANDERSON: Why don't your clients understand the new index fund?

FALCONE: It's a new fund, so they don't understand it. The information I send them is pretty complicated for a layperson.

ANDERSON: What steps could you take to make this fund easier for our clients and prospects to understand?

FALCONE: Maybe I could work up a thirty-second presentation that would give a nice overview of an index fund. This would enable me to make a quick pitch over the phone.

ANDERSON: Now you're making good sense. But I'm disappointed that an intelligent person like you didn't think of that before. Do you have a self-confidence problem when it comes to making quota on a new product?

FALCONE: I never thought I had a self-confidence problem until today's session with you.

ANDERSON: Whether or not you have a self-confidence problem, you can earn a lot more commissions by selling more of the new index fund.

FALCONE: Most people would have a self-confidence problem if they were going through what I am these days. It's not that easy concentrating on my work.

ANDERSON: I don't like to hear excuses, but I'll make an exception this time. What are you going through that makes it difficult to concentrate on your work, Jennifer?

FALCONE: My sister and I are pretty close, and she's in big trouble. I mean big trouble. She was down on her luck, so she started dealing in drugs. I warned her. My folks warned her, but she wouldn't listen. She got busted recently, and faces a ten-year prison term.

ANDERSON: Sorry to hear about your sister. But why feel so down? You weren't involved in her drug dealing, were you?

FALCONE: What's really dragging me down is that my sister used to tell me that I was her model. Her ideal. Some ideal. Her life is ruined.

ANDERSON: Now I understand why you are so down. However, let's meet again real soon to talk about your job performance.

1. Identify the strengths in Anderson's coaching technique.

2. Identify the areas for improvement in Anderson's coaching technique.

3. In what way does Anderson's motivational technique correspond to the effective use of expectancy theory?

Using the case you just analyzed as background material, do Leadership Skill-Building Exercise 10–3.

LEADERSHIP SKILL-BUILDING EXERCISE 10–3

The Financial Services Coach Role Play

Three months later, Derek Anderson calls Jennifer Falcone into his office to discuss her progress in selling the new index fund. Jennifer is now within 2 percent of making quota, and Derek wants to motivate her to surpass quota. One person plays the role of Derek, the other Jennifer. Derek is confident Jennifer can do even better, but Jennifer feels that Derek is unappreciative of the substantial progress she has made.

Before assuming the role of Jennifer, imagine how you would feel if you thought your immediate superior was unappreciative of your progress. Assert your feelings in your discussion with Derek. Before assuming the role of Derek, review the suggestions in this chapter about motivating and coaching skills.

Class members not participating in the role play observe the action, and then provide constructive feedback—in their best coaching style!

Creative Problem Solving and Leadership

*F*riends and coworkers were astonished when 30-year-old Jeff Bezos, a senior vice president at a thriving Wall Street fund, left his high-paying position. The geometric growth of Internet usage had prompted Bezos to think that his future would somehow be linked to the World Wide Web. In 1994, he composed a list of twenty products that were ideally suited to marketing online. After a year of research, Bezos concluded that selling books was an excellent choice. He reasoned that there are 1.3 million books in print, and the largest book-selling chain has only a 12 percent share of a market with $25 billion in annual sales. As a result, he established Amazon.com Inc., which through 1996 was experiencing a sales growth of 34 percent each month. Bezos reasoned that the world's largest bookstore has only 175,000 titles on the shelves, whereas Amazon.com offers 1.1 million. Furthermore, he thinks that no metropolitan area could support a bookstore of this magnitude.

To begin his business, Bezos and his wife headed to Seattle because of its high concentration of technical talent and excellent living conditions. Working from a rented home, Bezos and his first four employees set up shop in a garage, writing software to make the book-selling service possible. He knew he had to offer services that distinguished his company from other large booksellers. Bezos recognized that offering cappuccino and pastry over the Net was impossible, but that shopping at Amazon.com could still be fun. His slant was to give browsers a chance to write down what they thought about a particular book, and also to encourage authors and publishers to discuss their books on site. Another unique feature is a personal notification service called Eyes & Editors. It enables book lovers to fill out an electronic form stating their interests, and then be informed by E-mail when a new publication of that nature arrives.

People visiting www.amazon.com can search the extensive catalog by title, author, or subject key word. Customers get most books within five days after placing an order, although rare books take longer. Gift wrapping is available, and payment is by credit card. Web site visitors can browse through bestsellers and other books selected by staff members of Amazon.com. When an order is received, an employee notifies the right publisher or distributor, who then ships the book to Amazon's Seattle warehouse. Next comes shipment to the online customer. Time-pressed consumers enjoy the ease of ordering books. Another service offered by the company is to affiliate with other Web sites that might want to offer books on their specialty, such as white-water rafting. Amazon.com provides the shipping and order fulfillment, and the affiliated Web site receives a commission of 3 to 8 percent of revenues. With Bezos as CEO, the company has grown to 110 employees. A company outsider estimates that Amazon.com had gross sales of $10 million in its first year.[1]

The novel business formed by Jeff Bezos illustrates an important link between creativity and leadership. By thinking creatively, a person can form a new enterprise that can keep many engaged in productive activity. The role of a creative leader is to bring into existence ideas and things that did not exist previously or that existed in a different form. Leaders are not bound by current solutions to problems. Instead, they create images of other possibilities. For example, a leader might move a firm into an additional business or start a new department that offers another service.

This chapter emphasizes creativity development for the leader. It also explains the nature of creativity and creative people and examines the leader's role in establishing an atmosphere conducive to creativity among group members.

STEPS IN THE CREATIVE PROCESS

An important part of becoming more creative involves understanding the stages involved in **creativity,** which is generally defined as the production of novel and useful ideas. An attempt has been made to understand creativity more specifically as it pertains to the workplace. As defined by Richard

Woodman, John Sawyer, and Ricky Griffin, **organizational creativity** is the "creation of a valuable, useful new product, service, idea, procedure, or process by individuals working together in a complex social system."[2]

An old but well-accepted model of creativity can be applied to organizations. This model divides creative thinking into five stages,[3] as shown in Figure 11–1. Step 1 is *opportunity or problem recognition:* A person discovers that a new opportunity exists or a problem needs resolution. Thirty-five years ago an entrepreneurial leader, Robert Cowan, recognized a new opportunity and asked, "Why do business meetings have to be conducted in person? Why can't they connect through television images?"[4]

Step 2 is *immersion.* The individual concentrates on the problem and becomes immersed in it. He or she will recall and collect information that seems relevant, dreaming up alternatives without refining or evaluating them. Cowan grabbed every fact he could about teleconferencing. At one point he helped NASA and the University of Alaska produce the first videoconference by satellite. Cowan synthesized all his information into a book about teleconferencing.

Step 3 is *incubation.* The person keeps the assembled information in mind for a while. He or she does not appear to be working on the problem actively; however, the subconscious mind is still engaged. While the information is simmering, it is being arranged into meaningful new patterns. Cowan did not actively pursue his business videoconferencing idea for several years.

Step 4 is *insight.* The problem-conquering solution flashes into the person's mind at an unexpected time, such as on the verge of sleep, during a shower, or while running. Insight is also called the *Aha! experience:* All of a sudden something clicks. At one point Cowan suddenly thought of forming a teleconferencing business to exploit the potential of his idea.

Step 5 is *verification and application.* The individual sets out to prove that the creative solution has merit. Verification procedures include gathering supporting evidence, logical persuasion, and experimenting with new ideas. Application requires tenacity because most novel ideas are first rejected as being impractical. When banks refused to finance Cowan's start-up business, Cowan and his wife raised $45,000 from friends and obtained a second mort-

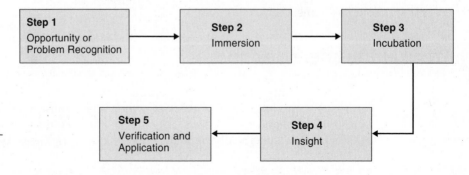

FIGURE 11–1

Steps in the Creative Process

gage on their house. Cowan did start his business, but he faced financial trouble. With his company on the verge of folding, Charles Schwab, the brokerage firm, hired Cowan's company to connect its 100 branch offices.

Note that the end product of Cowan's creative thinking was a business possibility rather than an invention. Nevertheless, businesspeople typically follow the same five steps of creative thought that inventors do. Even though creativity usually follows the same steps, it is not a mechanical process that can be turned on and off. Much of creativity is intricately woven into a person's intellect and personality. Furthermore, creativity varies among individuals, and creative people themselves have peaks and valleys in their creativity.[5]

CHARACTERISTICS OF CREATIVE LEADERS

Creative leaders, like creative workers of all types, are different in many ways from their less creative counterparts. As stated by Robert Kreitner and Angelo Kinicki, creative people often march to the beat of a different drummer.[6] They are devoted to their fields and enjoy intellectual stimulation. Creative leaders challenge the status quo, which leads them to seek improvements. The creative leader often observes, "There must be a better way." (Robert Cowan, for example, thought there must be a better way of conducting meetings that would not require many people to travel to a distant location.) Above all, creative people are mentally flexible, which allows them to overcome the traditional way of looking at problems.

The characteristics of creative people, including creative leaders, can be grouped into four areas: knowledge, intellectual abilities, personality, and social habits and upbringing.[7] These characteristics are described below and highlighted in Figure 11–2. Before studying this list, compare your thinking to that of creative people by doing the self-assessment exercise on page 277.

Knowledge

Creative problem solving requires a broad background of information, including facts and observations. Knowledge provides building blocks for generating and combining ideas. Davis Gilbert founded Electronic Recovery Systems, a company that has found its fortune in other people's discards. The Chicago-based company purchases discarded computers and breaks them down for the gold and other precious metals they contain. The company recovers the gold-bearing bits and pieces and then sells them to metal refiners. "We're kind of like the miner who takes out the ore," said Gilbert. "It's not cost-effective to refine a whole mountain, so they get out the ore to reduce the amount they have to refine. We're doing the same thing. We're basically 21st century gold miners."[8] To found this thriving company, Gilbert had to combine two basic ideas: one, that computers contain precious

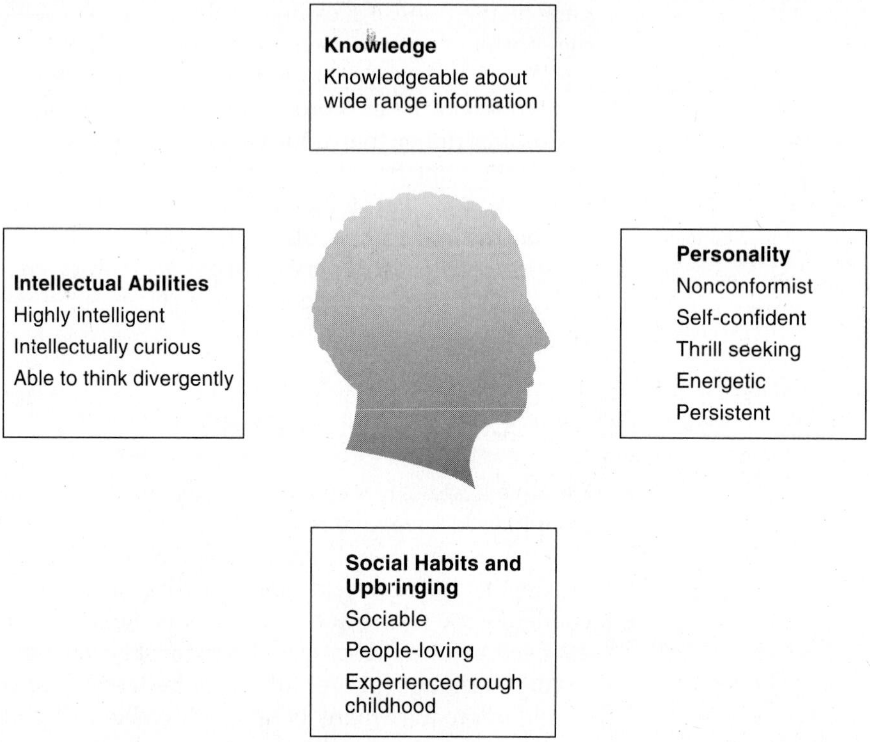

Knowledge
Knowledgeable about
wide range information

Intellectual Abilities
Highly intelligent
Intellectually curious
Able to think divergently

Personality
Nonconformist
Self-confident
Thrill seeking
Energetic
Persistent

**Social Habits and
Upbringing**
Sociable
People-loving
Experienced rough
childhood

FIGURE 11–2

**Characteristics of
Creative Leaders**

metals, and two, that mining for ore is the process that yields these precious metals. A less creative person might perceive obsolete and broken computers as worthless junk that will only clog landfills. What creative ideas do you have for salvaging old computers?

Intellectual Abilities

Intellectual abilities comprise such abilities as general intelligence and abstract reasoning. Creative problem solvers, particularly in business, tend to be bright, but not at the absolute top end of the brilliance scale. Extraordinarily high intelligence is not required in order to be creative, yet creative people are facile at generating creative solutions to problems in a short period of time. A paradox, however, is that one sometimes has to be highly intelligent to be hired for a position requiring creative work. Microsoft Corp., for example, hires only people whom the hiring manager evaluates as being outstandingly intelligent. The company uses standard measures of intelligence such as mental ability tests, grades in school, and past accomplishments. In addition, the company has developed its own set of interview questions that its managers think measure intelligence. In defense of

LEADERSHIP SELF-ASSESSMENT
EXERCISE 11–1 The Creative Personality Test

Directions: Describe each of the following statements as "mostly true" or "mostly false."

	Mostly True	Mostly False
1. It is generally a waste of time to read articles and books outside my immediate field of interest.	____	____
2. I frequently have the urge to suggest ways of improving products and services I use.	____	____
3. Reading fiction and visiting art museums are time wasters.	____	____
4. I am a person of very strong convictions. What is right is right; what is wrong is wrong.	____	____
5. I enjoy it when my boss hands me vague instructions.	____	____
6. Making order out of chaos is actually fun.	____	____
7. Only under extraordinary circumstances would I deviate from my To Do list (or other ways in which I plan my day).	____	____
8. Taking a different route to work is fun, even if it takes longer.	____	____
9. Rules and regulations should not be taken too seriously. Most rules can be broken under unusual circumstances.	____	____
10. Playing with a new idea is fun even if it doesn't benefit me in the end.	____	____
11. Some of my best ideas have come from building on the ideas of others.	____	____
12. In writing, I try to avoid the use of unusual words and word combinations.	____	____
13. I frequently jot down improvements in the job I would like to make in the future.	____	____

14. I prefer to avoid high-technology devices as much as possible.   ____ ____

15. I prefer writing personal notes or poems to loved ones rather than relying on greeting cards.   ____ ____

16. At one time or another in my life I have enjoyed doing puzzles.   ____ ____

17. If your thinking is clear, you will find the one best solution to a problem.   ____ ____

18. It is best to interact with coworkers who think much like you.   ____ ____

19. Detective work would have some appeal to me.   ____ ____

20. Tight controls over people and money are necessary to run a successful organization.   ____ ____

Scoring and interpretation: Give yourself a +1 for each answer in the creative direction for each statement, indicated as follows:

1. Mostly false	8. Mostly true	15. Mostly true
2. Mostly true	9. Mostly true	16. Mostly true
3. Mostly false	10. Mostly true	17. Mostly false
4. Mostly false	11. Mostly true	18. Mostly false
5. Mostly true	12. Mostly false	19. Mostly true
6. Mostly true	13. Mostly true	20. Mostly false
7. Mostly false	14. Mostly false	Total ____

Extremely high or low scores are the most meaningful. A score of 15 or more suggests that your personality and attitudes are similar to those of creative people, including creative leaders. A score of 8 or less suggests that you are more of an intellectual conformist at present. Don't be discouraged. Most people can develop in the direction of becoming more creative.

How does your score compare to your self-evaluation of your creativity? We suggest you also obtain feedback on your creativity from somebody familiar with your thinking and your work.

Microsoft's screening procedures, the ability to creatively develop software is closely associated with high raw intelligence.[9]

Creative people also maintain a youthful curiosity throughout their lives, and the curiosity is not centered just on their own field of expertise. Instead, their range of interests encompasses many areas of knowledge, and they are enthusiastic about puzzling problems. Creative people are also open and responsive to others' feelings and emotions.

Creative people show an identifiable intellectual style, being able to think divergently. They are able to expand the number of alternatives to a problem, thus moving away from a single solution. Yet the creative thinker also knows when it is time to narrow the number of useful solutions. For example, the divergent thinker might think of twenty-seven ways to reduce costs. Yet at some point he or she will have to move toward choosing the best of several cost-cutting approaches.

Personality

The emotional and other nonintellectual aspects of a person heavily influence creative problem solving. Creative people tend to have a positive self-image without being blindly self-confident. Because they are self-confident, creative people are able to cope with criticism of their ideas. They can tolerate the isolation necessary for developing ideas. Talking to others is a good source of ideas, yet at some point the creative problem solver has to work alone and concentrate.

Creative people are frequently nonconformists and do not need strong approval from the group. Many creative problem-solvers are thrill seekers, who find that developing imaginative solutions to problems is a source of thrills. Creative people are also persistent, which is especially important for the verification and application stage of creative thinking. Selling a creative idea to the right people requires considerable follow-up. Finally, creative people enjoy dealing with ambiguity and chaos. Less creative people become quickly frustrated when task descriptions are unclear and disorder exists.

Teresa M. Amabile studied research and development (R&D) scientists to obtain their view concerning the personality requirements for creativity. These scientists consistently identified the traits of persistence, curiosity, energy, and intellectual honesty as being important for creativity.[10] A number of other studies have shown that highly creative people tend to have an internal locus of control.[11] When creative people are faced with a difficult problem, they are likely to believe that they have the internal resources to find a creative solution.

Social Habits and Upbringing

Contrary to the stereotype, most creative people are not introverted loners or nerds. Many, especially those who become leaders, enjoy interacting with people and exchanging ideas. The majority of creative adults lacked a smooth and predictable environment during childhood. Family upheavals caused by financial problems, family feuds, and divorce are common occurrences. During their childhood, many people who became creative adults sought escape from family turmoil by pursuing ideas.

To fully understand the contribution of personal characteristics to creativity, we should return to the basic formula of human behavior presented in Chapter 1: $B = f (P \times E)$. In this context, certain personal characteristics may facilitate a leader's being creative, but the right environment is necessary to trigger creative behavior. Greg R. Oldham and Anne Cummings conducted a study with 171 employees from two manufacturing facilities. Creativity was measured by patent disclosures, contributions to an employee suggestion program, and supervisory ratings. It was found that the participants who produced the most creative work had creativity-relevant characteristics such as self-confidence and tolerance of ambiguity. It was also important, however, for employees to work on complex, challenging jobs, and to be supervised in a supportive, noncontrolling fashion.[12] The combination of the right personal characteristics with the right environmental conditions yielded the most creative output.

OVERCOMING TRADITIONAL THINKING AS A CREATIVITY STRATEGY

A unifying theme runs through all forms of creativity training and suggestions for creativity improvement: Creative problem solving requires an ability to overcome traditional thinking. The concept of *traditional thinking* is relative, but it generally refers to a standard and frequent way of finding a solution to a problem. A traditional solution to a problem is thus a modal or most frequent solution. For example, traditional thinking suggests that to increase revenue, a retail store should conduct a sale. Creative thinking would point toward other solutions. Borders Book Stores, a chain of upscale bookstores, increased revenues substantially by starting to offer audiotapes and CDs, and by opening cafés in the stores.

The creative person looks at problems in a new light and transcends conventional thinking about them. For many years, banks were unable to solve the problem of how to decrease the cost of customer withdrawals. They already knew how to decrease the cost of customer deposits: Night deposit devices enabled customers to deposit cash into a safe. Customers gained access with a key and deposited money into a mailbox-style drop. An inventor from outside the banking industry asked the right question: "Why not find a way to allow customers to deposit and withdraw money automatically?" This seminal thought led to the invention of the automatic teller machine (ATM).

The central task in becoming creative is to break down rigid thinking that blocks new ideas.[13] A conventional-thinking leader might accept the long-standing policy that spending more than $5,000 requires three levels of approval. A creative leader might ask, "Why do we need three levels of approval for spending $5,000? If we trust people enough to make them managers, why can't they have budget authorization to spend at least $10,000?"

Overcoming traditional thinking is so important to creative thinking that the process has been characterized in several different ways. Listed next are six concepts of creative thinking. These concepts have much in common and can be considered variations of the same theme. Distinguishing among them is not nearly as important as recognizing that they all carry the same message: Creative thinking requires nontraditional thinking.

1. *A creative person thinks outside the box.* A *box* in this sense is a category that confines and restricts thinking. Many executives have saved millions of company dollars by thinking outside the box—for example, abandoning the notion that headquarters must be located in a major city. Leadership Skill-Building Exercise 11–1 offers you an opportunity to "think outside the box."

2. *People who are not creative suffer from "hardening of the categories."* A noncreative person thinks categorically: "Only men can climb telephone poles"; "Only women can work in child care centers as caregivers."

3. *To be creative, one must develop new paradigms.* A paradigm is a model or framework. An example of a quality-inhibiting paradigm is that suppliers should be treated shabbily because they need the company more than the company needs them. In reality, creative companies form partnerships of mutual respect with suppliers. Developing a new paradigm can also benefit an organization by giving a business a new twist, thus

---

LEADERSHIP SKILL-BUILDING
EXERCISE 11–1 Thinking Outside the Box

Directions: Many people suffer from *functional fixedness*, in the sense that they can think of only one (or a fixed) function for an object, such as using a frying pan only for cooking. Visualize a table with three objects on top: a crayon, a box containing six thumbtacks, and a book of matches. Your problem is to explain how a candle can be mounted on the wall behind the table.

If you, or you and your team members, can think of a way to mount the candle on the wall, you are skillful at thinking outside the box, or overcoming functional fixedness. The solution to the problem appears on page 425.

For additional practice in overcoming functional fixedness, think of ten uses for a safety pin, a razor blade, a brick, and a wine bottle.

leading to a new source of revenues. The accompanying Leader in Action insert (page 283) describes a paradigm shift by a financial leader.

4. *Creativity requires overcoming traditional mental sets.* A **traditional mental set** is a conventional way of looking at things and placing them in familiar categories. One traditional mental set is that the only way for people to obtain the death benefit on their life insurance policy is to die. Several years ago an investor initiated the concept of *viatical settlement,* in which a person with a terminal illness sells his or her policy to an investor for about 80 percent of the policy value. When the person dies, the investor receives the death benefit from the insurance company. The sooner the person dies, the better the return on the investment (for the person who buys the policy from the ailing or aging person). Viatical settlements grew out of the AIDS epidemic, as many young people with no dependents and meager savings were faced with overwhelming medical bills. Today the concept has been extended to cancer patients and nursing home residents who prefer to cash in life insurance policies rather than cash in other assets. In the present form of viatical settlements, sellers and buyers are matched by a "living benefits" broker.[14]

5. *Creative people overcome traditional wisdom.* Traditional mental sets can also be regarded as conventional wisdom. Robert Cowan overcame the conventional wisdom that small businesses would never be interested in conducting conferences by video. An unusually productive example of overcoming traditional wisdom took place in the cellular telephone industry. For years the cellular phone companies had been in conflict with communities about the installation of the towers required for cellular phone connections. The conventional wisdom is that such towers interfere with the ambiance or architectural motif of a community. Somebody thought of the creative compromise of disguising cellular towers in structures wanted by a community. One such installation is a cellular tower hidden in the tower lights above Fenway Park in Boston. With even greater heights of creativity, Bell Atlantic agreed to build a replica of the damaged 1859 steeple of the United Methodist Church in the scenic town of Ipswich, Massachusetts, in exchange for hiding a cellular tower inside.[15] The willingness of cellular telephone companies to construct towers that blend in with the community architecture has substantially reduced conflict between the two parties.

6. *Creative people engage in lateral thinking in addition to vertical thinking.* **Vertical thinking** is an analytical, logical, process that results in few answers. The vertical, or critical, thinker is looking for the one best solution to a problem, much like solving an equation. In contrast, **lateral thinking** spreads out to find many different solutions to a problem. The vertical-thinking leader attempts to find the best possible return on investment in financial terms only. The lateral-, or creative, thinking leader might say, "A financial return on investment is desirable. But let's not restrict our thinking. Customer loyalty, quality, being a good

LEADER IN ACTION

Gary Wilson, Co-chairman of Northwest Airlines

Gary Wilson, now co-chairman and a major shareholder of Northwest Airlines, is considered a superstar among financial executives. He was a pacesetter in reformulating the job of the chief financial officer during the mid-1970s at Marriott Corporation. While at Marriott, he was the model of the CFO as an inventive manager and a creative and charismatic dealmaker who could find hidden value in a business firm. By formulating a new role, Wilson helped increase the CFO's contribution to an organization. At Marriott, he trained some of the most creative financial minds.

Wilson has always enjoyed glamour. His career climb began when he won a football scholarship to Duke University. He now lives in a palatial estate once owned by the daughter of movie mogul Louis B. Mayer. His neighbors include Barbra Streisand and Lillian Disney, the widow of Walt Disney. He dresses impeccably and has an impressive physical appearance.

During his days at Marriott, Wilson offered a continuous supply of unconventional ideas. He encouraged his team to look at problems in an unorthodox way. He says proudly, "I'll listen to any idea, no matter how nuts." While at the hotel chain, he developed financial strategies that created huge shareholder value. When Wilson was hired in 1974, Marriott was a small company that owned and operated hotels. The hotel business was highly profitable, but Marriott was experiencing slow growth because the company could not build hotels fast enough. Wilson then asked why a hotel chain could expand only by owning hotels that it had built.

As Wilson framed the problem, Marriott suffered from a shortage of capital. So he developed a plan to expand by using other people's money. To ensure consistent quality, Marriott kept building the hotels. Instead of owning them, however, it sold the properties to insurance companies, partnerships, and savings and loan associations. The company then signed contracts to operate the hotels it had sold. In line with Wilson's predictions, the management business showed explosive growth. By the early 1980s Marriott was building about $1 billion worth of hotels and other properties each year. In 1996, as Host Marriott Corporation, the company is still expanding and in sound financial health. It recently raised $550 million in convertible preferred securities to help continue its program of acquiring upscale and luxury full-service hotels.

Many major financial business deals today are derived from Wilson's approach of separating capital-intensive assets from highly profitable services (or separating ownership from operations).

Source: "The Big Daddy of CFOs," *Fortune*, November 13, 1995; "Host Marriott Corporation Raises $550 Million in Convertible Preferred Offering," www.hotel-online.com/Neo/News/1996, December 4, 1996.

corporate citizen, and job satisfaction are also important returns on investment."

Creativity expert Edward De Bono believes that creativity results from lateral thinking.[16] Lateral thinking will often proceed in illogical directions to apply new perceptions, insights, and points of entry to solve problems of extraordinary difficulty—such as how to build cellular telephone towers that don't irk community groups. To clarify the concept of lateral thinking further, see Figure 11–3, which presents more details about the difference between vertical and lateral thinking.

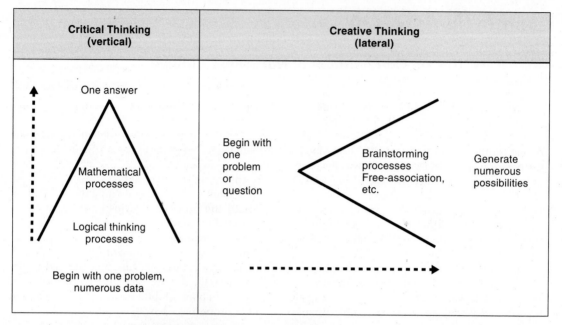

FIGURE 11–3

Vertical and Lateral Thinking

Source: From Robert E. Quinn, Sue R. Faerman, Michael P. Thompson, and Michael R. McGrath, Becoming a Master Manager: A Competency Framework. *Copyright © 1990. Reprinted by permission of John Wiley & Sons, Inc.*

ORGANIZATIONAL METHODS TO ENHANCE CREATIVITY

To enhance creative problem solving, the majority of organizations regularly engage in brainstorming. Many others also maintain suggestion programs to solicit creative ideas from employees. In recent years the size of the awards has decreased, yet some workers still receive cash awards for creative ideas approved by the suggestion committee. Many companies now believe that making creative suggestions is a regular part of a team member's position.[17] Here we focus on new developments in brainstorming and other creativity-enhancing methods. Programs of this nature are applied to actual problems, while at the same time they provide an opportunity to improve creative thinking.

The leader has a dual role in implementing creative problem-solving techniques: He or she facilitates group interaction and also provides a fair share of creative output. The six creativity-enhancing, problem-solving techniques described here are establishing idea quotas, brainstorming, the pet-peeve technique, the forced-association technique, the excursion method, and building a kitchen for the mind.

Establishing Idea Quotas

As with I-Power, described in Chapter 10, the leader can enhance creativity by simply establishing idea quotas. Although the vast majority of these ideas may not be capable of implementation, a few good ones will emerge. Thomas Edison, the man whose name is almost synonymous with creativity, set idea quotas for his workers. He established a personal quota of a minor invention every ten days and a major one every six months, which helped him achieve 1,093 patents during his career.[18] One reason idea quotas work is that they are a goal. Another is that an environmental need (in this case, the idea quota) is an excellent creativity stimulant. As we all know, "Necessity is the mother of invention."

Brainstorming

The best-known method for creativity improvement is brainstorming, which most of you have already done at some point. As a refresher, do Leadership Skill-Building Exercise 11–2 on page 286, which presents rules and guidelines for brainstorming.

A key aspect of brainstorming is that all ideas can be steppingstones and triggers for new and more useful ideas. Any idea might lead to other associations and connections. Thus, during the idea-generating part of brainstorming, potential solutions are not criticized or evaluated in any way, so that spontaneity is encouraged. The idea for an antitheft device for automobiles, The Club, is reported to have stemmed from brainstorming. One marketing person suggested that cars should have a portable steering wheel that the driver could remove after the car is parked. Somebody else suggested that the steering wheel be made inoperative, which led to the idea of an ultrastrong bar to lock the steering wheel in place. The Club, and its imitators, have become highly successful products; a version of The Club has been developed for securing doors.

Brainstorming continues to evolve as a method of creative problem solving. Two recent variations are the *6-3-5 method* and *visual brainstorming.* In the 6-3-5 method, six people take five minutes to write down three ideas each on a sheet of paper or large index card. After five minutes, the participants pass their papers or cards clockwise and add their own ideas to the new sheet. Continue the passing along and writing down of ideas until the sheets or cards get back to the people who originated them. Next, hold a group discussion of the merits of the various ideas.[19] During the discussion, it is likely that some members will modify their ideas or think of new ones because they will be stimulated by the list of eighteen ideas. Often, however, the list will contain many duplicate or similar ideas.

Visual brainstorming combines idea generation and drawing. Each member of a small group is assigned a concept quota and given a sketch pad. Participants are asked to draw their ideas as they emerge. The drawing technique will be favored by people who are more visual than verbal. Drawing

LEADERSHIP SKILL-BUILDING *EXERCISE 11–2* Brainstorming

Directions: First study the rules for brainstorming to refresh your memory. Then do the brainstorming exercise.

1. The ideal group size is five to seven people.

2. The expression of ideas should be spontaneous. All suggestions are welcome, even if they seem outlandish or outrageous.

3. Quantity and variety are important. The greater the number of ideas, the greater the likelihood of a breakthrough idea.

4. Group members should encourage combination and improvement of ideas. This process is called piggybacking or hitchhiking.

5. One person serves as the secretary and records ideas, writing them on a chalkboard or flipchart, or inputting them into a computer.

6. In many instances, a moderator can help keep the session on track by preventing one or two members from dominating the session. If the moderator takes notes, a secretary is not needed.

7. The session should not be overstructured; rules should not be followed too rigidly. Brainstorming is a spontaneous process.

Organize into groups to brainstorm one of the following problems:

1. How can a leader get more respect from group members?

2. How can a leader cut costs yet still maintain a productive and satisfied group?

3. For what useful purposes can a leader apply brainstorming?

is also useful because it helps participants defer judgment until their ideas are fully developed. In one application of the technique, tourists who ignored the speed limit were creating safety problems for a small town in the Florida Keys. Adding more patrol cars was one possible solution, but the municipality lacked the funds. Via visual brainstorming, the town's police chief arrived at a creative alternative solution. He drew a two-dimensional patrol car and installed it under a street light on the shoulder of the highway into town. The police chief achieved outstanding results. In addition to tourists slowing down their vehicles, the number of speeding violations by townspeople also plummeted.[20]

The Pet-Peeve Technique

An important part of quality leadership is for organizational units to find ways to continuously improve their service to external and internal customers. The **pet-peeve technique** is a method of brainstorming in which a group identifies all the possible complaints others might have about the group's organizational unit.[21] Through brainstorming, group members develop a list of complaints from any people who interact with their group. Sources of complaints include inside customers, outside customers, competitors, and suppliers.

Group members can prepare for the meeting by soliciting feedback on themselves from the various target groups. In keeping with the informal, breezy style of the pet-peeve group, feedback should be gathered informally. Rather than approaching target groups with a survey, members might tell others about the upcoming pet-peeve session, and then ask, "What complaints can you contribute?"

During the no-holds-barred brainstorming session, group members throw in some imaginary and some humorous complaints. Humorous complaints are especially important, for humor requires creative thinking. After all complaints have been aired, the group can process the information during a later session, at which they can draw up action plans to remedy the most serious problems.

A pet-peeve session in the human resources department of a small electronic appliance company generated the following complaints:

"A lot of people wonder what we are doing. They think we just fill out forms and create work for ourselves."

"Some line managers think our job is to find good reasons why they shouldn't hire their best job candidates."

"A lot of employees think we're the corporate ax carriers. We tell line management who to fire and whose job to eliminate."

"They call us the happiness people. They think our purpose is to keep everybody happy and create a big happy family."

"Job candidates from the outside think our job is to shred résumés. They think we throw away 90 percent of the résumés that arrive at the company."

As a result of these penetrating, albeit exaggerated, self-criticisms, the human resources department developed an effective action plan. The department leader arranged brief meetings with units throughout the organization to discuss the department's role and to answer questions.

Leadership Skill-Building Exercise 11–3 presents an opportunity to practice the pet-peeve technique.

The Forced-Association Technique

A widely used method of releasing creativity is the **forced-association technique**, in which individuals or groups solve a problem by making associations between the properties of two objects. An individual (working alone or

LEADERSHIP SKILL-BUILDING
EXERCISE 11–3 The Pet-Peeve Technique

Review the description of the pet-peeve technique given in the text. Break into groups of about five contributors each. Each group assumes the role of an organizational unit. (Pick one that is familiar to the group, either through direct contact or through secondhand knowledge. For example, you might assume the role of the auditing group of an accounting firm, the financial aid office at your school, or the service department of an automobile dealer.) Generate a number of real and imagined criticisms of your group. Take the two most serious criticisms and develop an action plan to move your group to a higher plane.

in a group) selects a word at random from a dictionary. Next, the person (or group) lists all the properties and attributes of this word.

Assume you randomly chose the word *pickle.* Among its attributes are "tasty," "green," "oblong," and "moderately priced." You then force-fit these properties and attributes to the problem you are facing. If you were trying to improve sunglasses, for example, making them "green" and "moderately priced" could be useful. The forced association is supposed to help solve the problem. A link is found between the properties of the random object and the properties of the problem object. An additional, supposedly true, example will help clarify this abstract process. A pharmaceutical company was investigating new ways of delivering medicine. In a forced-association session, someone picked *time bomb* from the dictionary. One of the key properties to emerge from the session was "slow release," which ultimately led to the development of "time capsules," medicine capsules that deliver medicine to the body over a period of time instead of all at once.[22]

The Excursion Method

The forced-association technique has many spinoffs. One of them is the **excursion method,** in which the problem solver makes word associations that relate to the problem. For instance, the leader of a company safety and health group wanted to increase the group's visibility. During a problem-solving meeting, team members were asked to "take an excursion with" (or free associate to) the word *visibility.*

Among the word associations were "big," "tall," "bright-colored," "shining light," "no fog," "sunny day," "media coverage," and "television." An indirect but powerful link between the word *television* and the problem flashed into the group leader's mind: What about becoming more visible by making a videotape showcasing the group? Copies of the videotape could then be sent to executives around the company, who could watch it at their leisure. Perhaps they could also encourage their staff members to watch the video.

The group ultimately prepared a videotape that explained the safety and health group's mission and some of its accomplishments. The video, in turn, led to more exposure, such as coverage in the company newsletter.

Equipping a Kitchen for the Mind

According to Mike Vance, the former dean of Disney University (the training program for The Walt Disney Company), every business needs a *kitchen for the mind*, a space designed to nurture creativity. The supplies can be ordinary items such as a chalkboard, flip charts, a coffeepot, a refrigerator, a pencil sharpener, and a personal computer with graphics software. Creativity rooms are also sometimes supplied with children's toys, such as dart guns, Frisbees, nerf balls, and stuffed animals. The purpose of the toys is to help people loosen up intellectually and emotionally, thus stimulating creative thinking. Many large corporations, including General Electric and Motorola, have established creative kitchens, often supplying them with VCRs and multimedia computers.

More important than the equipment within the kitchen for the mind is the existence of such a communal meeting place where people can get together to think creatively. Vance contends that even when people's resources are limited, they can still use their ingenuity to produce creative ideas.[23] As described in Chapter 9, the communal meeting place will simultaneously help develop teamwork.

Evaluation of Creativity Training

Very little research has been conducted to directly measure the results of creativity training. Research on creativity training, however, has provided useful insights into favorable conditions for such training. For creativity training to be effective, the environment and culture must be appropriate.[24] As an extreme example, creativity training will not help a person who is in a job setting where innovation is shunned. (More will be said about the right atmosphere for training toward the end of this chapter.)

A team of researchers trained manufacturing engineers to develop positive attitudes toward divergent (or lateral) thinking. The researchers found that training of work groups produced far superior carryover to the job than did training of individuals. A work group trained in divergent thinking thus seems to lead to social support of such thinking.[25] If the group were not favorably disposed toward divergent thinking, it would not receive sufficient reinforcement to be sustained.

SELF-HELP TECHNIQUES TO ENHANCE CREATIVE PROBLEM SOLVING

Leaders and others who want to solve problems more creatively can find hundreds of methods at their disposal. All of these methods aim to increase mental flexibility. A representative group of eight strategies and specific techniques for enhancing creative problem solving are presented below and outlined in Table 11–1. These strategies and techniques support and supplement the organizational programs described previously. An underlying contribution of these techniques is that they facilitate intuitive thinking. Intuition is not a mechanical process that can be learned directly, yet a person can develop the mental flexibility that enhances intuition.

Practicing Creativity-Enhancing Exercises

An established way to sharpen creative thinking is to regularly engage in activities that encourage flexible thinking. If you enjoy photography, put yourself on assignment to take a photograph illustrating a theme. You might, for example, take photographs illustrating the proper use of your company's product. Puzzles of all types are useful in stretching your imagination; many creative people regularly do crossword puzzles. Another mind stretcher is to force yourself to write jokes around a given theme. Can you create a joke about the creativity of a leader? One such joke follows:

> A quality assurance manager in an electronics firm rushed into the director of manufacturing's office. "We've got a terrible problem," he said. "Seventy-five percent of those new ink-jet printers produce blurry images. If we don't fix the problem right away, we won't be able to ship any orders, and the product will fail."
>
> The director of manufacturing arose from his desk cluttered with puzzles and new wave gadgets. With a bored expression, he replied: "Sorry, I can't help you. I'm into innovation, not operations."

Leadership Skill-Building Exercise 11–4 gives you an opportunity to practice creative thinking. Doing exercises of this nature enhances creative problem solving.

TABLE 11–1   Self-Help Techniques for Creativity Improvement

1. Practice creativity-enhancing exercises.
2. Stay alert to opportunities.
3. Use multiple senses when seeking solutions.
4. Maintain an enthusiastic attitude.
5. Speak to lead users.
6. Play "Business Jeopardy."
7. Maintain and use an idea notebook or computer file.
8. Play the roles of explorer, artist, judge, and lawyer.

LEADERSHIP SKILL-BUILDING
EXERCISE 11–4 **Word Hints to Creativity**

Directions: Find a fourth word that is related to the other three words in each row. *Example:*

poke   go   molasses   ____

The answer is *slow:* slow-poke, go slow, and slow as molasses. Now try these words:

1.	surprise	line	birthday	____
2.	base	snow	dance	____
3.	rat	blue	cottage	____
4.	nap	litter	call	____
5.	golf	foot	country	____
6.	house	weary	ape	____
7.	tiger	plate	news	____
8.	painting	bowl	nail	____
9.	jump	sea	priest	____
10.	maple	beet	loaf	____
11.	oak	show	plan	____
12.	light	village	golf	____
13.	merry	out	up	____
14.	jelly	green	kidney	____
15.	bulb	house	lamp	____

Scoring: Answers appear on page 426. If you were able to think of the "correct" word, or another plausible one, for ten or more of these words, your score compares favorably to that of creative individuals. More important than the score is the fact that you acquired some practice in making remote associations—a characteristic talent of creative people.

Source: This word hints test, developed by Eugene Raudsepp, is updated and adapted from "Ideas: Test Your Creativity," *Nation's Business* (June 1965), p. 80.

Staying Alert to Opportunities

The ability to spot opportunities that other people overlook characterizes creative leaders. Opportunity seeking is associated with entrepreneurial leadership because the entrepreneur might build an organization around an unmet consumer need. About a decade ago a man observed that most people had messy closets that were cramped for space. He built a successful company, California Closets, around this basic need. A leader within an organization can also be on the alert for an opportunity to bring about constructive change. A good example is the human resources manager at Digital Equipment Corp., who provided leadership within the company for recognizing the rights of gay and lesbian employees.

Using Multiple Senses When Seeking Solutions

Another way of becoming more mentally flexible—and therefore more creative—is to use multiple senses when searching for alternative solutions to a problem. Think in terms of the five basic senses—sight, sound, taste, touch, and smell—and any combination of the five. If possible, add the kinesthetic sense, which allows us to be aware of the movement and position of different parts of the body. Mike Vance and Diane Deacon, who recommend the tactic, think it is particularly appropriate for products or services that will be experienced broadly, such as a restaurant or retail store.[26]

To use the multiple-sense technique, visualize how a solution to your problem might look, sound, taste, feel, and smell, and how the body might be positioned while experiencing the solution. Suppose your assignment is to develop a theme and a motif for a booth to showcase your company's new product, an electric-powered home tractor, at a trade show. To gain attention for your tractor, seek answers to such questions as:

- What should the display look like?
- What sounds should the display emit?
- Should you give out food at the display to give the prospective dealers a taste sensation?
- What kind of feel should be built into the display?
- Should you accentuate the smell of new equipment and of freshly cut grass?
- Should you encourage dealers to sit on the tractor so they achieve the same kinesthetic sensation their customers might experience when riding the tractor?

By the time you have answered all of these questions, you may have arrived at a catchy theme. Even without a theme, you may have at least thought of an appropriate display for your electric-powered tractor.

Maintaining an Enthusiastic Attitude

The managerial leader faces a major hurdle in becoming a creative problem solver. He or she must resolve the conflict between being judicial and being imaginative. In many work situations, being judicial (or judgmental) is necessary. Situations calling for judicial thinking include reviewing proposed expenditures and inspecting products for quality or safety defects. Imaginative thinking is involved when searching for creative alternatives. Alex F. Osburn, a former advertising executive and the originator of brainstorming, notes how judgment and imagination are often in conflict:

> The fact that moods won't mix largely explains why the judicial and the creative tend to clash. The right mood for judicial thinking is largely negative. "What's wrong with this?. . . . No this won't work." Such reflexes are right and proper when trying to judge.
>
> In contrast, our creative thinking calls for a positive attitude. We have to be hopeful. We need enthusiasm. We have to encourage ourselves to the point of self-confidence. We have to beware of perfectionism lest it be abortive.[27]

The action step is therefore to project oneself into a positive frame of mind when attempting to be creative. The same principle applies when attempting to be creative about a judicial task. For instance, a leader might be faced with the task of looking for creative ways to cut costs. The manager would then have to think positively about thinking negatively!

Speaking to Lead Users

Part of a leader's role is to furnish breakthrough ideas. To obtain such an idea, consultant David Israel-Rosen suggests that you talk to lead users of your product or service. A lead user is a person at the leading edge of the industry. In a few years most of your other customers will be doing business in the same manner. Lead users constantly improve products to match them with new opportunities. Rosen thinks that many companies discourage customers from modifying products through such means as voiding warranties because of the modification. An example would be a customer adding a new feature to a machine.

According to Rosen, leading-edge users have produced inventions like the electron microscope, CAD-CAM engineering systems, and a host of consumer products. Another application of the leading-edge technique is to look for someone who does what you do but has a larger stake.[28] If you want to make durable tires, for instance, investigate what type of tires airplane manufacturers use; they have a considerable stake in tires that don't pop under heavy pressure.

Having People Play "Business Jeopardy"

Most puzzles and games enhance creativity. A particularly effective one is for group members to play a business version of the popular television show *Jeopardy*. Instead of playing questions and answers, the group plays answers and questions. Each person in turn gives an answer, for which group members must compose a question.[29] For example, one group member might give the answer, "Java." The *wrong* question for business purposes is "What is another name for coffee?" A *right* question for business purposes would be

"What is the name of one type of "software for the Internet?" As a warm-up activity to stimulate creative thinking, loosen up your mind, get together in a group, and play Business Jeopardy.

Maintaining and Using an Idea Notebook or Computer File

It is difficult to capitalize on creative ideas unless you keep a careful record of them. A creative idea trusted to memory may be forgotten in the press of everyday business. An important suggestion kept on your daily planner may become obscured. Creative ideas can lead to breakthroughs for your group and your career, so they deserve the dignity of a separate notebook or computer file. A cautious or forgetful person is advised to keep two copies of the idea book or computer file: one at home and one in the office.

Playing the Roles of Explorer, Artist, Judge, and Lawyer

Another creativity-improvement method incorporates many of the preceding methods. Say you want to enhance your creativity on the job. This method calls for you to adopt four roles in your thinking.[30] First, be an *explorer*. Speak to people in different fields and get ideas that can bring about innovations for your group. For example, if you manage a telecommunications group, speak to salespeople and manufacturing specialists.

Second, be an *artist* by stretching your imagination. Strive to spend about 5 percent of your day asking what-if questions. For example, the leader of a telecommunications group might ask, "What if some new research suggests that the extensive use of telecommunications devices is associated with high rates of cancer?" Also remember to challenge the commonly perceived rules in your field. A bank manager, for example, challenged why customers needed their cancelled checks returned each month. The questioning led to a new bank practice: returning cancelled checks only if the customer pays an additional fee.

Third, know when to be a *judge*. After developing some imaginative ideas, at some point you have to evaluate them. Do not be so critical that you discourage your own imaginative thinking. Be critical enough, however, so that you don't try to implement weak ideas. A managing partner in an established law firm formulated a plan for opening two storefront branches that would offer legal services to the public at low prices. The branches would advertise on radio, on television, and in newspapers. After thinking through her plan for several weeks, however, she dropped the idea. She decided that the storefront branches would most likely divert clients away from the parent firm, rather than create a new market.

Fourth, achieve results with your creative thinking by playing the role of *lawyer*. Negotiate and find ways to implement your ideas within your field or place of work. The explorer, artist, and judge stages of creative thought might take only a short time to develop a creative idea. Yet you may spend months or even years getting your breakthrough idea implemented. For example, many tax-preparation firms now give clients instant refunds in the amount of their anticipated tax refunds. It took a manager in a large tax-preparation firm a long time to convince top management of the merits of the idea.

ESTABLISHING A CLIMATE FOR CREATIVE THINKING

Leaders need to develop creative ideas of their own to improve productivity, quality, and satisfaction. Establishing a climate conducive to creative problem solving is another requirement of effective leadership. A foundation step in fostering organizational creativity is to establish a vision and mission that include creativity, such as, "We will become the most innovative provider of automobile undercare (mufflers, brakes, etc.) products and services in North America" [Monroe Muffler Brake]. Vision statements and mission statements set the pace, but they must be supported by the right climate and extensive use of the techniques described throughout this chapter.

The most influential step a leader can take to bring about creative problem solving is to develop a permissive atmosphere that encourages people to think freely. At the same time, organizational members must receive positive feedback and an occasional tangible reward for making innovative suggestions. Although extrinsic rewards enhance creativity, intrinsic motivators such as pride and the joy of accomplishment are still a more important contributor to creativity.[31]

At this point, do Leadership Diagnostic Activity 11–1. The instrument gives you an opportunity to ponder many of the management and leadership practices that encourage or discourage creative problem solving.

A study of research and development scientists conducted by Teresa M. Amabile and S. S. Gryskiewicz supports the importance of a permissive atmosphere for enhancing creativity. The researchers interviewed 120 R&D scientists, asking each of them to provide information about two critical incidents: one illustrating high creativity and one illustrating low creativity. In describing incidents of high creativity, about 74 percent of the scientists mentioned freedom to decide what to do and how to do one's work; freedom from constraints; and an open atmosphere.[32]

A maverick manager, as proposed by Donald W. Blohwiak, is precisely the type of leader who fosters creative problem solving among team members. Such a manager actively encourages group members to "color outside the lines" (which is similar to thinking outside the box). Maverick managers also seek ways to do new things and new ways to do old things.[33] At Xerox Corp., a leader who qualifies as a maverick manager challenged his team to simplify the company's billing system. Many customers received multiple

LEADERSHIP DIAGNOSTIC
ACTIVITY 11–1 Assessing the Climate for Innovation

Respond "mostly yes" or "mostly no" as to how well each of the following characteristics fits an organization familiar to you. If you are currently not familiar with an outside organization, respond to these statements in regard to your school.

	Mostly Yes	Mostly No
1. Creativity is encouraged here.	___	___
2. Our ability to function creatively is respected by the leadership.	___	___
3. Around here, people are allowed to try to solve the same problems in different ways.	___	___
4. The main function of members of this organization is to follow orders that come down through channels.	___	___
5. Around here, a person can get into a lot of trouble by being different.	___	___
6. This organization can be described as flexible and continually adapting to change.	___	___
7. A person can't do things that are too different around here without provoking anger.	___	___
8. The best way to get along in this organization is to think the way the rest of the group does.	___	___
9. People around here are expected to deal with problems in the same way.	___	___
10. This organization is open and responsive to change.	___	___
11. The people in charge around here usually get credit for others' ideas.	___	___
12. In this organization, we tend to stick to tried and true ways.	___	___
13. This place seems to be more concerned with the status quo than with change.	___	___
14. Assistance in developing new ideas is readily available.	___	___

15. There are adequate resources devoted to innovation in this organization.   ___   ___

16. There is adequate time available to pursue creative ideas here.   ___   ___

17. Lack of funding to pursue creative ideas is a problem in this organization.   ___   ___

18. Personnel shortages inhibit innovation in this organization.   ___   ___

19. This organization gives me free time to pursue creative ideas during the workday.   ___   ___

20. The reward system here encourages innovation.   ___   ___

21. This organization publicly recognizes those who are innovative.   ___   ___

22. The reward system here benefits mainly those who don't rock the boat.   ___   ___

Scoring and interpretation: The score in the direction of a climate for innovation is "mostly yes" for statements 1, 2, 3, 6, 10, 14, 15, 16, 19, 20, and 21, and "mostly no" for statements 4, 5, 7, 8, 9, 11, 12, 13, 17, 18, and 22. A score of 16 or higher suggests a climate well suited for innovation, 9 to 15 is about average, and 8 or below suggests a climate that inhibits innovation.

Source: From Susanne G. Scott and Reginald Bruce, "Determinants of Innovative Behavior: A Path Model of Individual Innovation in the Workplace," *Academy of Management Journal,* June 1994, p. 593. Used by permission of Academy of Management.

bills from Xerox each month. The manager welcomed all suggestions. Finally the accounts receivable department agreed upon procedures that enormously simplified the paperwork for customers.

Another strategy for enhancing creativity among team members is for the leader to avoid behavior and attitudes that block creativity. One such creativity blocker is an authoritarian—that is, inflexible and close-minded—attitude. Similarly, an attitude of *functional fixedness* will discourage creativity.[34] (Here the term *functional fixedness* refers to the belief that there is only one way to do something.) The manager should encourage team members to do things better and differently.

According to Michael Michalko, a widely quoted creativity consultant, *removing self-censors* is necessary in order to develop a climate for creativity. Self-censorship refers to the idea that many workers will fail to generate creative suggestions because they fear the consequences of contributing bad suggestions. To remove the self-censors that inhibit creativity, management must place more emphasis on quantity than on quality of employee ideas. Leaders and group members alike must trust that quantity will in fact produce quality. Developing a large quantity of ideas is an effective tactic because the base rate for workable ideas is generally so low. Only a small percentage of creative suggestions ever result in positive outcomes, so a large number of ideas must be generated to hatch a few good ones.[35] The idea quotas mentioned previously are an effective method for generating a large quantity of ideas.

A final organizational condition favoring creativity is the presence of peers and managers who can act as role models.[36] Organizational creativity is thus self-perpetuating. As the leaders bring more creative people into an organization, other people will be stimulated to think creatively.

Closely related to establishing organizational conditions favoring creativity is choosing effective methods for managing creative workers. The suggestions that follow supplement effective leadership and management practices in general.[37]

1. *Give creative people tools and resources that allow their work to stand out.* Creative workers have a high degree of self-motivation, and therefore want to achieve high-quality output. To achieve such high quality, they usually need adequate resources, such as state-of-the-art equipment and an ample travel budget for such purposes as conducting research.

2. *Provide ongoing recognition and appreciation.* Despite the high intrinsic motivation of creative workers, they also need extrinsic motivators. Inventors crave patents, photographers and painters want their work exhibited, and product development specialists desire companywide recognition. Memos of appreciation and oral praise are also effective motivators. An advertising executive notes that creative people are ego-driven.

3. *Give creative people flexibility and a minimum amount of structure.* Many creative workers regard heavy structure as the death knell of creativity. "Structure" for these workers means rules and regulations, many layers of approval, strict dress codes, fixed office hours, rigid assignments, and fill-in-the-blank paperwork. (Typically, the leader-manager will have to achieve a workable compromise in this area that stays within the framework of organizational policy. Regular office hours, for example, are a must for team assignments.)

4. *Employ creative people to manage and evaluate creative workers.* Managers of creative workers should have some creative ability of their own, so that they can understand creativity and be credible as leaders. Understanding the creative process is important for evaluating the creative contribution of others. What constitutes creative output is somewhat subjective, but the output can be tied to objective criteria. At Hallmark Cards Inc., for example, creativity is measured by such factors as how

well the creative work sold and how well it performed in a consumer preference test. In general, a manager's intuition about the potential contribution of a creative idea or product still weighs heavily in the evaluation.

SUMMARY

A creative leader brings forth ideas or things that did not exist previously, or that existed in a different form. The creative process has been divided into five steps: opportunity or problem recognition; immersion (the individual becomes immersed in the idea); incubation (the idea simmers); insight (a solution surfaces); and verification and application (the person supports and implements the idea).

Distinguishing characteristics of creative people fall into four categories: knowledge, intellectual abilities, personality, and social habits and upbringing. They possess extensive knowledge, good intellectual skills, intellectual curiosity, and a wide range of interests. Personality attributes of creative people include a positive self-image, tolerance for isolation, nonconformity, and the ability to tolerate ambiguity and chaos. Creative people also enjoy interacting with others. Many creative adults faced family problems during childhood. The right personal characteristics must interact with the right environment to produce creative problem solving.

A major strategy for becoming creative is to overcome traditional thinking, or a traditional mental set. Also, it is necessary to break down rigid thinking that blocks new ideas. A related idea is that creative people engage in lateral thinking in addition to vertical thinking. Lateral thinking seeks many different answers to problems, whereas vertical thinking looks for the one best answer.

Creative thinking can be enhanced by establishing idea quotas and brainstorming. A spinoff of brainstorming is the pet-peeve technique, in which a group of people think of all the possible complaints others might have about their unit. Another technique to facilitate creative thinking is to force associations between the properties of two objects. A similar technique, the excursion method, requires the problem solver to make word associations that relate to the problem. Some organizations also equip a kitchen for the mind, or a space designed for creativity. For creativity training to be effective, the environment and culture must be appropriate.

Self-help techniques to enhance creative problem solving include (1) practicing creativity-enhancing exercises, (2) staying alert to opportunities, (3) using multiple senses, (4) maintaining enthusiasm, (5) speaking to lead users (customers who make advanced use of the product), (6) playing "Business Jeopardy," (7) maintaining and using an idea notebook or computer file, and (8) playing the roles of explorer, artist, judge, and lawyer.

Establishing a climate conducive to creative problem solving is another requirement of effective leadership. A permissive atmosphere that encourages people to think freely facilitates creative problem solving. A maverick manager makes a contribution to creative thinking by encouraging group members to "color outside the lines." The leader must also avoid behavior and attitudes that block creativity. Self-censors to creativity can be reduced by emphasizing quantity rather than quality of suggestions. Managers should also act as role models for creativity.

Special attention should be paid to managing creative workers, including giving them the tools and resources they need in order to perform well. It is also important to provide ongoing appreciation and recognition, decrease structure, and have creative people evaluate their work.

KEY TERMS

Creativity	Vertical thinking	Forced-association technique
Organizational creativity	Lateral thinking	Excursion method
Traditional mental set	Pet-peeve technique	

GUIDELINES FOR ACTION AND SKILL DEVELOPMENT

To encourage creative problem solving among team members, the leader should avoid certain creativity dampeners and inhibitors, as implied in this chapter. Ten more of these creativity blockers are as follows:

1. Expressing attitudes that preserve the status quo by using such clichés as "Don't rock the boat"; "Don't make waves"; and "If it ain't broke, don't fix it"

2. Policing team members by every device imaginable

3. Saying yes to new ideas but not doing anything about them

4. Being the exclusive spokesperson for everything in the area of responsibility

5. Putting every idea through formal channels

6. Responding to most suggestions for change with a pained look and saying, "But that will cost *money*"

7. Promoting the "not-invented-here" syndrome (if the manager did not invent it, the manager will not consider it)

8. Being suspicious of any idea from below, because it's new and because it's from below

9. Treating problems as signs of incompetence and failure

10. Being free and open with criticism but stingy with praise[38]

DISCUSSION QUESTIONS AND ACTIVITIES

1. Why is it important for a leader to be a creative problem solver?

2. How might a person use information about the five stages of creative thought to become a more creative problem solver?

3. Find an example in a newspaper or magazine or on the Internet of creative problem solving by a leader. Be prepared to share your findings with classmates.

4. What relationship have you noticed between creativity and age?

5. In what way does your present program of study contribute to your ability to solve problems creatively?

6. The opinion has often been expressed that too much emphasis on teamwork inhibits creativity. What do you think of the merits of this argument?

7. Give an example of how you, or somebody you know, have thought "outside the box."

8. Why would playing games like Business Jeopardy enhance creativity?

9. What is your opinion of the importance of having people who are creative themselves evaluate the creative output of other workers?

10. Speak to the most creative person you know in any field, and find out if he or she uses any specific creativity-enhancing technique. Be prepared to bring your findings back to class.

LEADERSHIP CASE PROBLEM

Coping with the Clean Air Act

The Clean Air Act of 1990 requires states that have areas with unacceptable ozone and carbon monoxide levels to reduce air pollution. Parts of eleven states—California, Connecticut, Delaware, Illinois, Indiana, Maryland, New Jersey, New York, Pennsylvania, Texas, and Wisconsin—are considered to have unacceptable levels of these two pollutants. Various state officials have said that the Clean Air Act could affect approximately 5,000 employers and 3.5 million employees.

Given that automobiles are responsible for 90 percent of the carbon monoxide pollution, the act requires employers with more than 100 employees at a work site to reduce the number of autos (and trucks used as autos) arriving between 6:00 A.M. and 10:00 A.M. Companies with fewer than thirty-three employees arriving during that time are excluded. A key provision of the act relating to employers is called "Clean Transportation Alternatives." It reads as follows:

> The law requires the smoggiest cities to limit growth in vehicle travel by encouraging alternatives to solo driving. In areas where ozone levels exceed certain criteria, employers of 100 or more will be asked to find ways to increase the average number of passengers in each vehicle for commutes to work and during work-related driving trips.

The goal of the Clean Air Act is to increase the average passenger occupancy (APO) by 25 percent in states that have undesirable levels of pollutants. The APO is calculated by dividing the number of employees by the number of vehicles driven to work. Each company covered by the law must file a compliance plan with the state, clearly indicating how well it meets the average vehicle occupancy target. The states will then enforce these vehicle reduction plans.

At a Wisconsin company, a supervisor told a bookkeeper that he was not being a good citizen by riding to work in a sports utility vehicle all by himself. The bookkeeper responded, "I hate standing outside waiting for a ride when it's cold outside. Another problem is that I'm a smoker, and very few people want to ride with me. Besides that, it's my constitutional right to drive my own vehicle." The supervisor replied that he wished the worker would be less self-centered, and dropped the issue.

One method of complying with standards that has been tried is to charge employees for parking. The city of Bellevue, Washington, began charging for parking in 1989, when the city had only 200 parking spaces for 360 employees. The coordinator of the parking program at Bellevue said that charging was painful but effective.

Tom Hanlon is the marketing and sales director for the Transit Center, a New York–based public-private alliance to promote mass transit. He says, "Companies will look like the bad guys. They will have to govern how employees live outside the office."

1. What alternatives can you suggest for lowering the average passenger occupancy?

2. What alternatives can you suggest for monitoring the fact that employers are really lowering the APO?

3. What ways of reducing vehicle-created pollutants other than lowering the APO can you suggest?

4. What type of leadership can supervisors exert to deal with individual workers who resist changing their driving habits?

Source: Based on facts reported in Catherine Roman, "Business Copes with the Clean Air Conundrum," *Management Review*, pp. 34–37; "Motor Vehicles and the 1990 Clean Air Act," Fact Sheet OMS-11, www.epa.gov/docs/OMSWWW/11-vehs.html.

Communication and Conflict Resolution Skills

LEARNING OBJECTIVES

After studying this chapter, you should be able to

1. explain why good communication skills contribute to effective leadership.
2. describe the basics of inspirational and emotion-provoking communication.
3. describe the elements of supportive communication.
4. be sensitive to the importance of overcoming cross-cultural barriers to communication.
5. identify basic approaches to resolving conflict and negotiating.

*J*ack Welch, the oft-quoted CEO of General Electric Co., once said, "Leaders inspire people with clear visions of how things can be done better. Some managers, on the other hand, muddle things with pointless complexity and detail. They equate it with sophistication, with sounding smarter than anyone else. They inspire no one."[1] Welch's comment succinctly points to the relationship between communication skills and leadership effectiveness: effective communication skills contribute to inspirational leadership. Chapter 3 described how charismatic leaders are masterful oral communicators. This chapter expands upon this theme and also covers the contribution of nonverbal, written, and supportive communication. Furthermore, it describes how the ability to overcome cross-cultural communication barriers enhances leadership effectiveness. Finally, the chapter presents conflict resolution skills, because leaders spend a substantial amount of time resolving conflicts.

EVIDENCE ABOUT COMMUNICATION AND LEADERSHIP

Research evidence supports the conventional wisdom that effective leaders are also effective communicators. Based on his synthesis of studies, Bernard M. Bass found substantial evidence of a positive relationship between competence in communicating and satisfactory leadership and management performance. An interview study of 200 successful organizational leaders indicated that they had similar communication patterns. The leaders expanded their thinking regularly by actively soliciting new ideas and feedback from others. Furthermore, they continuously sought fresh information. They possessed the persuasive skills necessary to convince others of the quality of their ideas.[2]

An earlier study showed that high quality in oral communication skills facilitated leadership effectiveness. The subjects were 231 editorial workers, whose work involved abstracting technical publications, and their 15 assistant managers. Two leadership behaviors studied were explicitness in giving instruction and frequency of communication about job-related matters. Explicitness in giving instruction correlated significantly (.57) with group members' satisfaction with supervisory leadership. Frequency of communication, however, was not significantly related (.19) to satisfaction.[3]

Research has also been conducted on the contribution of nonverbal behavior to leadership effectiveness. One study suggested that when nonverbal messages contradict verbal messages, the listener tends to place more reliance on the nonverbal messages. A manager who talks about wanting to empower employees but looks bored during the discussion will be regarded as insincere and manipulative. To be effective, the leader must synchronize verbal and nonverbal behavior.[4]

Fred Luthans, Richard M. Hodgetts, and Stuart A. Rosenkrantz observed 178 managers as they carried out their day-by-day activities. They found that about 44 percent of the managers' activities could be considered routine communication—exchanging routine information and processing paperwork. An important conclusion was that communication activity made the biggest relative contribution to effectiveness, measured in terms of performance and satisfaction. The other activity categories were networking, traditional management, and human resource management.[5]

Despite the evident link between interpersonal communication and leadership effectiveness, a recent study suggests that companies are not communicating their mission, vision, and values as well as they might. An American Management Association survey of more than 10,000 U.S. manufacturing and service firms uncovered significant problems in the basis for effective communication at many firms.[6] One such finding was that a majority of managers and supervisors from different business functions were perceived to lack a high level of understanding of the company's mission, vision, and values. Furthermore, less than a third of the respondents agreed that their firm regularly sought feedback to make sure that messages were perceived as intended. A vice president at Monsanto Company expressed the problem in these terms: "We all think we're communicating more and better with each other because we now have E-mail, voice mail, and various other technologies. But I don't believe that's necessarily been the case at all."[7]

Although information technology may not always improve communication by leaders, this technology has had a meaningful impact on communication and coordination by leaders. By relying on information technology, leaders and managers can be in frequent contact with group members without being physically present. Managers can also be part of a **virtual office** in which employees work together as if they were part of a single office despite being physically separated. The most familiar tools of the virtual office are fax machines, modems, pagers, and cellular telephones. A more recent advance is the electronic assistant, a three-way combination of a computer, telephone, and voice recognition system. In response to the owner's voice command, an electronic assistant can telephone any number in its file system and can also relay messages.

Frequent contact with company employees, customers, and suppliers enhances coordination. At the same time, the manager can exercise leadership by inspiring, motivating, and persuading people more readily with this technology than by telephone and in-person contacts alone. Many leaders regularly send E-mail messages to motivate and inspire their constituents—locally, regionally, and internationally. The alternative is for the manager to communicate primarily when back at the office. A high-tech leader is never away from the office—even if he or she would like to be!

To focus your thinking on your communication effectiveness, complete Leadership Self-Assessment Exercise 12–1.

INSPIRATIONAL AND POWERFUL COMMUNICATION

Information about communicating persuasively and effectively is extensive. Here we focus on suggestions for creating the high-impact communication that contributes to effective leadership. Both formal and informal leaders must be persuasive and dynamic communicators. Effective communication often helps informal leaders be selected for formal leadership positions. Suggestions for becoming an inspirational and emotion-provoking communicator can be divided into two categories: (1) speaking and writing, and (2) nonverbal communication.

Speaking and Writing

Most of you are already familiar with the basics of effective spoken and written communication. Yet the basics—such as writing and speaking clearly,

LEADERSHIP SELF-ASSESSMENT
EXERCISE 12–1 A Test of Communication Effectiveness

The following scale consists of opposite descriptions of communication style. Between each pair is a 7-to-1 scale. Assess your communication style in terms of each pair of descriptions and circle the appropriate number. If you are not currently working as a manager, imagine how the situation would be based on your other work or social experience with people.

I think my communication with people who report to me:

Increases my credibility	7 6 5 4 3 2 1	Decreases my credibility
Is precise	7 6 5 4 3 2 1	Is imprecise
Is clear	7 6 5 4 3 2 1	Is unclear
Answers more questions than it raises	7 6 5 4 3 2 1	Raises more questions than it answers
Is effective	7 6 5 4 3 2 1	Is ineffective
Is competent	7 6 5 4 3 2 1	Is incompetent
Is productive	7 6 5 4 3 2 1	Is unproductive
Gets the results I want	7 6 5 4 3 2 1	Does not get the results I want
Is impressive	7 6 5 4 3 2 1	Is unimpressive
Creates a positive image of me	7 6 5 4 3 2 1	Creates a negative image of me
Is good	7 6 5 4 3 2 1	Is bad
Is skillful	7 6 5 4 3 2 1	Is unskillful
Is relaxed	7 6 5 4 3 2 1	Is strained
Is self-rewarding	7 6 5 4 3 2 1	Is not self-rewarding
Does not embarrass me	7 6 5 4 3 2 1	Does embarrass me

Total score _____ To find your total score, add the numbers you circled.

Interpretation: If your total score is 81 or above, you have analyzed yourself as a very effective communicator. If your total score is 59–80, you have analyzed yourself as an effective communicator. If your total score is 37–58, you have analyzed yourself as an ineffective communicator. If your total score is 15–46, you have analyzed yourself as a very ineffective communicator.

To increase the accuracy of your self-evaluation, ask another person to evaluate your on-the-job communication by taking this test. Many of the ideas contained in this chapter, and in books and articles about communication skills, will help you improve your communication effectiveness.

Source: Adapted from Lyle Sussman and Paul D. Krivnos, *Communication for Supervisors and Managers*, 1979, pp. 10–12. Used by permission of Mayfield Publishing.

maintaining eye contact, and not mumbling—are only starting points. The majority of effective leaders have an extra snap or panache in their communication style. The same energy and excitement is reflected in both speaking and writing. James M. Kouzes and Barry Z. Posner underscore the importance of colorful language in communicating a vision (one of the leader's most important functions), in these words:

> Language is among the most powerful methods for expressing a vision. Successful leaders use metaphors and figures of speech; they give examples, tell stories, and relate anecdotes; they draw word pictures; and they offer quotations and recite slogans.[8]

Group members and other constituents have more exposure to the spoken word of leaders. Nevertheless, with the increased use of E-mail and printed memos, the written word exerts considerable influence. Suggestions for dynamic and persuasive oral and written communication are presented below and outlined in Table 12–1. Before studying them, reread the speech by Martin Luther King, Jr., on page 78.

Use the Persuade Package of Influence Tactics.   One approach to being persuasive is to rely on research findings about which combination of influence tactics is likely to be effective across many situations. The **persuade package** is a small, standard set of influence tactics that leads the target to behave in a particular way. The package is really a mental framework about influencing others that directs the encoding, storage, and retrieval of information. Using a persuade package gives the influence agent a preference order for influence tactics.

Herman Aguinis and several associates conducted a study with college students in which the students were asked to rate the degree to which they believed the source would use each of four tactics in three situations. The four tactics were ingratiation, assertiveness, rationality, and exchange. The three situations were a landscaping company, a public relations department, and a manufacturing plant in which a supervisor wanted a subordinate to perform a task. Data analysis revealed that for all three situations, the preference order for use of influence tactics (the persuade package) was the same: ingratiation $\rightarrow$ rationality $\rightarrow$ assertiveness $\rightarrow$ exchange.[9] In other words, butter up, be logical, use moderate force, and then strike a bargain.

TABLE 12–1   Suggestions for Inspirational Speaking and Writing

1. Use the persuade package of influence tactics.
2. Use heavy-impact, embellishing language.
3. Use emotion-provoking words.
4. Use a power-oriented linguistic style.
5. Know exactly what you want.
6. Back up conclusions with data.
7. Minimize junk words and vocalized pauses.
8. Avoid or minimize common language errors.
9. Sell group members on the benefits of your suggestions.
10 Gear your message to the listener.
11. Explore the reasons for people's objections.
12. Front-load your message.
13. Write crisp, clear memos, letters, and reports.

Use Heavy-Impact, Embellishing Language.   Certain words used in the proper context give power and force to your speech. Used comfortably, naturally, and sincerely, these words can help you project the image of a self-confident person with leadership ability or potential. A mortgage officer at a bank made the following progress report to her manager:

> It's important that I fill you in on my recent activities. This bank's strategic plan is to get into the next generation of financial marketing. I've bought into the strategy, and it's working. Instead of simply selling commercial mortgages, I'm heavily into relationship banking. I've been building long-term symbiotic relations with some very big potential clients.
>
> So far, the short-term results I've achieved have been modest. But the long-term results could be mind boggling. We may soon become the dominant supplier of financial services to a key player in commercial real estate.

The mortgage officer framed her accomplishments and progress in buzzwords of interest to top management. She talked about supporting the corporate strategy, relationship banking, outstanding long-term results, and her company becoming a dominant supplier. Using powerful and upbeat language of this type enhances her leadership image. Yet if she had taken the embellishment too far, she might have appeared deceptive and devious.

Use Emotion-Provoking Words.   An expert persuasive tactic is to sprinkle your speech with emotion-provoking—and therefore powerful—words.

Emotion-provoking words bring forth images of exciting events. Examples of emotion-provoking and powerful words include *"outclassing* the competition," *"bonding* with customers," *"surpassing* previous profits," *"capturing* customer loyalty," and *"rebounding* from a downturn." It also helps to use words and phrases that connote power. Those now in vogue include *learning organization, virtual organization,* and *total customer satisfaction.* Leadership Skill-Building Exercise 12–1 illustrates one organizational leader's selective use of emotion-provoking words.

LEADERSHIP SKILL-BUILDING EXERCISE 12–1 Identifying Emotion-Provoking Words and Phrases

Directions: Identify the emotion-provoking words and phrases in the following excerpt from an interview with Thomas J. Usher, president of the U.S. Steel Group of USX Corporation, in which he expresses his views on the importance of quality in manufacturing. Compare your observations to those of other members of your class or study group. Also see the suggested answers to this exercise on pages 426–427.

Twenty years ago, in basic industries like steel, the terms "quality-driven" and "customer-driven" often were viewed more as trendy slogans than as daily blueprints for competitive success. But that viewpoint simply doesn't fly any more.

Today quality has become a given—you're expected to have good quality as a basic element of being in business. The question in business today is how to get at quality. How is quality defined? And does it make a competitive difference?

U.S. Steel is being turned around by building employee teams, empowering hourly workers, and giving everyone in the company a sense of purpose. We encourage worker involvement and worker innovation in a culture geared toward satisfying customers with the best steel products possible.

While we still have a long way to go, we're proud of where we stand and how far we've come on quality and efficiency. We don't take a back seat to the Japanese, Koreans, Germans, or anybody else. We continue to work on changing our culture to embrace quality. Suggestions and ideas flow between all levels of the organization. We've changed the way we think. We're becoming a purpose- and vision-driven company.

Source: Excerpted from "Thomas J. Usher: The 1993 William D. Gasser Distinguished Lectureship in Business" (Rochester Institute of Technology, College of Business brochure), March 16, 1993.

Use a Power-Oriented Linguistic Style.   A major part of being persuasive involves choosing the right **linguistic style,** a person's characteristic speaking pattern. According to Deborah Tannen, linguistic style involves such aspects as amount of directness, pacing and pausing, word choice, and the use of such communication devices as jokes, figures of speech, anecdotes, questions, and apologies.[10] A linguistic style is complex because it includes the culturally learned signals by which people communicate what they mean, along with how they interpret what others say and how they evaluate others. The complexity of linguistic style makes it difficult to offer specific prescriptions for using one that is power-oriented. Many of the elements of a power-oriented linguistic style are included in other suggestions made in this section of the chapter. Nevertheless, here are several components of a linguistic style that would give power and authority to the message sender in many situations:

- Downplay uncertainty. If you are not confident of your opinion or prediction, make a positive statement anyway, such as saying, "I know this new system will cure our inventory problems."
- Use the pronoun I to receive more credit for your ideas. (Of course, this could backfire in a team-based organization.)
- Minimize the number of questions you ask that imply that you lack information on a topic, such as, "What do you mean by an IPO?"
- Apologize infrequently, and particularly minimize saying, "I'm sorry."
- Offer negative feedback directly, rather than softening the feedback by first giving praise and then moving to the areas of criticism.
- Accept verbal opposition to your ideas as a business ritual rather than becoming upset when your ideas are challenged.
- Emphasize direct rather than indirect talk, such as saying, "I need your report by noon tomorrow," rather than, "I'm wondering if your report will be available by noon tomorrow."

Despite these interpretations of Tannen's work, she cautions that there is no one best way to communicate. How to project power and authority is often dependent upon the people involved, the organizational culture, the relative rank of the speakers, and other situational factors. The power-oriented linguistic style should be interpreted as a general guideline.

Know Exactly What You Want.   Your chances of selling an idea increase to the extent that you have clarified the idea in your own mind. The clearer and more committed you are at the outset of a selling or negotiating session, the stronger you are as a persuader. This is one of the many reasons why a leader with a vision is persuasive. In addition to knowing what you want, it is helpful to develop fallback positions. Consider what you might do if you cannot convince the other side to accept your first proposal. If plan A does not work, shift to plan B, then to plan C.[11]

Back Up Conclusions with Data.   You will be more persuasive if you support your spoken and written presentations with solid data. One approach to obtaining data is to collect it yourself—for example, by conducting a telephone survey of your customers or group members. The sales manager of an office supply company wanted to begin a delivery service for his many small customers, such as dental and real-estate offices. He telephoned a generous sampling of these accounts and found they would be willing to pay a premium price if delivery were included. The sales manager used these data to support his argument, thus convincing the company owner to approve the plan. He thus exercised leadership in providing a new service.

Published sources also provide convincing data for arguments. Supporting data for hundreds of arguments can be found in the business pages of newspapers, in business magazines and newspapers, and on the Internet. The *Statistical Abstract of the United States*, published annually, is an inexpensive yet trusted reference for thousands of arguments.

Relying too much on research has a potential disadvantage, though. Being too dependent on data could suggest that you have little faith in your intuition. For example, you might convey a weak impression if, when asked your opinion, you respond, "I can't answer until I collect some data." Leaders are generally decisive.

An important issue, then, is for the leader to find the right balance between relying on data versus using intuition alone when communicating an important point. One authority makes this observation:

> An effective leader does not willfully ignore relevant and available data just for the sake of looking decisive. Instead, he or she incorporates tentative conclusions based upon relevant data into a decisive action which may of necessity go beyond the available data.[12]

Minimize Junk Words and Vocalized Pauses.   Using colorful, powerful words enhances the perception that you are self-confident and have leadership qualities. Also, minimize the use of words and phrases that dilute the impact of your speech, such as "like," "you know," "you know what I mean," "he goes," (to mean he says), and "uhhhhhhh." Such junk words and vocalized pauses convey the impression of low self-confidence—especially in a professional setting—and detract from a sharp communication image.

An effective way to decrease the use of these extraneous words is to tape-record your side of a phone conversation and then play it back. (The latest voice mail systems enable the message sender to replay his or her message immediately.) Many people aren't aware that they use extraneous words until they hear recordings of their speech.

Avoid or Minimize Common Language Errors.   A good leader should be sure always to write and speak with grammatic precision to give the impression of being articulate and well-informed, thereby enhancing his or her leadership stature. Here are two examples of common language errors: "Just between you and I" is wrong; "just between you and me" is correct. *Irregardless* is a nonword; *regardless* is correct.

Another very common error is using the plural pronoun *they* to refer to a singular antecedent. For example, "The systems analyst said that *they* cannot help us" is incorrect. "The systems analyst said *she* cannot help us" is correct. Using *they* to refer to a singular antecedent has become so common in the English language that many people no longer make the distinction between singular and plural.[13] Some of these errors are subtle and are made so frequently that many people don't realize they're wrong—but again, avoiding grammatical errors may enhance a person's leadership stature.

When in doubt about a potential language error, consult a large dictionary. An authoritative guide for the leader (and anyone else) who chooses to use English accurately is *The Elements of Style* by William Strunk and E. B. White.[14]

Sell Group Members on the Benefits of Your Suggestions.   Leaders are constrained by the willingness of group members to take action on the leader's suggestions and initiatives. As a consequence, the leader must explain to group members how they can benefit from what he or she proposes. From the standpoint of expectancy theory, the leader attempts to increase the performance-to-outcome expectancies. In Tom Usher's situation, U.S. Steel employees were told that if they became part of the company quality movement, their job security would be enhanced. At the same time, Usher and other company executives held out a threat: Employees who could not accept the new way of doing business—such as being more responsive to customers—would lose their jobs.

Gear Your Message to the Listener.   An axiom of persuasive communication is that a speaker must adapt the message to the listener's interests and motivations. The company president visiting a manufacturing plant will receive careful attention—and build support—when he says that jobs will not be outsourced to another country. The same company president will receive the support of stockholders when he emphasizes how cost reductions will boost earnings per share and enlarge dividends.

Stephen P. Robbins, in his review of the evidence, concludes that the average intelligence level of the group is a key contingency factor in designing a persuasive message. People with high intelligence tend to be more influenced by messages based on strong, logical arguments. Bright people are also more likely to reject messages based on flawed logic.[15]

Explore the Reasons for People's Objections.   An important part of selling a product or an idea is to explore the reasons why the receiver is objecting to the message. After the objections are on the table, they can sometimes be overcome. The owner of a microelectronics company informed her staff that she had received an attractive offer to sell the company. Two of the key people, who were also major stockholders, said they would not consider selling their shares to a new owner. When the owner asked why, the objectors were concerned that they would lose their jobs after the takeover. The owner listened patiently. She then explained that she would demand job security for key staff members before agreeing to the sale.

Selling others on the benefit of a message capitalizes on the fact that many people act on the basis of self-interest. They want to know what's in it for them before they will buy an idea, product, or service, or move in a particular direction.

Front-load Your Message.   A persuasive speaker or writer places key ideas at the beginning of a conversation, memo, paragraph, or sentence.[16] Front-loaded messages are particularly important for leaders because people expect leaders to be forceful communicators. A front-loaded and powerful message might be "Cost reduction must be our immediate priority," which emphasizes that cost reduction is the major subject. It is clearly much more to the point than, for example, "All of us must reduce costs immediately."

One way to make sure messages are front-loaded is to use the active voice, making sure the subject of the sentence is doing the acting, not being acted upon. Compare the active (and front-loaded) message "Loyal workers should not take vacations during a company crisis" to the passive (non-front-loaded) message "Vacations should not be taken by loyal company workers during a crisis."

Write Crisp, Clear Memos, Letters, and Reports.   According to Michael Mercer, high achievers write more effective reports than do their less highly achieving counterparts. Mercer examined the business writing (memos, letters, and reports) of both high achievers and low achievers. He observed that high achievers' writing was distinctive in that it had more active verbs than passive verbs, more subheadings and subtitles, and shorter paragraphs.[17]

Nonverbal Communication

Effective leaders are masterful nonverbal as well as verbal communicators. Nonverbal communication is important because leadership involves emotion, which words alone cannot communicate convincingly. A major component of the emotional impact of a message is communicated nonverbally—perhaps up to 90 percent.[18] The classic study behind this observation has been misinterpreted to mean that 90 percent of communication is nonverbal. If this were true, facts, figures, and logic would make a minor contribution to communication, and acting skill would be much more important for getting across one's point of view.

A self-confident leader not only speaks and writes with assurance but also projects confidence through body position, gestures, and manner of speech. Not everybody interprets the same body language and other non-verbal signals in the same way, but some aspects of nonverbal behavior project a self-confident, leadership image in many situations.[19]

- Using an erect posture when walking, standing, or sitting. Slouching and slumping are almost universally interpreted as an indicator of low self-confidence.

- Standing up straight during a confrontation. Cowering is interpreted as a sign of low self-confidence and poor leadership qualities.

- Patting other people on the back, nodding slightly while patting.

- Standing with toes pointing outward rather than inward. Outward-pointing toes are usually perceived as indicators of superior status, whereas inward-pointing toes are perceived to indicate inferiority.

- Speaking at a moderate pace, with a loud, confident tone. People lacking in self-confidence tend to speak too rapidly or very slowly.

- Smiling frequently in a relaxed, natural-appearing manner.

- Maintaining eye contact with those around you.

A general approach to using nonverbal behavior that projects confidence is to have a goal of appearing self-confident and powerful. This type of auto-suggestion makes many of the behaviors seem automatic. For example, if you say, "I am going to display leadership qualities in this meeting," you will have taken an important step toward appearing confident.

Your external image also plays an important role in communicating messages to others. People pay more respect and grant more privileges to those they perceive as being well dressed and neatly groomed. Even on dress-down days, the majority of effective leaders will choose clothing that gives them an edge over others. Appearance includes more than the choice of clothing. Self-confidence is projected by such small items as

- Neatly pressed and sparkling clean clothing
- Freshly polished shoes
- Impeccable fingernails
- Clean jewelry in mint condition
- Well-maintained hair
- Good-looking teeth with a white or antique-white color
- A trace of cologne, perfume, or toilet water

What constitutes a powerful and self-confident external image is influenced not only by the organizational culture but by the culture in general. At a software development company, for example, powerful people might dress more casually than at an investment banking firm. Your verbal behavior, and the forms of nonverbal behavior previously discussed, contributes more to your leadership image than your clothing, providing you dress acceptably.

A subtle mode of nonverbal communication is the use of time. Guarding time as a precious resource will help you project an image of self-confidence and leadership. A statement such as, "I can devote fifteen minutes to your problem this Thursday at 4 P.M. " connotes confidence and being in control. (Too many of these statements, however, might make a person appear unapproachable and inconsiderate.) Other ways of projecting power through the use of time include such behaviors as being prompt for meetings, and starting and stopping meetings on time. It may also be helpful to make references to dates one year into the future and beyond, such as, "By 2002 we should have a 25 percent market share."[20]

We have been emphasizing how nonverbal behavior can be used to enhance powerful communication. Keep in mind also that being able to interpret nonverbal behavior contributes to effective leadership, as illustrated in the accompanying Leader in Action insert.

Now that you have refreshed your thoughts on effective verbal and nonverbal communication, do Leadership Skill-Building Exercise 12–2.

LEADER IN ACTION

Karen Vesper of Doorway Rug Service Interprets Nonverbal Behavior

Karen Vesper, the vice president of family-owned Doorway Rug Service Inc. in Buffalo, New York, carefully observed candidates for sales jobs in her company. "I was watching how they carried themselves, whether they made eye contact, whether they used animated hand movements," she explains. One prospect never opened his notebook. He asked only a few questions, then leaned back and sat quietly during the rest of the interview. Vesper did not invite him back. The behavior of one of the two people the company did hire was quite different. "She looked up all the time and made eye contact," said Vesper.

By watching the job candidates' mannerisms, Vesper was trying to evaluate how aggressive they would be as salespeople, as well as whether they would come across to potential customers as obnoxious or personable.

Vesper says she tries to monitor and control her body language when she goes on a sales call.

She has also profited from reading others' nonverbal cues in hiring and selling. She claims that her most useful clue is swallowing. A friend who inspects travelers for contraband at the Canadian border once told her that people who swallow before speaking have something to hide. A candidate who swallowed might be trying to hide facts about a major negative episode in his or her employment history. A customer prospect who swallowed might be trying to hide the fact that he or she didn't have the money to pay for the service, even though he or she was eager to sign up for it. She says, "I don't know whether body language is 100 percent accurate, but it gives you a better feel for the situation."

Source: Adapted from Mark Henricks, "More than Words: Brushing Up on Body Language May Give You Just the Competitive Edge You Need," *Entrepreneur*, August 1995, pp. 54–57.

LEADERSHIP SKILL-BUILDING
EXERCISE 12–2 Feedback on Verbal and Nonverbal Behavior

Ten volunteers have one week to prepare a three-minute presentation on a course-related subject of their choice. The topics of these presentations could be as far-reaching as "The Importance of the North American Free Trade Agreement," or "My Goals and Dreams." The class members who observe the presentations prepare feedback slips on 3 × 5 cards, describing how well the speakers communicated powerfully and inspirationally. One card per speaker is usually sufficient. Notations should be made for both verbal and nonverbal feedback.

Emphasis should be placed on positive feedback and constructive suggestions. Students pass the feedback cards along to the speakers. The cards can be anonymous to encourage frankness, but they should not be mean-spirited.

SUPPORTIVE COMMUNICATION

Communicating powerfully and inspirationally facilitates influencing and inspiring people. A more mellow type of communication is needed to implement the people-oriented aspects of a leader's role. A leader who uses supportive communication nurtures group members and brings out their best. Instead of dazzling them with a power presence, the leader is low-key and interested in the other person's agenda. **Supportive communication** is a communication style that delivers the message accurately and that supports or enhances the relationship between the two parties. The process has eight principles or characteristics, which have emerged from the work of many researchers.[21] They are described below and outlined in Table 12–2.

1. *Supportive communication is problem-oriented, not person-oriented.* Effective leaders and managers focus more on the problem than on the person when communicating with group members. Most people are more receptive to a discussion of what can be done to change a work method than to a discussion of what can be done to change them. Many people might readily agree that more alternative solutions to a problem are needed. Fewer people are willing to accept the message "You need to be more creative."

    A helpful adjunct to problem-oriented communication is for the leader or manager to encourage the other person to participate in a solution to the problem. In the example at hand, the leader might say, "Perhaps you can find a method that will generate more alternative solutions to the problem."

2. *Supportive communication is descriptive, not evaluative.* A closely related principle is that when a person's worth is being evaluated, he or she

TABLE 12–2   Principles and Characteristics of Supportive Communication

1. Problem-oriented, not person-oriented

2. Descriptive, not evaluative

3. Based on congruence, not incongruence

4. Focused on validating, rather than invalidating, people

5. Specific, not global

6. Conjunctive, not disjunctive

7. Owned, not disowned

8. Requires listening as well as sending messages

often becomes defensive. If a leader says to a group member, "You are a low-quality performer," the person will probably become defensive. The descriptive form of communication—for example, "I found errors in your last two reports that created problems"—allows the person to separate the errors from himself or herself. A supervisor's "I message" ("I found errors") is less accusatory than a "you message" ("You are a low-quality performer").

3. *Supportive communication is based on congruence, not incongruence.* A superior form of communication is **congruence,** the matching of verbal and nonverbal communication to what the sender is thinking and feeling. A leader is more credible when his or her nonverbal signals mesh with his or her spoken words. A chief executive officer might say to his staff, "I'm no longer concerned about the firm having to declare bankruptcy. Sales have improved substantially, and our costs are way down." If at the same time, the CEO is fidgeting and has a sickly, upset appearance, the message will not be convincing. In this case the leader's message doesn't fit; it is *incongruent.* If the CEO delivers the same message with a smile and a relaxed manner, his credibility will increase.

4. *Supportive communication validates rather than invalidates people.* Validating communication accepts the presence, uniqueness, and importance of the other person. Whether or not the person's ideas are totally accepted, he or she is acknowledged. During a meeting, the manager of internal auditing said to a recently hired auditor, "Your suggestion of bonus pay for auditors when they have to stay away from home more than two weekends has some merit. We can't act on your suggestion now, but please bring it up again in a future meeting." The young auditor felt encouraged to make other suggestions in the future. An invalidating communication would have been for the manager to flat out

ignore the auditor, or to make a snide comment such as "Your naiveté is showing. Nobody with much business experience would make such a bad suggestion."

5. *Supportive communication is specific, not global.* As described in Chapter 10, most people benefit more from specific than from global, or general, feedback. To illustrate, the statement "We have terrible customer service" is too general to be very useful. A more useful statement would be "Our customer satisfaction ratings are down 25 percent from previous years": It is more specific and provides an improvement target.

6. *Supportive communication is conjunctive, not disjunctive.* **Conjunctive communication** is linked logically to previous messages, thus enhancing communication. **Disjunctive communication** is not linked to the preceding messages, resulting in impaired communication. Conjunctive communication makes it easier for group members and other constituents to follow the leader's thoughts. David A. Whetton and Kim S. Cameron explain that communication can be disjunctive in three ways: (1) People might have unequal opportunity to speak because of interruptions and simultaneous speaking; (2) lengthy pauses are disjunctive because listeners lose the speaker's train of thought; and (3) communication is perceived as disjunctive when one person controls the topics. Many leaders, as well as group members, fail to relate their comments to the topics introduced by others.[22]

7. *Supportive communication is owned, not disowned.* Effective communicators take responsibility for what they say and do not attribute the authority behind their ideas to another person. The effective leader might say, "I want everybody to work eight extra hours per week during this crisis." The less effective leader might say, "The company wants everybody to work overtime." Other ways of disowning communication include using statements such as "they say," or "everybody thinks." Using the word *I* indicates that you strongly believe what you are saying.

8. *Supportive communication requires listening as well as sending messages.* Truly supportive communication requires active listening (as described in the discussion of coaching). The relationship between two parties cannot be enhanced unless each listens to the other. Furthermore, leaders cannot identify problems unless they listen carefully to group members. Listening is a fundamental management and leadership skill.

Supportive communication requires considerable practice, and must be integrated into one's leadership style to be implemented successfully. The coaching style of the leader finds supportive communication to be a natural way of relating to others. Leadership Skill-Building Exercise 12–3 gives you an opportunity to try out supportive communication.

LEADERSHIP SKILL-BUILDING EXERCISE 12–3 Supportive Communication

Six or seven students gather for a team meeting to discuss an important operational problem, such as finding new ways to reduce the cycle time required to complete their tasks, or deciding how to convince top management to expand the team budget. One person plays the role of the team leader. All the group members take turns at making both useful and apparently not-useful suggestions. The team leader, along with team members, will use supportive communication whenever ideas surface. Students not directly involved in the group role play will take note of the supportive (or nonsupportive) communication they observe so that they can provide feedback after the exercise. If class time allows, another team of six or seven students can repeat the group role play.

OVERCOMING CROSS-CULTURAL COMMUNICATION BARRIERS

Another communication challenge facing leaders and managers is to overcome communication barriers created by dealing with people from different cultures and subcultures. In today's workplace, leaders communicate with people from other countries, and with a more diverse group of people in their own country. The latter is particularly true in culturally diverse countries such as the United States and Canada. Because of this workplace diversity, leaders who can manage a multicultural and cross-cultural work force are in strong demand. Here we describe the role of attributions in helping to overcome cross-cultural communication barriers, and give some guidelines for overcoming them.

Attributions and Cross-Cultural Communication

A major underlying factor in overcoming cross-cultural communication barriers is to understand **attributions,** the judgments we make about the behavior and attitudes of others. As noted by Paul Hersey, Kenneth H. Blanchard, and Dewey E. Johnson, three factors affect the attributions or judgments we make.[23] (The judgments in attributions typically deal with interpretations of causation.) *Perception* refers to the various ways in which people interpret things in the outside world and how they react on the basis of these interpretations. For example, when visiting another city, you might see a large number of people on the street asking for money. During a business meeting in that city, one interpretation of this event that you might share is, "I guess you have a problem with a lot of lazy people in your city." Another interpretation of the same event might be, "My impression is that your town could benefit from economic expansion. A lot of people are still looking for work." When we are unfamiliar with another culture, it is more difficult to make accurate perceptions.

Stereotyping is evaluating an individual on the basis of our perception of the group or class to which he or she belongs. Although *stereotype* has a negative connotation, positive stereotypes can be useful in dealing with people from another culture. Suppose you stereotype Italians as being creative, artistic, and strongly interested in product design. On a business trip to Italy, you make many references to the design aspects of your product. So doing will foster communication with that group of Italians. Negative stereotypes, of course, can create substantial cross-cultural communication problems. A businesswoman from London visited a New York City affiliate during the winter. As she and three colleagues from the New York office entered a restaurant for dinner, the woman insisted on taking her overcoat to the table. She told the group, "I have been told that when visiting New York, you shouldn't let anything valuable out of your sight." Rapport between this woman and the group quickly deteriorated.

A third key attribution factor is *ethnocentrism*, the assumption that the ways of one's culture are the *best* ways of doing things. Displaying ethnocentrism can lead to complete communication breakdowns, such as an American's expressing pity for his work associates in Ireland because they are unable to watch NFL teams on Sunday.

Guidelines for Overcoming and Preventing Communication Barriers

In addition to being aware of the role of attributions, the leader attempting to communicate with members of a different culture should also follow certain guidelines. Implementing these guidelines will help overcome and prevent many communication problems.

1. *Be sensitive to the fact that cross-cultural communication barriers exist.*
   Awareness of these potential barriers is the first step in dealing with them. When dealing with a person of a different cultural background, solicit feedback to minimize cross-cultural barriers to communication. For example, investigate which types of praise or other rewards might be ineffective for a particular cultural group. In many instances, Asians newly arrived in the United States feel uncomfortable being praised in front of others, because in Asian cultures group performance is valued more than individual performance.

   Being alert to cultural differences in values, attitudes, and etiquette will help you communicate more effectively with people from different cultures. Observe carefully the following cultural mistakes.

   ■ Insisting on getting down to business quickly in most countries outside the United States. (In most countries, building a social relationship precedes closing a deal.)

- Misinterpreting "We'll consider it" as "Maybe" when spoken by a Japanese. (Japanese negotiators mean "No" when they say, "We'll consider it.")

- Misinterpreting "Yes" (*Hai*) during the course of conversation with a Japanese. (*Hai* only acknowledges that what has been said has been heard, and does not mean agreement.)

- Giving small gifts to Chinese when conducting business. (Chinese are offended by these gifts.)

- Not giving small gifts to Japanese when conducting business. (Japanese are offended by not receiving gifts.)

- Misinterpreting a British boss saying, "Perhaps you ought to think about this a little more" as an opportunity for you to revise your proposal. (In American terms, the Englishman is saying, "Your proposal is worthless.")

- Thinking that a businessperson from England is unenthusiastic when he or she says, "Not too bad at all." (English people under-state positive emotion.)

- Appearing in shirtsleeves at a business meeting in Germany. (Germans believe that a person is not exercising proper authority when he or she appears at a meeting in shirtsleeves.)

- Being overly rank-conscious in Scandinavian countries. (Scandinavians pay relatively little attention to a person's rung on the organizational ladder.)

- Appearing perturbed when somebody shows up late for a meeting in most countries outside the United States. (Time is much less valued outside the United States. Exceptions, however, include Germany and Scandinavia.)

- Pressuring an Asian job applicant or employee to brag about his or her accomplishments. (Boasting about his or her work achievements makes most Asians feel self-conscious. They prefer to let the record speak for itself.)

- Greeting a French customer or other business contact for the first time in a French-speaking country by saying, "Glad to meet you." (French is a polite language. It is preferable to say, "Glad to meet you, sir [or madame, or miss].")[24]

- In Saudi Arabia, asking about the spouse and family of a customer. However, in Mexico, it is considered courteous to make inquiries about the same topic.

- Interpreting the words "tabling a motion" in England to mean that the motion should be put away for a while, as in the United States. In England, "tabling" a motion means putting it on the table immediately for discussion.[25]

2. *Use straightforward language, and speak slowly and clearly.* When working with people who do not speak your language fluently, speak in an easy-to-understand manner. Minimize the use of idioms and analogies specific to your language. A systems analyst from New Delhi, India, left a performance review with her manager confused. The manager said, "I will be giving you more important assignments because I notice some good chemistry between us." The woman did not understand that *good chemistry* means *rapport,* and she did not ask for clarification because she did not want to appear uninformed.

   Speaking slowly is also important because even people who read and write a second language at an expert level may have difficulty catching some nuances of conversation. Facing the person from another culture directly also improves communication because your facial expressions and lips contribute to comprehension. And remember, there is no need to speak much louder.

3. *When the situation is appropriate, speak in the language of the people from another culture.* Americans who can speak another language are at a competitive advantage when dealing with businesspeople who speak that language. The language skill, however, must be more advanced than speaking a few basic words and phrases. A new twist in knowing another language has surged recently: As more deaf people have been integrated into the work force, knowing American Sign Language can be a real advantage to a leader when some of his or her constituents are deaf.

4. *Observe cross-cultural differences in etiquette.* Violating rules of etiquette without explanation can erect immediate communication barriers. A major rule of etiquette in many countries is that people address each other by last name unless they have worked with each other for a long time. Letitia Baldridge recommends explaining the difference in custom to prevent misunderstanding. Imagine this scenario in which you are working with a man from Germany, and you are speaking:

   Herr Schultz, in my country by now I would be calling you Heinrich and you would be calling me Charlie. Would you be comfortable with that? Because if you wouldn't, I would be glad to call you Herr Schultz until you tell me it's time to call you Heinrich.[26]

5. *Do not be diverted by style, accent, grammar, or personal appearance.* Although these superficial factors are all related to business success, they are difficult to interpret when judging a person from another culture. It is therefore better to judge the merits of the statement or behavior.[27] A highly intelligent worker from another culture may still be learning English and thus make basic mistakes. He or she might also not yet have developed a sensitivity to dress style in your culture.

6. *Be sensitive to differences in nonverbal communication.* A person from another culture may misinterpret nonverbal signals.[28] To use positive reinforcement, some managers will give a sideways hug to an employee

or will touch the employee's arm. People from some cultures resent touching from workmates and will be offended. Koreans in particular dislike being touched or touching others in a work setting. A more common cross-cultural communication error is for an American to symbolize OK by making a circle with the thumb and first finger. In some other cultures, including those of Spain and India, the "OK circle" symbolizes a vulgarity.

7. *Avoid racial or ethnic identification except when it is essential to communication.* Using a person's race or ethnicity as an adjective or other descriptor often suggests a negative stereotype.[29] For example, suppose a leader says, "I am proud of André. He is a very responsible African American customer service rep." One possible interpretation of this statement is that most African American customer service reps are not so responsible. Or, a leader might say, "We are happy to have Martha on our team. She is an easy-to-get-along-with British lady." A possible implication is that British women are usually not too easy to work with.

A general way to understand cross-cultural differences in nonverbal communication is to recognize that some cultures emphasize nonverbal communication more than others. People from high-context cultures are more sensitive to the surrounding circumstances or context of an event. As a result, they make extensive use of nonverbal communication. Among these high-context cultures are those of Asians, Hispanics, and African Americans. People from low-context cultures pay less attention to the context of an event and therefore make less use of nonverbal communication. Among these low-context cultures are those of northern Europeans and Swiss. Anglo-Americans are from a medium-context culture.[30] Many new members of the work force are from high-context cultures. Leaders from medium-context cultures must therefore learn to be extra responsive to nonverbal communication.

In dealing with people from a high-context culture, recognize that the people need to know how to place you in context in order to understand you better. People from a high-context culture will want to know something about your background and the company you represent. Without that knowledge, it may be difficult to establish good communication.[31]

THE LEADER'S ROLE IN RESOLVING CONFLICT AND NEGOTIATING

Leaders and managers spend considerable time resolving conflicts and negotiating. A frequent estimate is that they devote about 20 percent of their time to dealing with conflict. For example, according to Accountemps, managers spend roughly nine work weeks a year resolving employee personality clashes.[32] An extensive description of conflict resolution is more appropriate for the study of managerial skills than for the study of leadership skills because it has more to do with establishing equilibrium than with helping

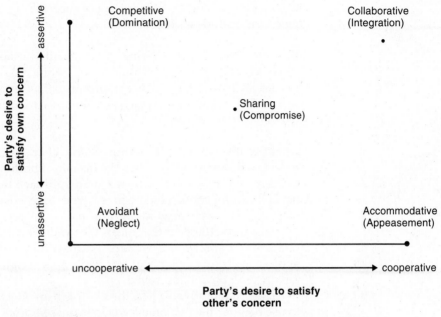

FIGURE 12–1

Conflict-Handling Styles According to the Degree of Cooperation and Assertiveness
Source: Marvin D. Dunnette, ed., Handbook of Industrial and Organizational Psychology, *p. 900 (Rand McNally). Copyright © 1976. Used by permission of Marvin D. Dunnette.*

the firm or organizational unit reach new heights. Here we focus on a basic framework for understanding conflict resolution styles, and a few suggestions for negotiating.

Conflict Management Styles

As shown in Figure 12–1, Kenneth Thomas identified five major styles of conflict management: competitive, accommodative, sharing, collaborative, and avoidant. Each style is based on a combination of satisfying one's own concerns (assertiveness) and satisfying the concerns of others (cooperativeness).[33]

Competitive Style.   The competitive style is a desire to win one's own concerns at the expense of the other party, or to dominate. A person with a competitive orientation is likely to engage in win-lose power struggles.

Accommodative Style.   The accommodative style favors appeasement, or satisfying the other's concerns without taking care of one's own. People with this orientation may be generous or self-sacrificing just to maintain a relationship. An irate customer might be accommodated with a full refund, "just to shut him (or her) up." The intent of such accommodation might also be to retain the customer's loyalty.

Sharing Style.   The sharing style is halfway between domination and appeasement. Sharers prefer moderate but incomplete satisfaction for both parties, which results in a compromise. The term *splitting the difference* reflects this orientation, which is commonly used in such activities as purchasing a house or car.

Collaborative Style.   In contrast to the other styles, the collaborative style reflects a desire to fully satisfy the desires of both parties. It is based on the underlying philosophy of the **win-win approach to conflict resolution,** the belief that after conflict has been resolved, both sides should gain something of value. The user of win-win approaches is genuinely concerned about arriving at a settlement that meets the needs of both parties, or at least does not badly damage the welfare of the other side. When collaborative approaches to resolving conflict are used, the relationships among the parties are built on and improved.

The collaborative style is the approach an effective leader is most likely to use because the outcome leads to increased productivity and satisfaction. The accompanying Leader in Action vignette illustrates this approach to conflict resolution.

Avoidant Style.   The avoider combines lack of cooperation and un-assertiveness. He or she is indifferent to the concerns of either party. The person may actually be withdrawing from the conflict or be relying upon fate. An example of an avoider is a manager who stays out of a conflict between two team members, leaving them to resolve their own differences.

People engaged in conflict resolution typically combine several of the five resolution styles to accomplish their purpose. For example, a generally effective approach to resolving conflict is to use forcing with regard to a cost that is important to oneself but unimportant to the opponent, and at the same time use accommodation for a cost that is unimportant to oneself but important to the opponent.[34] An experiment was conducted in which 116 Dutch police sergeants attempted to resolve conflicts with either a subordinate or a superior. One important finding was that an increase in problem solving (such as that found in collaboration) tended to enhance effectiveness if combined with considerable forcing, or domination, in dealing with a subordinate. Also in support of using a combination of tactics, the experiment showed that there is a *ladder of effectiveness* in using the conflict modes studied, as follows: forcing (dominating), avoiding, confronting, compromising, problem solving, and process controlling.[35]

Which mode or modes of conflict handling to use depends upon a number of variables, as presented in detail in Table 12–3. The major contingency factors are the importance of the conflict issue and the relative power of the opposing parties. An issue may be so important to a leader, such as prevent-

LEADER IN ACTION

Elizabeth Elton, Product Manager

Elizabeth Elton is a product manager for a pharmaceutical company. One of the products under her responsibility is zinc oxide ointment, which facilitates the healing of rashes, cuts, and abrasions. Several years ago, conflict over this product arose between manufacturing and sales.

Although the entire company had adopted a system of quality management , so far it had been implemented more directly in manufacturing. The head of the unit that manufactures zinc oxide ointment proudly claimed that defects in the product had been virtually eliminated. The sales director was proud of manufacturing's accomplishments in achieving total quality. Nevertheless, he maintained that the high product quality had led to a high manufacturing cost. In turn, the high cost had made it difficult to offer substantial discounts to distributors.

The head of sales presented convincing data that the company's product had lost substantial sales to house brands of zinc oxide. In retail outlets, the house brands were placed adjacent to the company brand, making it easy for the consumer to purchase by price.

Frequent mention was made in staff meetings of the struggle of having to produce a top-quality product that would compete against lower-priced brands of acceptable quality. Elton stepped into the conflict by working closely with manufacturing and sales to arrive at a mutually agreeable solution to resolving the conflict. She told the two unit heads that she agreed strongly with both of them—both quality *and* price are important. Elton then suggested that manufacturing should strive for quality, but at a price consumers are willing to pay. She also suggested that the sales manager should not abandon the idea that many consumers are willing to pay a slight premium for a name-brand pharmaceutical product.

The manufacturing group responded by finding a way to decrease the manufacturing cost 15 percent without a measurable impact on quality. The sales group then aggressively pushed the sales theme of quality and brand-name reliability, at a small price differential. Sales returned to a satisfactory level, and the manufacturing group was comfortable that the company did not slip backwards in offering a quality product.

ing his or her organization unit from being outsourced, that domination may be the most effective mode. At other times a leader may use the accommodating mode when the opposing side has much more power, and he or she may want to save domination for a more important issue in the future.

Negotiating and Bargaining

Conflicts can be considered situations calling for negotiating and bargaining, or conferring with another person in order to resolve a problem. When you are trying to negotiate a fair salary for yourself, you are simultaneously trying to resolve a conflict. At first the demands of the two parties may seem incompatible, but through negotiation a salary may emerge that satisfies both parties. Two general approaches to negotiation are *distributive bargaining* and *integrative bargaining*. In distributive bargaining, the two sides operate under zero-sum conditions. What one wins is at the expense of the other, and the purpose of bargaining is to distribute the resources. This is the commonsense

TABLE 12–3   Appropriate Situations for Using the Five Modes of Resolving Conflict

Conflict-Handling Mode	Appropriate Situation
Competing	1. When quick decisive action is vital, such as in an emergency 2. On important issues when unpopular actions need implementing, such as cost cutting, enforcing unpopular rules, or discipline 3. On issues vital to organization welfare when you know you are right 4. Against people who take advantage of noncompetitive behavior
Collaborating	1. To find an integrative solution when both sets of concerns are too important to be compromised 2. When your objective is to learn 3. To merge insights from people with different perspectives 4. To gain commitment by incorporating concerns into a consensus 5. To work through feelings that have interfered with a relationship
Compromising	1. When goals are important but not worth the effort or potential disruption of more assertive modes 2. When opponents with equal power are committed to mutually exclusive goals 3. To achieve temporary settlements of complex issues 4. To arrive at expedient solutions under time pressure 5. As a backup when collaboration or competition is unsuccessful
Avoiding	1. When an issue is trivial or more important issues are pressing 2. When you perceive no chance of satisfying your concern 3. When the potential disruption outweighs the benefits of a resolution 4. To let people cool down and regain perspective. 5. When gathering information supersedes making an immediate decision 6. When others can resolve the conflict more effectively
Accommodating	1. When you find you are wrong—to allow a better position to be heard, to learn, and to show your reasonableness 2. When issues are more important to others than to yourself—to satisfy others and maintain cooperation 3. To build social credits for later issues 4. To minimize the loss when you are outmatched and losing 5. When harmony and stability are especially important 6. To allow group members to develop by learning from mistakes

Source: Slightly adapted from Kenneth W. Thomas, "Toward Multidimensional Values in Teaching: The Example of Conflict Behaviors," *Academy of Management Review*, April 1977, p. 487. Used by permission of Academy of Management.

approach to negotiation. Integrative bargaining reflects the collaborative mode of managing conflict because it assumes that win-win solutions can be found. Table 12–4 outlines the differences between distributive and integrative bargaining. Following are several negotiation techniques leaders may need to have at their disposal.

Begin with a Plausible Demand or Offer.   Most people believe that compromise and allowing room for negotiation includes beginning with an extreme demand or offer. The theory is that the final compromise will be

TABLE 12–4   Distributive versus Integrative Bargaining

	Distributive Bargaining	*Integrative Bargaining*
Resources to be distributed	Fixed amount	Variable amount
Primary motivations of parties	To gain at the expense of the other side (I win, you lose)	To maximize gains for both sides (I win, you win)
Primary interests	180 degrees apart	Convergent or congruent
Focus of relationships	Short-term	Long-term

closer to the true demand or offer than if the negotiation were opened more realistically. But a plausible demand is better because it reflects good-faith bargaining. Also, if a third party has to resolve the conflict, a plausible demand or offer will receive more sympathy than an implausible one.

Focus on Interests, Not Position.   Rather than clinging to specific negotiating points, one should keep overall interests in mind and try to satisfy them. Remember that the true object of negotiation is to satisfy the underlying interests of both sides.

Here is how this strategy works: Your manager asks you to submit a proposal for increasing productivity. You see it as an opportunity to acquire an additional staff member. When you submit your ideas, you learn that management is really thinking about additional computerization, not additional staff. Instead of insisting on hiring a new worker, be flexible. Ask to be included in the decision making for acquiring an additional computer. You will reduce your workload (your true interest), and you may enjoy such secondary benefits as having helped the company increase productivity.[36]

Be Sensitive to International Differences in Negotiating Style.   A challenge facing the multicultural leader is how to negotiate successfully with people from other cultures. Frank L. Acuff notes that Americans often have a no-nonsense approach to negotiation. Key attitudes underlying the American approach to negotiation include:

"Tell it like it is."

"What's the bottom line?"

"Let's get it out."

A problem with this type of frankness and seeming impatience is that people from other cultures may interpret such remarks as rudeness. The adverse interpretation, in turn, may lead to a failed negotiation. Acuff gives a case example: "It is unlikely in Mexico or Japan that the other side is going to answer yes or no to any question. You will have to discern answers to questions through the context of what is being said rather than from the

LEADERSHIP SKILL-BUILDING
EXERCISE 12–4 Integrative Bargaining

The class is organized into groups of six, with each group being divided into two negotiating teams of three each. The members of the negotiating teams would like to find an integrative (win-win) solution to the issue separating the two sides. The team members are free to invent their own pressing issue, or choose one from among the following:

- Management wants to control costs by not giving cost-of-living adjustments in the upcoming year. The employee group believes that a cost-of-living adjustment is absolutely necessary for its welfare.

- The marketing team claims it could sell 250,000 units of a toaster wide enough to toast bagels if the toasters could be produced at $10 per unit. The manufacturing group says it would not be feasible to get the manufacturing cost below $15 per unit.

- Blockbuster Video would like to build in a new location that is adjacent to a historic district in one of the oldest cities in North America. The members of the town planning board would like the tax revenue and jobs that the Blockbuster store would bring, but they do not want a Blockbuster store adjacent to the historic district.

After the teams have arrived at their solutions through high-level negotiating techniques, the creative solutions can be shared with teammates.

more obvious direct cues that U.S. negotiators use."[37] By sizing up what constitutes an effective negotiating style, the negotiator stands a reasonable chance of achieving a collaborative solution.

Negotiating and bargaining, as with any other leadership and management skill, requires conceptual knowledge and practice. Leadership Skill-Building Exercise 12–4 gives you an opportunity to practice the highest form of negotiating and bargaining.

SUMMARY

Systematic observation and empirical research support the idea that effective leaders are also effective communicators. There is substantial evidence of a positive relationship between competence in communication and leadership performance. However, a survey has revealed that a top business executive may not be doing a good job of communicating the company's mission, vision, and values. Nonverbal skills are also important for leadership effectiveness.

Inspirational and powerful communication helps leaders carry out their roles. Suggestions for inspirational and powerful speaking and writing include the following: (1) Use the persuade package of influence tactics; (2) use heavy-impact, embellishing language; (3) use emotion-provoking words; (4) use a power-oriented linguistic style; (5) know exactly what you want; (6) back up conclusions with data; (7) minimize junk words and vocalized pauses; (8) avoid or minimize common language errors; (9) sell group members on the benefits of your suggestions; (10) gear your message to the listener; (11) explore the reasons for people's objections; (12) front-load your message; (13) write crisp, clear memos, letters, and reports.

Skill can also be developed in using nonverbal communication that connotes power, being in control, forcefulness, and self-confidence. Among the suggestions are to stand erect, speak at a moderate pace with a loud, clear tone, and smile frequently in a relaxed manner. A person's external image also plays an important part in communicating messages to others. People pay more respect and grant more privileges to those they perceive as being well dressed and neatly groomed.

Supportive communication enhances communication between two people and therefore contributes to leadership effectiveness. The process has identifiable principles and characteristics. Supportive communication is (1) problem-oriented, not person-oriented, (2) descriptive, not evaluative, (3) based on congruence, not incongruence, (4) focused on validating, rather than invalidating, people, (5) specific, not global, (6) conjunctive, not disjunctive, (7) owned, not disowned, and (8) characterized by intense listening.

Overcoming communication barriers created by dealing with people from different cultures is another leadership and management challenge. A major factor in overcoming cross-cultural barriers is to understand attributions—the judgments we make about the behaviors and attitudes of others. Three key factors in forming attributions are perception, stereotyping, and ethnocentrism. Guidelines for overcoming cross-cultural barriers include the following: (1) Be sensitive to the existence of cross-cultural barriers; (2) use straightforward language, and speak slowly and clearly; (3) when appropriate, speak in the language of the people from another culture; (4) observe cross-cultural differences in etiquette; (5) do not be diverted by differences in style, grammar, accent, or personal appearance; (6) be sensitive to differences in nonverbal communication; and (7) avoid racial or ethnic identification except when it is essential to communication.

A general way to understand cross-cultural differences in nonverbal communication is to recognize that some cultures emphasize nonverbal communication more than others. People from high-context cultures are more sensitive to the surrounding circumstances or context of an event.

Leaders and managers spend considerable time managing conflict. Five major styles of conflict management are as follows: competitive, accommodative, sharing, collaborative (win-win), and avoidant. Each style is based on a combination of satisfying one's own concerns (assertiveness) and satisfying the concerns of others (cooperativeness). When resolving conflict, people typically combine several of the five resolution styles to accomplish their purpose, such as combining dominating and accommodating. Which modes of conflict handling to use depends upon a number of variables, as presented in detail in Table 12–3.

Conflicts can be considered situations calling for negotiating and bargaining. Distributive bargaining and integrative bargaining are two general approaches to negotiation. In distributive bargaining, the two sides operate under zero-sum conditions. Integrative bargaining reflects the collaborative mode of managing conflict because it assumes that win-win solutions can be found. Specific negotiating techniques include the following: (1) Begin with a plausible demand or offer; (2) focus on interests, not positions; and (3) be sensitive to differences in negotiating style.

KEY TERMS

Virtual office	Congruence	Win-win approach to conflict
Persuade package	Conjunctive communication	resolution
Linguistic style	Disjunctive communication	
Supportive communication	Attributions	

GUIDELINES FOR ACTION AND SKILL DEVELOPMENT

Gay Lumsden and Donald Lumsden recommend a specific communications improvement program that can supplement the suggestions already made in this chapter.

1. **Seek congruity with your messages.** The information and feelings you communicate should be consistent with the verbal and nonverbal messages you use to send them.

2. **Ask for feedback from family, friends, coworkers, and managers.** Ask people who are familiar with your communication style about the congruence between your verbal and nonverbal messages.

3. **Observe others' responses.** Watch for positive, negative, and comprehending responses from others. Question how well your messages are received.

4. **Observe a videotape of yourself.** Obtain a videotape of yourself in daily conversation or making a presentation. Scrutinize your strengths and areas for development. Look for ways to appear more powerful and inspiring. Be particularly alert to voice quality, junk words, and weak expressions.

5. **Decide what to change.** Identify specific verbal and nonverbal behaviors you think you should change to enhance your communication effectiveness. Follow up by practicing the new or modified behaviors.[38]

DISCUSSION QUESTIONS AND ACTIVITIES

1. Now that you have studied this chapter, what are you going to do differently to improve your communication effectiveness as a leader?

2. Find an example of a powerful written message by a leader. Bring the information back to class to share with others.

3. Videotape a powerful spoken message delivered by a leader. If time and equipment permit, share your videotape with classmates.

4. What kinds of demands does the widespread use of electronic communication place on leaders in organizations?

5. How can you systematically determine if a given word is truly a "power word"?

6. Executive leaders in some large business corporations use videotapes of themselves to deliver important messages to large numbers of employees. From a leadership standpoint, what are the advantages and disadvantages of this means of communication?

7. Which leadership style or styles do you think most closely conform to supportive communication?

8. Think of three examples of positive ethnic stereotypes.

9. What adaptations should leaders make in their communication approaches to overcome potential communication barriers in dealing with the deaf?

10. Give two examples in which it would probably be effective for a leader to use the accommodative style of conflict handling.

LEADERSHIP CASE PROBLEM

Tough Day at Southern Tel

Chet Rivera, CEO at Southern Tel, thanked the human resources director for introducing him as the keynote speaker at the annual managers' meeting. Rivera began his presentation by talking about the progress the company had made during the last five years. He explained that the profits and return on investment were solid enough to satisfy the majority of the stockholders. He then leaned forward, held onto the lectern, and cleared his throat before continuing. Rivera quickly moved to the core of his presentation, in these words:

"But don't let our satisfactory financial progress make you complacent. We are treading water in an era when we must be splashing toward new records. Ever since the telephone industry has become deregulated, the competition is tougher than ever.

"Unshackle yourself from the Southern Tel of old. We are a company that has reinvented itself. We intend to lead the pack, not follow. We are forging our way into new technologies. We seek to maximize return on investment. Southern Tel has trimmed considerable fat, but we're still too bloated. We have a long way to go to sort out the doers of the future from the hangers on to the past.

"Those of you who can adapt to the new way of doing business in a competitive, deregulated world will have a job with us. Those of you whose thinking is not in line with our new corporate strategy will be asked to retire or find employment elsewhere. We have no place for the laggards, and for those who think in the past. Above all, we have no place for those managers who think we are doing customers a favor by providing them phone service.

"Be part of our new thinking or go find a compatible environment for yourself. I have no sympathy for those who lack commitment to our strategy, and for those who are not committed to excellence. Yet there will be a job for those of you who identify with the Southern Tel of today.

"We have undergone a major downsizing, but at the same time we have been hiring extensively. We are bringing on board people with the talent, energy, and mental strength to help make us a major player in the telecommunications revolution engulfing us.

"Make no mistake about it. We have plenty of room in this company for the ambitious, the visionaries, and those with cutting-edge skills. We have much less room for those without the essential skills we need.

"For many of you in this room, what I have said should be a cause for optimism.

"I have allotted five minutes for questions and answers."

Hardly a sound could be heard in the auditorium at Southern Tel for two minutes. After those two minutes, a loud buzz arose as the managers talked to each other nervously in groups of two and three.

1. What aspects of Rivera's talk contain inspirational language?

2. What aspects of Rivera's talk contain powerful language?

3. How would you evaluate Rivera's talk as a form of supportive communication?

Strategic Leadership

Gwenn Cagann spotted the specialty-coffee trend early enough to find a market niche and become a highly successful player in the field. In 1992, the former Colgate-Palmolive Co. marketing manager and a partner founded New World Coffee, Inc., which is now one of the most successful coffee-bar chains in the Northeast United States. In 1996, for example, New World Coffee acquired three Manhattan coffee bars and converted them to New World outlets. New World also opened two brand new stores using a recently completed new store prototype. The company is in close competition with Timothy's World Coffee, a Toronto-based chain. In New York, New World also competes directly with Starbucks, North America's leading roaster and coffee retailer.

To enter the coffee-bar chain field, Cagann developed a strategy for positioning New World Coffee between two big chains and countless single-store operations. Cagann entered the field well prepared. With a solid background in brand marketing, she formed a corporation with Ramin Kamfar, a colleague of her husband's at a New York investment bank. Cagann's responsibility was operations, marketing, and brand development. Kamfar's responsibility was finance and real estate. After raising $3.6 million from private investors, both quit their day jobs.

Part of Cagann's business strategy was to differentiate New World's style of roasting coffee from that used by the Starbucks chain, which she knew would be coming to town. "Like most West Coast roasters, their roasts are very dark, which tends to blur the distinctions between varietals." Cagann signed a ten-year exclusive agreement with a New Haven firm that supplies and roasts coffee from over forty countries. Cagann notes that New World became a presence because she and her partner focused on the business end of the specialty-coffee retail business.[1]

An important point illustrated by Gwenn Cagann's successful launching and sustaining of New World Coffee, Inc. is that a key leadership role is to form **strategy,** an organization's plan for achieving its mission and goals in its environment. Cagann thought of the concept for her successful chain of coffee bars—including how to differentiate New World from Starbucks—in order to create a thriving enterprise. In this chapter we approach strategic leadership by emphasizing the leader's role rather than focusing on strategy and strategic planning in great detail. Our approach is to first examine the nature of strategic leadership, followed by a review of the strategic management process. We then describe a sampling of strategies used by leaders to bring about organizational success, followed by descriptions of the leader's contribution to a firm achieving the strategies of quality and high technology.

THE NATURE OF STRATEGIC LEADERSHIP

Strategic leadership deals with the major purposes of an organization or an organizational unit, and thus differs more in level than in kind from leadership in general. We study strategic leadership separately because in practice it is the province of top-level executives. The term *strategic leadership* is sometimes considered synonymous with transformational leadership. For our purposes here, **strategic leadership** is the process of providing the direction and inspiration necessary to create, provide direction to, or sustain an organization. The founder of New World Coffee, Inc. provided strategic leadership because she developed a concept for an organization, grew the organization, and inspired large numbers of people to help her achieve her purpose.

Another perspective on strategic leadership is that it is the type of leadership necessary to effectively carry out strategic management. **Strategic management** refers to the process of ensuring a competitive fit between the organization and its environment. Strategic leadership is thus a complex of personal characteristics, thinking patterns, and effective management, all centering around the ability to think strategically. Do Leadership Self-Assessment Exercise 13–1 to explore your present orientation toward thinking strategically.

Our approach to understanding the nature of strategic leadership will be to describe certain associated characteristics, behaviors, and practices, as outlined in Table 13–1. The information about charismatic and transformational leadership presented in Chapter 3 is also relevant here.

LEADERSHIP SELF-ASSESSMENT
EXERCISE 13–1 Are You a Strategic Thinker?

Directions: Indicate your strength of agreement with each of the following statements: SD = strongly disagree; D = disagree; N = neutral; A = agree; SA = strongly agree.

	SD	D	N	A	SA
1. Every action I take on my job should somehow add value for our customers, our clients, or the public.	1	2	3	4	5
2. Let top management ponder the future; I have my own job to get done.	5	4	3	2	1
3. Strategic thinking is fluff. Somebody down the organization has to get the job done.	5	4	3	2	1
4. A company cannot become great without an exciting vision.	1	2	3	4	5
5. What I do on the job each day can affect the performance of the company many years into the future.	1	2	3	4	5
6. It's rather pointless to develop skills or acquire knowledge that cannot help you on the job within the next month.	5	4	3	2	1
7. Strategic planning should be carried out in a separate department rather than involving people throughout the organization.	5	4	3	2	1
8. It makes good sense for top management to frequently ask themselves the question, "What business are we really in?"	1	2	3	4	5
9. If a company does an outstanding job of satisfying its customers, there is very little need to worry about changing its mix of goods or services.	5	4	3	2	1
10. Organizational visions remind me of pipe dreams and hallucinations.	5	4	3	2	1

Scoring and interpretation: Find your total score by summing the point values for each question. A score of 42 to 50 suggests that you already think strategically, which should help you provide strategic leadership to others. Scores of 20 to 41 suggest a somewhat neutral, detached attitude toward thinking strategically. Scores of 10 to 19 suggest thinking that emphasizes the here and now and the short term. People scoring in this category are not yet ready to provide strategic leadership to group members.

TABLE 13–1   Components of Strategic Leadership

1. High-level cognitive activity by the leader
2. Gathering multiple inputs to formulate strategy
3. Anticipating and creating a future
4. Revolutionary thinking
5. Creating a vision

High-level Cognitive Activity by the Leader

Thinking strategically requires high-level cognitive skills, such as the ability to think conceptually, to absorb and make sense of a multitude of trends, and to condense all this information into a straightforward plan of action. The ability to process information and understand its consequences for the organization in its interaction with the environment is often referred to as *systems thinking*. In one analysis of the cognitive requirements of leadership, the work of management is divided into a system of seven levels within organizations. At each level there are qualitatively different task demands and skill requirements as one moves across higher and lower strata. A contributing factor is that the longer the time span incorporated into a manager's job, the greater the demands on intellectual ability.[2] A CEO, who might work with a twenty-five-year perspective, would therefore need to have greater problem-solving ability than a first-level supervisor, who typically has a one-week perspective.

According to the systems approach under consideration, the decisions required of first-level supervisors are less cognitively demanding than those typically encountered by executive decision makers. As one moves up the hierarchy, more problem-solving ability and imagination are required to effectively handle the task environment. To engage in strategic management and leadership, a person must therefore have conceptual prowess. An organization will be successful when the cognitive abilities of its leaders are a good fit with the nature of the work. This is one of many reasons why tests of problem-solving ability correlate positively with success in managerial work.[3] Creative problem solving is also important because the strategic leader has to develop alternative courses of action for shaping the organization. Furthermore, asking what-if questions requires imagination. For example, when Navistar was still called International Harvester, the CEO asked the question, "What if we got out of the farm equipment business?" In more recent years, the CEO of NeXT, Inc. asked, "What if we got out of the computer hardware business and concentrated on software?" Both CEOs decided to get out of their core businesses, which ultimately helped their firms survive.

Gathering Multiple Inputs to Formulate Strategy

Strategic leaders are often thought of as mystics who work independently and conjure up great schemes for the future. In reality, many strategic leaders arrive at their ideas for the organization's future by consulting with a wide range of interested parties, in a process similar to conducting research to create a vision. Strategy theorist Gary Hamel advises executives to make the strategy-creation process more democratic. He reasons that imagination is scarcer than resources. As a consequence, "We have to involve hundreds, if not thousands, of new voices in the strategy process if we want to increase the odds of seeing the future."[4]

A positive example of using participative management to formulate strategy is J.M. Smucker Co., the manufacturer of high-quality jams and jellies. President Richard K. Smucker enlisted a team of 140 employees (7 percent of the company's work force) who for more than six months devoted nearly half of their time to a major strategy exercise. Instead of having only the twelve top company executives working on the strategy, the 140-person team was used as ambassadors to solicit input from 2,000 employees. Strategy formulation was necessary because the company was encountering difficulty as it struggled to grow in a mature market. Smucker now has a dozen new product initiatives that are expected to double its revenues over the next five years. One of these initiatives is an alliance with Brach & Brock Confections Inc. to produce Smucker's jellybeans, the first of several co-branded products. The idea came from a team of workers who ordinarily would not participate in strategy formulation.[5]

A warning about the Smucker example: Some strategy theorists would dismiss it as incrementalism rather than true strategic leadership, such as moving the company into a new business or reinventing the future. Yet from a practical standpoint, pointing a company in a direction that will double its revenues even though it is competing in a mature business is effective strategic leadership.

Anticipating and Creating a Future

A major component of leadership is *direction setting*, which involves anticipating and sometimes creating a future for the enterprise or organizational unit. To set a direction is also to tell the organization what it should be doing. For example, during the mid-1990s, Lew Gerstner, the CEO at IBM, told his managers that the company should be getting a large share of its revenues from providing services (such as maintaining systems) instead of relying so heavily on selling products. The accompanying Leader in Action example presents a case history of how a leader set a new direction for selling the products of one of the world's best-known companies.

To set a productive direction for the future, the leader must accurately forecast or anticipate that future. An executive newsletter notes that "More than ever, insight into tomorrow is the difference between success and fail-

LEADER IN ACTION

Ron Zarrella Sets a New Direction for Selling GM Vehicles

General Motors Corp. vice president Ronald L. Zarrella was hired in December 1994 to bring an outsider's marketing expertise to improve the brand images of GM's divisions and products. Zarrella was the former president of Bausch & Lomb, and also has underwear manufacturing experience at Playtex Products, Inc. The GM divisions are Chevrolet, Buick, Oldsmobile, Pontiac, Cadillac, GMC Truck, and Saturn. In less than one year after taking office, Zarrella set a new direction for the sale of GM vehicles. His early decisions included eliminating plans for Cadillac to sell a luxury sport utility vehicle, and naming brand managers to help focus GM's overlapping brands. Zarrella also spearheaded the introduction of the Catera, a smaller Cadillac with European styling and manufacturing, aimed at younger, hipper buyers.

A marketing strategy aimed at sharpening brand images and reducing the number of GM dealers is for dealers to stop selling competitors' vehicles. In a news release and letter to dealers, Zarrella said that GM cars and trucks are not commodities and therefore should not be sold from facilities that sell competing brands. GM also intends to eliminate Cadillac and GMC Truck dealerships from rural markets and to specify preferred combinations of vehicles in dealerships that offer more than one GM product line. Zarrella indicated that in most cases it is preferable to have dealers handle only a single GM division's brands if the local market is strong enough to support this. The ideal situation would be for Chevrolet dealers to sell only Chevys, Buick dealers only Buicks, and so forth. The exception would be the Pontiac and GMC Truck brands, where the preferred pattern would be for the two brands to be sold by the same dealers. In situations where the market cannot support single-line GM dealers, Zarrella wants dealerships in these combinations:

- Buick–Pontiac–GMC Truck

- Oldsmobile with Cadillac, or with Chevrolet if Cadillac is not represented in the market.

- In rural areas, Chevrolet–Buick–Pontiac–Oldsmobile, with no presence of Cadillac or GMC Truck. Saturn dealerships would continue to offer only Saturn vehicles

In establishing these new configurations for vehicle sales, Zarrella said, "Each brand needs to be properly presented to the public through a renewed emphasis on having the right number of dealers, at the right locations, and of the right size" (Associated Press). The GM vice president recognizes that many GM veterans are skeptical that an outsider can effectively set new directions for the company. Yet top management continues to support his initiatives.

Source: Based on Mike McKesson, "GM Outlines Program to Focus Brands and Dealers," Associated Press story, October 10, 1995; "GM Learns to Love an Outsider," *Business Week*, July 3, 1995, p. 32; http://prn.branch.com/GMPAIN.HTM, January 8, 1997.

ure."[6] Insight into tomorrow can take many forms, such as a leader's making accurate forecasts about consumer preferences, customer demands, and the skill mix needed to operate tomorrow's organization. A truly visionary leader anticipates a future that many people do not think will come to pass. A classic example is that in the early days of xerography, market research indicated that most people polled saw no need for a product to replace carbon paper. (If you are unfamiliar with the term, find somebody over 40 to explain the meaning of *carbon paper.*) Leaders at both Federal Express Corporation and United Parcel Service anticipated a surge in worldwide demand for time-guaranteed delivery, thus setting the stage for an industry that has reached $30 billion per year.

Creating the future is a more forceful approach than anticipating the future. The leader, assisted by widespread participation of team members, creates conditions that do not already exist. He or she must ask questions about the shape of the industry in five to ten years, and decide how to ensure that the industry evolves in a way that is highly advantageous to the company. Furthermore, the leader must recognize the skills and capabilities that must be acquired now if the company is to occupy the industry high ground in the future. Another relevant issue is how the company can organize to capitalize upon opportunities that may not fit neatly within the current boundaries of organizational units.

To create the future, senior management must develop a process for pulling together the collective wisdom of the organization. According to Gary Hamel and C. K. Prahalad, concern for the future and a sense of where opportunities lie are not the exclusive province of top management. Instead, people from all levels within the organization can help define the future. For example, in 1990, Electronic Data Systems Corp. (EDS) created a Corporate Change Team. Whatever ideas emerged from the team would be submitted to senior leaders within EDS, referred to as the Leadership Council. From around the world, 150 EDS managers, thirty at a time, gathered at company headquarters to begin creating the future. After an enormously time-consuming process (estimated at 30,000 person-hours) involving the input of 2,000 employees, EDS developed a new strategy that can be highlighted in three words: globalize, informationalize, and individualize.[7]

Creating the future has also been conceptualized as reinventing an industry. Entrepreneurial leaders frequently engage in such activity. Prahalad explains that the shoe industry is a good example of reinvention. Nike and Reebok have fundamentally reinvented their industry, and consequently are fast-growing businesses in a mature industry. One factor is that they have changed the price-performance relationship in the industry. (Have you priced high-end basketball shoes recently?) Both companies have introduced very high technology, new materials, large-scale advertising, and global brands. None of these factors were so pronounced previously in the shoe industry.[8] Reinventing an industry, however, can have ethical consequences that are not part of Prahalad's analysis. Many critics of the sports-shoe industry are concerned that child labor is employed in the manufacture of Nike shoes, and that both brands have created a high demand for a product that many of its consumers can ill afford. There have been many reported instances of young people assaulting others to steal their new athletic shoes. Another ethical concern is that college athletes are forced to promote these brands but receive no compensation. Yet their coaches receive extraordinary fees for outfitting the team in a given manufacturer's brand.

Revolutionary Thinking

Using even stronger terms than *reinventing the future*, a recent analysis by Hamel characterizes strategy as being revolutionary.[9] According to Hamel, corporations are reaching the limits of incrementalism. Incremental improvements include squeezing costs, introducing a new product a few weeks earlier, enhancing quality a notch, responding more quickly to customer inquiries, and capturing another point of market share. To be an industry leader, a company's leaders must think in revolutionary terms. Revolutionary companies, such as the Charles Schwab Corporation, Dell Computer Corporation, and Swatch, create the rules for others to follow. As explained by Hamel, any strategy that does not seriously challenge the status quo should not even be considered a strategy. What passes for strategy in most companies is often sterile and unimaginative. An effective leader thinks in revolutionary terms, partly by ferreting out revolutionary ideas that are harbored somewhere within the firm. What constitutes a *revolutionary* idea, however, is subjective. Is selling computers by telephone (Dell Computer) really revolutionary? Selling all sorts of merchandise by phone—for example, mattresses (1-800-Mattress)—predated selling computers the same way.

For strategic leadership to be revolutionary, it would have to redefine products and services, market space, and even the entire industry. Suggestions for achieving this exalted status are described next. Leaders implement these suggestions themselves or motivate others to join them in the effort.

Reconceiving a Product or Service.   To reconceive a product or service, the company begins by radically improving the value equation. The value equation refers to how many units of money buy how many units of value. Many electronic products now deliver substantially more value for the dollar. Ten years ago it would have cost about $3,000 retail to purchase the equivalent of a laser printer that costs $600 today. Another way to reconceive a product or service is to separate core benefits (function) from the ways in which the benefits are woven into a product or service (form). For example, one of the functions of a credit card is to assure the merchant that the customer whose name appears on the card is the same person who is presenting the card. Yet by changing the form of assurance, such as using handprints, voiceprints, or retinal scans, a new niche in the industry can be created. (Only a highly creative person would conceive of such an idea.)

Reconceiving a product or service can also be accomplished through *joy of use*. "We now want our products and services to be whimsical, tactile, and just plain fun."[10] Any company that can incorporate joy of use into a product or service might become an industry revolutionary. Some very successful restaurants in recent years, such as Planet Hollywood and several owned by fashion models, are a combination of pop-culture museum and eatery.

Redefining Market Space.   One approach to redefining market space is to *push the bounds of universality,* or focus on the widest possible market. An excellent example is the way single-use cameras have made access to photography practically universal. Among the almost unlimited users of single-use cameras (about $7.00 retail) are children at birthday parties, skiers who don't want to risk losing or damaging their expensive 35mm cameras, and people who have an urgent need to take photos, but whose primary camera is broken. Another way a leader can redefine market space is to *strive for individuality* in offering a product or service. Product leaders at Saturn conceived of the idea of allowing customers to *customize* their vehicles by choosing their personal combination of options. The car is then ordered from the factory with the customer's specific option package, and it arrives in the showroom as a unique vehicle. Although this movement in the direction of individuality has not decimated the competition, it has contributed to Saturn's distinctiveness.

A third way of redefining market space is to *increase accessibility* in ways such as selling through cyberspace, as www.amazon.com does. First Direct, the fastest-growing bank in Great Britain, can be accessed only by telephone. Yet it was opening 10,000 new accounts per month in 1995, and the average daily balance was ten times higher than that of customers at its parent bank, Midland Bank PLC.

Redrawing Industry Boundaries.   Leaders in even basic industries are redefining and redrawing industry boundaries. One tactic is to *rescale industries,* such as local industries going regional and national industries going global. Remember Wayne Huizenga and his national chains of garbage disposal services and used-car lots? Have you visited your neighborhood SuperCuts? Strategic thinkers have also rescaled toward smallness, such as bed-and-breakfast inns, microbreweries, and local bakeries. *Compressing the supply chain* by eliminating intermediaries is another way of redrawing boundaries. Buying clubs (e.g., Sam's Club and BJ's Wholesale Club), which are essentially warehouses converted into stores, have eliminated many traditional retail stores.

Driving convergence also helps the strategic leader redraw industry boundaries. To compete successfully, many companies now offer integrated service outside of their traditional business. For example, Merrill Lynch & Company, Inc. offers many banking services, such as checking accounts, home equity loans, and credit cards. Most large supermarkets offer hot meals for takeout.

The nine strategies embedded in the above description contribute to making business strategy revolutionary, thus enhancing strategic leadership. We caution again that these ideas are not all revolutionary. Several of them fall into the category of creative thinking that recycles old ideas, such as striving for individuality. Custom clothiers (a form of striving for individuality) have been around for at least 300 years. Several of the ideas can also be criticized in terms of social responsibility. An outstanding strategic leader creates jobs and growth rather than focusing on ways to eliminate jobs through such means as driving out intermediaries.

Creating a Vision

We have already mentioned vision in several places, including the description in Chapter 3 of the vision component of charismatic leadership. Here we examine the concept of vision in more depth because visions are an integral part of strategic leadership. Although the term *vision* in relation to leadership has achieved common-use status, it is really a multifaceted concept. Laurie Larwood and her associates conducted a study in which 331 chief executives in one national and three regional samples were asked about the content and structure of their organizational visions.[11] The executives came from firms that were in a variety of industries and that ranged in size from $1 million to $1 billion in sales per year.

The chief executives were asked to write a brief, one-sentence statement of their organizational vision. Participants in the study were also asked to analyze the statements by applying twenty-six descriptors from a list the researchers provided. Each descriptor was rated on a 1-to-5 scale from "very little" to "very much." Among the terms used to describe the vision were "action-oriented," "responsive to competition," "product of leadership," "strategic," "directs effort," and "risky." Factor analysis reduced the twenty-six descriptors to seven identifiable factors:

1. Vision formulation
2. Implementation
3. Innovative realism
4. General
5. Detailed
6. Risk taking
7. Profit-oriented

The visions based on these factors extended from six months to more than twenty years with an average of sixty-four months. The current visions (those in use at the time of the study) were retained between three months and twenty years, with an average of seventy-four months. Another important aspect of the study was to relate this analysis of visions to previous research. The factor results were thought to provide good support for what is known about visions. Of major importance, the concept of a vision as involving far-reaching strategic planning (factor 1) and the ability and willingness to share with others (factor 2) was supported. Innovative realism (factor 3) includes items considered important to visionary and charismatic leadership.

Another conclusion from the study is also relevant for strategic leadership: Executives with a triple emphasis on long-term strategy, wide communication and acceptance of their visions, and operational realism or style are the most likely to be successful in creating change within their organizations. One reason for this conclusion is that this group of executives scored highest on a question about perceived firm change.[12]

The executive leaders who agreed to participate in the study just cited all came from firms with established visions. Yet, according to one analysis, only one in twenty business firms has an explicitly stated vision, and fewer than one in a hundred has a vision that has been communicated to the firm's people.[13] The study about communication cited at the beginning of Chapter 12 also reported the need for wider communication of visions. A strategic leader not only formulates a vision, often assisted by many organizational members, but also communicates the vision and then implements it in other ways. Chief Executive Bob Haas at Levi Strauss & Co. provides a good example of a strategic leader who is able to implement a vision.

Top management at Levi Strauss has developed an *aspirations statement* that is close to a vision because it describes what the company wants to become. The statement begins, "to sustain commercial success as a global marketing company of branded career apparel." Also included is the statement, "Above all we want satisfaction from accomplishment and friendships, balanced personal and professional lives, and to have fun in our endeavors." To turn this aspiration into reality, Haas uses a variety of tactics, including the following:

- He tells people, "You don't work *for* Levi's, you work for yourselves; you just happen to work *at* Levi's."

- At the San Francisco headquarters, some departments supply every worker with a few "You Are Great" or "Aspiration" coupons, which they can hand out to other workers for a job well done. The recipient gets on-the-spot recognition and then can trade in the coupon for $25 or a gift certificate. Levi Strauss employees found it awkward to give out these coupons, because the recipients often downplayed the magnitude of their accomplishments. To circumvent this problem, the company now has neutral messengers, such as human resource specialists, deliver the awards.[14]

Although the tactics at Levi Strauss appear more like basic human relations than strategic leadership, they illustrate an important point. Somebody has to implement strategic initiatives on a daily basis on an operational level, often involving entry-level workers.

THE STRATEGIC PLANNING MODEL

The emphasis in this chapter is on the leadership aspects of strategy. It is important, however, to review the basic planning model that many leaders follow in developing strategy. **Strategic planning** encompasses those activities that lead to the statement of goals and objectives and the choice of strategies to achieve them. Under ideal circumstances, a firm arrives at its strategy after completing strategic planning. In practice, many executive leaders choose a strategy prior to strategic planning. Once the firm has the strategy, a plan is developed to implement it.

A representative strategic planning model is presented in Figure 13–1. Do not interpret its five steps as a rigid sequence. In reality, several of the steps might be taken simultaneously. A leader-manager using the planning model would pursue the steps described next.

1. *Analyze the environment* to understand such factors as the characteristics of the industry, product demand, prevailing technology, and government regulations. This analysis requires substantial time and effort. Some of the information needed is available in computer databases and through skillful browsing of the Internet.

2. *Analyze the organization* to understand its position in the market, financial status, technical skills, structure, and work force. A well-managed company has much of this information on hand.

3. *Determine the skills necessary for success,* such as the ability to reach customers readily or to understand what customers really want. The owners of New World Coffee, Inc., for example, modify their stores based on the customer mix—whether customers are mostly businesspeople in a hurry or neighborhood people stopping at a coffee bar to relax. The neighborhood shops offer more baked goods to take out.

4. *Assess the problems and opportunities* that could influence the strategic decision. Ron Zarrella pushed for a sportier, hipper Cadillac because its market share among younger people was rapidly diminishing. As many dealers joked ghoulishly, "We have too many *last time* buyers (seniors who would never need to purchase another automobile)." A SWOT analysis as described in Leadership Skill-Building Exercise 13–1 is a standard tool for assessing problems and opportunities, or doing a situational analysis.

5. *Develop, evaluate, and select alternative strategies* to take advantage of opportunities. Because firms have limited resources, they are forced to select one or two strategies to implement. The strategic leader plays a major role here by selecting which strategic alternative to choose after collecting input from staffers.

The final outcomes of strategic planning are statements of mission and vision, strategy, and policy. Specifying a mission answers the question, "What business are we really in?" A firm's mission may not be apparent to the casual observer. For example, in recent years Packard Bell NEC, Inc. has been the first or second leading manufacturer of personal computers in the United States, selling almost entirely through retail stores. Yet, according to

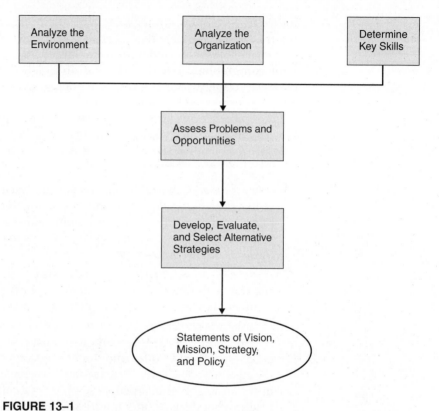

FIGURE 13–1

The Strategic Planning Model

one business analyst, "Packard Bell is not a PC company, it's a consumer-electronics company."[15]

Strategic planning is primarily the responsibility of top management, assisted by planning specialists. Yet, as mentioned previously, today's strategic leaders solicit input from managers and other workers at all levels, and even from company outsiders, when formulating strategy. Lower-ranking people can make important contributions because they are usually closer to available information about product performance, customer relations, competitive actions, and delivery problems.

Strategic planning has its skeptics, yet it is still widely practiced in organizations of all types and sizes. The larger the organization, however, the more likely it is that leaders will engage in strategic planning. Research has been done to determine whether the widespread faith in strategic planning is justified. A recent example is a study by James W. Dean, Jr., and Mark P. Sharfman that investigated the contribution of strategic planning to decision-making effectiveness. The researchers studied fifty-two decisions in twenty-four companies to determine if procedural rationality (such as

LEADERSHIP SKILL-BUILDING
EXERCISE 13–1 How to Conduct a SWOT Analysis

In both strategic planning and other situations, managers and leaders can benefit from conducting a SWOT analysis—they must consider the *strengths, weaknesses, opportunities,* and *threats* in a given situation.

Strengths. What are the good points about a particular alternative? Use your judgment and intuition. Ask knowledgeable people.

Weaknesses. Consider the risks of pursuing a particular course of action, such as subcontracting work to a low-wage country (outsourcing). Again, use your judgment and ask knowledgeable people.

Opportunities. Think of the opportunities that welcome you if you choose a promising strategic alternative, such as creating a culturally diverse customer base. Use your imagination and visualize the possibilities.

Threats. There's a downside to every alternative, so think ahead to allow for contingency planning. Ask people who may have tried in the past what you are attempting now. But don't be dissuaded by the naysayers, heel draggers, and pessimists. To quote Nike, "Just do it."

Now that you have read the basics of conducting a SWOT analysis, gather in small groups to conduct one. Develop a scenario for a SWOT analysis, such as the group starting a chain of coffee shops, pet-care service centers, or treatment centers for on-line addictions. Or, conduct a SWOT analysis for reorganizing a company that is hierarchical to make it team-based. Since you will probably have mostly hypothetical data to work with, you will have to rely heavily on your imagination. Group leaders might share the results of the SWOT analysis with the rest of the class.

using the strategic planning model) and political behavior influence the effectiveness of strategic decisions. A decision was considered strategic if it determined the overall direction of the firm. Rationality and political behavior were measured by questionnaires, and decision effectiveness was measured by interviewing executives to obtain effectiveness ratings. Among the various types of strategic decisions studied were restructuring, new product, marketing strategy, human resource strategy, and quality.[16]

A major finding was that procedural rationality and political behavior were significantly related to the effectiveness of strategic decisions. Managers who collected information and used analytical techniques (such as the strategic planning model) were more effective than those who did not. Managers who emphasized power plays or pushed hidden agendas (negative aspects of organizational politics) were less effective than those who avoided these techniques.

A SAMPLING OF BUSINESS STRATEGIES FORMULATED BY LEADERS

We have been focusing on the process by which leaders and managers make strategic decisions. Also of interest to leaders and potential leaders is the content of such decisions, with an emphasis on the actual business strategies. Business strategies are often classified according to their focus of impact: corporate level, business level, or functional level. Corporate-level strategy asks, "What business are we in?" Business-level strategy asks, "How do we compete?" And functional-level strategy asks, "How do we support the business-level strategy?"[17] As you will see, some of the business strategies listed next might cut across more than one of these three levels. You may recognize the first three of these strategies as the generic strategies espoused by the well-recognized business strategist Michael Porter.[18]

1. *Differentiation.* A differentiation strategy attempts to offer a product or service that is perceived by the customer as being different from available alternatives. The organization may use advertising, distinctive features, exceptional service, or new technology to gain this perception of uniqueness. The stunning appearance of Acer personal computers is part of the company's differentiation strategy. The extraordinary success of Swatch watches was based on a strategy of producing a watch that had a dramatically different face at a competitive price. What differentiates one of your favorite products?

2. *Cost leadership.* A basic strategy is to produce a product or service at a low cost in order to lower the selling price and gain market share. Wal-Mart is a master at cost leadership because the company's massive buying power enables it to receive huge price concessions from suppliers. At times a company will shift to a cost leadership strategy when a product does not sell as well as expected. Digital Equipment Corp. tried for years to convince computer makers to build desktop computers and high-end servers around the powerful Alpha microprocessor, with limited success. In late 1996, leaders at Digital lowered the price of the chips by 29 percent in the hope of gaining greater market share.[19]

3. *Focus.* In a focus strategy, the organization concentrates on a specific regional market or buyer group. To gain market share, the company will use either a differentiation or a cost leadership approach in a targeted market. One of the most successful financial services firms in the United States, USAA, has a concentrated market of military personnel, former military personnel, and their dependents or former dependents. The automobile insurance unit has a smaller percentage of claims to pay than competitors do because of the stable and conservative nature of its policy holders. As a consequence, net premiums are lower, further increasing customer loyalty.

4. *Imitation.* If you cannot be imaginative, why not imitate the best? The entire PC clone industry is based on an imitation strategy. The imitation

strategy has two key components: strategic followership and learning by watching. The company waits for the right time to introduce a lower-priced competitor. Benchmarking is a form of learning by watching.[20]

5. *Forming strategic alliances.* An increasingly popular business strategy is to form alliances, or share resources, with other companies to exploit a market opportunity. A strategic alliance is also known as a virtual corporation. The highly successful Advanced Photo System cameras were the result of teamwork by Kodak, Fuji, Canon, Minolta, and Nikon. Working together, even though they were rivals on many products, the companies were able to achieve outstanding success. Another buzzword for forming strategic alliances is for companies to *co-evolve*. Instead of acting as solo players, the companies use the resources of others.

6. *High speed.* High-speed managers focus on speed in all of their business activities, including product development, sales response, and customer service. Knowing that "time is money," they choose time as a competitive resource. It is important to get products to market quickly because the competition might get there first. One of the many reasons for IBM's phenomenal success in 1996 and 1997 is that under Lew Gerstner's leadership, the company has shortened the cycle time on most of its products and services.

7. *Global diversification.* A widely practiced business strategy, especially with products, is to diversify globally in order to expand business. Even several restaurant chains, such as McDonald's and Pizza Hut, employ a diversification strategy. Global diversification is such a widely accepted strategy that the burden of proof would be on a business leader who shunned globalization.

8. *Sticking to core competencies.* Many firms of all sizes believe they will prosper if they confine their efforts to the activities they perform best—their core competencies. Thomas C. McDermott, the president of Goulds Pumps, Inc., said his company was going to expand overseas by strategic acquisitions. Nevertheless, he insisted on companies that were either in or related to the pump business. He said, "We're going back to our knitting."[21] (Goulds had strayed from its core competencies in the past.)

9. *Paying attention to white-space opportunity.* A recently articulated business strategy is for the leaders to identify new areas of growth opportunity that have been neglected because they do not comfortably match the capabilities of existing business units. Martinez at Sears, Roebuck & Co. hired strategy consultants to help the company identify white-space opportunities. It was proposed that by segmenting the do-it-yourself market and focusing on easy-to-do home projects, Sears could avoid head-to-head competition with Home Depot and other major players in the home-improvement market. The freestanding hardware stores mentioned in Chapter 1 exemplify one such white space.[22]

10. *Growth.* A fundamental business strategy is to grow an organization. One of the many reasons that growth enhances success is that it leads to brand recognition. A leader can use growth as a motivational tactic because workers will rally around the prospects of growth. They also much prefer growth to a cost-containment and downsizing strategy. The Guidelines for Action and Skill Development present suggestions for implementing a growth strategy.

All of the above business strategies contribute to the master strategy of listening to customers, identifying their needs, and figuring out how to satisfy them. Although every leader is aware of this all-encompassing strategy, many business failures can be attributed to letting it slip from attention.

LEADERSHIP AND TOTAL QUALITY

In recent years, achieving quality has become a minimum requirement of companies and other types of organization if they are to compete successfully. Leaders thus continue to emphasize quality even if there is less explicit emphasis today on **total quality management (TQM).** The term refers to a management system for improving performance throughout the firm by maximizing customer satisfaction and making continuous improvements based on extensive employee involvement.

Quality is included in this chapter because it can rightfully be considered a leadership strategy. One reason that quality is considered a strategy is that it contributes to competitive advantage in cost and differentiation. According to James W. Dean, Jr., and James R. Evans, "Companies that aspire to world-class status reach the highest level of evolution where quality becomes an integral part of the overall strategic plan and is viewed as a central operating strategy."[23]

Max De Pree, the former CEO of furniture maker Herman Miller, Inc., and now a management author, says that an important leadership responsibility is the cultivation and maintenance of a sense of quality in the organization.[24] Our focus on quality here is to describe several major actions that leaders can take to promote quality throughout the organization and to facilitate the implementation of quality. The accompanying Leader in Action vignette gives a feel for the type of activities engaged in by a leader of a medium-size company who wants to foster quality.

At its best, quality management is a transformation in the way an organization manages. Leadership focuses on the continuous improvement of operations, functions, and especially work processes. *Demonstrating top-level commitment* is the most important contributor to the successful implementation of any quality improvement effort. Many quality experts maintain that quality management must be a top-down process, integrated into the corporate culture.[25] Quality must be included in the organization's strategy and

LEADER IN ACTION

■ Nicholas Juskiw Leads Trident to a Malcolm Baldridge Award

Back in March 1988, Nicholas Juskiw attended a two-day seminar on total quality management organized by Xerox Corp. for its suppliers. It was the beginning of a quest that would make his company—Trident Precision Manufacturing, Inc. of Webster, N.Y.—one of four 1996 winners of the Malcolm Baldridge Award. "It was almost a religious feeling for me," said Juskiw, the owner, president, and chief executive of Trident. "I saw the problem-solving and quality improvement processes, and the videos for the team activity and how Xerox was starting to fight back the Japanese."

Trident is a small contract manufacturer with about 170 employees. The company produces components and assemblies for several major manufacturers, including Xerox, IBM, and Eastman Kodak Company. Although the company was successful, Juskiw wanted to improve its internal operations. The employee turnover and scrap rates were worse than industry standards. Trident was operating by crisis management. "Everything was run, run, run as fast as you can to deliver parts," said Juskiw. The company had no long-range plan, no business plan, and not even an employee handbook. TQM provided the company a systematic approach that it could use to focus on growth.

Juskiw chose the theme of "Excellence in Motion" to improve the company. Implementing the theme included extensive training of senior management and employees, building teams to solve company problems, benchmarking, and creating a family atmosphere through employee activities and recognition. All the managers and supervisors spent fourteen months writing a TQM strategy, a move that involved both top and middle managers in the quality process.

The strategic plan identified five basic goals: supplier partnerships, employee satisfaction, operational performance, customer satisfaction, and shareholder value for its sole owner, Juskiw. To demonstrate its commitment, Trident put a mobile home on the grounds where classes could be conducted, and eventually built a training room. Each employee was cross-trained to perform at least two and sometimes three job functions, a move that improved job security and gave management more flexibility, explain Trident officials. Worker-management teams were formed to tackle production problems and improve the manufacturing process. For example, one team organized the dies used in manufacturing, which had previously been strewn about the plant.

Trident reinforces its quality program by recognizing employees, both as a group and individually. The training room is lined with charts showing the progress of each team, quality ratings from customers, sales, and other statistics. Also, the company newsletter gives "Atta-Boys/Girls" awards for specific employee contributions. Juskiw also encourages a family atmosphere. He regularly walks through the plant and he knows all employees and most of their family members.

April V. Lusk, Trident's total quality administrator, believes that all managers and supervisors must set an example, particularly in a small company. "There are advantages to TQM if you're small in the sense that you can see things change," she said. "But at the same time from a management point of view you have to be constantly utilizing those behaviors because everyone can see you."

Source: Adapted and excerpted from Jill A. Zelickson, "Quest for Excellence: Trident's 8-year Odyssey Leads to Baldridge Award," *Monday's Business*, Rochester *Democrat and Chronicle/Times-Union*, November 18, 1996, pp. 1, 7. Reprinted by permission.

mission statement, and every manager and organizational unit must be responsible for quality. A mission statement contributes substantially to creating a *corporate culture of quality*. This is important because significant quality improvement requires an upheaval in the corporate culture. If the corporate culture does not embody quality, any quality improvement efforts will probably be shallow and short-lived.

Continuous improvement as a way of life is one of the dominant values in a corporate culture of quality. The quest for continuous improvement is closely associated with **kaizen**, a philosophy of gradual improvement in personal and work life. Doing Leadership Skill-Building Exercise 13–2 will give you additional insights into the nature of a corporate culture that favors quality. You can also use the instrument contained in the exercise as a diagnostic tool. To achieve total quality, leaders must *empower employees to fix and prevent problems*. Equally important, group members have to accept the authority and become involved in the improvement process. Empowerment is important because it may enhance motivation and release creative energy.

Although achieving high quality is intrinsically rewarding, the contribution of financial rewards to achieving high quality cannot be dismissed. Leaders can strengthen the impact of quality management by *championing a link between quality performance and pay*. Employees are more likely to respond favorably to a leader's quality initiatives if they receive high pay for achieving high quality.[26] A bold quality-enhancing leadership practice is to *establish extraordinarily difficult quality targets for group members, and then insist that they find a way to attain them*. Many companies have established one of two close-to-impossible goals: the zero-defects standard or the 6-sigma quality standard (see Figure 13–2). Well-known business leaders such as George Fisher at Eastman Kodak Company and Larry Bossidy at AlliedSignal, Inc. describe the progress of their firm in terms of how close workers are getting to the 6-sigma standard. Neither leader believes that his company has yet achieved this exalted state of quality.

Quality management has been integrated into many business strategies and has contributed to many business turnarounds. Maintaining high quality standards, such as ISO 9000, also enables many companies to stay on other companies' preferred supplier lists. Yet leaders must be aware of a major potential problem with quality management. Advocates of quality management often become preoccupied with the process of achieving high quality and overlook the fact that they may be making quality improvements that customers are not willing to pay for. The process becomes more important than the content.[27] Quality is often said to pay for itself in terms of increased customer demand and loyalty. In reality, a firm can lose market share when it invests too much money in enhancing quality. Motorola, Inc., one of the world leaders in the quality movement (it invented 6-sigma), began to lose some share of cellular telephones to lower-price competition in the late 1990s.

LEADERSHIP SKILL-BUILDING
EXERCISE 13–2 Do You Have the Right Corporate Culture for TQM?

Directions: To evaluate whether your company has a culture that is ideally suited to total quality, check whether the description in the left-hand or the right-hand column best describes your firm. Confer with another person who works for the same employer to increase the accuracy of your ratings. If you are not currently working, speak to someone who is employed and evaluate his or her company. It would be helpful to interview more than one person from the same organization.

TQM Companies	*Traditional Companies*
___ Driven by customer needs	___ Driven by company wants
___ Prevention of problems before they happen	___ Detection of problems after the fact
___ Nothing less than 100 percent will do	___ Established maximum acceptable levels of error, waste
___ Committed to quality at the source	___ Belief that inspection is key to quality
___ Cooperative, interdepartmental teams	___ Autonomous, independent departments
___ High employee participation—empowered work force	___ Top-down, management-directed work force
___ Long-term staying power a primary goal.	___ Short-term profit a primary goal.

Interpretation: Seven check marks in the left-hand column would indicate that the firm you have evaluated is probably a world-class quality company. Seven check marks in the right-hand column suggests that the company you have evaluated might be at a competitive disadvantage in a quality-conscious economy. Check marks to the right can also be used as indicators of a need for organizational improvement.

Source: "Total Quality Management: A Step-by-Step Guide to Making TQM Work for You," National Seminars brochure, 1992.

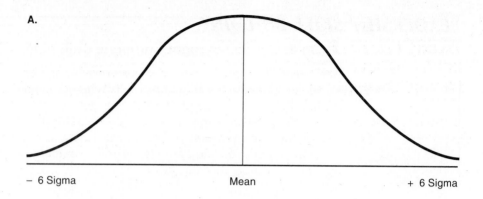

A.

− 6 Sigma   Mean   + 6 Sigma

B. 6 – Sigma translates into 99.999997% error free

C. 6 – Sigma =   3.4 defect

1 million opportunities

Note: The Greek letter *sigma* is the symbol for standard deviation.

FIGURE 13–2

The Meaning of the 6-Sigma Quality Standard

LEADERSHIP PRACTICES THAT FOSTER A TECHNOLOGY STRATEGY

Another aspect of strategic leadership is to foster an advanced-technology environment. In this regard, the leader's task is to inspire appropriate use of advanced technology. As the term is used here, **technology** refers to all the tools and ideas available for extending the physical and mental reach of people.[28] Using a shopping cart to restock returned merchandise in a supermarket is an example of using low technology. Using computers to communicate with staffers at various locations around the world is an example of using advanced (or high) technology. Leadership Self-Assessment Exercise 13–2 will help you think through your attitudes toward advanced technology.

Choosing an Appropriate Technological Strategy

An executive leader of a company or a strategic business unit may have the authority to choose a technological strategy. Choosing the most appropriate strategy greatly influences the success of the organization or unit. Technology plays a major role in four business strategies,[29] as described next.

First to Market.   Being first to market is an offensive strategy with high potential rewards but high risk. New entrepreneurial high-tech firms are

LEADERSHIP SELF-ASSESSMENT
EXERCISE 13–2 Attitudes Toward Technology

Directions: Indicate your strength of agreement with each of the following statements: strongly disagree, SD; disagree, D; neutral, N; agree, A; strongly agree, SA.

		SD	D	N	A	SA
1.	Few organizations can succeed without continually moving toward higher forms of technology.	(1)	(2)	(3)	(4)	(5)
2.	I regularly use high-technology devices at home, such as a camcorder, CD player, or personal computer.	(1)	(2)	(3)	(4)	(5)
3.	When I use a personal computer or camcorder, I make frequent use of the advanced features.	(1)	(2)	(3)	(4)	(5)
4.	I enjoy interacting with technical people.	(1)	(2)	(3)	(4)	(5)
5.	Electronic gadgets in the workplace have contributed very little to productivity.	(5)	(4)	(3)	(2)	(1)
6.	During a downsizing, the first area I would recommend for layoffs would be the research and development group.	(5)	(4)	(3)	(2)	(1)
7.	The contribution of technology to society is overrated.	(5)	(4)	(3)	(2)	(1)
8.	Placed in an executive position, I would keep a computer on my desk and use it regularly.	(1)	(2)	(3)	(4)	(5)
9.	Most of the great business firms of the world are high-tech companies.	(1)	(2)	(3)	(4)	(5)
10.	Most technical people are nerds.	(5)	(4)	(3)	(2)	(1)

Total score: _____

Scoring and interpretation: Find your total score by summing the point values. A score of 40 to 50 suggests very positive attitudes toward technology and technical people. Scores of 20 to 39 suggest a somewhat neutral, detached attitude toward technology and technical people; scores of 10 to 19 suggest negative attitudes.

This quiz is linked to skill development. To lead an organization or subunit toward effective use of technology, you should have favorable attitudes toward technology and technical people. If you scored 19 or lower, you would need to become more interested in advanced technology to inspire others to make good use of it.

likely to use this strategy, as are more progressive, established firms such as Hewlett-Packard. Sometimes the competitive advantage can be sustained through patents and proprietary knowledge. Creative marketing people may be required to stimulate demand. Classic first-to-market products include Polaroid's instant camera and the Sony Walkman.

Fast Follower and Overtaker.   After the pioneering firm has demonstrated that a market for the product exists, the fast follower swoops in with a similar product developed through innovative imitation. General Electric used the fast-follower strategy to enter the market for computerized axial tomography (CAT) scanners. The original CAT scanner was developed by Electrical and Musical Industries (EMI) of the United Kingdom.

Cost Minimization.   With the cost minimization strategy, a company finds a way to reduce the cost of manufacturing a mass-produced product with standard features. Japanese and other Pacific Rim companies succeeded in overtaking the U.S. consumer electronics industry by becoming low-cost producers of high-tech devices.

Market Niche.   New high-tech ventures searching to develop a unique competence employ the market-niche strategy. To succeed, the market niche must be chosen carefully and adhered to rigorously. Michael Dell of Dell Computer Corp. found a marketing niche for a high-tech product by marketing good-quality computers through the mail.

Investing Heavily in Training

Leaders play a key role in fostering a high-technology environment by advocating a heavy investment in training. Continuous training is necessary if a company is to become and to remain a high-tech firm. Several years ago, Fred Smith, the founder of Federal Express, said, "The most significant strategic investment we are making right now is a massive training and retraining effort to adapt for the next generation of technology."[30] Part of "FedEx's" continuing success in a competitive market can be attributed to its sophisticated, high-tech package-routing system.

Establishing a Reward System for Innovation

Advances in technology are, by definition, innovations. To encourage a stream of innovations, company leadership must establish a reward system for creative contributions. Part of the reward system can be intrinsic, such as rewarding the innovator with additional exciting assignments. Another intrinsic reward is to grant innovative people more freedom to pursue work that is of interest to them. More freedom means fewer controls in terms of tight budgets and accountability for short-term results.

SUMMARY

Strategic leadership deals with the major purposes of an organization or organizational unit, and provides the direction and inspiration necessary to create, provide direction to, or sustain an organization. As described here, strategic leadership has five important components: (1) high-level cognitive activity by the leader; (2) gathering multiple inputs to formulate strategy; (3) anticipating and creating a future; (4) revolutionary thinking; and (5) creating a vision. Revolutionary thinking includes reconceiving a product or service, redefining market space, and redrawing industry boundaries.

Creating a vision is an integral part of strategic leadership. One study found that visions contain seven identifiable factors: vision formulation, implementation, innovative realism, general, detailed, risk taking, and profit orientation. The visions based on these factors extended from six months to more than twenty years, with an average of sixty-four months. After formulating a vision, the leader should be involved in its communication and implementation.

Many leaders follow a model in developing strategy that includes the following steps: analyzing the environment, analyzing the organization, determining the skills necessary for success, assessing problems and opportunities, and selecting alternatives to take advantage of opportunities. Strategic planning leads to statements of mission and vision, strategy, and policy. A SWOT analysis is a standard tool for assessing problems and opportunities. According to one study, procedural rationality contributes to the effectiveness of strategic decisions.

Strategic leaders use many different types of business strategies, including the following: (1) differentiation, (2) cost leadership, (3) focus on a specific regional market or buyer group, (4) imitation, (5) forming strategic alliances, (6) high speed, (7) global diversification, (8) sticking to core competencies, (9) paying attention to white-space opportunities, and (10) growth.

Leaders continue to emphasize quality as a strategy because it contributes to competitive advantage in cost and differentiation. At its best, quality management is a transformation in the way an organization manages. Key quality initiatives include (1) demonstrating top-level commitment, (2) creating a corporate culture of quality, (3) empowering employees to fix and prevent problems; (4) championing a link between quality performance and pay, and (5) establishing extraordinarily difficult quality targets for group members.

Another aspect of strategic leadership is to foster an advanced-technology environment. Technology plays a major role in four business strategies: first to market, fast follower and overtaker, cost minimization, and market niche. The technology-minded leader should also invest heavily in training and establish a reward system for innovation.

KEY TERMS

Strategy	Strategic planning	Kaizen
Strategic leadership	Total quality management	Technology
Strategic management	(TQM)	

GUIDELINES FOR ACTION AND SKILL DEVELOPMENT

Larry Bossidy, the highly acclaimed CEO of AlliedSignal Corp., the aerospace and auto parts conglomerate, offers the following suggestions for achieving a growth strategy:

1. **Cut the fat.** The first step is boosting productivity because only the lean grow profitably.

2. **Set killer goals.** Extraordinary stretch targets motivate staffers far better than reasonable ones.

3. **Grow through globalization.** New, sizzling markets like China and India are difficult to navigate but worth the risk because of their large potential payoff.

4. **Multiply new products.** Even in stable, mature businesses, innovation produces growth.

5. **Make niche acquisitions.** Search for small sprinters that add key products you do not already manufacture.

6. **Claw your way to victory.** No excuse making. Push managers relentlessly to meet your growth goals.[30]

DISCUSSION QUESTIONS AND ACTIVITIES

1. Why does Gwenn Cagann at New World Coffee qualify as a *strategic leader?*

2. Why is strategic leadership thought to have the same meaning as transformational leadership?

3. Many top level-managers say that they want lower-ranking managers to think strategically. How can a middle manager "think strategically"?

4. What sources of information should a leader use to find helpful input for formulating strategy?

5. What does it really mean for a leader to "create a future"?

6. Use media sources and interviews and conversations with auto salespeople to find out if Ronald Zarrella's strategy for GM is helping the company.

7. Working by yourself or with several team members, provide a recent example of revolutionary thinking by a company.

8. What makes sticking to core competencies an effective business strategy in many situations?

9. How ethical is it if for a leader to encourage group members to set next-to-impossible quality standards?

10. How important is it for a leader in a high-technology company to regularly use a computer himself or herself?

LEADERSHIP CASE PROBLEM

Acer Carves Out a Competitive Edge

The Acer Group is a personal computer company based in Taiwan. It has had such phenomenal success in recent years that its founder and CEO, Stan Shih, has become a celebrity throughout Asia. The Acer personal computer is now seventh in the world, as measured by the total number of desktops, laptops, and notebooks sold. The company's monitors occupy the number three position. In 1996 Acer had over 15,000 employees directly or indirectly supporting eighty offices operating in thirty-eight countries, with dealers placed in more than 100 nations. In 1995, sales were US$ 5.825 billion, net income was US$ 413 million, and revenue growth over the previous year was more than 80 percent. The company sells more than 4 million PCs each year. One of its fastest-growing markets is the United States, where the company now has 7 percent of the personal computer market. A major goal of the Acer Group is "21 in 21"—having twenty-one publicly listed companies in the twenty-first century. In a step toward this goal, the Acer Computer International Ltd. Region business unit has become a fully independent, publicly listed operation.

Shih believes that much of the success of the Acer Group can be attributed directly to a few simple, fresh ideas. He says, "Fresh ideas are both rare and precious, but their true value can only be determined through implementation. For this reason, simple ideas are of the best because they can be applied to the broadest range of circumstances. Acer's most powerful and successful strategies are based on simple, powerful, and fresh ideas, ideas which can be implemented easily and consistently on a global basis" ("Acer. A Fresh Perspective," p. 2).

Shih challenges the competition with a new way of producing PCs. Acer's competitors typically buy their memory chips, drives, monitors, and other components from original equipment manufacturers (OEMs), whose trademarks rarely appear on the assembled package. Intel's Pentium chip is a notable exception. Acer manufactures the components and assembles them into computers that carry its brand name. Yet the company began as an OEM and still makes components and complete products, such as notebooks, for other manufacturers.

Acer manufactures almost all components itself, and thus is not dependent upon a network of diverse OEMs. Shih believes that as a result, retail customers are assured of a uniformity of quality. He explains, "We turn out PCs the way McDonald's makes hamburgers" (*Fortune*, p. 188).

To get where it is today, the Acer Group has gone through two different phases of development, and is now in a third phase. Phase one was 1976–1985, and mostly involved with commercializing microprocessor technology. Phase two was 1986–1995, and focused mostly on globalization. Phase three is 1996–2005, which has involved and will involve building world-renowned brand awareness. Company executives believe that brand recognition becomes critically important as Acer becomes more deeply involved in consumer electronics markets. The company intends to become more consumer-oriented and market-driven in the future.

Shih believes that an information technology company the size of Acer could never be managed effectively from one central location. To stay fast and flexible, top management delegates responsibility to a network of autonomous business units (BUs). The company also believes that the quality of leadership in each independent location is vital to the success of the Acer Group overall. Most of the BU heads have over fifteen years of experience working within the Acer organization. Another reason for the organization into business units is to provide maximum flexibility and responsiveness to change to deal with the dynamic business environment of information technology.

Speed, cost, and value are the three core competencies the Acer Group uses to create the corporation's major competitive advantages. *Speed* is defined as fast time to market with new products and fast responses to change in the industry. *Cost* includes minimizing overhead, inventory reduction, and risk management. Controlling costs also means frugality in daily operations, including such minor items as executives writing memos on the back of old reports (when they are not using E-mail). *Value* means giving customers something of importance to them, and the company believes that providing real value to customers leads directly to new opportunities to enter new markets. The company likes to depict its competitive advantages on Stan Shih's smiling curve. On the left side of a chart, value is added through component design and production. On the right side, value is added through marketing, distribution, and localized assembly. The middle of the curve shows that little value gets added by the simple assembly of PC systems. Acer selects only those opportunities that allow it to provide real value and become a market segment leader. To ensure that the Acer Group would achieve sustainable long-term growth and success, three key strategic initiatives were created: the global brand, local touch philosophy; the client-server organizational structure; and the fast-food business model.

Global brand, local touch. The company recognizes that a well-known brand name can provide a positive image for both the company and its product. On the local level, independent business operations promote the Acer brand as they strive to meet the unique needs of their local customers. Local efforts create a strong positive image in the minds of their target audiences, letting them feel that Acer is a company that understands their unique local need and cares about them.

Client-server organization. Although they are independent in terms of operations and decision making, each BU also enjoys the benefits of belonging to a network of companies sharing a cohesive, overall strategic direction. Centralized component design and production provides cost advantages because of greater economies of scale. Regionalized marketing teams adapt the product offerings to the local market and develop their own plans to attain leadership in a market segment. Top management believes that this type of organizational structure fosters quick decision making and fast implementation, enabling the company to stay responsive to fast-changing local markets.

Fast-food business model. Based on the same strategy used by global restaurant chains, Acer's fast-food business model call for final product assembly operations to be performed at Uniload sites located around the world. Components are classified as either perishable or nonperishable. Perishable motherboards, memory, hard disk drives, and related components are sent via air transport to ensure fast delivery. Nonperishable PC housings and floppy disk drives, for example, are shipped via slower sea transport. Perishable components may also be sourced locally, from approved vendors, to expedite the process even faster.

Shih believes that the global brand, local touch philosophy leverages both global and local resources while focusing attention where it belongs—on the customer's needs. Also important is the mission statement launched in June 1995: Provide fresh technology to be enjoyed by everyone, everywhere. To Acer, *fresh* means the best—high-value, low-risk, user-friendly technology that is affordable by everyone and that has a longer useful life span. Fresh ideas are also very powerful when applied to business strategy. Top management believes that keeping the company fresh is the only way to compete successfully in the rapidly changing information technology industry. Shih has vigorously pursued a strategy of making original products rather than following the traditional pattern of copycat Taiwan manufacturers. He has steadily invested in making original products under the Acer brand name.

Changing the World of Home Computing. Acer leadership believes that innovation is a big part of what the company is all about and that because of Acer's innovative ability, on September 5, 1995, the world of home computing was changed forever. In Acer's leaders' opinion, the launch of the Acer Aspire line of multimedia home PCs rocked the industry, setting a new standard for another product category. Working closely with a famous California design firm, Acer America created the revolutionary new Aspire look. The housing resembles a modern charcoal-colored television receiver, with emerald trim. Acer's product expertise was applied to develop the tooling and internal PC technology. A company spokesperson said, "The Acer Aspire is a shining example of the Acer Group's unique combination of a deep resource base plus flexible strategic design and organizational structure" ("Acer. A Fresh Perspective"). The

company intends to continually update, refine, and develop the Aspire line. Management believes that staying close to its customers to fully understand their changing needs is the only way Acer will be able to continue to stay one step ahead of the competition. One of Shih's major goals is to challenge Japanese dominance of the consumer electronics market. He also wants to double Acer's size to $10 billion annually by the turn of the century.

1. What is your evaluation of Stan Shih as a strategic leader?

2. Identify at least five business strategies used by Acer.

3. What recommendations can you make to the executive team at Acer to help them achieve their goals and maintain their prosperity?

Source: "Acer. A Fresh Perspective: Celebrating 20 Years of Achievement, 1976–1996," www.ipb.acer.com.tw/ai/ profile, January 6, 1997; based on information reported in Louis Kraar, "Acer's Edge: PCs to Go," Fortune, October 30, 1995, pp. 187–204.

International and Culturally Diverse Aspects of Leadership

LEARNING OBJECTIVES

After studying this chapter, you should be able to

1. explain the potential ethical and competitive advantage from leading and managing diversity.
2. describe how cross-cultural factors influence leadership practice.
3. summarize characteristics and behaviors important for leading diverse groups.
4. pinpoint leadership initiatives to enhance valuing diversity.
5. outline a plan for developing the multicultural organization.
6. outline a plan for achieving leadership diversity within the organization.

*J*eanne Engel, the vice president of a machine shop in Toronto, Ontario (Canada), told the company president, "Wish me luck. I'm headed off to Montreal. I'm trying to get some subcontract business from Chrysler of Canada. Business is approaching overcapacity for them, and we're hurting. I've been speaking French every chance I've had for the last two weeks. I want to be prepared for my meeting with Girard Balfour, the plant manager I'll be dealing with. "

"Jeanne, is that really necessary?" asked Max Fairbanks, the machine shop owner. "All businesspeople in Quebec speak English fluently."

"*Absolument,*" said Engel. "Yet even if Monsieur Balfour speaks English perfectly, remember one fact. I'm selling, not buying. I'm trying to please, not be pleased."

The exchange between Jeanne Engel and her boss presents an important message about cross-cultural relations and influence in today's world. Engel knows through both experience and intuition that speaking the language of a person from another culture can give one a competitive edge—especially when selling. In a broader sense, Engel demonstrates that sensitivity to, and an appreciation of, cultural diversity improves working relationships.

The modern leader must be multicultural because corporate success, profit, and growth depend increasingly on the management of a diverse work force.[1] For example, the average age of the American worker is increasing, and white males now constitute less than 50 percent of the work force. An increasing number of new entrants to the work force are women and people of color. The diversity umbrella in the work force encompasses such groups as men, women, people of color, white people, able-bodied people, the physically disabled, gay males, lesbians, the old, the young, married people with children, unmarried people with children, and single parents. These groups want their leaders and coworkers to treat them with respect, dignity, fairness, and sensitivity.

Not only is the work force becoming more diverse, but business has become increasingly global. Small and medium-size firms, as well as corporate giants, are increasingly dependent on trade with other countries. An estimated 10 to 15 percent of jobs in the United States depend on imports or exports. Furthermore, most manufactured goods contain components from more than one country. For reasons like these, Warren Bennis, Jagdish Parikh, and Ronnie Lessem argue that ethnocentrism is "out" and international citizenry is "in." Leaders and managers now have to place themselves within a continually expanding global ecosystem and learn how to survive and prosper within this environment.[2]

Our approach to cultural diversity both within and across countries emphasizes the leadership perspective. Key topics include the ethical and competitive advantage of managing for diversity, cultural factors influencing leadership practices, and the attributes of leaders that are important for leading diverse groups. The chapter also discusses organizational approaches leaders can take to enhance valuing diversity, develop the multicultural organization, and create a more diverse group of leaders. The underlying theme is that effective leadership of diverse people requires a sensitivity to and enjoyment of cultural differences.

THE ADVANTAGES OF MANAGING FOR DIVERSITY

The ethical and social responsibility goals of leaders and their organizations include providing adequately for members of the diverse work force. Ethics is involved because treating people fairly is considered morally right from the *deontological* view of ethics. The deontological approach is based on universal principles such as honesty, fairness, justice, and respect for persons and property. Leaders who ascribe to this view of ethics would therefore feel compelled to use merit as a basis for making human resource decisions.

A firm that embraces diversity is also behaving in a socially responsible manner. Both ethics and social responsibility relate to the goodness and morality of leaders and organizations, but social responsibility is a broader concept that relates to an organization's impact on society, beyond doing what is legal or ethical.[3] A leader, for example, who chose to hire five culturally disadvantaged, unemployed people would be acting in a socially responsible manner. Hiring these people would transfer responsibility for their economic welfare from the state or private charity to the employer. (Some would argue that unless hiring these people is cost-effective, the company is neglecting its responsibility to shareholders.)

The many spheres of activity that managing for diversity encompasses are shown in Figure 14–1. According to Taylor H. Cox and Stacy Blake, managing for diversity also brings the firm a competitive advantage.[4] Here we

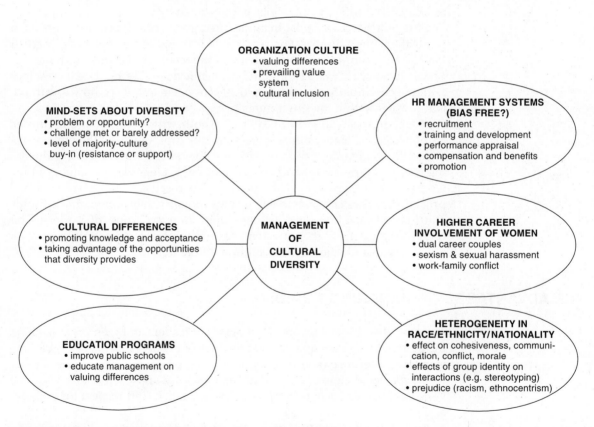

FIGURE 14–1

Spheres of Activity in the Management of Cultural Diversity

Source: Taylor H. Cox and Stacy Blake, "Managing for Cultural Diversity: Implications for Organizational Competitiveness," Academy of Management Executive, *August 1991, p. 46. Used by permission.*

review the arguments of Cox and Blake, along with more recent evidence and opinion, about the competitive advantage of diversity.

An important cost argument can be presented for providing effective leadership to the management of diversity. As organizations become more diverse, the cost of managing diversity poorly will increase. Turnover and absenteeism are often higher among women and racioethnic minorities than among white males. Job satisfaction is also lower for minorities, even among those with MBA degrees. More effective management of diversity may increase the job satisfaction of diverse groups, thus decreasing turnover and absenteeism and their associated costs. At one point, Ortho Pharmaceutical Corporation estimated its accumulated savings to be $500,000, primarily from reduced turnover among women and ethnic minorities.[5]

Companies with a favorable record in managing diversity are at a distinct advantage in recruiting and retaining talented people. Those companies with a favorable reputation for welcoming diversity attract the strongest job candidates among women and racioethnic minorities. Anita Rowe explains that companies need an inclusive environment to attract the best of any group. "People look at an organization and say if there's no one like me, do I want to work there?"[6]

Managing diversity well also offers a marketing advantage. A representational work force facilitates selling goods and services. A key factor is that a multicultural group of decision makers may be at an advantage in reaching a multicultural market. For example, Avon Products, Inc., faced low profitability in its inner-city markets. The company then gave African American and Hispanic managers considerable authority over these markets. Soon the inner-city markets became highly profitable for Avon. Another marketing advantage is that many people from these same groups may prefer to buy from a company with a good reputation for managing diversity.

Heterogeneity in the work force may also offer a company a creativity advantage. Creative solutions to problems are more likely to be reached when a diverse group attacks a problem. A study of organizational innovation suggested that innovative companies had above-average records on reducing racism, sexism, and classism. In addition, they tended to employ more women and other minorities than did less innovative companies.[7]

Closely related to the creativity advantage, managing diversity well has the potential to improve problem solving and decision making. Decision quality appears to be best when the group is neither excessively homogeneous nor overly heterogeneous. With a culturally diverse group present, there is less likelihood of groupthink. (Groupthink, as you will recall, occurs when a group tries so hard to be cohesive that it loses its faculty for critical self-analysis.)

The results of empirical research on heterogeneity in groups suggest that diversity offers both a substantial advantage for organizations and a formidable challenge. Some research suggests that a diverse group is likely to consider a greater range of perspectives and to generate more high-quality solutions than a homogeneous group. Yet the greater the amount of diversity within an organizational subunit, the less cohesive the group. The result may be dissatisfaction and turnover. According to Frances J. Milliken and Luis L. Martins, diversity thus appears to be a double-edge sword: It increases both the opportunity for creativity and the likelihood that group members will be dissatisfied and fail to identify with the group.[8]

Managing diversity can also offer the advantage of system flexibility. Cox and Blake argue that bilingual people have higher levels of divergent thinking and cognitive flexibility. Both characteristics enhance flexible thinking. Another argument is that managing diversity fosters less standardization of policies and procedures, leading to more fluidity and adaptability.

Systems thinking about the potential advantages of diversity has been pushed one step further. According to David A. Thomas and Robin J. Ely, organizations can sometimes use identity-group differences to assist organizational learning, growth, and renewal. The process involves incorporating employees' perspectives into the main work of the organization. For example, the law firm of Dewey & Levin hired its first female Hispanic attorney with the expectation that she would bring in clients from her own community and demonstrate the firm's commitment to representing women. Yet an even greater advantage emerged: The new attorney introduced ideas about what kind of cases the firm should tackle, such as challenging English-only policies. Valuing diversity thus helped shape the nature of the firm's work.[9]

To raise your level of awareness about how to capitalize upon the potential advantages of diversity, do Leadership Skill-Building Exercise 14–1.

LEADERSHIP SKILL-BUILDING
EXERCISE 14–1 Capitalizing on Diversity

The class organizes into small groups of about six students who assume the roles of the top management team of a medium-size manufacturing or service company. Being socially aware, ethical, and modern in its thinking, your company already has a highly diverse work force. Yet somehow, your company isn't any more profitable than the competition. As the company leaders (yourself a diverse group), today you will work on the problem of how to better capitalize on the cultural diversity within your company. Working for about fifteen minutes, develop a few concrete ideas to enable your company to capitalize upon diversity. After the problem solving has been completed, the team leaders might present their ideas to the other groups.

CULTURAL FACTORS INFLUENCING LEADERSHIP PRACTICE

A **multicultural leader** is a leader with the skills and attitudes to relate effectively to and motivate people across race, gender, age, social attitudes, and lifestyles. To influence, motivate, and inspire culturally diverse people, the leader must be aware of overt and subtle cultural differences. Such culturally based differences are generalizations, but they function as starting points in the leader's attempt to lead a person from another culture. For example, many Asians are self-conscious about being praised in front of the group because they feel that individual attention clashes with their desire to maintain group harmony. A manager might refrain from praising an Asian group member before the group until he or she understands that group member's preferences. The manager is likely to find that many Asians welcome praise in front of peers, especially when working outside their homeland.

Here we examine three topics that help a leader learn how to manage in a culturally diverse workplace: (1) understanding key dimensions of differences in cultural values; (2) applying a motivational model across cultural groups; and (3) understanding cross-cultural differences in leadership style.

Key Dimensions of Differences in Cultural Values

One way to understand how national cultures differ is to examine their values. Here we examine seven different values and how selected nationalities relate to them. Geert Hofstede identified the first five value dimensions in research spanning eighteen years, involving over 160,000 people from over sixty countries.[10] The qualitative research of Arvind V. Phatak identified the other two values.[11] A summary of these values is described next, and outlined in Figure 14–2.

1. *Individualism/collectivism.* At one end of the continuum is **individualism**, a mental set in which people see themselves first as individuals and believe their own interests and values take priority. **Collectivism**, at the other end of the continuum, is a feeling that the group and society should receive top priority. Members of a society that value individualism are more concerned with their careers than with the good of the firm. Members of a society who value collectivism, on the other hand, are typically more concerned with the organization than with themselves. Individualistic cultures include the United States, Canada, and Great Britain; collectivistic cultures include Japan, Hong Kong, Mexico, and Greece.

2. *Power distance.* The extent to which employees accept the idea that members of an organization have different levels of power is referred to as **power distance**. In a high-power-distance culture, the boss makes many decisions simply because he or she is boss, and group members readily comply. In a low-power-distance culture, employees do not readily

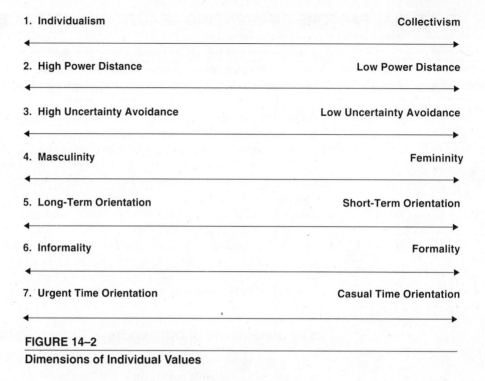

FIGURE 14–2

Dimensions of Individual Values

recognize a power hierarchy. They accept directions only when they think the boss is right or when they feel threatened. High-power-distance cultures include France, Spain, Japan, and Mexico. Low-power-distance cultures include the United States, Israel, Germany, and Ireland.

3. *Uncertainty avoidance.* People who accept the unknown, and tolerate risk and unconventional behavior, are said to have low **uncertainty avoidance**. In other words, these people are not afraid to face the unknown. A society ranked high in uncertainty avoidance contains a majority of people who want predictable and certain futures. Low-uncertainty-avoidance cultures include the United States, Canada, and Australia. At the other end of the continuum, workers in Israel, Japan, Italy, and Argentina value certainty and predictability more highly.

4. *Masculinity/femininity.* The terms *masculinity* and *femininity* are now considered sexist in relation to work. Nevertheless, Hofstede used the terms to refer to the useful distinction between materialism and concern for personal welfare. In this context, **masculinity** refers to an emphasis on assertiveness and the acquisition of money and material objects, and a deemphasis on caring for others. At the other end of the continuum is **femininity,** which refers to an emphasis on personal relationships, concern for others, and a high quality of life. "Masculine" countries

include Japan and Italy, whereas "feminine" cultures include Sweden and Denmark.

5. *Long-term orientation/short-term orientation.* Workers from a culture with a **long-term orientation** maintain a long-range perspective, and thus are thrifty and do not demand quick returns on their investments. A **short-term orientation** is characterized by a demand for immediate results, and a propensity not to save. Pacific Rim countries are noted for their long-term orientation. In contrast, the cultures of the United States and Canada are characterized by a more short-term orientation.

6. *Formality/informality.* A country that values **formality** attaches considerable importance to tradition, ceremony, social rules, and rank. In contrast, **informality** refers to a casual attitude toward tradition, ceremony, social rules, and rank. Workers in Latin American countries highly value formality, such as lavish public receptions and processions. American and Canadian workers are much more informal.

7. *Urgent time orientation/casual time orientation.* Long- and short-term orientations focus mostly on planning and investment. Another time-related value dimension is how much importance a person attaches to time. People with an **urgent time orientation** perceive time as a scarce resource and tend to be impatient. People with a **casual time orientation** view time as an unlimited and unending resource and tend to be patient. Americans are noted for their urgent time orientation. They frequently impose deadlines and are eager to "get down to business." Asians and Middle Easterners, in contrast, are patient negotiators. In fact, businesspersons in the Middle East are known to allow a business meeting to run over while another visitor waits outside the office.

How might a manager use information about cultural differences in values to become a more effective leader? A starting point would be to recognize that a person's national values might influence his or her behavior. Assume that a leader wants to influence a person with a low-power-distance orientation to strive for peak performance. The "low-power" person will not spring into action just because the boss makes the suggestion. Instead, the leader needs to patiently explain the personal payoffs of achieving peak performance. Another example is a leader who wants to improve quality and therefore hires people who value collectivism. A backup tactic would be to counsel people who value individualism on the merits of collective action, and thereby achieve high quality. Leadership Self-Assessment Exercise 14–1 will help you think about how values can moderate (or influence) work performance.

The accompanying Leader in Action insert illustrates how national values indirectly enter into forming effective working relationships with people from another culture. As you read the insert, look for evidence indicating the importance of being aware of the importance of values. Refer back to the same Leader in Action insert when you read the section on cultural sensitivity.

LEADERSHIP SELF-ASSESSMENT
EXERCISE 14–1 Charting Your Cultural Value Profile

Directions: For each of the seven value dimensions, circle the number that most accurately fits your standing on the dimension. For example, if you perceive yourself to be "highly concerned for others," circle the 7 on the fourth dimension.

1. Individualism   Collectivism

   1   2   3   4   5   6   7

2. High Power Distance   Low Power Distance

   1   2   3   4   5   6   7

3. High Uncertainty Avoidance   Low Uncertainty Avoidance

   1   2   3   4   5   6   7

4. Materialism (masculinity)   Concern for Others (femininity)

   1   2   3   4   5   6   7

5. Long-Term Orientation   Short-Term Orientation

   1   2   3   4   5   6   7

6. Informality   Formality

   1   2   3   4   5   6   7

7. Urgent Time Orientation   Casual Time Orientation

   1   2   3   4   5   6   7

Scoring and interpretation: After circling one number for each dimension, use a felt-tip pen to connect the circles; this gives you a *profile of cultural values*. Do not be concerned if your marker cuts through the names of the dimensions. Compare your profile to others in class. Should time allow, develop a class profile by computing the class average for each of the seven dimensions and then connecting the points. If the sample size is large enough, compare the cultural value profiles of Westerners and Easterners.

One possible link to leadership development is to hypothesize which type of profile would be the most responsive and which would be the least responsive to your leadership.

Applying a Motivational Theory Across Cultural Groups

As we have seen, motivating people is a major leadership function. What would happen if we were to apply a motivation theory to various cultural groups? Here we take another look at the expectancy theory of motivation,

LEADER IN ACTION

Y. C. Tsien Advises American and Chinese Businesspeople to Engage in Mutual Understanding

Y. C. Tsien is the general manager and founder of Deh Hsing International Inc., a firm of international business advisers in Fairport, New York. He has observed that after American and Chinese businesspeople have signed an agreement, they often find implementation frustrating despite mutual good intentions. He thinks that both sides may be at fault for not being aware of the other's culture and business practices. A blending of the two systems and values is necessary for a successful operation in China. Tsien offers several anecdotes based on his experiences.

■ During a business meeting between the Chinese general manager of a joint venture and the president of the American parent company, there was confusion on how sales should be recorded for a particular quarter. The American wanted the sale to be recorded because the product had been shipped. The Chinese did not consider it a sale because the joint venture had not received payment. This illustrates the difference between accrual and cash accounting systems.

■ In a meeting, the senior executive of a U.S. manufacturer came fully prepared with an overhead projector and hard copies of the presentation, while the head of a Chinese government agency read from handwritten notes. Both sides made well-prepared and reasoned presentations, but it was extremely difficult to follow the Chinese presentations, even with a good interpreter.

Tsien advises that is not enough for American managers to be trained in Chinese culture and business practice. If an American company wants to succeed in China, it should also train its Chinese staff on how to deal with Americans. The training should cover American culture, basic business terms, and the American company's corporate values and expectations of its employees. The Chinese staff should be encouraged to be more direct with Americans—argue and disagree if necessary. The Chinese are well known for saying no indirectly. The neophyte American manager in China would probably not understand the true meaning of, "It has been extremely fatiguing to sell your products with the current specifications, but we shall continue to exert maximum effort."

According to Tsien, doing business in China will not become easy even if both American and Chinese staffs are trained in each other's culture and business practice. But mutual frustration should be greatly reduced and the quality of communication should also improve significantly.

Source: From Y. C. Tsien, "Key to Success Lies in Mutual Understanding," Rochester *Democrat and Chronicle*, November 24, 1996, p. 15A. Reprinted by permission.

which provides detailed guidelines for leaders. Doing so will illustrate the principle that some aspects of motivation theory apply across cultures, whereas other aspects most be modified. Two aspects of expectancy theory are especially important for understanding cross-cultural differences in motivation: perception of individual control over the environment, and appropriateness of rewards.

Environmental Control.   As analyzed by Nancy J. Adler, expectancy theories depend on the extent to which workers believe they have control over the outcome of their efforts, and how much faith they have in leaders to deliver rewards.[12] The assumption that workers believe they have control over their own fate may be culturally dependent. In countries where individualism dominates, employees may believe more strongly that they can influence performance and outcomes. In collectivist societies, such as Taiwan and Japan, the ties between the individual and the organization have a moral component. In the United States and similar cultures, many people believe that "where there is a will, there is a way."

Adler argues that the reasons that people in individualistic societies become committed to organizations are quite different reasons from those of people in collectivist societies. An employee in an individualistic culture (such as the United States, Canada, or Germany) is more likely to ask, "What's in it for me?" before responding to a motivational thrust. Employees with collectivistic values commit themselves to the organization more because of ties with managers and coworkers than because of intrinsic job factors or individual incentives.

Despite the cultural generalization, the leader must be alert to individual and subcultural differences. Many Japanese workers are becoming less loyal to their employers and thus more self-centered and eager for individual recognition. Workers from rural areas in the United States are much more collectivist than their counterparts from large cities. One of the many reasons Saturn Motors located its plant in Tennessee is the presence of a more harmonious and loyal work force.

Appropriateness of Rewards.   Expectancy theories are universal because the motivator must search for rewards that have valence for individual employees. Leaders themselves must analyze the type and level of rewards that have the highest valence for individuals. The appropriateness of rewards is most strongly tied to individual differences, yet cultural differences are also important. A classic study by David Sirota and M. J. Greenwood investigated the work goals of 19,000 employees in a multinational electrical equipment manufacturer.[13] (Goals are related to rewards because people are motivated to achieve rewards that enable them to achieve their goals.) Results were reported for twenty-five countries in which a minimum of forty employees were surveyed.

The five most important goals related to achievement. Next in importance were the immediate environment, general aspects of the organization, and employment conditions, such as compensation and work hours. Many significant differences in goal importance were found among the various countries. Workers from English-speaking countries, for example, placed more emphasis on individual achievement and less emphasis on job security. (In the current era, job security would probably have a much higher valence because of the decrease in full-time, permanent jobs in many countries.)

Many American managers have mistakenly assumed that a reward with a high valence among American workers will also have a high valence among workers from other cultures. In one situation, raising the salary of a particular group of Mexican workers motivated them to work fewer rather than more hours. A spokesperson for the Mexican workers said, "We can now make enough money to live and enjoy life in less time than previously. Now, we do not have to work so many hours."[14]

Cross-Cultural Differences in Leadership Style

In recent years several management researchers and writers have looked for evidence of differences in leadership and management style across cultures or searched for the dominant style in a particular culture. Roland Calori and Bruno Dufour conducted one such investigation by conducting in-depth interviews with fifty-two top executives from some of Western Europe's best-known firms.[15] In spite of differences across Europe, it was found that European firms share some common management philosophies and practices. Four common characteristics were noted among managers and leaders in prominent European firms.

1. *A greater orientation toward people.* Compared to their U.S. and Japanese counterparts, European managers are more likely to believe that they share a common inclination to foster the fulfillment of people. As the European business leaders see it, in the United States, profits dominate everything, and people are considered a resource that you can take or leave. In Japan, evidence is surfacing of mental and physical harassment of employees in an attempt to force them to resign as their employers face stiffer competition.

2. *A higher level of internal negotiation.* European managers invest considerable time negotiating inside the firm—between different levels of management, between management and the workers, with trade unions, and between headquarters and divisions or subsidiaries. U.S. executives tend to be more top-down in making major decisions, while Japanese managers typically strive for consensus management.

3. *Greater skill in managing international diversity.* Based on the interviews, the researchers concluded that European managers have an ability to recognize diversity. They respect and appreciate diversity, and have developed skill in managing it to advantage. (Of course, this edge is disappearing as Americans take courses in leadership!) European managers generally respect the host country, and are less imperialistic than the Americans and Japanese, who have a tendency to export their way of thinking.

4. *European managers are capable of managing between extremes.* Management philosophies and styles in the United States and Japan are often

characterized as lying at the extremes on certain dimensions, such as the short-term perspective of Americans versus the long-term perspective of Japanese. If a European style of management exists, it is halfway between the extremes of the U.S. and Japanese styles on various leadership dimensions such as extent of concern for human resources.

Identifying typical European styles of management and leadership may be helpful in relating to European managers and group members. If a group of European workers are accustomed to considerable negotiation, they will expect such behavior from a North American manager on assignment in Europe. Nevertheless, cultural stereotypes are limited because they do not take into account differences within a culture. For example, American managers who practice empowerment are strongly oriented toward a negotiating style. Another consideration is that as leadership and management knowledge continues to be disseminated widely, effective managers from different geographic regions may develop similar styles. One of the executives in the study under consideration put it this way: "The real difference will be between the best companies (wherever they come from), between the best management practices and mediocre management practices. Management in the world and in Europe will be homogeneous at its best."[16]

CULTURAL SENSITIVITY

Some managers are more effective at leading diverse groups than others, depending on their characteristics and behaviors. The traits and behaviors described in Chapters 2, 3, and 4 would equip a person to lead diverse groups, but cultural sensitivity is also essential for inspiring people from cultures other than one's own. Leaders, as well as others, attempting to influence a person from a foreign country, must be alert to possible cultural differences. Thus the leader must be willing to acquire knowledge about local customs and learn to speak the native language at least passably.

A cross-cultural leader must be patient, adaptable, flexible, and willing to listen and learn. All these characteristics are part of **cultural sensitivity**, an awareness of and a willingness to investigate the reasons why people of another culture act as they do.[17] A person with cultural sensitivity will recognize certain nuances in customs that will help build better relationships with people in his or her "adopted" cultures. Table 14–1 presents a sampling of appropriate and less appropriate behaviors in a variety of countries. (These are suggestions, not absolute rules.)

Sensitivity is the most important characteristic for leading people from other cultures because cultural stereotypes rarely provide entirely reliable guides for dealing with others. An American manager, for example, might expect Asian group members to accept his or her directives immediately because Asians are known to defer to authority. Nevertheless, an individual Asian might need considerable convincing before accepting authority. The

TABLE 14–1   Protocol Do's and Don'ts

Region and Country	Do's	Don'ts
EUROPE Great Britain	DO hold your fork (tines pointed down) in the left hand and your knife in the right hand throughout the meal.	DON'T ask personal questions. The British protect their privacy.
	DO say please and thank you—often.	DON'T gossip about royalty.
France	DO be punctual for appointments.	DON'T expect to complete any work during the French two-hour lunch.
	DO shake hands (a short, quick pump) when greeting, being introduced, and leaving. Only close friends kiss cheeks.	DON'T try to do business during August—*les vacances* (vacation time).
Italy	DO write business correspondence in Italian for priority attention.	DON'T eat too much pasta, as it is not the main course.
	DO make appointments between 10 A.M. and 11 A.M., or after 3 P.M.	DON'T hand out business cards freely. Italians use them infrequently.
Spain	DO write business correspondence in English, unless your Spanish is impeccable.	DON'T expect punctuality. Your appointments will arrive 20–30 minutes late.
	DO take business lunches at 2:30 P.M. and dinner at 9 P.M. or 10 P.M. Be prepared to dine until midnight, or later if chatter flows.	DON'T make the American sign for "okay" with your thumb and forefinger. In Spain, this is vulgar.
ASIA Japan	DO find a highly respected third party to act as your introducer to the lower-ranking person you need to work with	DON'T attempt to get a deal going by directly approaching a target who is below the top level in the organization.
China	DO print your business cards and stationery without black borders.	DON'T use black borders because in China, black is associated with death.
Korea	DO say "yes," "perhaps," or "I will carefully consider your suggestion."	DON'T say "no." Koreans feel it is important to have visitors leave with good feelings.
MEXICO AND LATIN AMERICA Mexico	DO meet two or three times before expecting to consummate a deal.	DON'T fly into a Mexican city in the morning and expect to close a deal by lunch.
Brazil	DO create a good impression by expressing an interest in the Portuguese language.	DON'T attempt to impress Brazilians by speaking a few words of Spanish; Portuguese is the official language of Brazil.

Source: Dorothy Manning of International Business Protocol, cited in Heidi J. LaFleche, "When in Rome," *TWA Ambassador,* October 1990, p. 69; William Pantalon III, "Kodak Author: Asia a Gold Mine," Rochester *Democrat & Chronicle,* September 25, 1995, p. 5B; Carla Johnson, "Cultural Sensitivity Adds Up to Good Business Sense," *HRMagazine,* November 1995, pp. 82–83.

link to leadership here is that cultural sensitivity helps one become a multi-cultural leader.

Problems of cultural misunderstanding that leaders should be aware of cluster in five areas.[18] *Language* differences create problems because U.S. workers (most of whom are monolingual) can become frustrated by coworkers' accents and limited English skills. Non-English speakers may feel that they do not fit well into the team. Differences in *religion* are the source of many misunderstandings. In many cultures, religion dominates life in ways that Americans find difficult to comprehend. *Work habits* vary enough across cultures to create friction and frustration. Employees in some cultures are unwilling to spend personal time on work. Problems can also stem from office rituals. An international manager noted, "Here in the UAR (United Arab Republic), everyone has to shake hands and have tea or coffee first thing in the morning—which wastes a lot of time according to American standards."[19]

Women's roles may differ considerably from those in the United States. Women in many countries may not have the same independence or access to education and higher-level jobs as American women. Workers from various countries may therefore have difficulty accepting the authority of an American manager who is female. *Personal appearance and behavior* varies considerably across cultures. Grooming, office attire, eating habits, and nonverbal communication may deviate significantly from the U.S. standards. Many workers around the world may perceive American workers as overfriendly, aggressive, or rude.

Cultural sensitivity is enhanced by diversity training (or valuing differences training), and also by simply listening carefully and observing. A key principle is to be flexible when dealing with people from other cultures. An excellent example is the attitude of Zhang Xin Sheng, the mayor of Suzho, China, whose strategic goal is to make Westerners feel comfortable in his city. Zhang says in fluent English, "It's not necessary to use chopsticks. A knife and fork are okay."[20] The accompanying Leader in Action vignette describes how one company helps people from various cultures to work together harmoniously.

LEADERSHIP INITIATIVES

For organizations to value diversity, top management must be committed to it as well. The commitment is clearest when valuing diversity is embedded in organizational strategy. A true diversity strategy should encourage all employees to contribute their unique talents, skills, and expertise to the organization's operations, independent of race, gender, ethnic background, and any other definable difference. Organizational leaders sometimes formulate strategy with the input of a wide range of organizational members. In addition, leaders should take the initiative to assure that dozens of other activities are implemented to support the diversity strategy.

LEADER IN ACTION

Chris Dennis at Grace Cocoa Builds a Cross-Cultural Understanding

Grace Cocoa is an $800 million company that processes more than 12 percent of the world's cocoa for industrial companies, primarily those producing baked goods and confectionery. In the early 1990s, the company realized that it needed to attain a more global focus. The company had to be capable of implementing changes to keep pace with the rapidly evolving business environment. Chris Dennis, vice president, human resources, was asked by Grace to be its change agent to transform its divisions into one company with one culture.

"We could have implemented a standard training program," says Dennis, "but we knew what would happen: People would go through the program and go back to their offices and do nothing with what they learned." With assistance from a consulting firm, Dennis created a program called the Grace Leadership Forum. One of its key elements is to take people from different disciplines and put them into five-member teams to solve specific problems.

The teams are made up of Grace Cocoa employees from all over the world, including the United States, Canada, France, Spain, Singapore, Ecuador, the Netherlands, and the Ivory Coast. Team members are given twenty-four days of training spread over six months. Essentially, the team works for a project client (the person or group within the company whose problem is being solved). Although the project client gives the team guidance and suggestions, the team is expected to work as an independent entity. Not only do the team members come from different countries, no two members on any team may come from the same functional background.

Given that the team members come not only from different divisions but from different coun-

tries, they learn how to deal with cultural diversity. "We wanted to accomplish two things. First, we wanted people to understand other cultures. Second, we wanted people to understand how other cultures saw them," explains Dennis. "We don't expect each team member to understand each culture completely. You can't teach culture—but you *can* make people aware of the impression they convey to others."

Team members are encouraged to personally examine cultural issues in the countries where they are meeting. "Our teams have explored what it is like to be black in the United States, what it's like to be a woman in Holland, and how religion influences the Singaporeans," notes Dennis. Another strategy Grace Cocoa uses is to assign people to problems outside their usual disciplines. "Our goal is to improve people's leadership skills," notes Dennis. "Through our team structure, participants learn problem-solving techniques that can be applied to a variety of functions, not just their area of expertise. The key emphasis is on management development—how to make money without worrying about it."

Since its inception, the Grace Cocoa Leadership Forum has done more than give people from different cultures the opportunity to work together. The team's suggestions have saved the company several million dollars, with anticipated continued savings in the millions. "We knew we had to find a method to connect Grace Cocoa worldwide and combine them culturally into one," says Dennis. "It looks as though we've found the right direction."

Four hundred human resource professionals responded to a survey to determine the kinds of diversity policies that existed in their organizations. The firms included manufacturers, service firms, retailers and wholesalers, government agencies, health care providers, and educational institutions. In the firms studied, certain employee groups represented current and future priorities for accommodating special needs. Minorities and women represented the highest priority groups; disabled and older employees represented the next priority; functionally illiterate employees received the lowest priority.[21] As shown in Table 14–2, the diversity policies and programs were divided into four categories: building a diversity culture, educational initiatives, career support, and accommodating special needs.

A diversity policy not shown in Table 14–2 is developing an employee base to match the customer base. For example, if 20 percent of a company's athletic shoes are sold to young black males, then about 20 percent of the employees should be young black males. Digital Equipment Corp. was the first business firm to strive to achieve this balance. Kinney Shoes is another firm that is striving to match the employee base with the customer base.

Diversity (or valuing differences) training has become a widely used, though controversial, method for enhancing diversity within organizations. The purpose of **valuing differences training** is to bring about workplace harmony by teaching people how to get along better with diverse work associates. Quite often the program is aimed at minimizing open expressions of racism and sexism. All forms of valuing differences training center around increasing people's awareness of and empathy for people who are different from themselves in some noticeable way.

Training sessions in valuing differences focus on the ways in which men and women, or people of different races, reflect different values, attitudes, and cultural background. These sessions can vary from several hours to several days or longer. Sometimes the program is confrontational, sometimes not. As described by diversity consultant R. Roosevelt Thomas Jr., the objectives of valuing differences training include one or more of the following:[22]

- Fostering awareness and acceptance of individual differences
- Helping participants understand their own feelings and attitudes about people who are "different"
- Exploring how differences might be tapped as assets in the workplace
- Enhancing work relations between people who are different from one another

An essential part of relating more effectively to diverse groups is to empathize with their point of view. To help training participants develop empathy, representatives of various groups explain their feelings related to workplace issues. Leadership Skill-Building Exercise 14–2 gives you the opportunity to engage in an effective diversity training exercise.

Leaders of diversity training exercises are cautioned to guard against encouraging participants to be too confrontational and expressing too much

TABLE 14–2   Managing Diversity Policies Within a Variety of Private and Public Employers

Policy/Program	% Policy Exists	% Need Policy/ *Need to Do More
Building a Valuing-Diversity Culture		
Discussion groups to promote tolerance and understanding	49.9	75.1*
Diversity training for supervisors	38.0	74.5
Efforts to change corporate culture to value differences	37.0	61.4
Team building for diverse groups that must work together	35.3	68.8
Diversity task force to recommend policy changes where needed	34.6	44.9
Holding managers accountable for increasing diversity in managerial ranks	32.7	65.5
Awareness training to reduce prejudice	11.6	26.2
Educational Initiatives		
Incentives for younger workers to complete their education	65.5	72.7
Basic education classes (Reading, Math)	29.8	57.1
Classes in English for non-English-speaking employees	21.4	64.8
Career Support		
Minority internships	58.1	62.2
Networking among minority groups	41.7	70.3
Programs to steer women and minorities into "pivotal" jobs—key positions critical to rapid advancement	25.7	61.8
Specific goals to diversify middle and upper management	27.7	57.1
Accommodating Special Needs		
Scheduled days off to accommodate religious preferences	58.2	40.5
Policies to hire retirees for temporary assignments	45.1	51.6
Day-care arrangements or benefits	24.5	48.8
Work-at-home arrangements	19.5	32.7
Job redesign to accommodate disabled employees	17.3	49.4
Translation of written materials (manuals, newsletters) into several languages	12.6	21.0

Source: Benson Rosen and Kay Lovelace, "Piecing Together the Diversity Puzzle," *HRMagazine*, June 1991, p. 82. Reprinted with the permission of *HRMagazine*, published by the Society for Human Resource Management, Alexandria, VA.

LEADERSHIP SKILL-BUILDING EXERCISE 14–2 The Diversity Circle

Some diversity trainers use the *diversity circle* exercise to help workers appreciate diversity and overcome misperceptions. The exercise adapts well for classroom use. Form a group of about ten students. Arrange your chairs into a circle, and put one additional chair in the center of the circle. A "diverse" group member volunteers to sit in the center chair and become the first "awareness subject." Because most people are diverse in some way, most people are eligible to occupy the center chair.

The person in the center tells the others how he or she has felt about being diverse or different and how people have reacted to his or her diversity. For example, an Inuit described how fellow workers were hesitant to ask him out for a beer, worrying whether he could handle alcohol.

An equally effective alternative to the procedure just described is for each class member to come up in front of the class to describe a significant way in which he or she is different. After each class member has presented, a discussion might be held of observations and interpretations.

hostility. Companies have found that when employees are too blunt during these sessions, it may be difficult to patch up interpersonal relations in the work group later on. Key themes of negative reactions to diversity-training programs are charges of "political correctness" and "white-male bashing." Based on a review of relevant studies and theory, Patricia L. Nemetz and Sandra L. Christensen concluded that diversity training is most likely to lead to behavioral and attitudinal change under three conditions: (1) Participants have not yet committed to strong views of their own based on long-standing paradigms; (2) a conflicting informal influence (such as peer pressure) is not present; and (3) the organizational culture supports a well-defined ideal of multiculturalism.[23]

DEVELOPING THE MULTICULTURAL ORGANIZATION

The leadership initiatives just reviewed strongly contribute to valuing diversity. An even more comprehensive strategy is to establish a **multicultural organization**. Such a firm values cultural diversity and is willing to encourage and even capitalize on such diversity. Developing a multicultural organization helps achieve the benefits of valuing diversity described previously. In addition, the multicultural organization helps avoid problems stemming from diversity, such as increased turnover, interpersonal conflict, and communication breakdowns.[24]

According to Taylor Cox, Jr., the multicultural organization has six key characteristics, all requiring effective leadership to achieve. These characteristics are shown in Figure 14–3 and summarized next.

1. *Creating pluralism.* In a pluralistic organization, both minority- and majority-group members are influential in creating behavioral norms, values, and policies. Valuing diversity training is a major technique for achieving pluralism. Another useful technique is to encourage employees to be conversant in a second language spoken by many coworkers, customers, or both.

2. *Creating full structural integration.* The objective of full structural integration is a zero correlation between culture-group identity and job status —that is, no one should be assigned to a specific job just because of his or her ethnicity or gender. One approach to achieving full structural integration is to upgrade the education of minority group members where needed. Affirmative action programs and career development programs also help achieve integration. The firm's performance appraisal and reward systems should reinforce the importance of effectively managing for diversity. Employers linking pay to performance on diversity management objectives include Baxter Health Care, Amtrak, Merck & Co., and Coca-Cola.

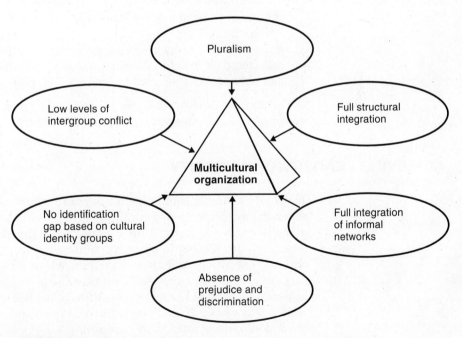

FIGURE 14–3

The Multicultural Organization

3. *Creating full integration of informal networks.* Minorities are often excluded from informal networks, making it difficult for them to achieve career advancement. Several things can help integrate informal networks: company-sponsored mentoring programs that target minorities; company-sponsored social events that minorities are encouraged to attend; and the creation of minority associations and support groups within an organization, provided they do not foster a "minority-versus-majority" attitude. Xerox Corp.'s Hispanic Professional Association is a positive example of a minority association within a company.

4. *Creating a bias-free organization.* Bias and prejudice create discrimination, so organizational efforts to reduce bias help prevent discrimination. Northern Telecom, for example, offers a sixteen-hour program designed to help employees identify and modify cultural biases and prejudices. Some companies create task forces that monitor organizational policy and practices for evidence of unfairness.

5. *Organizational identification.* In a multicultural organization, there is a zero correlation between the cultural identity group and levels of organizational identification. This would mean, for example, that Asians would identify as strongly with the organization as would white males. All the techniques mentioned in the other five steps help foster such strong identification.

6. *Minimizing intergroup conflict.* To achieve a multicultural organization, conflict must be at healthy levels. Cox believes that the most effective approach to minimizing conflict among cultural groups is to collect and share data about sensitive issues. Corning Incorporated, for example, collected data to help white males understand that diversity programs had not adversely affected their promotion rates.

Leadership Self-Assessment Exercise 14–2 gives you an opportunity to examine your attitudes toward valuing diversity.

ACHIEVING LEADERSHIP DIVERSITY

To achieve a multicultural organization, firms must also practice **leadership diversity**, the presence of a culturally heterogeneous cadre of leaders. Many global firms based in the United States have already achieved leadership diversity with respect to ethnicity. Among the most visible of these international executives is Eckhard Pfeiffer, who you will recall is the chief executive officer of Compaq Computer Corp. Sex is another key area for leadership diversity. Currently four-fifths of the 500 largest companies in the United States have at least one woman on the board of directors. Yet eighty-three companies, mostly in computing, engineering, automaking, and wholesaling, do not have a woman on the board of directors. An average of 30 percent of the companies with at least three women on the board of directors also have women in high-level management positions.[25]

LEADERSHIP SELF-ASSESSMENT
EXERCISE 14–2 How Much Do I Value Diversity?

Directions: Rate yourself on your responses to the statements below. Use a scale of 1 to 5 to rate how strongly you agree with the statements, with 1 being for low agreement and 5 being high.

1. I regularly assess my strengths and weaknesses and consciously work toward my goals.

2. I am interested in the ideas of people who do not think as I think, and I respect their opinions even when I disagree with them.

3. Some of my friends or associates are different from me in age, race, gender, physical abilities, economic status, and education.

4. If I were at a party with people outside of my own group, I would go out of my way to meet them.

5. I do not need to understand everything going on around me. I tolerate ambiguity.

6. I am able to change course quickly. I readily change my plans or expectations to adapt to a new situation.

7. I recognize that I am a product of my upbringing and my way is not the only way.

8. I am patient and flexible. I can accept different ways of getting a job done as long as the results are good.

9. I am always asking questions, reading, exploring. I am curious about new things, people, and places.

10. I am interested in human dynamics and often find myself thinking, "what's really going on here?"

11. I can see two sides on most issues.

12. I have made mistakes and I have learned from them.

13. In an unfamiliar situation, I watch and listen before acting.

14. I listen carefully.

15. When I am lost, I ask for directions.

16. When I don't understand what someone is saying, I ask for clarification.

17. I sincerely do not want to offend others.

18. I like people and accept them as they are.

19. I am sensitive to the feelings of others and observe their reactions when I am talking.

20. I am aware of my prejudices and consciously try to control my assumptions about people.

Scoring: Total your answers. If your score is 80 or above, you probably value diversity and are able to manage people who are different from yourself—but you certainly have room for improvement. If your score is below 50 you probably experience much difficulty managing diversity and could benefit from further training.

Source: Teacher's Trainer's Guide, *Valuing Diversity*®, Part I, "Managing Differences." Used by permission of Griggs Productions, San Francisco, CA.

To increase leadership diversity, several companies have developed fast-track programs for minority-group members who display the potential and motivation to succeed in leadership positions. A program designed by Juanita Cox-Burton creates a linkage between Caucasian male leaders and employees at all levels who have demonstrated leadership on or off the job. During monthly two-day sessions, participants broaden their knowledge of company operations, learn how to demonstrate their strengths, and develop skills necessary for advancement. Although the program was originally developed for women of color, it has now been expanded to members of other groups who are demographically different from the people in power.[26]

A general framework for increasing leadership diversity has been developed by Ann M. Morrison. Based on interviews with over 200 managers at sixteen exemplary organizations, she has identified the best practices for encouraging the advancement of the new leaders: white women and people of color. Morrison provides five steps an organization can take to achieve leadership diversity.[27]

Step 1: Discover and rediscover diversity problems in the organization. To begin, analyze barriers to achieving diversity goals. Interview a cross section of women and minority-group employees. Interviews should be conducted periodically to demonstrate that achieving leadership diversity is not a one-time program. Search to uncover barriers to the selection of minorities and women, including unnecessary job standards such as weight or height requirements that may not be valid. A height or weight requirement might exclude women or people from Pacific Rim countries. (If a person is blocked from an entry-level position, her or his chances of becoming a supervisor are also blocked.)

Step 2: Strengthen top-management commitment. The same axiom of organizational improvement surfaces again. Without top management commitment, long-lasting changes are unlikely to occur. To show commitment to diversity, a male Caucasian CEO might hire a 250-pound, 55-year-old Native American male who uses a wheelchair as his administrative assistant.

Step 3: Choose solutions to fit a balanced strategy. Bringing about leadership diversity requires sensitivity and tact. For example, top management might have to deal with the puzzlement and anger of a middle-aged white male who wonders why a woman of color with half his seniority is becoming his boss! The key principles underlying Morrison's guidelines are flexibility, patience, training, and communication.

Step 4: Demand results and revisit the goals. Success in diversity management should be measured by objective standards, much like profit margins and quality goals. The company should go beyond quantifying human resource decisions, such as how many people in which demographic group get promoted. Human resource decisions must also be tied to productivity factors, such as evaluating the effectiveness of the new leaders. Unless the new leader group is composed of highly competent people, the leadership diversity program will invite skepticism.

Step 5: Use building blocks to maintain momentum. Although step 5 is a summary of the entire leadership diversity program, it has a theme of its own. Each successful outcome in the program makes the next step easier. At one manufacturer, a Latino woman became the vice president of marketing. Her initiatives improved sales. Shortly thereafter, managers throughout the company became much more receptive to identifying more women and minority-group members as future leaders.[28]

SUMMARY

The modern leader must be multicultural because corporate success, profit, and growth depend increasingly on the management of a diverse work force. The ethical and social responsibility goals of leaders and their organizations include providing adequately for the members of the diverse work force.

Managing for diversity brings a competitive advantage to the firm in several ways. Costs may be lower because minorities and women become more satisfied. A marketing advantage accrues because a representational work force facilitates selling goods and services. A heterogeneous group of workers may be more creative and may improve problem solving and decision making. A more diverse work force may also be more flexible, leading to system flexibility and fostering organizational learning and growth. A factor opposing these advantages is that diversity within a group may lead to dissatisfaction and failure to identify with the group.

To influence, motivate, and inspire culturally diverse people, the leader must be aware of overt and subtle cultural differences. Differences in cultural values help explain differences among people. Seven of these values are as follows: degree of individualism or collectivism; power distance (how much the power hierarchy is accepted); uncertainty avoidance; masculinity versus femininity (materialism and aggressiveness versus concern for others); long-term versus short-term orientation; degree of formality; and time orientation.

Understanding differences between cultural groups is important for applying motivational techniques. For example, when applying expectancy theory, we must recognize that cultures differ in how much control they perceive to have over the environment. Also, appropriate rewards (those with high valence) have to be selected for each cultural group.

Another way to understand how culture influences leadership is to compare leadership styles across cultural groups. One study identified four common characteristics among managers, with European managers in general taking an intermediate position between U.S. and Japanese managers. The European managers were found to have a greater orientation toward people, to negotiate more internally, to have greater skill in managing international diversity, and to be capable of managing between extremes of certain dimensions.

Cultural sensitivity is essential for inspiring people from different cultures. Part of this sensitivity is the leader's willingness to acquire knowledge about local customs and to learn to speak the native language. A person with cultural sensitivity will recognize certain nuances in customs that help him or her build better relationships with people from different cultures. Cultural misunderstandings tend to cluster in five key areas: language differences, religious differences, work habits, women's roles, and personal appearance and behavior.

Top management commitment to valuing diversity is clearest when valuing diversity is embedded in organizational strategy. Specific leadership initiatives for valuing diversity can be divided into four categories: building a diversity culture, educational initiatives, career

support, and accommodating special needs. It is also important to develop an employee base to match the customer base. Diversity training (or valuing differences training) is a widely used, though controversial, method for enhancing diversity within organizations. The purpose of such training is to bring about workplace harmony by teaching people how to get along better with diverse work associates.

A comprehensive strategy for valuing diversity is to establish a multicultural organization. Such a firm values cultural diversity and is willing to encourage such diversity. A multicultural organization has six key characteristics: pluralism; full structural integration; full integration of informal networks; absence of prejudice and discrimination; organizational identification among all workers; and low levels of intergroup conflict.

To achieve a multicultural organization, firms must also practice leadership diversity—the presence of a culturally heterogeneous cadre of leaders. To increase leadership diversity, several companies have developed fast-track programs for minority-group members who display the potential and motivation to succeed in leadership positions. A five-step approach has been proposed to achieve leadership diversity. It includes identifying diversity problems, strengthening top management commitment, choosing solutions to fit a balanced strategy, demanding good results and revisiting the goals, and using building blocks to maintain momentum.

KEY TERMS

Multicultural leader	Femininity	Casual time orientation
Individualism	Long-term orientation	Cultural sensitivity
Collectivism	Short-term orientation	Valuing differences training
Power distance	Formality	Multicultural organization
Uncertainty avoidance	Informality	Leadership diversity
Masculinity	Urgent time orientation	

GUIDELINES FOR ACTION AND SKILL DEVELOPMENT

An important goal of a diverse workplace is for people from varied backgrounds to be able to work together smoothly. Much of the information in this chapter would support such a goal. In addition, consider these basic suggestions to make it easier for diverse people to work together smoothly:

- Make an effort to include everyone in social functions. Certain reserved individuals might not know how to enter into these activities. A worker whose religion forbids drinking can still be encouraged to join other staffers after work if it is pointed out that not everyone is expected to consume alcohol.

- Demonstrate your commitment to a diverse workplace by not playing favorites. Treat all employees with respect and understanding, including giving them all honest feedback. If you assume that someone cannot perform well because of a cultural stereotype, you are depriving that person of a chance to improve and excel.

- Be familiar with at least the basics of equal employment opportunity legislation, including (if you are governed by U.S. law) the Civil Rights Act, the Americans with Disabilities Act, and the Family and Medical Leave Act. Familiarity with such legislation will help you understand what accommodations you should or should not automatically make.[29]

DISCUSSION QUESTIONS AND ACTIVITIES

1. Since the U.S. work force is becoming increasingly Hispanic, should managers all be required to speak and read Spanish?

2. How does the concept of diversity in organizations relate to *political correctness*?

3. What actions might a leader take to show that his or her interest in diversity goes beyond rhetoric?

4. How does a culturally heterogeneous staff contribute to the leader's ability to make effective decisions?

5. Would it be fair for a sales manager to exclude a candidate for a sales job because the candidate was raised in a country with a casual time orientation?

6. Much of the information on cultural sensitivity published in the United States centers around Americans adjusting to the cultural values of other people. What adaptations in behaviors should workers from other countries make when they visit the United States?

7. How does the aphorism, "When in Rome, do as the Romans do" relate to cultural sensitivity?

8. What tasteful steps might a company take to demonstrate to the public that it is a multicultural organization?

9. Some deaf people maintain that top leaders in most organizations should use sign language in addition to speech when they address a large audience. How important do you think it is for organizational leaders to be able to sign, even if they have full hearing?

10. Find an article, book, or Internet reference, or interview a business leader, to help you answer the question, "How can I prepare myself to become a leader in a multicultural organization?"

LEADERSHIP CASE PROBLEM

"We're Working in Chicago, Not Stockholm"

Naomi Green, the manager of collections at Oakdale Street Bank and Trust, was beginning to feel challenged by Sven Olsen, one of the credit representatives on her staff. Although Green had rated Olsen's performance as satisfactory for each of his first three evaluations, he was making life difficult for her as a manager and leader. During one staff meeting, for example, Olsen asked for a few minutes to discuss an important issue. Somewhat surprised by Olsen's request, Green nevertheless said that she welcomed his input. With a serious facial expression, Olsen said:

"Naomi, the way I see it, you are appointed by the bank to do the best job you can of helping the group accomplish its job. Your role as the manager is to make it easier for us—the people who do the actual work in this department—to get the job done. We need your help to do a good job."

Green interrupted, "That's one way of looking at my role. But go ahead."

Olsen continued, "Yes, that is the way I look at your role. Here are some of the things I think you should be doing to help us, the staff members, do a better job. First, you are making too many decisions by yourself. Before you make any important decision, you should consult us. Second, we the staff members should evaluate your performance every six months. In this way, you can learn better what you are doing right and wrong.

"Third, we would like full disclosure of what you speak about with your boss and the other managers. We have a right to know about all important information that could affect us and our work."

Green responded, "You are certainly putting me on the spot. I'll give some careful thought to your requests."

Ten days later, one Tuesday morning, Green was planning her day and getting ready for a staff meeting at 11 that morning. Into her office walked Olsen—again without a prior appointment. Feeling a little taken aback, Naomi asked, "How can I help you, Sven?"

Olsen replied, "I need you to do something for me right away. I'm leaving this afternoon for a trip to Springfield. One of our delinquent accounts is still too far behind schedule. Phone calls and faxes haven't worked. I need to make an in-person visit."

"If that's what needs to be done," responded Green. "Go ahead and make the trip. I assume you will be gone just one night."

"Please let me finish," said Olsen. "You have to authorize me a cash advance. I'm out of cash. I'll need about $350 to cover everything.

"Also, so long as I'm here, we might as well schedule my next performance review. I want to know how big my raise will be so I can make some plans with my wife to buy a new Volvo."

"Okay, Sven, I'll sign your advance voucher. And I can give you next Friday at 3 P.M. for the performance review. But quite frankly, I don't like the demanding tone in your voice. You act as if I work for you, not the other way around."

"I don't think it matters who's the boss," said Olsen. "We're supposed to work as a team to get the job done. Back in Sweden, that's the way it goes. Maybe you Americans get a little uptight."

"Sven, you and I will have to talk some more when I'm not so busy. I appreciate Scandinavian management as much as you do. But we're working in Chicago, not Stockholm."

1. What does this case problem reveal about managing cultural diversity?

2. What cultural value is Sven Olsen expressing?

3. Evaluate the extent of Naomi Green's cultural sensitivity.

4. What, if anything, should Green do about the different perceptions she and Olsen have about the role and authority of the leader?

Leadership Development, Succession, and the Future

LEARNING OBJECTIVES

After studying this chapter, you should be able to

1. explain how leaders develop through self-awareness and self-discipline.
2. explain how leaders develop through education, experience, and mentoring.
3. summarize the nature of leadership development programs.
4. describe a process for evaluating the outcomes of leadership development efforts.
5. describe the nature of leadership succession.
6. understand three major leadership challenges of the future: cultivating a learning organization, cultivating good followers, and maintaining trust.

At the conclusion of a leadership development workshop, the counselor said to the materials-handling manager of a small manufacturing company: "The feedback we've collected on your impact as a leader is generally positive. Yet we do see some areas for growth. The positive theme is that you're an energetic guy whose enthusiasm is contagious. According to the group, you express yourself in a colorful way. Several of the people at the workshop said they would enjoy working for you."

"Well, what didn't they like about my leadership impact?" asked the manager nervously.

"A few of the people were concerned that you don't process feedback at a deep level," replied the counselor. "No doubt you listen to what people think of you, but you don't take it a step further. You don't take a deeper look at the way you operate. You don't ask if you should be operating in a profoundly different way. You neglect to ask whether you are working on the right problems."

The exchange between the leadership development counselor and the manager illustrates only one of the many ways in which leaders attempt to improve their effectiveness. The information presented earlier in this book also deals with enhancing leadership effectiveness. Each chapter has included information and activities designed to enhance present or future leadership effectiveness. This chapter describes the processes organizations use to develop present and future leaders. (It also describes an important part of leadership self-development.) Such activities and processes are typically referred to as leadership development, leadership training, or management development.

Leadership and management development are substantial activities. An estimated 22 percent of the $30 billion annual corporate training budget is invested in managers.[1] Perhaps 10 percent of this $6.6 billion is devoted to programs aimed specifically at developing leaders.

In addition to describing various approaches to leadership development, we also examine two related topics. Leadership succession is included here because an important part of leadership development is being groomed for promotion. The text concludes with an overview of the substantial leadership challenges of the future. Leaders must develop to meet these challenges.

DEVELOPMENT THROUGH SELF-AWARENESS AND SELF-DISCIPLINE

Leadership development is often perceived in terms of education and training, job experience, and coaching. Nevertheless, self-help also contributes heavily to developing leadership capabilities. Self-help takes many forms, including working on one's own to improve communication skills, to develop charisma, and to model effective leaders. Two major components of leadership self-development are self-awareness and self-discipline.

Leadership Development Through Self-Awareness

An important mechanism underlying self-development is **self-awareness**, insightfully processing feedback about oneself to improve personal effectiveness. For example, a managerial leader might observe that three key group members left her group over a six-month time span. The leader might defensively dismiss this fact with an analysis such as, "I guess we just don't pay well enough to keep good people." Her first analysis might be correct. With a self-awareness orientation, however, the leader would dig deeper for the reasons behind the turnover. She might ask herself, "Is there something in my leadership approach that creates turnover problems?" She might ask for exit-interview data to sharpen her perceptions about her leadership approach.

Chris Argyris has coined the terms "single-loop learning" and "double-loop learning" to differentiate between levels of self-awareness.[2] **Single-loop learning** occurs when learners seek minimum feedback that might substantially confront their basic ideas or actions. As in the example of the high-turnover leader, single-loop learners engage in defensive thinking. Argyris offers the example of a thermostat that automatically turns on the heat whenever the room temperature drops below 68 degrees Fahrenheit (20 degrees Celsius).

Double-loop learning is an in-depth type of learning that occurs when people use feedback to confront the validity of the goal or the values implicit in the situation. The leader mentioned above was engaged in double-loop learning, when she questioned the efficacy of her leadership approach. To achieve double-loop learning, one must minimize defensive thinking. Argyris explains that a double-loop learning thermostat would ask, "Why am I set at 68 degrees?" The thermostat would then ask whether another temperature might more economically achieve the goal of heating the room. Figure 15–1 illustrates the difference between single-loop and double-loop learning.

An important contribution of double-loop learning is that it enables the leader to learn and profit from setbacks. Interpreting the reason that a setback occurred may help the leader to do better the next time. Faced with a group in crisis, a leader might establish a vision of better days ahead for group members. The leader observes that the vision leads to no observable changes in performance and behavior. Perhaps the group was not ready for a vision. In a comparable situation in the future, the leader might hold back on formulating a vision until the group is headed out of the crisis. Double-loop learning was shown by Louis Gerstner, the IBM chairman, who had previously held key leadership posts at two other major firms that faced financial troubles. When asked by analysts in 1993 why he had not yet formulated an Olympian strategy for IBM's future, Gerstner replied: "The last thing IBM needs right now is a vision. What it needs are tough-minded business strategies for each of its businesses."[3] Several years later, when IBM had regained a powerful forward thrust and was setting record profits, Gerstner talked in visionary terms about IBM being the leader in the dawning world of networked computing and electronic commerce. The same phenomenon is referred to as a network-centric world.[4]

Leadership Development Through Self-Discipline

As with other types of personal development, leadership development requires considerable self-discipline. In the present context, **self-discipline** is mobilizing one's effort and energy to stay focused on attaining an important goal. Self-discipline is required for most forms of leadership development. Assume, for example, that a leader is convinced that active listening is an important leadership behavior. The leader reads about active listening and also attends a workshop on the subject. After the reading and workshop are completed, the leader will need to concentrate diligently in order to remember to listen actively. Self-discipline is particularly necessary because

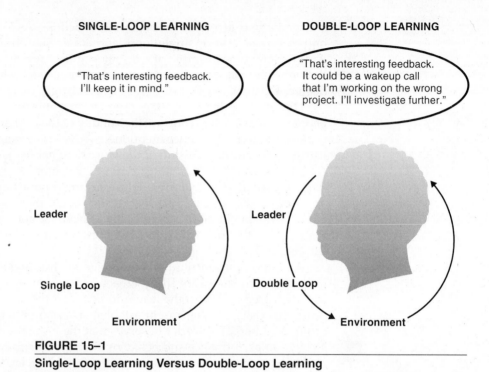

FIGURE 15–1

Single-Loop Learning Versus Double-Loop Learning

the pressures of everyday activities often divert a person's attention from personal development.

Self-discipline plays an important role in the continuous monitoring of one's behavior to ensure that needed self-development occurs. After one identifies a developmental need, it is necessary to periodically review whether one is making the necessary improvements. Assume that a person recognizes the developmental need to become a more colorful communicator as a way of enhancing charisma. The person would need self-discipline to make the conscious effort to communicate more colorfully when placed in an appropriate situation. Leadership Self-Assessment Exercise 15–1 contains an interpersonal skills checklist that will help you identify your own developmental needs related to interpersonal relationships.

DEVELOPMENT THROUGH EDUCATION, EXPERIENCE, AND MENTORING

Much of leadership development takes place through means other than self-awareness and self-discipline or leadership development programs. Leadership is such a comprehensive process that almost any life activity can help people

LEADERSHIP SELF-ASSESSMENT
EXERCISE 15–1 The Interpersonal Skills Checklist

Directions: Below are a number of specific aspects of behavior that suggest that a person needs to improve his or her interpersonal skills related to leadership and influence. Check each statement that is generally true for you. You can add to the reliability of this exercise by asking one or two other people who know you well to rate you. Then compare your self-analysis with their analysis of you.

Developmental Needs and Areas for Improvement

1. I'm too shy and reserved. ____

2. I bully and intimidate others too frequently. ____

3. I tell others what they want to hear rather than emphasizing the truth. ____

4. I have trouble expressing my feelings. ____

5. I make negative comments about group members too readily. ____

6. Very few people pay attention to the ideas I contribute during a meeting. ____

7. My personality isn't colorful enough. ____

8. People find me boring. ____

9. I pay too little attention to the meaning behind what team members and coworkers are saying. ____

10. It is very difficult for me to criticize others. ____

11. I'm too serious most of the time. ____

12. I avoid controversy in dealing with others. ____

13. I don't get my point across well. ____

14. It's difficult for me to make small talk with others. ____

15. I boast too much about my accomplishments. ____

16. I strive too much for individual recognition instead of looking to credit the team. ____

17. Self-confidence is my weak point. ____

18. My spoken messages are too bland. ____

19. My written messages are too bland. ____

20. I read people poorly.   ____

21. _____

    (Fill in your own statement.)   ____

Now that you (and perhaps one or two others) have identified specific behaviors that may require change, draw up an action plan. Describe briefly a plan of attack for bringing about the change you hope to achieve for each statement that is checked. Ideas might come from personal development books or from human relations and leadership development workshops.[4] After formulating an action plan, you will need self-discipline for its successful implementation. For example, if you checked, "People find me boring," you might want to expand your fund of knowledge by extensive reading and by talking to dynamic people. You will then need the self-discipline to continue your quest for ideas and to incorporate some of these ideas into your conversation.

---

prepare for a leadership role. The president and owner of a large residential and commercial heating and cooling company made these comments:

> One of my best preparations for running a company came from my early days as a waiter. I learned how to handle difficult people and how to accept compliments. I also learned how to persuade people to make choices on the menu that gave them pleasure and increased the restaurant's profits. Those lessons are all important in running a $45 million business.

Three important life and work experiences that contribute to leadership development are education, experience as a leader, and mentoring. Let's look at the link between each of these three factors and leadership.

Education

Education generally refers to acquiring knowledge without concern about its immediate application. If a potential leader studies mathematics, the logical reasoning acquired might someday help him or her solve a complex problem facing the organization. As a result, the leader's stature is enhanced. Formal education is positively correlated with achieving managerial and leadership positions. Furthermore, there is a positive relationship between amount of formal education and level of leadership position attained.

Bernard M. Bass has concluded that educational credentials, demonstrated by degrees in engineering, law, or business administration, provide avenues to success in business leadership.[5] The correlation between education and leadership status, however, may not reflect causation. Many people get the opportunity to hold a business leadership position *only if* they have achieved a specified level of education. A more important issue than the statistical association between leadership and formal education is *how* education contributes to leadership effectiveness.

Most high-level leaders are intelligent, well-informed people who gather knowledge throughout their career. The knowledge that accrues from formal education and self-study provides them with information for innovative problem solving. Being intellectually alert also contributes to exerting influence through logical persuasion.

Experience

On-the-job experience is an obvious contributor to leadership effectiveness. Without experience, knowledge cannot readily be converted into skills. For example, you will need experience to put into practice the appropriate influence tactics you studied in Chapter 8. Leadership experience also helps build skills and insights that a person may not have formally studied. Pepsico CEO Wayne Calloway dramatizes the importance of experience in these words: "Among the elements of teaching leadership, 80% is experience. Our first line of offense is just to put them in the job."[6] Here we look at two important aspects of experience: sources of experience and the importance of broad experience.

Sources of Experience.   The two major developmental factors in any work situation are work associates and the task itself.[7] Work associates can help a person develop in myriad ways. An immediate superior can be a positive or negative model of effective leadership. You might observe how your boss skillfully confronts a quality problem during a staff meeting. You observe carefully and plan to use a similar technique when it becomes necessary for you to confront a problem with a group. In contrast, assume that your boss's confrontational approach backfires—the group becomes defensive and recalcitrant. You have learned how *not* to confront. Members of upper management, peers, and reporting staff can also help a worker profit from experience. For example, by trial and error the worker might learn which type of praise is best for influencing others.

Work-related tasks can also contribute to leadership development because part of a leader's role is to be an effective and innovative problem solver. The tasks that do most to foster development are those that are more complex and ambiguous than a person has faced previously. Starting a new activity for a firm, such as establishing a dealer network, exemplifies a developmental experience.

Steven Kerr, the chief learning officer (a.k.a. director of management development and training) at GE, says that the majority of peak learning experiences in relation to leadership occur on the job—and through serendipity, not planning. He also notes, however, that serendipity is more likely to occur when people are assigned a carefully planned series of varied and challenging work assignments characterized by heavy responsibility and a risk of failure.[8]

Broad Experience.   Many aspects of leadership are situational. A sound approach to improving leadership effectiveness is therefore to gain managerial experience in different settings. An aspirant to executive leadership is well advised to gain management experience in at least two different organizational functions, such as marketing and operations. Daphna F. Raskas and Donald C. Hambrick use the term *multifunctional managerial development* to refer to the process of achieving broad experience. **Multifunctional managerial development** is an organization's intentional efforts to enhance the effectiveness of managers by giving them experience in multiple functions within the organization.[9]

As shown in Figure 15–2, the most modest level of commitment to multifunctional management development would be for managers merely to study other functions. Studying other functions, however, is quite useful because it provides a person with the necessary background to profit from experience. Participation in multifunctional task forces indicates more commitment to the acquisition of breadth.

The highest level of commitment is complete mobility across functions. Hewlett-Packard represents this approach through its *career maze* program. For example, an employee may begin in product design, and then move on to assignments in marketing, manufacturing, customer service, purchasing, human resources, and so forth. Employees judged to have leadership potential are the most likely to be offered the career maze.

Achieving broad experience fits well with the current emphasis on growth through learning new skills rather than a preoccupation with vertical mobility. A successful manufacturing company studied by Michael Beer, Russell Eisenstadt, and Bert Spector gives its most promising managers lateral transfers, including experience in the human resources department. The company also uses its most innovative manufacturing facilities as "hothouses" for developing managers. The innovative units become leadership development centers for the company.[10]

- **HIGH COMMITMENT**

- **Complete mobility across functions, i.e., "career maze"**

- **Temporary (six-month to two-year) assignments outside the person's "home function"**

- **Brief, orientational rotation through functions**

- **Exposure to other functions on task forces project teams**

- **Classroom education about other functions**

- **LOW COMMITMENT**

FIGURE 15–2

Continuum of Practical Options for Multifunctional Managerial Development

Source: Reprinted by permission of the publisher, from Organizational Dynamics, *Autumn/1992, © 1992. American Management Association, New York. All rights reserved.*

Mentoring

Another experience-based way to develop leadership capability is to be coached by an experienced, knowledgeable leader. Quite often this person is a **mentor**, a more experienced person who develops a protégé's abilities through tutoring, coaching, guidance, and emotional support. The mentor, a trusted counselor and guide, is typically a person's manager. However, a mentor can also be a staff professional or coworker. An emotional tie exists between the protégé (or apprentice) and the mentor.

Mentoring is traditionally thought of as an informal relationship based on compatibility between two personalities. Nevertheless, a current study found that thirty-one out of seventy-nine supervisory protégés were classified as formal protégés.[11] Also, several large organizations such as the Internal Revenue Service, Hewlett-Packard (H-P), and IBM have experimented with formal matches between the mentor and the protégé. Sometimes the junior manager or professional is given a choice of mentors. The standard approach to finding a mentor is to make oneself visible through outstanding job performance and volunteering for assignments. Like other friendships, mentoring is based on a spark or chemical attraction between two people— even if the mentor and protégé are immediate manager and group member.

Mentors enhance the careers of protégés in many ways, such as recommending them for promotion and helping them establish valuable contacts. Of interest here is how a mentor can help you become a better leader. The mentor can serve as a model of effective (or sometimes ineffective) leadership. A high level of mentor involvement is to coach the apprentice on how he or she handles certain leadership assignments. The mentor is usually not physically present when the protégé is practicing leadership. A substitute is for the protégé to recap a leadership situation and ask for a critique. Wendy Lopez, who is the data processing manager for a payroll services firm, recounts a mentoring session with her boss about a leadership incident:

> I explained to Max [her mentor and the vice president of administration] that I had some trouble motivating my supervisors to pitch in with weekend work. We had received a surge of new clients because many firms had decided to downsize their own payroll departments. Our group was having trouble adjusting to the new workload. Instead of operations running smoothly, things were a little spastic. Although I tried to explain the importance of getting out the work, the supervisors were still dragging their heels a little.
>
> Max reviewed the incident with me. He told me that I might have helped the supervisors take a broader view of what this new business meant to the firm. Max felt I didn't communicate clearly enough how the future of our firm was at stake. He also suggested that I should have been more specific about how pitching in during an emergency would benefit the supervisors financially.
>
> With Max's coaching behind me, I did a much better job of enlisting cooperation the next time an emergency surfaced.

Despite the many advantages of mentoring for leadership development, Stuart Levine, CEO of Dale Carnegie & Associates, believes that patterning yourself after a business leader you admire is a common mistake. The likely outcome is that you will end up becoming an inferior imitation of your role model (who is often a mentor). As a result, some of your own best strengths will be diminished.[12]

The accompanying Leader in Action vignette includes much experience-based information about leadership development, including the role of mentoring. Also, to help you capitalize on experience as a source of leadership development, do Leadership Skill-Building Exercise 15–1.

LEADERSHIP DEVELOPMENT PROGRAMS

A time-honored strategy for developing prospective, new, and practicing leaders is to enroll prospective leaders in leadership development programs. These programs typically focus on such topics as personal growth, leadership style, strategy formulation, influence, motivation, and persuasive communication. Outdoor and wilderness training, as described in Chapter 9, is

LEADERSHIP SKILL-BUILDING
EXERCISE 15–1 **Maintaining a Personal Leadership Journal**

A potentially important aid in your development as a leader is to maintain a journal or diary of your leadership experiences. Make a journal entry within twenty-four hours after you carried out a significant leadership action, or failed to do so when the opportunity arose. You will therefore have entries dealing with leadership opportunities capitalized upon and those missed. An example: "A few of my neighbors were complaining about exhaust fumes from a restaurant blowing directly into our apartments. I volunteered to take up the problem with the restaurant manager and the town board." Or, in contrast: "A few of my neighbors . . . apartments. I thought to myself that someone else should take care of the problem. My time is too valuable."

Also include in your journal such entries as feedback you receive on your leadership ability, leadership traits you appear to be developing, key leadership concepts you learn about, and leadership books and articles you intend to read. You might also want to record observations about significant acts of leadership or leadership blunders that you have observed in others, either firsthand or through the media.

Review your journal monthly, and make note of any progress you think you have made in developing your leadership skills. Also consider preparing a graph of your leadership skill development. The vertical axis can represent skill level on a 1-to-100 scale, and the horizontal axis might be divided into time intervals, such as calendar quarters.

one important type of leadership training. Many management development programs are also aimed at leadership development. The difference, however, is that management development programs offer courses that cover hundreds of topics within the functions of planning, organizing, controlling, and leading. Table 15–1 lists a sample of leadership development programs.

Key Characteristics of a Leadership Development Program

Developing and training leaders is far more complex than merely sending aspiring leaders to a one-week seminar. The leadership development program has to be appropriately sponsored, carefully designed, and professionally executed. Marshall Whitmire and Philip R. Nienstedt have formulated such an approach to leadership development, as outlined in Table 15–2 and summarized below.[13]

1. *Involve executives and secure their sponsorship.* For a leadership training program to receive high priority, top executives must set the program's tone and objectives. They should also sponsor implementation, as is done with the four-week executive program at General Electric.

2. *Target career transitions.* Managers at different levels should receive different types of leadership training. The Honeywell system, for example, targets training for current general managers, directors, and middle managers. Programs provide different leadership emphases for these three groups. General managers might have a workshop on vision setting and organizational change, whereas motivation and coaching might be a better fit for the other two groups.

3. *Address current and future organizational needs.* A company moving swiftly toward globalization would provide training on global leadership skills, such as developing the multicultural organization and adapting to rapid change.

4. *Use an appropriate model.* Leadership skills are often instilled better when they are taught in a solid conceptual framework. Several of the frameworks presented in this text are often used in leadership development, including the situational leadership model, SuperLeadership, and the leader-member participation model.

5. *Support individual improvement with diagnostic tools.* Many leadership development programs include self-evaluation with assessment instruments like those presented throughout this text. In addition to self-evaluation, other people who know the participant also complete the forms. In one program at the Center for Creative Leadership, about nine work associates complete an inventory on various dimensions of leadership for each participant. Particularly meaningful are significant discrepancies between self-perceptions and perceptions by others. (You will recall the description of 360-degree feedback in Chapter 4.)

TABLE 15–1   A Sampling of Leadership Development Programs Offered by Universities and Training and Development Firms

The Executive Program (four-week program for senior executives involved in the strategic management of their firms)

Developing a Vision for Your Organization

Strategic Leadership

Becoming a Multicultural Leader

How to Make Presentations with Confidence and Power

The Looking Glass (management simulation)

Team-Building Skills for Managers

Leadership and Team Development for Managerial Success

Outdoor Training

Developing Effective Leadership

Excellence in Leadership

Business Ethics and the Professional Manager

The Learning Organization: A New Approach to Leading Your Company

Note: Organizations offering such seminars and courses include the Michigan Business School, the Wharton School of the University of Pennsylvania, the American Management Association, and the Center for Creative Leadership.

TABLE 15–2   Characteristics of a Comprehensive Leadership Development Program

1. Involve executives and secure their sponsorship
2. Target career transitions
3. Address current and future organizational needs
4. Use an appropriate model
5. Support individual improvement with diagnostic tools
6. Ensure practical and relevant content
7. Emphasize interpersonal relations and teamwork
8. Conclude with individual action plans

Source: Developed from information in Marshall Whitmire and Philip R. Nienstedt, "Lead Leaders into the '90s," *Personnel Journal,* May 1991, pp. 80–85.

6. *Ensure practical and relevant content.* Many leadership development programs present participants with problems closely related to those found on the job; an example of such a program is the Pittsburgh Global Alliance for Leadership. The alliance consists of four companies and the University of Pittsburgh's Joseph M. Katz Graduate School of Business. Each company and the university select a team of three to five people to work on a significant problem that affects the bottom line. Teams consisting of company managers and business professors begin work on the problem on the job. The managers then spend two weeks in residence at the university and complete the project when they return to the workplace. Later, team members present their solutions or approaches to the problem to senior management.[14]

7. *Emphasize interpersonal relationships and teamwork.* Many leadership development programs emphasize team building and outdoor training because leaders at every level must have good interpersonal and teamwork skills.

8. *Conclude with individual action plans.* In a high-quality leadership program, attendees must develop personalized action plans for improvement (such as those requested in Leadership Skill-Building Exercise 15–1). At Motorola, participants prepare a self-letter describing personal changes to which they are willing to commit.

Types of Leadership Development Programs

In practice, the various programs for developing leaders often overlap. For ease of comprehension, however, we'll divide these programs into four categories: personal growth; feedback on traits and style; developing conceptual skills; and simulations. Figure 15–3 places these types of leadership development programs on a continuum. As the figure shows, personal growth approaches are most clearly related to leadership development, whereas simulations overlap considerably with management development.

Personal Growth. Leadership development programs that focus on personal growth assume that leaders are deeply in touch with their personal dreams and talents, and that they will act to fulfill them. Therefore, if people can get in touch with their inner desires and fulfill them, they will become leaders. A tacit assumption in personal-growth training programs is that leadership is almost a calling. Jay Conger captures the essence of personal-growth programs in these words:

> Using outdoor-adventure activities and psychological exercises, personal growth programs induce participants to reflect on their behaviors (such as their orientation toward risk or personal intimacy) and on their personal values and desires. They also empower participants through experiences that teach them to take responsibility for their situations—rather than blame problems on the job on outside influences or events.[15]

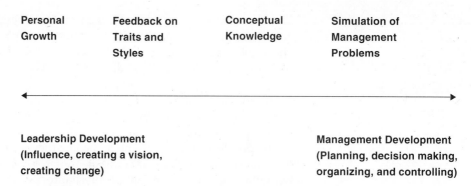

FIGURE 15–3

Types of Leadership Development Programs

Personal-growth leadership development programs have burgeoned in popularity. (Conger is concerned, however, that they are based on an overly simple conceptualization of leadership.) Most of these programs are established and implemented by business entrepreneurs rather than by professionals in human behavior. The Pecos River Learning Center near Santa Fe, New Mexico, offers a well-known leadership program of this type. Two principal aims of the program are developing skills in risk taking and teamwork.

Feedback on Traits and Style.   A long-standing, yet continually evolving, type of leadership development is to receive systematic feedback on one's personal traits and leadership style. The assertiveness and leadership style tests (Chapters 2 and 5) are representative feedback instruments. As mentioned in relation to diagnostic instruments, self-feedback is supplemented by feedback from workplace associates who complete similar forms. An excerpt follows from a feedback session with a counselor about a discrepancy between self-feedback and feedback from others:

> Your self-feedback suggests that one of your key strengths is sensitivity to people and compassion. I suspect you are quite interested in being sensitive and compassionate. The feedback from others, however, rates you quite low on sensitivity and compassion. Let's see if we can discover the reason for this discrepancy.

The manager in question discovered that part of his problem was that his body language was inconsistent with his thoughts and actions. For example, he gave encouragement in a manner that was perceived as cold and aloof. By improving his body language—so that he was perceived as sensitive and compassionate—the manager improved his relationships with people.

Conceptual Knowledge.   A standard university approach to leadership development is to equip people with a conceptual understanding of leadership. The concepts are typically supplemented by experiential activities such as role playing and cases. Nonuniversity learning firms such as the American Management Association and TPG/Learning Systems also offer conceptually based leadership development programs. Conceptual knowledge is very important because it alerts the leader to information that will make a difference in leadership. For example, if a person studies how a leader brings about transformations, he or she can put these ideas into practice.

The Leadership Challenge program developed by James M. Kouzes and Barry Z. Posner (and stemming from the book of the same name) presents a useful set of concepts for stimulating leadership thinking. The five core practices common to successful leaders are as follows:

1. Challenge the process (don't accept the status quo).
2. Inspire a shared vision.
3. Enable others to act (much like empowerment).
4. Model the way (serve as a positive model).
5. Encourage the heart (leadership involves passion and commitment).[16]

The accompanying Leaders in Action box presents a glimpse of life at the world's most prestigious leadership development program. It combines conceptual knowledge about management with some opportunities for personal growth.

Simulations of Leadership and Management Problems. Another standard approach to leadership development is to give participants an opportunity to work on a problem that simulates a real organization. Many simulations are computerized, and others reflect the typical scenario of managers making decisions without much assistance from a computer. The Looking Glass, developed by the Center for Creative Leadership, is a carefully constructed simulation of problems facing a real glass manufacturer. (The term *Looking Glass* indicates that participants reflect on their behavior and action, and receive feedback.) The simulation strives to bring the office into the classroom by simulating a real job challenge followed by debriefing.

A dominant feature of the Looking Glass is the unrelenting pressure inherent in the simulation. By compressing various organizational roles and demands into six hours, the Looking Glass creates the sense of urgency that many leaders and managers face on the job. Other features of executive life incorporated into the simulation are

Coming to grips with a new, unfamiliar position

Exercising leadership in the face of organizational constraints

Being persuasive and influential in the absence of formal authority[17]

The debriefing that follows the simulation is supportive rather than negative and critical. Feedback is based on the observations of peers and trained observers. Many participants in the Looking Glass report that they achieved insight into the human side of management, including the importance of giving effective feedback and resolving conflict.

LEADERS IN ACTION

Life at the Advanced Management Program of Harvard University

The Harvard University Advanced Management Program is geared to the future chief executives and chief financial officers of the world. During the three-month program, class members live in dormitories, away from spouses, significant others, and children. They are given firm instructions not to call the office. Program participants must work exceedingly hard, reveal their weaknesses, and showcase their strengths.

The program, which runs twice a year, requires courage and self-confidence. George Harvin, vice president of Roses Stores Inc., says, "You get put into an environment where you are totally intimidated by everything—by the Harvard name; by being with the top-level folks from very large, successful companies, from all industries, cultures and from many different countries. And you find out how you measure up."

Participants are required to have fifteen to twenty-five years of business experience. Firms carefully choose who will attend and leave little choice to the designate. Being among the 150 participants indicates that a person is on the fast track to the top. The company must invest over $30,000 in tuition per person for the program. In addition, the company must do without the manager's contribution for a quarter of a year.

Jeannette Wagner, one of the two women in her class in 1983, says, "Your boss has to decide to do without your brains for three months and decide not to bug you while you are there." When Wagner attended, she was senior vice president of Estee Lauder International Inc. She is now president.

The key subject areas are finance, marketing, operations, and negotiating. Placing the managers in a situation of fierce competition in these courses helps them develop leadership skills.

Almost half the class members are from countries outside North America. Consequently, a network is developed among people who may be politically important to each other in the future. Many friendships develop as a result of enforced, close living; in the dormitories, eight single rooms are grouped around a common living room. Business deals are often made during the course because the participants occupy such high-level positions.

Despite the seriousness of the program, many of the participants get together during late evenings to hold spontaneous parties. Claude Zinngrabe, chairman of Prudential Home Building Investors Inc., recalls fondly a midnight session of singing "Hey Jude" next to a Scotsman playing the piano.

Source: Based on facts reported in Barbara Lyne, "Harvard University's Fast-Track Boot Camp for Rising Executives," *The New York Times* syndicated story, May 31, 1992.

EVALUATION OF LEADERSHIP DEVELOPMENT EFFORTS

A comprehensive approach to leadership development would include a rigorous evaluation of the consequences of having participated in a developmental experience. Executives and human resource professionals would ask such tough questions as the following:

Do people who receive mentoring actually become more effective leaders?

Do leaders who attend outdoor training become better team leaders than (1) those who do not attend the training, or (2) those whose "team development" consists of playing softball with the office gang?

Does the Advanced Management Program at Harvard improve the decision-making skills of participants?

The evaluation of training and development programs is a comprehensive topic that includes such considerations as the design of experiments, and the development of accurate outcome measures.[18] Here we examine the traditional approach to evaluating training and development outcomes and an approach that is better adapted to leadership development.

The Traditional Approach to Evaluation

The traditional approach to the evaluation of leadership training and development programs would first specify the program objectives. After training was completed, measurements would be made of the extent to which those objectives were met.[19] Two sets of outcomes are especially relevant. First, an assessment is made of the extent to which the participants acquired new skills during the program. For example, did the seminar participants acquire new skills in giving supportive feedback? Second, an assessment is made of whether the organization has become more effective as a result of this new skill acquisition. Did the bottom line improve because of the new skills? For example, has supportive feedback by leaders resulted in higher quality and profits?

A more rigorous approach to the evaluation of leadership training and development would include an experiment, as shown in Table 15–3. The experimental group would consist of the participants in the development program. Before-and-after measures of skills would be taken to determine if improvements took place. Outcome measures from the experimental group would then be compared to those from two control or contrast groups. All three groups would be composed of people similar in education, intelligence, job level, job experience, and so forth. People in one control group would receive no special development. Members of the second control group would receive a different kind of development. Instead of training in giving supportive feedback, they might be trained in memo writing. The purpose of the second control (or contrast) group is to determine if training in supportive feedback has an edge over simply sending people to any sensible training program.

TABLE 15–3   Evaluating Leadership Development Through the Experimental Method

	Pretraining Measures	Training	Posttraining Measures
Experimental group	Yes	Supportive feedback	Yes
Control group I	Yes	None	Yes
Control group II	Yes	Memo writing	Yes

The traditional method of evaluation is best suited to evaluating structured, definable skills, such as running software or performing a breakeven analysis. Leadership training and development, however, involves much broader, less structured behaviors, such as inspiring others and identifying problems. Another problem is that few organizations would be willing to randomly assign managers to expensive and time-consuming leadership development programs.

Domains of Impact of a Leadership Development Program

Researchers at the Center for Creative Leadership decided that the traditional approach to the evaluation of training and development was inadequate for their purposes. Development programs aim to discover and advance individual potential, especially in interpersonal relationships. These programs are highly personal in nature and will benefit different people in different ways. After participating in the same development program, one leader might become more visionary, whereas another might become more attuned to empowerment.

Members of the Center for Creative Leadership decided to evaluate their Looking Glass program (LGI) by asking, "How did it leave its mark?" rather than, "Did it leave this particular mark?" Specifically, the researchers asked four questions that covered important **domains of impact** (ranges of possible effects) that a program might have:[20]

1. *What did participants learn from LGI?* Open-ended questions were asked about learning outcomes for the development program. The responses related to the domains of *knowledge* (concepts and content) and *self-objectivity* (learning about individual limitations and strengths).

2. *What impact did the program have on participants' self-objectivity?* Asking about self-objectivity is meaningful because most leadership development programs purport to help participants achieve sharpened self-insights. The participants in the programs themselves, along with their peers and superiors, can be asked to contribute input about the participant's self-objectivity after he or she attended the program.

3. *How was behavior back on the job affected?* Both interviews and questionnaires are used to assess behavioral changes stemming from participation in the Looking Glass program. For example, group members might be asked if the leader had become more adept at helping the group resolve a high-pressure problem such as meeting a challenging deadline.

4. *Was there a relationship between enhanced self-objectivity and behavior change back on the job?* Rather than evaluating the results of the program, this question is aimed at understanding the relationship between two domains (self-objectivity and behavior). The relationship between the two domains might work in this way: A leader develops enhanced

insight into her sarcastic behavior when a group member makes a mistake. Back on the job, she softens her sarcasm. Constructive change has therefore taken place, whether or not this change can be translated into bottom-line results.

Answering these four questions evaluates the essence of the Looking Glass Program. Nevertheless, many top executives will still want to know how improvement in the domains of impact leads to improved productivity and quality.

LEADERSHIP SUCCESSION

In a well-managed organization, replacements for retiring and dismissed executives are chosen through **leadership succession**, an orderly process of identifying and grooming people to replace executives. Succession planning is linked to leadership development in two important ways. First, being groomed as a successor is part of leadership development through enriched experience. Second, the process of choosing and fostering a successor's development is part of a manager's own development. In a book written for CEOs, Thomas Horton urges them to identify one or more successors before retiring or leaving for other reasons.[21] Identifying a replacement can be regarded as a professional commitment.

Our approach to understanding the leadership aspects of succession focuses on four topics: (1) how the balance of power influences the selection of a successor; (2) how organizational performance influences the choice of a successor; (3) succession planning at GE; and (4) the emotional aspects of leadership succession.

Balance of Power and the Selection of a Successor

In large business firms, the selection of a specific successor to the CEO is heavily influenced by the relative power of the CEO and the board of directors. Edward J. Zajac and James D. Westphal studied 232 voluntary and involuntary CEO successions in large industrial and service firms. For each succession, the researchers compared selected demographic characteristics (functional background, age, and education in terms of degree type and college or university attended) of the outgoing and successor CEOs. Power was measured in various ways, including an executive's being rated as powerful if he or she held both the CEO and board chairperson positions. Another measure of relative power was the tenure of the board compared with that of the CEO.

A key finding was that the organizational balance of power was a good predictor of the demographic characteristics of the CEO. More powerful boards were more likely to change the CEO characteristics in the direction of their own demographic profile. For example, when the CEO was also board chairperson, the age, functional background, and education of the successor resembled those of the incumbent CEO. Conversely, if the board possessed more power than the incumbent CEO, the newly appointed executive tended to be more similar to the board members in age, functional background, and education. Also, demographic characteristics of outside successors tended to be different from those of their predecessors, yet similar to those of the members of the board.[22] In short, the good-old-boy and good-old-gal system still operates for people who hold the balance of power.

Organizational Performance and the Choice of a Successor

A key factor in deciding to choose an outsider to succeed an incumbent CEO is organizational performance. When board members, and quite often other stockholders, believe that an organization is performing poorly or is far from reaching its potential, an outsider is likely to be recruited as the new CEO. Furthermore, the outsider may be from a different industry. An outsider is often recruited when the organization is performing poorly because insiders are thought to be too closely identified with the CEO's failed strategies and policies. An outsider also has the advantage of not having emotional ties to insiders and therefore may be willing to make necessary replacements. An outsider from another industry may be sought to bring in a fresh perspective on how to deal with the company's problems.

A dramatic example of bringing in a complete outsider to help turn around a troubled giant, occurred in 1996. AT&T chose John R. Walter as its new president and the likely successor to incumbent CEO Bob Allen. Walter had spent his entire career at R.R. Donnelley & Sons Company, the world's largest commercial printing company. Allen was selected for his proven ability to transform a mammoth old-line company that was challenged by new technologies and new markets.[23] Yet Walter left AT&T in 1997 when he was not officially named as Allen's successor.

Despite the anecdotal evidence just described about poor organizational performance being associated with bringing in an outside leader, certain contingency factors should be taken into account. An analysis of 472 succession events indicated that poor performance leads to outsider selection only when sociopolitical forces are weak. One factor (or force) prompting the selection of an outsider is the lack of an heir apparent. Another factor is that when the executive holds only the CEO title and is not also chairperson, a replacement might be brought in from the outside.[24] Observe that in the study reported above, an influential factor in leadership succession was also whether an executive held the dual position of CEO and board chairperson.

Succession Planning at General Electric

General Electric is often noted for its progressive and thorough management techniques. Its system for identifying and developing talent is considered exemplary. Much of this activity is linked closely to succession planning. Board members are closely involved in an ongoing evaluation of the company's 130 highest-ranking managers. Twice a year, directors scrutinize about fifteen of these people. The information they use comes from lengthy interviews with the managers, their managers, former associates, and group members. Directors investigate the managers' strengths and weaknesses, make suggestions for leadership development, and discuss future assignments. Should the day arrive when a manager must be chosen to replace a higher-level manager, the board will be prepared to make an independent decision rather than giving automatic approval to an insider's recommendations.[25]

Key advantages of the GE system for identifying successors are that it is based on multiple opinions and that it tracks longitudinal performance. Yet the system may still be replete with political biases. The board members, for example, are not exempt from giving high ratings to the people they like the best or to people who have personal characteristics similar to theirs.

The Emotional Aspects of Leadership Succession

Leadership succession should not be regarded as a detached, objective management process. Even financially independent executives are likely to experience an emotional loss when they are replaced, such as yearning for the power and position they once possessed. Leadership succession in family-owned firms is a highly emotional process for many reasons. Family members may fight over who is best qualified to take the helm, or the owner and founder may not feel that any family member is qualified. An intensely emotional situation exists when the owner would like a family member to succeed him or her, yet no family member is willing. The business may therefore have to be sold or simply abandoned; in any case, its identity will be lost.

The emotional aspects of leadership succession are also evident when a business founder is replaced by another leader, whether or not the enterprise is a family business. Jane Plitt, a business consultant, has noted that a founder's leaving can be "one of the highest traumas that can be experienced by a company. When it is done successfully, it is really a major accomplishment."[26] After the sale of his or her company, the business founder often stays on in some capacity, such as a consultant or chairperson. Watching the new owner manage the business can be uncomfortable for the founder. The issue transcends concerns about delegation. The entrepreneurial leader is typically emotionally involved in the firm he or she has founded, and finds it difficult to look on while somebody else operates the firm. Plitt offers the following advice for the business founder who stays on, yet is succeeded by another person who has a bigger formal leadership role:

- *Flexibility.* The founder must remember that his or her role is different in the new structure. And the new leader must recall that the business wouldn't be there without the founder.
- *Clarity.* A new manager can actually make things worse by being too sensitive around the founder. New leaders should make it clear that they are in charge, but do so with sensitivity and tact.
- *Perspective.* Keep in mind the shared goals of both the new and the old leaders. Both want the business to succeed.[27]

To the extent that the leader of an enterprise of any size is highly charismatic, many organizational members will experience some emotional pain in the form of a perceived loss when he or she leaves. The new leadership must therefore work hard to gain the trust and respect of employees who identified with the predecessor.

LEADING EDGE AND FUTURE CHALLENGES

An essential part of developing as a leader is to become sensitive to and prepare for leading-edge and future challenges. Many leading-edge challenges, such as being a multicultural leader and providing strategic leadership, have been discussed in previous chapters. Here we highlight three aspects of leadership that are important now, but will probably mushroom in importance during the next decade: cultivating a learning organization, helping group members to become good followers, and maintaining trust.

Cultivating a Learning Organization

For several years now, leaders have been urged to help their organizations better adapt to their environment by being more effective learners, much like double-loop learning. A **learning organization** is one that is skilled at creating, acquiring, and transferring knowledge, and at modifying behavior to reflect new knowledge and insights.[28] The emphasis on helping others learn at a deep level is most likely to continue in an era of heavy competition and environmental turbulence. Peter Vail refers to such turbulence as *permanent white water.*[29] To cultivate a learning organization, leaders must act as models of learning themselves, and also engage in actions that facilitate organizational learning.

A Procter & Gamble (P&G) plant in Lima, Ohio, exemplifies a learning organization. The plant is 30 percent more productive than comparable facilities. Every worker in the plant is encouraged to keep learning. Technicians are skilled in managing their activities, and managers are skilled in performing technical tasks. The organization is described as organic because teams organize and reorganize themselves frequently to meet current challenges. Frequent job rotation and role switching also encourages learning. On a given issue, a team member might assume a leadership role. Pay is based on skill (which by definition requires learning), and workers shift frequently between line and staff assignments. Managers spend considerable time developing group members, including acting as mentors.[30]

A major challenge in creating a learning organization is that the concept covers so much ground, and is perceived in many different ways by researchers and executives. Here we identify major leadership initiatives that enhance a learning organization. Understanding them will help you grasp the concept of what a leader might do to enhance organizational learning.[31] To begin with, a top-level leader should *create a strategic intent to learn.* Organizational learning then becomes a vehicle for gaining competitive advantage. *Creating a shared vision* enhances learning as organization members develop a common purpose and commitment to having the organization keep learning. If workers at all levels believe that the company is headed toward greatness, they will be motivated to learn to help deliver greatness.

Systems thinking is almost synonymous with organizational learning. The leader helps organization members regard the organization as a system in which everybody's work affects the activities of everybody else. Systems thinking also means keeping the big picture foremost in everybody's mind and being keenly aware of the external environment. In addition to the big picture of systems thinking, the leader must encourage the little picture of *personal mastery of the job.* As team members gain personal mastery of their jobs, they contribute to *team learning,* which is also an essential part of a learning organization. Team learning centers around collective problem solving, in which members freely share information and opinions to facilitate problem solving. Team learning is widely practiced today, with Hewlett-Packard being an outstanding example. Even such tasks as finding new ways to enhance the delivery of products are subject to team learning, as encouraged by team leaders.

Learning from failure contributes immensely to a learning organization. A company that diversified into an area unsuccessfully might analyze why it failed and then not repeat the same mistake. *Encouraging continuous experimentation* is another important practice for crafting a learning strategy. The leader encourages workers to learn from competitors, customers, suppliers, and other units within the organization. For example, a division of Johnson & Johnson developed a profitable line of specialty contact lenses (Accuvue) based on a suggestion from an employee who worked in an entirely different division. The path to a profitable product was rocky, yet J&J leadership was willing to experiment for a long-range gain.

A final perspective on the learning organization is that the leader must encourage organizational members to think creatively—to imagine possibilities that do not already exist. Instead of merely adapting to the environment, the organization engages in the type of breakthrough thinking described in our previous discussions of creativity and strategic leadership.

Helping Group Members to Become Good Followers

According to Stephen A. Laser, the single greatest problem facing leaders today is one that is rarely brought to light—getting people to want to accept leadership.[32] As we mentioned at the outset of this book, the word *follower* suffers from political incorrectness. Nevertheless, to be an effective leader, one needs good followers. Most of the topics in our study of leadership so far have been aimed at inspiring, motivating, and influencing group members to want to achieve organizational goals. It is also valuable, however, to mention effective group member characteristics that facilitate followership. As observed by Robert E. Kelley, effective followers share four essential qualities.[33]

1. *Self-management.* The key to being a good follower is to think for oneself and to work well without close supervision. Effective group members see themselves as being as capable as their leaders. You will recall that the goal of SuperLeadership is to facilitate self-management.

2. *Commitment.* Effective followers are committed to something beyond themselves, be it a cause, product, department, organization, idea, or value. To a committed group member, the leader facilitates making progress toward achieving a goal.

3. *Competence and focus.* Effective followers build their competence and focus their efforts for maximum impact. Competence centers around mastering skills that will be useful to the organization. Less effective group members rarely take the initiative to engage in training and development.

4. *Courage.* Effective followers establish themselves as independent, critical thinkers and will fight for what they believe is right. A good follower, for example, might challenge the company's policy of taking ninety days to make good on accounts payable, or recruiting key people almost exclusively from people with demographic characteristics similar to those of top management.

The above list is illustrative, since almost any positive human quality would contribute directly or indirectly to being an effective group member or follower. Another way of framing the qualities of effective followers is that such followers display the personal characteristics and qualities of leaders. Although leaders cannot be expected to change the personalities of group members, they can take steps to encourage the above qualities. Interventions such as coaching, SuperLeadership, supportive communication, and frequent feedback would support effective followership. Leadership Skill-Building Exercise 15–2 will give you more insight into the multidimensional nature of effective group membership.

LEADERSHIP SKILL-BUILDING
EXERCISE 15–2 The Followership Evaluation Form

Should you be the leader of a relatively stable group, use the following set of standards as material for group discussion. Get the group members' opinions on the validity of these statements as indicators of being an effective group member or follower. As we cautioned previously, the term *follower* has negative connotations for many despite its use in the professional literature. The terms *team member* and *group member* fit the times better.

Outstanding

a. Loyal, effective team player with a contagious positive attitude

b. Ready and willing to accept and act on tasks, even on short notice or under pressure

c. Spurs the team to remain positive in confusing or changing situations

d. Readily volunteers in a way that makes a difference

e. Offers supportive suggestions that the chain of command adopts

f. Facilitates team progress

g. Adopts unpopular higher headquarters decision as own

h. Regards peers well and is well regarded by peers

i. Acts for the good of the team

Excellent

a. Effective team player

b. Accepts and acts on assigned tasks

c. Volunteers in useful ways

d. Remains positive when the situation is confused or changing

e. Offers suggestions, but supports the chain of command

f. Helps the team make progress

g. Properly executes unpopular headquarters decisions

h. Gets along with peers

i. Gets own share of work done

j. Acts for the good of the team

Needs Improvement

a. Does not contribute much to team morale or effectiveness

b. Reluctant or unwilling to accept assigned tasks

c. Does not volunteer or does so ineffectively or superficially

d. Visibly upset by confusing or changing situations; tends to aggravate the situation

e. Does not offer helpful suggestions or argues with the chain of command, thereby hindering team progress

f. Fails to execute higher headquarters decisions properly and/or openly complains about or blames the higher headquarters

g. Has trouble getting along with some peers

h. Needs help from others to get own share of work done

i. Acts primarily for reasons of personal gain

j. Expects more of others when in charge than is willing to produce when others are in charge

Source: Adapted from material in Cadet Command Regulation 145-3, "Army Reserve Officers' Training Corps: Precommissioning Training and Leadership Development," U.S. Army Cadet Command, Fort Monroe, Va., March 1996.

Maintaining Trust

Generating trust as an effective leadership behavior has already been mentioned directly and indirectly several times in our study of leadership. We conclude with another look at trust because it has been identified by a panel of academics and other experts as one of the essential attributes of leadership for the new millennium. Leaders must be trustworthy, and they must also trust group members. Given that so many people distrust business leaders, as well as political leaders, gaining and maintaining trust is a substantial challenge.[34] The following trust builders are worthy of a leader or prospective leader's attention and implementation:

- Make your behavior consistent with your intentions. Practice what you preach and set the example. Let others know of your intentions and invite feedback on how well you are achieving them.

- When your organization or organizational unit encounters a problem, move into a problem-solving mode instead of looking to blame others for what went wrong.

- Honor confidences. One incident of passing along confidential information results in a permanent loss of trust by the person whose confidence was violated.

- Maintain a high level of integrity. Building a reputation for doing what you think is morally right in spite of the political consequences will enhance your integrity.[35]

It takes a leader a long time to build trust, yet one brief incident of untrustworthy behavior can permanently destroy it. Leaders are usually allowed a fair share of honest mistakes. In contrast, dishonest mistakes quickly erode leadership effectiveness.

Leadership Skill-Building Exercise 15–3 may give you a few good insights into the type of leader you are becoming.

LEADERSHIP SKILL-BUILDING
EXERCISE 15–3 Building for the Future

Our final skill-building exercise, the use of a feedback circle, encompasses many aspects of leadership covered in this and the previous fourteen chapters. Ten members of the class arrange their chairs in a circle. One person is selected as the feedback "target," and the other nine people take turns giving him or her supportive feedback. Assume it is "Ralph's" turn. Each person in the circle gives Ralph two pieces of feedback: (a) his best leadership attribute, and (b) how he needs to develop for the future. The feedback should take about thirty seconds per feedback giver. After receiving input from all the circle members, Ralph is free to comment. It is then the next person's turn to be the feedback target.

Class members who are not in the circle observe the dynamics of what is happening, and report their observations after the circle finishes. With diligence, the whole process will take about ninety minutes. If time permits, a new feedback circle can form. Alternatively, the class can break into several circles that operate simultaneously, or run just one circle with ten volunteers.

SUMMARY

Leadership and management development are widely practiced in a variety of organizations and take many forms, including self-development. Self-awareness involves the insightful processing of feedback about oneself to improve personal effectiveness. Single-loop learning occurs when learners seek minimum feedback that may substantially confront their basic ideas or actions. Double-loop learning occurs when people use feedback to confront the validity of the goal or values implicit in the situation; it enables the leader to learn and profit from failure.

Leadership development requires considerable self-discipline. For example, self-discipline is needed to monitor one's behavior to ensure that needed self-development takes place.

Education, leadership experience, and mentoring are all major contributors to leadership development. Most high-level leaders are intelligent, well-informed people who gather knowledge throughout their career. Two important aspects of leadership experience are work associates and the task itself (such as a complex and ambiguous assignment). Broad experience is important for leadership development, as suggested by multifunctional managerial development. A mentor is a more experienced person who develops a protégé's ability through tutoring, coaching, guidance, and emotional support. Mentors can serve as a model of effective (or ineffective) leadership and can coach protégés in leadership skills. Many mentors are formally assigned to their roles. A caution has been expressed that patterning yourself after a mentor can be a mistake because you might become an inferior imitation.

A comprehensive leadership development program includes certain key features: executive involvement; targeting career transitions;

addressing current and future organization needs; an appropriate model; diagnostic tools; practical and relevant content; emphasis on interpersonal relations and teamwork; and individual action plans.

Personal-growth experiences for leadership development assume that leaders are deeply in touch with their personal dreams and talents and will act to fulfill them. Outdoor training exemplifies a personal-growth experience. A standard university approach to leadership development is to equip people with a conceptual understanding of leadership. The concepts, such as those included in the Leadership Challenge, can then be applied to leadership situations. Simulations are another standard approach to leadership development, as exemplified by the Looking Glass. The simulation includes practice in exercising leadership in the face of organizational constraints, and supportive feedback on performance.

The traditional approach to the evaluation of leadership development programs includes specifying objectives and then measuring whether they were met. Measures of organizational outcomes, such as increased profits, might also be made. A more rigorous approach to evaluation would be based on an experimental design. An alternative approach to evaluation is to examine the domains of impact (ranges of possible effects) a program might have. Among these domains are concepts and content, self-objectivity, and behavior.

Leadership succession (or succession planning) is linked to leadership development because being groomed as a successor contributes to development. Also, selecting and grooming a successor is part of a leader's development. One study found that more powerful boards of directors were more likely to choose a new CEO with a demographic profile more in line with their own. More powerful CEOs chose successors much like themselves. An outsider is more likely to be chosen as a successor when the organization is performing poorly, particularly when sociopolitical forces are weak. General Electric is an example of rigorous success planning. Leadership succession is highly emotional for the leader being replaced, especially when a founder sells a business.

Three key leadership challenges that are particularly relevant for the future are maintaining a learning organization, helping group members develop followership skills, and maintaining trust. Major leadership initiatives for creating a learning organization include creating a strategic intent to learn, creating a shared vision, and encouraging systems thinking and continuous experimentation. Good followership skills include self-management, commitment, competence and focus, and courage. Maintaining trust is a key leadership requirement for the new millennium and can be attained through such means as making one's behavior and intentions consistent, and acting with integrity.

KEY TERMS

Self-awareness	Multifunctional managerial development	Leadership succession
Single-loop learning		Learning organization
Double-loop learning	Mentor	
Self-discipline	Domains of impact	

GUIDELINES FOR ACTION AND SKILL DEVELOPMENT

An important method for enhancing both the acceptance and the effectiveness of leadership development is *needs analysis*, the diagnosis of needs for development. Conducting a needs analysis is based on the idea that there are individual differences among leaders and future leaders. For example, Jennifer might have excellent conceptual knowledge about leadership, but limited team experience. She might be a good candidate for outdoor training. Jack might be an excellent team leader with limited conceptual knowledge. He might be a good candidate for a leadership development program concentrating on formal knowledge about leadership. Sources of data for assessing leadership developmental needs include the following:

1. Self-perceptions of developmental needs, including the results of many of the diagnostic instruments presented in this text

2. Perceptions by superiors, subordinates, and peers of the person's developmental needs

3. Psychological evaluation of developmental needs

4. A statement of organizational needs for development, such as the importance of leaders who can deal effectively with diversity (within company, with customers, and globally)

Multiple sources of data are useful because of possible errors in perception, biases, and favoritism.

DISCUSSION QUESTIONS AND ACTIVITIES

1. Many executives believe that playing team sports helps a person develop as a leader. Based on your knowledge of leadership development, where do you stand on this issue?

2. How can a person increase self-awareness?

3. Give an example from your own life in which you engaged in double-loop learning, or in which you *should have* engaged in such learning.

4. How can a person begin capitalizing on the advantages of multifunctional managerial development early in his or her career?

5. How seriously should people in business take the advice of a leadership expert from the U.S. Marine Corps?

6. Should the managers who perform the best in a simulation be considered the most eligible for promotion? Why or why not?

7. What do you perceive as the difference between employee training and organizational learning?

8. What role does appearance play in gaining the trust of team members?

9. Assume that you were responsible for selecting a leadership development program for your organization. What questions would you ask a potential provider of these services?

10. Ask an experienced leader what he or she thinks is the most effective method of developing leadership skills. Bring your findings back to class.

LEADERSHIP CASE PROBLEM

The Troubled Mentor

During her junior year as a management major, Karen Stiles decided that she wanted to become a human resources professional. After consulting with her professors and speaking to practitioners in the field, Stiles decided that a sensible method of entry into human resources would involve several components. She would first obtain several years of work experience in a line function, then work full-time on an MBA. With line experience and an MBA behind her, she would then seek a human resources position.

Stiles's plan worked well. After graduating from college, she found a position selling payroll services and bookkeeping services to small and medium-size companies. Her employer, Custom Services Inc., was growing rapidly. Stiles also had the opportunity to sell human resources services, such as benefit programs and human resource manuals. Each year she met her sales objectives, and she received above-average performance evaluations. Toward the end of her third year with the company, Karen informed her boss, Larry LeMayo, that she planned to resign so that she could attend graduate school full-time to obtain an MBA.

After listening to her plans, LeMayo said, "Karen, you've been a wonderful performer. The company would hate to lose you. Elizabeth (LeMayo's manager) has the same high opinion of you that I do. You have good sales skills, and we think you also have leadership skills. I would like to think of your obtaining an MBA as a leave of absence, not a resignation. In my opinion, you have a promising future at Custom Services. We anticipate fabulous growth during the next decade that will create good opportunities for people of your caliber.

"Let me speak to Elizabeth (Palamore). I'm sure she will want to talk to you before you resign or take a leave of absence."

The next day Stiles met with Palamore, who reinforced LeMayo's sentiments and went a little further. Elizabeth Palamore said to Karen, "I believe strongly that you have a great future in our company. You have already told us that you want to get into human resources. Our company is growing so rapidly that we will soon have a full-fledged human resources department reporting to me. If you return after getting your MBA, I can pretty much guarantee you a slot in our human resources department. Depending on when you return and how big the department needs to be, you might be appointed as a supervisor. When might you be returning?"

Karen responded, "I should get my MBA within twelve months, including summer session. Since I majored in management, the admissions counselor said I can get a four-course waiver."

"The timing would be perfect," said Elizabeth. "And I also have something else in mind for you. I would like to be your mentor. During your leave of absence, let's do lunch at least once a month. And maybe you could do a few spot assignments for the company during your absence. Maybe you could call on a few potential accounts that we think you could handle particularly well."

"I'm astounded to hear all this good news," said Karen. "And I consider it a big-time compliment that you want to be my mentor. I accept your offer."

During Karen's leave, the mentoring went as planned. Karen and Elizabeth met periodically for lunch, and they often discussed how Karen could apply the knowledge she was acquiring to help Custom Services upon her return. Karen also worked about three days per month for the company during her absence.

When Karen rejoined the firm, she was offered a dual position as the training and staffing coordinator, reporting to the human resources manager. At the same time she kept in regular contact with Elizabeth, to the point that Karen soon acquired the descriptor of "Elizabeth's protégé." Karen felt a little uncomfortable being considered somebody's protégé, yet she felt that on balance it was good for her career. From time to time Elizabeth would delegate a task to Karen without first checking with Karen's manager. Some friction developed between Karen and her boss, but the latter did not blame Karen.

Karen performed well in her human resources slot, and within one year Elizabeth hinted that Karen might soon be promoted to supervisor, with a staff of three professionals and one office assistant. At about this time, Karen began to notice a subtle shift in her relationship with Elizabeth, who slowly was becoming more dependent upon Karen. Elizabeth would often telephone Karen at nights and on weekends to talk about personal problems, such as an investment turned sour, and marital problems.

At the office, Karen began to hear negative rumors about Elizabeth's leadership skills and her personal integrity. One rumor she heard was that Elizabeth had diverted $20,000 of company money to cover a margin stock account. The story was that Elizabeth had returned the money before the external auditors discovered it was missing, thus avoiding dismissal or other punishment. Another rumor Karen heard was that Elizabeth became inebriated at a top-management retreat, and made a few insulting

comments about the CEO's leadership capabilities. Also of concern to Karen was a rumor that Elizabeth had asked two temporary workers for kickbacks should she recommend them for full-time positions with the firm.

One day at lunch, Todd Iverson, a company sales representative, said half-jokingly to Karen, "Your old buddies in the sales department are thinking of throwing a good-bye party for you when you follow Elizabeth out the door. People are wondering what wrongdoings you might be involved in, since you are so closely aligned with Elizabeth."

After returning from lunch, Karen found a message from Elizabeth in her E-mail: "Can we get together for a drink after work? I really need your advice on several issues."

Karen started wondering what to do about her relationship with Elizabeth in general, and how she should respond to the E-mail. She thought to herself, "If my mentor is in trouble, does that mean I'm in trouble? Or am I in bigger trouble if I try to jump ship? Or, should I just ignore all these vicious rumors?"

1. What has this case got to do with leadership?

2. What recommendations can you make to Karen for managing her relationship with her mentor?

3. What, if any, actions should management be taking with respect to Elizabeth Palamore?

4. What is your evaluation of the path Karen has chosen to develop her career as a leader?

ENDNOTES

Chapter 1

1. "Sears Takes Aim at Small Hardware Stores," Associated Press and staff reports story in Rochester *Democrat and Chronicle,* July 21, 1996, pp. 1E, 6E; Patricia Sellers, "Sears: In With the New," *Fortune,* October 16, 1995, pp. 96–98.
2. W. Chan Kim and Renee A. Maubourgne, "Parables of Leadership," *Harvard Business Review,* July–August 1992, p. 123.
3. Derived from a literature review in Bernard M. Bass, *Bass & Stogdill's Handbook of Leadership: Theory, Research, & Managerial Applications* (New York: The Free Press, 1990), pp. 11–18.
4. Peter Block, *Stewardship: Choosing Service over Self-Interest* (San Francisco: Berrett-Koehler Publishers, 1993), pp. 27–32.
5. Ibid., pp. 29–31.
6. John P. Kotter, *A Force for Change: How Leadership Differs from Management* (New York: The Free Press, 1990); Warren Bennis, *An Invented Life: Reflections on Leadership and Change* (Reading, Mass.: Addison-Wesley, 1993); David A. Whetten and Kim S. Cameron, *Developing Management Skills,* 3rd ed. (New York: HarperCollins, 1995), p. 16.
7. Edwin A. Locke and associates, *The Essence of Leadership: The Four Keys to Leading Successfully* (New York: Lexington/Macmillan, 1991), p. 4.
8. The information about the positive impact of leadership on organizational performance is based on Bass, *Bass & Stogdill's Handbook,* pp. 6–10.
9. Gary A. Yukl, *Leadership in Organizations,* 3rd ed. (Englewood Cliffs, N.J.: Prentice-Hall, 1994), pp. 384–387.
10. Jon P. Howell, David E. Bowen, Peter W. Dorfman, Steven Kerr, and Philip Podaskoff, "Substitutes for Leadership: Effective Alternatives to Ineffective Leadership," *Organizational Dynamics,* Summer 1990, p. 23.
11. Ibid., pp. 26–27.
12. Bass, *Bass & Stogdill's Handbook,* p. 686.
13. Jeffrey Pfeffer, "The Ambiguity of Leadership," *Academy of Management Review,* April 1977, pp. 104–112.
14. Henry Mintzberg, *The Nature of Managerial Work* (New York: Harper & Row, 1973); Kenneth Graham, Jr., and William M. Mihal, *The CMD Managerial Job Analysis Inventory* (Rochester, N.Y.: Rochester Institute of Technology, Center for Management Development, 1987), pp. 2–6.
15. Christopher A. Bartlett and Sumantra Ghosal, "Changing the Role of Top Management: Beyond Systems to People," *Harvard Business Review,* May–June 1995, pp. 132–133.
16. Thomas A. Stewart, "The Nine Dilemmas Leaders Face," *Fortune,* March 18, 1996, pp. 112–113.
17. Yukl, *Leadership in Organizations,* pp. 15–18; Locke and associates, *The Essence of Leadership,* pp. 6–11; James G. Hunt, *Leadership: A New Synthesis* (Newbury Park, Calif.: Sage Publications, 1991); John A. Wagner III and John R. Hollenbeck, *Management of Organizational Behavior,* Englewood Cliffs, N.J.: Prentice-Hall, 1992), pp. 441–442.
18. Paul Hersey, Kenneth H. Blanchard, and Dewey E. Johson, *Management of Organizational Behavior: Utilizing Human Resources* (Upper Saddle River, N.J.: Prentice-Hall, 1996), p. 91.
19. Stephen P. Robbins, *Managing Today!* (Upper Saddle River, N.J.: Prentice-Hall, 1997), pp. 418–420.
20. Bass, *Bass & Stogdill's Handbook.*

Chapter 2

1. William Patalon III, "Fisher at Center Stage," Rochester *Democrat and Chronicle,* October 30, 1994, p. 14A.
2. Edwin A. Locke and associates, *The Essence of Leadership: The Four Keys to Leading Successfully* (New York: Lexington/Macmillan, 1991), pp. 13–34; Shelley A. Kirkpatrick and Edwin A. Locke, "Leadership: Do Traits Matter?" *The Executive,* May 1991, pp. 48–60.
3. Carol J. Loomis, "Citicorp: John Reed's Second Act," *Fortune,* April 29, 1996, pp. 90–91.
4. Julie Cohen Mason, "Leading the Way Into the 21st Century," *Management Review,* October 1992, p. 19.
5. Richard M. Hodgetts, "A Conversation with Warren Bennis on Leadership in the Midst of Downsizing," *Organizational Dynamics,* Summer 1996, p. 75.
6. Morgan W. McCall, Jr., and Michael M. Lombardo, *Off the Track: Why and How Successful Leaders Get Derailed,* Technical Report No. 21 (Greensboro, N.C.: Center for Creative Leadership, 1983), p. 11.
7. Bernard M. Bass, *Bass & Stogdill's Handbook of Leadership: Theory, Research, & Managerial Applications,* 3rd ed. (New York: The Free Press, 1990), p. 90.
8. Locke and associates, *The Essence of Leadership,* p. 55.
9. "The Hot Seat: Leadership in the 90s Is a Different Ball Game," *Executive Strategies,* September 1992, p. 1.

10. "Why Leaders Laugh," *Executive Strategies*, November 1995, p. 3.
11. Quoted in "Leadership Concepts," *Executive Strategies*, July 9, 1991, p. 1.
12. Chris Piotrowski and Terry R. Armstrong, "The CEO: Analysis of the CNN Telecast 'Pinnacle,'" *Psychological Reports*, 65, 1989, pp. 435–438.
13. Kirkpatrick and Locke, "Leadership: Do Traits Matter?" pp. 51–52.
14. Jeffrey Pfeffer, *Managing with Power: Politics and Influence in Organizations* (Boston: Harvard Business School Press, 1992), p. 172.
15. Ellen Van Velsor and Jean Brittain Leslie, "Why Executives Derail: Perspectives Across Time and Cultures," *Academy of Management Executive*, November 1995, pp. 62–72.
16. Avis L. Johnson, Fred Luthans, and Harry W. Hennessey, "The Role of Locus of Control in Leader Influence Behavior," *Personnel Psychology*, Spring 1984, p. 70.
17. Peter Koestenbaum, *Leadership: The Inner Side of Greatness* (San Francisco: Jossey-Bass, 1991).
18. Warren Bennis and Burt Nanus, "The Leadership Tightrope," *Success*, March 1985, p. 28.
19. David C. McLelland and Richard Boyatzis, "Leadership Motive Pattern and Long-Term Success in Management," *Journal of Applied Psychology*, December 1982, p. 727.
20. Locke and associates, *The Essence of Leadership*, p. 22.
21. Ibid., p. 22.
22. John B. Miner, Normal R. Smith, and Jeffrey S. Bracker, "Role of Entrepreneurial Task Motivation in the Growth of Technologically Innovative Firms," *Journal of Applied Psychology*, August 1989, p. 554.
23. Cited in Mason, "Leading the Way into the 21st Century," p. 18.
24. Fred E. Fiedler and Joseph E. Garcia, *New Approaches to Effective Leadership: Cognitive Resources and Organizational Performance* (New York: Wiley, 1987); Robert P. Vecchio, "Theoretical and Empirical Examination of Cognitive Resource Theory," *Journal of Applied Psychology*, April 1990, p. 141.
25. Vecchio, "Theoretical and Empirical Examination of Cognitive Resource Theory," pp. 141–147; Vecchio, "Cognitive Resource Theory: Issues for Specifying a Test of the Theory," *Journal of Applied Psychology*, June 1992, p. 66.
26. Charles M. Farkas and Suzy Wetlaufer, "The Ways Chief Executive Officers Lead," *Harvard Business Review*, May–June 1996, p. 112.
27. Manfred F. R. Kets de Vries, "The Leadership Mystique," *Academy of Management Executive*, August 1994, p. 74.
28. Ray J. Friant, Jr., "Leadership Training for Long-Term Results," *Management Review*, July 1991, p. 50.
29. Kirkpatrick and Locke, "Leadership: Do Traits Matter?" p. 59.
30. Frances Hesselbein, Marshall Goldsmith, and Richard Beckhard (eds.), *The Leader of the Future* (San Francisco: Jossey-Bass, 1996).
31. Gary A. Yukl, *Leadership in Organizations*, 3rd ed. (Englewood Cliffs, N.J.: Prentice-Hall, 1994), pp. 278–279.
32. Abridged and adapted from Robert E. Alberti and Michael L. Emmons, *Your Perfect Right: A Guide to Assertive Behavior* (San Luis Obispo, Calif.: Impact Publishers, 1970), Chapter 2.

Chapter 3

1. "ValuJet Comes Flying Back," Associated Press story, September 15, 1996; "ValuJet Airlines," www.valujet.com/tale.html, October 21, 1996.
2. Jay A. Conger, Rabindra N. Kanungo, and associates, *Charismatic Leadership* (San Francisco: Jossey-Bass, 1988).
3. Jay A. Conger, *The Charismatic Leader: Behind the Mystique of Exceptional Leadership* (San Francisco: Jossey-Bass, 1989).
4. Eugene Schmuckler, book review in *Personnel Psychology*, Winter 1989, p. 881.
5. Robert J. House, "A 1976 Theory of Charismatic Leadership," in J. G. Hunt and L. L. Larson (eds.), *Leadership: The Cutting Edge* (Carbondale: Southern Illinois University Press, 1977), pp. 189–207.
6. Jeffrey D. Kudisch, Mark L. Poteet, Gregory H. Dobbins, Michael C. Rush, and Joyce E. A. Russell, "Expert Power, Referent Power, and Charisma: Toward the Resolution of a Theoretical Debate," *Journal of Business and Psychology*, Winter 1995, pp. 177–195.
7. Jane A. Halpert, "The Dimensionality of Charisma," *Journal of Business Psychology*, Summer 1990, p. 401.
8. Conger, Kanungo, and associates, *Charismatic Leadership*; Bernard M. Bass, *Bass & Stogdill's Handbook of Leadership: Theory, Research, & Managerial Applications*, 3rd ed. (New York: The Free Press, 1990), pp. 185–186.
9. "Colin Powell: Four-Star CEO?" *Business Week*, November 27, 1995, p. 40.
10. Jane M. Howell and Bruce Avolio, "The Ethics of Charismatic Leadership: Submission or Liberation?" *The Executive*, May 1992, pp. 43–52; Patricia Sellers, "What Exactly Is Charisma?" *Fortune*, January 15, 1996, pp. 72–75.
11. Laurie Larwood, Cecilia M. Falbe, Mark P. Kriger, and Paul Miesing, "Structure and Meaning of Organizational Vision," *Academy of Management Journal*, June 1995, pp. 740–769.
12. Andrew Kupfer, "Craig Sees an Internet in the Sky," *Fortune*, May 27, 1996, p. 64.
13. Howell and Avolio, "The Ethics of Charismatic Leadership," p. 46.
14. Noel Tichy and Christopher DeRose, "Roger Enrico's Master Class," *Fortune*, November 27, 1995, p. 106.
15. Jay A. Conger, "Inspiring Others: The Language of Leadership," *The Executive*, February 1991, p. 39.
16. Ibid., p. 39.
17. "Management by Anecdote," *Success*, December 1992, p. 35.
18. John J. Hater and Bernard M. Bass, "Superiors' Evaluations and Subordinates' Perceptions of Transformational and Transactional Leadership," *Journal of Applied Psychology*, November 1988, p. 695; Noel M. Tichy and Mary Anne Devanna, *The Transformational Leader* (New York: Wiley, 1990).

19. Peter Koestenbaum, *Leadership: The Inner Side of Greatness* (San Francisco: Jossey-Bass, 1991).
20. Alan J. Dubinsky, Francis J. Yammarino, and Marvin A. Jolson, "An Examination of Linkages Between Personal Characteristics and Dimensions of Transformational Leadership," *Journal of Business and Psychology,* Spring 1995, p. 316.
21. Based on literature review in Dubinsky, Yammarino, and Jolson, "An Examination of Linkages," pp. 316–318.
22. Hater and Bass, "Superiors' Evaluations and Subordinates' Perceptions," p. 701.
23. Ibid.
24. Jane M. Howell and Bruce J. Avolio, "Transformational Leadership, Transactional Leadership, Locus of Control, and Support for Innovation: Key Predictors of Consolidated-Business-Unit Performance," *Journal of Applied Psychology,* December 1993, pp. 891–902.
25. Warren G. Bennis and Burt Nanus, *Leaders: Strategies for Taking Charge* (New York: Harper & Row, 1985), p. 223.
26. Robert C. Tucker, "The Theory of Charismatic Leadership," *Daedalus,* Summer 1968, pp. 731–756.
27. Howell and Avolio, "The Ethics of Charismatic Leadership," pp. 52–53.
28. Daniel Sankowsky, "The Charismatic Leader as Narcissist: Understanding the Abuse of Power," *Organizational Dynamics,* Spring 1995, p. 57.
29. Roger Dawson, *Secrets of Power Persuasion: Everything You'll Need to Get Anything You'll Ever Want* (Englewood Cliffs, N.J.: Prentice-Hall, 1992), pp. 179–194.

Chapter 4

1. Eric Pooley, "One Good Apple," *Time,* January 19, 1996, pp. 54–56; Elizabeth Lesly, "A Safer New York City," *Business Week,* December 11, 1995, pp. 81–84.
2. Ralph M. Stogdill and Alvin E. Coons (eds.), *Leader Behavior: Its Description and Measurement* (Columbus: The Ohio State University Bureau of Business Research, 1957); Carroll L. Shartle, *Executive Performance and Leadership* (Englewood Cliffs, N.J.: Prentice-Hall, 1956).
3. Andrew W. Halpin, "The Observed Leader Behavior and Ideal Leader of Aircraft Commanders and School Superintendents," in Stogdill and Coons, *Leader Behavior,* p. 64.
4. Rensis Likert, *New Patterns of Management* (New York: McGraw-Hill, 1961); Arnold S. Tannenbaum, *Social Psychology of the Work Organization* (Monterey, Calif.: Wadsworth, 1966).
5. John P. Kotter, "What Leaders Really Do," *Harvard Business Review,* May–June 1990, pp. 104–105.
6. Both quotes are from Karl Albrecht, *The Northbound Train: Finding the Purpose, Setting the Direction, Shaping the Destiny of Your Organization* (New York: AMACOM, 1994).
7. Tim Smart, "GE's Money Machine: How Its Emphasis on Performance Built a Colossus of Finance," *Business Week,* March 8, 1993, p. 64.
8. Thomas J. Peters and Robert H. Waterman, Jr., *In Search of Excellence: Lessons from America's Best-Run Companies* (New York: Harper & Row, 1982).

9. Cited in Jay A. Conger, *Learning to Lead: The Art of Transforming Managers into Leaders* (San Francisco: Jossey-Bass, 1992), pp. 130, 131.
10. "Général Invente le Téléphone de l'an 2000," *Enterprise (Le Figaro),* February 22, 1993, p. 7.
11. "Masters of the Game: CEOs Who Succeed in Business When Times Are Really Trying," *Business Week,* October 12, 1992, pp. 113–114.
12. Kotter, "What Leaders Really Do," pp. 105–106.
13. Jenny C. McCune, "Polishing the Apple," *Management Review,* September 1996, pp. 47–48.
14. Conger, *Learning to Lead,* p. 131.
15. David S. Brown, "Manager's New Job Is Concert Building," *HRMagazine,* September 1990, p. 42.
16. Conger, *Learning to Lead,* p. 149.
17. Kotter, "What Leaders Really Do," p. 107.
18. Don Dinkmeyer and Dan Eckstein, *Leadership by Encouragement* (Delray Beach, Fla.: St. Lucie Press, 1995).
19. "Covey Proposes: Principle-Based Leadership," *Management Review,* September 1995, p. 21.
20. Charles C. Manz and Henry P. Sims, Jr., "SuperLeadership: Beyond the Myth of Heroic Leadership," *Organizational Dynamics,* Spring 1991, p. 18.
21. Charles C. Manz, "Helping Yourself and Others to Master Self-Leadership," *Supervisory Management,* November 1991, p. 9.
22. Robert Hoffman, "Ten Reasons Why You Should Use 360-Degree Feedback," *HRMagazine,* April 1995, p. 84.
23. Ibid.
24. Gary Yukl, *Leadership In Organizations,* 3rd ed. (Englewood Cliffs, N.J.: Prentice-Hall, 1994), p. 71.

Chapter 5

1. Ronald Henkoff, "P & G: New and Improved!" *Fortune,* October 14, 1996, p. 152.
2. Kurt Lewin and Ronald Lippitt, "An Experimental Approach to the Study of Autocracy and Democracy: A Preliminary Note," *Sociometry,* No. 1, 1938, pp. 292–300.
3. Robert Tannenbaum and Warren H. Schmidt, "How to Choose a Leadership Pattern," *Harvard Business Review,* May–June 1973, pp. 162–164, 166–168.
4. "Turnaround Is Fair Play," *Management Review,* July 1995, p. 26; Joseph Nocera, "Confessions of a Corporate Killer," *Fortune,* September 30, 1996, p. 200.
5. "Consensus v. Leadership: Balancing the Two Today," *Executive Strategies,* April 1995, p. 9.
6. Donna Brown, "Why Participative Management Won't Work Here," *Management Review,* June 1992, p. 42.
7. Ibid., p. 44. See also John A. Wagner III, "Participation's Effect on Performance and Satisfaction: A Reconsideration of Research Evidence," *Academy of Management Review,* April 1994, p. 451.
8. Robert R. Blake and Anne Adams McCarse, *Leadership Dilemmas and Solutions* (Houston: Gulf Publishing, 1991).
9. Robert R. Blake and Jane S. Mouton, *The New Managerial Grid* (Houston: Gulf Publishing, 1978).
10. Bruce M. Fisher and Jack E. Edwards, "Consideration and Initiating Structure and Their Relationships with Leader Effectiveness: A Meta-Analysis," *Academy of Management Best Papers Proceedings,* 1988, p. 204.

11. Based in part on Michael Warshaw, "The Mind-Style of the Entrepreneur," *Success,* April 1993, pp. 28–33; Franck A. deChambeau and Fredericka Mackenzie, "Intrapreneurship," *Personnel Journal,* July 1986, p. 40.

12. Cited in Warshaw, "The Mind-Style of the Entrepreneur," p. 30.

13. Wilson L. Harrell, "Aggression: It's the Entrepreneur's Insurance," *Success,* April 1993, p. 8.

14. Gary N. Powell, "The Effects of Sex and Gender on Recruitment," *Academy of Management Review,* October 1987, pp. 731–743.

15. Judy Rosener, "Ways Women Lead," *Harvard Business Review,* November–December, 1990, pp. 119–125.

16. Quoted in Roz Morris, "Management: Why Women Are Leading the Way," in Michel Syrett and Clare Hogg (eds.), *Frontiers of Leadership* (Oxford, England: Blackwell Publishers, 1992), p. 271.

17. Cited in "Debate: Ways Men and Women Lead," *Harvard Business Review,* January–February 1991, p. 151.

18. James A. Autry, *Life and Work: A Manager's Search for Meaning* (New York: William Morrow, 1994).

19. Debra Phillips, "The Gender Gap," *Entrepreneur,* May 1995, pp. 110, 111.

20. Jan Grant, "Women as Managers: What They Can Offer Organizations," *Organizational Dynamics,* Winter 1988.

21. Bernard M. Bass, *Bass & Stogdill's Handbook of Leadership: Theory, Research, & Managerial Applications,* 3rd ed. (New York: The Free Press, 1990), p. 725.

22. Adam Zagorin, "Short-Shirted in Maine," *Time,* June 3, 1996, p. 58.

23. Cited in Phillips, "The Gender Gap," p. 112.

24. Paul Hersey, Kenneth H. Blanchard, and Dewey E. Johnson, *Management of Organizational Behavior: Utilizing Human Resources,* 7th ed. (Upper Saddle River, N.J.: Prentice-Hall, 1996), p. 91.

25. Ralph M. Stogdill, "Historical Trends in Leadership Theory and Research," *Journal of Contemporary Business,* Autumn 1974, p. 7.

26. Thomas R. Horton, *The CEO Paradox: The Privilege and Accountability of Leadership* (New York: AMACOM, 1992), p. 115.

27. Peter Burrows, "The Man in the Disk Driver's Seat," *Business Week,* March 18, 1996, p. 72.

28. "Directive Management or Not," *Working Smart,* December 1992, p. 3.

Chapter 6

1. Patricia Sellers, "Wal-Mart's Big Man Puts Blockbuster on Fast-Forward," *Fortune,* November 25, 1996, pp. 111–113.

2. Donald M. Moretti, Carol L. Morken, and Jeanne M. Borkowski, "Profile of the American CEO: Comparing *Inc.* and *Fortune* Executives," *Journal of Business and Psychology,* Winter 1991, pp. 193–205.

3. Fred E. Fiedler, Martin H. Chemers, and Linda Mahar, *Improving Leadership Effectiveness: The Leader Match Concept,* 2nd ed. (New York: Wiley, 1994); E. Leroy Plumlee, "A Visit with Fred Fiedler," *Management Newsletter* (published by Houghton Mifflin), December 1989, pp. 2–7.

4. Plumlee, "A Visit with Fred Fiedler," p. 4.

5. Chester A. Schriesheim, Bennett J. Tepper, and Linda A. Tetrault, "Least Preferred Co-Worker Score, Situational Control, and Leadership Effectiveness: A Meta-Analysis of Contingency Model Performance Predictions," *Journal of Applied Psychology,* August 1994, pp. 561–573.

6. Robert J. House, "A Path-Goal Theory of Leader Effectiveness," *Administrative Science Quarterly,* September 1971, pp. 321–338; Robert T. Keller, "A Test of the Path-Goal Theory of Leadership with Need for Clarity as a Moderator in Research and Development Organizations," *Journal of Applied Psychology,* April 1989, pp. 208–212; Robert J. House and Terence R. Mitchell, "Path-Goal Theory of Leadership," *Journal of Contemporary Business,* Autumn 1974, pp. 81–97.

7. House and Mitchell, "Path-Goal Theory," p. 84; Bernard M. Bass, *Bass & Stogdill's Handbook of Leadership: Theory, Research, and Managerial Applications,* 3rd ed. (New York: The Free Press, 1990), p. 633.

8. Robert Kreitner, *Management,* 5th ed. (Boston: Houghton Mifflin, 1992), p. 466.

9. Paul Hersey, Kenneth H. Blanchard, and Dewey E. Johnson, *Management of Organizational Behavior: Utilizing Human Resources,* 7th ed. (Upper Saddle River, N.J.: Prentice-Hall, 1996), pp. 188–223.

10. Bass, *Bass & Stogdill's Handbook,* p. 493.

11. Robert P. Vecchio, "Situational Leadership Theory: An Examination of a Prescriptive Theory," *Journal of Applied Psychology,* August 1987, pp. 444–451.

12. Victor H. Vroom, "A New Look at Managerial Decision Making," *Organizational Dynamics,* Spring 1973, pp. 66–80; Victor H. Vroom and Arthur G. Jago, *The New Leadership: Managing Participation in Organizations* (Englewood Cliffs, N.J.: Prentice-Hall, 1988).

13. Madeline F. Heilman, Harvey A. Hornstein, Jack H. Cage, and Judith K. Herschlag, "Reactions to Prescribed Leader Behavior as a Function of Role Perspective: The Case for the Vroom–Yetton Normative Model of Leadership," *Journal of Applied Psychology,* February 1982, pp. 523–532; Richard H. G. Field and Robert J. House, "A Test of the Vroom–Yetton Model Using Manager and Subordinate Reports," *Journal of Applied Psychology,* June 1990, pp. 362–366.

14. Charles M. Farkas and Suzy Wetlaufer, "The Ways Chief Executive Officers Lead," *Harvard Business Review,* May–June 1996, pp. 110–122; Charles M. Farkas and Philippe De Backer, *Maximum Leadership: The World's Leading CEOs Share Their Five Strategies for Success* (New York: Henry Holt, 1996).

15. Farkas and Wetlaufer, "The Way Chief Executive Officers Lead," p. 116.

16. "How Situational Leadership Fits into Today's Organizations," *Supervisory Management,* February 1996, p. 3.

Chapter 7

1. "Riley Leaves Knicks in Power Dispute," Associated Press story, June 16, 1995.

2. Kathleen M. Eisenhardt and L. J. Bourgeois III, "Politics of Strategic Decision Making in High-Velocity

Environments: Toward a Midrange Theory," *Academy of Management Journal,* December 1988, p. 737.

3. John R. P. French and Bertram Raven, "The Basis of Social Power," in Dorwin Cartwright (ed.), *Studies in Social Power* (Ann Arbor, Mich.: Institute for Social Research, 1969); Timothy R. Hinkin and Chester A. Schrieschein, "Power and Influence: The View from Below," *Personnel,* May 1988, pp. 47–50.

4. Marshall Loeb, "The Bad Boss Gets a New Life," *Fortune,* May 27, 1996, p. 192.

5. Gary Yukl and Cecilia M. Falbe, "Importance of Different Power Sources in Downward and Lateral Relations," *Journal of Applied Psychology,* June 1991, p. 416.

6. Sydney Finkelstein, "Power in Top Management Teams: Dimensions, Measurement, and Validation," *Academy of Management Journal,* August 1992, p. 510.

7. Abraham L. Gitlow, *Being the Boss: The Importance of Leadership and Power* (Homewood, Ill.: Business One–Irwin, 1991).

8. Finkelstein, "Power in Top Management Teams," p. 508.

9. Jeffrey Pfeffer, *Managing with Power: Power and Influence in Organizations* (Boston: Harvard Business School Press, 1992), pp. 100–101.

10. Morgan McCall, Jr., *Power, Influence, and Authority: The Hazards of Carrying a Sword* (Greensboro, N.C.: Center for Creative Leadership, 1978), p. 5.

11. William Rothschild, *Risktaker, Caretaker, Surgeon, Undertaker: The Four Faces of Strategic Leadership* (New York: Wiley, 1993).

12. C. R. Hinings, D. J. Hickson, C. A. Lee, R. E. Schneck, and J. M. Pennings, "Strategic Contingencies Theory of Intraorganizational Power," *Administrative Science Quarterly,* 1971, pp. 216–229.

13. Herminia Ibarra, "Network Centrality, Power, and Innovation Involvement: Determinants of Technical and Administrative Roles," *Academy of Management Journal,* June 1993, pp. 471–501.

14. Leanne E. Atwater and Francis J. Yammarino, "Bases of Power in Relation to Leader Behavior: A Field Investigation," *Journal of Business and Psychology,* Fall 1996, pp. 3–22.

15. A good example is Robert C. Ford and Myron D. Fottler, "Empowerment: A Matter of Degree," *Academy of Management Executive,* August 1995, pp. 21–31.

16. Gretchen M. Spreitzer, "Psychological Empowerment in the Workplace: Dimensions, Measurement, and Validation," *Academy of Management Journal,* October 1995, pp. 1442–1465.

17. Jay A. Conger, "Leadership: The Art of Empowering Others," *Academy of Management Executive,* February 1989, pp. 17–25; Frank Shipper and Charles C. Manz," "Employee Self-Management Without Formally Designated Teams: An Alternative Road to Empowerment," *Organizational Dynamics,* Winter 1992, p. 59.

18. Several of the ideas in this section are based on David A. Whetton and Kim S. Cameron, *Developing Management Skills,* 3rd ed. (New York: HarperCollins, 1995), pp. 504–513; Thomas R. Horton, "Delegation and Team Building: No Solo Acts Please," *Management Review,* September 1992, pp. 58–61.

19. Joseph T. Straub, "Reversing Reverse Delegation," *Getting Results,* September 1996, pp. 6–7.

20. Eisenhardt and Bourgeois, "Politics of Strategic Decision Making," pp. 737–770.

21. Gregory Moorhead and Ricky W. Griffin, *Organizational Behavior: Managing People and Organizations,* 4th ed. (Boston: Houghton Mifflin, 1995), p. 329.

22. Gerald Biberman, "Personality Characteristics and Work Attitudes of Persons with High, Moderate, and Low Political Tendencies," *Psychological Reports,* Vol. 57, 1985, p. 1309.

23. Marshall Schminke, "A Dispositional Approach to Understanding Individual Power in Organizations," *Journal of Business and Psychology* Fall 1992, pp. 63–79.

24. Jeffrey Pfeffer, "Power and Resource Allocation in Organizations," in Barry M. Staw and Gerald R. Salancik (eds.), *New Dimensions in Organizational Behavior* (Chicago: St. Clair Press, 1977), p. 239.

25. Gerald R. Ferris and Thomas R. King, "Politics in Human Resources Decisions: A Walk on the Dark Side," *Organizational Dynamics,* Autumn 1991, p. 60.

26. Tom Peters, "Power," *Success,* November 1994, p. 34.

27. Eugene Schmuckler, book review in *Personnel Psychology,* Summer 1982, p. 497.

28. William H. Newman, *Administrative Action: The Techniques of Organization and Management* (Englewood Cliffs, N.J.: Prentice-Hall, 1963), p. 90.

29. Andrew J. DuBrin, *Stand Out! 330 Ways for Gaining the Edge with Bosses, Co-workers, Subordinates and Customers* (Englewood Cliffs, N.J.: Prentice-Hall, 1993).

30. "The Corporate Elite: Chief Executives of the *Business Week* 1000," *Business Week,* October 19, 1990, p. 11.

31. A good example is Sandy J. Wayne and Robert C. Liden, "Effects of Impression Management on Performance Ratings," *Academy of Management Journal,* February 1995, pp. 232–260.

32. "Career 'Insurance' Protects DP Professionals from Setbacks, Encourages Growth," *Data Management,* June 1986, p. 33.

33. Peters, "Power," p. 34.

34. "How to Win at Organizational Politics—Without Being Unethical or Sacrificing Your Self-Respect," report published by *Research Institute Personal Report,* 1985, p. 4.

35. "Did Apple Shoot the Messenger?" *Business Week,* October 16, 1995, p. 43.

36. Moorhead and Griffin, *Management,* p. 341.

37. Robert P. Vecchio, *Organizational Behavior,* 2nd ed. (Hinsdale, Ill.: Dryden, 1991), p. 282.

38. Gary A. Yukl, *Leadership in Organizations,* 2nd ed. (Englewood Cliffs, N.J.: Prentice-Hall, 1989), p. 44.

Chapter 8

1. Ira Sager, "How IBM Became a Growth Company Again," *Business Week,* December 9, 1996, pp. 154–158.

2. Allan R. Cohen, Stephen L. Fink, Hermon Gadon, and Robin. D. Willits, *Effective Behavior in Organizations: Cases, Concepts, and Student Experiences,* 5th ed. (Homewood, Ill.: Irwin, 1992), p. 139.

3. This section follows closely Gary Yukl, *Leadership in Organizations,* 3rd ed. (Englewood Cliffs, N.J.: Prentice-Hall, 1994), pp. 229–232.

4. James L. Bowditch and Anthony F. Buono, *A Primer of Organizational Behavior,* 4th ed. (New York: Wiley, 1997), pp. 4–5.
5. R. Bruce McAfee and Betty J. Ricks, "Leadership by Example: 'Do as I Do!'" *Management Solutions,* August 1986, p. 10.
6. Gary Yukl and J. Bruce Tracey, "Consequences of Influence Tactics Used with Subordinates, Peers, and the Boss," *Journal of Applied Psychology,* August 1992, p. 526.
7. Mitchell S. Nesler, Herman Aguinis, Brian M. Quigley, and James T. Tedeschi, "The Effect of Credibility on Perceived Power," *Journal of Applied Social Psychology,* 1993, 23, 17, pp. 1407–1425.
8. Bernard Keys and Thomas Case, "How to Become an Influential Manager," *Academy of Management Executive,* November 1990, p. 44.
9. "Build Power and Influence," *Executive Strategies,* June 19, 1990, p. 6.
10. Adapted from ibid., pp. 45–46.
11. Gary Yukl, *Skills for Managers and Leaders: Text, Cases, and Exercises* (Englewood Cliffs, N.J.: Prentice-Hall, 1990), pp. 58–62.
12. Jeffrey Pfeffer, *Managing with Power: Power and Influence in Organizations* (Boston: Harvard Business School Press, 1992), p. 224.
13. Yukl, *Skills for Managers and Leaders,* p. 65.
14. Andrew J. DuBrin, "Sex Differences in Endorsement of Influence Tactics and Political Behavior Tendencies," *Journal of Business and Psychology,* Fall 1989, p. 10.
15. Bernard M. Bass, *Bass & Stogdill's Handbook of Leadership: Theory, Research, & Managerial Applications,* 3rd ed. (New York: The Free Press, 1990), p. 134.
16. David M. Buss, Mary Gomes, Dolly S. Higgins, and Karen Lauterbach, "Tactics of Manipulation," *Journal of Personality and Social Psychology,* December 1987, p. 1222.
17. Chad T. Lewis, Joseph E. Garcia, and Sarah M. Jobs, *Managerial Skills in Organizations* (Boston: Allyn & Bacon, 1990), p. 234.
18. Buss et al., "Tactics of Manipulation," p. 1222.
19. Gary Yukl and Cecilia M. Falbe, "Influence Tactics and Objectives in Upward, Downward, and Lateral Influence Attempts," *Journal of Applied Psychology,* April 1990, p. 133.
20. Buss et al., "Tactics of Manipulation," p. 1222.
21. David Kipnis and Stuart M. Schmidt, "Intraorganizational Influence Tactics: Explorations in Getting One's Way," *Journal of Applied Psychology,* August 1980, p. 445.
22. Comment contributed by anonymous reviewer and professor of organizational behavior, September 1996.
23. Yukl and Tracey, "Consequences of Influence Tactics," pp. 525–535.
24. Yukl, *Leadership in Organizations,* p. 234.
25. Keys and Case, "How to Become an Influential Manager," p. 46.
26. David Kipnis and Stuart M. Schmidt, "Upward Influence Styles: Relationships with Performance Evaluations, Salary, and Stress," *Administrative Science Quarterly,* 1988, pp. 528–542.
27. Keys and Case, "How to Become an Influential Manager," p. 48.

Chapter 9

1. Sandra Phillips, "Teams Facilitate Change at Turbulent Plant," *Personnel Journal,* October 1994, pp. 110–119.
2. Edwin A. Locke and associates, *The Essence of Leadership: The Four Keys to Leading Successfully* (New York: Lexington/Macmillan, 1991), p. 94.
3. Jon R. Katzenbach and Douglas K. Smith, "The Discipline of Teams," *Harvard Business Review,* March–April 1993, p. 112.
4. Ibid.
5. Meredith Belbin, "Solo Leader/Team Leader: Antithesis in Style and Structure," in Michel Syrett and Clare Hogg (eds.), *Frontiers of Leadership* (Oxford, England: Blackwell Publishers, 1992), p. 271.
6. William D. Hitt, *The Leader-Manager: Guidelines for Action* (Columbus, Ohio: Battelle Press, 1988), pp. 68–69.
7. Justin Martin, "The Man Who Boogied Away a Billion," *Fortune,* December 23, 1996, p. 137.
8. Peter F. Drucker, "The Coming of the New Organization," *Harvard Business Review,* January–February 1988, pp. 45–53; Richard S. Wellins, William C. Byham, and George R. Dixon, *Inside Teams: How 20 World-Class Organizations Are Winning Through Teamwork* (San Francisco: Jossey-Bass, 1994).
9. Ibid.
10. Ellen Hart, "Top Teams," *Management Review,* February 1996, p. 90.
11. Irving L. Janus, *Victims of Groupthink: A Psychological Study of Foreign Policy Decisions and Fiascoes* (Boston: Houghton Mifflin, 1972); Glen Whyte, "Groupthink Reconsidered," *Academy of Management Review,* January 1989, pp. 40–56.
12. Kenneth Labich, "Elite Teams," *Fortune,* February 19, 1996, p. 90.
13. Shari Caudron, "Teamwork Takes Work," *Personnel Journal,* February 1994, p. 45.
14. Ibid.; Andrew J. DuBrin, *The Reengineering Survival Guide: Managing and Succeeding in the Changing Workplace* (Cincinnati, Ohio: Thomson Executive Press, 1996), pp. 129–144.
15. Robert Fisher and Bo Thomas, *Real Dream Teams: Seven Practices That Enable Ordinary People to Achieve Extraordinary Results as Team Leaders* (Delray Beach, Fla: St. Lucie Press, 1995).
16. Dean Tjosvold and Mary M. Tjosvold, *The Emerging Leader: Ways to a Stronger Team* (New York: Lexington/Macmillan, 1993).
17. William A. Cohen, *The Art of the Leader* (Englewood Cliffs, N.J.: Prentice-Hall, 1990).
18. Mike Vance and Diane Deacon, *Think Out of the Box* (Franklin Lakes, N.J.: Career Press, 1995).
19. Paul S. George, "Teamwork Without Tears," *Personnel Journal,* November 1987, p. 129.
20. Clive Goodworth, "Some Thoughts on Creating a Team," in Syrett and Hogg, *Frontiers of Leadership,* p. 472.
21. Susan Sonnesyn Brooks, "Managing a Horizontal Revolution," *HRMagazine,* June 1995, p. 56.
22. Katzenbach and Smith, "The Discipline of Teams," p. 118.

23. Stephenie Overman, "Saturn Teams Working and Profiting," *HRMagazine*, March 1995, p. 72.

24. "Building Teamwork Takes Some Effort," Rochester *Democrat and Chronicle*, September 23, 1993, p. 8B.

25. Katzenbach and Smith, "The Discipline of Teams," p. 119.

26. Lee G. Bolman and Terrence E. Deal, "What Makes a Team Work?" *Organizational Dynamics*, Autumn 1992, pp. 40–41.

27. Ibid., pp. 41–42.

28. Edward Glassman, "Self-Directed Team Building Without a Consultant," *Supervisory Management*, March 1992, p. 6.

29. Frank Shipper and Charles C. Manz, "Employee Self-Management Without Formally Designed Teams: An Alternative Road to Empowerment," *Organizational Dynamics*, Winter 1992, p. 59.

30. Charles C. Manz and Henry P. Sims, Jr., "Leading Workers to Lead Themselves: The External Leadership of Self-Managing Work Teams," *Administrative Science Quarterly*, March 1987, p. 118.

31. Stratford Sherman, "Secret of HP's 'Muddled' Team," *Fortune*, March 18, 1996, p. 120.

32. Jennifer J. Laabs, "Team Training Goes Outdoors," *Personnel Journal*, June 1991, p. 59.

33. Jay A. Conger, *Learning to Lead: The Art of Transforming Managers into Leaders* (San Francisco: Jossey-Bass, 1992), p. 159.

34. George Graen and J. F. Cashman, "A Role Making Model of Leadership in Formal Organizations: A Developmental Approach," in J. G. Hunt and L. L. Larson (eds.), *Leadership Frontiers* (Kent, Ohio: Kent State University Press, 1975), pp. 143–165.

35. Robert P. Vecchio, "Are You IN or OUT with Your Boss?" *Business Horizons*, 1987, pp. 76–78.

36. Randall P. Settoon, Nathan Bennett, and Robert C. Liden, "Social Exchange in Organizations: Perceived Organizational Support, Leader-Member Exchange, and Employee Reciprocity," *Journal of Applied Psychology*, June 1996, pp. 219–227.

37. Pamela Tierney and Talya N. Bauer, "A Longitudinal Assessment of LMX on Extra-Role Behavior," *Academy of Management Best Papers Proceedings*, 1996, pp. 298–302.

38. Robert C. Liden, Sandy J. Wayne, and Dean Stilwell, "A Longitudinal Study on the Early Development of Leader-Member Exchanges," *Journal of Applied Psychology*, August 1993, pp. 662–674.

39. Robert J. Waterman, Jr., "The Power of Teamwork," in Syrett and Hogg, *Frontiers of Leadership*, pp. 487–488.

40. Deborah Harrington-Mackin, *The Team Building Tool Kit: Tips, Tactics and Rules for Effective Workplace Teams* (New York: AMACOM, 1994).

Chapter 10

1. Roger D. Evered and James C. Selman, "Coaching and the Art of Management," *Organizational Dynamics*, Autumn 1989, p. 16.

2. An original version of expectancy theory applied to work motivation is Victor H. Vroom, *Work and Motivation* (New York: Wiley, 1964). Also see Anthony J. Mento, Edwin A. Locke, and Howard J. Klein, "Relationship of Goal Level to Valence and Instrumentality," *Journal of Applied Psychology*, August 1992, pp. 395–405.

3. Wendelien Van Eerde and Henk Thierry, "Vroom's Expectancy Models and Work-Related Criteria: A Meta-Analysis," *Journal of Applied Psychology*, October 1996, pp. 548–556.

4. David A. Nadler and Edward E. Lawler III, "Motivation: A Diagnostic Approach," in J. Richard Hackman, Edward E. Lawler III, and Lyman W. Porter (eds.), *Perspectives on Behavior in Organizations*, 2nd ed. (New York: McGraw-Hill, 1983), pp. 67–78; James A. F. Stoner and R. Edward Freeman, *Management*, 4th ed. (Englewood Cliffs, N.J.: Prentice-Hall, 1989), p. 448.

5. Book review in *Personnel Psychology*, Winter 1991, p. 872.

6. Edwin A. Locke and Gary P. Latham, *A Theory of Goal Setting and Task Performance* (Englewood Cliffs, N.J.: Prentice-Hall, 1990).

7. P. Christopher Earley and Terri Lituchy, "Delineating Goal and Efficacy Effects: A Test of Three Models," *Journal of Applied Psychology*, February 1991, p. 83.

8. A representative example is presented by Fred Luthans, Robert Paul, and Lew Taylor in "The Impact of Contingent Reinforcement on Retail Salespersons' Performance Behaviors: A Replicated Field Experiment," *Journal of Organizational Behavior Management*, Spring/Summer 1985, pp. 25–35.

9. An authoritative source on the use of behavior modification in organizations is Fred Luthans and Robert Kreitner, *Organizational Behavior Modification and Beyond: An Operant and Social Learning Approach* (Glenview, Ill.: Scott, Foresman, 1984).

10. Fred Luthans, *Organizational Behavior*, 6th ed. (New York: McGraw-Hill, 1992), p. 237.

11. Florence M. Stone and Randi T. Sachs, *The High-Value Manager: Developing the Core Competencies Your Organization Demands* (New York: AMACOM, 1995), pp. 142–143.

12. William D. Hitt, *The Leader-Manager: Guidelines for Action* (Columbus, Ohio: Battelle Press, 1988), pp. 186–187.

13. Evered and Selman, "Coaching and the Art of Management," p. 15.

14. Ibid., pp. 27–28.

15. Sharon Aurelio and John P. Kennedy, Jr., "Performance Coaching: A Key to Effectiveness," *Supervisory Management*, August 1991, pp. 1–2.

16. Hitt, *The Leader-Manager*, pp. 186–187.

17. Ibid., pp. 187–188.

18. Richard J. Walsh, "Ten Basic Counseling Skills," *Supervisory Management*, November 1990, p. 6.

19. Marilyn J. Darling, "Coaching People Through Difficult Times," *HRManagement*, November 1994, pp. 70–73.

20. For example, see Dick Grote, *Discipline Without Punishment: The Proven Strategy That Turns Problem Employees into Superior Performers* (New York: AMACOM, 1995).

21. Gerald M. Sturman, "The Supervisor as Career 'Coach,'" *Supervisory Management*, November 1990, p. 6.

Chapter 11

1. Based on facts as reported in Michael H. Martin, "The Next Big Thing: A Bookstore?" *Fortune*, December 9, 1996, pp. 168–170; Tom Stein, "Masters of the Web," *Success*, December 1996, pp. 30–32; www.amazon.com, December 26, 1996.
2. Richard W. Woodman, John E. Sawyer, and Ricky W. Griffin, "Toward a Theory of Organizational Creativity," *Academy of Management Review*, April 1993, p. 293.
3. G. Wallas, *The Art of Thought* (New York: Harcourt Brace, 1926).
4. Anna Esaki-Smith and Michael Warshaw, "Renegades 1993: Creating the Future," *Success*, January/February 1993), p. 36.
5. Teresa M. Amabile, "The Social Psychology of Creativity: A Componential Conceptualization," *Journal of Personality and Social Psychology*, August 1993, pp. 357–376.
6. Robert Kreitner and Angelo Kinicki, *Organizational Behavior*, 2nd ed. (Homewood, Ill.: Irwin, 1992), p. 579.
7. Robert T. Godfrey, "Tapping Employees' Creativity," *Supervisory Management*, February 1986, pp. 17–18; John A. Gover, Royce R. Ronning, and Cecil R. Reynolds (eds.), *Handbook of Creativity* (New York: Plenum Press, 1989), p. 10; Pamela Smith, "Mix Skepticism, Humor, a Rocky Childhood—and Presto! Creativity," *Business Week*, September 30, 1985, p. 81.
8. David Dishneau, "Gold Mining In Old Computers," Associated Press story, January 14, 1996.
9. Randall E. Stross, "Microsoft's Big Advantage—Hiring Only the Supersmart," *Fortune*, November 25, 1996, pp. 159–162.
10. Teresa M. Amabile, "A Model of Creativity in Organizations," in Barry M. Staw and Lawrence L. Cummings (eds.), *Research in Organizational Behavior*, Vol. 10 (Greenwich, Conn.: JAI Press, 1988), pp. 123–167.
11. Woodman, Sawyer, and Griffin, "Toward a Theory of Organizational Creativity," p. 298.
12. Greg R. Oldham and Anne Cummings, "Employee Creativity: Personal and Contextual Factors at Work," *Academy of Management Journal*, June 1996, pp. 607–634.
13. Alan J. Rowe and James D. Boulgarides, *Managerial Decision Making: A Guide to Successful Business Decisions* (New York: Macmillan, 1992), p. 172.
14. "Death Futures Growing," *Toledo Blade*, May 14, 1995.
15. "Cellular Phone Towers Put On Some Clever Disguises," Associated Press story, July 9, 1996.
16. Edward De Bono, *Serious Creativity: Using the Power of Lateral Thinking to Create New Ideas* (New York: Harper-Collins, 1993).
17. Kathleen Driscoll, "Capturing Employee Ideas," Rochester *Democrat and Chronicle*, February 28, 1994, p. 1D.
18. Richard Lally, "How to Produce More Creative Ideas," *Getting Results*, November 1996, p. 6.
19. "Brainstorm Better Ideas with the 6-3-5 Method," *Manager's Intelligence Report*, undated sample distributed in September 1996.
20. Lally, "How to Produce More Creative Ideas," p. 7.
21. Anne Sagen, "Creativity Tools: Versatile Problem Solvers That Can Double as Fun and Games," *Supervisory Management*, October 1991, pp. 1–2.
22. Edward Glassman, "Creative Problem Solving: New Techniques," *Supervisory Management*, March 1989, p. 16.
23. Robert McGarvey, "Turn It On: Creativity Is Crucial to Your Business' Success," *Entrepreneur*, November 1996, p. 156.
24. Woodman, Sawyer, and Griffin, "Toward a Theory of Organizational Creativity," p. 305.
25. M. Basadur, George B. Graen, and S. G. Green, "Training in Creative Problem-Solving: Effects on Ideation and Problem Finding and Solving in an Industrial Research Organization," *Organizational Behavior and Human Performance*, Vol. 30, 1988, pp. 41–70.
26. Mike Vance and Diane Deacon, *Think Out of the Box* (Franklin Lakes, N.J.: Career Press, 1995).
27. Quoted in "Breakthrough Ideas," *Success*, October 1987, p. 50.
28. "Breakthrough Ideas," *Success*, October 1990, p. 38.
29. Contributed by anonymous reviewer, 1996.
30. "Be a Creative Problem Solver," *Executive Strategies*, June 6, 1989, pp. 1–2.
31. Teresa M. Amabile, *Growing Up Creative* (Buffalo, N.Y.: CEF Press, 1989).
32. Teresa M. Amabile and S. S. Gryskiewicz, *Creativity in the R & D Laboratory* (Greensboro, N.C.: Center for Creative Leadership, 1987).
33. Donald W. Blohwiak, *Mavericks! How to Lead Your Staff to Think Like Einstein, Create Like da Vinci and Invent Like Edison* (Homewood, Ill.: Business One–Irwin, 1992).
34. Robert E. Quinn, Sue R. Faerman, Michael P. Thompson, and Michael R. McGrath, *Becoming a Master Manager: A Competency Framework* (New York: Wiley, 1990), p. 255.
35. Quoted in Lally, "How to Produce More Creative Ideas," p. 6.
36. Amabile, "The Social Psychology of Creativity."
37. Shari Caudron, "Strategies for Managing Creative Workers," *Personnel Journal*, December 1994, pp. 104–113.
38. Gareth Morgan, *Creative Organization Theory: A Resourcebook* (Newbury Park, Calif: Sage, 1990); Rosabeth Moss Kanter, *The Change Masters* (New York: Simon and Schuster, 1983).

Solution to Leadership Skill-Building Exercise 11–1, Thinking Outside the Box

Affix the small box to the wall with the thumbtacks. Then place the candle on top of the box. Strengthen the attachment by dripping some wax from the candle, lighting it with the matches. You can strengthen the bond by inserting a thumbtack from underneath, going through the underside of the top of the box.

Solutions to Leadership Skill-Building Exercise 11–4, Word Hints to Creativity

1. party	5. club	9. high	13. make
2. ball	6. dog	10. sugar	14. bean
3. cheese	7. paper	11. floor	15. light
4. cat	8. finger	12. green	

Chapter 12

1. Frank Sonnenberg, "Internal Communication: Turning Talk into Action," *Supervisory Management*, September 1992, p. 9.
2. Bernard M. Bass, *Bass & Stogdill's Handbook of Leadership: Theory, Research, & Managerial Applications*, 3rd ed. (New York: The Free Press, 1990), p. 111.
3. Richard J. Klimoski and Noreen J. Hayes, "Leader Behavior and Subordinate Motivation," *Personnel Psychology*, Autumn 1980, pp. 543–555.
4. M. Remland, "Leadership Impressions and Nonverbal Communications in a Superior-Subordinate Interaction," *Journal of Business Communication*, Vol. 18, No. 3, 1981, pp. 17–29.
5. Fred Luthans, Richard M. Hodgetts, and Stuart A. Rosenkrantz, *Real Managers* (Cambridge, Mass.: Ballinger, 1988), p. 68.
6. Peter Lowy and Byron Reimus, "Ready, Aim, Communicate!" *Management Review*, July 1996, pp. 40–43.
7. Ibid., p. 40.
8. James M. Kouzes and Barry Z. Posner, *The Leadership Challenge: How to Get Extraordinary Things Done in Organizations* (San Francisco: Jossey-Bass, 1987), p. 118.
9. Herman Aguinis, Mitchell S. Nesler, Megumi Hosoda, and James T. Tedeschi, "The Use of Influence Tactics in Persuasion," *Journal of Social Psychology*, Vol. 134, No. 4, 1994, pp. 429–438.
10. Deborah Tannen, "The Power of Talk: Who Gets Heard and Why," *Harvard Business Review*, September–October 1995, pp. 138–148.
11. Jimmy Calano and Jeff Salzman, "Persuasiveness: Make It Your 'Power Booster,'" *Working Woman*, October 1988, p. 124.
12. Personal communication from anonymous reviewer, September 1993.
13. Several of these examples are from "Avoid These Top Ten Language Errors," *Working Smart*, October 1991, p. 8.
14. William Strunk Jr. and E. B. White, *The Elements of Style*, 3rd ed. (New York: Macmillan, 1979).
15. Stephen P. Robbins, *Training in Interpersonal Skills: TIPS for Managing People at Work* (Englewood Cliffs, N.J.: Prentice-Hall, 1989), p. 155.
16. Sherry Sweetham, "How to Organize Your Thoughts for Better Communication," *Personnel*, March 1986, p. 39.
17. Michael W. Mercer, "How to Make a Fantastic Impression," *HRMagazine*, March 1993, p. 49.
18. Albert Mehrabian and M. Wiener, "Decoding of Inconsistent Communications," *Journal of Personality and Social Psychology*, Vol. 6, 1947, pp. 109–114.
19. Several of the ideas here are from "Body Language," *Executive Strategies*, April 17, 1990, p. 4; *Body Language for Business Success* (New York: National Institute for Business Management, 1989), pp. 28–29.
20. Andrew J. DuBrin, *Ten Minute Guide to Effective Leadership* (New York: Simon and Schuster, 1997), Chapter 5.
21. The literature is reviewed in David A. Whetton and Kim S. Cameron, *Developing Management Skills*, 3rd ed. (New York: HarperCollins, 1995), pp. 255–275; Chad T. Lewis, Joseph E. Garcia, and Sarah M. Jones, *Managerial Skills in Organizations* (Boston: Allyn & Bacon, 1990), p. 24.
22. Whetton and Cameron, *Developing Management Skills*, pp. 265–266.
23. Paul Hersey, Kenneth H. Blanchard, and Dewey E. Johnson, *Management of Organizational Behavior: Utilizing Human Resources* (Upper Saddle River, N.J.: Prentice-Hall, 1996), pp. 354–355.
24. Sandra Thiederman, "Overcoming Cultural and Language Barriers," *Personnel Journal*, December 1988, pp. 38–40; Sylvie Overnoy, "Cet Eté Je Pars Toute Seule," *Cosmopolitan* (International Edition), July 1992, pp. 91–92.
25. The last two items are from Lennie Copeland, "Training Americans to Do Business Overseas," *Training*, July 1993, p. 12.
26. "Letitia Baldrige: Arbiter of Business Manners and Mores," *Management Review*, April 1992, p. 50.
27. David P. Tulin, "Enhance Your Multi-cultural Communication Skills," *Managing Diversity*, Vol. 1, 1992, p. 5.
28. Roger E. Axtell, *Gestures: The Do's and Taboos of Body Language Around the World* (New York: Wiley, 1991).
29. "Cross Cultural Communication: An Essential Dimension of Effective Education," *Northwest Regional Educational Laboratory: CNORSE*—www.nwrel.org/cnorse.
30. Jim Kennedy and Anna Everest, "Put Diversity in Context," *Personnel Journal*, September 1991, pp. 50–52.
31. Lowell H. Lamberton and Leslie Minor, *Human Relations: Strategies for Success* (Chicago: Irwin/Mirror Press, 1995), p. 124.
32. Cited in "Best Tips," *Working Smart*, July 1996, p. 1.
33. Kenneth Thomas, "Conflict and Conflict Management," in Marvin D. Dunnette (ed.), *Handbook of Industrial and Organizational Psychology* (Chicago: Rand McNally, 1976), pp. 900–922.
34. Elizabeth A. Mannix, Leigh L. Thompson, and Max H. Bazerman, "Negotiation in Small Groups," *Journal of Applied Psychology*, June 1989, pp. 508–517.
35. Evert van de Vliert, Martin C. Euwema, and Sipke E. Huismans, "Managing Conflict with a Subordinate or a Superior: Effectiveness of Conglomerated Behavior," *Journal of Applied Psychology*, April 1995, pp. 271–281.
36. "Negotiating Without Giving In," *Executive Strategies*, September 19, 1989, p. 6.
37. Frank Acuff, *The World Class Negotiator: An Indispensable Guide for Anyone Doing Business with Those from a Foreign Culture* (New York: AMACOM, 1992).
38. Adapted from Gay Lumsden and Donald Lumsden, *Communicating in Groups and Teams: Sharing Leadership* (Belmont, Calif.: Wadsworth, 1993), p. 233.

Solution to Leadership Skill-Building Exercise 12–1, Identifying Emotion-Provoking Words and Phrases

quality-driven
customer-driven
viewpoint simply doesn't fly anymore
empowering hourly workers

best steel products possible
take a back seat to
we're becoming a purpose- and vision-driven company.

Chapter 13

1. Linda Lee Small, "Starbucks Wars," *Working Woman*, January 1996, pp. 25–27; "Fresh Cup: In the 'Hood'," www.freshcup.com/Aug96/aug-hood.shtml.
2. Robert L. Phillips and James G. Hunt (eds.), *Strategic Leadership: A Multiorganizational-Level Perspective* (Westport, Conn.: Quorum Books, 1992).
3. Bruce J. Avolio and David A. Waldman, "An Examination of Age and Cognitive Test Performance Across Job Complexity and Occupational Types," *Journal of Applied Psychology*, February 1990, pp. 43–50.
4. John A. Byrne, "Three of the Busiest New Strategists," *Business Week*, August 26, 1996, p. 50.
5. "Strategic Planning: After a Decade of Gritty Downsizing, Big Thinkers Are Back in Corporate Vogue," *Business Week*, August 26, 1996, p. 52.
6. Les Harrison, "The Competitive Edge: Capitalizing on Change," *Executive Focus*, January 1996, p. 35.
7. Gary Hamel and C. K. Prahalad, "Competing for the Future," *Harvard Business Review*, July–August 1994, pp. 127–128.
8. "A Strategy Session with C. K. Prahalad," *Management Review*, April 1995, pp. 50–51.
9. Gary Hamel, "Strategy as Revolution," *Harvard Business Review*, July–August 1996, pp. 69–82.
10. Ibid., p. 72.
11. Laurie Larwood, Cecilia M. Falbe, Mark P. Kriger, and Paul Miesing, "Structure and Meaning of Organizational Vision," *Academy of Management Journal*, June 1995, pp. 740–769.
12. Ibid., p. 765.
13. Joseph W. Quigley, *Vision: How Leaders Develop It, Share It, Sustain It* (New York: McGraw-Hill, 1993).
14. Robert J. Waterman, Jr., *What America Does Right: Learning from Companies That Put People First* (New York: W. W. Norton, 1994).
15. Larry Armstrong, "More Red Meat, Please," *Business Week*, May 22, 1995, p. 134.
16. James W. Dean, Jr., and Mark P. Sharfman, "Does Decision Process Matter? A Study of Strategic Decision-Making Effectiveness," *Academy of Management Journal*, April 1996, pp. 368–396.
17. Milton Leontiades, *Strategies for Diversification and Change* (Boston: Little, Brown, 1980), p. 63.
18. Michael Porter, *Competitive Strategy* (New York: The Free Press, 1980), pp. 36–46.
19. Paul C. Judge, "Digital's Struggle to Save Its Alpha Chip," *Business Week*, December 30, 1996, p. 44
20. Michele Kremen Bolton, "Imitation Versus Innovation: Lessons to Be Learned from the Japanese," *Organizational Dynamics*, Winter 1993, pp. 30–45.
21. Personal communication, May 1995.
22. "Strategic Planning," *Business Week*, August 26, 1996, p. 52.
23. James W. Dean, Jr., and James R. Evans, *Total Quality: Management, Organization, and Strategy* (Minneapolis/St. Paul: West, 1994), p. 260.
24. Max De Pree, "A Sense of Quality," *Executive Excellence*, September 1996, p. 12.
25. Thomas H. Berry, *Managing the Total Quality Transformation* (New York: McGraw-Hill, 1991).
26. Patricia Zingheim and Jay R. Schuster, "Linking Quality and Pay," *HRMagazine*, December 1992, pp. 55–59.
27. Richard Reed, David J. Lemak, and Joseph C. Montgomery, "Beyond Process: TQM Content and Firm Performance," *Academy of Management Review*, January 1996, p. 174.
28. Robert Kreitner, *Management*, 5th ed. (Boston: Houghton Mifflin, 1992), p. G9.
29. Pier A. Abetti, "Technology: A Key Strategic Resource," *Management Review*, February 1989, pp. 38–39.
30. Cited in "Tom Peters on Managing Technology," *Management Review*, February 1989, p. 39.
31. Quoted in Shawn Tully, "So, Mr. Bossidy, We Know You Can Cut. Now Show Us How to Grow," *Fortune*, August 21, 1995, p. 78.

Chapter 14

1. Cresencio Torres and Mary Bruxelles, "Capitalizing on Global Diversity," *HRMagazine*, December 1992, p. 32.
2. Warren Bennis, Jagdish Parikh, and Ronnie Lessem, *Beyond Leadership: Balancing Economics, Ethics, and Ecology* (Oxford, England: Blackwell, 1994).
3. Gregory M. Bounds, Gregory H. Dobbins, and Oscar S. Fowler, *Management: A Total Quality Perspective* (Cincinnati: South-Western College Publishing, 1995), p. 150.
4. Taylor H. Cox and Stacy Blake, "Managing Cultural Diversity: Implications for Organizational Competitiveness," *Academy of Management Executive*, August 1991, pp. 45–56.
5. Julianne Bailey, "How to Be Different but Equal," *Savvy Woman*, November 1989, p. 47 (cited in Cox and Blake, "Managing Cultural Diversity," p. 48).
6. Genvieve Capowski, "Managing Diversity," *Management Review*, June 1996, p. 15.
7. Rosabeth Moss Kanter, *The Change Masters* (New York: Simon and Schuster, 1983).
8. Frances J. Milliken and Luis L. Martins, "Searching for Common Threads: Understanding the Multiple Effects of Diversity in Organizational Groups," *Academy of Management Review*, April 1996, p. 403.
9. David A. Thomas and Robin J. Ely, "Making Differences Matter: A New Paradigm for Managing Diversity," *Harvard Business Review*, September–October 1996, pp. 79–90.
10. Geert Hofstede, *Culture's Consequences: International Differences in Work-Related Values* (Beverly Hills, Calif.: Sage, 1980); updated and expanded in "A Conversation with Geert Hofstede" (interview by Richard Hodgetts), *Organizational Dynamics*, Spring 1993, pp. 53–61.
11. Arvind V. Phatak, *International Dimensions of Management* (Boston: Kent, 1983), pp. 22–26.
12. Our analysis of expectancy theory across cultures is based on Nancy J. Adler, *International Dimensions of Organizational Behavior*, 2nd ed. (Cincinnati: South-Western College Publishing, 1991), pp. 157–160.

13. David Sirota and M. J. Greenwood, "Understanding Your Overseas Workforce," *Harvard Business Review*, January–February 1971, pp. 53–60.
14. Adler, *International Dimensions of Organizational Behavior*, p. 159.
15. Roland Calori and Bruno Dufour, "Management European Style," *Academy of Management Executive*, August 1995, pp. 61–71.
16. Ibid., p. 70.
17. Phatak, *International Dimensions of Management*, p. 167.
18. Carla Joinson, "Cultural Sensitivity Adds Up to Good Business Sense," *HRMagazine*, November 1995, pp. 83–85.
19. Ibid., p. 84.
20. Louis Kraar, "Need a Friend in Asia? Try the Singapore Connection," *Fortune*, March 4, 1996, p. 180.
21. Bensen Rosen and Kay Lovelace, "Piecing Together the Diversity Puzzle," *HRMagazine*, June 1991, pp. 78–84.
22. R. Roosevelt Thomas Jr., *Beyond Race and Gender: Unleashing the Power of Your Total Work Force by Managing Diversity* (New York: AMACOM, 1991), p. 25.
23. Patricia L. Nemetz and Sandra L. Christensen, "The Challenge of Cultural Diversity: Harnessing a Diversity of Views to Understand Multiculturalism," *Academy of Management Review*, April 1996, p. 455.
24. Taylor Cox, Jr., "The Multicultural Organization," *Academy of Management Executive*, May 1991, p. 34.
25. "Leaders Reflect Board Diversity," Associated Press story, December 15, 1996.
26. Karen Hildebrand, "Use Leadership Training to Increase Diversity," *HRMagazine*, August 1996, pp. 53–54.
27. Ann M. Morrison, *The New Leaders: Guidelines for Leadership Diversity in America* (San Francisco: Jossey-Bass, 1992).
28. Ibid.; John W. Hodges, "Practical Strategies for Leading Diversity," *HRMagazine*, May 1993, pp. 17–19.
29. "Diversity: Getting Past Stereotypes," *Supervisory Management*, August 1995, p. 6.

Chapter 15

1. Based on information presented by Thomas Amirault in *Occupational Outlook Quarterly* (Washington, D.C.: U. S. Bureau of Labor Statistics, 1993).
2. Chris Argyris, "Teaching Smart People How to Learn," *Harvard Business Review*, May–June 1991, pp. 99–109.
3. Steve Lohr, "IBM Racks Up $8-Billion Loss," *New York Times Service (Toronto Globe and Mail)*, July 28, 1993, p. B7.
4. Ira Sager, "The View from IBM," *Business Week*, October 30, 1995, p. 142.
5. Bernard M. Bass, *Bass & Stogdill's Handbook of Leadership: Theory, Research, & Managerial Applications*, 3rd ed. (New York: The Free Press, 1990), p. 173.
6. Stratford Sherman, "How Tomorrow's Best Leaders Are Learning Their Stuff," *Fortune*, November 27, 1995, p. 93.
7. Richard L. Hughes, Robert C. Ginnett, and Gordon J. Curphy, *Leadership: Enhancing the Lessons of Experience* (Burr Ridge, Ill.: Irwin, 1993), pp. 33–36.
8. Sherman, "How Tomorrow's Best Leaders Are Learning Their Stuff," p. 93.

9. Daphna F. Raskas and Donald C. Hambrick, "Multifunctional Managerial Development: A Framework for Evaluating the Options," *Organizational Dynamics*, Autumn 1992, p. 5.
10. Michael Beer, Russell Eisenstadt, and Bert Spector, *The Critical Path to Corporate Renewal* (Boston: Harvard Business School Press, 1995).
11. Bennett J. Tepper, "Upward Maintenance Tactics in Supervisory Mentoring and Nonmentoring Relationships," *Academy of Management Journal*, August 1995, p. 1195.
12. "The Leader in You: What It Takes, How to Get It," *Executive Strategies*, April 1994, p. 9.
13. Marshall Whitmire and Philip R. Nienstedt, "Lead Leaders into the '90s," *Personnel Journal*, May 1991, pp. 80–85.
14. Ellen Hoffman, "Not for Future CEOs Only," *USAir Magazine*, April 1996, p. 22.
15. Jay A. Conger, *Learning to Lead: The Art of Transforming Managers into Leaders* (San Francisco: Jossey-Bass, 1992), pp. 46–48. See also Jay A. Conger, "Personal Growth Training: Snake Oil or Pathway to Leadership?" *Organizational Dynamics*, Summer 1993, pp. 19–30.
16. James M. Kouzes and Barry Z. Posner, *The Leadership Challenge: How to Get Extraordinary Things Done in Organizations*, 2nd ed. (San Francisco: Jossey-Bass, 1995).
17. Ellen Van Velsol, Marian Ruderman, and Dianne Phillips, "The Lessons That Matter," *Issues & Observations*, Spring 1989, pp. 6–7.
18. William R. Tracey, *Designing Training and Development Systems* (New York: AMACOM, 1992); Bass, *Bass & Stogdill's Handbook*, pp. 807–856.
19. A. Dianne Phillips, "Taking a Good Look at Development," *Issues & Observations*, Summer 1990, pp. 1–2.
20. Ibid., pp. 3–4.
21. Thomas R. Horton, *The CEO Paradox: The Privilege and Accountability of Leadership* (New York: AMACOM, 1992).
22. Edward J. Zajac and James D. Westphal, "Who Shall Succeed? How CEO/Board Preferences and Power Affect the Choice of New CEOs," *Academy of Management Journal*, February 1996, pp. 64–90.
23. Catherine Arnst and Richard A. Melcher, "Why AT&T Made an Outside Call," *Business Week*, November 4, 1996, pp. 36–37.
24. Albert A. Cannella, Jr., and Michael Lubatkin, "Succession as a Sociopolitical Process: Internal Impediments to Outside Selection," *Academy of Management Journal*, August 1993, pp. 763–793.
25. Linda Grant, "GE: The Envelope, Please," *Fortune*, June 26, 1995, pp. 89–90.
26. Mark Helm, "Giving Up the Helm: Tackling Transition When Founders Step Aside," Rochester *Democrat and Chronicle*, December 16, 1996, pp. 1D, 6D.
27. Ibid., p. 6D.
28. David A. Garvin, "Building a Learning Organization," *Harvard Business Review*, July–August 1993, p. 80.
29. Peter B. Vail, *Learning as a Way of Being: Strategies for Survival in a World of Permanent White Water* (San Francisco: Jossey-Bass, 1996).
30. Robert H. Waterman, Jr., "A Model of Learning," *Executive Excellence*, September 1996, p. 4.

31. Frank J. Barrett, "Creating Appreciative Learning Cultures," *Organizational Dynamics*, Autumn 1995, pp. 36–49; John W. Slocum, Jr., Michael McGill, and David T. Lei, "The New Learning Strategy: Anytime, Anything, Anywhere," *Organizational Dynamics*, Autumn 1994, pp. 33–48; Peter M. Senge, *The Fifth Discipline* (New York: Doubleday, 1990).

32. Book review in *Personnel Psychology*, Winter 1996, p. 993.

33. Robert E. Kelley, "In Praise of Followers," *Harvard Business Review*, November–December 1988, pp. 142–148.

34. Genevieve Capowski, "Anatomy of a Leader: Where Are the Leaders of Tomorrow?" *Management Review*, March 1994, p. 15.

35. Robert Glaser, "Paving the Road to Trust," *HRFocus*, January 1997, p. 5.

Glossary

Achievement motivation Finding joy in accomplishment for its own sake.

Assertiveness Forthrightness in expressing demands, opinions, feelings, and attitudes.

Attributions The judgments we make about the behavior and attitudes of others.

Attribution theory The process of attributing causality to events.

Autocratic leader A person in charge who retains most of the authority for himself or herself.

Bandwagon technique A manipulative approach emphasizing that "everybody else is doing it."

Behavior modification An attempt to change behavior by manipulating rewards and punishment.

Behavior shaping Rewarding any response in the right direction and then rewarding only the closest approximation.

Blemish A simple game in which the manager always finds a flaw in a group member's work.

Casual time orientation The view that time is an unlimited and unending resource, leading toward extreme patience.

Centrality The extent to which a unit's activities are linked into the system of organized activities.

Charisma A special quality of leaders whose purposes, powers, and extraordinary determination differentiate them from others.

Coalition A specific arrangement of parties working together to combine their power.

Coercive power The power to punish for noncompliance; power based on fear.

Cognitive factors Problem solving and intellectual skills.

Cognitive resource theory A theory of leadership emphasizing that intelligent and competent leaders make more effective plans, decisions, and strategies than do leaders with less intelligence or competence.

Collectivism A belief that the group and society should receive top priority.

Commitment The highest degree of success when a leader exerts influence.

Compliance Partial success of an influence attempt by a leader.

Concert building A conception of the leader's role that involves both aligning and mobilizing.

Congruence The matching of verbal and nonverbal communication to what the sender is thinking and feeling.

Conjunctive communication Communication that is linked logically to previous messages, thus enhancing communication.

Consensus leader The person in charge who encourages group discussion about an issue and then makes a decision that reflects general agreement and will be supported by group members.

Consideration The degree to which the leader creates an environment of emotional support, warmth, friendliness, and trust.

Consultative leader A person in charge who confers with group members before making a decision.

Contingency approach to leadership The contention that leaders are most effective when they make their behavior contingent upon situational forces, including group member characteristics.

Contingency theory of leadership An explanation of leadership specifying the conditions under which a particular style of leadership will be effective.

Cooperation theory A belief in cooperation and collaboration rather than competitiveness as a strategy for building teamwork.

Creativity The production of novel and useful ideas.

Cultural sensitivity An awareness of and a willingness to investigate the reasons why people of another culture act as they do.

Debasement The act of demeaning or insulting oneself to control the behavior of another person.

Delegation The assignment of formal authority and responsibility for accomplishing a specific task to another person.

Democratic leader A person in charge who confers final authority on the group.

Disjunctive communication Communication that is not linked to the preceding messages, resulting in impaired communication.

Domains of impact   In management development, the ranges of possible effects that a program might have.

Double-loop learning   An in-depth style of learning that occurs when people use feedback to confront the validity of the goal or the values implicit in the situation.

Drive   A propensity to put forth high energy into achieving goals, and persistence in applying that energy.

Effective leader   One whose actions facilitate group members' attainment of productivity, quality, and satisfaction.

Emotional stability   The ability to control emotions to the point that one's emotional responses are appropriate to the occasion.

Empathy   The ability to place oneself in another's frame of reference.

Employee-centered leader   One who encourages subordinate participation in goal setting and other work decisions.

Empowerment   Passing decision-making authority and responsibility from managers to group members.

Excursion method   A creative problem-solving technique in which the problem solver makes word associations that relate to the problem.

Expectancy   The probability assigned by the individual that effort will lead to correct performance of the task.

Expectancy theory   A theory of motivation based on the premise that the amount of effort people expend depends on how much reward they expect to get in return.

Expert power   The ability to influence others because of one's specialized knowledge, skills, or abilities.

Expertise approach   A belief that the leader's most important responsibility is providing an area of expertise that will be a source of competitive advantage.

Farsightedness   The ability to understand the long-range implications of actions and policies.

Femininity   In Hofstede's research, an emphasis on personal relationships, concern for others, and a high quality of life.

Flexibility   The ability to adjust to different situations.

Forced-association technique   A method of releasing creativity in which individuals or groups solve a problem by making associations between the properties of two objects.

Formality   The attachment of considerable importance to tradition, ceremony, social rules, and rank.

Free-rein leader   A person in charge who turns over virtually all authority and control to the group.

Game   A repeated series of exchanges between people that seems plausible but has a hidden agenda or purpose.

Goal   What a person is trying to accomplish.

Great person theory   See **Trait approach.**

Groupthink   A deterioration of mental efficiency, reality testing, and moral judgment in the interest of group solidarity.

High tolerance for frustration   The ability to cope with the blocking of goal attainment.

Individualism   A mental set in which people see themselves first as individuals and believe their own interests and values take priority.

Influence   The ability to affect the behavior of others in a particular direction.

Informality   A casual attitude toward tradition, ceremony, social rules, and rank.

Information power   Power stemming from formal control over the information people need to do their work.

Initiating structure   The degree to which the leader organizes and defines relationships in the group by activities such as assigning specific tasks, specifying procedures to be followed, scheduling work, and clarifying expectations of team members.

Initiative   The quality of being a self-starter; ability to take action without support and stimulation from others.

Insight   A depth of understanding that requires considerable intuition and common sense.

Instrumentality   The probability assigned by the individual that performance will lead to certain outcomes.

Internal locus of control   The belief that one is the primary cause of events happening to oneself.

Kaizen   A philosophy of gradual improvement in personal and work life that has become part of the philosophy of total quality management.

Lateral thinking   A thinking process that spreads out to find many different solutions to a problem.

Leader   A person who inspires confidence and support among the people who are needed to achieve organizational goals.

Leader irrelevance   The position that leaders' actions have almost no impact on most organizational outcomes.

Leader-match concept   The proposition that leadership effectiveness depends on matching leaders to situations in which they can exercise more control.

Leader-member exchange model (or **vertical dyad linkage model**)   A model positing that leaders develop unique working relationships with subordinates, thereby creating in-groups and out-groups.

Leadership   The ability to inspire confidence and support among the people who are needed to achieve organizational goals.

Leadership diversity   The presence of a culturally heterogeneous cadre of leaders.

Leadership effectiveness   Attaining desirable outcomes such as productivity, quality, and satisfaction in a given situation.

Leadership Grid®   (formerly the **Managerial Grid**) A framework for specifying the concern for the production and people dimensions of leadership simultaneously.

Leadership polarity   The disparity in views of leaders: They are revered or vastly unpopular, but people rarely feel neutral.

Leadership power   The exercise of position power.

Leadership style   The relatively consistent pattern of behavior that characterizes a leader.

Leadership succession   An orderly process of identifying and grooming people to replace executives.

Leading by example   Influencing others by acting as a positive role model.

Learning organization   An organization that is skilled at creating, acquiring, and transferring knowledge, and at modifying behavior to reflect new knowledge and insights.

Legitimate power   Power granted by the organization.

Linguistic style   A person's characteristic speaking pattern.

Long-term orientation   A long-range perspective by workers, who thus are thrifty and do not demand quick returns on investments.

Machiavellians   People in the workplace who ruthlessly manipulate others.

Management by anecdote   The technique of inspiring and instructing group members by telling fascinating stories.

Masculinity   In Hofstede's research, an emphasis on assertiveness and the acquisition of money and material objects, and a deemphasis on caring for others.

Mentor   A more experienced person who develops a protégé's abilities through tutoring, coaching, guidance, and emotional support.

Micromanagement   The close monitoring of most aspects of group member activities by the manager or leader.

Mission statement   A firm's formal statement of its general field, purposes, values, and direction.

Multicultural leader   A leader with the skills and attitudes to relate effectively to and motivate people across race, gender, age, social attitudes, and lifestyles.

Multicultural organization   A firm that values cultural diversity and is willing to encourage and even capitalize on such diversity.

Multifunctional managerial development   An organization's intentional efforts to enhance the effectiveness of managers by giving them experience in multiple functions within the organization.

Normative decision model   An approach that views leadership as a decision-making process and specifies what a leader ought to do in a given situation.

Organizational creativity   The creation of novel and useful ideas and products that pertain to the workplace.

Organizational politics   Informal approaches to gaining power through means other than merit or luck.

Outcome   Anything that might stem from performance, such as a reward.

Participative leader   A person in charge who shares decision making with group members.

Partnership   A relationship between leaders and group members in which power is approximately balanced.

Path-goal theory   An explanation of leadership effectiveness that specifies what the leader must do to achieve high productivity and morale in a given situation.

Personalized charismatic   One who exercises few restraints on the use of power, in order to best serve his or her own interests.

Personal power   Power derived from the person rather than from the organization.

Persuade package   A small, standard set of influence tactics that leads the target to behave in a particular way.

Pet-peeve technique   A group method of identifying all the possible complaints others might have about one's organizational unit.

Politics   The various methods people use to attain or maintain power and gain other advantages.

Power   The potential or ability to influence decisions and control resources.

Power distance   The extent to which employees accept the idea that the members of an organization have different levels of power.

Prestige power   The power stemming from one's status and reputation.

Production-centered leader   One who sets tight work standards, organizes tasks carefully, prescribes the work methods to be followed, and supervises closely.

Readiness   In situational leadership, the extent to which a group member has the ability and willingness to accomplish a specific task.

Referent power   The ability to influence others that stems from the leader's desirable traits and characteristics.

Relationship behavior   The extent to which the leader engages in two-way or multiway communication.

Resistance   The state that occurs when an influence attempt by a leader is unsuccessful.

Resource dependence perspective   The view that an organization requires a continuing flow of human resources, money, customers and clients, technological inputs, and materials to continue to function.

Reward power   The authority to give employees rewards for compliance.

Self-awareness   Insightfully processing feedback about oneself to improve personal effectiveness.

Self-discipline   The ability to mobilize one's efforts and energy to stay focused on attaining an important goal.

Sensitivity to others   Empathy with group members; an understanding of who they are, what their position on issues is, and how to best communicate with and influence them.

Short-term orientation   A focus by workers on immediate results, and a propensity not to save.

Silent treatment   A means of influence characterized by saying nothing, sulking, or other forms of passivity.

Single-loop learning   A situation in which learners seek minimum feedback that might substantially confront their basic ideas or actions.

Situational leadership model   A model that explains how to match leadership style to the readiness of the group members.

Socialized charismatic   A leader who restrains the use of power in order to benefit others.

Social loafing   Shirking individual responsibility in a group setting.

Social responsibility   The idea that organizations have an obligation to groups in society other than owners or stockholders and beyond that prescribed by law or union contract.

Strategic contingency theory   An explanation of sources of power suggesting that units best able to cope with the firm's critical problems and uncertainties acquire relatively large amounts of power.

Strategic leadership   The process of providing the direction and inspiration necessary to create, provide direction to, or sustain an organization.

Strategic management   The process of ensuring a competitive fit between the organization and its environment.

Strategic planning   Those activities that lead to the statement of goals and objectives and the choice of strategies to achieve them.

Strategy   An organization's plan for achieving its mission and goals in its environment.

Substitutes for leadership   Factors in the work environment that provide guidance and incentives to perform, making the leader's role almost superfluous.

SuperLeader   One who leads others to lead themselves.

Supportive communication   A communication style that delivers the message accurately and that supports or enhances the relationship between the two parties.

Systemic thinking   Seeing patterns and the invisible fabrics of interrelated actions that may take years to surface.

Task behavior   The extent to which the leader spells out the duties and responsibilities of an individual or group.

Team   A small number of people with complementary skills who are committed to a common purpose, set of performance goals, and approach, for which they hold themselves accountable.

Teamwork   An understanding and commitment to group goals on the part of all team members.

Technology   All the tools and ideas available for extending the physical and mental reach of people.

360-degree feedback   A formal evaluation of superiors based on input from people who work for and with them, sometimes including customers and suppliers.

Total quality management (TQM)   A management system for improving performance throughout the firm by maximizing customer satisfaction and making continuous improvements based on extensive employee involvement.

Traditional mental set   A conventional way of looking at things and placing them in familiar categories.

Trait approach (or great person theory)   The observation that leadership effectiveness depends on certain personal attributes such as self-confidence.

Transactional leader   A manager who mostly carries on transactions with people, such as taking care of administrative work and offering rewards for good performance.

Transformational leader   A leader who brings about positive, major changes in an organization.

Uncertainty avoidance   A dislike of—and evasion of—the unknown.

Universal theory of leadership   The belief that certain personal characteristics and skills contribute to leadership effectiveness in many situations.

Upward appeal   A means of influence in which the leader enlists a person with more formal authority to do the influencing.

Urgent time organization   A view of time as a scarce resource, leading to impatience.

Valence   The worth or attractiveness of an outcome.

Valuing differences training   A type of training designed to bring about workplace harmony by teaching people how to get along better with diverse work associates.

Vertical dyad linkage model.   *See* **Leader-member exchange model.**

Vertical thinking   An analytical, logical process that results in few answers.

Virtual corporation   A temporary network of independent firms linked by information technology to share skills, costs, and access to each other's markets.

Virtual office   A situation in which employees work together as if they were part of a single office despite being physically separated.

Vision   The ability to imagine different and better conditions and the ways to achieve them.

Vroom–Yetton–Jago model   *See* **Normative decision model.**

Win-win approach to conflict resolution   The belief that after conflict has been resolved, both sides should gain something of value.

Work ethic   A firm belief in the dignity of work.

Name Index

434

Organization Index

Subject Index